Logic and Rhetoric in England, 1500-1700

Logic and Rhetoric
in England, 1500-1700

By Wilbur Samuel Howell

ELOQUENTIA   LOGICA

NEW YORK / RUSSELL & RUSSELL

Preface

THIS book is intended as a chapter in the history of ideas. Its particular purpose is to describe the ideas that Englishmen of the Renaissance held towards their method of producing discourses for the needs of their civilization. Political, cultural, intellectual, and literary historians have repeatedly interested themselves in the writings of the Renaissance, and have of course considered those writings to be the basic evidence upon which our own knowledge of the sixteenth and seventeenth centuries ultimately depends. My history is devoted, not to another account of the contents of those writings, but to a new interpretation of the theories that governed their production. Thus I seek here to trace historically the methods recognized by the Renaissance Englishman as the laws of authorship.

In its widest sense, authorship means the profession of making anything. In a narrower sense, it means the profession of producing any kind of literary work, poetical or non-poetical, oral or written. As I have just used the term in reference to the subject of this book, it means the profession of producing written or oral works of the non-poetical kind. In other words, I am not here endeavoring to give an account of the theories governing the production of Renaissance poetry, fiction, and drama; I am confining myself instead, for reasons set forth in Chapter 1 of this book, to theories that govern arguments, expositions, lectures, speeches, letters, and sermons. In the Renaissance these latter discourses were produced in accordance with the principles that made up the disciplines of logic and rhetoric. The chief treatises on logic and rhetoric in England between 1500 and 1700 have therefore become the primary data of my present history. I have tried to examine all of these data. I have sought to classify them into families, to describe their general characteristics, to identify their authors, to inquire into their origins, to indicate the presuppositions upon which they rest, and to interpret them as part of a social, political, intellectual, and religious context.

If the Renaissance may be considered the period which witnessed at one and the same time the death of medievalism and the first beginnings of modernism, then all ideas in that period become of special interest, so far at least as they give us the opportunity to see in them their ancient and their new aspects, ranged side by side as for comparison and thus made capable of telling us more about the nature of the old and the new than either one by itself had ever been able to do before or would ever be able to do again. Certainly the Renaissance ideas about logic and rhetoric exhibit the tendency to illuminate the basic nature of ancient and modern thought. Thus the history of these ideas may help us to see what classical rhetoric and logic had come to mean at the time of the Renaissance; what the world which these two arts served had come to be; and why that world had acquired new responsibilities which in turn demanded changes in the orientation of these two arts. From this history we can hope to derive a better understanding of the theories of communication in our twentieth-century world, and perhaps a deeper respect for the classical theories which governed western European civilization from the age of Pericles to that of William and Mary.

This book contains traces of my previous attempts to tell the story of English rhetoric. For example, a condensed account of the subject dealt with below in Chapter 3 appeared under the title, "English Backgrounds of Rhetoric," in *History of Speech Education in America: Background Studies* (New York: Appleton-Century-Crofts, Inc., 1954), a volume published under the auspices of the Speech Association of America. I prepared the condensed account shortly before I began to write Chapter 3. Thus it was perhaps inevitable that both versions would be similar in respect to many details of organization and wording. At any rate, such similarities will be found to exist. I should like to say, however, that Chapter 3 aims to cover the subject of traditional rhetoric much more thoroughly than I was able to do in the condensed account. I should also like to say, in acknowledging some points of similarity between Chapter 4 and an essay of mine entitled "Ramus and English Rhetoric: 1574-1681" (*The Quarterly Journal of Speech*, xxxvii, 299-310), that Chapter 4 is intended to do thoroughly what I briefly outlined in that essay.

In the preparation of this book I have received many forms of assistance, and I should like in gratitude to acknowledge them now. The Trustees of the John Simon Guggenheim Memorial Foundation granted me a Fellowship in the academic year 1948-1949 for research in the field of English and American rhetorical and poetic theory. As a result of that Fellowship, and of a sabbatical leave simultaneously awarded me by the Trustees of Princeton University, I was able to complete my study of rhetoric and poetics in the English Renaissance, and to make real progress in the study of Renaissance logic. These studies were conducted chiefly at the Bodleian

Library, the British Museum, and the Huntington Library. Two years thereafter, the Trustees of the Huntington Library awarded me a Fellowship for a year of residence and study at that incomparable institution. At the same time, the University Research Committee of Princeton University granted me funds to help me defray living expenses in California during my tenure as Fellow at the Huntington Library. This latter arrangement, and the others previously mentioned, were greatly facilitated by the warm and effective support of the late Donald A. Stauffer, Chairman of the Department of English at Princeton University. To him I shall always owe a particular debt of gratitude. I also owe a particular debt of gratitude to Godfrey Davies, Chairman of the Research Group of the Huntington Library, who believed in the worth of this project and helped to arrange the Huntington Fellowship that permitted me to do much of the actual writing of this book. In addition, I wish to offer thankful acknowledgment to the Princeton University Research Fund for two subsidies guaranteeing the transcription and publication of my manuscript; to Mrs. Miriam T. Winterbottom for her aid in typing the manuscript and reading proof; to Benjamin F. Houston of Princeton University Press for his helpful assistance in interpreting the manuscript to the printer and in working out efficient editorial procedures; and to Lane Cooper, Harry Caplan, Herbert A. Wichelns, Charles G. Osgood, and Whitney J. Oates for various kinds of support and encouragement. Finally, I should like to thank my wife for her affectionate help in all stages of this endeavor.

Wilbur Samuel Howell

Contents

Logic and Rhetoric in England, 1500-1700

CHAPTER 1

Introduction

Logic, conceived today as the science of validity of thought, and as the term for the canons and criteria that explain trustworthy inferences, was in the English Renaissance a theory not so much of thought as of statement. For all practical purposes, the distinction between thoughts and statements is not a very real distinction, since the latter are merely the reflection of the former, and the former cannot be examined without recourse to the latter. But what distinction there is consists in a differentiation between mental phenomena and linguistic phenomena, the assumption being that the thing to which either set of phenomena refers is reality itself. Logicians of the twentieth century are primarily interested in mental phenomena as an interpretation of the realities of man's environment, and in that part of mental phenomena which we call valid or invalid inference. Logicians of the English Renaissance were primarily interested in statements as a reflection of man's inferences, and in the problem of the valid and invalid statement. Thus Renaissance logic concerned itself chiefly with the statements made by men in their efforts to achieve a valid verbalization of reality. Since such statements were the work of scholars and scientists, not of laymen, Renaissance logic founded itself upon scholarly and scientific discourse and was in fact the theory of communication in the world of learning. The data upon which this theory rested were all learned tractates of that and earlier times. The theory itself attempted on the one hand to explain the nature of these tractates, as to language, sentence structure, and organization, and on the other to offer assistance to the learner in his effort to master learned communication, as part of his entrance fee to the scientific and philosophical world.

Rhetoric, popularly taken today as a term for the sort of style you happen personally to dislike, was less subjectively construed in England during the sixteenth and seventeenth centuries. Rhetoric was then regarded as the theory behind the statements intended for the populace. Since the populace consisted of laymen, or of people not learned in the subject being treated by a speaker or writer, and since the speaker or writer by his very office was to some extent a master of the real technicalities of his subject, rhetoric was regarded as the theory of communication between the learned and the lay world or between expert and layman. Over and over again in logical and rhetorical treatises of the English Renaissance, logic is compared to the closed fist and rhetoric to the open hand, this metaphor being borrowed from Zeno through Cicero and Quintilian to explain the preoccupation of logic with the tight discourses of the philosopher, and the preoccupation of rhetoric with the more open discourses of orator and popularizer. The fact that this metaphor gives both arts the same flesh and blood, the same defensive and offensive function, and the same skeletal structure, is merely an indication of the conviction of Renaissance learning that logic and rhetoric are the two great arts of communication, and that the complete theory of communication is largely identified, not with one, not with the other, but with both.

There was one important aspect of communication, however, which logic and rhetoric did not seek fully to explain or to teach during the sixteenth and seventeenth centuries. That aspect was concerned with what we might call poetic, as opposed to scientific or popular discourse. Englishmen of these two centuries did not waste their time in the vain effort to deny to poetry a primarily communicative function. Nor had the science of aesthetics yet been invented to insulate poetry from any contact with logic and rhetoric. Instead, poetry was considered to be the third great form of communication, open and popular but not fully explained by rhetoric, concise and lean but not fully explained by logic. So far as critics of that time postulated a difference between poetry, on the one hand, and logical and rhetorical discourse, on the other, their thinking might be described by saying that the two latter kinds of discourse were respectively considered to be closed and open, according to Zeno's analogy, whereas the former was regarded as having both characteristics at once. That is, poetry was thought to be a form of communication which, because it habitually used the medium of story and characterization, spoke two simultaneous languages, one in terms of a plot simple enough to hold children from play, and the other in terms of a humanistic meaning so subtle and complex that it held old men from the chimney corner.

The difference between the figurative and the literal statement might be said to be a partial clue to the distinction drawn by Renaissance critics between poetry and its two companion forms, but this distinction meant, of course, that rhetorical and logical discourse in

being declared literal was not therefore denied the resources of figurative language. Figurative language was considered rather to be a
means of carrying out a literal as well as a figurative intention, and
thus the figures of speech were part of the machinery of scientific,
of popular, and of poetic discourse, and were assigned formally and
without equivocation to rhetoric during the Renaissance. Again, the
difference between the feigned history and the real history, between
fiction and fact, might be said to be a partial clue to the difference
between poetry and the other two branches of discourse, but again
this distinction meant history to be broadly representative of scientific and popular discourse in its desire to be at once exact and popular, whereas feigned history or fiction, whether in prose or verse,
was broadly representative of poetic discourse in its desire to convey
meaning through indications of story and character. Still again, the
difference between the imitative and non-imitative discourse was in
part the distinction between poetry and its two companion forms,
but this distinction meant that the imitation of life as proposed by
poetry was in reality an attempt to create in language a posture of
imagined affairs to convey significance about an observer's awareness
of analogous postures in his own real affairs, whereas nonimitative
discourse dealt directly with real affairs without the intrusion of the
imagined postures.

Although poetry must be accepted as part of the communicative
structure of the Renaissance world, and although the theory of poetry
underwent changes between 1500 and 1700, it is not my present purpose to deal with it. I propose instead to describe what happened in
those years to logic and rhetoric in England. The great change which
occurred in poetical theory in the Renaissance was that the value of
the new poetry was asserted more and more warmly and with increasing effect. In other words, poetics more and more warmly sanctioned as valid art those works which achieved their effect without
necessarily imitating in close fashion the subject matter, the themes,
and the metrical patterns of the ancient world of Homer and Virgil.
This change had its parallel in logic, where the interest in general
accumulated wisdom as the starting point for man's thinking about
his world was gradually lost, and an interest in direct observation of
reality as the starting point was gradually established. Meanwhile,
a similar change was taking place in rhetoric, as men lost faith in
ancient devices for finding arguments ready made in systems of commonplaces or accepted opinions and came more and more to accept

[5]

the necessity for a direct and exhaustive study of the individual case as the best means of finding arguments that would have a lasting effect upon the hearer. But these parallel changes in poetical theory and its companion disciplines, while indicative that a great cultural revolution like the Renaissance will have similar effects in similar fields of learning, do not provide a satisfactory historical pattern for a close examination of Renaissance logic and rhetoric. The historical pattern so far as logic and rhetoric are concerned is best described as that in which there was at first an accepted tradition, then a reform, then a counterreform, and finally a resultant new tradition. Since poetical theory in the Renaissance does not exhibit this pattern, except in some degree, a treatment of it in connection with logic and rhetoric might force it to assume an unwarrantable configuration without gaining any compensating advantage save that of a more direct appeal to literary scholars than may be possible in a work devoted exclusively to a chapter in the history of the theory of nonpoetical communication.

The accepted tradition in English logic during the first seventy years of the sixteenth century is best described by saying that the logical treatises of Aristotle, as construed by commentators of the ancient pagan world and by their Christian and Mohammedan successors, were the ruling authorities. Scholastic logic is the term given to this tradition by historians of logic who lived in the period covered by the present study, and I shall use this term as they used it. Scholastic logic has a continuous history in England between the age of Alcuin, first English logician, and the middle of the sixteenth century, when this subject was given a representative treatment in the Latin language by John Seton and its first treatment in the English language by Thomas Wilson and Ralph Lever. To this logic I shall devote the second chapter of this book.

During the period in which scholastic logic was in the ascendancy in England, rhetorical theory in that country is perhaps best termed traditional. This traditional rhetoric is made up of three distinct patterns, unified as to basic concepts and ultimate origin, but diverse as to points of emphasis. These three patterns will be the subject of my third chapter.

The first of these patterns I shall call the Ciceronian. Ciceronian rhetoric exists wherever rhetoric is made to consist of all or most of the five operations anciently assigned to it by Cicero and Quintilian, these five operations being designated as invention, arrangement, style, memory, and delivery. These five operations were first identified with English rhetorical learning by Alcuin, who wrote a Latin version of Ciceronian rhetoric in the late eighth century. At the middle of the sixteenth century, Ciceronian rhetoric, which had already been converted in part into the English language, received a full-length treatment in that medium by Thomas Wilson, shortly after he wrote the first English version of scholastic logic. Thus Wilson like Alcuin will play a dual role in my present story.

The second pattern of traditional rhetoric I shall call the stylistic. Stylistic rhetoric is committed to all of the five operations just enumerated, but it chooses to select the third, style, for treatment. Stylistic rhetoric begins in English learning with the Venerable Bede, whose *Liber de Schematibus et Tropis*, written at the beginning of the eighth century, deals in Latin with an important part of the Ciceronian theory of oratorical style. From that date until the 1680's, this form of rhetorical learning had its adherents in England, the later ones of whom converted the doctrine of the tropes and the figures into English, as Wilson had done with scholastic logic and Ciceronian rhetoric.

The third pattern of traditional rhetoric I shall call the formulary. Formulary rhetoric was designed to foster the five operations which Ciceronian rhetoric made essential parts of the training of speakers and writers, but it carried out this purpose, not by the study of precepts, but by the study of examples. The first full-grown formulary rhetoric to be written in English was produced in 1563 by Richard Rainolde, and to this treatise we shall turn later when we deal with formulary rhetoric in connection with the whole subject of traditional rhetoric in England before 1570.

A revolt against scholastic logic and traditional rhetoric occurred in England between 1574 and 1600. This revolt was based upon the educational reforms of the celebrated Frenchman, Pierre de la Ramée, better known by his Latin name Petrus (or Peter) Ramus. An earlier revolt against scholastic logic, that of Ramon Lull in the thirteenth century, had considerable vogue on the European continent during the fifteen-hundreds, but it appears not to have influenced Englishmen to any extent, whereas Ramus dominated English logic in the late sixteenth century and held an English following of some importance during most of the seventeenth century. Ramus's revolt against scholasticism and tradition resulted in a logic and a rhetoric that may be called Ramistic. Ramistic logic was the work of

Ramus himself, and thus it deserves to bear his name and no other. His colleague, Omer Talon, or Audomarus Talaeus, was author of the rhetorical system that carries out the Ramistic reform of that branch of the liberal arts, and thus Ramistic rhetoric, as a body of doctrine examined in the present study, has to be understood as having a double authorship. Ramistic logic and rhetoric will be discussed together in the fourth chapter of the present study.

My fifth chapter will deal with the Systematics. This term occurs in a brief history of logic written early in the seventeenth century where it refers to that movement which sought to restore scholasticism without ignoring the validity of some of Ramus's reforms. The Systematics were influential during a large part of the seventeenth century, even if they did not succeed in terminating the vogue of Ramus in England. Their logic was written for the most part in Latin, although there is one good example of it in English. It had its minor branches, as one of its advocates took occasion to differ with another, but by and large it sought to occupy middle ground between scholastic and Ramistic logic.

While the Systematics were endeavoring to establish a reformed scholasticism in logic, a corresponding movement in English rhetoric can be observed. This movement will also be discussed in my fifth chapter, and I shall call its authors the Neo-Ciceronians. Neo-Ciceronian rhetoric was the result of an attempt to restore the earlier traditional rhetoric without ignoring some of the reforms proposed by Ramus. As the earlier traditional rhetoric had three distinct patterns, so did Neo-Ciceronian rhetoric, and I shall deal with them severally in Chapter 5.

Towards the end of the seventeenth century, a logic emerged which was critical not only of the Systematics but also of the Ramists. This logic found its first expression in English when the famous *Port-Royal Logic* was published in an English version in 1685, although three Latin editions of that work had already been published by that time in England and had already made English learning aware of what was to become a new tradition in logical theory. *The Port-Royal Logic* was still being published in English versions and used in English universities as late as the 1870's, and thus it may serve to illustrate accepted English thinking on this subject up to the time of John Stuart Mill's *System of Logic*. At any rate, *The Port-Royal Logic* is the most modern of logics produced in the seventeenth century, and to it I shall devote a considerable part of my sixth chapter.

That sixth chapter will also be concerned with those developments in the seventeenth century which pointed towards a new rhetoric. The first of these developments occurred early in the century with the publication of Bacon's *Advancement of Learning*. This remarkable work, which influenced English learning of the seventeenth century as did no other contemporary work, contained some ideas on rhetoric which were in opposition not only to Ramistic theory but also to the traditional rhetoric of the early Renaissance. This opposition grew as the seventeenth century advanced. The Royal Society, which carried out scientific investigations in the manner proposed by Bacon, and which was to some extent the finest result of Bacon's pioneering thought, had finally to develop a system of communication suited to the transfer of information from one scientist to another, and from scientist to public, and the rhetorical theory which underlies that system is a step towards the creation of a new rhetoric. Other developments of the same sort occurred later in the century, and they will be noticed as the sixth chapter unfolds.

As I have indicated already, the theory of communication as expressed in logic and rhetoric was throughout the Renaissance a response to the communicative needs of English society of that time, and thus it is not to be considered in a vacuum, but in complex relation to the culture surrounding it. Ramon Lull made his celebrated attack on Aristotelian logic during the thirteenth century because he wanted to convert Mohammedans to Christianity, not by the sword but by the syllogism, and he conceived of Aristotelian logic as too complex for that purpose. Ramus's attack on scholasticism and traditional rhetoric was motivated also by his desire to simplify overly complex instruments. Both of these reformers were articulating misgivings which the society around them shared, and both were seeking to bring learning into a closer relation with the practical needs which it exists to satisfy. So it always is. A theory of communication is an organic part of a culture. As the culture changes, so will the theory change. The scholastic logic and the traditional rhetoric of the early sixteenth century were an expression of late medieval times, and were suited to those times. Had those times continued without change, scholastic logic and traditional rhetoric would not have come under attack by the Ramists, and would not have emerged from the collision with Ramism as modified versions of their former selves.

[9]

Had the seventeenth century remained static to the end, *The Port-Royal Logic* and the new rhetoric would not have emerged to rival and at length to supplant Neo-Ciceronian rhetoric and the logic of the Systematics.

The forces at work to change the theory of communication during the English Renaissance may be indicated briefly. One force developed as men came to see that the old deductive sciences could not offer a sufficient explanation of a world discovered through observation of nature, and thus it came about, not that logic changed from an emphasis on deduction to an emphasis on induction, but that concrete descriptions of reality came to be admitted to the status of sciences alongside the older generalizations of moralist and theologian. Those concrete descriptions of reality did not have a ready-made vocabulary in which to express themselves, and could not fully utilize the ready-made vocabulary constructed from the ten categories of scholastic logic. Thus scholastic logic began to fail as a guide to learned communication, and the reformers began to move in.

Another force developed as the stable aristocracy of the late medieval world began to lose its political power, and the middle class began to assert its authority. That aristocracy did not have to conciliate the commoners whenever a crisis developed in political life. Instead, the commoners had at all times to conciliate the aristocrats, and thus stylistic rhetoric, which taught that the everyday pattern of speech must be avoided at all costs in formal discourse, and the unusual pattern adopted, was a perfect expression of the middle period of the sixteenth century. But England of the seventeenth century beheaded one king and deposed another, with the result that, by 1688, the middle class had established itself as a powerful force; and the new rhetoric had to abandon the unusual pattern of speech that would delight the aristocrat, and to teach the everyday pattern that would convince the commoner. Thus a new political structure made an old theory of popular appeal unworkable, and again the reformers moved in.

A third force came from the Reformation. The Catholic world of the Middle Ages was bound together by a system of agreements that made it necessary for a speaker to proceed only so far as to link a given proposal to those agreements. Thus the old rhetoric of the commonplaces—the old rhetoric which defined invention less as the discovery of something new than as the recalling of the proper element among the old—was admirably suited to such a stable world.

But the Reformation brought many of the old agreements under debate, and created many doubts where only a few had existed before. Ramus, himself a convert to Protestantism, simplified scholastic logic and traditional rhetoric in order to sharpen the tools which an age of controversy had to use. Then Protestantism itself began to lose its solid structure and to disintegrate into an established church and the sects. Preachers in the sects often had great fervor and no training. Preachers in the established church often had great training and no fervor. Congregations began to drift towards the sects. Thus the rhetoric of the tropes and figures, the rhetoric which had sought to say things in unusual ways in order to persuade, found itself failing to convince the people that religious belief was a serious matter. Thus preachers in the established church began to question the elaborate rhetoric of style, as Fénelon questioned it in seventeenth-century France and as Glanvill did in seventeenth-century England. And out of their questioning emerged a new theory of communication as between preacher and layman, quite harmonious in its basic purpose with the new political rhetoric and the new logic of the learned world.

CHAPTER 2

Scholastic Logic

I. Thomas Wilson's *Rule of Reason*

THE first logic that Englishmen could read in their own native language was "Imprinted at London by Richard Grafton, printer to the Kynges Maiestie" in the year 1551, and bore the title, *The rule of Reason, conteinyng the Arte of Logique, set forth in Englishe*. Its author, Thomas Wilson, was well prepared for his pioneering task. He had taken his degree as bachelor of arts at King's College, Cambridge, in 1545-46, and had studied Greek under Sir John Cheke of King's on his way to the master's degree conferred upon him in 1549. Since the first edition of the *Rule of Reason* appeared only three years after he took the latter degree, the work was probably in the process of composition during his maturer years at Cambridge. He implies as much, at any rate, in the prefatory letter which dedicates the *Rule of Reason* to his sovereign, the young king Edward VI. There he refers to his work as "parte of suche fruictes as haue growne in a poore studentes gardin."[1] So far as the *Rule of Reason* is concerned, those fruits were the harvest of Wilson's logical studies at Cambridge and of his reading of the six treatises that make up what has been called since the fifteenth century the *Organon* of Aristotle.[2] Wilson's ability in Greek was later shown in his translation of seven orations of Demosthenes, which, as the earliest English version of that author, is deemed to have attained "a high level of scholarship."[3] The *Rule of Reason*

[1] *Rule of Reason* (London, 1551), sig. A2v.
[2] These six treatises are usually given the following Latin and English titles: 1) *Categoriae*, that is *The Categories* (or *The Predicaments*); 2) *De Interpretatione* or *Perihermeniae*, that is, *On Interpretation*; 3) *Analytica Priora*, that is, *The Prior Analytics* (or *Concerning Syllogism*); 4) *Analytica Posteriora*, that is, *The Posterior Analytics* (or *Concerning Demonstration*); 5) *Topica*, that is, *The Topics*; and 6) *De Sophisticis Elenchis*, that is, *The Sophistical Elenchi*. Excellent translations of these treatises are to be found in *The Works of Aristotle Translated into English*, ed. W. D. Ross (Oxford, 1928), 1. See also Octavius Freire Owen, *The Organon, or Logical Treatises, of Aristotle. With the Introduction of Porphyry. Literally Translated, with Notes, Syllogistic Examples, Analysis, and Introduction* (Bohn's Classical Library, London, 1853).
[3] *Dictionary of National Biography*, s.v. Wilson, Thomas (1525?-1581). This translation of Demosthenes bears the following title and colophon: "The three Orations of Demosthenes chiefe Orator among the Grecians, in fauour of the Olynthians, a people in Thracia, novv called Romania: with those his fovver Orations titled expressely & by name against king Philip of Macedonie . . . By Thomas Wylson Doctor of the ciuill lavves. Imprinted at London by Henrie Denham . . . Anno Domini 1570."

is not a translation of Aristotle's *Organon*. But it is an attempt to render into English the main concepts and terms of the *Organon*, as those concepts and terms had come to be understood in the Renaissance; and it too is of good quality as a work of learning.

Richard Grafton, the printer of the *Rule of Reason*, was one of those who sought to encourage Wilson in writing it. Grafton had previously interested himself in such pioneering ventures as the distribution of Coverdale's English Bible and the publication of the first Book of Common Prayer.[4] Wilson himself mentions in the dedicatory epistle of the *Rule of Reason* that Grafton had not only provoked him to create an English logic, but had done him services during his student days and at various later times.

That dedicatory epistle is full of the elation of the man who sees himself as the founder of a tradition. My work, he tells the king, represents an attempt "to ioyne an acquaintaunce betwiene Logique, and my countrymen, from the whiche they haue bene hetherto barred, by tongues unacquaynted."[5] He wants the king to respect his labor in bringing so noble a mystery into so noble a country. He stresses, however, that he does not regard himself as a cunning logician; "but because no Englishman untill now hath gone through with this enterprise, I haue thought mete to declare that it maie be done." He adds: "And yet herein I professe to be but as a spurre or a whet stone, to sharpe the pennes of someother, that they may polishe, and perfect, that I haue rudely and grossely entered."[6]

Earlier in the letter he speaks of the effect he hopes his treatise will have, and he lays stress upon his patriotic motive:

This fruict being of a straunge kynde (such as no Englishe grounde hath before this time, and in this sorte by any tyllage brought forth,) maie perhaps at the first tasting, seme somewhat rough, and harshe in the mouth, because of the straungenesse: but after a litle use, and familiar accustomyng thereunto, I doubt not but thesame wil waxe euery one daie more pleasaunt then other. But in simple and plaine woordes to declare unto your Maiestie, wherein my witt and earnest endeuour hath at this season trauailed: I haue assaied through my diligence to make Logique as familiar to Thenglishe man, as by diuerse mennes industries the most parte of the other the liberall Sciences are.[7]

---

[4] *Dictionary of National Biography*, s.v. Grafton, Richard (d. 1572?).
[5] *Rule of Reason*, sig. A3v-A4r.   [6] *Ibid.*, sig. A4v.
[7] *Ibid.*, sig. A2v-A3r.

The liberal sciences were, of course, the seven liberal arts, within which early Renaissance learning was enclosed, so far as most of the formal curriculum of school and university was concerned. Shortly after Wilson begins to expound logic, he interrupts himself for a moment to insert what he calls "A brief declaration in meter, of the vii, liberal artes, vvherin Logique is comprehended as one of theim," and these verses are of interest as showing the stress placed upon the mastery of communication in the educational program of the sixteenth century:

> Grammer dothe teache to vtter vvordes.
> To speake bothe apt and playne,
> Logique by art settes furth the truth,
> And doth tel vs vvhat is vayne.
> Rethorique at large paintes vvel the cause,
> And makes that seme right gay,
> Vvhiche Logique spake but at a vvorde,
> And taught as by the vvay.
> Musicke vvith tunes, delites the eare,
> And makes vs thinke it heauen,
> Arithmetique by number can make
> Reconinges to be eauen.
> Geometry thinges thicke and brode,
> Measures by Line and Square,
> Astronomy by sterres doth tel,
> Of foule and else of fayre.[8]

Perhaps Wilson has a figurative intention in assigning two lines of these verses to each one of the liberal arts except rhetoric, which in tribute to its largeness of wordage is given four. At any rate, when he comes soon after to speak of the accepted difference between logical and rhetorical discourse, he makes the two disagree only in respect to economy of words. He observes:

Bothe these Artes are much like sauing that Logique is occupied aboute all matters, and doeth playnly and nakedly setfurthe with apt wordes the summe of thinges by the way of Argumentacion. Againe of the other side Rethorique useth gay painted Sentences, and setteth furth those matters with fresh colours and goodly ornamentes, and that at large. Insomuche, that Zeno beyng asked the difference betwene Logique and Rethorique, made answere by Demonstration of

[8] *Ibid.*, sig. B2r.

his Hande, declaring that when his hande was closed, it resembled Logique, when it was open and stretched out, it was like Rethorique.[9]

Scholastic logic as a system of precepts for the teaching of learned communication had come during the sixteenth century to divide itself into two procedures, one of which was called invention and the other, judgment or disposition. Invention, or *inventio* as it was expressed in Latin, consisted of the methods by which debatable propositions could be analyzed to determine what could be said for or against them. Judgment or disposition, termed *iudicium* in Latin, consisted in methods of arranging words into propositions, propositions into syllogisms or inductions, and syllogisms or inductions into whole discourses. Taken together, these two procedures constituted a machinery of analysis and synthesis on the level of language—a machinery for assembling materials to prove the truth of an assertion and for combining those materials into complex discourses. Actually these two procedures are the organizing principle of Aristotle's *Topics*, where seven books are devoted to the processes of analyzing dialectical propositions, and the eighth book, to the process of combining and using them. The same two procedures, with invention again outranking disposition in the amount of space assigned to it, were the structural members of Cicero's *Topics*, the treatise which the Roman orator intended as a digest of Aristotle's similar work.[10] Boethius also recognized these procedures in his *De Differentiis Topicis* as the two parts of ancient Aristotelian logic.[11] Thereafter, examples of this particular interpretation of Aristotle and Cicero are a common feature of logical theory. Hugh of St. Victor and John of Salisbury conceive of logic as having these two parts,[12] and their opinions were in turn widely respected by later scholastics.

But so far as Thomas Wilson's generation is concerned, the chief authority for this bipartite division of logic was Rudolph Agricola.

[9] *Ibid.*, sig. B3r-B3v. The comparison of dialectic to the closed fist and rhetoric to the open hand was attributed to Zeno of Citium, founder of Stoicism, by Cicero (*Orator*, 32.113, and *De Finibus*, 2.6.17), and later by Quintilian (*Institutio Oratoria*, 2.20.7) and by Sextus Empiricus (*Adversus Mathematicos*, 2.7). For a discussion of various appearances of this analogy in the Renaissance, see Wilbur S. Howell, "Nathaniel Carpenter's Place in the Controversy between Dialectic and Rhetoric," *Speech Monographs*, I (1934), 20-41.

[10] Cicero, *Topics*, §§ 1-8.

[11] For a convenient reprint of this work of Boethius, see J.-P. Migne, *Patrologia Latina* (Paris, 1844-1905), LXIV, 1173. Boethius's words are: "Omnis ratio disserendi, quam logicen Peripatetici veteres appellavere, in duas distribuitur partes, unam inveniendi, alteram judicandi."

[12] See Charles Sears Baldwin, *Medieval Rhetoric and Poetic* (New York, 1928), pp. 154, 156 note 16, 164.

Agricola, who lived between 1443 and 1485, was professor of philosophy at Heidelberg in his later years. According to his biographers, he saw Erasmus when the latter was only ten years of age, and
he predicted the child's future greatness.[13] Agricola is considered a
major figure in the learned world of the early Renaissance. His most
influential work, written during the fourteen-seventies or eighties, is
called *De Inventione Dialectica*. It stresses invention and judgment
as the two parts of logic;[14] it follows Aristotle and Cicero in preferring invention to judgment as the subject for detailed and systematic treatment; and it certainly was instrumental in inducing
logicians of the sixteenth century to adopt Aristotle's *Topics* rather
than other treatises of the *Organon* as guide to the main divisions of
logical theory. Wilson is merely reflecting the influence of Agricola
when he begins his *Rule of Reason* with the following definitions of
the two parts of logic:

> The first parte standeth in framing of thinges aptlye together, in knit-
> ting woordes, for the purpose accordingly, and in Latin is called
> *Iudicium*. The second parte consisteth in finding out matter, and
> searching stuffe agreable to the cause, and in Latine is called *Inuentio*.[15]

Cicero's *Topics*, as an authoritative Latin interpretation of Aristotle's parallel treatise, was of course a work on dialectic rather than
logic. In Aristotle's *Organon*, dialectic is that branch of logic which
"reasons from opinions that are generally accepted"[16] in matters
where strict scientific demonstration is not applicable as an instrument in the quest for truth. In other words, Aristotle made dialectic
a kind of logic of opinion, whereas rigid demonstration was the logic
of science. But of course the method used in determining what the
best opinion may be in a given case resembled the method used in

[13] *Biographie Universelle, Ancienne et Moderne*, s.v. Agricola, Rodolphe; *Nouvelle Biographie Générale*, s.v. Agricola, Rodophe.

[14] See *Rodolphi Agricolae Phrisij, de inuentione dialectica libri tres, cum scholijs Ioannis Matthaei Phrissemij* (Parisiis: Apud Simonem Colinaeum, 1538), pp. 7, 93, 149, 391-392. This work was published many times at continental presses during the six-teenth century. A copy of one of the earliest editions, *Rodolphi Agricole Phrisij Dialec-tica* (Louanii: In aedibus T. Martini, 1515), is at the British Museum. Other editions appeared at the following places: Cologne, 1518, 1520, 1523, 1527, 1528, 1535, 1538, 1539, 1542, 1543, 1548, 1552, 1557, 1563, 1570, 1579; Strasbourg, 1521; Paris, 1529, 1533, 1534, 1535, 1538, 1542, 1554, 1558; Venice, 1559. An Italian version was pub-lished at Venice in 1567.

[15] *Rule of Reason*, sig. B1r.

[16] Aristotle, *Topica*, 100ᵃ 30. Translation by W. A. Pickard-Cambridge in *The Works of Aristotle*, ed. Ross, 1. For an instructive account of Aristotle's distinction be-tween logic and dialectic, see Owen, *The Organon*, 11, 357-359.

determining truth in science, and thus dialectic and logic were differentiated by Aristotle rather in field of application than in basic internal structure. To scholastic logic, however, this Aristotelian distinction between dialectic and logic tended to vanish altogether, especially among those logicians who made logic consist of the procedures of invention and judgment as anciently assigned to dialectic. Thus it is not surprising that Wilson identifies dialectic with logic. He does this, not as one who considered the identification a matter of controversy in the learned world, but as one who considered the identification acceptable to everyone. In fact, he does it in an aside, when he is discoursing upon the distinction between logic and sophistry:

> Logique otherwise called Dialecte (for they are bothe one) is an Arte to try the corne from the chaffe, the truthe from euery falshed, by defining the nature of any thing, by diuiding the same, and also by knitting together true Argumentes and untwining all knotty Subtiltees that are bothe false, and wrongfully framed together.[17]

The next major topic in Wilson's *Rule of Reason*, and a major topic in the whole corpus of scholastic logic, is that of the predicables, otherwise called "the fiue common words."[18] These five common words are terms for the five predicates that propositions have, not in a grammatical but in a scientific sense. That is to say, any statement qualifies for admission into learning when it can be classified as a statement of genus, of species, of difference, of property, or of accident. A statement that cannot be so classified may be true and helpful, but it is not a proper scientific statement, and thus it cannot be given status in the world of science.

These five terms are probably as unfamiliar to the modern mind as they were in Wilson's day to Englishmen who knew no Latin. But Latin scholars of the sixteenth century would have recognized these five words as a development of four of the main terms in Aristotle's *Topics*. All dialectical propositions, in Aristotle's view, are propositions of accident, of genus, of property, or of definition. Since definition involves mention of the differences between the thing being defined and other species of the same genus,[19] we can see how Aristotle's four terms are in reality as comprehensive as the five predicables of scholastic logic. Aristotle makes these four kinds of propositions the four heads of his treatment of dialectical invention, accident

[17] *Rule of Reason*, sig. B2v. [18] *Ibid.*, sig. B4r.
[19] Aristotle, *Topica*, VI. 1, 5-6.

being the subject of Books II and III of the *Topics*, genus of Book IV, property of Book V, and definition of Books VI and VII. The scholastic logicians made their five parallel terms a part of the treatment of dialectical judgment, not invention, although they also recognized the importance of the predicables as a background for the discovery of subject matter.[20]

Wilson's enumeration of the seven places of invention inhering in the substance or nature of things involves four of the concepts previously discussed by him as predicables, and thus he too suggests that the predicables belong under invention as well as under judgment. But primarily, he thinks, "they are good to iudge the knitting of wordes, and to se what thing may truely be ioyned to other, for there is no Proposition, nor yet ioining together of any sentence (accordyng to the common order of nature) but they alwayes agre to these aboue rehersed Predicables."[21] Moreover, they may be used to separate permanently true from occasionally true propositions. If a proposition joins a species to its genus, and states how the species differs from the genus, and what property the species has, and these steps are correctly taken, the proposition is permanently true. Wilson's own words are as follows:

> Therfore when a proposition is made from the kynde, to the general, to his difference, or propertie: it is euermore an undoubted true proposition, as this. *Homo est animal ratione praeditum, loquendi facultatem habens.* A man is a liuing creature endewed with reason, hauing aptnesse by nature to speake.[22]

Here a species (man) is properly associated with its genus (animal), and is then properly differentiated from other members of that genus by a differentia (the gift of reason), and is finally given a true property (the aptness to speak). If, however, a proposition associates a species with an accident, as in the statement, *homo est albus* (some men are white), the proposition will not be true of all men, or it may not be true of a white man at all times. "Therfore," concludes Wilson, "it is good to be knowen, when you haue a Proposition, whether it be undoubted true, for euermore, or els maye be false at any tyme."[23]

Another major topic in Wilson's *Rule of Reason*, as in scholastic logic as a whole, is that of the categories or, as they were oftener

[20] See below, pp. 26-27, 53.
[22] *Ibid.*, sig. C3r.
[21] *Rule of Reason*, sig. C2v.
[23] *Ibid.*, sig. C3r-C3v.

called, the predicaments. These are the subject of Aristotle's *Categories*, which is ordinarily made the first treatise in the *Organon*. The question of the precise meaning of these categories, as Aristotle discusses them, has occasioned much difference of opinion among his many interpreters.[24] Wilson's view, however, is basically representative of that of his age. He calls the categories or predicaments "general wordes," as opposed to the five predicables, or "common wordes." The difference between the latter and the former, he says, is "that the Predicables, set forth the largenesse of wordes," whereas "the Predicamentes do name the verey nature of thynges, declaryng (and that substantially) what they are in very deede."[25] Thus the predicables may be described as those words which define and delimit the boundaries of scientific statements; the predicaments, as those words which name the possible scientific conceptions men may have as to the nature of reality. In other words, if a statement gains admission into science only when its predicate declares the genus, the species, the difference, the property, or the accident of its subject, then a concept gains admission into science only when it is a concept belonging under one of the basic aspects of things.

Substance and accident are the two great categories or predicaments, in Wilson's view. A concept of substance is a concept of a thing as having about it something absolutely essential to its being or nature—something without which that thing could not be what it is. A concept of accident, on the other hand, is a concept of a thing as having about it something always or usually associated with it, but not absolutely essential to its being or nature. Concepts of accident are nine in number. These nine, added to the concept of substance, make up the ten predicaments of scholastic logic, and these ten are of course equivalent to the famous ten categories analyzed in the first treatise of Aristotle's *Organon*. Wilson gives these ten categories their familiar Latin terms and his own experimental and tentative English terms, as follows:

1.	Substantia.	The Substance.
2.	Quantitas.	The Quantite.
3.	Qualitas.	The Qualitee.
4.	Relatiua	The Relacion.
5.	Actio.	The maner of doing.
6.	Passio.	The Suffring.

[24] For an instructive note on this problem, see Owen, *The Organon*, I, 1.
[25] *Rule of Reason*, sig. C4v.

7.	Quando.	When.
8.	Vbi.	Where.
9.	Situs.	The Settelling.
10.	Habitus.	The appareiling.[26]

Although scholastic logic is content to treat the ten predicaments as only in part definable, and thus as never susceptible of precise verbal analysis, a few illustrative comments may help to reveal their general function. We might say that the category of substance contains a concept of the substance of each thing known or knowable—that it acts as a repository of man's knowledge about the substance of all things. "As for an example," says Wilson, "if ye will knowe what a man is, you must haue recourse to the place of *substantia*, and there ye shall learne by the same place that man is a liuyng creature endued with reason."[27] Again, the category of quality contains the concepts of the qualities of each thing known or knowable. The quality of virtue in men, for example, is "a constant habite of the mind, makyng them praise worthye in whom it is."[28] Still again, the category of relation contains the concepts of relations of things to things. If you visit this category, it will tell you, among other items, that "he is a father, that hath a sonne, he is a maister, that hath a seruaunt, and so forthe in the reaste."[29] The business of science is to store these categories with concepts, as things are studied, and their substance and their accidents are discovered and catalogued. The business of a particular science is to study things properly belonging to it, and to ascertain about those particular things what concepts of substance and of accident are truly applicable. The business of logic is in part to decide the total number of categories to be used in classifying all concepts, as a librarian might decide the total number of terms to be used in classifying by subject all books under his jurisdiction. "Therfore," observes Wilson, with the young logician in mind, "ye muste nedes haue these Predicamentes readye, that whan so euer ye wyll define any worde, or geue a natural name unto it, ye may come to this store house, and take stuffe at wyll."[30] To put the matter in another way, there is a general vocabulary throughout the world of learning, over and above the particular vocabulary of a given science, and that general vocabulary must be mastered before the world of learning can be known, as that vocabulary must be used if a specialist in one field is to communicate with a specialist in an-

[26] *Ibid.*, sig. C5v.   [27] *Ibid.*, sig. D7r.   [28] *Ibid.*, sig. D7r.
[29] *Ibid.*, sig. D7r.   [30] *Ibid.*, sig. D7r.

other. The ten categories were the key terms in that vocabulary. Taken with the five common words, or predicables, they constituted in scholastic logic a kind of basic English of the intellectual world— a vocabulary for scientific communication incorporated into the theory of scientific communication.

Another major topic in scholastic logic and in Wilson's *Rule of Reason* is that of definition and division. This requires little explanation, since those processes, as understood then, are known by the same terms today. Wilson's summary of the two processes is as good as any. He says: "As a definition therfore dothe declare what a thyng is, so the diuision sheweth howe many thynges are contayned in the same."[31] The fundamental necessity of these two processes in dialectic had been remarked by Plato.[32] Wilson mentions this Platonic requirement as he prepares to make the statement just quoted.

Method was to become an important concept in Ramus's reform of scholastic logic, as we shall see in Chapter 4. But of course that concept, less fully developed than in Ramus, was a part of the tradition that he labored to change. Like other expounders of the tradition, Wilson devotes some space to method, apparently with the first chapter of the second book of *The Posterior Analytics* in mind, where Aristotle discusses the four forms of inquiry. To Wilson, method is "the maner of handeling a single Question, and the readie waie howe to teache and sette forth any thyng plainlie, and in order, asit'should be, in latine *Methodus*."[33] Aristotle's obscure and condensed version of the four forms of inquiry becomes in Wilson a clear but possibly redundant discussion of eight forms, even as Cicero's *Topics*, through a process of developing Aristotle's implications, yields five forms of general inquiry and three forms of finite inquiry.[34] Wilson's program is indicated by saying that things are to be examined by inquiring into their existence, their nature, their parts, their causes, their effects, their concomitants, their opposites, and their witnesses.[35] In covering the actual manner of setting forth the results of an examination, Wilson briefly advises that exposition should begin with the general and descend to the parts, as Cicero had done in *De Officiis* and as Aristotle had done in the *Ethics*. Thus

[31] *Ibid.*, sig. E1v.
[32] In *Phaedrus*, 265-266; see Lane Cooper, *Plato Phaedrus, Ion, Gorgias, and Symposium, with passages from the Republic and Laws Translated into English* (London, New York, Toronto, 1938), pp. 53-54.
[33] *Rule of Reason*, sig. E4v.   [34] Cicero, *Topics*, §§ 79-91.
[35] *Rule of Reason*, sig. E4v-E6r.

Wilson discusses method by identifying it in part with dialectical arrangement and in part with dialectical invention—an emphasis that Ramus modified by limiting method to arrangement alone.

Wilson's next topic is the proposition. His discussion of this element of logic follows Aristotle's *De Interpretatione* in substance and the scholastic logicians in terminology and form of presentation. He defines a proposition as "a perfite sentence spoken by the Indicatiue mode, signifiyng either a trewe thyng, or a false, without al ambiguitie, or doubtfulness. As thus, ewery man is a liar."[36] He next proceeds to speak of the logical subject and predicate of a proposition. Then he treats of the various kinds of propositions (general, particular, indefinite, singular); then of opposition among propositions; then of categorical and hypothetical propositions, and of the kinds of conversion or of reversal of subject and predicate.

The topic of argument brings to a close Wilson's discussion of judgment as the initial procedure of logic. "An argument," he says, "is a waie to proue how one thyng is gathered by another, and to shewe that thyng, whiche is doubtfull, by that whiche is not doubtfull."[37] Four kinds of argument are then distinguished by him, and the Latin terms which he uses indicate that the English vocabulary had not yet learned to speak of them with ease. The first kind Wilson calls *Syllogismus*; the second, *Enthymema*; the third, *Inductio* or Induction; and the fourth, *Exemplum* or Example. This part of scholastic logic is based in Wilson and elsewhere upon the two books of Aristotle's *Prior Analytics*. Wilson would have been less than human if in this honored subject matter he had been more than traditional. He speaks of the parts and terms of the syllogism, and in calling the middle term "the double repete," the major term "the term at large," and the minor term "the several term," he reminds us again that he is blazing a trail through a new land, without having found in these instances at least the path that later generations of Englishmen will follow. He calls the enthymeme the half argument, and thinks of it as a syllogism with one of its three propositions missing. His conception of induction is not so much improper as restricted. He says:

An Induction, is a kynde of Argument when we gather sufficiently a nombre of propre names, and there upon make the conclusion uniuersall, as thus.

[36] *Ibid.*, sig. E7r.   [37] *Ibid.*, sig. F6v.

Rhenyshe wine heateth,
Maluesey heateth,
Frenchewine heateth, neither is there any wyne that doth the
    contrary:
Ergo all wine heateth.[38]

Similar to induction is example. "An example," he says, "is a maner
of Argumentation, where one thyng is proued by an other, for the
likenes, that is found to be in them both. . . ."[39] And he illustrates
this form as follows:

> If Marcus Attilius Regulus had rather lose his life, then not kepe
> promise with his enemie, then shoulde euery man beyng taken prisoner
> kepe promise with his enemy.

Having finished with example, Wilson brings his discussion of
argument to a close with a mention of the sorites and the dilemma
as special forms of the syllogism and with an exposition of five rules
for the knitting together of propositions.

His next topic is "the second part of Logique, called Inuentio, that
is to saie, the fyndyng out of an argument."[40] Invention, as one of
the two main procedures in the process of composing a learned discourse, involves a plan for the systematic discovery of subject matter.
If it be suggested at this point that the discovery of subject matter
normally precedes its arrangement, and thus that invention as a
topic in logic ought normally to precede rather than follow disposition or judgment, the reply is that the same line of reasoning occurred to Wilson and the other scholastic logicians, even though they
usually treated judgment first. Wilson justifies himself for placing
judgment before invention by saying that you have to know how to
order an argument before you seek for it, and that anyway "a reason
is easlier found then fashioned."[41] This attitude is a significant phenomenon in intellectual history. It really is a way of saying that
subject matter presents fewer difficulties than organization, so far as
composition is concerned. A society which takes such an attitude must
be by implication a society that is satisfied with its traditional wisdom
and knows where to find it. It must be a society that does not stress
the virtues of an exhaustive examination of nature so much as the
virtues of clarity in form. No guilt should be attached to either of
these tendencies. Each is of value, and each is with us at any moment

[38] *Ibid.*, sig. H5v.   [39] *Ibid.*, sig. H6v.   [40] *Ibid.*, sig. J4v.
[41] *Ibid.*, sig. B1v.

of time, guarding us against the excesses of the other. But the great shift which occurred in men's thinking between 1500 and 1700 was in part a shift from the preponderant emphasis upon traditional wisdom to the preponderant emphasis upon new discoveries, and this shift is nowhere better illustrated than in the transition from Wilson's belief in the relative ease of discovery to the modern belief in its relative difficulty.

Invention in scholastic logic was a process in which an author found subject matter by connecting his mind with the traditional wisdom of his race and by allowing that contact to induce a flow of ideas from the general store into himself. This process involved his knowing what were called "the places." Nowhere is scholastic logic more attractive than in Wilson's definition of a place, and he deserves to be quoted at some length on this point:

> A Place is the restyng corner of an argument, or els a marke whiche giueth warnyng to our memory what we maie speake probablie, either in one parte, or the other, upon all causes that fall in question. Those that be good hare finders will sone finde the hare by her fourme. For when they se the grounde beaten flatte round aboute, and faire to the sight: thei haue a narrow gesse by al likelihod that the hare was there a litle before. Likewyse the hontesman in huntyng the foxe, wil sone espie when he seeth a hole, whether it be a foxe borough, or not. So he that will take profite in this parte of logique, must be like a hunter, and learne by labour to knowe the boroughes. For these places be nothyng els but couertes or boroughes, wherein if any one searche diligentlie, he maie fynde game at pleasure. And although perhappes one place fayle him, yet shal he finde a dousen other places, to accomplishe his purpose. Therfore if any one will do good in this kynde, he must go from place to place, and by serching euery borough, he shall haue his purpose undoubtedlie in moste part of them if not in all.[42]

The great source for all speculation about the places, so far as scholastic logic is concerned, is Aristotle's *Topics*, although Cicero's similar work, which condenses and systematizes Aristotle, provides a Latin terminology that had great influence upon Boethius and the scholastics.[43] Cicero classifies the places of logic as intrinsic and ex-

[42] *Ibid.*, sig. J5v-J6r.

[43] Boethius wrote extensively upon Aristotelian logic. He commented upon the entire *Organon: The Categories, On Interpretation, Prior Analytics, Posterior Analytics, Topics,* and *Sophistical Elenchi.* He also commented upon Porphyry's comment upon Aristotle, and he wrote a commentary in six books on Cicero's *Topics.* The logical writings of Boethius are conveniently collected in Migne, *Patrologia Latina,* LXIV, 9-1216.

trinsic. Under the former head he evolves a final list of sixteen distinct places, whereas under the latter he speaks only of argument from authority, this entire head being devoted to what were called non-artistic proofs, or proofs not invented by recourse to the places.[44] Wilson's procedure in respect to the classification of the places illustrates both the sacrosanctity and the flexibility of this branch of learning. Wilson follows Cicero in designating two great groups of places, the inward and the outward. He follows Cicero in respect to the terms used and the functions assigned to many of the actual places described in these groups. But he does not follow Cicero's limiting of the places to sixteen, or Cicero's allotting of them all to the first of the two great headings.[45]

We are fortunate in having from Wilson's first English logic a concrete demonstration of the way in which the places were envisaged as useful in the religious controversies of the time. Wilson poses the question whether it be lawful for a priest to have a wife or no. He undertakes to examine this question by taking the two key words "priest" and "wife" to the places, and by seeing whether the conclusions obtained from the places in respect to one of these words agree with the conclusions obtained in respect to the other. His assumption is that where there is agreement between the conclusions reached in the case of priest and the conclusions reached in the case of wife, then to that extent the proposition that it is lawful for a priest to have a wife is good. Where there is disagreement, of course, the proposition is not good. Wilson's own description of this assumption is as follows:

> For where as the places agree (that is to saie, al thinges are referred to yᵉ one, that are referred to the other) there the proposition is good, and the latter part of the proposition, is truly spoken of the first. But where the places do not agree (that is to saie, some thynges are referred to the one worde, that are not referred to the other) there the thynges themselues cannot agree.[46]

Wilson's procedure is to examine priesthood within nineteen differ-

---

[44] Cicero, *Topics*, §§ 8-24.

[45] In the final analysis, Wilson would seem to allow fifteen places, although his first illustration of the use of the places as a system names exactly sixteen, and his second illustration names nineteen. In reality some of these nineteen are species of genera named among the original fifteen, and some of the original fifteen are dismissed as inapplicable to the second illustration. The first illustration concerns the word king; the second, the words priest and wife.

[46] At this point, I quote from the 1552 edition of *The rule of Reason*, fol. 114r.

ent places, such as that of definition, of genus, of species, of property, of whole, of parts, etc. Then he examines wifehood under the same aspects. Then he notes wherein there is agreement between the conclusions assembled for priesthood and for wifehood, and shows how these conclusions may yield arguments for and against the lawfulness of marriage among the clergy. Wilson's own conviction is that it is lawful for a priest to marry, and his discussion does not conceal that prejudice. Thus his machinery of analysis does not so much permit him to discover what attitude is right as to defend adequately the attitude that he had previously judged to be right.

A few samples of Wilson's analysis will show how he himself conceived of the actual use of the procedure of invention. His definition of priest is as follows:

> A Preacher is a clerke or shepeherd whiche wil geue his life for his shepe, enstructed to sette forth the kynddome of God, and desierouse to lyue vertuousely: a faithfull, and a wise steward whom the lord doth set ouer his house, that he maie geue the householde seruauntes meate, in due time.[47]

Wilson's definition of wife comes later, after the nineteen places have been visited for ideas about priests. That definition reads:

> A wife, is a woman that is lawfully receiued into the felouship of life, for ye encrease or gettyng of chyldren, and to auoide fornication.[48]

Wilson's use of these two definitions is indicated at the end of his examination of wifehood under the nineteen aspects. He says:

> Nowe that we haue drawen these wordes, the preacher, and the wife, after this sort, throughout the places, so far as we could: we shuld cōpare them together, and se wherein thei do agre, and wherein they varie. Let vs compare the definitions together, and we shal finde somwhat euen there, where these wordes be (desiryng to lyue vertuously) whiche shall geue light for an argument, as thus.

> Whosoeuer desireth to liue vertuously,
>   must mary a wyfe.
> Euery true preacher of Goddes word
>   desireth to liue vertuously
> Ergo euery true Preacher must mary a wife.[49]

Wilson indicates that if his adversary denies the major premise of this argument, the conclusion collapses unless some help can be found

---

[47] *Ibid.*, fol. 114r-114v.   [48] *Ibid.*, fol. 117r.   [49] *Ibid.*, fol. 119r.

in the definition of wife. That help is forthcoming in the statement that a wife is married for the increase of children, and for the avoidance of fornication. Thus Wilson confronts his adversary with a new argument:

> Whosoeuer desireth to liue vertuously,
> desireth to auoide fornication.
> Whosoeuer desireth to auoyde fornication,
> desireth mariage.
> Ergo whosoeuer desireth to lyue vertuously,
> desiereth mariage.[50]

Thus does Wilson illustrate the use of the place of definition in respect to the two words, priest and wife. He next illustrates the place of genus or "generall worde":

> Againe the generall worde of both these definitions geueth lyght for an argument. Euery wyfe is a woman, euery Preacher is a man, and nature hath ordeyned that man and woman may liue in mariage, (if they be so disposed) of what degre, cōdition, or state, so euer they be, nothyng in al the scriptures to the contrarye. Therfore I may reason thus.
>
> What soeuer is man, that same maie marie a woman by gods ordinaunce.
> Euery preacher is a man
> Ergo euery preacher maie marie a woman by gods ordinaunce.[51]

Three of the other places which figure in this illustration of the nature of logical invention are those of time, place, and "thynges annexed."[52] If these appear to be reminiscent of three of the ten predicaments discussed by Wilson as a major part of logical judgment, and if therefore invention and judgment as the two parts of scholastic logic begin to seem curiously redundant in subject matter, I can only reply that this tautology was perfectly obvious to the scholastic logicians themselves. Indeed, Wilson takes the trouble to point it out. He says as he analyzes the places of time, place, and things annexed:

> And these thre are nothing els, than the thre predicamentes or moste generall places, whiche I rehersed before.

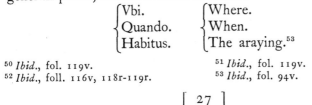

Vbi.	Where.
Quando.	When.
Habitus.	The araying.[53]

[50] *Ibid.*, fol. 119v. [51] *Ibid.*, fol. 119v.
[52] *Ibid.*, foll. 116v, 118r-119r. [53] *Ibid.*, fol. 94v.

But the acknowledgment that one main part of logic duplicated the other was not enough, as things turned out. The tautology had to be removed. And it was Ramus who attempted, as we shall see, to remove such tautologies as this, and to make invention and judgment nonoverlapping parts of logic.

The final topic in Wilson's system of logic is that of fallacies. He introduces it by summarizing what he had previously covered, and by adding:

> I wil frō hēce furth, set out the maner of deceiptfull argumentes, called in Latine, *Repraehensiones*, or *fallaces conclusiunculae*, euen as Aristotle hath set thē furth.[54]

These words are a reminder that this part of scholastic logic derives its materials from *The Sophistical Elenchi*, which is the sixth and final treatise in Aristotle's *Organon*. From that source Wilson selects for main emphasis the lore of the six types of deceitful arguments that depend on diction, and the seven that are independent of diction. His illustrations reflect the religious controversies of his time, not of Aristotle's. But he strikes a merry note at the end of his work by setting forth "to delite the reader" a series of witty fallacies "called trappyng argumētes." These he names as Crocodilites, Antistrephon, Ceratinae, Asistaton, Cacosistaton, Vtis, and Pseudomenos.[55]

The second of these, which means the turning of an argument back upon an opponent, is illustrated by Wilson from Aulus Gellius. According to Wilson, Gellius relates that Pythagoras gave lessons in eloquence to a young man named Euathlus.[56] The bargain between them was that Euathlus must give Pythagoras a great sum of money, half at the beginning of their association, and the other half when Euathlus won his first case in court as a result of his training under Pythagoras. It appears that Euathlus repeatedly postponed the day of that first case, and after a while Pythagoras brought suit against him for the other half of his fee. Pythagoras then went into court and his words to his opponent are quoted thus by Wilson:

> If thou art cast in the law, I haue wonne by vertue of the lawe: if thou art not cast, but gettest the ouerhande by iudgement of these

[54] *Ibid.*, fol. 123v.　　　　　[55] *Ibid.*, fol. 170r.

[56] See Aulus Gellius, *Noctes Atticae*, 5.10. In Gellius, however, the figures in this story are Protagoras and Euathlus. Diogenes Laertius, *De Vita et Moribus Philosophorum Libri X*, 9.56, also tells this story about Protagoras, but much more briefly than does Gellius. The same story is told with Corax, the inventor of the art of rhetoric, in place of Protagoras; see Sextus Empiricus, *Adversus Mathematicos*, 2.96-99.

men, yet muste I haue it neuerthelesse, because our bargain was so made, when I first began to teach the.[57]

This argument appeared to delight Euathlus. He pointed out to Pythagoras that he could escape from its toils by hiring an advocate to plead his case, whereupon he himself could not yet be charged with having legally incurred the obligation to pay the rest of the fee, if the verdict went in his favor. But he preferred, he said, to plead his own case, and he would do so by turning the argument of Pythagoras against him, and thus would escape from the debt altogether. Wilson quotes him as follows:

> For if you be cast in the law, I haue wonne by vertue of the lawe, & so I owe you nothyng. If you be not cast, but gette the ouerhand of me, by the iudgement of these mē: then according to my bargain, I shal pay you nothyng because I haue not gotten the ouerhād in iudgement.[58]

Wilson observes that the young scholar in this instance gave his master a bone to gnaw, and beat him with his own rod. For the judges, fearing to decide one way or the other, postponed the case to another time.

Now that the *Rule of Reason* has been discussed in full, our next task is to comment upon its antecedents. These will constitute a kind of history of scholastic logic in England from the time of its earliest formulation by an Englishman to the time of Wilson's vernacular treatise. As we leave the *Rule of Reason*, we might remark that it enjoyed a considerable success for about thirty years after the date of its first edition in 1551—as indication that Grafton, the printer, had correctly diagnosed public reaction when he initially urged Wilson to prepare it for publication. It was reprinted in 1552, 1553, 1563, 1567, and 1580. Thereafter it apparently ceased to command public interest, and it has never received further editions. Traces of it can be found in Thomas Blundeville's *The Arte of Logicke*, published in 1599, itself an attempt to teach logic to Englishmen who knew no Latin. But Blundeville, as we shall see later, apparently does not feel it an advantage to acknowledge his borrowings from Wilson.[59] The chief reason why Wilson lost favor rapidly after 1567 is that Ramistic logic made its appearance in England in the fifteen-seventies and ended the reign of scholastic logic as we see it in Wilson

---

[57] *Rule of Reason* (1552), fol. 172r.   [58] *Ibid.*, fol. 172v.
[59] See below, p. 288.

and his predecessors. When the inevitable reaction set in against Ramus, as we see it setting in with Blundeville, logicians did not then go back to Wilson's generation for their inspiration, since even anti-Ramists could not deny the validity of some of Ramus's criticisms of scholastic logic. Thus the *Rule of Reason* did not long survive after Wilson's death, which occurred in 1581. But by virtue of its position as the first logic to be written in English, it will always have an honorable place in the intellectual history of the Anglo-Saxons.

A last interesting fact about the *Rule of Reason* should be mentioned in closing this account of it. As it gained new material in the editions that followed the first, it acquired something on one occasion to give it a special interest to later historians of the English drama. That occasion came as a result of the edition of 1553. There, in connection with his discussion of the fallacy of ambiguity, which is the second of the six types of deceitful argument depending on diction, Wilson adds to the three old illustrations in the earlier editions a remarkable new one in the form of a 35-line quotation which he identifies as from "an entrelude made by Nicolas Vdal."[60] This quotation is an address to a "maistresse Custaûce" by one "Roisterdoister," which, read according to one system of punctuation, has highly derogatory implications for the lady in question, and, read according to another system, highly complimentary implications. For almost three hundred years after the date of that edition of the *Rule of Reason*, it was commonly accepted that Wilson's 35-line quotation from an interlude by Udall represented the only specimen of Udall's dramatic works to have been preserved.[61] But in 1818 a printed copy of an anonymous old play was discovered and presented to Eton College, the school where Thomas Wilson had prepared for Cambridge. Also in 1818 that old play was given a new edition under the title, *Ralph Royster Doyster*.[62] It was not long until scholars became

[60] Wilson's 35-line quotation appears at foll. 67r-68r of the 1563 and the 1567 editions of the *Rule of Reason*. It appears in the 1553 edition at sig. S2v, according to Walter Wilson Greg in the Malone Society reprint of *Roister Doister* (Printed for the Malone Society by John Johnson at the Oxford University Press, 1934 [1935]), p. v. I have not seen the 1553 edition.

[61] For a typical expression of this view, see Anthony à Wood, *Athenae Oxonienses*, ed. Philip Bliss (London, 1813-1820), I, 213-214.

[62] For a convenient summary of the bibliographical history of this play, see Nicholas Udall, *Roister Doister*, ed. Edward Arber (English Reprints, Vol. XVII, London, 1869), p. 8. This summary by Arber accepts John Payne Collier as rightful claimant to the honor of being the first to connect Wilson's quotation with the letter to Mistress Custance in *Ralph Royster Doyster*. William Durrant Cooper, *Ralph Roister Doister, A*

aware that the 35-line illustration of ambiguity in Wilson's *Rule of Reason* was in fact a quotation from the anonymous old play, *Ralph Royster Doyster*, and that, since Wilson had attributed his quotation to Nicholas Udall, the anonymous old play must be one of Udall's lost dramas. Thus did scholarship give real substance to what had been the shadowy dramatic reputation of Udall; thus was the now-famous early comedy given an author in the person of a man solidly distinguished in other fields. And the means to this happy end was Thomas Wilson's English logic. Incidentally, the 35-line quotation in Wilson is the letter which in the Udall play Royster Doyster had had a scrivener write for him as part of his campaign to become the husband of Mistress Custance. As interpreted by the scrivener, the letter complimented Mistress Custance in terms at once fulsome and persuasive; but as read by Mathew Merygreeke to the lady herself, it was derogatory if not slanderous.[63] The words were the same in each case. The meaning, as in poetry in general, changed with the character and environment of the reader.

Comedy, By Nicholas Udall. And The Tragedie of Gorboduc (London, Printed for the Shakespeare Society, 1847), p. vi, also supports Collier's claim. Later opinion is less indulgent to Collier; see "Roister Doister," ed. Ewald Flügel, in *Representative English Comedies*, ed. Charles Mills Gayley (New York, 1903-1914), I, 97-98.

[63] The scrivener's letter appears in *Ralph Royster Doyster*, Act III, Scenes 4 & 5. (In the Malone Society reprint, lines 1074-1108 and 1239-1273.)

II. Backgrounds of Scholasticism

SEVEN and a half centuries before the date of Thomas Wilson's translation of scholastic logic into native English speech, another Englishman, whose name was Alcuin, wrote a treatise on dialectic in Latin, thus becoming the first English logician of record. That treatise, formally entitled *De Dialectica*, was composed in France, probably about the year 794, as part of Alcuin's campaign to build an educational system throughout the empire of his patron and friend Charlemagne.[1] It was Charlemagne who had in the first instance invited Alcuin to come to France in the capacity of a kind of minister of education. It was Charlemagne who took an active interest in Alcuin's efforts to establish in France a learning that would suit the needs of the Frankish pulpit, law court, and imperial administration. It was Charlemagne who lent his own great prestige to the cause of letters by allowing Alcuin on occasion to present treatises in which learned doctrine was arranged in the form of a dialogue between the emperor himself and the English scholar. One treatise so presented by Alcuin is on rhetoric, and it will be discussed later as the earliest full treatment of Ciceronian rhetoric by an Englishman. Alcuin's *De Dialectica* is another treatise so presented, and it serves to begin our present discussion of English logic.

When Alcuin took up his residence at the court of Charlemagne, he was about forty-seven years of age, and already distinguished as the most learned Englishman since Bede. Alcuin was born in 735, the year of Bede's death, and was educated at York in a school established by Egbert, one of Bede's pupils. That school enjoyed an immense prestige during the eighth century. Professor Laistner has said of it that, for nearly fifty years after its founding, it was "the leading home of culture in western Europe."[2] The fact that it was founded by one of Bede's pupils is enough to account for its early fame; and Alcuin's connection with it as student, teacher, and librarian is enough to explain its fame during the years of his own

---

[1] The most convenient edition of Alcuin's *De Dialectica* is that in Migne, *Patrologia Latina*, CI, 951-976, upon which my present discussion is based, and which I cite by chapter and page (i.e., column) number.—Since the opening speech of *De Dialectica* (1.951) identifies that work as an immediate continuation of Alcuin's *De Rhetorica*, and since the latter is known to have been written in the year 794, the former may be given the same date. For a discussion of the date of *De Rhetorica*, see Wilbur S. Howell, *The Rhetoric of Alcuin and Charlemagne* (Princeton, 1941), pp. 5-8.

[2] M. L. W. Laistner, *Thought and Letters in Western Europe A.D. 500 to 900* (London, 1931), p. 150.

pre-eminence in European learning as master of the palace school at Charlemagne's court. Before the time of Bede and Alcuin, the literary output of England had been meagre indeed, and English writings on the theory of literature had been nonexistent, save for Aldhelm's treatise on rhythm and metrics, *De Septenario*, usually called the *Letter to Acircius*.[3] But a new era began with Bede, during whose lifetime the great English epic *Beowulf*, the earliest considerable poetic achievement in any of the modern languages, is usually assumed to have been composed.[4] Bede wrote three small works having to do with literary theory: the *Liber de Orthographia*, the *Liber de Arte Metrica*, and the *Liber de Schematibus et Tropis*.[5] The last of these is a treatise on devices of rhetorical style, and it ranks as the earliest fragment of Ciceronian rhetorical theory to have come from the pen of an Englishman, although Alcuin must be regarded as the first of his countrymen to teach the full Ciceronian doctrine. I shall examine Bede's little work on style when I come later to speak of stylistic rhetoric in England. At present it is sufficient to observe that Bede and to some small extent Aldhelm created a fabric of literary speculation for later English learning to complete, and that Alcuin, in the generation which followed Bede, began to complete that fabric in his *De Rhetorica* and *De Dialectica*, both of which must be counted as theories of communication, the one being devoted to the open and the other to the closed discourse.

Early in *De Dialectica*, Alcuin himself distinguishes between dialectic and rhetoric in terms of Zeno's ancient metaphor of closed fist and open hand, even as we have seen Wilson doing centuries later in his vernacular logic. Alcuin's pupil Charlemagne asks: "What are dialectic and rhetoric to each other?" Alcuin replies without acknowledgments to Zeno:

> Dialectic is to rhetoric as the closed fist is to the distended palm in a man's hand. The former manner of arguing draws conclusions in brief speech; the latter runs about through fields of fluency in copious

---

[3] See Laistner, *Thought and Letters*, pp. 104-129, for an excellent brief account of English learning to the time of Bede's death. See also J. W. H. Atkins, *English Literary Criticism: The Medieval Phase* (New York and Cambridge, England, 1943), pp. 36-51, cited below as *The Medieval Phase*; also Jack D. A. Ogilvy, "Anglo-Latin Scholarship, 597-780," The University of Colorado Studies, XXII (1934-1935), pp. 327-340.

[4] See George K. Anderson, *The Literature of the Anglo-Saxons* (Princeton, 1949), pp. 82-83.

[5] These works are printed in Migne, *Patrologia Latina*, XC, 123-186. The *Liber de Schematibus et Tropis* is also in Carolus Halm, *Rhetores Latini Minores* (Leipzig, 1863), pp. 607-618.

speech. The former restrains its words; the latter is lavish with them. If indeed dialectic is the more enlarged in respect to the invention of subject matter, rhetoric is nevertheless the more fluent in respect to the expressing of what has been invented. The former searches out the few and the studious; the latter usually advances toward the multitude.[6]

Just before he makes this distinction between dialectic and rhetoric, Alcuin at Charlemagne's request divides philosophy into three parts, that is, into physics, ethics, and logic. Each of these parts is then divided into species, and logic, as the science concerned with the theory of judging rightly, is given two species, dialectic and rhetoric.[7] Thus logic in the sense in which Alcuin uses the term is to be defined by the definitions, divisions, and ultimate principles of dialectical and rhetorical theory. Thus logic does not receive at his hands a separate analysis as a science; how he regards it must be gathered instead from the disciplines which he treats as its two branches.

His *De Dialectica*, conceived at the outset as the theory of learned communication, is developed in such a way that at the end we can understand why it was considered to be so far up to date as to be given two editions in the sixteenth and three in the seventeenth centuries.[8] Indeed, Alcuin's dialectical system would not have been an anachronism in the Cambridge of Thomas Wilson's time, although it is by no means as detailed as was scholastic logic of the Renaissance, nor is it divided into invention and judgment, as was the custom among the followers of Agricola. What Alcuin does is to distinguish five principal points of emphasis in dialectical theory, and to build his discussion upon them.

The first of these points he calls initially "isagogae," that is, "introductions," thus associating this part of his work with Porphyry's famous *Isagoge*, written during the third century A.D. to introduce readers of Aristotle's *Categories* to a knowledge of the basic classes

[6] *De Dialectica*, 1.953. Translation mine.

[7] *Ibid.*, 1.952. Alcuin's words are as follows:
C. Logica in quot species dividitur?
A. In duas, in dialecticam et rhetoricam.

[8] The two sixteenth-century editions were by Menrad Molther at Haguenau and Paris in 1529 and by Matthieu Galen at Douai in 1563 and 1564. For further details, see Howell, *Rhetoric of Alcuin*, pp. 10-12. The three seventeenth-century editions were by Henricus Canisius (in *Antiquae Lectionis Tomus I-VI*, Ingolstadt, 1601-1604), by André Duchesne (in *B. Flacci Albini sive Alchwini Opera*, Paris, 1617), and by Matthaeus Weiss (in *Ad Logicam sive Organum Aristotelis Introductio*, Salzburg, 1629).

of propositions discussed by Aristotle in Chapters 4, 5, and 6 of the first book of his *Topics*. In Alcuin, as in Porphyry, the term "introduction" covers the same concepts which Thomas Wilson was to call the predicables or the five common words. Thus Alcuin under his first heading defines and illustrates genus, species, differentia, accident, and property.[9]

His second point of emphasis is the "categoriae" or, in Thomas Wilson's English, the predicaments. Alcuin anticipates Wilson by classifying these as of substance or of accident, the latter group being composed of nine categories which combine with the category of substance to make the ten in Aristotle's original list.[10] Alcuin's Latin terms for these categories are parallel in six cases to those which Wilson offers as the basis of his English terms. In the other four cases, Alcuin uses close synonyms of the terms indicated by Wilson. To these ten terms, Alcuin devotes eight chapters of his short treatise, thus giving this aspect of dialectic more than a third of his total space.

His remaining points of emphasis are the argument or syllogism, the place or topic, and the proposition. The last one of these, which is Alcuin's concluding subject, embraces doctrine descended from the second treatise in Aristotle's *Organon*, that is, the treatise *On Interpretation*; and it is illogically placed in Alcuin's scheme, since a discussion of propositions ought normally to precede the analysis of the way in which propositions combine to form syllogisms and other arguments. There are other criticisms to be made of the last three points of Alcuin's *De Dialectica*, and indeed of the treatise as a whole. For one thing, it is decidedly skimpy, particularly in its treatment of the syllogism. For another thing, it is often naive in the way it uses examples. And again, it is superficial rather than profound in its presentation of dialectical principles, as one of its editors has remarked.[11] But when these valid criticisms are registered, we should still remain aware that this first logic by an Englishman contains the basic concepts of Aristotelian logic, and transmits to its readers a fair outline of the outline of Aristotle's *Organon*.

These basic concepts, to be sure, did not come to Alcuin from his own direct study of Aristotle's logical system. They came to him instead from various intermediate sources. Of the sixteen chapters into which his treatise is divided in its edition by Migne, the first two and

---

[9] *De Dialectica*, 2.953-954. [10] *Ibid.*, 3.954-955.
[11] Matthaeus Weiss, whose criticism to this effect is cited in the headnote of the edition I have been referring to here.

the last four are partly or entirely made up of passages borrowed by him from the section on dialectic in Isidore's *Etymologiae*, whereas the remaining ten chapters belong in doctrine and direct phraseology to the same section of Isidore, to Boethius's *De Differentiis Topicis*, and pre-eminently to the *Categoriae Decem*, a work of uncertain authorship supposed in Alcuin's time to be a translation by Saint Augustine of Aristotle's *Categoriae*.[12] Alcuin mentions Porphyry at the end of his second chapter and occasionally brings in the name of Aristotle, but the other sources just mentioned are sufficient to account for almost every word of his *De Dialectica*. Thus he is more of a compiler than an independent theorist in this aspect of his total achievement, as indeed were his successors in English logic for some time to come.

Between the ninth and the mid-sixteenth centuries, a logic not unlike Alcuin's prevailed in English learning as the universities of Oxford and Cambridge developed from shadowy beginnings, and as the seven liberal arts, one of which was of course dialectic or logic, became the established form of higher education. These seven odd centuries witnessed many minor shifts in emphasis in logical theory, as western scholarship gradually uncovered forgotten details of

[12] The following table shows the sources of Alcuin's *De Dialectica*. The numbers at the left refer to chapter numbers in the text in Migne. The Latin phrases are chapter titles appearing in the same text. At the right are references to Alcuin's sources, chapter by chapter, with corresponding references to the texts of those sources as printed in Migne.

I	De Philosophia et Partibus Eius. Isidore, *Etymologiae*, 2.22, 23, 24; Migne, LXXXII, 140-142.
II	De Isagogis. *Ibid.*, 2.25; Migne, LXXXII, 142-143.
III	De Categoriis. Pseudo-Augustine, *Categoriae Decem*, chs. 8, 2, 3, 5, 9; Migne, XXXII, 1421 et seq.
IV	De Quantitate. *Ibid.*, ch. 10; Migne, XXXII, 1427-1430.
V	De Ad Aliquid. *Ibid.*, ch. 11; Migne, XXXII, 1430-1431.
VI	De Qualitate. *Ibid.*, ch. 12; Migne, XXXII, 1432-1435.
VII	De Facere et Pati. *Ibid.*, ch. 13; Migne, XXXII, 1435-1436.
VIII	De Jacere. *Ibid.*, ch. 14; Migne, XXXII, 1436.
IX	De Ubi et Quando. *Ibid.*, ch. 15; Migne, XXXII, 1436.
X	De Habere. *Ibid.*, ch. 16; Migne, XXXII, 1436-1437.
XI	De Contrariis vel Oppositis. Isidore, *Etymologiae*, 2. 31; Migne, LXXXII, 153-154. Pseudo-Augustine, *Categoriae Decem*, chs. 18-20; Migne, XXXII, 1437-1439.
XII	De Argumentis. Boethius, *De Differentiis Topicis*, Bk. I; Migne, LXIV, 1174-1175. Isidore, *Etymologiae*, 2. 28; Migne, LXXXII, 146.
XIII	De Modis Diffinitionum. Isidore, *Etymologiae*, 2. 29; Migne, LXXXII, 148.
XIV	De Speciebus Diffinitionum. *Ibid.*, 2. 29; Migne, LXXXII, 148-150.
XV	De Topicis. *Ibid.*, 2. 30; Migne, LXXXII, 151-153.
XVI	De Perihermeniis. *Ibid.*, 2. 27; Migne, LXXXII, 145-146.

For a slightly different analysis of the sources of Alcuin's *De Dialectica*, see Max Manitius, *Geschichte der Lateinischen Literatur des Mittelalters* (Munich, 1911-1931), I, 283-284.

Aristotelian logic, and as the great Arabic students of Aristotle's *Organon*, Al-Farabi in the tenth century, Avicenna in the eleventh, and Averroës in the twelfth, transmitted their knowledge of Aristotelianism through the iron curtain between the Moslem and Christian world, and made the west freshly aware of the Greek basis of its Latin culture.[13] But my present field is the Renaissance, and thus I shall not dwell so much upon the different shadings of medieval scholastic logic, as upon the major figures and works in English logic before the period of Thomas Wilson.

According to Anthony à Wood, famous historian of Oxford, the first logician at that university was John, a monk of St. David's, possibly to be identified with Johannes Scotus.[14] Wood bases his statement upon the testimony of Brian Twyne, earliest Oxford historian, who says that John was the first lecturer at Oxford under an endowment established there by King Alfred around 879. Twyne also says that John's lectures were based upon the logic of Aristotle and Averroës. It is a temptation to regard this story with sentimental indulgence, because Johannes Scotus, the great Irish scholar and candidate for the honor of being the earliest scholastic philosopher, had previously spent a large part of his life in France, where, like Alcuin before him, he had been summoned by a French king to take charge of the court school of that country, and where, like Alcuin, he had lived to establish himself as the most learned Briton of his time. But Twyne's story rests upon untrustworthy evidence, and cannot now be accepted.[15] Nor is it possible any longer to accept on the basis of the same evidence the belief that the first college, University, was founded at Oxford in Alfred's reign. The first endowment of University College is now regarded as having been established in 1249, although educational activity of some sort began at Oxford early in the previous century. Twyne's story, moreover, involves a strange anachronism—a lecturer on logic at Oxford in 879 would have been unable to interpret Averroës, who was not born until 1126.

In the latter half of the century in which Averroës was at work in Moslem Spain on his commentaries on Aristotle, the seven liberal

---

[13] For the history of logic in western Europe in these centuries, see Carl von Prantl, *Geschichte der Logik in Abendlande* (Leipzig, 1855-1870); also Barthélemy Hauréau, *Histoire de la Philosophie Scolastique* (Paris, 1872-1880); also Philotheus Boehner, *Medieval Logic An Outline of Its Development from 1250 to c. 1400* (Chicago, 1952).

[14] Anthony à Wood, *The History and Antiquities of the University of Oxford, in two Books*, ed. John Gutch (Oxford, 1792-1796), II, 820.

[15] On this point, see *Dictionary of National Biography*, s.v. Twyne, Brian (1579?-1644).

arts became the foundation of the growing educational activity at both Cambridge and Oxford, with the result that logic began to acquire a place of genuine importance in higher learning in England.[16] That same half-century witnessed the composition of one of the great medieval treatises on logic, John of Salisbury's *Metalogicon*. John of Salisbury was mentioned earlier in these pages for his division of logic into invention and judgment. Baldwin calls his *Metalogicon* "a unified and carefully coherent presentation of all teaching that deals with words."[17] "So far as is known," remarks another critic of the *Metalogicon*, "this is the first work of the Middle Ages in northern Europe in which the complete *Organon* of Aristotle is used."[18] John was born in England but educated in France between 1136 and 1148 under the opposing influences of the nominalists and realists.[19] His chief master in the camp of the former was Abelard; later he studied under Abelard's opponents, especially the distinguished logician Gilbert de la Porrée, author of the *Liber de Sex Principiis*, which long remained famous as a commentary on six of Aristotle's ten categories.[20] Hugh of St. Victor is not usually mentioned among John's teachers in France, but it is worth remembering that Hugh was professor of theology in the famous school of St. Victor in Paris from 1133 to his death in 1140, and that John not only mentions him in the *Metalogicon* but follows him in considering invention and judgment to be the parts of dialectic.[21] Apart from his contribution to logic, John was distinguished as an ecclesiastical executive under successive archbishops of Canterbury, and he underwent the ordeal of witnessing the assassination of one of them, his friend Thomas à Becket, at the hands of determined opponents of the exercise of political power by the church. John died in 1180 at Chartres, where he had spent his last four years as bishop of that cathedral.

[16] James Bass Mullinger, *The University of Cambridge* (Cambridge, 1873-1911), I, 342-343.

[17] *Medieval Rhetoric and Poetic*, p. 156. For a detailed digest of the *Metalogicon*, see this same source, pp. 158-172; see also Atkins, *The Medieval Phase*, pp. 59-90. The *Metalogicon* was completed in 1159. The best edition is that of Clement C. J. Webb, *Ioannis Saresberiensis Episcopi Carnotensis Metalogicon, Libri IIII* (Oxford, 1929). The work is also in Migne, *Patrologia Latina*, CXCIX, 823-946.

[18] Thus S. Harrison Thomson in a review of Webb's edition of the *Metalogicon* in *Speculum*, V (January 1930), 133.

[19] For a good brief sketch of his life, see *Dictionary of National Biography*, s.v. John of Salisbury.

[20] This work is printed in Migne, *Patrologia Latina*, CLXXXVIII, 1257-1270. For a brief account of the author, see *Biographie Universelle*, s.v. Gilbert de la Porrée.

[21] For a brief indication of John's indebtedness to Hugh, see Baldwin, *Medieval Rhetoric and Poetic*, p. 156, note 16. For a sketch of Hugh's life, see *Biographie Universelle*, s.v. Hugues de Saint-Victor.

The next century produced Alexander of Hales, an English philosopher who was later considered to be important enough in the history of logic to be called the father of the scholastics.[22] His great work, the *Summa Theologiae*, completed after his death by his colleagues in the Franciscan order, shows his knowledge of the Arab interpreters of Aristotle, but is not primarily a treatise in our present field. His contemporary, Edmund Rich, who became archbishop of Canterbury and later was canonized as St. Edmund, has a stronger connection with English logic of the thirteenth century; in fact, he is said to have been "the first to expound the *Sophistici Elenchi* at Oxford."[23] Rich's pupil, Robert Grosseteste, bishop of Lincoln, and first chancellor of Oxford, also expounded parts of Aristotle's *Organon* at that university, and left behind commentaries on *The Categories*, *The Sophistical Elenchi*, and *The Posterior Analytics*, the last of which was published at Naples perhaps as early as 1473, and at Venice on several occasions later in the same century.[24]

But for the great thirteenth-century work on logic, we must turn, not to an English author, but to a Frenchman, Vincent of Beauvais, and to his vast encyclopaedia, the *Speculum Majus*, thought to have been completed around 1250. One of the three divisions of the original *Speculum Majus* is the *Speculum Doctrinale*; and Book IV of the latter is devoted to logic, rhetoric, and poetics, logic being given 98 chapters, rhetoric 10, and poetics 23.[25] Vincent's method is to

[22] Alexander is given this title in the early seventeenth century by Robert Sanderson, *Logicae Artis Compendivm* (Oxford, 1618), p. 119.

[23] See John Edwin Sandys, *A History of Classical Scholarship*, 3rd edn. (Cambridge, 1921), I, 574, 592.

[24] *Ibid.*, pp. 575-576. Grosseteste's Latin text of *The Posterior Analytics* and his commentary thereon, as published at Naples between 1473 and 1478 by Sixtus Riessinger, was accompanied by the following treatises, all in Latin: 1) Porphyry's *Isagoge*, with the commentary of Boethius; 2) Aristotle's *The Categories*, also with the commentary of Boethius; 3) Gilbert de la Porrée's *Liber de Sex Principiis*, with the commentary of Albertus Magnus; and 4) Aristotle's *On Interpretation*. A copy of this work is in the Huntington Library.

Grosseteste is identified in the table of contents at the beginning of this volume as follows: "Posterior editio de Analecticis Aristotelis & interpretatio Linconiensis viri summi." He is identified in much the same way at the head of his text of Aristotle and in a Latin quatrain before the text begins; also in much the same way at the end of the text. Anthony à Wood, *History and Antiquities of Oxford*, ed. Gutch, I, 199, attributes this spelling of Grosseteste's name to the mistake that a foreigner would make with the Latin form of Lincoln. Wood notes just before that most authors call Grosseteste "Linconiensis" without any additional explanation.

[25] My analysis of the *Speculum Doctrinale* is based upon two fifteenth-century editions, one believed to have been done at Strasbourg by the R-printer about 1472, and the other known to have been done at Nuremberg by Anton Koberger in 1486. Copies of both of these editions are in the Huntington Library. The two are alike in respect to division of subject matter into books and chapters, and in respect to text. The edition

quote excerpts from the writers considered by him to have pre-eminent authority in these three fields, and to arrange the excerpts in a continuous and comprehensive discussion, so that each field is represented by its best subject matter and its ablest spokesmen. Now and then Vincent departs from this routine by adding a chapter or paragraph of his own composing. His treatment of poetics in the company of logic and rhetoric is his way of indicating that he is following Al-Farabi, Arab commentator on Aristotle, in respect to the classification of poetic theory as the last of the parts of logic. In fact, Vincent quotes Al-Farabi's *Liber de Divisione Scientiarum* to this effect at the beginning of his account of the poetical art.[26] Alcuin, as we have seen, thought of dialectic and rhetoric as the two parts of logic, and John of Salisbury extended this simple classification to include also within logical theory the discipline of grammar, with poetics as one of its aspects.[27] Thus Vincent merely adds the authority of Al-Farabi to this established trend in logical theory. His discussion of poetics as the last part of logic will not seem completely antique today if we remember that poetics in his time and later was considered to be that part of the theory of communication which dealt with veiled discourse, whereas rhetoric and logic completed the theory of communication by dealing respectively with the open and the closed discourse.

Vincent's treatment of logic is in the full scholastic tradition. After five chapters of preliminary comment on the purposes and parts of this science, he selects as his headings such customary topics as the predicables, the categories, propositions, syllogism, induction, places of dialectic, demonstration, dialectical proof, problems, definition, division, and fallacies. His primary authority is Aristotle. He quotes Latinized passages from each one of the six works of the *Organon: The Categories, On Interpretation, The Prior Analytics, The Posterior Analytics, The Topics,* and *The Sophistical Elenchi.* He also quotes now and then from Aristotle's other works. He makes no secret of the origin of these quotations, taking care at the beginning or in the course of each chapter to indicate by Latin title the Aristotelian work upon which he depends at that point. Wherever the

---

published at Douai in 1624 puts the discussion of logic, rhetoric, and poetics into Book III instead of Book IV; see Baldwin, *Medieval Rhetoric and Poetic,* pp. 174-175. For a brief outline of the Douai text of the entire *Speculum Majus,* see *The Encyclopaedia Britannica,* 11th edn., s.v. Vincent of Beauvais.

[26] *Speculum Doctrinale* [Strasbourg, 1472], Bk. IV, Ch. 109. For a translation of a large part of this chapter, see Baldwin, *Medieval Rhetoric and Poetic,* pp. 175-176.

[27] For John's classification of the disciplines in the Trivium, see the convenient table in Baldwin, *Medieval Rhetoric and Poetic,* p. 157.

source is someone else, he indicates as much, and these indications involve names which we have encountered before. For example, he quotes passages from Isidore's *Etymologiae*, Richard of St. Victor's *Excerptionum*, Al-Farabi's *Liber de Divisione Scientiarum*, Boethius's *De Differentiis Topicis* and *Liber de Divisione*, Porphyry's *Isagoge*, Gilbert de la Porrée's *Liber de Sex Principiis*, and Themistius's *Paraphrases of Aristotle*, with Isidore, Boethius, and Gilbert being cited most often.

One theme to appear not only in Vincent's scholastic logic but also in the logic which Ramus produced three hundred years later as a protest against scholasticism is that of Aristotle's three laws. Vincent devotes Chapter 53 of his treatise on logic to these three laws, which he calls "that which concerns all," "that which is through itself," and "that which is universal." Vincent's Latin terms for these laws appear as the title to that chapter: "De hoc qd' est de oī & p se & vniuersale." His previous chapter consists of passages located by him "in li. posterio[rum]," that is, in Aristotle's *The Posterior Analytics*, and the same source, although not specifically cited, provides him with all the passages that make up Chapter 53. As the three laws occur in *The Posterior Analytics*, they are indications of the nature of propositions which befit the necessary demonstrations of science.[28] Aristotle's view is that truly scientific propositions can be recognized by three characteristics, and must possess these characteristics. Vincent takes the same view. But his explanation of them is a condensation of Aristotle, and Aristotle is so elliptical at this point that his chapter on the three characteristics is one of the most difficult in the entire *Organon*. Thus my present rationalization of these characteristics, or laws, is to be accepted, not as a final statement of Aristotle's meaning, but as an attempt to arrange his obscure clues into a pattern that best seems to interpret them.

The first law, called "de omni" by Vincent and other Latin commentators on Aristotle, appears to indicate that the predicate of the strictly scientific proposition must be true of every case of the subject. Aristotle's illustrations of this law are incomplete, and Vincent's still more so. But the language of both suggests that a proposition violates

---

[28] See Aristotle, *The Posterior Analytics*, Bk. I, Ch. 4. Owen's translation of this chapter in his *Organon, or Logical Treatises, of Aristotle*, I, 253-256, has some helpful commentary upon the meaning of Aristotle's three phrases, that is, of "το κατὰ παντὸς" as the equivalent of "de omni," "τὸ καθ' αὐτό" as the equivalent of "per se" and "το καθόλου" as the equivalent of "universale." See also G. R. G. Mure's clear translation of this difficult chapter in *The Works of Aristotle*, ed. Ross, I, 73ᵃ-74ᵃ.

this first law when the subject and predicate belong together in some instances but not in others. For example, if we say that any three-sided figure having angles equal to two right angles is an isosceles triangle, our proposition violates this first law, not by giving an isosceles triangle three sides, or three angles equal to two right angles, but by failing to place within the subject something which must always be there if that subject is to be true of every case of isosceles triangle. The additional something is that two of its sides must be equal. Thus the subject (three-sided figure having angles equal to two right angles) and the predicate (isosceles triangle) belong together, but not in every case—not, for example, in the case where three sides are equal, or in the case where the three sides are unequal, for in those cases, our triangle is not an isosceles.

The second law, called "per se" in Latin versions of Aristotle, as in the version followed by Vincent, appears to mean that the predicate of a strict logical proposition must be harmonious within itself no less than harmonious with its subject. Aristotle discusses this law by oblique indications. Thus Vincent's excerpts from him are not conducive to an understanding of the original text. What appears to be meant is that a proposition fails to conform to this second law when its predicate postulates among its own parts a harmony that does not really exist or a disharmony that is contrary to fact. For example, if we say that any number is either odd or prime, our predicate deals with two essential attributes of number, and thus is satisfactory to that extent, but it deals with them unharmoniously, inasmuch as the attribute of oddness and the attribute of primeness cannot be defined in terms of each other. Odd can be defined in terms of even; prime in terms of composite. Only when the attributes in a predicate stand in such opposition to each other that one excludes the other, as odd excludes even, can we postulate opposition between them in reference to the subject to which they belong.

The third law, called "universale" by Aristotle's Latin commentators and by Vincent, appears to mean that the predicate of any strictly logical proposition must belong to its subject in a proximate as opposed to a remote relation. Thus if we say that any linear structure having angles equal to two right angles is a geometrical figure, our predicate applies to our subject, not in a proximate but in a remote sense, as the more general term "figure" includes the more specific term "triangle" without regard to those things in the subject which make the latter term more strictly applicable than the former.

Thus Aristotle's three laws, as a description of the nature of the propositions we should encounter in strictly scientific literature, as for example in mathematical writings, would seem to indicate that a logical predicate of a proposition must belong to every instance of its subject, must be harmonious within itself, and must represent the proximate class of its subject. What Aristotle probably wanted these laws to say is that our statements are important, inasmuch as they set our minds at work to infer other statements; and that therefore, if these latter are not to get completely out of hand, completely at variance with reality, we must be very careful about our formulation of them and of the original statements that prepared the way for them. His three laws are in other words three ways of being careful that statements yield no more than they should in the way of inferences and suggestions.

Our basic statements, which should be the most sharply scrutinized and carefully formulated of all our utterances, constitute in the aggregate what Aristotle meant by science. Logic was to him the corpus of doctrine relating to the process of getting those basic statements properly conceived and expressed. In some fields, say geometry, for instance, our basic statements could conform to the three laws just discussed. But in other fields, like law, politics, and ethics, our statements could not achieve an exactitude that extended to the utmost limits of the three laws, and thus these latter statements had to be classed as opinion, not science. To Aristotle, dialectic was the corpus of doctrine relating to the process of getting such opinion conceived, organized, and expressed. Beyond logic and dialectic were two other aspects of argument, called by Aristotle eristic or contentious argument, on the one hand, and sophistries or deceitful arguments, on the other. The latter of these aspects we would today probably identify as the profitable misreasonings of politics or commerce, whereas the former are misreasonings employed in seminar or theater or academic chair to test hypotheses or display wit or develop skill in the processes of debate and controversy.[29]

Vincent's own approach to these matters is as Aristotelian as he could make it. Not only does he discuss the three laws by relevant quotations from *The Posterior Analytics*, as we have observed; he also places just before that discussion a series of quotations from

[29] For Aristotle's enumeration of these four types of argument, see *The Topics*, Bk. I, Ch. I. The translation by W. A. Pickard-Cambridge in Vol. I of *The Works of Aristotle*, ed. Ross, is particularly good.

Aristotle's *Topics* on the subject of logical demonstration, dialectical reasoning, contentious argument, and false syllogisms, thereby establishing an Aristotelian basis for the last forty-seven chapters of his logic.[30] Moreover, immediately after his recognition of the four types of argument, and immediately before his discussion of the three laws, he quotes (Chapter 52) from *The Posterior Analytics*, as I noted earlier, and arranges these quotations to constitute an explanation of logical demonstration and its materials, as contrasted with the three other types of proof or argument.

The period in which Vincent produced his *Speculum Majus* is also the period of Roger Bacon's *Opus Majus*. This latter work, says Whewell in an oft-quoted passage, "may be considered as, at the same time, the *Encyclopedia* and the *Novum Organon* of the thirteenth century."[31] These words do not exaggerate the importance of the *Opus Majus* as a summary of learning and a vision of things to come in the history of science. For many reasons, as Burke has observed, "the *Opus Majus* must ever remain one of the few truly great works of human genius."[32] Judgments as complimentary as these should not blind us to the fact, however, that the *Opus Majus* does not rank with Vincent's *Speculum Doctrinale* as a contribution to logical theory or as an influence upon the scholastic logicians of the Renaissance. Indeed, Bacon's brief account of logic, showing his grasp of Aristotle's *Posterior Analytics* and *Categories*, showing also his insight into the commentary of Averroës upon Aristotle, and into Al-Farabi's *Liber de Divisione Scientiarum*, is dedicated, not to the exposition of logical theory, but to the argument that "the whole excellence of logic depends on mathematics."[33] It is not surprising, therefore, that the *Opus Majus* devotes to mathematics the space ordinarily reserved in such treatises to logical theorizing. Moreover, the *Opus Majus* was not given a printed edition until 1733, whereas Vincent's *Speculum Doctrinale* appeared several times at the earliest printing presses of Europe, and was known during the late fifteenth

[30] See *Speculum Doctrinale*, Bk. IV, Ch. 51. This chapter, as Vincent indicates, depends upon Aristotle, "in thopicis," that is, upon *The Topics*, Bk. I, Ch. I.

[31] William Whewell, *History of The Inductive Sciences*, 3rd edn. (London, 1857), I, 368. The sense of Whewell's statement is quoted by Sandys, *History of Classical Scholarship*, I, 590, and by R. Adamson in the account of Roger Bacon in the *Dictionary of National Biography*.

[32] Robert Belle Burke, *The Opus Majus of Roger Bacon A Translation* (Philadelphia, 1928), I, xii.

[33] *Ibid.*, I, 120. Bacon's account of logic covers the two and a half pages that precede this quotation in Burke's translation, whereas the account of mathematics covers three hundred following pages.

century wherever printed books were collected. By a strange mis-carriage of justice, those earliest presses were meanwhile publishing only those works of Roger Bacon that had about them the aura of sorcery and black magic. Thus his popular reputation, as shown to-wards the end of the sixteenth century in Robert Greene's successful drama, *Friar Bacon and Friar Bungay*, is that of an alchemist rather than that of a prophet or philosopher.

Robert Grosseteste's commentary on *The Posterior Analytics* of Aristotle, which has already been mentioned as having appeared in print at Naples perhaps as early as 1473, deserves to be called the first treatise on logic by an Englishman in the history of printed books. Vincent's *Speculum Doctrinale* no doubt preceded it in print by at least a year, but Vincent does not belong, of course, in the cata-logue of English logicians, except as an influence from without.[34] Grosseteste's little work on logic, and Vincent's more considerable one, had both appeared in first editions before the introduction of printing into England by Caxton in 1476. The first Latin logic by an Englishman to be printed at an English press is Roger Swines-head's *Tractatus Logici*, believed to have been produced by Theo-doric Rood at the first printing press at Oxford in 1483.[35] Swines-head, a shadowy figure in English logic, whose last name is often given as Swiset or Suiseth, and whose first name is sometimes made Richard rather than Roger, was a fellow of Merton College, Oxford, and flourished in the second quarter of the fourteenth century, as an associate of a group of Merton scholars particularly interested in mathematics, astronomy, and logical disputation.[36] In the same year in which Swineshead's *Tractatus Logici* was published, another Latin treatise on the same subject, the *Scriptum super Libros Veteros Logice*, by Antonius Andreae, of the Franciscan order, appeared at

[34] The earliest edition of the *Speculum Doctrinale* is acknowledged to be that at Strasbourg around 1472. See above, p. 39, note 25.

[35] I have not seen a copy of this work. For bibliographical descriptions of it, see Falconer Madan, *Oxford Books* (Oxford, 1895-1931), I, 3; also E. Gordon Duff, *Fifteenth Century English Books* ([Oxford], 1917), p. 78. The volume contains 19 treatises, each with the word "Tractatus" in the title, the whole being "strung together to form a systematic work on Logic," says Madan. These facts would seem to suggest that *Tractatus Logici* ought to be the proper bibliographical title of the work, rather than the English *Logic* preferred by Madan and Duff. The seventeenth treatise is signed, "Et sic finiuntur insolubilia swynishede," but, says Madan, "he was probably only the author of that part." The entire nineteen treatises in this volume, including one called *Topics*, are however, ascribed to Swineshead by Anthony à Wood, *History and An-tiquities of Oxford*, ed. Gutch, I, 419.

[36] See F. M. Powicke, *The Medieval Books of Merton College* (Oxford, 1931), pp. 25, 26, 27. See also *Dictionary of National Biography*, s.v. Swineshead, Richard.

St. Albans.[37] Andreae, known otherwise for the disarming and persuasive way in which he explained the doctrines of his master, Johannes Duns Scotus, was by birth a Spaniard and by date a member of the generation between Grosseteste and Vincent, on the one side, and Swineshead, on the other.[38] Thus the earliest Latin logic printed anywhere from an English author, the earliest Latin logic printed in England from a foreign author, and the earliest Latin logic printed in England from an English author, all represented the thinking of the period between the middle years of the thirteenth and the middle years of the fourteenth centuries, and all were first published as the fifteenth century was drawing to its remarkable end.

While these events were occurring one by one, a development of high promise but of small intrinsic value took place in English logical theory. This development constituted the first printed attempts to transmit logical doctrine through the medium of native English speech. Thomas Wilson, as has been said, is the author of the first logic in English; but seventy years before he published the *Rule of Reason*, logic delivered herself of two brief English speeches, both of which were designed rather to awaken interest in herself than to develop her doctrine in a systematic way. These speeches are usually assigned to the year 1480 or 1481 as their date of publication. One is in verse and the other in prose. Let us look briefly at each.

No doubt the first in point of time is that contained in the rambling allegorical poem, *De Curia Sapiencie*, now better known as *The Court of Sapience*, which was published at Caxton's famous press in Westminster perhaps in 1480, perhaps in 1481.[39] The poem recounts

---

[37] I have not seen the St. Albans edition of this work. But it is apparently a slight abridgment of the edition published at Venice in 1477 and 1480, the latter of which I have seen in the copy at the Huntington Library. The Venice edition of 1480 contains the following treatises: *Scriptum super librum Porphirii; Scriptum super librum predicamentorum Aristotelis; Scriptum super librum sex principiorum; Scriptum super libros pyermenias; Scriptum super librum divisionum Boecii*. The St. Albans edition, as described by Duff, *Fifteenth Century English Books*, p. 7, ends with the words, "Explicit scriptū Antonii in sua logica veneciis correctum." Immediately before these final words is a passage which falls, not on the last page of the Venice edition of 1480, but on the last page but three. Thus the Venice edition of 1480 contains at this point some matter not found in the St. Albans edition. This Venice edition also contains at the beginning about two pages of text which the St. Albans edition omits. Later issues of this work appeared at Venice in 1492, 1496, 1508, 1509, and 1517.

[38] Grosseteste died in 1253, Vincent in 1264, Swineshead about a century later. Andreae flourished in the late thirteenth and early fourteenth centuries; see *Nouvelle Biographie Générale*, s.v. Andrès, Antoine.

[39] The poem is in English, although its first edition is customarily listed under the Latin title, *De Curia Sapiencie*. It is attributed by Stephen Hawes to John Lydgate. See

the adventures of the poet in forsaking the world and entering upon the contemplative life. The episode of chief concern to the present discussion is that in which the poet visits the castle of sapience and encounters the seven ladies, symbolizing the seven liberal arts. The second of these ladies is "Dame Dialetica." Although we meet her as a person, we are informed in a kind of stage direction as we approach her parlor that a "breuis tractatus de Dialetica" is about to begin. This brief treatise occupies seven stanzas, each of seven lines, and its chief interest for us is that it mentions the terms used by Dame Dialetica in teaching her art to her own clerks and scholars.[40] We are informed that "latyne was hyr langage," and indeed her parlor is decorated with such argumentative formulas as "differt," "scire," and "incipit," while her pupils often chorus "Tu es asinus." But the poet describes her subject matter in English terms, and perhaps his is the earliest attempt to give his countrymen a taste of the printed English vocabulary of logic. Thus "quatkyn," "proposicion," "diuisioun," "subiect," "couple," "predicate," "subalterne," "contradiccion," "Equipollens," "conuersioun," "Silogismes," "sophyms," "vniuersals," "predicamentes," "topykes," "principals," "Elynkes," are the important words he mentions,[41] and these, awkward or familiar as they may now seem to be in relation to our established idiom, were in their time a novel experiment.

At about the time of the appearance of *The Court of Sapience* in its earliest edition, the first encyclopaedia in English, the *Mirrour of the World or thymage of the same*, came also from Caxton's press. This work represents Caxton's own translation of a French prose work, *Sensuit le livre de clergie nomme lymage du monde*, compiled around 1245 by a Frenchman now identified as Gossouin.[42] Caxton's

---

his *The Pastime of Pleasure*, ed. William Edward Mead, Early English Text Society, Original Series, No. 173 (London, 1928 [for 1927]), p. 56, line 1357. The second edition, titled *The Courte of Sapyence*, appeared at London in 1510. The only modern edition, *The Court of Sapience Spät-Mittelenglisches Allegorisch-Didaktisches Visiongedicht*, ed. Dr. Robert Spindler, in Beiträge zur Englischen Philologie, VI (Leipzig, 1927), is the basis of my present discussion and contains (pp. 97-114) a survey of the question of authorship of the poem.

[40] See Spindler, pp. 196-198 [stanzas 264-270].

[41] Judging by the variant reading given for line 1872 by Spindler, I suggest that "principals" refers to Gilbert de la Porrée's *Liber de Sex Principiis*. "Predicamentes," "topykes," and "Elynkes," refer of course to Aristotle's *Categories*, *Topics*, and *The Sophistical Elenchi*. The other terms are all to be located in these treatises or elsewhere in the *Organon*. For additional information about the origin of these stanzas on logic, see Curt Ferdinand Bühler, *The Sources of the Court of Sapience*, Beiträge zur Englischen Philologie, XXIII (1932), pp. 71-74.

[42] For details regarding publication date, source, composition date, and authorship of

Mirrour gives an English account of the seven sciences, the entire chapter on logic being as follows:

> The secōde science is logyke whyche is called dyaletyque. This science proueth the .pro. and the .contra. That is to saye the verite or trouthe and otherwyse. And it preueth wherby shal be knowen the trewe fro the fals and the good fro the euyll. So veryly that for the good was created heuen and maad And on the contrarye wyse for the euyll was helle maad and establisshyd whiche is horryble stynkyng and re-doubtable.[43]

This statement of the moral as well as scientific end of logic is not accompanied by any analysis of logical means, any recommendation as to logical procedures. The third edition of the *Mirrour*, published by Laurence Andrewe at London in or around 1527, rectifies this defect by enlarging the account of logic to 93 lines of text, as contrasted to 13 lines in the edition just quoted, and by offering technical definitions and illustrations of such logical instruments as the proposition, the argument, definition, and description.[44] Beyond this point, however, the English vocabulary of logic did not progress until Wilson published his *Rule of Reason*.

Along with the interesting attempt in *The Court of Sapience* to render logical terms into English speech and into the still more unaccustomed medium of verse, we should here notice an early sixteenth-century poem, Stephen Hawes's *The Pastime of Pleasure*. Like *The Court* before it, *The Pastime* is a didactic allegory. As

---

this work, see *Caxton's Mirrour of the World*, ed. Oliver H. Prior, Early English Text Society, Extra Series, cx (London, 1913 [for 1912]), pp. v-x.

[43] [William Caxton], *Mirrour of the World or thymage of the same* ([Westminster, 1481]), sig. C4v. From the Huntington Library photostat of their own original copy.

[44] The third edition is called *The myrrour: & dyscrypcyon of the worlde with many meruaylles*. Its colophon reads: "Enprynted by me Laurence Andrewe dwellynge in fletestrete at the sygne of the goldē crosse by flete brydge." It bears no date, but is assigned tentatively to the year 1527 by the British Museum catalogue. The seven chapters between Ch. 7 and Ch. 13 deal with the seven liberal arts, as had the same chapters in the two earlier editions. But, as the following table shows, the edition of 1527 rearranges the order of the seven arts and adds new material to that contained in the earlier texts:

Edition of 1481		*Edition of 1527?*	
Ch. 7 (On grammar)	21 lines	Ch. 7 (On grammar)	72 lines
Ch. 8 (On logic)	13 lines	Ch. 8 (On rhetoric)	84 lines
Ch. 9 (On rhetoric)	23 lines	Ch. 9 (On logic)	93 lines
Ch. 10 (On arithmetic)	23 lines	Ch. 10 (On geometry)	166 lines
Ch. 11 (On geometry)	14 lines	Ch. 11 (On arithmetic)	273 lines
Ch. 12 (On music)	41 lines	Ch. 12 (On music)	71 lines
Ch. 13 (On astronomy)	115 lines	Ch. 13 (On astronomy)	138 lines

critics have pointed out, it represents a course of training in the seven liberal arts as the proper preparation for the life of an ideal knight and as a necessary step in winning a fair lady of higher degree than the suitor.[45] Although its account of rhetoric is of more interest historically and otherwise than is its account of logic, the latter deserves mention as a continuation of Caxton's emphasis upon the moral end of this science—upon its relevance to the quest for salvation. The lady who dwells in the bright chamber of logic summarizes the virtues of her science in these words:

> So by logyke is good perceyueraunce
> To deuyde the good and the euyll a sondre
> It is alway at mannes pleasaunce
> To take the good and cast the euyll vnder
> Yf god made hell it is therof no wonder
> For to punysshe man that hadde intellygence
> To knowe good from yll by trewe experyence.[46]

There are five other stanzas like this, each having seven lines, and each being devoted in part or wholly to the praise of logic as the science of discerning, by argumentation grounded on reason, who are friends or foes, and what is false or true, right or wrong, in this wretched world. These stanzas are part of the defective first edition of *The Pastime*, as published by Wynkyn de Worde at London in 1509; and of course they figure in the improved editions published in 1517, 1554, and 1555.[47] Thus they were available for a half-century as a reminder to readers that learning in logic is conducive to the good life and to success in love.

That same half-century not only produced Wilson's *Rule of Reason* as the first fully developed vernacular logic; it also produced John Seton's *Dialectica*, the first Latin textbook on logic to be published in England, and the first response in English logical theory to the enormously popular sixteenth-century continental work, Rudolph Agricola's *De Inventione Dialectica*. Agricola has been previously mentioned as a logician of the fifteenth century, and his *De Inventione Dialectica* as a work which gave wide currency to ancient

---

[45] See *The Pastime of Pleasure*, ed. Mead, p. xliii. For a discussion of the relation of *The Court of Sapience* to *The Pastime of Pleasure*, see Whitney Wells, "Stephen Hawes and *The Court of Sapience*," *The Review of English Studies*, VI (1930), 284-294.

[46] *The Pastime of Pleasure*, ed. Mead, p. 29 [lines 631-637].

[47] A discussion of all editions of this poem will be found in Mead's reprint, pp. xxix-xli. See his first note, p. xxx, for a precise indication of the missing lines in the 1509 edition.

theory that the two parts of dialectic are invention and disposition.[48] Speaking of Agricola's influence at Cambridge in the period before 1545, Mullinger says that "his treatise on logic became a text-book in our own university."[49] As for the European attitude towards *De Inventione Dialectica*, Mullinger is quite right in remarking that the treatise "appears to have been one of the most popular of the two or three manuals that, up to the time of Seton, superseded for a time the purely scholastic logic."[50]

John Seton was educated at St. John's College, Cambridge, where he earned the degree of bachelor of arts in 1528 and that of master of arts in 1532, and where he served an appointment as fellow, during which time he taught philosophy. Later he studied divinity, and was awarded his doctorate in that subject at Cambridge in 1544. A Roman Catholic, he held several ecclesiastical posts for the next decade, but he eventually left England as a result of the religious troubles of the period between the death of Henry VIII and the early days of Elizabeth's reign. He died at Rome in 1567. His *Dialectica* was first published in 1545. According to his biographer, Thompson Cooper, "this work was extensively circulated in manuscript among students long before it appeared in print, and for nearly a century it was recognized as the standard treatise on logic."[51] The popularity of the *Dialectica* was due in large part, however, to Peter Carter, also a graduate of St. John's, Cambridge, who brought out *In Johannis Setoni Dialecticam Annotationes* at London in the fifteen-sixties,[52] and whose *Dialectica Ioannis Setoni Cantabrigiensis, annotationibus Petri Carteri*, as published at London in 1572 and many times thereafter, kept Seton's logical doctrine alive for the next seventy years.[53] My present discussion of Seton's *Dialectica* is based upon the popular text as edited and annotated by Carter,[54] since this joint work is in point of influence superior to its predecessor.

[48] See above, p. 16.
[49] Mullinger, *University of Cambridge*, I, 410.
[50] *Ibid.*, I, 413.
[51] *Dictionary of National Biography*, s.v. Seton, John.
[52] In 1563, according to the *Dictionary of National Biography*, s.v. Carter, Peter. The work is entered in the Stationers' Registers during the year 1562-1563; see Edward Arber, *A Transcript of the Registers of the Company of Stationers* (London and Birmingham, 1875-1894), I, 208. A copy dated London, 1568, is held at the library of Trinity College, Dublin.
[53] After the London edition of 1572, the *Dialectica* of Seton and Carter appeared in 1574, 1577, 1584, 1611, 1617, 1631, 1639.
[54] The title page of the edition I cite throughout my present discussion reads: "Dialectica Ioannis Setoni Cantabrigiensis, annotationibus Petri Carteri, vt clarissimis ita

The *Dialectica* is divided into four sections or books, the first three of which deal with judgment or disposition as a main part of logic, whereas the final section deals with invention as the other main part. The reason for this disproportionate emphasis upon disposition, as stated in words clearly attributed by Carter to Seton, is that Agricola had treated invention with fulness and fluency, and that Seton himself would therefore undertake to speak of what remained.[55] Carter elaborates this position by saying that Seton had largely confined his work to disposition on the theory that dialectic chiefly treats that subject[56]—a theory, by the way, which Cicero had attributed to the Stoics and had himself rejected.[57] To Carter, the practice of emphasizing disposition more than invention apparently seems justified, because he makes no attempt to change Seton's original decision to give only the last of his four main sections to the latter subject. But Carter does recognize in his annotations that invention is prior to disposition in the order of nature, as matter is prior to form, and he credits this sentiment to Boethius.[58]

As for the relation of dialectic to rhetoric and to logic, Carter adheres to traditional scholastic views. Zeno's ancient metaphor is in his mind if not in his exact words when he says: "Dialectic is the art of disputing, Rhetoric the art of speaking, the latter being more copious, the former, more compressed."[59] Thus both arts bear a relation to the parent discipline of logic, although Carter stresses only the connection between logic and dialectic, and disposes them towards each other as whole to part.[60] This opinion, which he attributes

---

breuissimis explicata. Hvic Accessit, ob Artium ingenuarum inter se cognationem, Guilielmi Buclaei Arithmetica. Londini, Excudebant Gerardus Dewes & Henricus Marsh, ex assignatione Thomae Marsh. Anno Salutis. 1584. Cvm Privilegio." In this edition, which I consulted at the Huntington Library, Seton's text is distinguished from Carter's notes by printed marginal indications, "Seton" designating the former, and "Car." the latter.

[55] The text reads at this point: "Dialectica est artificium, docens de quauis materia probabiliter disserere, hanc in duas secant partes, nimirum, inueniendi & iudicandi de priori diligenter & satis copiosè scripsit Rhodulphus: de altero verò nos (volente Deo) dicere aggrediemur." (sig. A2r.) This section is designated in the margin as Seton's. Carter's name does not appear until sig. A3r, where a heading announces for the first time the presence of his annotations.

[56] Says Carter, sig. A3r: "Setonus inscripsit librum suum de iudicio, quia praecipuè eam Dialectices partem tractat."

[57] *Topica*, §§6-7. See also above, p. 15.

[58] Sig. A3r.

[59] Sig. A3v. The text reads: "Ars disserendi Dialectica est, ars dicendi Rhetorica est: haec enim latior est, illa est strictior." Translation mine here and below.

[60] Sig. A3v. The text: "Dialectica affecta est ad Logicam, tanquam pars ad totum. Coelius secundus." "Coelius secundus" refers to Coelius Secundus Curio or Curion (1503-

to Coelius Secundus Curio, might as handily have been attributed to Alcuin, or to Isidore, among others.[61] It represents, of course, a view unlike that of Wilson, who thought of dialectic and logic as identical.[62] But nevertheless it has deep roots in scholastic logic, and it was not one of the opinions which seemed to matter much one way or the other in the early sixteenth century.

As Seton and Carter proceed with their four books of doctrine, they follow a scheme suggested by the conventional arrangement of the various treatises in Aristotle's *Organon*. Thus Book I deals with the simplest ingredients of learned discourse, that is, with terms, and these require as the chief points of emphasis a discussion of the five predicables and the ten categories. It will be recalled at this point that the ten categories are the subject of the treatise ordinarily placed first in the *Organon*, and that Porphyry's *Isagoge*, as an introduction to that first treatise, gave special currency to the concept of the five predicables. Seton and Carter handle these big points of emphasis in the style of scholastic logic. What they say of the general difference between predicable and category is worth quoting, if only to remind ourselves that scholastic logic, as the theory of learned discourse, considered it important to deal not only with the basic methods of reasoning and organization, but also with the·basic vocabulary in which all learning was to be expressed. Here are their exact words:

> Concerning the difference in theory between
> arranging words into categories and predicables.

Words are arranged together in predicables whenever they are being examined along with other words. As "virtue" in respect to "man" is accident; in respect to "condition," species; in respect to "temperance," genus. Words are arranged together in categories, whenever they are being examined in and for themselves. As "virtue" examined without any other regard is quality.[63]

Book II in Seton and Carter's scheme deals with propositions, even as *De Interpretatione*, conventional second treatise in the *Organon*,

---

1569), professor of belles-lettres at Basel, whose *Logices Elementorum Libri Quatuor* (Basel, 1567) is, I assume, the work from which Carter drew these words. But I have not been able to check this source.

[61] See above, pp. 34, 36.   [62] See above, p. 17.

[63] Sig. B8v. The Latin text, headed "De Prędicamentis," reads:

De diuersa ratione collocandarum vocum in praedicamentis, & praedicabilibus.
Voces collocantur in praedicabilibus, quemadmodum cum aliis considerantur. Vt, virtus respectu hominis, accidens est: Respectu habitus, species; respectu temperantiae, genus. Voces collocantur in praedicamentis, quemadmodum per se considerantur: vt, virtus sine alterius respectu est in qualitate.

takes up the same subject. The transitional sentence with which Book II opens is attributed to Seton himself by his collaborator, and it shows that the order of progress through the subject of logic is here envisaged as an order of increasing complexity, the proposition being a unit composed of simpler elements called terms, and being therefore more difficult to manage than is any one of its components.[64] The subject matter of Book II is afforded by the analysis of the parts of propositions (subject, predicate, copula), the types of propositions (categorical and hypothetical), the forms of opposition between propositions, the forms of equivalence among propositions, the nature of definition and description, and the nature of division. Discourse and its problems are everywhere in the authors' minds. Even poetry is given a passing glance in the passage on description. The authors say:

> Description is twofold, poetical and dialectical. In poetical description the genus is omitted for the most part, and the opposite is done in dialectical description. Description sets out a thing appropriately—that is, it is convertible with the process of delineating.[65]

But redundancies develop. Thus in discussing definition, Seton and Carter run through the places to show how definition can be accomplished by recourse to the differentia, the property, the whole, the part, the conjugate form, and so on; yet in Book IV, where invention is discussed, the same places are again the heads of discussion, and the same doctrine has to be covered again.

The subject matter of Book III is argumentation—the process of combining logical propositions so that a fully articulated act of thought, a complete inference or demonstration, is created. This aspect of logic is considered in Aristotle's *Prior Analytics*, it will be remembered, and that treatise is usually the third element in the *Organon*. To Seton and Carter, dialectic has a special interest in the structures of reasoning. "The highest goal of this art," they say, "to which everything else in it tends, is argumentation, and we have destined the third book to the explanation of it." They add: "First, therefore, it ought to be shown what argumentation is; next, how

[64] See sig. F6v for the beginning of Book II and for the wording of this transitional sentence.

[65] Sig. K1r. The Latin text reads at this point:
Descriptio duplex. Poetica. Dialectica.
In poetica descriptione maxima ex parte omittitur genus, è contrà sit in Dialectica descriptione.
Descriptio rem appositè explicat, id est, cōuertitur cum descriptio.

many basic forms it has; and lastly, what are its affiliated types."[66] Book III follows this tripartite plan. Argumentation is defined as reasoning in which specific propositions are laid down and a specific conclusion drawn from them. It is a verbal process, to be distinguished from argument, which is not fully verbalized.[67] The basic forms of argumentation are enumerated as syllogism, induction, enthymeme, and example.[68] In the discussion of syllogism, a table is put in to show what terms were assigned to the members of the syllogism by Aristotle, Cicero, Quintilian, Themistius, Boethius, and Agricola.[69] Induction is defined as an act of argument from many particulars to one universal, or an act of progression from parts to whole.[70] The enthymeme stands as an imperfect syllogism, only one of the two premises being given to justify the conclusion, as when it is argued that no science is designed without use, and therefore dialectic is not designed without use.[71] An argument from example is a demonstration in which one particular is proved from another on account of some resemblance between them, as when we say that the touching of moist gypsum or white clay easily induces it to take whatever form you like, and that therefore rude minds are capable of every discipline.[72]

As for the affiliated types of argumentation, these are discussed here and there during the exposition of the four main types. Perhaps chief among the affiliates is the rhetorical syllogism. This is conceived as a movement in five distinct parts, first being the statement of the major premise, then the citing of proof for it, then the statement of the minor premise, then the citing of proof for it, and finally, the statement of the conclusion. The explanation and illustration of these steps are borrowed by Seton and Carter from Cicero's *De Inventione*, 1.33.58-59.[73] Rhetorical induction is also made an affiliated type of argumentation, and it is differentiated from dialectical induction as a probable conclusion based upon cases differs from a necessary conclusion based upon cases.[74] Still another affiliated type is the dilemma, and with it Book III ends.

[66] Sig. LIV. The Latin text reads: "Svmmus huius artis scopus, ad quem omnia diriguntur, est argumentatio. Cui explicandȩ tertium librū destinauimus. Primùm ergo quid argumentatio, deinde quotuplex sit, postremò quae ei affinia sunt demonstrandum est."
[67] Sig. L3r.   [68] Sig. L3v.   [69] Sig. L4v.
[70] Sig. N8v. The Latin definition is: "Inductio est argumentatio à pluribus singularibus ad vniuersale: vel à partibus ad totum progressio."
[71] Sig. O3r.   [72] Sig. O5r.   [73] Sig. N5v.
[74] Sig. O2r.

Book IV, as indicated earlier, deals with invention, the second main part of dialectic, and proceeds to classify, enumerate, and discuss all of the places in which argumentative materials could be found. This section of dialectical theory depends ultimately, of course, upon Aristotle's *Topics*, usually arranged as the fifth book of the *Organon*. The places are indicated in tabular form by Seton and Carter as being divided into two main classes, the internal and the external, each of which is further divided and subdivided until thirty-three places are ultimately specified.[75]

Seton and Carter's *Dialectica* is virtually the last major document in the history of scholastic logic in England. Even as it appeared in 1572, new influences were beginning to be felt among English logicians, and the chief of these influences was to be Ramistic logic, already on the threshold of being given an English translation and a Latin edition for the first time at an English press. This historical fact sheds some interesting light upon the complimentary verses which Thomas Drant wrote as a preface to Carter's annotations of Seton. These verses are a catalogue of the names of famous logicians of the past, and of the place of Thomas Wilson, John Seton, and Peter Carter on that roll. Ramus is also there, although not in such a way as to suggest that his dialectic might one day supplant on English soil the scholastic logic celebrated by Drant. The verses which contain Drant's references to Seton and Carter, Wilson and Ramus, run as follows:

> Yet helpful is Ramus, as if he alone were the
> fruit-bearer,
> Thrusts he forth grape-clusters joyful, with
> Phoebus smiling the while.
> The force of examples adorns him, as do also
> finiteness and use,
> Art also adorns him, and maxims, and luminous
> order.
> Nothing sweet to have tasted in fruits of that
> very rame.
> Our Wilson has spoken in accents of our very
> country,
> The Britannic Muse praises him still for his
> pioneering:

[75] Sig. P1r.

Nor, Seton, is your labor done in an ignoble
fashion,
Nor Carter, is yours: grace lies in both of your
works.[76]

[76] Sig. A4v. The Latin text reads:

Vtilis ast Ramus, quasi solus fructifer esset,
Protrudit laetos (Phoebo ridente) racemos.
Hunc exemplorum virtus, hunc finis, & vsus,
Hunc ars & voces ornant & lucidus ordo.
Fructibus istius Rami, nil dulcidus esu.
Wilsonus nostras, nostrati voce locutus
Claret adhuc nouitate rei, Musaque Britanna:
Nec (Setone) tuum plane est ignobile factum,
Nec (Cartere) tuum: decus est vtroque labore.

The play on the word "ramus," which as a common noun means "branch," "bough," "twig," etc., is not easily rendered into English. The rare English word "rame," meaning "branch of a tree" is the only possibility I can find for Drant's playful and difficult Latin.

III. Witcraft

RALPH LEVER's *The Arte of Reason, rightly termed, Witcraft*, published at London in 1573, has the interesting distinction of being the second full-fledged logic in English, the final English logic in the tradition of pre-Ramistic scholasticism, and a work which, had things turned out a bit differently, might have stood where Wilson's *Rule of Reason* stands as the first complete logic in our language.[1] In view of Lever's theory of the proper terminology for English logic, he might have changed the whole vocabulary of this science in the English-speaking world, had his *Witcraft* preceded Wilson's more conservative work and gained for itself the authority that any original effort usually commands. At any rate, my account of scholastic logic in England would be incomplete without reference to Lever, and would lack some elements of color that only his peculiar approach to his subject can impart. Thus to him I now turn in bringing this chapter to a close.

Lever's career was parallel to Wilson's in many ways. Both were born in the middle years of the decade between 1520 and 1530. Both were educated at Cambridge, where Wilson attended King's College, and Lever, St. John's. Both were undergraduates at about the same time, Wilson being awarded his bachelor's degree in arts in 1545-46, and Lever his two years later. The same time interval separated them when they both took their master's degree at Cambridge three years after their first degree. For a time both were in the service of noble families, Wilson as tutor of the sons of the Duchess of Suffolk, and Lever as tutor of Walter, first earl of Essex, to whom he later dedicated his *Witcraft*. Both were in exile from England during the bitter reign of Mary Tudor. Both had a connection with Durham, Lever being appointed canon of that cathedral in 1567, and Wilson lay dean in 1580. Wilson's biographer comments that Ralph Lever protested against Wilson's being given this appointment, apparently on the ground that the post should have gone to a professional churchman.[2] Both men held doctoral degrees, Wilson from Ferrera

---

[1] The title page reads: "The Arte of Reason, rightly termed, Witcraft, teaching a perfect way to argue and dispute. Made by Raphe Leuer. Seene and allowed, according to the order appointed in the Queenes Maiesties Iniunctions. Imprinted at London, by H. Bynneman, dwelling in Knightrider streate, at the signe of the Mermayde. Anno. 1573. These Bookes are to be solde at his Shop at the Northvvest dore of Paules church." My references below are to the Huntington Library photostat of their own copy of this work. So far as I know, the 1573 edition is the only one ever made.

[2] *Dictionary of National Biography*, s.v. Wilson, Thomas (1525?-1581). Ralph Lever's biography in the same work does not refer to this interesting fact.

and Lever from Cambridge. As has been said, both wrote complete English logics, and were the two first to do so. Finally, both died in the first half of the decade between 1580 and 1590, Wilson being then famous as privy councillor and secretary of state, whereas Lever was at least of solid standing as holder of successive ecclesiastical posts and as master of Sherburn Hospital in Durham.

There is some reason to believe that Lever became interested in the project of writing a logic in English shortly after his undergraduate days at Cambridge, even as Wilson had done. In the dedicatory letter in *Witcraft*, as he bestows his work upon the earl of Essex, Lever says that "Martine Bucer read ouer this arte, in his old days, and renevved in his age, the rules that he learned thereof in his youth."[3] This remark appears to place the date of the completion of *Witcraft* sometime in the period between 1549 and 1551, even though the work was not published until more than twenty years thereafter. As evidence that *Witcraft* belongs to this two-year period, there is the circumstance of Bucer's having been regius professor of divinity at Cambridge between the autumn of 1549 and the time of his death on February 28, 1551, whereas his earlier career had been spent on the continent as an advocate of Protestantism and an associate of Luther. So far as Lever is concerned, the same two-year period was that in which he held an appointment as fellow of St. John's, Cambridge, and worked to complete the studies for his master's degree. Thus this period is the only time when Bucer's path could have crossed Lever's in such a way as to make it possible for the former to "read ouer" the latter's art of reason.

As additional evidence that *Witcraft* belongs to this two-year period, there is the circumstance of Lever's endeavoring in "The Forespeache" of his work "To proue that the arte of Reasoning may be taught in englishe."[4] Lever's whole discussion of this point appears to fit historically into the period before 1551, but not into the period that followed. For in 1551, as noted earlier, Wilson's *Rule of Reason* was published, and it was popular enough to have had four later editions before Lever's *Witcraft* appeared in print.[5] Now, Lever does not refer to the *Rule of Reason* as an unsatisfactory first step in the attempt to teach logic in English. What is more striking, he does not mention Wilson's pioneering work anywhere in the preface or text of *Witcraft*, even though, as I said, Wilson had been an older contemporary of his at Cambridge, and had conspicuously succeeded

[3] *Witcraft*, sig. *3r.   [4] Sig. *4r.   [5] See above, p. 29.

long before *Witcraft* was published in accomplishing the very purpose which Lever himself was attempting. These omissions make it difficult to believe that the main body of *Witcraft* was written after Wilson's *Rule of Reason* was published. Coupled with the reference to Bucer's having read the work in his old age, Lever's complete silence on the subject of Wilson offers strong proof that *Witcraft* was already in something like final form at the very moment when the *Rule of Reason* captured the honor of being the first logic in English. Only an author who has been beaten to the press by a rival can fully appreciate what Lever's frustration must have been when the *Rule of Reason* appeared in 1551. But Lever gained second honors at least by putting out *Witcraft* when he did. All he probably added to the manuscript Bucer had seen were the dedicatory letter and the concluding section of "The Forespeache." This concluding section, which ends with the words, "Farewell from Duresme, the .24. of Nouember, 1572,"[6] contains a spirited denunciation of one W. F., who had edited Lever's *The Philosopher's Game* in 1563 without Lever's authorization and without respecting Lever's manuscript.[7] This denunciation and the dedicatory letter with its reference to Lever's period of service as tutor of Essex could not have been written before 1563, but everything else in *Witcraft* could have been and undoubtedly was the product of the period between 1549 and 1551.

Lever's approach to the task of creating an English logic where none as yet existed was ingenious and radical. Most scholars in his position would have created an English vocabulary out of the forms of the established Latin vocabulary. In fact, Wilson was then doing this very thing in preparing his *Rule of Reason* for the press. Thus he was referring to his subject as logic or dialectic, and to its cognate subject as rhetoric, as if Latin words could become English almost

---

[6] Sig. **4r.

[7] *The Most Noble auncient, and learned playe, called the Philosophers game*, by Rafe Leuer and augmented by W. F. (London, [1563]), is devoted to the description of a game called "the battell of numbers" as played on "a doble chesse bord" (sig. A1r, A2r). "W. F." is identified as William Fulke by Lever's biographer in the *Dictionary of National Biography*; but he should be identified as William Fullwood, according to the better authority of the Huntington Library Catalogue. The Huntington Catalogue, s.v. Fullwood, William, points out that the verses on the fifteenth page (which are entitled "The bookes verdicte" and fall on the page preceding the text) are an acrostic, with the first letter in each line combining to read "VV I L Y A M F V L V O D." This William Fullwood was the one who published at London in 1568 *The Enimie of Idlenesse*, discussed below (pp. 143-145) as one of the early formulary rhetorics in England.

without change. Thus too he was creating for logic an English vocabulary made up of such terms as predicables, predicaments, definition,
proposition, subject, predicate, and so on, where his every term had
a form derived from its Latin equivalent. But Lever would have
none of this. In his preface he states a less expected theory regarding
the problem of an English logic:

> Therefore consider the case as it is: An arte is to be taughte in that
> toung, in whiche it was neuer written afore. Nowe the question lyeth,
> whether it were better to borrowe termes of some other toung, in
> whiche this sayde Arte hath bene written: and by a litle chaunge of
> pronouncing, to séeke to make them Englishe wordes, whiche are
> none in déede: or else of simple vsual wordes, to make compounded
> termes, whose seuerall partes considered alone, are familiar and
> knowne to all english men?[8]

The second of these options is the one chosen by Lever. He believes
himself to be close to the genius of our language in making this
choice, as he himself observes:

> As for deuising of newe termes, and compoūding of wordes, our
> tongue hath a speciall grace, wherein it excelleth many other, & is
> comparable with the best. The cause is, for that the moste parte of
> Englyshe woordes are shorte, and stande on one sillable a péece. So
> that two or thrée of them are ofte times fitly ioyned in one.[9]

Thus does Lever expound his theory of an English terminology
for logic. But even with this theory in mind, the reader is not fully
prepared for what he finds later in the actual text of *Witcraft*. He
finds nothing unexpected in the way of doctrine, to be sure. Lever
arranges his doctrine into four books, precisely as Seton had done,
the three first books being devoted to judgment or disposition, and
the last, to invention. Moreover, in progressing through these two
grand divisions of logic, Lever goes from simpler to more complex
units of discourse, speaking in Book I of words, in Book II of propositions, in Book III of inductive and deductive arguments, and in
Book IV of the places or topics. But the reader in assimilating this
conventional scholastic doctrine finds himself in contact with an
amazing terminology. Lever's preface contains several anticipations
of his vocabulary, and one of the best is the passage in which he gives
his reader a first taste of what is to come. After stating his preference
for a familiar English vocabulary, he says:

[8] *Witcraft*, sig. *5v-*6r.   [9] *Ibid.*, sig. *5r-*5v.

For trial hereof, I wish you to aske of an english man, who vnder-
standeth neither Greek nor Latin, what he conceiueth in his mind,
when he heareth this word a backset, and what he doth conceiue when
he heareth this terme a Predicate. And doubtlesse he must confesse,
if he consider ý matter aright or haue any sharpnesse of wit at al,
that by a backset, he conceiueth a thing that muste be set after, and
by a predicate, that he doth vnderstande nothing at all. The like shall
fall foorth when comparison is made, betwixt any of our new termes
compounded of true english words, and the inkhorne termes deriued
of straunge and forain languages.[10]

A preference for "backset" as opposed to "predicate" is a fair
sample of the prevailing direction of Lever's vocabulary. "Logic" or
"dialectic" as terms for the subject he is treating disappear in favor
of "witcraft." "Rhetoric" as a term for the other branch of the theory
of communication disappears in favor of "spéechcrafte." "Astronomy," on the few occasions when it is mentioned, disappears in favor
of "starcraft." Thus Lever says at one point: "For if it be wel sayd,
learning is not gotten with ease: it is also well sayd: witcraft is not
gotten with ease, spéechcrafte, starcraft, Physike, lawe, or any other
kind of learning."[11] In his table of special terms at the end of his
work, he defines his subject as follows:

Witcrafte. . . . If those names be always accompted the best, which
doe moste playnly teache the hearer the meanyng of the thyng, that
they are appoynted to expresse: doubtelesse neyther Logicke, nor
Dialect can be thought so fit an Englishe worde to expresse and set
foorth the Arte of reason by, as Witcraft is, seeing that Wit in oure
mother toung is oft taken for reason: and crafte is the aunciente
English woorde, whereby wée haue vsed to expresse an Arte: whiche
two wordes knit together in Witcrafte, doe signifie the Arte that
teacheth witte and reason.[12]

This principle is everywhere in evidence. Thus, for "category"
Lever has "storehouse"; for "proposition," "saying"; for "declara-
tive proposition," "shewsay"; for "definition," "saywhat"; for "affirmation," "yeasay"; for "negation," "naysay"; for "induction,"
"reason by example"; for "deduction," "reason by rule"; for "premise," "foresaye"; and for "conclusion," "endsay."

A final example will show how strange this language is today,
despite its origin in simple English words. Here is a rule covering
the relation of the elements in a logical proposition to each other:

[10] *Ibid.*, sig. *6r.　　　[11] *Ibid.*, p. 150.　　　[12] *Ibid.*, pp. 238-239.

> If the backset be sayd of the foreset, and be neyther his sayewhat, propretie, nor difference: then it is an Inbeer. For that we count an Inbeer, which being in a thing, is neyther his saywhat, propretie, kinde, nor difference.[13]

When there was no established vocabulary for English logic, this rule would doubtless have sounded as unfamiliar in a Latinized English as in Lever's Saxon English. But today Lever's English is almost completely unintelligible, and would have to be turned into the very inkhorn terms he despised in order to yield its meaning. What he is saying is this:

> If the predicate is said of the subject, and is neither the definition, the property, nor the differentia, of the subject, then it is an accident. For that we count as accident, which being in a thing, is neither that thing's definition, property, genus, nor differentia.

Like the other logicians in the scholastic tradition, Lever follows Aristotle as his ultimate authority. Unlike many of them, Lever is explicit on this point. He says in his preface:

> Now to let euerie writer haue his deserued praise, I confesse (to them that desire to knowe whom I folow) that in my thrée firste bookes, I onely folow Aristotle: both for matter, & also for order.[14]

Aristotle, he adds, far surpasses all profane writers in the truth of his substance and the plainness of his manner. Who these profane writers are, Lever does not say. But he describes them in general terms as follows:

> As for Ciceronians & suger tongued fellowes, which labour more for finenes of speach, then for knowledge of good matter, they oft speake much to small purpose, and shaking foorth a number of choise words, and picked sentences, they hinder good learning, wyth their fond chatte.[15]

As for Lever's authority in the final book of *Witcraft*, he confesses himself to be independent of those who have written on invention, even though he pays tribute to the method of invention advocated in Aristotle's *Topics*. His words are:

> But in my fourth booke, which intreateth of the places, & sheweth a way how to prouide store of arguments: I haue thought good neither fully to folow Aristotle: nor yet anye other that I haue seene. For

[13] *Ibid.*, p. 73.   [14] *Ibid.*, sig. **ır-**ıv.   [15] *Ibid.*, sig. **ıv.

Aristotles inuention serueth best, for vniuersitie men, when a question is broughte to some generall issue, as to proue that the backset is, or is not, the saywhat, the kinde, the propertie, or the Inbeer of the foreset. Howbeit, men vse in disputing or writing, to argue to and fro, neuer bringing the matter that lyeth in question, to anye of these foure generall issues.[16]

One of the last things Lever says in his preface is that he may one day supplement *Witcraft* by a work on the faults of reasoning.[17] He is obviously thinking at that point of Aristotle's *Sophistical Elenchi* as the final treatise in the *Organon,* and of the desirability of covering the subject of fallacies himself, so that his own English logic would extend at last over the entire territory assigned to it by Aristotle. It is interesting to think that if Lever had applied his theory of logical terminology to fallacies, the English language would have had in the sixteenth century as unusual a work on that subject as Bentham finally wrote in the beginning of the nineteenth century, although Lever's approach would certainly have been less profound than Bentham's. But Lever apparently never completed the task of putting the *Organon* into an English vocabulary. Still, except for the section on fallacies, he covers Aristotle's logical writings in round terms, and thus gives us an odd monument to stand at the end of the scholastic period in English logic.

[16] *Ibid.,* sig. **1v-**2r.   [17] *Ibid.,* sig. **4r.

CHAPTER 3

Traditional Rhetoric: The Three Patterns

I. Origin and Boundaries

ETWEEN the year 700 and the year 1573, rhetoric flourished continuously in England as that branch of the theory of communication in which directions were set down, and observations made, for the guidance of speakers or writers whose audience was the populace and whose purpose was instruction or persuasion by means not primarily connected with the use of fictions.[1]

As indicated earlier, the directions and observations which made up rhetoric during this period of eight hundred odd years are perhaps best termed traditional. It is a temptation to call them scholastic, and thus to speak of scholastic rhetoric as the companion of scholastic logic. But the term "scholastic" as connected with rhetoric would imply, not only a sort of rhetoric that was the product of a profound deference to authority, not only the sort that reduced the theory of communication to a stiff and formal method, but also the sort wherein deference to authority would mean deference to Aristotle. After all, these three meanings are always in our minds when we speak of scholasticism in logic. Although the first two meanings would describe the rhetoric I am speaking of in this chapter, the last would not, except in a remote sense. In other words, it is not accurate to say that Aristotle is the authority behind English rhetoric in the period before 1573.[2] As we have seen, he taught Englishmen logic in that time, and it might be added that he was the great teacher of logic in western Europe during the whole period between his own era and

---

[1] For various parts of this period rhetoric has been discussed historically by the following authors: E. E. Hale, Jr., "Ideas on Rhetoric in the Sixteenth Century," *Publications of the Modern Language Association*, XVIII (1903), 424-444; R. C. Jebb, "Rhetoric," in *The Encyclopaedia Britannica*, 11th edn.; Donald Lemen Clark, *Rhetoric and Poetry in the Renaissance* (New York, 1922); Baldwin, *Medieval Rhetoric and Poetic*; William Phillips Sandford, *English Theories of Public Address, 1530-1828* (The Ohio State University, 1929); William Garrett Crane, *Wit and Rhetoric in the Renaissance* (New York, 1937); Thomas Whitfield Baldwin, *William Shakspere's Small Latine & Lesse Greeke* (Urbana, 1944), II, 1-238; J. W. H. Atkins, *English Literary Criticism: The Renascence* (London, 1947), pp. 66-101, cited below as *The Renascence*; Sister Miriam Joseph, *Shakespeare's Use of the Arts of Language* (New York, 1947); Wilbur S. Howell, "English Backgrounds of Rhetoric," *History of Speech Education in America* (New York: Appleton-Century-Crofts, 1954), pp. 3-47.

[2] For a thorough investigation of this question, see Lee Sisson Hultzén, "Aristotle's *Rhetoric* in England to 1600" (Unpbl. diss., Cornell University, 1932).

that of the Renaissance. But Cicero, who was a profound student of Aristotelian logic and rhetoric, formulated from that and other sources a rhetorical system to which all rhetorical instruction in western Europe during the period now under discussion must be referred. Thus Cicero was the great teacher of rhetoric in western Christendom while scholastic logic held sway, and I should not like to deprive him of that title by calling his doctrines scholastic. The term "traditional rhetoric," as a substitute, suggests, of course, a doctrine transmitted orally from teacher to pupil and from generation to generation. It suggests also, not so much a theory composed of generalizations constantly revised by reference to practice, as a body of ritualistic conventions that have forgotten their original contact with the real world. Neither of these implications is intended in the present chapter. Traditional rhetoric was constantly being reformulated in writing during the eight hundred odd years now under analysis, and those reformulations are the basic documents I shall discuss. Moreover, traditional rhetoric did not become a body of rituals insulated from the needs of successive generations of speakers and writers. Speaking in the law court, in the pulpit, and in the council of state, as well as writing to dignitaries or to friends or to congregations, are continuing activities. Rhetorical theory was originally developed to teach them, and always bears a relation to them. In the period here being considered, these activities prevented rhetoric from losing contact with the world. What I should like the term "traditional rhetoric" to mean is that system of precepts which, as delivered in writing from teacher to student and from generation to generation in England between 700 and 1573, owed its authority to the teachings and prestige of Cicero, and needed in that entire period only a few minor revisions to keep it abreast of the needs of the times.

Traditional rhetoric, as I mentioned above in Chapter 1, has three patterns, the Ciceronian, the stylistic, and the formulary. Each of these will now receive attention. The Ciceronian pattern cannot be connected with the works of Englishmen until almost a century after the appearance on English soil of the stylistic pattern, but nevertheless the Ciceronian pattern, as the most comprehensive of the forms in which the teachings of Cicero made themselves felt, will be discussed first. The formulary pattern, so far as the English record is concerned, did not appear until late in the period under discussion here, and even when it did appear, it never became very popular. But it deserves some treatment, nevertheless, and I shall consider it in the final section of the present chapter.

II. The Five Great Arts

CICERONIAN rhetoric in the form which it assumed in Cicero's own works is best described as an art made up of five arts. These five arts or five procedures constitute the complex act of producing a communication intended for the popular audience, and Cicero designates these procedures as invention, arrangement, style, memory, and delivery. In *De Inventione*, the first work which Cicero wrote on the subject of rhetoric, he defined these five procedures as he and his later disciples generally conceived of them, and these definitions are brief enough for quotation here:

> Invention is the discovery of valid or seemingly valid arguments to render one's cause plausible. Arrangement is the distribution of arguments thus discovered in the proper order. Expression [that is, *elocutio*, Cicero's term for style] is the fitting of the proper language to the invented matter. Memory is the firm mental grasp of matter and words. Delivery is the control of voice and body in a manner suitable to the dignity of the subject matter and the style.[1]

Cicero's *De Inventione* discusses only the first of these five procedures, although, had it been completed, it would have covered the others as well. The earliest extant Latin treatment of the doctrine involved in these five procedures is that found in *Ad C. Herennium Libri Quattuor De Arte Rhetorica*, usually called the *Rhetorica ad Herennium*. During the Middle Ages the *Rhetorica ad Herennium* was ascribed to Cicero, and was often called the *Rhetorica Secunda* or *Rhetorica Nova* to distinguish it from Cicero's *De Inventione*, which was called the *Rhetorica Prima* or *Rhetorica Vetus*.[2] Nowadays the *Rhetorica ad Herennium* is not accepted as Cicero's work, but nobody disputes the great similarity between it and Cicero's *De Inventione*, so far as the latter goes. Nor is it unfair to assume that the two works would have been closely alike throughout, if Cicero had completed *De Inventione*.

In his other major writings on rhetoric, Cicero holds to these five procedures as his basic terms, whether he deals with them all, as in *De Oratore* and *De Partitione Oratoria*, or mainly with the third

---

[1] Cicero, *De Inventione*, 1.7.9, trans. H. M. Hubbell (The Loeb Classical Library, Cambridge, Mass. and London, 1949), pp. 19-21.

[2] Edmond Faral, *Les Arts Poétiques du XIIe et du XIIIe Siècle* (Paris, 1924), p. 49; also Atkins, *The Medieval Phase*, p. 116; also below, p. 77.

one, style, as in *Orator*.[3] The following words from his *Brutus*, spoken by himself as he and Brutus and Atticus converse about rhetoric on his own lawn near a statue of Plato, show his enduring regard for eloquence as the product of these five faculties:

> Well then, . . . to praise eloquence, to set forth its power and the honours which it brings to those who have it, is not my present purpose, nor is it necessary. However, this one thing I venture to affirm without fear of contradiction, that whether it is a product of rules and theory, or a technique dependent on practice, or on natural gifts, it is one attainment amongst all others of unique difficulty. For of the five elements of which, as we say, it is made up, each one is in its own right a great art. One may guess therefore what power is inherent in an art made up of five great arts, and what difficulty it presents.[4]

An art made up of five great arts—this is the Ciceronian thesis about rhetoric. The most thorough commentary in ancient Roman times upon these five arts, as treated by Cicero and many lesser writers, is Quintilian's *Institutio Oratoria*, written towards the end of the first century A.D. "The art of oratory, as taught by most authorities, and those the best," says Quintilian, "consists of five parts:— *invention, arrangement, expression, memory,* and *delivery* or *action* (the two latter terms being used synonymously)."[5] Of the twelve books of his learned and important *Institutio Oratoria*, Books 3, 4, 5, and 6 deal with *inventio* and constitute a summary of all previous thinking upon this first and most difficult of the tasks of the speaker and writer; Book 7 deals with *dispositio*; Books 8, 9, 10, and the first chapter of 11 deal with *elocutio*, usually considered the procedure that demanded almost as much space in rhetorical theory as *inventio*; and Book 11 in its other two chapters deals respectively with *memoria* and *pronuntiatio*. Thus Quintilian adheres to the practice of the best authorities. The first two and the final books of his work are concerned with the earliest phases of the training of

---

[3] Cicero's constant reference to these five terms is a feature of all his writings on rhetoric. For samples of his use of them, see *De Oratore*, 1.28.128; 1.31.142; 1.42.187; 2.19.79; 2.85.350; see also *De Partitione Oratoria*, 1.3, and *Orator*, 14.43-55.

[4] *Brutus*, 6.25, trans. G. L. Hendrickson (The Loeb Classical Library, Cambridge, Mass. and London, 1939), pp. 35-37.

[5] *Institutio Oratoria*, 3.3.1, trans. H. E. Butler (The Loeb Classical Library, London and New York, 1933), I, 383. Italics are Butler's. Quintilian's own words are: "Omnis autem orandi ratio, ut plurimi maximique auctores tradiderunt, quinque partibus constat, inventione, dispositione, elocutione, memoria, pronuntiatione sive actione, utroque enim modo dicitur."

speaker and writer, and with the later phases of the career of the orator in society. Cicero is the authority whom Quintilian undoubtedly admires most; but there are many other rhetoricians mentioned in his pages, some famous and others little known, whose opinions are quoted and sometimes disputed as he proceeds with his discussion of the five procedures constituting the Ciceronian theory of rhetoric.

Invention, as the process of discovering valid or seemingly valid arguments to render one's case plausible, sounds at first like an invitation to master the appearances rather than the realities of tight and honest proof. Actually, however, it was an invitation to speaker or writer to find the best of available materials, wherever they might be. Some of these available materials would be documentary evidence, eyewitness testimony, confessions, and the like. Perhaps on occasion such proofs as these would be sufficient. The art of rhetoric, according to the ancient idea, did not extend to the discovery or use of such proofs as these, which were called non-artistic, in the sense that they were there to start with, and had only to be used, not discovered by a theoretical process. Rhetorical invention was concerned rather with the theoretical process by which proofs not there to start with could be discovered or uncovered. These proofs were called artistic, not because they were considered more ingenious if less convincing than the others, but simply because they were regarded as being subject to discovery by a theoretical means that was always available for that use. Aristotle's *Rhetoric* makes something of the difference between non-artistic and artistic proofs, the latter being in fact considered to be the only proof that belonged properly to rhetorical theory, inasmuch as theory could be no guide to the discovery of the former. Says Aristotle in a passage that was to have great influence:

> Of the modes of persuasion some belong strictly to the art of rhetoric and some do not. By the latter I mean such things as are not supplied by the speaker but are there at the outset—witnesses, evidence given under torture, written contracts, and so on. By the former I mean such as we can ourselves construct by means of the principles of rhetoric. The one kind has merely to be used, the other has to be invented.[6]

This distinction between non-artistic and artistic proofs was accepted by Cicero and Quintilian as an important dividing line, on one

[6] *Rhetoric*, 1355[b] 36ff., trans. W. Rhys Roberts in *The Works of Aristotle*, ed. Ross, XI.

side of which lay relatively unpredictable materials, varying greatly in weight and number from case to case, while on the other side lay the relatively predictable materials that tended to be of constant application to all sorts of cases, and that could usually be brought to light by systematic analysis.[7] Rhetorical invention meant the process of systematic analysis which would produce these circumstantial materials, or proofs based upon constant factors in every case. If a murderer could be convicted by impeccable eyewitness testimony, supplemented by his confession, and by other tangible direct evidence, then rhetorical theory could offer little help to the prosecutor, who would be able to gain his point simply by using these overwhelming direct means. But if there were no eyewitnesses, no confession, not much tangible direct evidence, but nevertheless a victim and the probability of a crime, rhetorical theory could offer some help by pointing to those collateral facts which, in the common experience of mankind, are usually or always a kind of proof of the main fact at issue.

Our modern distinction between direct and indirect evidence is parallel to the ancient distinction between non-artistic and artistic proofs. Incidentally, one great difference between ancient and modern rhetorical theory is that ancient peoples, less experienced than man has since become in the methods of investigating all aspects of his physical environment, tended to decide doubtful issues upon collateral or indirect evidence, and to believe in the validity of their decisions, with the result that ancient rhetorical theory stressed the system by which indirect evidence was to be assembled; whereas modern peoples have less faith in collateral evidence, and more taste for decisions based upon direct evidence, with the result that modern rhetorical theory has abandoned the ancient system of invention, and replaced it with techniques for the discovery of direct evidence in every case at issue. At any rate, the ancient system of invention, as planned by Aristotle and elaborated by later theorists, chiefly Cicero and Quintilian, survived and answered men's needs until the time of the Renaissance, when it began to lose favor and to be supplanted by modes of assembling factual data in connection with the process of deliberation and decision.

Cicero's *De Inventione,* in giving an authoritative account of the ancient system of rhetorical invention, obliges the speaker to assemble

---

[7] See *De Inventione,* 2.14.47; *De Oratore,* 2.27.116-117; also *Institutio Oratoria,* 5.1.1.

proof by making three large decisions about the case which becomes his to argue. One of these decisions requires that the case be classified as to the kinds of oratory in use in human affairs. There were three kinds of oratory in use in ancient Greece and Rome: the demonstrative or eulogistic, the deliberative or political, and the judicial or forensic. Each of these types had its own set of customary moral issues. Thus demonstrative oratory was addressed to questions of honor or dishonor; deliberative oratory, to questions of expediency or inexpediency; judicial oratory, to questions of justice or injustice. If we assume that any man who thinks at all would have assembled a store of ideas upon these questions, then we may suggest to him that that store is one place for research whenever he has to make a speech, and that his research should begin by determining which of the three sections of that store his subject will most intimately concern.[8]

Another of the decisions which the speaker has to make in assembling proof for his case requires him to classify his subject as to the types of positions involved in disputes. This decision is connected with a system of elaborate technicalities, the key term in which is *constitutio* in the earliest Latin rhetorics like *De Inventione* and the *Rhetorica ad Herennium*, and *status* in later works like Quintilian's *Institutio Oratoria*.[9] These two terms, and others sometimes preferred in place of them, represent the theory that disputes arise as the result of a conflict between someone's allegation and someone else's reply, and that, because allegations and replies tend to be limited to a few types, disputants tend therefore to take one of a small number of fixed positions in conducting arguments. The precise number of the positions available to disputants varies from one ancient rhetorical theorist to another. In *De Inventione*, Cicero says that four positions are available whenever speakers debate upon traditional meanings of things said or done; and he also says that there are five quasi-positions available whenever debates arise upon the meanings of written documents.[10] If, for example, an allegation is made that the speaker

[8] For Cicero's discussion of these three types of oratory in connection with the task of rhetorical invention, see *De Inventione*, 1.5,7; 2.4.12-13; 2.23-39; 2.51.155-178.

[9] The best ancient discussion of the meaning of *constitutio* and *status* in rhetorical theory is that in Quintilian, *Institutio Oratoria*, 3.6.

[10] *De Inventione*, 1.8.10; 1.12.17. The term "quasi-position" as a name for the category of disputes arising over the interpretation of texts is suggested by Cicero's own language in the *Topics*, §95. For a discussion of this category and its companion, the true position, see Howell, *Rhetoric of Alcuin*, pp. 36-37. For Cicero's analysis of the four positions and the five quasi-positions, see *De Inventione*, 1.8.10-16; 1.12.17-18; 2.4-39; 2.40.116-154.

committed a certain crime, and the speaker denies that he committed it, he has taken a position called conjectural by Cicero, and positions of this kind are defended (or attacked) in certain fixed ways. If the allegation is that the speaker committed a certain act constituting robbery, and the speaker denies that his act does constitute robbery, he takes what Cicero calls the definitive position, and positions of this kind are defended (or attacked) in certain fixed ways. The other two of these four positions are called the general and the procedural, the former being the locality in which the question concerns the justice or injustice of an act, and the latter, the locality in which questions arise as to whether a given court or tribunal has jurisdiction in the case under debate.

As for the five quasi-positions, they are assumed at various times in debates over things written. Suppose, for example, that there is a discrepancy between what written words say and what their author apparently meant. Or suppose that there is a discrepancy between one and another written rule for cases of a given kind. Or suppose that what has been written is subject to two or more interpretations. Or suppose that what has been written does not quite fit the case to which it is applied. Or suppose that what is written contains a key term that is left undefined. All of these causes of dispute exist wherever there also exists any document to limit or prescribe human action. For each of these five types of dispute, as for each of the preceding four, the attack and defense are subject to description in advance, and rhetorical theory undertakes to supply that description as a means of enabling the speaker to make the second of the three large decisions required of him by the system of inventing artistic proofs.

The third decision required of the speaker forces him to consider the successive steps necessary for persuasive presentation of any subject. The common experience of mankind indicates that in the presentation of any subject the interest of the hearer should first be aroused. Then the subject should be made understandable in terms of the events which have made its discussion necessary. Next, the argument about to be launched in connection with the subject should be stated in round terms, so that an audience will appreciate what position the speaker takes, and to what propositions his proof will be answerable. Next, the proof of those propositions should be advanced, and any contrary propositions that the speaker's opponent could uphold should be destroyed or refuted. Finally, the sentiments and emotions of the hearer should be aroused in connection with the human implications of the proof. These six steps permitted the ancient rhetoricians to discuss, as one of the big topics in rhetorical invention, the successive parts of the classical oration, usually enumerated as introduction, narration, division, proof, refutation, and conclusion.[11]

The tendency to treat the six parts of the oration under the heading of invention was not without its limitations, so far as the ancient rhetoricians were concerned. For if rhetoric was made to consist of the five procedures that Cicero declared it to have, and if the first of these procedures, that is, invention, received so wide a treatment as to include the six parts of the oration, what was to be said when the second procedure, arrangement, came up for discussion? Cicero's *De Inventione* contains no answer to this question—it treats the six parts of an oration under the heading of invention, and breaks off at that point, leaving arrangement, style, memory, and delivery untouched. The earliest Latin treatise to attempt to answer the question is the *Rhetorica ad Herennium*. The *Rhetorica ad Herennium* analyzes the six parts of the oration when it discusses invention; and then, when it comes to arrangement, as the second main part of rhetoric, it says in effect that arrangement in theory consists of placing in each part of the oration what should be placed there, whereas arrangement in actual practice consists in knowing under what circumstances to omit one or more of the standard parts of the oration or when to rearrange their standard order.[12] In other words, this authoritative treatise handles arrangement by recognizing it as an independent part of rhetoric and by explaining it later as a subordinate part of one of the other independent parts.

As for style, memory, and delivery, they were given their due share of attention in ancient rhetoric, after arrangement had been treated thus ambiguously. Style, as the third part of Cicero's program, was usually considered to be next to invention in importance, and was thus treated more fully than arrangement, memory, or delivery. The kind of treatment style received in such treatises as the *Rhetorica ad Herennium*, the *Orator*, and the *Institutio Oratoria* will be indicated later when I speak of the stylistic pattern of English rhetoric. Memory and delivery will also be explained later, as these main topics emerge in English versions of the full Ciceronian pattern. Incidentally, memory has an unusual subject matter connected with it in

---

[11] For Cicero's discussion of the six parts of the oration in connection with the task of rhetorical invention, see *De Inventione*, 1.14-56.

[12] *Rhetorica ad Herennium*, 3.9-10.

treatises on rhetoric in ancient times and in the Renaissance, but it was not given as much space in rhetorical theory as invention and style received; whereas delivery, which concerned the use of the voice and body in pronouncing an oral message to an audience, was considered to be of overwhelming importance in the process of communication but was not thought to be particularly susceptible to theoretical treatment.

Many English rhetorics in the period between 700 and 1573 deal with the theory of popular communication by emphasizing some or all of the five procedures just described. Whenever these procedures or a majority of them are mentioned by Englishmen as the basic concepts of rhetoric, and are then treated in such a way as to stress the special importance of invention, the rhetoric thus created becomes Ciceronian in the present sense in which I am using the term.

Alcuin's *De Rhetorica* has already been mentioned as the first work by an Englishman to deal with the five procedures of Ciceronian rhetoric. In turning now to this work to examine what Ciceronian rhetoric looked like in its earliest appearance in English learning, I should like to emphasize again that Alcuin wrote it in the year 794 as a dialogue between himself and Charlemagne not only to improve rhetorical instruction throughout the Carolingian empire but also to provide his readers with the precepts of one of the grand divisions of logic, the other division being covered by his *De Dialectica*.[13] I might add that *De Rhetorica* is an attractive little work, quite apart from the interest it holds as the first statement by an Englishman of Cicero's theory of popular communication; and that, as a work of scholarship, it captures more of the spirit of Cicero than the *De Dialectica* captures of the spirit of Aristotle.

Alcuin's treatment of rhetorical invention is in reality an abridgment of Cicero's entire *De Inventione*.[14] Whole passages from the Ciceronian treatise are taken over and pieced together by Alcuin in such fashion that he gives his readers a fair outline of all the material in that source. Thus he indicates the three kinds of oratory and their customary moral issues. Thus he speaks in some detail of the four

---

[13] See above, pp. 32-36, especially note 7. The Latin text and an English translation of Alcuin's treatise on rhetoric, which is formally called *Disputatio de Rhetorica et de Virtutibus Sapientissimi Regis Karli et Albini Magistri*, may be found in Howell, *Rhetoric of Alcuin*. For other editions of the Latin text, see Migne, *Patrologia Latina*, CI, 919-950, and Halm, *Rhetores Latini Minores*, pp. 523-550.

[14] For particulars regarding this and other sources of *De Rhetorica*, see Howell, *Rhetoric of Alcuin*, pp. 22-33, 159-169.

positions and the five quasi-positions. Thus he emphasizes the six parts of the oration and the materials and objectives of each part. His discussion of the six parts of the oration covers almost twice as much space as he allots to the nine positions, and a little more than four times as much space as he allots to the three kinds of oratory.[15] Moreover, these topics, as the principal part of his discussion of invention, are given more care than he bestows in the aggregate upon arrangement, style, memory, and delivery as the other parts of rhetoric.

For his treatment of these other parts, Alcuin depends upon a rhetorician of the fourth century A.D. named Julius Victor, whose *Ars Rhetorica* had dealt with the subject of Ciceronian rhetoric, and whose explanation of arrangement, style, memory, and delivery was made up of doctrine from Cicero's *Orator* and *De Oratore*, and from Quintilian's *Institutio Oratoria*.[16] Thus Alcuin's treatise remains Ciceronian even when he comes to the end of *De Inventione* and has no other work by Cicero available for use. To arrangement Alcuin devotes little space, since he felt that he had already covered most of that subject when he spoke of the six parts of an oration, and would cover the rest when he spoke of the ordering of words in sentences as a part of style.[17] Nor does he have anything to say of memory, except to stress that Cicero had called it indispensable for a speaker, and that practice and an abstemious life would improve it.[18] As for style, Alcuin speaks of it in such fashion as to indicate only a fraction of that part of Ciceronian theory; but, even so, style ranks next after invention in the amount of space he devotes to it. Delivery he handles by quoting Cicero's opinion of its importance, and by borrowing from Victor some observations that stem from the treatment given this part of rhetoric in Cicero's *De Oratore* and Quintilian's *Institutio Oratoria*.[19]

"With the death of Alcuin," remarks Atkins, "the tradition of learning in England underwent a prolonged eclipse."[20] This observation applies with particular force to Ciceronian rhetoric, for it was a long time after Alcuin's era that interest in the five procedures began

---

[15] Alcuin discusses the three kinds of oratory and related topics from line 88 to line 103 and from line 1199 to 1286 of his text as edited by Howell. The discussion of the nine positions extends in the same text from line 123 to line 395, whereas the six parts of the oration are discussed from line 470 to line 935.

[16] See Howell, *Rhetoric of Alcuin*, pp. 28-33, 167-168.

[17] *Ibid.*, p. 130 [lines 975-985].   [18] *Ibid.*, pp. 136-138 [lines 1070-1083].

[19] *Ibid.*, pp. 138-140 [lines 1092-1134].   [20] *The Medieval Phase*, p. 59.

to reassert itself in written works. Meanwhile, the educational system in England undoubtedly made some attempt to train students in the art of communication, and thus undoubtedly provided some sort of instruction in rhetoric and logic, as well as in grammar. But whether instruction in rhetoric in English schools involved the five procedures of Ciceronian rhetoric, as set forth by such an author as Alcuin, or the stylistic theory of the ancients, as interpreted by Bede and others, is a question not finally answered for the period between 800 and 1200. Nor is it easy to say confidently that a university in any real sense existed at either Oxford or Cambridge during the greater part of that period. There is a tradition, as I mentioned before, which dates the founding of Oxford from the reign of King Alfred, and which represents that monarch as having instituted and endowed lectureships there in almost every faculty about the year 879, Asser of St. David's being recorded as first royal lecturer in grammar and rhetoric.[21] Asser might well have been a teacher of these subjects somewhere in Alfred's realm, but royal support for Oxford and Cambridge as universities did not apparently begin until long after that time, and thus Asser's connection with what could properly be called a royal foundation or even a university in the formal sense is completely unsubstantiated.[22]

Early in the thirteenth century, the procedures of Ciceronian rhetoric reappeared in English learning. This development, however, occurred under the auspices of poetical as opposed to rhetorical theory, and thus was somewhat outside of the Ciceronian tradition as interpreted by Alcuin. The writer who converted Ciceronian terminology to the uses of the art of poetry was Geoffrey of Vinsauf, a shadowy figure in the history of his times, who is believed to be of English origin and to have received his education in part at St. Frideswide's priory in Oxford, and in part in France and Italy, where he spent most of his life. It was his *Poetria Nova*, composed sometime between 1208 and 1213, that discussed the tasks of the poet under the headings of Ciceronian rhetoric, with the doctrine of style featured more than that of invention and disposition.[23] The example which he

---

[21] For the names of these ancient and royal lecturers, see Anthony à Wood, *History and Antiquities of Oxford*, ed. Gutch, II, 819-820. See also above, p. 37.

[22] See Mullinger, *University of Cambridge*, I, 81, note 1.

[23] The text of the *Poetria Nova* is found in Faral, *Les Arts Poétiques du XIIᵉ et du XIIIᵉ Siècle*, pp. 197-262; see the same work, pp. 194-197, for an analysis of the *Poetria Nova*, and pp. 15-33 for a discussion of Geoffrey of Vinsauf; see pp. 28-33 for an analysis of the question of the date of the *Poetria Nova*, which Faral finally places between 1208 and 1213.

set was followed in the early sixteenth century by Stephen Hawes, who has the distinction not only of converting the key terms of the *Rhetorica ad Herennium* and of *De Inventione* to the uses of poetry more fully than Geoffrey had done, but also of being the first Englishman to render those terms and a part of their doctrine into English. Some notion of Geoffrey's *Poetria Nova* can be gained from Hawes, and thus I shall not pause here to discuss it, despite its importance in the history of Ciceronian rhetoric in England. It should be mentioned, however, that Geoffrey is not alone in his time in thinking of the business of the writer as an offshoot of the business of the orator and of Ciceronian rhetoric. Giraldus Cambrensis, a Welsh contemporary of Geoffrey, indicates that the task of the writer necessarily involves the processes of invention, arrangement, and style, and thus he shows his awareness of Ciceronian theory even though he mentions it more to endorse its applicability to writing than to explain its doctrine.[24]

So far as the thirteenth century is concerned, French learning provides a closer approach to the original Ciceronian pattern of rhetoric than does English learning in the *Poetria Nova* of Geoffrey of Vinsauf. Vincent of Beauvais's *Speculum Doctrinale* may be cited in support of this statement. I have already mentioned the *Speculum Doctrinale* as one of the three parts of Vincent's colossal encyclopaedia, the *Speculum Majus*, and as a work which devotes all of Book IV to a discussion of logic, rhetoric, and poetics, with logic receiving 98 chapters, rhetoric 10, and poetics 23.[25] Book III, by the way, is given over to grammar, and this subject is treated in 193 chapters, the last three of which deal respectively with the schemes, the tropes, and certain other figures, among them allegory. Thus Vincent follows Isidore in treating certain matters of rhetorical style under the heading of grammar, and Bede does the same thing, as I shall mention later in speaking of the origins of stylistic rhetoric in England.[26] But whereas Isidore also treated the subject of poetry as in large part the property of grammar, and whereas Geoffrey treated poetry in terms of rhetoric, thus creating what Atkins calls "a treatise on rhetoric as applied to poetry,"[27] Vincent keeps largely to the ancient Ciceronian terms in speaking of rhetoric, and, as I indicated above, he associates poetics with logic, giving the art of poetry ex-

[24] Atkins, *The Medieval Phase*, p. 93.
[25] See above, pp. 39-44.
[26] See below, pp. 116-119.   [27] *The Medieval Phase*, p. 97.

tensive discussion through passages identified by him as in part written by himself and in part borrowed from the *Etymologiae* of Isidore and the *Mythologiae* of Fulgentius, with Cicero's *De Oratore* being quoted briefly once.[28]

In the chapters allotted to rhetoric, Vincent identifies his discussion as a tissue of excerpts from the *Etymologiae* of Isidore, *De Differentiis Topicis* of Boethius, the *Institutio Oratoria* of Quintilian, and *De Oratore*, the *Rhetorica Secunda*, and the *Rhetorica Prima* of Cicero.[29] Indeed, there is scarcely a word in Vincent's entire discussion that is not part of a direct quotation from one of these authorities. Boethius and Isidore supply two-thirds of his material, or 236 lines of text; next to them in importance is the *Rhetorica Prima* of Cicero, which supplies 68 lines of text; and least quoted of all are the *Institutio Oratoria*, *De Oratore*, and the *Rhetorica Secunda*, the contributions from which amount in sum to 43 lines of text divided almost equally among the three works.[30] By means of his sources, Vincent presents the following materials: 1) a definition of rhetoric; 2) a distinction between rhetoric and dialectic; 3) a brief explanation of the five parts of rhetoric; 4) a discussion of invention in terms of the parts of an oration, the kinds of oratory, the kinds of positions, the nature of the rhetorical syllogism, the kinds of rhetorical places; and 5) a brief discussion of style. An example of his method may be seen in his first chapter, which he calls *De Arte Rhetorica*:

Isidore as above.

Rhetoric is the science of speaking well on civil questions for the purpose of persuading by a just and good copiousness in respect to the interactions of events and persons. Indeed, rhetoric was the term in Greece for copiousness of speaking. For among the Greeks speaking is called *rhesis*, and the orator, *rhetor*.

Boethius in the *Topics*, Book IV.

[28] Of the 23 chapters allotted by Vincent to the discussion of poetry, he acknowledges Isidore to be his authority in chs. 110, 111, 112, 113, 127, 128, 129, 130, and 131. He acknowledges Cicero to be his authority in the first part of ch. 127. Fulgentius he acknowledges as authority in chs. 124, 125, and 126. He acknowledges himself as author of chs. 109, 114, 115, 116, 117, 118, 119, 120, 121, 122, and 123, although his method of moralizing fables in these chapters is obviously based upon that exemplified in the passages he quotes from Fulgentius.

[29] The *Rhetorica Secunda* is the *Rhetorica ad Herennium*, which Vincent thought to be Cicero's. The *Rhetorica Prima* is Cicero's *De Inventione*. See above, p. 66.

[30] Vincent's ten chapters on rhetoric in *Speculum Doctrinale* (Nuremberg, 1486), Book IV, Chs. 99-108, amount to 352 full lines of text, 347 of which are identified by him as quotations from his sources.

Rhetoric differs from dialectic because dialectic mostly considers theses, that is, questions without surroundings in time and place. And if at any time dialectic takes up for dispute questions with surroundings in time and place, it uses them not mainly but entirely in connection with the thesis upon which it is discoursing. In truth, rhetoric treats of and discourses upon hypotheses, that is, questions with a multitude of surroundings in time and place, and if at any time it brings up a thesis, it uses it in connection with its hypothesis. These are its surroundings: Who? What? Where? By whose help? Why? In what manner? At what time?

Moreover, dialectic is carried on by interrogations and responses, whereas rhetoric flows along on an appropriate subject without interruption.

Again, dialectic makes use of the complete syllogism, whereas rhetoric is content with the brevity of the enthymeme.

Once again, the orator has beyond his adversary a judge who decides between the two disputants, whereas in truth the very one who sits as adversary renders a quasi verdict against the dialectician by the way he responds. Thus every difference between orator and dialectician is constituted either in subject matter, or use, or end. I say "end" because the orator attempts indeed to persuade the judge, whereas the dialectician attempts to extort from his adversary what is wanted.[31]

Although Vincent's theory of rhetoric, like his theory of logic, cannot be strictly classed as part of the history of these two subjects in England, yet his treatment of both arts would have been familiar and influential in England at most times between the age of Alcuin and that of Thomas Wilson. Thus I have not hesitated to allow him to figure in my account of scholastic logic and of traditional rhetoric in English learning, even as the English authors to whom I have been referring are also the property of the intellectual history of France or of other regions of western Europe, no less than of England. Several generations after Vincent's time, he would still have been accepted throughout Europe as an authority on the rhetoric then current. Indeed, the chapters on rhetoric in the *Speculum Doctrinale* are not unlike the first treatise on Ciceronian rhetoric to be

---

[31] *Speculum Doctrinale*, Bk. IV, Ch. 99. Translation mine. The texts here used were printed at Strasbourg about 1472 and at Nuremberg in 1486. See above, p. 39, note 25. The reference to Isidore is to the *Etymologiae*, 2.1.1 (in Migne, *Patrologia Latina*, LXXXII, 123). The reference to Boethius is to De *Differentiis Topicis*, Book IV (in Migne, *Patrologia Latina*, LXIV, 1205-1206).

printed at an English press, despite the fact that the latter work was written over two centuries after the former. Curiously enough, the author of this first rhetoric in the history of English printing was an Italian monk, not an Englishman, and the work itself was written in Latin while he was teaching theology at Cambridge University. The *Nova Rhetorica*, as this work is usually called, is more complete than Vincent's chapters on rhetoric in respect to Cicero's five terms. Both works, however, belong to each other's period as readily as to their own.

The *Nova Rhetorica*, which appeared at Caxton's press in Westminster around 1479, and at the press of "the Schoolmaster Printer" in St. Albans in 1480, had for author a man who in English would be called Brother Laurence William of Savona, of the Minor Order, doctor of sacred theology; but his official name as recorded in reference books and library catalogues appears as Lorenzo Guglielmo Traversagni.[32] Traversagni was born of aristocratic parents in Savona, Italy, in the year 1422. At the age of twenty, already well schooled in grammar, logic, rhetoric, and secular literature, he was received into the Franciscan (or Minor) Order in his native town, where he pursued his studies further during his early monastic life, his teacher being Marco Vigirio, bishop of Noli, who soon conferred upon him the title of doctor. Then he studied for the next few years at the same place under Francesco dalla Rovere, who afterwards became Pope Sixtus IV. His active career from his twenty-fifth to his seventieth year was spent as a traveling scholar, teacher, and writer. He studied logic, philosophy, theology, and canon law at Padua and Bologna; he lectured on theology at Cambridge, Paris, and Toulouse; he wrote many books on such subjects as prayer, the contemplative and active life, matrimony, the triumph of Christ, the eternal life, and chastity, in addition of course to his *Nova Rhetorica*, which

---

[32] My present discussion of the *Nova Rhetorica* is based upon the Huntington Library's microfilm of an original specimen of the St. Albans edition of 1480 at the Bodleian Library. This copy begins as follows: "Fratris laurencij guilelmi de saona ordiuis [sic] mino[rum] sacre theologie doctoris prohemiũ in nouam rethoricam." Its colophon reads: "Inpressum fuit hoc presens opus Rethorice facultatis apud villã sancti Albani. Anno domini. Mº. CCCC. LXXX." For additional information about this edition and that made by Caxton somewhat earlier, see William Blades, *The Biography and Typography of William Caxton, England's First Printer* (London and Strasbourg, 1877), pp. 216-219; also Duff, *Fifteenth Century English Books*, p. 102; also Isak Collijn, *Kataloge der Inkunabeln der Schwedischen Öffentlichen Bibliotheken II. Katalog der Inkunabeln der Kgl. Universitäts-Bibliothek zu Uppsala* (Uppsala, 1907), p. 232; also *British Museum General Catalogue of Printed Books*, s.v. Traversanus (Laurentius Gulielmus).

was the only one of his treatises to be printed. He tells us at the conclusion of that work of his having finished it July 6, 1478, at Cambridge. At that time he would have been fifty-six years of age. His teaching career on foreign soil ended at Toulouse when he was seventy. Thereafter he lived in the Franciscan monastery of his native Savona, engaging himself in teaching, writing, collecting books, and giving financial support from his own purse for various architectural improvements in his cloister. He is reported to have been occupied in enlarging one of his earlier works as late as the seventy-eighth year of his life. One of the most complete of the biographical sketches of him says that he died on the fifth day of the third month of the year 1503, at the age of 81, and was buried in the church of St. Francis of Savona, having bequeathed to his monastery the sum of 300 crowns and what must have been a considerable library of books he had assembled by himself.[33]

Traversagni's *Nova Rhetorica* is thoroughly Ciceronian in the sense in which that term is here being used. It is divided into an introduction and three books, the whole work being composed of 362 pages. The introduction begins by recalling the present uses and the past greatness of eloquence as an instrument in practical affairs and a subject in learning; the final words of the third book refer to the precepts of rhetoric as a treasure to be adapted to sacred speaking. What lies between this beginning and end is a thorough discussion of the five procedures of Ciceronian rhetoric. Early in Book I Traversagni quotes a passage from Boethius in which the latter enumerates these five procedures.[34] Traversagni goes on to define each procedure by borrowing his definitions from the *Rhetorica ad Herennium*, which he had mentioned shortly before as Cicero's.[35] Invention occupies the rest of Book I and most of Book II. What Traversagni does is to discuss this important subject by considering how to devise materials for each of the six parts of the oration as these parts appear in

---

[33] Giovanni Vincenzo Verzellino, *Delle Memorie Particolari e Specialmente Degli Uomini Illustri della Città di Savona*, ed. Andrea Astengo (Savona, 1890-1891), I, 400-401. In the same volume, pp. 520-521, there is an account of Traversagni in Latin, which supplements to some extent the account in Italian just cited. I have relied almost completely upon these two accounts for the information I have given here. But I have also consulted Lucas Waddingus, *Scriptores Ordinis Minorum*, editio novissima (Rome, 1906-1921), I, 158; III, 167; and Blades, *Biography and Typography of Caxton*, pp. 218-219.

[34] *Nova Rhetorica* (St. Albans, 1480), sig. A8v. Traversagni's reference is to Boethius, *De Differentiis Topicis*, IV (in Migne, *Patrologia Latina*, LXIV, 1208).

[35] Compare *Nova Rhetorica*, sig. A8v, and *Rhetorica ad Herennium*, 1.2.

each of the three kinds of oratory. Thus Book I deals with the exordium, narration, division, proof, refutation, and conclusion, these topics being related to the forensic oration, and being defined in the language used in a similar connection in the *Rhetorica ad Herennium*.[36] Book II, so far as it treats invention, adds doctrine that applies to deliberative and demonstrative oratory. Arrangement is disposed of briefly in the closing pages of that same book, and in Book III, style receives great attention, with memory and delivery allotted short but standard treatment. In the discussion of style, Traversagni mentions such illustrious fathers as Jerome and Augustine, but his examples of stylistic devices are drawn mainly from the Bible, thus demonstrating how pagan rhetoric could be accommodated to sacred utterances.

Six years after Traversagni's death, the terms of Ciceronian rhetoric were expressed for the first time in the English language, and thus the way was prepared for the later vernacular rhetorics of Cox and Wilson. Stephen Hawes's *Pastime of Pleasure* is the work in which this development took place. I have already mentioned the *Pastime* in connection with the early vernacular history of English logic, and also in connection with the attempt of Geoffrey of Vinsauf to write poetical theory in terms of rhetoric.[37] Now I should like to show how Hawes converts Ciceronian rhetoric to the uses of the theory of poetry, and what the particular combination amounts to on this occasion.

In the course of his training in the seven liberal arts, and immediately after his indoctrination by the lady who taught logic, the hero of the *Pastime of Pleasure* ascends one more flight of stairs in the Tower of Doctrine and enters the chamber of Dame "Rethoryke." The instruction which this lady gives the hero is not designed to make him an orator. In fact, he kneels before her murmuring "O gylted goddesse of the hygh renowne,"[38] and asks that his tongue be painted with her royal flowers, so that he may succeed in gladdening his auditors and in having power "to moralyse thy lytterall censes trewe."[39] These are the ends of poet and critic, not of lawyer, politician, or preacher. But why not? The hero of the *Pastime* is after all a poet in quest of a beautiful lady, and he has the right to ask rhet-

---

[36] Compare *Nova Rhetorica*, sigs. A8v-B1r, and *Rhetorica ad Herennium*, 1.3.
[37] See above, pp. 48-49, 76.
[38] *The Pastime of Pleasure*, ed. Mead, p. 31 [line 668].
[39] *Ibid.*, p. 31 [line 677].

oric to teach her doctrine according to his particular needs. So she responds to his needs by outlining in Ciceronian terms what she has to teach:

> Fyue partes hath rethoryke for to werke trewe
> Without whiche fyue there can be no sentence
> For these fyue do well euermore renue
> The mater parfyte with good intellygence
> Who that wyll se them with all his dylygence
> Here folowenge I shall them specyfy
> Accordynge well all vnto myne ordynary.[40]

And, having used the insistence of repetition to stress the precise number of the parts of her subject, she proceeds to specify them as "inuencyon," "dysposycyon," "elocucyon," "pronuncyacyon," and "memoratyfe."[41] All of these terms, so familiar in the training of an orator, enter her explanation one after another in such fashion as to make them serve the special problems of the poet.

First she speaks of "inuencyon." This she describes as the product of five inward faculties of the mind: "comyn wytte," "ymagyna-cyon," "fantasy," "good estymacyon," and "retentyfe memory."[42] Her discussion of these faculties as parts of invention presupposes the instruction about them that the hero is later to receive in the pavilion of Dame Astronomy, and thus my present analysis of the five wits as applied to poetry rests upon both of these two sections of the *Pastime*. Common wit is in ordinary life the faculty of experiencing perceptions, of discerning "all thynges in generall."[43] As ap-

---

[40] *Ibid.*, p. 32 [lines 694-700].

[41] *Ibid.*, pp. 33 [line 701]; 37 [line 821]; 40 [line 904]; 50 [line 1189]; 52 [line 1240].

Hawes's account of rhetoric extends from line 652 to line 1295, a total of 644 lines. These are distributed as follows:

To preliminaries	652-700	that is 49
To invention	701-819	that is 119
To disposition	820-903	that is 84
To elocution	904-1183	that is 280
To pronunciation	1184-1239	that is 56
To memory	1240-1288	that is 49
To conclusion	1289-1295	that is 7

[42] *Ibid.*, pp. 33-35. Mead regards these five faculties, not as parts of invention, but as parts of rhetoric, although he also believes the five parts of rhetoric in Hawes's scheme to be invention, arrangement, style, memory, and delivery; see pp. xxi, lvi. His latter view is correct. The former is not. He appears to have gone astray through his failure to see the structural importance of line 703, and through his failure to construe line 704 as a comment on line 703, not on line 701.

[43] *Ibid.*, p. 110 [line 2842].

plied to the task of the poet, common wit chooses and joins poetic perceptions.[44] Imagination, as the faculty of bringing wholeness of feeling to the things selected by perception, becomes in poetry the power to cloak a truth in a dark fiction:

> For often vnder a fayre fayned fable
> A trouthe appereth gretely profytable.[45]

It was the power to imagine this sort of fable that made the famous poets of antiquity so wise and inventive:

> Theyr obscure reason fayre and sugratyfe
> Pronounced trouthe vnder cloudy fygures
> By the inuencyon of theyr fatall scryptures.[46]

Fantasy, the third faculty that ministers to invention, is the mental visualization of an object of perception and imagination, even as this faculty for the general run of men acts "to brynge to fynysshement" what the imagination produces.[47] Fourth in the poetic process is estimation, or judgment, a logical gift, by which causation is determined, quantity and quality ascertained, space, time, and other circumstances calculated.[48] Lastly the poetic process involves retentive memory, the faculty which enables the poet to retain inwardly the sum of his poetical matter while his reason gives it approval and his written language gives it outward form.[49]

Nothing in Hawes's account of poetic invention trespasses upon the doctrine of rhetorical invention in Cicero and his disciples; and yet we would have to admit that there is a process of poetic as of rhetorical invention, and that this process, while it has one configuration in poetry and another in oratory, is in both cases a quest for the materials of composition, and thus is justifiably called in both cases by the same term.

When Hawes speaks, however, of disposition or arrangement as it affects poetry, his account does trespass somewhat upon the theory of arranging an oration. Thus Dame Rethoryke teaches this part of her subject to the hero of the *Pastime* by recognizing it as a preeminent characteristic of eloquence, and as a process of imparting

---

[44] *Ibid.*, p. 33 [lines 706-707].
[45] *Ibid.*, p. 34 [lines 713-714]; cf. p. 110 [lines 2843-2846].
[46] *Ibid.*, p. 34 [lines 719-721].
[47] *Ibid.*, p. 34 [lines 722-735]; cf. p. 110 [lines 2847-2849].
[48] *Ibid.*, p. 34 [lines 736-749]; cf. p. 110 [lines 2850-2856].
[49] *Ibid.*, p. 35 [lines 750-763]; cf. p. 111 [lines 2857-2863].

meaning to matter, and often of deciding between the form of narration or that of argumentation.[50] These two latter terms are close to the import of narration and proof as parts of the classical oration, and Dame Rethoryke offers some cryptic observations on the occasions when one or the other is to be preferred. The rest of her disquisition upon this second part of rhetoric is more in the vein of eulogy than of instruction. Her last observation laments the rudeness of those who lack appreciation for order in discourse:

> So dull they are that they can not fynde
> This ryall arte for to perceyue in mynde.

We would ordinarily expect a treatment of style as the third part of rhetoric to enumerate the kinds of style and to explain the figures of speech and thought. Nor would we be surprised if much of that treatment applied as well to poetry as to oratory, since all the arts of discourse have points of style in common. Dame Rethoryke begins her remarks upon style as if she were going to follow these conventional lines. But as she continues, she soon limits herself to the fable and the figure as keys to poetic symbolism, and thus her treatment of style has more application to poetry than to oratory. She discusses the possible interpretations of the fable of Atlas, the Centaurs, Pluto, Hercules;[51] she speaks of the four rivers, that is, of poetry as it creates understanding of ourselves, as it offers symbolic solutions to human problems, as it profits us by its novelty, as it sheds a glow of light upon our rudeness;[52] and she mentions Virgil, Cicero, and Lydgate as examples of the styles of which she approves.[53]

The treatment of "pronuncyacyon" by Dame Rethoryke is interesting not only as the first English version of doctrine belonging to this part of rhetoric, but also as an attempt to treat briefly the delivery of speeches and the oral interpretation of poetry. The standards of delivery both for speaker and reader are formulated by considering the audience. An audience of high estate, for example, requires the speaker to be obedient and cultivated, if he would have a sympathetic hearing. As for the custom of poets in telling their tales, it consists in avoiding rudeness and in being gentle and seemly, since the ends of speech are to refine manners and remove folly.

[50] *Ibid.,* p. 37 [lines 820-903].
[51] *Ibid.,* p. 43 [lines 988-1050].
[52] *Ibid.,* p. 45 [lines 1051-1141].
[53] *Ibid.,* p. 49 [lines 1161-1176].

Thus does Dame Rethoryke condense into a few lines her advice to poets who read their works aloud. She concludes as follows:

I can not wryte to moche for theyr sake
Them to laude for my tyme is shorte
And the mater longe whiche I must reporte.[54]

Of all the parts of her subject mentioned by Dame Rethoryke for the instruction of her disciple, memory is the one in which she comes closest to the doctrine of Ciceronian rhetoric as it applies to the orator.

The doctrine of memory, as set forth in the *Rhetorica ad Herennium* and as usually mentioned and discussed in other ancient works on rhetoric, involved the notion of the natural memory, as a faculty possessed by all men, and of the cultivated memory, as the faculty that resulted when the natural memory was trained. The memory system as developed by the ancient rhetoricians to train speakers to remember their speeches during delivery involved two key concepts, called respectively the places and the images.[55] According to Cicero, the distinguished poet Simonides of Ceos was the inventor of this system, and Cicero thus states the theory behind it as developed by Simonides out of a personal experience in which he had been able to identify mutilated corpses by his ability to recall where they had each been sitting at a banquet table before the roof fell in and crushed them beyond recognition:

He inferred that persons desiring to train this faculty must select localities and form mental images of the facts they wish to remember and store those images in the localities, with the result that the arrangement of the localities will preserve the order of the facts, and the images of the facts will designate the facts themselves, and we shall employ the localities and images respectively as a wax writing tablet and the letters written on it.[56]

The places chosen by a speaker as the basis of his own particular memory system could be any set of physical arrangements—the rooms of a house, the floors of a public building, the stages of a long

---

[54] *Ibid.*, p. 52 [lines 1237-1239].

[55] See *Rhetorica ad Herennium*, 3.16-24, and Quintilian, *Institutio Oratoria*, 11.2.1-26, for representative accounts of the process by which the memory could be trained. The two key concepts are thus stated in the former of these two works (3.16): "Constat igitur artificiosa memoria ex locis et imaginibus." For these same two terms in Quintilian, see *Institutio Oratoria*, 11.2.21-22.

[56] *De Oratore*, 2.86.354, trans. E. W. Sutton and H. Rackham (The Loeb Classical Library, Cambridge, Mass. and London, 1942), I, 467.

journey, the components of a rampart, the sections of a picture, or the signs of the zodiac.[57] The images to be stored in those places are also the subject of individual choice, and should be selected so as to be naturally associated with the ideas in a particular speech. For example, images could be drawn from military weapons, if the speech concerned military affairs. Now by storing the images within the system of places, and by visualizing himself as visiting the places one by one, the speaker would find each place holding its image, and each image suggesting the ideas previously connected with it in his mind, with the result that a constant flow of ideas would occur, and a fluent speech would be produced.

Dame Rethoryke applies this ancient memory system to the needs of the poet reciting his poems aloud to an audience. She suggests that he envisage his leathern wallet as a convenient system of places, and go through it mentally to remind himself of the images stored in its various compartments and associated with their respective tales. Her words are these:

> Yf to the orature many a sundry tale
> One after other treatably be tolde
> Than sundry ymages in his closed male
> Eache for a mater he doth than well holde
> Lyke to the tale he doth than so beholde
> And inwarde a recapytulacyon
> Of eche ymage the moralyzacyon
>
> Whiche be the tales he grounded pryuely
> Vpon these ymages sygnyfycacyon
> And whan tyme is for hym to specyfy
> All his tales by demonstracyon
> In due ordre maner and reason
> Than eche ymage inwarde dyrectly
> The oratoure doth take full properly
>
> So is enprynted in his propre mynde
> Euery tale with hole resemblaunce
> By this ymage he dooth his mater fynde
> Eche after other withouten varyaunce
> Who to this arte wyll gyue attendaunce
> As therof to knowe the perfytenes
> In the poetes scole he must haue intres.[58]

[57] These suggestions about the choice of places are from Quintilian, *Institutio Oratoria*, 11.2.18-22.

[58] *Pastime*, p. 52 [lines 1247-1267].

Thus does Dame Rethoryke complete her task of combining the terms of Ciceronian rhetoric with the requirements of the poet's profession, as she had no doubt been taught to do by the *Poetria Nova* of Geoffrey of Vinsauf, and as the *Rhetorica ad Herennium* had in turn taught Geoffrey to do, when he decided to analyze the problem of poetic communication in the accents of ancient rhetorical instruction.[59]

In his pioneer essay on sixteenth-century English rhetorical theory prefacing his edition of Leonard Cox's *The Arte or Crafte of Rhethoryke*, Frederic Ives Carpenter implies that Caxton's translation of the *Mirrour of the World* is perhaps the first printed account of Cicero's five terms to appear in English.[60] Actually, however, the first two editions of the *Mirrour*, one of which is usually dated at Caxton's press at Westminster around 1481, and the other at the same press around 1490, contain no hint of Ciceronian terminology in their very brief accounts of rhetoric as the third of the seven liberal arts. In fact, those accounts do nothing but indicate that righteousness, reason, and arranging of words are involved in rhetoric, and that rhetoric is connected not only with the process of framing and applying laws and decrees, but also with the desire to earn salvation by working in the cause of right.[61] Not until the third edition of the *Mirrour* at the press of Laurence Andrewe in London around 1527 does that work discuss rhetoric in Cicero's five terms. Even then, however, its treatment of invention, arrangement, and style is little more in each case than a definition, although memory is discussed

[59] The connection between the account of rhetoric in Hawes's *Pastime* and the account of poetry in Geoffrey's *Poetria Nova* has not to my knowledge been worked out. But the kinship between the two works in respect to rhetorical theory can be established not only by pointing to their structural similarities but also by regarding *The Court of Sapyence* as a means of connecting Hawes to Geoffrey. Hawes believed the *Court* to be the work of Lydgate, and his reverence for Lydgate is repeatedly expressed; see *Pastime*, p. 56 [lines 1357, 1373]; also Whitney Wells, "Stephen Hawes and *The Court of Sapience*," *The Review of English Studies*, VI (1930), 284-294. The *Court* in its brief account of rhetoric advises the reader to go for further instruction "to Tria Sunt, And to Galfryde, the poete lawreate"; (ed. Spindler, p. 199 [lines 1914-1915]). The "Tria Sunt" appears to refer to the prose version of Geoffrey's *Poetria Nova*, whereas the mention of Geoffrey as poet laureate might be a covert reference to the poetic version of the same work; see C. F. Bühler, *The Sources of the Court of Sapience*, Beiträge zur Englischen Philologie, XXIII (1932), p. 76. Thus some reason exists for believing that Hawes on the authority of the *Court* would accept Geoffrey as the master of his own master, and would thus have sentimental connections with the idea of converting Ciceronian rhetoric to the uses of poetry.

[60] Leonard Cox, *The Arte or Crafte of Rhethoryke*, ed. Frederic Ives Carpenter (Chicago, 1899), p. 25.

[61] *Caxton's Mirrour*, ed. Prior, pp. 35-36.

[87]

at some little length, and pronunciation receives definite emphasis. Now by 1527 Hawes's *Pastime*, with its fuller English account of Cicero's five terms, had already gone through two editions, and thus it deserves the honor in respect to those terms that Carpenter by strong implication assigns to the *Mirrour*. The *Mirrour* is more accurately numbered as the second of the appearances of Ciceronian rhetoric in an English version.

The first two editions of Caxton's *Mirrour* are available to any modern reader in Prior's reprint, to which I have already made various references. But copies of the expanded third edition cannot be consulted except at a few libraries, and thus some quotations from its treatment of rhetoric may be helpful as a supplement to the passage quoted by Carpenter to show what he means when he refers to the *Mirrour* as containing "perhaps the first printed account of rhetoric in English."[62] As I just indicated, the third edition of the *Mirrour* treats invention, arrangement, and style, by giving little more than brief definitions of them, and these definitions are included in Carpenter's quotation from that work. But the subject of memory receives really interesting treatment in that same edition. Here is the way the entire subject is handled as a part of rhetoric:

¶ Ars memoratiua / Or memory /

¶ The fourth thynge is memory, as whan thou haste dysposed how thou shalt elygantly vtter thy mater / Than thou must deuise a way to kepe it in thy mynde for fere of oblyuion whan thou sholdest pronow̄unce it / which mememory standeth in .11. thynges / that is to say memory naturall / & memory artyficyall / memory naturall / is that which god hath gyuen to euery man /

¶ Memory Artyfycyall is that which men cal Ars memoratiua / The crafte of memory / by which craft thou mayste wryte a thynge in thy mynde / & set it in thy mynde as euydētly as thou mayst rede and se the wordes whych thou wrytest with ynke vpon parchemēt or paper / Therfore in this arte of memory thou muste haue places which shal be to the lyke as it were perchenent or paper to wryte vpon / Also instede of thy lettres thou must ymagyn Images to set in the same places / Therfore fyrst thou shalt chose thy places fyrste As in some greate hous that thou knowest well / and begyn at a certayn place of that hous / & marke som poste / corner / or wall / beynge. there as they stande arow / and within .x. or .xii. fote and

[32] *Op. cit.*, p. 25.

not past .xx. fote asōder marke som other poste or wall // and so alway procedyng forthe one way tyll thou haue marked or notyd .C. or .CC. places / or as many as thou canste haue /

¶ Also in this crafte as I sayde before thou must haue euer ymags of corporall thynges that thou muste se with thyn eye whiche thou muste ymagyn in thy mynde that thou seest them sette in the places

¶ And so of euery corporall thynge thou muste ymagyn that thou seest the same comporall thyng in the place /

¶ As whan thou wylte remembre a man / a horse / a byrde / a fysshe / or suche other to Imagyn that thou seest the same man / hors / byrde / or fisshe / in thy place and so of euery corporall thyng / But yf thou canst not haue a corporall ymage of the same thynge / as yf thou woldest remembre a thynge whyche is of it selfe no bodely nor corporall thyng but incorporall / That thou muste yet take an ymage therfore that is a corporall thynge / As yf thou woldest remēber thys word / to rede / than thou maist ymagyn one lokynge on a boke / or for this word. walk / to ymagin a payre of legges / or for this worde wysedome an olde man wyth a whyt hed so that euery ymage must be a bodely & a corporal thyng.[63]

This same edition of the *Mirrour* also has an account of pronunciation which is brief enough for quotation here and which will serve to indicate some of the doctrine connected with the Ciceronian discussion of delivery as the last part of rhetoric:

¶ The fyfte thynge is pronūciacyō which is but to modder and to ordre thy voyce & thy body acordynge to the wordes & to the scyēce /

¶ The voyce must haue strength / sharpnes / & temperaunce.

¶ Countenaunce is the orderynge of thy face / as whan thou spekyst of a mery mater to shew a laughyng and mery countenaunce /

¶ And whan thou spekyst of a pytefull mater to shew a lamentable countenaunce & a heuy /

¶ And whan thou spekest of a weyghty cause or mater to shewe a sad and a solempne countenaunce

¶Gesture is not only in excersisyng one parte of the body but ī euery outward mēber of the body / as in hede / armes / & leggs / and

---

[63] *The myrrour: & dyscrypscyon of the worlde with many meruaylles* ([London, 1527?]), sig. D3r-D3v. From the Huntington Library photostat of their own original copy. Spelling, abbreviating, and pointing are reproduced here to conform to that original.

other vtt' partes / Therfore to euery mater that thou shalt vtt' thou must haue quemēt gesture / as whā thou spekest of a solēpne mat' to stāde vp ryghte with lytell meuynge of thy body / but poyntynge it with thy fore fynger /

¶ And whan thou spekyst of any cruell mater or yrefull cause to bende thy fyst and shake thyn arme / And whan thou spekyst of any heuenly or godly thynges to loke vp & poīte towarde the skye with thy finger /

¶ And whā thou spekest of any gentilnes /myldenes / or humylyte / to ley thy handes vpon thy breste / & whā thou spekest of any holy mater or deuocyon to holde vp thy handes./[64]

Thus did the third edition of Caxton's *Mirrour* deal with memory and delivery as the last two parts of rhetoric. Its treatment of the first three parts was less extended, as I have said, but no less faithful to the main intent of Ciceronian teaching.

Next after it in the historical sequence of Ciceronian rhetorics in English stands Leonard Cox's *Rhethoryke*, which first appeared at London around 1530, and which was given a second edition at the same place in 1532. Cox's *Rhethoryke* marks the third appearance of Ciceronian theory in the vernacular. But it has two other larger distinctions. First of all, it is the earliest English textbook on rhetoric to be published anywhere, and so it deserves a special place in the literary history of Anglo-Saxon civilization. Secondly, it is the first systematic attempt to acquaint English readers with the original rhetorical content of the Ciceronian doctrine of invention, and so it is a milestone on the long road towards the vernacularization of classical learning.

At the time when Cox wrote his *Rhethoryke*, he was a schoolmaster at Reading. He indicates this fact in the epistle dedicating his work to "the reuerende father in god & his singuler good lorde the lorde Hugh Faryngton Abbot of Redynge."[65] In the same letter he says that he owes his position to the Abbot, whose ancestors had

---

[64] *Ibid.*, sig. D3v-D4r.

[65] Leonard Cox, *The Art or crafte of Rhetoryke* (London, 1532), sig. A2v. From the Huntington Library photostat of their own copy of the 1532 edition. I have not seen the first edition, which bears no date and has been assigned by Carpenter (*op. cit.*, pp. 10, 12, 19) to the year 1530 or thereabouts. The *British Museum General Catalogue of Printed Books* (London and Beccles, 1949) tentatively gives the first edition the date of 1529, although in 1886 the *Catalogue* dated it 1524, as did the *Short-Title Catalogue* in 1926. Carpenter's reprint is based upon both early editions, but the first edition is his preferred authority.

founded the very school in which he is now serving; and he goes on to declare that he has long been considering ways in which he could show his patron how much he appreciated what the latter had done for him. Then he adds:

> And whan I had thus long prepensed in my mynde what thynge I myght best chose out: non offred it selfe more conuenyent to the profyte of yonge studentes (which your good lordshyp hath alwayes tenderly fauoured / and also meter to my [pro]fession: than to make som proper werke of the right pleasaunt and persuadible art of Rhetorique whiche as it is very necessary to all suche as wyll either be Aduocates and Proctours in the law: or els apte to be sent in theyr Prynces Ambassades or to be techers of goddē worde in suche maner as may be moost sensible & accepte to theyr audience and finally to all them hauynge any thyng to purpose or to speke afore any companye (what someuer they be).[66]

This declaration of the uses of the art of rhetoric in law, statecraft, and the ministry, as well as on numerous occasions of private life, is typical of the whole rhetorical tradition in the Latin world from Cicero to Traversagni, and is thus worthy to appear in the first rhetorical textbook to bear Cicero's teachings to English boys in their own tongue. So is Cox's analysis of the social needs his work is designed to meet:

> So contraryly I se no science that is lesse taught & declared to Scolers which ought chiefly after the knowlege of Gramer ones had to be instructe in this facultie without the whiche oftentymes the rude vtteraunce of the Aduocate greatly hindereth and apeyreth his clietes cause. Likewise the vnapt disposicion of the precher (in orderyng his mater) confoundeth the memory of his herers and briefly in declarynge of maters: for lacke of inuencion and order with due elocucion: great tediousnes is engendred to the multitude beyng present by occasion wherof the speker is many tymes ere he haue ended his tale: either left almost aloon to his no litle confusiō: or els (which is a lyke rebuke to hym) the audience falleth for werynes of his ineloquent language fast on slepe.[67]

The remedy for these shortcomings, Cox implies, is to be found in proper instruction in rhetoric. It is to provide such instruction, he declares, that "I haue partly translated out of a werke of Rhetorique wryten in the Latin tongue: and partly compyled of myn owne: and

[66] *Rhetoryke* (1532), sig. A2v. [67] *Ibid.*, sig. A2v-A3r.

so made a lytle treatyse in maner of an Introductyon into this afore-sayd Science: and that in our Englysshe tongue."[68] Two Latin sources openly referred to by Cox in his little treatise are Cicero's *De Inventione* and Trapezuntius's *Rhetoricorum Libri Quinque*.[69] But, as Carpenter was the first to point out, the "werke of Rhetorique wryten in the Latin tongue" from which Cox partly translated to form his own work is Melanchthon's *Institutiones Rhetoricae*.[70]

Melanchthon's *Institutiones Rhetoricae* partitions rhetoric under the headings of invention, judgment, arrangement, and style.[71] The second of these terms seems to be out of place as a part of the rhetoric of the Ciceronian tradition; but actually that term is not so much out of place as unnecessary. As a concept in the classical theory of communication, judgment refers to the second of the two parts of dialectic, invention being the other part, as I have already shown;[72] and judgment in dialectical theory, it will be remembered from my earlier discussion, is equivalent in function to arrangement or disposition in rhetoric. Thus it would seem that, if arrangement is counted a part of rhetorical theory, nothing would be gained by claiming judgment as an added part, since both of these concepts involve the problem of literary structure, and to handle them both in the same work is to invite the charge of redundancy. To be sure, there were rhetorical theorists in antiquity who insisted that rhetoric had six parts, and who found the sixth part by adding judgment to the five parts approved by Cicero. Quintilian mentions these theorists, and even discusses to some extent the meaning they assigned to judgment as a part of rhetoric.[73] But his own opinion is that what is said under judgment when it is treated separately overlaps what has to be said anyway under invention, arrangement, style, and even delivery, and therefore Cicero's five parts are to be preferred to the suggested six. Nevertheless, Melanchthon chooses to count both judgment and arrangement as parts of rhetoric, perhaps in imitation of the theorists mentioned by Quintilian, or perhaps in an attempt to indicate that rhetorical theory needed to be strengthened by additions that belonged properly under a dialectical concept.

[68] *Ibid.*, sig. A3r.
[69] *Ibid.*, sigs. E7v, F6r, F6v.
[70] Carpenter, p. 29.
[71] In Carpenter's edition of Cox's *Rhethoryke*, pp. 91-102, are printed extracts from Melanchthon's *Institutiones Rhetoricae*; for the latter's partitioning of rhetoric under these four heads, see p. 91.
[72] See above, pp. 15-16.
[73] *Institutio Oratoria*, 3.3.5-7; 6.5.1-4.

Cox defines rhetoric as having the four procedures that Melanchthon had assigned to it.[74] He limits himself, however, to invention, commenting both at the beginning and end of his work that this procedure is hardest of the four to master.[75] He takes the trouble to point out, moreover, that in thus limiting himself, he has "folowed ye facion of Tulli who made a seuerall werke of inuencion."[76]

As for his actual treatment of the first part of rhetoric, Cox agrees somewhat more closely with the method followed in the *Rhetorica ad Herennium* than with Cicero's method in *De Inventione*, especially in connection with the doctrine of the positions of argument. These positions are discussed by Cox under three main headings, after the manner of the *Rhetorica ad Herennium*,[77] although the basic terms which evolve from his classification are in close agreement with those in *De Inventione*, where the positions are classed somewhat differently, as I indicated earlier in this chapter.[78] Moreover, even as the *Rhetorica ad Herennium* follows the general plan of discussing each of the kinds of oratory in relation to each of the several parts of the oration, with the result that the terms for the parts of the oration recur as each kind of oratory is described, so also does Cox; yet in the final analysis his doctrine amounts to that presented a bit differently by Cicero's *De Inventione*. Incidentally, by treating the parts of the oration under invention, Cox manages as the classical theorists did to cover the most important aspect of the doctrine of rhetorical arrangement without having to take it up directly.

There is, however, one slight peculiarity in Cox's theory of invention, and it deserves notice in this history. It arises when Cox speaks of the precise number of classes into which rhetorical discourses fall. On this point he observes that there are "foure causes or for the more playnnes foure kyndes of Oracions."[79] These he immediately enumerates as "Logycall," "Demonstratiue," "Deliberatiue," and "Judiciall"; and he adds that "these thre last be properly called spices or kyndes of oracions."[80] Now, in dealing with four kinds of oratory rather than the conventional three as I discussed them earlier,[81] Cox departs from the *Rhetorica ad Herennium* and

---

[74] *Rhetoryke* (1532), sig. A4r-A4v.
[75] *Ibid.*, sigs. A4v, F6r.
[76] *Ibid.*, sig. F6r.
[77] *Ibid.*, sig. D7r; see also *Rhetorica ad Herennium*, 1.11.
[78] See above, pp. 70-71.
[79] *Rhetoryke*, sig. A5r.
[80] *Ibid.*, sig. A5v.   [81] See above, pp. 69-70.

also from *De Inventione*.[82] Moreover, in what he says of the method of invention to be followed in logical orations, he draws his material from the theory of dialectical invention, taking the position that logical questions appear both in dialectic and in rhetoric, and hence need some attention in the latter science, even though what is said of them there must be borrowed from the former.[83] In other words, Cox extends the scope of Ciceronian rhetoric somewhat, and then fortifies the theory of rhetorical invention by additions from the parallel theory in dialectic. But he does not alter the traditional relation of these two arts to each other. In fact, his distinction between them, phrased as follows, is in the spirit of his time:

> For this is the dyfference that is betwene these two sciences that the Logician in dysputynge obserueth certayne rules for the settynge of his wordes being solicitous that there be spokē no more nor no lesse than the thynge requyreth & that it be euin as plaily spokē as it is thought. But the Rhethorician seketh about & boroweth where he can asmoche as he may for to make the symple and playne Logicall argumentes gaye & delectable to the eare. So than the sure iugement of argumentes or reasons must be lerned of the logician but the crafte to set thē out with pleasaunt figures and to delate the mater belongeth to the Rhetorician.[84]

Twice in his treatise on rhetoric Cox mentions his desire to do something further with that subject. His dedicatory epistle draws to a close with the avowal that he trusts "by the ayde of almyghty god to endyte other werkes bothe in this faculty and other to the laude of the hygh godhed."[85] At the very end of his work, in his conclusion as author, he speaks of his having treated invention, the chief part of rhetoric, and of his being willing, if the present book succeeds, to "assay my selfe in yᵉ other partes & so make & accōplyssh yᵉ hole werke."[86] Apparently his resolution to write another work on rhetoric had not been abandoned by 1540, because in a letter dated May 23 of that year he mentions his plan to write a work to be called the *Erotemata Rhetorica*.[87] Possibly that would have been the more complete treatise which he promised at the end of his earlier one; possibly also it would have been a further translation from Melanch-

---

[82] *Rhetorica ad Herennium*, 1.2; *De Inventione*, 1.5.7. See also Quintilian, *Institutio Oratoria*, 3.4.1-16, where the dispute over the number of kinds of oratory is discussed.

[83] *Rhetoryke*, sig. A6r, A8v.

[84] *Ibid.*, sigs. A8v-B1r.

[85] *Ibid.*, sig. A3v.   [86] *Ibid.*, sig. F6r.

[87] *Rhethoryke*, ed. Carpenter, pp. 15-16, 21.

thon, since Cox's projected title suggests his desire to identify his new work with that famous author, who had called one of his own works the *Erotemata Dialectices*. But Cox appears never to have finished or at any rate to have published a second work on rhetoric.

Among the circumstances which led Cox to take a special interest in Melanchthon, there is at least one possibility to be emphasized. Cox took his bachelor's degree at Cambridge University around 1528, and thus was an undergraduate when William Paget, who must have been about Cox's age, is said to have delivered a course of lectures in his own college at Cambridge on Melanchthon's rhetorical theory.[88] Since Paget appears to have left Cambridge before taking his bachelor's degree, we may assume that his lectures on Melanchthon were not part of the authorized curriculum. But they are evidence of undergraduate interest in that particular author, and Cox's own *Rhethoryke* reflects that same interest on a maturer and more professional level.

Despite the fact that Cox does not go beyond the theory of rhetorical invention, Ciceronian rhetoric was represented by him in its most important aspect. Its other aspects were not long in finding new English interpreters. About sixteen years after the date of the second edition of Cox's *Rhethoryke*, and some five years before the date of Thomas Wilson's great English version of the doctrine belonging to all five terms of the Ciceronian rhetorical formula, the ancient theory of memory was made the subject of a separate work for the first time in English, and thus did Ciceronian rhetoric receive its first important supplement since Cox's treatise on invention. Robert Copland, a printer who had learned his trade under Caxton and Wynkyn de Worde, was author of this supplement. He named his work *The Art of Memory, that otherwyse is called the "Phenix."* His title page describes it as "A boke very behouefull and profytable to all professours of scyences. Grammaryens / Rethoryciens Dialectyke / Legystes / Phylosophres & Theologiens." The colophon indicates that the work was printed at London by William Middleton, and that it was a translation "out of french in to englyshe by Roberte Coplande."[89] "For asmuch as many (ī th[is] tyme moderne

[88] The date of Cox's Cambridge degree is not of record. He was incorporated B.A. at Oxford on Feb. 19, 1529-30, as one who already held the same degree from Cambridge. See *Dictionary of National Biography*, s.v. Cox, Leonard. For mention of Paget's lectures at Cambridge, see Mullinger, *University of Cambridge*, I, 563; also *Dictionary of National Biography*, s.v. Paget, William (1505-1563).

[89] No date is given on the title page or colophon. The *Short-Title Catalogue* assigns

ý ṕsētly rēneth) be of a slow memory & late mynded," avows the prologue, "this lytell boke was made & composed, for to gyue and presēt it to all people, albeit that at the begynnynge it was dyrected to the Italyke nacion." The work thus identified by Copland as his ultimate source is in reality a small Latin treatise by Petrus Ravennas, also called Pietro Tommai, an Italian scholar, who died in 1508 after having served for a time as lecturer on canon law at the University of Padua. Tommai's little book was first published at Venice in 1491 as *Foenix Dñi Petri Rauēnatis Memoriae Magistri*;[90] under that same title and others it was republished several times at European presses during the sixteenth century.

The prologue of Copland's translation says that the original Italian author had had no teacher of the art of memory, "but ý it came to hym by inuencion throughe the socour and help of god that lyghtned and inspired his spyrite." What this means is that the original author was merely inventor of ways in which the old memory system of Ciceronian rhetoric could be worked out in practical terms. In other words, Tommai accepted the basic concepts of places and images as his starting point, and proceeded to suggest things to be used for them, his method being to reduce his doctrine to a few main conclusions, each of which had its special rules. Here is a sample of his formulations as Copland renders them into English:

> The fyrste conclusyon shalbe suche. This arte is, and consysteth of places and magnytudes. The places be as cardes or scrolls or other thynges for to wrytte in. The ymages be ý symylytudes of the thynges that we wyll retayne in mynde. Than I wyl fyrst [pre]pare my carde wherin we may colloke & order ý ymages in places.[91]

The rules which follow this first conclusion indicate what type of physical objects may serve as places, and how they are to be chosen:

---

the work tentatively to the year 1548. My present discussion of it is based upon the Huntington Library photostat of the copy at Cambridge University Library.

[90] The Huntington Library owns a copy of this edition under the title just given. The text itself begins: "Artificiosa Memoria Clarissimi Iuris Vtrius[que] Doctoris & militis domini Petri Rauēnatis Iura Canonica ordinarie de sero legentis in Celeberrimo Gymnasio Patauino in hoc libello continetur." The colophon reads: "Bernardinus de Choris de Cremona Impressor delectus Impressit Venetias Die. X. Ianuarii. M. ccccxci." This edition is cited below as *Foenix*.

[91] *The Art of Memory*, sig. A2v-A3r. Tommai states the first conclusion as follows: "Prima erit Conclusio: Ars ista constat ex locis & imaginibus: loca sunt tanq̄ charta seu alia materia in qua scribimus: Imagines sunt similitudines rerū quas memoriae uolumus cōmendare. Chartam ergo primū parabo in qua imagines collocare possimus." *Foenix*, sig. B3r.

And for the foundacion of this fyrst cōclusyon I wyll put foure rules. The fyrste is this. The places are the wyndowes set in walles, pyllers, & anglets, with other lyke. The .II. rule is. The places ought nat to be to nere togyther nor to fare a sōder. . . . The .III. rule is suche. But it is vayne as me semeth. For it is the opynyon of talkers that the places ought nat to be made where as mē do haunt, as in churche and comyn places. For it suffyseth to haue sene church vacaunt wher as people walke nat alway and in that hath ben taught ý cōtrary experyence. whyche is the mayster of those thynges. The .IIII. rule is th[is]. That the places be nat to hye. For I wyl that the men set for the ymages or in the steade of ymages may touch the places, ý whiche I haue iudged as behouefull.[92]

In illustration of these rules, Tommai says that he selects a church well known to himself, considers its parts, walks through it three or four times, and then returns to his own house. There he endeavors to remember the things he has seen. He recalls something on the right side of the gate along the path that leads to the right aisle and the high altar, and this he ordains as his first place. His second place he fixes upon the wall next to the first, but five or six feet off. These places are chosen either for some unusual feature they may possess, say a pillar in a window, or for some unusual feature they may be imagined to possess. Each place is fixed along the route through the church and back to the entrance gate. Thus is a system of places created for the later reception of images. Says Tommai of his own system:

But bicause ý I haue wylled to surmoūt all the men of Itally by habundaūce of thynges and holy scryptures, in Canone lawe and Cyuyl, and in other authoritees of many thynges, whyle that I was but yonge adolescent I haue prepared a C. M. places. And now I haue added to them ý other .x. M. places wherin I haue put the thynges which are to say & vtter by my selfe, so ý they be prompt-emēts whan I wyll experyment the vertues and strengthes of my memory.[93]

[92] *The Art of Memory*, sig. A3r-A3v. The Latin text reads at this point: "Et pro fundamento huius primae conclusionis quatuor regulas pono. Prima est haec: loca sunt fenestrae in parietibus positae colūnae anguli & quae his similia sunt. Secūda sit regula: loca non debent esse nimium uicina aut nimium distātia. Tertia sit regula uana ut mihi uidetur est opinio dicentium loca fieri non debere ubi sit hominum frequentia: ut in ecclesiis aut in plateis; nam ecclesiam quādo[que] uacuā uidisse sufficit non enim semper ibi hominum deambulatio uisa fuit & in hoc experientia quae est rerū magistra cōtrarium docuit. Quarta sit regula: loca nō sint alta quia uolui [que] homines pro imaginibus positi loca tangere possint quod utile semper iudicaui." *Foenix*, sig. B3r.

[93] *The Art of Memory*, sig. A4v.

Having established his system of places, Tommai was apparently quite successful in its use. He relates that when he was young, he found himself in the company of certain noblemen, and it was proposed that a list of names be read off, whereupon he would recall them. As each name was called, Tommai associated it with the image of a friend of his having a similar name, and stored each image in his system of places. Then, with the list complete, he mentally visited his places, and from the images in them he recalled the names.[94]

The rest of Tommai's work as Copland translates it is given over to practical hints on systems of places and types of images. The alphabet is suggested as one system of places, each letter being conceived as a fair maiden, with whom something to be memorized can be associated. Parts of the body, patterns of vocal sounds, arrangements of colors, and systems of enumeration, are among the possibilities considered, and the practical needs of preachers, lawyers, and professors are kept in mind throughout.

However useful Copland wanted his *Art of Memory* to be in the fraternity of talkers, he nevertheless does not present it as a subdivision of rhetorical theory or as a conventional topic in the Ciceronian program for oratorical training. Thus to readers of its own time, the *Art* would probably not have appeared to belong to the family which also claimed Cox's *Rhethoryke*, particularly since the latter did not include memory among rhetorical interests. But Copland does belong to that family, as we can see, and so it is entirely appropriate to include his *Art* in the sequence of English versions of the Ciceronian program, even though Thomas Wilson's *The Arte of Rhetorique* is in a more obvious sense the next work after Cox in this sequence, and is moreover the greatest Ciceronian rhetoric in English, short of a direct translation of the works of the Latin master himself.

Wilson published his *Rhetorique* in 1553, just two years after he had made history by putting out the first English logic.[95] The opinion persists among scholars that the first edition of the *Rhetorique* is incomplete, and that the edition of 1560 is the true *editio princeps*.[96]

---

[94] *Ibid.*, sig. A5v.

[95] The title page of the first edition reads: "The Arte of Rhetorique, for the vse of all suche as are studious of Eloquence, sette forth in English, by Thomas Wilson. Anno Domini. M. D. LIII. Mense Ianuarij." The Huntington Library has a copy of the first edition; also of the second edition (London, 1560), the third (London, 1562), and the seventh (London, 1584).

[96] Thus Atkins, *The Renascence*, p. 74, refers to Wilson's *Rhetorique* as published in 1553 and completed in 1560. Atkins borrowed this opinion from *Wilson's Arte of Rhet-*

But in reality the latter contains only about four pages of material not found in the former, as Russell Wagner has shown, and those four pages are made up, not of additional doctrine, but of examples.[97] Thus 1553 may be accepted as the year in which the earliest complete English account of the rhetorical doctrine connected with all five parts of the Ciceronian theory of oratory appeared in print.

The *Rhetorique* was prepared by Wilson in accordance with a promise that he had made a year earlier to John Dudley, known to history as Duke of Northumberland, who was at that time the power behind the young king Edward VI, and was later beheaded by Queen Mary because of his attempt to secure the throne for Lady Jane Grey. Wilson mentions his promise to the duke in the epistle which dedicates the *Rhetorique* to him:

> I therefore, commend to your Lordshippes tuition and patronage, this treatise of Rhetorique, to the ende that ye may get some furtheraunce by the same, & I also be discharged of my faithfull promise, this last yere made vnto you.

Since the duke had been named chancellor of Cambridge early in the year 1552, and since Wilson, as a quite recent graduate of that university, was just then beginning to achieve some reputation from his *Rule of Reason*, it may be that an interview between Wilson and the nobleman had been initiated by the latter soon after he assumed the chancellorship. The dedicatory epistle prefixed to the *Rhetorique* suggests at any rate that Wilson's "faithfull promise" had been given at a meeting between them:

> For, whereas it pleased you among other talke of learning, earnestly to wish, that ye might one day see the preceptes of Rhetorique, set forth by me in English, as I had erst done the rules of Logicke: hauing in my countrey this last Sommer, a quiet time of vacation, with the right worshipfull Sir Edward Dimmoke Knight: I trauailed so much, as my leasure might serue thereunto, not onely to declare my good heart, to the satisfying of your request in that behalfe, but also through that your motion, to helpe the towardnesse of some other, not so well furnished as your Lordship is.

---

orique *1560*, ed. George Herbert Mair ([Oxford], 1909), p. xxxv. Incidentally, Mair's edition of the *Rhetorique* is the only modern version easily available to students; for convenience I shall refer my discussion to it.

[97] Russell Halderman Wagner, "Thomas Wilson's Arte of Rhetorique An Abstract of a Dissertation Presented to the Faculty of the Graduate School of Cornell University for the Degree of Doctor of Philosophy, July, 1928," *Cornell University Abstracts of Theses*, II.

Invention is the subject to which Wilson devotes the lion's share of attention, as did his Ciceronian predecessors. Like them he speaks of the three kinds of oratory;[98] in analyzing the third kind, that is, the forensic speech, he discusses the positions of argument;[99] he also explains the parts of an oration, and considers the applicability of each part to each kind of speech.[100] His treatment of the positions of argument follows the classification adopted by Cox and sanctioned by the *Rhetorica ad Herennium*; and so he speaks of three main positions or "States." But it turns out in the end that he covers nine separate ones in all, more or less in the fashion of Cicero in *De Inventione*. Wilson shows traces of confusion in this part of his interpretation of classical doctrine, particularly when he first explains what the legal state is.[101] His other main topics in the theory of invention are handled more securely, however, and in general it may be said that he gives the first adequate English account of that theory to be found anywhere.

As a recognized writer in the field of logic, and thus as an authority on dialectical invention, Wilson handles the problem of rhetorical invention with a special awareness of the connections between philosophical and popular expression. At the very beginning of his discussion of rhetorical invention, before he has proceeded beyond a brief definition of the term, he says that the "places of *Logique*, giue good occasion to finde out plentifull matter."[102] He adds at once: "And therefore, they that will proue any cause, and seeke onely to teach thereby the trueth, must search out the places of *Logique*, and no doubt they shall finde much plentie." But this plain indication that the machinery of dialectical invention is useful in the similar procedure of rhetoric is not the only sign of Wilson's concern for the integration of the disciplines of communication. After he proposes four rhetorical places for proving that abstractions or inanimate things are worthy of praise, he immediately sees the places of logic as available for the same purpose, and thus he conceives of dialectical

[98] *Rhetorique*, pp. 11-99.
[99] *Ibid.*, pp. 86-99.
[100] *Ibid.*, pp. 7, 99-156.
[101] *Ibid.*, p. 89. At this point, Wilson regards the legal state as if it did not turn upon the meaning of written language—as if it applied, for example, to cases in which a given offense is called manslaughter by the defendant and murder by the prosecutor. Later (pp. 94-97) he regards the legal state as applying to cases which concern the interpretation of a written law or text. Only the latter interpretation is justified by the *Rhetorica ad Herennium*, from which Wilson's classification of states is derived.
[102] *Ibid.*, p. 6.

invention as a substitute form of rhetorical invention on a different level of application. His exact words are:

> Many learned will haue recourse to the places of *Logicke*, in steede of these fower places, when they take in hand to commend any such matter. The which places if they make them serue, rather to commende the matter, then onely to teach men the trueth of it, it were wel done, and Oratour like, for seing a man wholly bestoweth his witte to play the Oratour, he should chiefly seeke to compasse that, which he en-tendeth, and not doe that only which he neuer minded, for by plaine teaching, the *Logician* shewes himselfe, by large amplification, and beautifying of his cause, the *Rhetorician* is alwaies knowne.[103]

Wilson then lists six of the places of logic, and comments that they are possibly more basic than the four rhetorical places he had just enumerated. What he means by this can be gathered later when in speaking of proof as a part of the oration he says: "Therfore I wish that euery man should desire, & seeke to haue his *Logique* perfit, before he looke to profite in *Rhetorique*, considering the ground and confirmation of causes, is for the most part gathered out of *Logique*."[104]

Thus does Wilson recognize two theories of invention, the one dialectical and the other rhetorical, the one for proving and teach-ing plainly, the other for commending, amplifying, and giving beauty to a cause. But when he comes in the *Rhetorique* to the doctrine of arrangement or disposition, which was of course not only the second part of that subject in the Ciceronian scheme, but also the second part of scholastic dialectic as Wilson himself among others had con-ceived of it, he does not indicate differences or relations between dia-lectical and rhetorical arrangement, any more than he had done at the same point in his *Rule of Reason*. He speaks rather of two kinds of rhetorical arrangement, one natural, the other discretionary.[105] Nat-ural arrangement turns out to be the distributing of materials among the parts of the oration. Since Wilson had spoken of that under in-vention, he devotes little additional space to it now. Discretional arrangement turns out to be that which results from a calculation of what the time, the place, the audience, and the subject matter may require. Calculations of this sort would not have special analogues in dialectic, where the learned audience and learned subject are pre-supposed; nor would the dialectician have recourse to the theory of

[103] *Ibid.*, p. 23.   [104] *Ibid.*, p. 113.   [105] *Ibid.*, p. 158.

the parts of an oration, except as he might use the theory of oratorical proof to guide him in constructing his argument. Hence Wilson was not obliged to discuss rhetorical arrangement in the light of the theory of dialectical arrangement. Nevertheless it would have been an imaginative extension of classical doctrine if he had elected to consider those two kinds of organization with some thought of their similarities and differences.

Elocution or style, as the third of the procedures of Ciceronian rhetoric, receives far less of Wilson's total space than does invention, but nevertheless he contrives it to rank next after invention in spatial emphasis. In other words, he gives most of his first two books to invention, and most of his third and last book to style, thus appearing to say that these two procedures are much more important than the others, and that style is much less important than invention. He protects himself, however, from an appearance of hostility to style by paying high tribute to it in his own words and in those of Cicero, and by averring it to be the one quality that distinguishes an orator from other wise men:

> For whereas Inuention helpeth to finde matter, and Disposition serueth to place arguments: Elocution getteth words to set forth inuention, and with such beautie commendeth the matter, that reason semeth to be clad in Purple, walking afore both bare and naked. Therefore *Tullie* saieth well, to finde out reason and aptly to frame it, is the part of a wiseman, but to commende it by wordes and with gorgious talke to tell our conceipt, that is onely proper to an Oratour.[106]

The true heads of Wilson's discussion of style are enumerated as plainness, aptness, composition, and exornation.[107] The famous protest against "straunge ynkehorne termes" or "outlandish English" is pointed at those who affect French or Italian or Latin forms of speech in preference to "their mothers language," and it occurs in connection with his sprightly treatment of the first of these topics.[108] Aptness and composition are handled briefly as terms respectively concerning appropriateness of wording and pleasantness of sound in putting words together.[109] Under exornation, the last major heading of this section of his work, Wilson discusses the three kinds of style, as well as the tropes, the schemes, and the colors.[110]

[106] *Ibid.*, p. 160. Cf. Cicero, *Orator*, 14.44; 19.61.
[107] *Ibid.*, p. 162.
[108] *Ibid.*, pp. 162-165.
[109] *Ibid.*, pp. 165-169.   [110] *Ibid.*, pp. 169-208.

Although Wilson's account of the classical theory of memory is by no means the first in English, as I have already shown, it is superior to its predecessors in fidelity to its Latin sources and in expository skill. Moreover, Wilson's account supplements the classical theory by drawing upon current medical and psychological ideas to locate the memory "in the hinder part" of the head, and to explain a good memory as the product of a proper balance among qualities of moisture, dryness, cold, and heat in the brain. Thus Wilson says, "Children therefore being ouer moyst, and old men ouer drie, haue neuer good memories." As for what the proper balance should be, Wilson states himself as follows: "For such as be hot and moist, do sone conceiue matters, but they keepe not long. Again, they that be colde and drie, doe hardly conceiue, but they keepe it surely when they once haue it."[111] Wilson's medical theory of memory, which he openly attributes to the "Phisitions,"[112] is reminiscent of the thinking that produced in Hawes's account of poetic invention the description of the five inward faculties of the mind. At any rate, Wilson speaks of "the common sence," "iudgement," and "memorie," although he does not mention the faculties of imagination and fantasy, both of which figure prominently in Hawes's list.

When he turns from these considerations to the classical theory of memory, Wilson proceeds to use the chief terms of the similar theory in the *Rhetorica ad Herennium*. Thus he divides memory into the natural and the artificial;[113] he retells the story of Simonides and his identification of the mutilated victims after the collapse of the roof at the house of Scopas; and he comes then to the concepts of the place and the image, which he defines and illustrates. His theory is contained in the following four propositions:

I   The places of Memorie are resembled vnto Waxe and Paper.
II   Images are compted like vnto Letters or a Seale.
III The placing of these Images, is like vnto wordes written.
IIII The vtterance and vsing of them, is like vnto reading.[114]

In order that these propositions may be fully understood, Wilson uses a somewhat preposterous example:

My friend (whom I tooke euer to bee an honest man) is accused of theft, of adulterie, of ryot, of manslaughter, and of treason: if I would keepe these wordes in my remembrance, and rehearse them in

[111] *Ibid.*, p. 210.   [112] *Ibid.*, p. 209.
[113] *Ibid.*, p. 211.   [114] *Ibid.*, p. 214.

order as they were spoken, I must appoint fiue places, the which I had neede to haue so perfectly in my memorie, as could be possible. As for example, I will make these in my Chamber. A doore, a window, a presse, a bedstead, and a chimney. Now in the doore, I wil set *Cacus* the theefe, or some such notable verlet. In the windowe I will place *Venus*. In the Presse I will put *Apitius* that famous Glutton. In the Bedstead I will set Richard the third King of England, or some notable murtherer. In the Chimney I will place the blacke Smith, or some other notable Traitour. That if one repete these places, and these Images twise or thrise together, no doubt though he haue but a meane memorie, he shall carie away the wordes rehearsed with ease. And like as he may doe with these fiue words, so may he doe with fiue score, if he haue places fresh in his remembraunce, and doe but vse himselfe to this trade one fortnight together.[115]

Wilson's final topic, pronunciation or delivery, is no longer than his discussion of disposition, and thus is one of the two briefest parts of his theory of oratory. He sees delivery as so important that pleasantness in the sound of the speaker's voice and graciousness in his bearing may well overcome defects in his subject matter. He then remarks that, "as the sounde of a good instrument stirreth the hearers, and mooueth much delite, so a cleare sounding voyce, comforteth much our deintie eares, with much sweete melodie, and causeth vs to allow the matter, rather for the reporters sake, then the reporter for the matters sake."[116] He at once goes on to paraphrase the famous saying of Demosthenes that the first quality in oratory is pronunciation, the second, pronunciation, and the third, pronunciation.[117] He then divides pronunciation into two headings, voice and gesture, and concludes this part of rhetoric, and indeed his treatise, with a discussion of each.[118] His comments on faults in English pronunciation in his own day are protests against shrillness, hoarseness, throatiness, cackling, loudness, whining, frowning, and a multitude of other habits of speech. What he says about training children to pronounce distinctly has interest in the history of manners:

[115] *Ibid.*, p. 215.
[116] *Ibid.*, p. 218.
[117] For this saying in Cicero, see *Orator*, 17.56, *Brutus*, 38.142, and *De Oratore*, 3.56.213. Wilson undoubtedly quotes the story from *De Oratore*, for he adds the incident about Aeschines as Cicero gives it at that same point, and the incident about Demosthenes's practicing with pebbles under his tongue as Cicero gives it earlier in that same work, that is, in *De Oratore*, 1.61.260-261.
[118] *Rhetorique*, pp. 218-221. Cf. *Rhetorica ad Herennium*, 3.11.19.

Musicians in England haue vsed to put gagges in childrens mouthes, that they might pronounce distinctly, but now with the losse and lacke of Musick, the loue also is gone of bringing vp children to speake plainly.[119]

In his *Rhetorique* as a whole, Wilson is bent not only upon giving an English version of Ciceronian theory, but also upon naturalizing that theory and making it at home in England. There are illustrations of this latter tendency throughout the work. Thus in analyzing Cicero's dictum that a universal proposition is always implied in a particular, he says:

> As for example. If I shall aske this question, whether it bee lawfull for William Conquerour to inuade England, and win it by force of Armour, I must also consider this, whether it bee lawfull for any man to vsurpe power, or it bee not lawful.[120]

Thus again in illustrating the ancient commonplaces from which a eulogist would draw material for praising a noble personage, Wilson shows how English speakers would use realm or shire as topics. He says:

> To bee an English man borne, is much more honor then to bee a Scot, because that by these men, worthie Prowesses haue beene done, and greater affaires by them attempted, then haue beene done by any other.
> The Shire or Towne helpeth somewhat, towardes the encrease of honor: As it is much better to bee borne in Paris, then in Picardie: in London then in Lincolne. For that both the ayre is better, the people more ciuill, and the wealth much greater, and the men for the most part more wise.[121]

Thus again, in illustrating a eulogy to a noble personage, Wilson writes a model speech of his own in praise of two young nobles, Henry, second duke of Suffolk, and Charles, the third duke, whom he had tutored, and whose death had occurred July 14, 1551, in an epidemic of the sweating disease.[122] Again, Wilson's letter to the grief-stricken mother of these young men is put in to illustrate the deliberative address designed to give comfort.[123] Still again, Wilson writes an example of a forensic speech in which a soldier, fresh from the wars, is accused of murdering a worthy English farmer, and one

[119] *Ibid.*, p. 219.   [120] *Ibid.*, p. 2.
[121] *Ibid.*, pp. 12-13.   [122] *Ibid.*, pp. 14-17, 66, 68.
[123] *Ibid.*, pp. 66-85. For Wilson's other references to these two youths, see pp. 127, 184.

line of proof developed against the soldier is that his reputation is evil, he having been bred "among the men of Tinsdale & Riddesdale, where pillage is good purchase, and murthering is coumpted manhood."[124] Again, to illustrate pretentious "inke pot termes" in style, Wilson prints a letter devised by a Lincolnshire man, "Ioannes Octo," in applying for a vacant benefice through the intermediation of a gentleman who might possibly have influence with the Lord Chancellor.[125] And (to give one final example) Wilson suggests the following as a specimen of synecdoche:

> All Cambridge sorrowed for the death of *Bucer*, meaning the most part. All England reioyceth that Pilgrimage is banished, and Idolatrie for euer abolished: and yet all England is not glad but the most part.[126]

Wilson's *Rhetorique* should not be dismissed from consideration without some recognition of its special concern for sermon-making. As we have seen, Wilson discusses invention in part by emphasizing the three ancient types of oratory, the demonstrative, the deliberative, and the judicial. These forms of popular communication had respectively developed from the public ceremony, the political assembly, and the court of law. In Wilson's day these ancient forms of discourse were all in use, and thus a training in rhetoric had to provide indoctrination in each of them while indicating what extensions or modifications had been made in each since classical times. Deliberative oratory had declined in importance during the period of the Roman Empire,[127] and by the middle of the sixteenth century had not yet regained its dominant position among the three forms. Wilson reflects this state of affairs by illustrating deliberative oratory as the private counsel we might give a friend in an effort to induce him to study the laws of England, or as the epistle we might write either to persuade a young man to marriage or to comfort a mother on the death of her sons.[128] Judicial oratory was flourishing in Wilson's day, and he illustrates it without modifying or extending classical doc-

[124] *Ibid.*, p. 93.

[125] *Ibid.*, p. 163. In the 1553 edition of the *Rhetorique* this letter is not identified as having been written by a Lincolnshire man signing himself "Ioannes Octo." But it has nevertheless an English setting.

[126] *Ibid.*, p. 174.

[127] For an excellent discussion of this subject, see Harry Caplan, "The Decay of Eloquence at Rome in the First Century," *Studies in Speech and Drama in Honor of Alexander M. Drummond* (Ithaca, 1944), pp. 295-325.

[128] *Rhetorique*, pp. 31-39, 39-63, 66-85.

trine.[129] Demonstrative or ceremonial oratory was also flourishing. Wilson illustrates it by writing a commendation of the two young nobles, to which I referred earlier. He also illustrates it by adding a discourse in praise of King David for the killing of Goliath, and by throwing in a discourse in praise of Justice.[130] These two latter are close to sermons in substance and tone, although Wilson does not offer them as pure examples of this type of demonstrative oratory. What he does instead is to make frequent references to preaching throughout his *Rhetorique*, thus indicating unmistakably the application of rhetorical principles to pulpit oratory.

For example, in speaking of the oration as having the functions of teaching, delighting, and persuading, he pauses to emphasize the second of these uses by warning that "except men finde delite, they will not long abide."[131] He adds:

And that is the reason, that men commonly tarie the ende of a merie Play, and cannot abide the halfe hearing of a sower checking Sermon. Therefore euen these auncient Preachers, must now and then play the fooles in the pulpit, to serue the tickle eares of their fleting audience, or els they are like sometimes to preach to the bare walles, for though their spirite bee apt, and our will prone, yet our flesh is so heauie, and humours so ouerwhelme vs, that we cannot without refreshing, long abide to heare any one thing.[132]

For another example, when Wilson discusses the judicial speech with its ancient doctrine of positions of argument, he defines the Latin terms *constitutio* or *status* as "the chiefe ground of a matter, and the principall point whereunto both he that speaketh should referre his whole wit, and they that heare should chiefly marke";[133] and unexpectedly he elaborates his definition by reference to pulpit, not courtroom:

A Preacher taketh in hande to shewe what prayer is, and how needfull for man to call vpon God: now he should euer remember this his matter, applying his reasons whollie and fullie to this end, that the hearers may both knowe the nature of prayer, and the needfulnesse of prayer. The which when he hath done, his promise is fulfilled, his time well bestowed, and the hearers well instructed.

Another application of rhetorical doctrine to pulpit oratory occurs in Wilson's treatment of the introduction of speeches, where he

---

[129] *Ibid.*, pp. 92-94.   [130] *Ibid.*, pp. 14-17, 18-21, 23-29.
[131] *Ibid.*, p. 3.   [132] *Ibid.*, pp. 3-4.   [133] *Ibid.*, p. 88.

makes special mention of "Enteraunces apt for Preachers."[134] Still
another application occurs in connection with his discussion of narration as the second part of the speech.[135] Later, in his discussion of
style, he specifically disapproves of a rhymed sermon he recalls having heard:

> I heard a preacher deliting much in this kind of composition, who
> vsed so often to ende his sentences with wordes like vnto that which
> went before, that in my iudgement there was not a dozen sentences
> in his whole sermon, but they ended all in Rime for the most parte.
> Some not best disposed, wished the Preacher a Lute, that with his
> rimed sermon he might vse some pleasant melody, and so the people
> might take pleasure diuers waies, and dance if they list.[136]

He reverts later to rhymed sermons when he discusses the figures
of *similiter desinens* and *similiter cadens*, and at that point he speaks
of the liking of the people of St. Augustine's time for rhymed sentences and orations made ballad wise, even as judges were reported
by Tacitus to have been driven to use the same sort of "Minstrels
elocution."[137]

As for the sources of Wilson's *Rhetorique*, the best modern authority is Russell Wagner. He has stated that the *Rhetorica ad
Herennium*, doubtless considered by Wilson to be Cicero's, was one
of Wilson's chief authorities, and that Wilson also drew to some extent upon Cicero's *De Inventione, De Oratore, De Partitione Oratoria,* and *Brutus,* as well as upon Quintilian's *Institutio Oratoria.*
In addition to these basic treatises in the Ciceronian pattern, Wilson
was possibly obligated to Cox's *Rhethoryke,* observes Wagner, and
obviously went to Erasmus "for leading ideals, for detailed matter,
and for examples and critical dicta."[138] Incidentally, the epistle designed to persuade a young gentleman to marriage, already mentioned as an illustration of deliberative discourse, is one of Wilson's
borrowings from Erasmus, as he himself acknowledges. Many of
Wilson's readers had probably seen that epistle before, inasmuch as
Richard Taverner had also translated and published it in 1536 or
1537 as *A right frutefull Epystle deuysed by the moste excellent
clerke Erasmus in laude and praise of matrimony.*[139]

---

[134] *Ibid.,* p. 105.   [135] *Ibid.,* p. 108.   [136] *Ibid.,* p. 168.
[137] *Ibid.,* pp. 202-203.
[138] Russell Halderman Wagner, "Wilson and his Sources," *The Quarterly Journal of
Speech,* XV (1929), 530-532.
[139] On this point see Charles Read Baskervill, "Taverner's *Garden of Wisdom* and the
Apophthegmata of Erasmus," *Studies in Philology,* XXIX (April 1932), 149-150.

By way of a necessary supplement to the sources identified by Wagner, I should like to list Richard Sherry's *A Treatise of Schemes and Tropes*. This work, first published in 1550, was, like Wilson's *Rhetorique*, the first complete treatise on its subject in English, and it will be discussed in the next section of this chapter when I speak of the stylistic pattern of traditional rhetoric. But it should be mentioned now as having supplied Wilson with English phraseology and with illustrations for his treatment of the three kinds of style, for his definitions of figure, of scheme, of *gradatio*, and for his clarification of such stylistic concepts as aptness, metaphor, abusion, metonymy, transumption, periphrasis, epenthesis, syncope, proparalepsis, apocope, *extenuatio*, and *dissolutum*.[140]

Wilson's *Rhetorique* enjoyed great popularity for an entire generation after its first publication in 1553. It appeared in a second edition at London in 1560, supplemented by "A Prologue to the Reader," in which Wilson expresses his bitterness at the misfortunes which his *Rule of Reason* and his *Rhetorique* had recently brought upon him. Having fled from England after 1553 to escape persecution by the Catholic regime of Queen Mary, Wilson had taken refuge in Italy, only to have his two famous works pronounced heretical by Rome, and himself imprisoned and tortured. His "Prologue" speaks bitingly of the verdict of the Inquisition against him, and he angrily refuses, now that he is back in England, to correct his *Rhetorique* in its second edition, because, as he says, "If the Sonne

---

[140] The following table, which refers to Mair's edition of the *Rhetorique*, and to the first edition of Sherry's *Treatise* (London, 1550), indicates the topics wherein similarities between the two works are to be found:

Topic	Wilson	Sherry
"audience of sheepe"	p. 166	sig. C2r
"three maner of stiles"	p. 169	sig. B3r
"figure"	p. 170	sig. B5r
"metaphore"	pp. 172-173	sig. C4v-C5r
"abusion"	pp. 174-175	sig. C5r
"metonymia"	p. 175	sig. C5v
"transumption"	p. 175	sig. C5r-C5v
"periphrasis"	pp. 175-176	sig. C6v
"scheme"	p. 176	sig. B5r
"epenthesis"	p. 177	sig. B6r
"syncope"	p. 177	sig. B6r
"proparalepsis"	p. 177	sig. B6r
"apocope"	p. 177	sig. B6r
"extenuatio"	pp. 180-181	sig. D7r*
"gradatio"	p. 204	sig. D5v
"dissolutum"	p. 205	sig. D6v

* Wilson illustrates "extenuatio" with the form used by Sherry to illustrate "diminutio."

were the occasion of the Fathers imprisonment, would not the Father bee offended with him thinke you?" He even uses the "Prologue" as an opportunity to warn the public not to read such a subversive treatise as his *Rhetorique* is, since "if the world should turne (as God forbid) they were most like to weepe, that in all pointes would followe it." But the world did not turn. England remained Protestant; Wilson lived to become prominent in Queen Elizabeth's government; and his *Rhetorique* did not bring persecution to its readers. It was given a third edition in 1562, a fourth in 1563, and a fifth in 1567. Then for more than a decade it seems to have lost public favor, as Ramistic logic and rhetoric began to monopolize the spotlight in England. But despite the steady growth of Ramism in England after 1574, Wilson's *Rhetorique* had another term of popularity somewhat later, since it was given successive printings in 1580, 1584, and 1585. But with the latest of these dates its bibliographical history ended until the time of Mair's reprint of 1909.[141] Ciceronian rhetoric was revived in England by Thomas Vicars just forty years after Wilson's death in 1581, as we shall see in a later chapter, and that revival was one of the early signs of English dissatisfaction with Ramism. Still, the Ciceronianism that developed as a protest against Ramus was not devoid of the marks of the latter's philosophy, and thus it cannot be regarded as a mere continuation of Wilson's traditional scheme. Indeed, Wilson's *Rhetorique* is better accepted as a great summary of late medieval Ciceronianism in England than as an influence upon English Neo-Ciceronianism in the seventeenth century.

In bringing to a close this account of Ciceronian rhetoric in England before the complete emergence of the English Ramists, I should like to turn from lay to sacred rhetoric and mention a work that is historically interesting as one of the earliest English treatises to be devoted exclusively to the art of preaching. This treatise was written originally in Latin by Andreas Gerardus Hyperius, and published in 1555 at Dortmund as *De Formandis Concionibus Sacris, seu De Interpretatione Scripturarum Populari Libri II*. Later it was translated into English by John Ludham and published at London in 1577 under the title, *The Practise of preaching, Otherwise Called The Pathway to the Pulpet: Conteyning an excellent Method how to frame Diuine Sermons*. The author, Andreas Gerardus or André Gerhard, whose surname Hyperius is the Latin word for his native

---

[141] My list of editions of Wilson's *Rhetorique* is based upon entries in the *Short-Title Catalogue*, s.v. Wilson, Sir Thomas.

Ypres, was an influential Protestant theologian of the sixteenth century.[142] He studied at the University of Paris between 1528 and 1535; he lived in England from 1536 to 1540; he became professor of theology at Marburg in 1542, and held that post until his death in 1564. He wrote on dialectic, rhetoric, and other subjects, as well as on preaching. The John Ludham who translated Gerhard's work on preaching into English was graduated from St. John's College, Cambridge, with the degree of bachelor of arts in 1563-64, and served as vicar of Wethersfield in Essex from 1570 to 1613, when he died.[143]

The *Practise of preaching* is divided into two books, each of which describes itself as a treatise "Of framing of Diuine Sermons, or populer interpretation of the Scriptures."[144] The word "popular" receives great emphasis throughout the work, for Hyperius believes that there are two kinds of theological discourses, one addressed to the expert and the other to the layman, and he intends his treatise to be the theory of the latter kind. His first chapter begins with a clear statement of this distinction:

> No man doubteth but that there bee two maner of wayes of interpreting the scriptures vsed of skilfull diuines, the one *Scholastical*, peculyer to yᵉ scholes, yᵉ other *Popular* pertayning to the people. That one is apt for the assembles of learned men and young students somedeale profited in good letters: This other is altogether applied to instructe the confused multitude, wherin are very many rude, ignoraunt and vnlearned. The first is exercised within the narrowe compasse of the Scholes: The seconde taketh place in the large and spacious temples. The one strict and straight laced, sauoring *Philosophicall* solytarinesse and seueritie: The other stretched forth, franck and at lybertie, yea and delightinge in the light and (as ye would say) in the court of Orators. In yᵉ are mani things exacted after the rule of *Logical* breuitie and simplicitie: In this, *Rhetoricall* bountie and furniture ministreth much grace and decencie.[145]

As a theory to be followed by preachers who speak to the people, the *Practise of preaching* bases itself upon the terms of the pagan rhetoric of Cicero, but in such a way as to show that Hyperius has

---

[142] *Nouvelle Biographie Générale*, s.v. Hyperius, André Gerhard; also Alexander Chalmers, *The General Biographical Dictionary*, s.v. Hyperius, Gerard Andrew.

[143] John Venn and J. A. Venn, *Alumni Cantabrigienses* (Cambridge, 1922-1951), Pt. I, s.v. Ludham or Luddam, John. Cited below by title alone.

[144] Andreas Gerhard Hyperius, *The Practise of preaching*, Englished by Iohn Ludham (London, 1577), foll. 1r, 50v. My present discussion is based on the copy in the Huntington Library.

[145] *Ibid.*, fol. 1r.

an independent mind and an awareness of the differences between the orator and the pulpit speaker. The following passages beautifully illustrate his traditionalism and his originality:

> That many thinges are common to to [sic] the Preacher with the Orator, Sainct *Augustine* in his fourth Booke of Christian doctrine, doth copiously declare. Therfore, the partes of an Orator, whiche are accounted of some to be, *Inuention, Disposition, Elocution, Memory*, and *Pronounciation*, may rightlye be called also the partes of a Preacher. Yea and these thrée: *to Teache, to Delight, to Turne*: Likewise againe the thrée kyndes of speakyng, *Loftye, Base, Meane*: Moreouer, the whole craft of varienge the Oration by *Schemes* and *Tropes*, pertaineth indifferently to the Preacher and Orator, as Sainct *Augustine* in the same booke doth wittily confesse and learnedly proue. To be short, whatsoeuer is necessarie to the Preacher in disposition, Elocution, and Memorye, the *Rhetoritians* haue exactlye taught all that in their woorkhouses: wherfore (in my opinion) the Preachers may most conuenientlye learne those partes out of them. Certainly, he that hath béene somdeale exercised in the Scholes of the *Rhetoritians* before he be receiued into the order of Preachers, shall come much more apte and better furnished then many other, and may be bolde to hope, that he shall accomplish somwhat in the Church, worthy of prayse and commendation.[146]

Having marked out arrangement, style, and memory as the three parts of Ciceronian theory of special application to preaching, Hyperius now indicates why delivery and invention are less applicable:

> But pronounciation, for as much as it is now far otherwyse vsed, then it was in times past, and that all thinges ought with greater grauitie, yea maiestie, to bee done in the Temple then in the courte (to the whiche onely the *Rhetoritians* somtime informed theyr Disciples) agayne, syth euery Prouince and euery language hath hys proper *decorum* and comelynesse both in Pronounciation and gesture, which in an other place woulde not so well bee lyked off: It shall be good for the Preacher, not to searche the arte of Pronouncinge out of the Scholes of auncient Orators, but to endeuour hymselfe rather to imitate those Maisters, whom hee perceiueth, aboue the residue, to bee commended for their excellent grace and dexteritie, in Pronounciation and behauiour, especially in theyr owne natiue Countrye and region.
>
> By all these thinges it may appeare, that the Preacher hath many

[146] *Ibid.*, fol. 9r-9v.

poyntes, chiefly in Inuention, wherein he differeth from the Orator. whiche thinge séeinge it is so, it shall be our part, in opening of Inuention, to employ a specyall labour and dilygence. Albeit, in the meane time, if wee shall perceiue any thing to happen by the way as touching disposition, néedful to be marked, we wyll in no wyse dissemble it.[147]

The whole subsequent work is a development of this attitude towards the five parts of Ciceronian rhetoric. Hyperius takes very seriously his remark that the preacher should go to the ancient rhetoricians for the theory of style and memory, for on these topics he offers none of the traditional doctrine. As for delivery, he devotes to it a part of the final chapter of his second book without special regard for ancient doctrine. To arrangement he gives nine chapters of Book I, although that much space does not seem to be promised in the concluding words of the passage just quoted. These nine chapters develop the thesis that in a sermon "The parts commonly receiued are in nūber seuen, yᵉ is to say: *reding of the sacred scripture, Inuocatiō, Exordiū, propositiō or diuisio, Confirmation, Confutation, cōclusiō.*"[148] The discussion which this thesis receives from Hyperius is very close indeed to the Ciceronian doctrine of the parts of an oration, after due allowances are made for what Hyperius regards as necessary differences between the oration and the sermon. It even appears to be true that Hyperius, like Cicero, regards this part of rhetorical theory as a phase of the concept of invention, despite its obvious bearing upon arrangement. But Hyperius, as he acknowledges, does not follow Cicero closely in treating the other aspects of invention; he stays within the Ciceronian tradition, while creating new doctrine to conform to the special needs of the preacher.

One of the innovations of Hyperius concerns the doctrine of the kinds of sermons. He says, "I fréely confesse that I can in no wise fancy theyr iudgement, that endeuour to bringe, those thrée kindes of cases, I meane *Demonstratiue, Delibratiue,* and *Iudiciall,* oute of the prophane market place, into the sacred and reuerend Churche, and set them forth, vnto preachers to be immitated and folowed."[149] As a substitute for this aspect of Ciceronian theory, Hyperius proposes that sermons are of five kinds: 1) those of doctrine, in which all true principles and opinions are confirmed; 2) those of redargution, in which false and erroneous opinions are refuted; 3) those of

---

[147] *Ibid.,* fol. 9v.   [148] *Ibid.,* fol. 22r.   [149] *Ibid.,* fol. 17v.

institution or instruction, which teach how life and manners are made godly; 4) those of correction, which reprove corrupt manners; and 5) those of consolation, which offer comfort.[150] These five kinds of sermons provide the main topics for Hyperius's second book, in which the doctrinal sermon receives nine chapters of treatment, and the other four kinds receive one chapter each, whereas other topics, including delivery, receive only three chapters of the total.

Another of the innovations of Hyperius concerns that large section of Ciceronian doctrine devoted to the positions of argument. Hyperius says that the "*State* is a bréefe sūme of the whole matter, wherof a man purposeth to speake, and euen the argument and fountaine of the whole oration."[151] But having adopted the conventional definition, he proceeds to apply it to pulpit oratory by enumerating five states, one for each of his five kinds of sermons. For example, a sermon on the proposition that the pains of hell are a reality refutes an erroneous opinion, and thus contains a state "redargutiue." A sermon which condemns the envious, the vainglorious, or the riotous, contains a state "correctiue." And a sermon showing that a Christian ought to live devoutly contains a state "instructiue."

The only other innovation of Hyperius that I shall discuss here concerns the doctrine of places. Once again Hyperius alters the conventional doctrine for the sake of having his theory more adequately interpret the facts of preaching. All the places used in sermons, he says, are divided into two forms or orders, one called theological or divine places, the other, philosophical places.[152] The theological places, which show the preacher how and after what sort he may gather out of the scriptures the chief commonplaces touching all the doctrine of piety and of faith, and all the duties of charity and hope, turn out to be five in number, one for each of the five kinds of sermons.[153] The philosophical places or the places of logical invention, out of which are derived apt arguments to describe and set forth the nature and force of the thing under discussion, turn out to be twenty-eight in number, and to involve such concepts as definition, general kind, species, difference, property, division, whole, parts, matter, form, efficient, end, events, effects, subject, circumstances, comparatives, and opposites.[154] These are rehearsed but not discussed by Hyperius; in fact, instead of treating them at length, he refers his

---

[150] *Ibid.*, foll. 18r-18v, 20r.   [151] *Ibid.*, fol. 21r.
[152] *Ibid.*, fol. 54v.   [153] *Ibid.*, foll. 54v-58r.
[154] *Ibid.*, foll. 54v, 58r-59r.

preacher to the logician for further help in this particular matter.

Hyperius's theory of preaching is enthusiastically hailed by Michel Nicolas as the first complete work, and at the same time as one of the best, on the art of the pulpit.[155] The first half of this verdict is ambiguous in the extreme, for there were many treatises on preaching in the period before 1555, and one of the best of these, St. Augustine's *De Doctrina Christiana*, is openly admired by Hyperius, as is indicated in a passage quoted above.[156] Moreover, these earlier treatises are not all incomplete, even when they select for major emphasis a restricted aspect of their subject. But the other half of Nicolas's verdict is fully acceptable. The sacred rhetoric of Hyperius, as Ludham's translation repeatedly demonstrates, is a fresh and stimulating application of Ciceronian theory to the problems of sermon-making, and while it preserves machinery that was to be discarded by such later writers as Fénelon, it is unquestionably one of the best works of its kind in the Ciceronian tradition. The English pulpit was fortunate to have it available in popular form by 1577 as a full statement of the position that was already under attack by the Ramists.

[155] *Nouvelle Biographie Générale*, s.v. Hyperius.

[156] For a discussion of theories of preaching in the period between 1100 and 1500, and for a translation of one of those theories, see Harry Caplan, "A Late Medieval Tractate on Preaching," *Studies in Rhetoric and Public Speaking in honor of James Albert Winans* (New York, 1925), pp. 61-91. For a list of theories of preaching during the thirteenth, fourteenth, and fifteenth centuries, see the same author's *Mediaeval "Artes Praedicandi" A Hand-List* and *Mediaeval "Artes Praedicandi" A Supplementary Hand-List*, Cornell Studies in Classical Philology, XXIV (Ithaca, 1934); XXV (Ithaca, 1936).

III. The Rhetoric of Style

STYLISTIC rhetoric, as a recognizable and distinctive pattern of traditional rhetorical theory in England, has two main characteristics. First of all, it is openly committed to the doctrine of style as the most important aspect of training in communication. Secondly, it is openly mindful that invention, arrangement, memory, and delivery, or combinations of two or more of them, conceived in sum as Cicero had anciently dictated, were also legitimate parts of the full rhetorical discipline.

Readers of Cicero's *Orator* will recall that its major emphasis is upon style, although it gives some degree of recognition to the other parts of the Ciceronian formula.[1] Thus the *Orator* is important as a source book in the history of traditional stylistic rhetoric, although the fourth book of the *Rhetorica ad Herennium*, the third book of *De Oratore*, and the eighth and ninth books of Quintilian's *Institutio Oratoria* all contain a full treatment of style as the verbal aspect of the speaker's total problem, and all are sources along with the *Orator* in the development of the stylistic pattern in England.

The first treatise by an Englishman in this field, as I mentioned before, is the Venerable Bede's *Liber de Schematibus et Tropis*.[2] Bede is presumed to have written this work in 701 or 702.[3] As its title suggests, it undertakes to deal with the Latin theory of *elocutio*, not in its entirety, but in one of its main divisions, that of stylistic devices. Thus Bede enumerates twenty-nine schemes and forty-one tropes, but he succeeds in condensing these into seventeen of the former and thirteen of the latter, whereupon he defines each and illustrates it from the Bible, except in one case where his example is from the Christian poet Sedulius.[4] It must be confessed that his treatise is more of a dictionary of terms than a discourse upon the problem of achieving effectiveness in style; and yet, as the first treatise of its kind by an Englishman, it represents an interesting and persistent theory as to what it is that constitutes real distinction of utterance.

---

[1] See *Orator*, 14.43-44; 15.50-53; 17.54-61.

[2] See above, pp. 7, 33. For information about recent editions of Bede's little work, see p. 33, note 5.

[3] The evidence on this matter is indicated in M. L. W. Laistner, *A Hand-List of Bede Manuscripts* (Ithaca, 1943), pp. 131-132.

[4] For the sources of Bede's illustrations, see the notes on the text of the *Liber* in Halm, *Rhetores Latini Minores*, pp. 607-618. See also M. L. W. Laistner, "The Library of the Venerable Bede," in *Bede His Life, Times, and Writings*, ed. A. Hamilton Thompson (Oxford, 1935), p. 241.

That theory consists in the assumption that good style is a deliberate and systematic repudiation of the speech of everyday life. In other words, good style results only from word orders that stand opposed to the patterns of common speech. The schemes and the tropes are the two categories into which those orders fall, and thus Bede's definitions of these basic concepts emphasize that each is an attempt to get away from what is ordinary in usage. He says:

> On many occasions in writings it is customary for the sake of elegance that the order of words as they are formulated should be contrived in some other way than that adhered to by the people in their speech. These contrivances the Greek grammarians call schemes, whereas we may rightly term them attire or form or figure, because through them as a distinct method speech may be dressed up and adorned. On other occasions, it is customary for a locution called the trope to be devised. This is done by changing a word from its proper signification to an unaccustomed but similar case on account of necessity or adornment. And indeed the Greeks pride themselves upon having been the discoverers of such schemes and tropes.[5]

It is suggestive to speculate upon the cultural implications of a rhetorical theory which equates true elegance and hence true effectiveness with a system of studied departures from the established pattern of everyday speech. Such a theory appears to be the normal concomitant of a social and political situation in which the holders of power are hereditary aristocrats who must be conciliated by the commoners if the latter are to gain privileges for themselves. In a situation like that, persuasive forms of speech would emerge as agreeable forms; and agreeable forms would be those which sound agreeable to the aristocratic holders of power. What forms could sound more agreeable to the aristocrat than those which originated in a repudiation of the speech of the lower classes? Would not such forms remind him of the superiority of his own origin and thus be a way of softening his will by the subtle inducements of flattery? Would not the patterns of ordinary speech, if used by a commoner in seeking advantage from a great lord, be a way of showing contempt for the august person addressed? And would not that implication of contempt be enough to secure the prompt denial of the advantage sought? Speaking of the use of rhymed sentences as one of the uncommon patterns of speech, Thomas Wilson said in his *Rhetorique*, "Yea,

[5] Bede, *Liber*, in Halm, p. 607. Translation mine.

great Lordes would thinke themselues contemned, if learned men (when they speake before them) sought not to speake in this sort."[6] These words imply that the schemes and the tropes are the functional rhetoric of any aristocratic state or society, and that learned men as commoners and rhetoricians in aristocratic states must formulate rhetorical theory upon that principle. And this implication is borne out by the history of rhetoric in England. For the schemes and the tropes were especially popular in the feudal and monarchial periods of English history, and became less important with the growth of parliamentary government.

Bede's definitions of the schemes and the tropes, and also his subsequent treatment of them, came to him from the thirty-sixth and thirty-seventh chapters of Book I of Isidore's *Etymologiae*.[7] These chapters, by the way, are part of Isidore's treatment of grammar, and Book II of his same work deals with rhetoric and dialectic.[8] The fact that Bede's treatise on the schemes and tropes comes from Isidore's *De Grammatica* rather than from a regular work on rhetoric might lead to the supposition that it should be classed, not as a rhetoric, but as a grammar. Indeed, this very supposition apparently troubled Halm when he reedited the minor Latin rhetorics that had formed the basis of the famous *Antiqui Rhetores Latini* as put out earlier by Pithou and again by Capperonnier. At any rate, Halm admitted Bede's *Liber* to a place in his collection with open reluctance, and he intimated that he would willingly have left it out if he had not been more or less obligated to include in his work whatever his two predecessors had allowed in theirs.[9] He might, however, have spared himself this anxiety. In actual fact, the schemes and the tropes are not more grammatical than rhetorical. Their history proves that they are grammatical in Donatus and Charisius, rhetorical in the *Rhetorica ad Herennium, Orator, De Oratore,* and *Institutio, Oratoria,* both grammatical and rhetorical in English stylistic rhetorics of the sixteenth century, and purely and emphatically rhetorical in the reformed rhetoric of Ramus. Thus they should occasion no apology to those who regard Bede's treatment of them as a work on rhetoric.

Bede's failure to include in his *Liber* such other topics as those of

---

[6] Mair's edition, p. 203.

[7] See Laistner, "The Library of the Venerable Bede," in Thompson, p. 241.

[8] For Isidore's *De Grammatica* and *De Rhetorica*, see Migne, *Patrologia Latina,* LXXXII, 73-124, 123-140; for his *De Rhetorica* alone, see Halm, pp. 505-522.

[9] Halm, p. xv.

the virtues, vices, and kinds of style should not be construed to mean that he was ignorant of the broad Latin doctrine of *elocutio*. Nor should it be assumed that, because he does not specifically mention style as one of the five parts of rhetoric, he therefore was unaware of the full extent of the Ciceronian program. He knew both of these matters beyond question. Although Cicero's rhetorical writings were not a part of the considerable library to which he had access,[10] he did of course know and use Isidore's *Etymologiae*, and that work lists the five conventional parts of rhetoric, and treats style as the third part, only a few pages beyond its disquisition on the schemes and tropes as components of grammar.

Between the eighth and the fifteenth centuries, stylistic rhetoric appears to have attracted more favor in England than did the full Ciceronian formula, despite the fact that Alcuin's work in the latter vein was of greater intrinsic value than was Bede's in the former. In that long stretch of time a few names are of importance in the history of stylistic theory. One of the earliest after Alcuin is John of Salisbury. His *Metalogicon* has already been mentioned as an early scholastic logic by an English author, and as a work in which logic is divided into invention and disposition, according to a tradition that went back to Aristotle's *Topics*.[11] It would be within reason for a man who equated logic with these two procedures to regard rhetoric as having no province except that of style and delivery. And that appears to have been John's position, although he does not treat rhetoric specifically, except as his advice on what constitutes good writing emphasizes matters of style above other considerations.[12]

Soon after the time of John of Salisbury, the Ciceronian formula for rhetoric, as we have seen, passed over into poetic theory and became the framework of Geoffrey of Vinsauf's *Poetria Nova*; and when that formula was again restored to rhetorical theory in Stephen Hawes's *Pastime of Pleasure*, it carried back with it much of the poetic content and poetic presuppositions that Geoffrey had given it.[13] In addition to his *Poetria Nova*, Geoffrey wrote a little treatise called the *Summa de Coloribus Rhetoricis*,[14] which limits itself to the de-

---

[10] For a catalogue of authors and works in Bede's library, see Laistner, "The Library of the Venerable Bede," in Thompson, pp. 263-266.

[11] See above, pp. 15, 38.

[12] Atkins, *The Medieval Phase*, p. 75; also Baldwin, *Medieval Rhetoric and Poetic*, pp. 156-172.

[13] See above, pp. 81-87.

[14] For an analysis of this work and typical extracts from it, see Faral, *Les Arts Poétiques*, pp. 321-327.

vices of style, as did Bede's *Liber,* and thus by strong implication holds rhetoric to the third part of Cicero's formula. If Geoffrey's theory of a rhetorical poetic and a stylistic rhetoric was typical of the early years of the thirteenth century, the same conditions must have been still in existence some fifty years later. John of Garland, an Englishman of that later date, composed a treatise entitled *Poetria* and another called *Exempla Honestae Vitae.* The first of these is an adaptation of the doctrine of rhetorical style to poetics, with some faint recognition of such other rhetorical procedures as invention, arrangement, memory, and delivery.[15] The second is described by Atkins as "a text-book treating of the use of the rhetorical figures." Atkins adds: "It supplies sixty-four illustrations of such devices, giving to each its appropriate name; but it represents nothing more than the conventional treatment of such matters found in other collections of a similar kind."[16]

The teaching of stylistic rhetoric in an English classroom was pictured around 1481 in *The Court of Sapience,* the learned poetic allegory which I mentioned earlier in connection with the first attempts to express logical doctrine in English.[17] It will be remembered that the hero of *The Court* visits the castle of sapience where dwell the seven ladies, who represent the seven liberal arts. After he quits the parlor of Dame "Dialetica," he goes next to "Dame Rethoryke, Modyr of Eloquence," and in six seven-line stanzas, which amount, as a Latin headnote in the text says, to a "breuis tractatus de Rethorica," he describes the effect of Dame Rhetoric upon the pupils before her, the actual heads of the doctrine she is teaching them, the authorities upon whom she appears to him to rely, and the great prose writers and poets to whom her instruction refers.[18]

Delight rather than conviction best describes the mood of the pupils of Dame Rhetoric, according to the report we are given. The hero of *The Court* exclaims as he sees her at work:

> And many a clerke had lust hyr for to here;
> Hyr speche to theym was parfyte sustynaunce,
> Yche worde of hyr depuryd was so clere
> And enlumynyd wyth so parfyte plesaunce,
> That heuyn hit was to here her beau parlaunce;

[15] See Baldwin, *Medieval Rhetoric and Poetic,* pp. 191-195.
[16] *The Medieval Phase,* p. 97.
[17] See above, pp. 46-47.
[18] *The Court of Sapience,* ed. Spindler, pp. 198-200.

> Her termes gay of facound souerayne
> Cacemphaton in noo poynt myght dysteyne.

If the last two of these lines seem negative in declaring that sovereign eloquence is never discolored by what is ill-sounding or obscene, the earlier lines are at least something of a positive program. And their climactic reference to the musical sound of perfect speech represents of course a main tenet of the program of a rhetoric limited predominantly to style.

The actual heads of the doctrine which Dame Rhetoric teaches her pupils are systematically reminiscent of ancient stylistic theory. Says her poet-observer:

> She taught theym all the craft of endytyng,
> Whyche vyces bene that shuld auoyded be,
> Whyche ben the coloures gay of that konnyng,
> Theyre difference and eke theyre propurte;
> Yche thyng endyted how hit shuld peyntyd be;
> Dystinccion she gan clare and discus,
> Whyche ys coma, colon, periodus.

First to be noticed in this list is the topic of the vices of style, and these, as enumerated by Quintilian, not only involved cacemphaton but such other things as meanness or extravagance, meagerness, sameness, superfluous elaboration, perverse affectation, and the like.[19] Second in the list are the colors, under which fall the schemes and the tropes. Third is the topic of painting, which quite possibly refers to the concept of illustration and word picture discussed with special detail by Quintilian as ἐνάργεια, that is, *enargia* or vivid description.[20] And last are the "coma," the "colon," and the "periodus," which must be construed as referring, not to marks of punctuation, but to the whole question of rhythm in style. In Cicero, and again in Quintilian, the *comma* or *incisum* is a thought expressed in something less than a full sentence, possibly in a phrase; the *colon* or *membrum* is a thought expressed likewise in something less than a complete sentence, and in something more than a phrase, say in a clause; and the *periodus* or *circuitus* is a thought expressed in a complete sentence, usually made up of four *cola*, this number being possibly reminiscent of the ancient use of περίοδος to designate the complete circuit of the four Grecian games, the most memorable of which were the Olympics.[21]

---

[19] See *Institutio Oratoria*, 8.3.44-60.   [20] *Ibid.*, 8.3.61-81.
[21] See *Orator*, 61.204-206; 62.211-214; 66.223-226. Also *Institutio Oratoria*, 9.4.22-45,

As for the authorities upon whom Dame Rhetoric relies in her teaching of stylistic rhetoric, her poet-observer mentions "Galfryde" and "Januense," that is, Geoffrey of Vinsauf and Balbus de Janua.[22] The former of these, as we know, wrote not only on Cicero's five procedures in his *Poetria Nova*, but also on style alone in his *Summa de Coloribus Rhetoricis*. The latter, Balbus, wrote on the schemes and tropes in the fourth book of his *Catholicon*, which is a treatise on Latin grammar and vocabulary. In addition to these two authorities, the poet-observer mentions Cicero as master of Dame Rhetoric; in fact, Cicero is "The chosyn spowse vnto thys lady fre," and in him "Thys gyltyd craft of glory ys content." The poet-observer then mentions that works on law and science are sources of the knowledge needed to express oneself beautifully, and here as elsewhere he follows the Ciceronian doctrine of *elocutio*. His description of the work of Dame Rhetoric closes with the observation that she is concerned with "prose and metyr of all kynde," and he then enumerates some of the prose writers and poets to whom she refers her doctrine, the most notable being Homer, Virgil, Ovid, and Horace.[23]

The passage concerning Dame Rhetoric in *The Court* is notable as the first printed English account of the doctrine of stylistic rhetoric and of the act of teaching it in a classroom. Dame Rhetoric uses Latin textbooks and Latin examples; the clerks who are her pupils would expect her actual instruction to be in Latin; indeed, around 1481, when *The Court* was first published, there were no English textbooks on rhetoric, and English itself, as the medium of preliminary instruction and the instrument for teaching Latin, had replaced French in the schools of England only about a century before. But although Latin may have been the language overheard by the poet-observer as he visited the parlor of Dame Rhetoric in the castle of sapience, he transmits his own impressions in English, and thus he becomes more interesting in a historical sense than he is usually considered to be as a poet.

The vogue of stylistic rhetoric in the schools of England during

---

122-130. C. F. Bühler regards these three terms as references to marks of punctuation, and thinks the inclusion of them as a part of rhetoric is unusual. See his *The Sources of the Court of Sapience*, Beiträge zur Englischen Philologie, XXIII (1932), p. 75. But actually these terms have a most prominent position in Cicero's and Quintilian's theory of oratorical rhythm.

[22] See Bühler, *op. cit.*, pp. 75-76.

[23] Bühler, *loc. cit.*, notes that the list of exemplary writers in *The Court* corresponds to the similar list in the *Laborintus* of Évrard l'Allemand.

the sixteenth century is indicated about seventy years after the first edition of *The Court* by John Jewel's *Oratio contra Rhetoricam*.[24] This little work is one of the earliest of the extant literary efforts of Jewel, who in Elizabeth's reign was to become the bishop of Salisbury and the greatest early apologist for the position of the English church against Roman Catholicism. Between 1544 and 1552 Jewel served as praelector in humanities and rhetoric at Corpus Christi College in Oxford. The *Oratio contra Rhetoricam* was delivered around the year 1548 before all the members of Corpus Christi, and it is doubtless the most elaborate of the lectures pronounced by Jewel during his praelectorship. It is not so much an attack on rhetoric, however, as an ingenious and ironical condemnation of what rhetoric had come to mean in the schools and at Oxford. And what rhetoric had come to mean was that speaking must be done in such a way as to appear systematically opposed to the ordinary habits of communication.

Early in his oration Jewel announces his own determination to abandon the study of rhetoric and take up poetry. Perhaps he means by this only that his subsequent lectures will concern the humanities as his past ones have concerned rhetoric. Perhaps he is merely lending interest to a mundane transition by giving it an air of crisis and renunciation. But at any rate he conducts his speech as if he had had a genuine change of heart towards rhetoric, and really believed his own statement that "the whole time which thus far we have devoted to eloquence has been wasted and worse than wasted."

As this thesis develops, Jewel makes it evident that there is a kind of speaking which is worthy of study, and that this worthy kind has lost the name of rhetoric, although it still possesses the greatest value and dignity. "For if in speaking," says he, "we seek this (as we certainly do), that we may be understood by others with whom we deal, who can discover a better mode of speech than to speak intelligibly, simply, and clearly? What need of art? What need of childish ornaments?" He adds:

> Truth, indeed, is clear and simple; it has small need of the armament of the tongue or of eloquence. If it is perspicuous and plain, it has enough support in itself; it does not require flowers of artful speech.

[24] My discussion of the *Oratio contra Rhetoricam* and all my quotations from it depend upon Hoyt H. Hudson's translation and comment. See his "Jewel's Oration against Rhetoric: A Translation," *The Quarterly Journal of Speech*, XIV (1928), 374-392.

If it is obscure and unpropitious, it will not be brought to light in vociferation and flow of words.

Jewel is not so naive as to want to imply that man is born with the ready-made capacity to be fully understandable in speech. Nor does he mean that truth is easily found and easily communicated, and that intelligibility, simplicity, and clarity are possessions of everyone, if only art keeps out of the way. What he does mean is that the business of learning to be clear, simple, and understandable does not in his time concern the rhetoricians, who are preoccupied instead with the business of teaching the flowers of speech and the artifices of delivery. These flowers and artifices as the exclusive concern of rhetoric are what Jewel is renouncing. The picture he draws later of the rhetoric of his time bears this out. Speaking of the insolence, trickery, and slander of oratory, he says:

> Such courses the orators undertake and profess: they have only so much right on their side as they have tongue and impudence. For if they trust to the truth and equity of their cause, why do they flee simplicity and an ordinary mode of speech? Why pursue all these verbal graces, these obscurities and pedantries? Why for free and un-trammeled discourse contrive feet, rhythm, and like fetters? Why go into battle with hints, conjectures, opinions, fables, and rumors? Why devise so many snares for captivating our ears? What do they want of these tropes, figures of speech, *schemata*, and what they call "colors" (to me they seem rather *shades*),—epanorthoses, antimetaboles, suspensions, catachreses, enigmas, extenuations, premunitions, exclamations, aposiopeses, apologies, circumlocutions, diminutions, and hyperboles? Why fill the forum with cries, vociferations, and tears? Why call down the gods from heaven? Why raise the shades from the underworld? Why have buildings, temples, columns, tombs, and stones cry out? What do they want of such faces? Why that thrashing about of the body? Why that sudden contraction? that waving of arms? that slapping of the thigh? that stamp of the foot? Why is it they speak not with the mouth, not with the tongue, not with the jaws, but with the hand, fingers, joints, arms, face, and the whole body? For idle men have fashioned all these things for themselves, and they become much more conversant with this arsenal than with the subject itself and with truth. O gentle triflers, who will never in your whole lives, I know, lack a subject of study!

It was only a short time after this outburst against ornamental rhetoric, as the sixteenth century was reaching its midpoint, that the first English textbook on the schemes and tropes, and on stylistic rhetoric in general, was printed. This textbook is Richard Sherry's *Treatise of Schemes and Tropes,* published at London in 1550.[25] A graduate of Magdalen College, Oxford, in 1527, Sherry had been appointed headmaster of Magdalen College School in 1534 after taking his master's degree at Oxford in the meantime. His headmastership ended in 1540. Ten years later, at the request of Thomas Brooke, to whom he dedicated the work, he put into his mother tongue the stylistic lore that he had formerly taught to his pupils in Latin.

The realization that his English readers would find his vocabulary unfamiliar, and might therefore reject his work without fair consideration, led him in the opening words of his dedicatory epistle to try to prevent such an outcome by associating it with rashness and frivolity, and by intimating that an opposite outcome would be a sign of modernity. He says:

> I doubt not but that the title of this treatise all straunge vnto our Englyshe eares, wil cause some men at the fyrst syghte to maruayle what the matter of it should meane: yea, and peraduenture if they be rashe of iudgement, to cal it some newe fangle, and so casting it hastily from thē, wil not once vouch safe to reade it: and if they do, yet perceiuynge nothing to be therin that pleaseth their phansy, wyl count it but a tryfle, & a tale of Robynhoode. But of thys sorte as I doubte not to fynde manye, so perhaps there wyll be other, whiche moued with the noueltye thereof, wyll thynke it worthye to be looked vpon, and se what is contained therin. These words, *Scheme* and *Trope,* are not vsed in our Englishe tongue, neither bene they Englyshe wordes. No more be manye whiche nowe in oure tyme be made by continual vse, very familier to most men, and come so often in speakyng, that aswel is knowen amongest vs the meanyng of them, as if they had bene of oure owne natiue broode.[26]

[25] The title page reads: "A treatise of Schemes & Tropes very profytable for the better vnderstanding of good authors, gathered out of the best Grammarians & Oratours by Rychard Sherry Londoner. Whervnto is added a declamacion, That chyldren euen strayt frō their infancie should be well and gently broughte vp in learnynge. Written fyrst in Latin by the most excellent and famous Clearke, Erasmus of Roterodame." The dedicatory letter ends thus: "Geuen at London the .XIII. day of Decembre. Anno. M. D. L." There is no date on the title page. The colophon reads: "Imprynted at London by John Day dwellinge ouer Aldersgate, beneth saint Martyns. And are to be sold at his shop by the litle conduit in Chepesyde at the sygne of the Resurrection. Cum priuilegio ad imprimendum solum. Per septennium."

[26] *A treatise of Schemes & Tropes* (London, 1550), sig. A1v-A2r.

The motives which led him to undertake his pioneering venture are revealed later in the dedicatory epistle. Speaking in defense of English not only as the language of such famous authors as Gower, Chaucer, Lydgate, Elyot, and Wyatt, but also as a vocabulary capable of receiving all kinds of sciences and all manner of thoughts, Sherry goes on to say that he is qualified to discuss the schemes and tropes "bicause longe ago, I was well a quaynted wyth them, when I red them to other in ȳ Latin"; and he adds that, since "they holpe me verye muche in the exposicion of good authoures, I was so muche the more ready to make them speak English: partli, to renew the pleasure of mine old studies, and partelye to satysfy your request."[27] He next recalls that the "famous clarke Rodulphus Agricola" had urged all men to translate into their own tongue whatever they read in another, that being the way to perceive the strength and weakness of utterance. As for the attitude of the learned world towards the subject of his present work, Sherry remarks:

> No lerned nacion hath there bene but ȳ learned in it haue written of schemes & fygures, which thei wold not haue don, except thei had perceyued the valewe.[28]

Sherry emphasizes on three occasions that he is writing upon the schemes and tropes as a topic of style, and that he is writing on style as the third part of the whole Ciceronian program. The first occasion arises in the dedicatory epistle as he speaks of the schemes and tropes as aids in the interpretation of great writing:

> For thys darre I saye, no eloquente wryter maye be perceiued as he shulde be, wythoute the knowledge of them: for asmuche as al togethers they belonge to Eloquucion, whyche is the thyrde and pryncipall parte of rhetorique.[29]

The second occasion arises at the beginning of the actual text of his work, where Sherry prints the following headnote:

> Schemes and Tropes.
> A briefe note of eloquciō, the third
> parte of Rhetoricke, wherunto
> all Figures and Tropes be
> referred.[30]

On the third occasion, Sherry is speaking of style and its relation to the other parts of rhetoric. He says:

[27] *Ibid.*, sig. A4v.   [28] *Ibid.*, sig. A5r.   [29] *Ibid.*, sig. A6v.   [30] *Ibid.*, sig. B1r.

Tullye and Quintilian thoughte that inuencion and disposiciō were the partes of a wytty and prudent man, but eloquence of an oratour. For howe to finde out matter, and set it in order, may be comen to all men, whyche eyther make abridgementes of the excellent workes of aunciente wryters, and put histories in remēbraunce, or that speake of anye matter them selues; but to vtter the mynde aptely, distinctly, and ornately, is a gyft geuen to very fewe.[31]

It is important to notice these statements that the schemes and the tropes are merely a part of style, and that style is third among the five parts of rhetoric. They constitute proof that Sherry belongs among writers on traditional stylistic rhetoric, not among disciples of the reformed stylistic rhetoric of Ramus, whose influence in Europe began to mount after 1543. The Ramists, as we shall see in greater detail later, considered rhetoric to have only two parts, style and delivery, as opposed to five parts under the ancient program; and style they considered to have only two parts, the schemes and the tropes, as opposed to the larger content of the doctrine of *elocutio* under Cicero, Thomas Wilson, and Sherry. It would have been unusual for Sherry to be influenced by the Ramists as early as 1550, since their doctrine was young and untraveled at that date. But the title of Sherry's work invites us to think that he conceives of rhetoric as the Ramists did, and to avoid such a misunderstanding we must take into account his repeated declarations of faith in the older arrangements of Cicero.

Sherry's treatise covers style by speaking of words used singly and words used in combination. Under the first heading he speaks of clearness and of the faults of barbarism and solecism. Under the second heading he lumps everything else: the three kinds of style (the great, the small, the mean, that is, the middle); the schemes, which require a discussion of three things—figures, faults, virtues; the tropes, which are particularly useful as ornaments; the first order of rhetorical figures, which include larger aspects of style like repetition, antithesis, and climax; the ornaments of sentences, which include still larger aspects like partition, enumeration, rhetorical description or *enargia*, amplification, hyperbole, proofs, examples, parables, images, and so on.

The heart of Sherry's work is, however, the topic of the schemes and the tropes, as his title indicates. To him, as to Bede, the schemes

---

[31] *Ibid.*, sig. B1v-B2r.

and the tropes are verbal arrangements that differ from what is customary and accepted, and thus they advertise the theory that true effectiveness in speech proceeds, not from its accurate correspondence to states of reality, but from its lack of resemblance to the idiom of ordinary life. This theory is implied in Sherry's key definitions:

> Scheme is a Greke worde, and signifyeth properlye the maner of gesture that daunsers vse to make, whē they haue won the best game, but by translacion is taken for the fourme, fashion, and shape of anye thynge expressed in wrytynge or payntinge: and is taken here now of vs for the fashion of a word, sayynge, or sentence, otherwyse wrytten or spoken then after the vulgar and comen vsage, and that thre sūdry waies: by figure, faute, vertue.

Figure.

> Fygure, of Scheme ȳ fyrst part, is a behaueoure, maner, or fashion eyther of sentence, oracion, or wordes after some new wyse, other thē men do commenlye vse to wryte or speake: and is of two sortes. Dianoias, that is of sentence, and Lexeos of worde.[32]

> Figure Lexeos, or of worde, is when in speakyng or wrytyng any thynge touchynge the wordes is made newe or straunge, otherwyse then after ȳ comen custume: & is of 11. kyndes, diccion, & construccion.[33]

> Vertue, or as we saye, a grace & dygnitye in speakynge, the thyrde kynde of Scheme, is when the sentence is bewtyfied and lyfte vp aboue the comen maner of speaking of the people. Of it be two kyndes: Proprietie, and garnyshyng.[34]

Tropes.

> Emonge authors manye tymes vnder the name of figures, Tropes also be comprehended: Neuerthelesse ther is a notable difference betwixt thē. In figure is no alteracion in the wordes frō their proper significacions, but only is the oracion & sētence made by thē more plesaūt, sharpe & vehemēt, after ȳ affecciō of him that speketh or writeth: to ȳ which vse although tropes also do serue, yet properlye be they so called, because in them for necessitye or garnyshynge, there is a mouynge and chaungynge of a worde and sentence, from theyr owne significaciō into another, whych may agre wyth it by a similitude.[35]

As individual schemes and tropes are enumerated and exemplified, the thesis that each represents a departure from the ordinary pattern of speech becomes more and more evident.

[32] *Ibid.*, sig. B5r.   [33] *Ibid.*, sig. B5v.   [34] *Ibid.*, sig. C3r.
[35] *Ibid.*, sig. C4r-C4v.

The first actual schemes listed by Sherry are the figures of diction. He calls the second one of these by its Greek term *Apheresis*, and by its Latin term *Ablatio*. This figure, he indicates, is produced when we remove a syllable or letter from the beginning of any word without changing the sense in which it is used, except apparently as our action adds an element of surprise or interest to the ordinary meaning of the term. Sherry's illustration of this figure does not represent good reasoning about the derivation of the English word he discusses, but it does represent the nature of the figure he wants to explain. He takes the English word "pentis," which means a small shed with sloping roof erected against another building, or by extension, any structure with a sloping roof, say a window awning. Actually, this word, now surviving as "penthouse," came from the Latin word "appendere" meaning "to belong to." But Sherry argues that the word "pentis" was originally the Greek word "epenthesis," and that the Greek word not only had its first letter, "e," removed by speakers seeking to alter its familiar pattern under the figure of *Apheresis*, but also had its middle syllable, "hes," removed for the same purpose under the figure of *Syncope*, with the result that "pentis" came into being at the hands of seekers of novelty in style. The whole of Sherry's explanation deserves quotation:

> Apheresis   2 *Ablatio*, the takynge awaye of a letter or sillable from the begynnynge of a worde, of a letter, when we say: The pēthesis of thys house is to low, for the epenthesis. Wher note this ȳ word pēthesis is a greke worde, & yet is vsed as an englishe, as many mo be, and is called a pentis by these figures, Sincope and Apheresis, the whole word beynge as is before, epenthesis, so called because it is betwyxt ȳ lyght & vs, as in al occupiers shops cōmenlie it is.[36]

The "occupiers shops" mentioned in the closing words of this quotation are of course merchants' shops of any sort. The "pentis" or "awning" in such shops would be between the occupants and the light outside. The Greek word "ἐπένθεσις" means "the insertion of a letter" and by metaphor any insertion between something and something else. Still, the English word "pentis" does not happen to come from "ἐπένθεσις," although the figure of Apheresis and of Syncope would be admirably illustrated by it if Sherry's argument were etymologically sound.

[36] *Ibid.*, sig. B5v-B6r.

As we have already seen by Sherry's definition of the trope, there is an element of necessity as well as of ornament about its use, and thus it does not seem to represent a purely wilful departure from the language of ordinary life as do the two schemes just discussed. Nevertheless in Sherry's analysis of this aspect of style, the implication is plain not only that tropes involve the use of words in some orbit outside of their usual ones, but also that, when these departures from the ordinary are made, the motive is often ornament rather than necessity. Metaphor, the first of the tropes listed by Sherry, is defined as "*Translatio*, translacion, that is a worde translated from the thynge that it properlye signifieth, vnto a nother whych may agre with it by a similitude."[37] He adds: "And among all vertues of speeche, this is the chyefe." Now when Sherry illustrates that form of metaphor which represents the use of a physical term to designate a mental happening, he has ornament rather than necessity in mind, since in each of the cases he cites, the metaphor is strictly speaking unnecessary, as he points out by showing what literal term would be available if one did not want to decorate the ordinary expression. He says:

Translacions be diuerse.
Some frō the body to the mynd, as: I haue but lately tasted the Hebrue tonge, for newely begunne it. Also I smell where aboute you go, for I perceyue.

Most of his other illustrations of tropes indicate that he is discussing them, not on the primitive level where man has to use them, but on the sophisticated level where man uses them to exhibit his wit and learning. On this level, of course, they are conspicuous departures from the speech of the people, inasmuch as tropes in popular speech are more a matter of instinct than design.

One other example may be cited to show how pervasive in Sherry's treatise is idea that figures are departures from ordinary patterns of communication. In speaking of the first order of rhetorical figures, Sherry comes at length to that called *Homoeoteleuton* or *Similiter desinens*, that is, like ending, or rhyme. Rhyme as an arrangement of language is not part of ordinary speech. It is rather a contrivance for making a thought seem out of the ordinary. Sherry's examples are rather feeble, as indeed were the rhymed sermons condemned by

[37] *Ibid.*, sig. C4v.

Thomas Wilson.[38] But their status as departures from common speech is unmistakable. Says Sherry:

> Homoteleto. *Similiter desinens*, endynge al alyke, when words or sentēces haue alyke endyng, as: Thou dareste do fylth-ely, and studiest to speke baudely. Content thy selfe w̄ thy state, in thy herte do no man hate, be not the cause of stryfe and bate.[39]

As this review of Sherry's pioneering work draws to an end, I should like to mention that he is quite explicit about the sources upon which his treatise is based. He speaks in his dedicatory letter of having prepared himself for his task by reading sundry treatises, some written long ago, and some in his own day.[40] He declares, however, of his definitions and examples:

> I haue not translated them orderly out of anye one author, but run-ninge as I sayde thorowe many, and vsyng myne owne iudgement, haue broughte them into this body as you se, and set them in so playne an order, that redelye maye be founde the figure, and the vse where-vnto it serueth.[41]

From the authors and works explicitly mentioned by Sherry in his dedicatory letter and in the *Treatise* itself, it would appear that he places primary reliance upon such modern writings as Rudolph Agricola's *De Inventione Dialectica*, Petrus Mosellanus's *Tabulae de Schematibus et Tropis*, Thomas Linacre's *Rudimentes Grammatices*, and Erasmus's *De Duplici Copia Verborum ac Rerum* and *The Preacher*; whereas for the ancients he goes to Quintilian's *Institutio Oratoria*, to Cicero's *Orator*, *De Oratore*, and *De Partitione Oratoria*, and to Aristotle's *Topics* and possibly his *Rhetoric*.[42]

"But if God spare me lyfe," says Sherry after apologizing for the inadequacies of his *Treatise*, "I truste hereafter to make it an intro-ducciō, wherbi our youth not onlye shall saue that moste precious Jewell, Time, whyle they wander by them selues, readynge at all

---

[38] See above, p. 108.
[39] *Treatise of Schemes and Tropes*, sig. D5v.
[40] *Ibid.*, sig. A5r.   [41] *Ibid.*, sig. A6r.
[42] In speaking of the places of logic and rhetoric, Sherry says in part: "These be commen to the Oratours with the Logicians, albeit Aristotle hathe seperatelye written of them in hys Topickes, and in his Rethorickes hathe not touched thē, and they profite much both to iudgement, and to endightynge, but the varietie of authors hath made the handlynge of them sumwhat darke, because amonge them selues they can not wel agre, neyther of the names, neyther of the number, neyther of the order." Sig. F4v. This passage, it seems, contains his only reference to Aristotle's *Rhetoric*.

aduentures sundry and varyous authors: but that also thei shalbe able better to vnderstande and iudge of the goodlye gyftes and ornamentes in mooste famous and eloquente oratoures."[43] The promise indicated in these words was in some measure fulfilled by the publication at London in 1555 of Sherry's *Treatise of the Figures of Grammer and Rhetorike*.[44] This work is dedicated to William Paget, Baron of Beaudesert, whom I mentioned earlier as an advocate of Melanchthon's rhetorical theory when Paget and Leonard Cox were at Cambridge together.[45] Sherry introduced four new features in his revised edition: he made "figure" his key word, and proceeded to discuss figures of grammar, figures of rhetoric called tropes, and figures of rhetoric called schemes; he put the topic of the three kinds of style at the end rather than near the beginning of his treatise; he presented his material in such fashion that a Latin discussion of a given topic preceded an identical English discussion of it, the work as a whole being thus an almost invariable alternation of Latin and English passages; and finally he abandoned as his one big illustration the theme from Erasmus on the subject of the education of children, and substituted for it an English version of Cicero's oration for Marcus Marcellus. There are other differences between his first and his second edition, but none that places the basic philosophy of the former in a new light.

At one point in the first edition of his *Treatise*, Sherry remarks that the man who goes into a goodly garden garnished with herbs and flowers, and only beholds them, without knowing what they are called, does not have the pleasure of him who also knows the names and properties of everything he sees.[46] This image may have suggested something to Henry Peacham. At any rate, Peacham published at London in 1577 *The Garden of Eloquence Conteyning the Figures of Grammer and Rhetorick*;[47] and this work, more extensive

---

[43] *Ibid.*, sig. A7v-A8r.

[44] The title page reads: "A Treatise of the Figures of Grammer and Rhetorike, profitable for al that be studious of Eloquence, and in especiall for suche as in Grammer scholes doe reade moste eloquente Poetes and Oratours: Whereunto is ioygned the oration which Cicero made to Cesar, geuing thankes vnto him for pardonyng, and restoring again of that noble mā Marcus Marcellus, sette foorth by Richarde Sherrye Londonar. Londini in aedibus Ricardi Totteli. Cum priuilegio ad imprimendum solum." No date is given on the title page. The colophon reads: "Imprinted at London in Fletestrete within Temple barre, at the sygne of the hand and starre by Richarde Tottill. the .1111. daye of Maye, the yeare of oure Lorde. M D L V. Cum priuilegio ad imprimendum solum."

[45] See above, p. 95.

[46] Sig. A8r-A8v.

[47] The title page reads: "The Garden of Eloquence Conteyning the Figures of Gram-

than Sherry's two earlier efforts in the same field, brings to full maturity the English stylistic theory of rhetoric.

"Figure" is the key term in Peacham's *Garden*, as it was in Sherry's second edition. Peacham begins his work with the following definitions:

The names of Figures.

Figures of the Grecians, are called *Tropes* and *Schemates*, and of the Latines, Fygures Exornations, Lightes, Colours, and Ornaments of spéech. *Cicero* who supposed them to be named of the Grecians *Schemates*, as a iesture and countenaunce of spéech, called them *Concinnitie*, that is propernesse, aptnesse, featnesse, also conformations, formes, and fashions, comprising all ornamentes of spéech vnder one name.

A Figure what it is.

A Figure is a fashion of words, Oration, or sentence, made new by Arte, tourning from the common manner and custome of wryting or speaking.[48]

With the definition of figure clearly set forth in these terms, Peacham proceeds to divide his subject into its parts and elements. A given figure, he says, is either a trope or a "schemate." A trope is either of a word or of a sentence, there being nine of the former and ten of the latter. A given "schemate," meanwhile, is either grammatical or rhetorical. Grammatical "schemates" number fifty-six in all, fourteen of them being orthographical, and forty-two, syntactical. Rhetorical "schemates," the most numerous class, embrace twenty-four that pertain to words, twenty-six that pertain to sentences, and sixty-six that pertain to amplification.[49] Thus his work as a whole deals with one hundred and ninety-one terms, each of which is defined, then divided where necessary into species, and finally illustrated by the Bible, by classical literature, and by homemade examples.

It may seem strange that human energy should be applied so diligently to this interminable enumeration of stylistic devices, when

---

mer and Rhetorick, from whence maye bee gathered all manner of Flowers, Coulors, Ornaments Exornations, Formes and Fashions of speech, very profitable for all those that be studious of Eloquence, and that reade most Eloquent Poets and Orators, and also helpeth much for the better vnderstanding of the holy Scriptures. Set foorth in Englishe, by Henry Pecham Minister. Anno. 1577. Imprinted at London, in Fleetestrete, beneath the Conduite, at the Signe of Saint Iohn Euaungelist, by H. Iackson."

[48] *Garden of Eloquence*, sig. B1r.

[49] *Ibid.*, sig. B1r. Peacham's table indicates twenty-five rhetorical schemes of the sentence, but actually he names twenty-six later. His table indicates sixty schemes of amplification, but his later discussion includes sixty-six.

the subject of communication offers more philosophic and more hu-
mane approaches, particularly in the regions where persuasion is considered, and the means of persuasion are studied as matters of logic,
emotion, and morality. But even though we admit that Peacham and
his school appear more concerned with the husks than with the ker-
nels of style, we should nevertheless credit them with some philosophic conception of what they were doing—a conception which im-
parts a measure of interest to their otherwise mechanical routine.
They conceived of wisdom and eloquence as the two forces which
hold society together and maintain civilization. They conceived of
oratory as the union of these two forces and as the organ of leadership. They conceived of wisdom as the force which man never elected
to do without, whereas eloquence was the force which he might under-
rate and disparage in moments of pride and confidence. Thus eloquence had to be cultivated as a special power, and the study of eloquence became the study of the forms of speech, wisdom having
already guaranteed that the substance of speech was present as raw
material. This philosophy was expressed by Peacham in the dedicatory letter of the revised edition of the *Garden*, published at London
in 1593. Speaking there of the power of wisdom and the prudent art
of persuasion, he says that "so mighty is the power of this happie
vnion, (I meane of wisdom & eloquence) that by the one the Orator
forceth, and by the other he allureth, and by both so worketh, that
what he commendeth is beloued, what he dispraiseth is abhorred,
what he perswadeth is obeied, & what he disswadeth is auoided: so
that he is in a maner the emperour of mens minds & affections, and
next to the omnipotent God in the power of perswasion, by grace, &
diuine assistance." Peacham adds:

> The principal instrumēts of mans help in this wonderfull effect, are
> those figures and formes of speech cōnteined in this booke, which are
> the frutefull branches of eloquution, and the mightie streames of elo-
> quence: whose vtilitie, power, and vertue, I cannot sufficiently com-
> mēd, but speaking by similitude, I say they are as stars to giue light,
> as cordials to comfort, as harmony to delight, as pitiful spectacles to
> moue sorrowfull passions, and as orient colours to beautifie reason.[50]

Implicit in this philosophy is the assumption that the orator is an
emperor under the rule of God, and that his subjects are not so much
the common people as the aristocrat and temporal king, whose au-

[50] *The Garden of Eloqvence* (London, 1593), sig. AB3v-AB4r. This work has recently been made available in a facsimile reproduction with an Introduction by William
G. Crane (Gainesville, Florida: Scholars' Facsimiles & Reprints, 1954).

thority is unquestioned, and whose hearts are won only by the forms of speech "differing from the vulgar maner and custome of writing or speaking."[51]

The reader of the first edition of the *Garden of Eloquence* is often aware that Peacham's analysis of the figures of grammar and rhetoric depends upon the first edition of Sherry's *Treatise*. Sometimes the dependence is so direct that a passage in Peacham is virtually a copy of the similar passage in Sherry. For example, Peacham's long illustration of the second kind of *expolitio* is closely similar to Sherry's illustration of "expolicion," despite the fact that Sherry mentions Erasmus as his source, whereas Peacham mentions Cornificius as his.[52] Incidentally, "expolitio" is the figure in which a speaker says the same thing in many diverse ways, as though many things were being said. In addition to this borrowing, there are in the early edition of the *Garden* other passages which bear a close resemblance to corresponding passages in Sherry's first edition, and must therefore have been transferred deliberately from one to the other.[53]

It is also apparent that Peacham's first edition borrows at least once from the second edition of Sherry. The passage in which this borrowing occurs is meant to illustrate the rhetorical device of *partitio*, and I shall quote what Peacham and then Sherry have to say on this point, not only to show the resemblance between them, but also to indicate their thinking upon one of the largest and most im-

---

[51] *Ibid.*, p. 1. Notice that these words differ somewhat from those used by Peacham in 1577 and quoted above, p. 133. The main difference is that "vulgar" has replaced "common."

[52] Compare the *Treatise* (1550), sig. F7r-F8v, with the *Garden* (1577), sig. Q1r-Q2r.

[53] The following are examples:

Sherry: "Also I smell where aboute you go, for I perceyue." (sig. C4v)

Peacham: ". . . also, I smell whereabout you goe, for, perceaue whereabout you goe . . ." (sig. B3v)

Sherry: "By that goeth before, the thynge that foloweth, as: He set hys spurres to hys horse, for he rode a pace, or fled faste awaye." (sig. C6r)

Peacham: "Thinges following, by thinges going before, as to say, he put to his Spurres, meaning hée roade apace. . ." (sig. C3v)

Sherry: "By that ẏ foloweth, the thinge wente before, as: I got it wyth the swete of my face, for w̄ my labour." (sig. C6r)

Peacham: "Contrariwyse, thinges going before, by thinges following, as *Genesis*. 3. In the sweate of thy face, shalte thou eate thy breade, for, with labour shalt thou eate thy bread, which goeth before sweate. . ." (sig. C3v)

Sherry: "Sarcasmus. *Amara irrisio*, is a bitter sporting a mocke of our enemye, or a maner of iestyng or scoffinge bytynglye, a nyppyng tawnte, as: The Jewes sayde to Christ, he saued other, but he could not saue hym selfe." (sig. C7v)

Peacham: "Sarcasmus, is a bitter kinde of mocke, or dispytefull frumpe, vsed of an enemy, such as the Jewes vsed to Christ hāging on ẏ Crosse, now sayd they, let him come downe from the Crosse and saue himselfe, that saued others: Also, he saued others, himselfe he cannot saue." (sig. D3v)

portant of the rhetorical figures—those figures which, as Peacham defines them, "doe take a way the wearinesse of our common and dayly speach, and doe fashion a pleasant, sharpe, euident and gallant kinde of speaking, giuing vnto matters great strength, perspecuitie and grace. . . ."[54] Here then is Peacham on *partitio*:

> *Partitio*, when the whole is deuyded into partes, and then it is called Partitien, as if you might say, he is well séene in all Sciences, this generall saying you may declare by partes, thus. He perfitely knoweth all the painefull rules of Grammer, the pleasaunt Flowers of Rhetoricke, the subtilties of Logitians, the secretes of naturall Philosophy, the difficultie of Wisedome supernaturall, the pleasaunt Fables of Poets, the Mathematicall demonstrations, the motions of Starres, the cunning reasons of numbers, the description of the worlde, the measuring of the earth, the situations, names, distaunces of Countries, Cities, Mountaynes, Riuers, Fountaynes, and Wildernesses, the properties of Soyles, the déepe misteries of Diuinitie, the difference of harmonies, the consent of tunes, histories, olde and newe, antiquities, nouelties, Gréeke, Latine and Hebrew. Finally, whatsoeuer good learning hath bene founde and taught of good Authors, all that hath this man perceyued, knowne and remembred.[55]

In his first edition Sherry uses this same general thesis to illustrate *partitio*;[56] but it is from the wording of his second edition that Peacham borrows, as we can see at once if we compare the quotation just given with the following words from Sherry's revised treatise:

> Partition is, when that that might be spoken generally, is more largely declared by partes. As if we would say: he is perfectly seen in al sciences. Thys sentence thou mayest declare by partes in this wise. He knoweth merueylously well the fables of Poetes, the flowers of Rhetorique, the painefull rules of Grammer, the subtilties of Logitians, the secretes of natural philosophy, the hardnes of wisedom supernatural, the misteries of diuinitie, the mathematicall demonstrations, the mocions of starres, the reasons of nūbers, the measuring of ý earth, the situations, names, and spaces of Cities, Mountaynes, Floudes, and Fountaynes, the dyfference, and harmonies of Tunes, histories olde, and newe: antiquities, nouelties, Greke and Latine: finally whatsoeuer good learnyng hath been founde and taught of good authours, all that wholy hath this one man perfitlye perceyued, knowen, and remembred.[57]

---

[54] *Garden of Eloquence* (1577), sig. H4v.
[55] *Ibid.*, sig. R3v.   [56] *Treatise of Schemes & Tropes*, sig. D7v-D8r.
[57] *Treatise of the Figures of Grammer and Rhetorike*, fol. xli.

In addition to Sherry, Peacham relies very heavily upon Susenbrotus's *Epitome Troporum ac Schematum,* and upon such other authorities as Erasmus's *De Duplici Copia Verborum ac Rerum,* Quintilian's *Institutio Oratoria,* and the anonymous *Rhetorica ad Herennium,* which Peacham attributes to Cornificius.[58] Peacham draws also from Cicero and probably from the other sources mentioned by Sherry, all of whom would be likely to influence any traditional stylistic rhetoric of the second half of the sixteenth century. There is even some reason to believe that the second edition of Peacham's *Garden* was influenced indirectly by the reformed rhetoric of Ramus. As we shall see in the next chapter, Ramus taught that all schemes and tropes were strictly the property of rhetoric, and should never be counted as belonging in part to grammar. In fact, the assigning of the tropes and schemes to rhetoric rather than to grammar was a point of real emphasis in Ramus's concept of the liberal arts. In his first edition of 1577, Peacham pays no attention to this point of emphasis, his schemes being distributed between grammar and rhetoric, as I indicated above. But by 1593, when Peacham published his revised edition of the *Garden,* England had been so far converted to Ramistic rhetoric that even a traditionalist like Peacham was to some extent affected. Thus it is not surprising to find that this second edition abandons the distinction between grammatical and rhetorical schemes, and omits from consideration many of the schemes which the first edition had classed as grammatical.

The *Garden* is the last English treatise on the tropes and the figures to appear in print before 1584, when the earliest English version of Ramistic rhetoric was published. Thus my survey of English stylistic rhetoric as a separate pattern of traditional theory ends with Peacham. Stylistic rhetoric continued to be influential in England for the following century, but not in the exact form it had had in the works we have been considering. What form it took after the days of Sherry and Peacham has been suggested already, and will be discussed more at length when Ramistic rhetoric has been analyzed. Meanwhile, a few words need to be said on the subject of formulary rhetoric, the third and last of the traditional patterns of rhetorical theory in England.

[58] For references by Peacham to these two latter works, see the *Garden of Eloquence* (1577), sigs. A2v, A3r, E1v, Q1r, Q2r. Peacham's debt to Susenbrotus, Sherry, Erasmus, and other sources is discussed in full detail by William G. Crane in the Introduction to his recent facsimile reprint of the *Garden.*

IV. Models for Imitation

FORMULARY rhetoric is made up of compositions drawn to illustrate rhetorical principles and presented as models for students to imitate in the process of developing themselves for the tasks of communication.

Rhetorical education has always rested upon the assumption that practice in communication is necessary for the development of proficiency, and that the best possible practice consists in performing exercises like those required in the actual processes of civilized life. Sometimes these exercises are performed by students in conscious imitation of models, and sometimes in conscious attempts to produce an original piece of work according to previously studied rules. Traditional English rhetoric of the Ciceronian and stylistic pattern is designed to provide the necessary rules for the latter of these two methods, whereas formulary rhetoric has the other of these methods in mind, and aims to provide models for imitation.

There is, of course, an element of formulary rhetoric in each of the two streams of theory already discussed. Thomas Wilson's *Rhetorique*, as I mentioned earlier,[1] contains model discourses to illustrate a forensic speech, and the various kinds of eulogies, as well as the letter of advice and of consolation. Sherry also presented model discourses in company with each edition of his pioneering English version of stylistic rhetoric, the first edition containing a theme by Erasmus on the education of children, and the second, a speech by Cicero to Caesar.[2] But full-blown illustrations like these are not by any means the only models to occur in works of the Ciceronian and the stylistic pattern. In particular, each scheme and trope offered an opportunity for copious illustration from the Bible and classical literature, with the result that all treatises on figurative language contain hundreds of model ornaments for imitation.

As an entity by itself rather than as an ingredient of rhetorical theory, formulary rhetoric began its vernacular development in England in the second quarter of the sixteenth century. Its origin would appear to be in several popular collections of materials drawn from the ancient classics. One of the earliest of these collections was Nicholas Udall's *Flovres for Latine Spekynge Selected and gathered oute of Terence, and the same translated in to Englysshe*, published at London in 1533. Udall's work not only included Latin passages from

---

[1] See above, pp. 105-107.
[2] See above, pp. 125, note 25, 132, note 44.

Terence and an English translation of them, but also notes on Terence's vocabulary and grammar. Richard Taverner's *The garden of wysdom* and *The secōde booke of the Garden of wysedome*, which were separately published at London in 1539, are collections of witty sayings of ancient Greek and Latin princes, philosophers, and other renowned personages, and would of course serve admirably as models for pithy and sententious discourse.[3] The same purpose would also be served by Taverner's *Proverbes or adagies with newe addicions gathered out of the Chiliades of Erasmus*, likewise published at London in 1539. This work is organized so as to give a Latin proverb, an English translation of it, and a full explanation of it in English, these latter two units being translations from Erasmus's Latin. Another work of the same general pattern and purpose is the *Flores aliquot sententiarum ex variis collecti scriptoribus*, also called *The flowres of sencies gathered out of sundry wryters by Erasmus in Latine and Englished by Rychard Taverner*, published at London in 1540.[4] And of course Nicholas Udall's translation of Erasmus's *Apophthegmes* (London, 1542) should be mentioned not only as a work drawn from the source that gave Taverner his *Garden*, but also as one more indication of the popularity of Erasmus in England in the fifteen-thirties and forties.

These collections cannot be claimed as true formulary rhetorics. They are addressed primarily to young students, and are intended not only to supply ideas and models for school exercises but also to provide wise saws and ancient instances for developing youthful character and intellect. They do not aim, however, to present models to illustrate systematically the various types of discourse, and thus they can hardly be said to introduce students to all or most of the situations in which communications pass back and forth in the course of human living. The true formulary rhetoric differs from these collections in having its selections cover some or most of the occasions for discourse, and in providing that these selections will teach good rhetorical form no less than sound concepts.

[3] Charles Read Baskervill, "Taverner's *Garden of Wisdom* and the *Apophthegmata* of Erasmus," *Studies in Philology*, XXIX (April 1932), 153-159, has shown that most of the material in Taverner's *Garden*, and about two-thirds of the material in *The second booke of the Garden*, are translated from the *Apophthegmata* of Erasmus. Baskervill also clarifies the bibliographical history of these two works.

[4] Baskervill, *op. cit.*, pp. 151-152, indicates that this work was originally published in 1540, and is a translation by Taverner of a small section of the *Opuscula aliquot* of Erasmus, not of the latter's *Apophthegmata*. I have seen only the 1550 edition in photostat at the Huntington Library.

The first English work to conform fully to these specifications is Richard Rainolde's *A booke called the Foundacion of Rhetorike*, published at London in 1563. This work, as Professor Johnson has shown in the essay that accompanies his facsimile reprint of Rainolde's original text, is mainly an English adaptation of Reinhard Lorich's Latin version of Aphthonius's *Progymnasmata*.[5] Aphthonius is one of the three great names in the field of ancient formulary rhetoric, the others being Theon and Hermogenes. Not much is known of them, but each is remembered for his collection of model discourses for use in rhetorical instruction, and each called his collection the *Progymnasmata*, that is, *Preparatory Exercises*. Theon and Hermogenes lived in the second century of our era, and Aphthonius in the late fourth century.[6] Their model discourses are grouped under such terms as *narration, proof, refutation,* and *commonplace,* and are obviously meant to constitute preparation for the later study of the full rhetorical discipline in its theoretical phases.

Rainolde's opening address "To the Reader" lends point to the *Rhetorike* in four ways. First of all, it associates the work with the famous man Aphthonius, who "wrote in Greke of soche declamacions, to enstructe the studentes thereof, with all facilitie to grounde in them, a moste plentious and riche vein of eloquence." Secondly, it states Rainolde's belief in preparatory exercises—"No man is able to inuente a more profitable waie and order, to instructe any one in the exquisite and absolute perfeccion, of wisedome and eloquence, then *Aphthonius, Quintilianus* and *Hermogenes.*" Thirdly, it recalls that such exercises had helped the great Tully, "whose Eloquence and vertue all tymes extolled, and the ofspryng of all ages worthilie aduaunceth." Fourthly, it indicates that Rainolde is writing with an eye to England's present needs—"because as yet the verie grounde of Rhetorike, is not heretofore intreated of, as concernyng these exercises, though in fewe yeres past, a learned woorke of Rhetorike is compiled and made in the Englishe toungue, of one, who floweth in all excellencie of arte, who in iudgement is profounde, in wisedome and eloquence moste famous." This last statement, with its handsome tribute to the worth of Thomas Wilson's *Rhetorique,* gives us a flash of insight into the movement in Elizabethan England to cre-

---

[5] *The Foundacion of Rhetorike by Richard Rainolde,* ed. Francis R. Johnson (New York: Scholars' Facsimiles & Reprints, 1945), pp. xiv-xvii.

[6] For sketches of these three rhetoricians, see William Smith, *A Dictionary of Greek and Roman Biography and Mythology,* s.v. Aphthonius of Antioch, Hermogenes 6, Theon, literary 5.

ate a vernacular learning, and to adapt ancient rhetorical methods to England's expanding civilization.

The text of Rainolde's *Rhetorike* opens with explanatory comment on man's logical and rhetorical faculties, and on logic and rhetoric as the sciences designed to instruct and adorn them. As groundwork for his distinction between these two sciences, Rainolde depends upon a familiar analogy:

> *Zeno* the Philosopher comparing *Rhetorike* and *Logike*, doeth as-similate and liken them to the hand of man. *Logike* is like saith he to the fiste, for euen as the fiste closeth and shutteth into one, the iointes and partes of the hande, & with mightie force and strength, wrappeth and closeth in thynges apprehended: So *Logike* for the deepe and profounde knowlege, that is reposed and buried in it, in soche sort of municion and strength fortified, in few wordes taketh soche force and might by argumente, that excepte like equalitée in like art and knowledge doe mate it, in vain the disputacion shalbe, and the repulse of thaduersarie readie. *Rhetorike* is like to the hand set at large, wherein euery part and ioint is manifeste, and euery vaine as braunches of trées sette at scope and libertée. So of like sorte, *Rhet-orike* in moste ample and large maner, dilateth and setteth out small thynges or woordes, in soche sorte, with soche aboundaunce and plentuousnes, bothe of woordes and wittie inuencion, with soche good-lie disposicion, in soche a infinite sorte, with soche pleasauntnes of Oracion, that the moste stonie and hard hartes, can not but bee in-censed, inflamed, and moued thereto.[7]

Rainolde does not attempt to make the verbal power of rhetoric appear more desirable than the lean wisdom of logic. It is rather the union of both in some few men that makes for true benefit in the commonwealth; and he enumerates the great orators of Greece and Rome as examples of this union. Demosthenes in particular commands his attention, and he mentions how Philip of Macedon had sought to trap Athens into surrendering her orators to him in the interest of tranquility, and how Demosthenes had defeated Philip's design by delivering an oration based upon the fable of the shepherds who surrendered their dogs to the wolves in a pact of peace, and of the wolves who immediately afterwards devoured the flocks of the shepherds. This fable recalls several others to Rainolde, some of which have an English setting. His talk of fables leads him then to say that orations are made not only upon them, but also upon such

[7] Fol. 1r-1v.

other exercises as the narration, the *chria*, the sentence, the confutation, the confirmation, the commonplace, the praising, the dispraising, the comparison, the *ethopeia*, the description, the thesis, and the advocacy or the opposing of a law. He adds:

> Of euery one of these, a goodlie Oraciō maie be made these exercises are called of the Grekes *Progimnasmata*, of the Latines, profitable introduccions, or fore exercises, to attain greater arte and knowlege in *Rhetorike*, and bicause, for the easie capacitée and facilitée of the learner, to attain greater knowledge in *Rhetorike*, thei are right profitable and necessarie: Therefore I title this booke, to bee the foundaciō of *Rhetorike*, the exercises being *Progimnasmata*.[8]

The nineteen compositions which follow this statement are model speeches upon each of the exercises previously enumerated by Rainolde. He gives two speeches to illustrate the fable; five to illustrate narration; and one to illustrate each of the other twelve exercises. Some of the model speeches run to nine or ten pages; others, to six or eight; the shortest, to a half-page. Each model is preceded by comments and suggestions on the composition of that particular form. Also, most models are divided into clearly marked sections or parts. For example, the speech to illustrate confutation, which is on the subject, "It is not like to be true, that is said of the battaill of Troie," is divided into six parts. The first censures all poets as liars; the second states Homer's theory of the cause of the Trojan war; the third reduces that theory to a matter of doubt; the fourth, to an incredibility; the fifth, to an impossibility and an unlikelihood; and the sixth, to an unseemly and unprofitable notion.[9]

Rainolde's *Rhetorike* appears not to have been published between the date of its first edition and the date of Professor Johnson's facsimile reprint in 1945. There are two reasons for Rainolde's lack of a public during the crucial early years of that interval of time. First, the kind of rhetoric that he represented did not have much of a chance to become popular in the schools of England at the time when it was first introduced; for Ramism was then about to have its biggest vogue, and was on the verge of crowding out traditional rhetoric, which Rainolde accepted as his premise. Secondly, the exercises of Aphthonius in the Latin version of Reinhard Lorich were often published in England after 1572, and that Latin version probably satisfied what demand there was for formulary rhetoric on the elementary

[8] Fol. 4r-4v.   [9] Foll. xxv r-xxviii v.

levels of instruction, where Rainolde's English adaptation of Lorich would probably not have been popular with schoolmasters.[10]

The last formulary rhetoric to receive attention before we turn to Ramus was written by William Fullwood, a member not of the profession of scholars and teachers, but of the company of merchant tailors of London. Fullwood has figured before in this history. He was the W. F. who brought out in 1563 an edition of Ralph Lever's *The Philosopher's Game*, thus incurring the displeasure of that author, as Lever himself testified later in his *Witcraft*.[11] A year before his edition of *The Philosopher's Game*, Fullwood published at London *The Castel of Memorie*, his own translation of the medical treatise *De Memoria* by Guglielmo Grataroli, which contains as its seventh chapter a discussion of the memory system outlined in the *Rhetorica ad Herennium*.[12] Fullwood's formulary rhetoric, first published at London in 1568, is called *The Enimie of Idlenesse*, and is dedicated "To the right worshipfull the Maister, Wardens, and Company of the Marchant Tayllors of London."[13] It contains a collection of precepts on letter writing, and a collection of sample letters on all sorts of topics and occasions, the whole being intended, not for the educated class, but for the ambitious tradesman and merchant. This intention, indeed, is expressed at one point in Fullwood's dedicatory epistle, which is in verse:

> For know you sure, I meane not I the cunning clerks to teach:
> But rather to the vnlearned sort a few precepts to preach.[14]

[10] For an account of editions of Lorich in England, see Johnson's reprint of Rainolde, pp. xiii-xiv. Donald Lemen Clark, "The Rise and Fall of Progymnasmata in Sixteenth and Seventeenth Century Grammar Schools," *Speech Monographs*, XIX (1952), 259-263, should also be consulted about editions of Lorich in England and Europe.

[11] See above, p. 59.

[12] Fullwood's *Castel of Memorie* had a second edition in 1563, and a third in 1573. A copy of the 1573 edition is in the Huntington Library. Its seventh chapter contains 7 leaves (14 pages) and extends from sig. F5v to sig. G4v. Its title reads: "The seuenth Chapter treateth in fewe wordes of locall or artificiall Memorie." The previous chapters deal with such topics as the location of the memory, what impairs and damages it, what assists it, what medicines are available for curing or strengthening it, and what philosophical principles govern it.

[13] The title page reads: "The Enimie of Idlenesse: Teaching the maner and stile how to endite, compose and write all sorts of Epistles and Letters: as well by answer, as otherwise. Deuided iuto foure Bokes, no lesse plesaunt than profitable. Set forth in English by William Fulwood Marchant, &c. The Contentes hereof appere in the Table at the latter ende of the Booke.
> An Enimie to Idlenesse,
> A frend to Exercise:
> By practise of the prudent pen,
> Loe here before thine eyes.
Imprinted at London by Henry Bynneman, for Leonard Maylord. Anno 1568."

[14] *Enimie of Idlenesse* (London, 1568), sig. A3v.

Later, in verses purporting to express his book's verdict upon itself, Fullwood indicates that its true utility will be declared by merchants, lawyers, and people of all degrees, rich and poor, but chiefly and above all by lovers.

The first of the four books into which the *Enimie of Idlenesse* is divided sets forth certain principles of letter writing, and provides many examples of those principles. Fullwood offers advice on the addressing of letters to one's superiors, one's equals, and one's inferiors; he divides letters into those "of Doctrine, of Myrth, or of Grauitie."[15] An illustration of the letter of mirth contains a traveler's report that the Turks delight much in song, and provide themselves with an ample supply of it by having singers go to cold climates where their songs are frozen and sent back to be reproduced by being thawed out at later celebrations.[16] In a curious analogy between letter writing and logical doctrine, Fullwood indicates that a letter is properly divided into three parts, the cause, the intent, and the consequence, even as the logical argument "consisteth of the *Maior*, the *Minor*, and Conclusion. . ."[17] He thus explains the analogy:

> The cause is in place of the *Maior*, which moueth or constrayneth vs to write to an other, willing to signifie vnto him our mynde: The intent is in steade of the *Minor*, whereby we gyue him to vnderstande what our mynde is by Epistle or letter. The consequent or conclusion is of it selfe sufficiently knowne.[18]

Following this are examples of the way in which these three parts are revealed in actual letters. Four parts are suggested for letters of recommendation, and three parts again for "expositiue letters, certifying the vvitnesse or notyce of a thing."[19] Book I closes with the discussion and illustration of a great many other types of letters, such as those of congratulation, rejoicing, exhortation, invective, and the like.

Book II is a collection of letters by famous men to each other. Politian is represented most often, sixteen of his letters being printed; but Fullwood also includes letters by various other celebrities, among them Pico della Mirandola, Ficino, and Pope Innocent VIII.

Book III is also composed entirely of specimen letters, but it contains no historical correspondence, being devoted instead to letters showing how to reply to a son, a father, a husband, a wife, a brother, a sister, a daughter, a mother, a social equal, a business associate, and friend.

---

[15] *Ibid.*, fol. 8r.   [16] *Ibid.*, fol. 9r-9v.   [17] *Ibid.*, fol. 10r.
[18] *Ibid.*, fol. 10v.   [19] *Ibid.*, fol. 46v.

In Book IV, the emphasis shifts to love letters "as well in Verse as in Prose."[20] Here lovers request favors of their ladies, and the ladies make answer. One lover ingeniously presses his suit under the guise of telling the story of Pygmalion, his letter being headed as follows:

> A secrete Louer writes his will
> By story of *Pigmalions* ill.[21]

Following this are other love letters in verse; but this entire book, despite the obvious appeal of its subject matter, contains only 28 pages, whereas Book III contains 53, Book II, 29, and Book I, 179.

In the three closing decades of the sixteenth century there were other formulary rhetorics published in English at English presses for the benefit of secretaries, lawyers, preachers, and private citizens. These rhetorics, however, belong chronologically to the period that followed the invasion of Ramistic doctrine into English learning, and thus I shall not discuss them at this present time. They will receive brief notice after my next chapter, where the Ramistic invasion is chronicled.

[20] *Ibid.*, fol. 131v.   [21] *Ibid.*, fol. 139v.

CHAPTER 4

The English Ramists

I. Ramus's Reform of Dialectic and Rhetoric

PIERRE DE LA RAMÉE, also known as Peter Ramus, was born in the Catholic faith in the year 1515 at the little village of Cuth in Vermandois in the north of France; and he died at Paris on August 26, 1572, as a Protestant victim of what came to be called the massacre of St. Bartholomew's Day.[1] His life was as stormy as the times in which he lived. At the age of 21, after a struggle for an education at Paris against the discouragements of poverty and lack of family assistance, he was awarded his degree of master of arts as a result of his defense of the bold thesis that all things affirmed on the authority of Aristotle are overelaborate, contrived, artificial.[2] Although this was more of an attack upon works

---

[1] For the best biography of Ramus, see Charles Waddington, *Ramus (Pierre de la Ramée) sa vie, ses écrits et ses opinions* (Paris, 1855). This work grew out of Waddington's earlier Latin biography, *De Petri Rami Vita, Scriptis, Philosophia* (Paris, 1848), published under the name of Waddington-Kastus. For a somewhat shorter French account, see Charles Desmaze, *P. Ramus Professeur au Collège de France sa vie, ses écrits, sa mort 1515-1572* (Paris, 1864). See also the brief life by Gustave Rigollot in *Nouvelle Biographie Générale*, s.v. Ramus, Pierre.

The best English life is by Frank Pierrepont Graves, *Peter Ramus and the Educational Reformation of the Sixteenth Century* (New York, 1912). For recent discussions of Ramus's influence, see Hardin Craig, *The Enchanted Glass* (New York, 1936), pp. 142-159; Crane, *Wit and Rhetoric in the Renaissance*, pp. 51, 55-57; Perry Miller, *The New England Mind* (New York, 1939), pp. 111-180, 312-330, 493-501; Baldwin, *William Shakspere's Small Latine & Lesse Greeke*, II, 4-68; Harold S. Wilson and Clarence A. Forbes, *Gabriel Harvey's "Ciceronianus,"* University of Nebraska Studies: Studies in the Humanities No. 4 (Lincoln, 1945), pp. 1-34, 107-139; Rosemond Tuve, *Elizabethan and Metaphysical Imagery* (Chicago, 1947), pp. 331-353; Sister Miriam Joseph, *Shakespeare's Use of the Arts of Language*, pp. 3-40; Donald Lemen Clark, *John Milton at St. Paul's School* (New York, 1948), pp. 76-77, 160-161, 179.

For special studies of Ramus, see the following: Leon Howard, " 'The Invention' of Milton's 'Great Argument': A Study of the Logic of 'God's Ways to Men,' " *The Huntington Library Quarterly*, IX (February 1946), 149-173; Norman E. Nelson, *Peter Ramus and the Confusion of Logic, Rhetoric, and Poetry*, The University of Michigan Contributions in Modern Philology, No. 2 (Ann Arbor, 1947); P. A. Duhamel, "The Logic and Rhetoric of Peter Ramus," *Modern Philology*, XLVI (February 1949), 163-171; J. Milton French, "Milton, Ramus, and Edward Phillips," *Modern Philology*, XLVII (November 1949), 82-87; Wilbur S. Howell, "Ramus and English Rhetoric: 1574-1681," *The Quarterly Journal of Speech*, XXXVII (1951), 299-310; Walter J. Ong, S.J., "Hobbes and Talon's Ramist Rhetoric in English," *Transactions of the Cambridge Bibliographical Society*, I (1949-1953), 260-269.

[2] Waddington, *Ramus*, pp. 28-29. For a good discussion of the proper English translation of Ramus's thesis, see P. Albert Duhamel, "Milton's Alleged Ramism," *PMLA*, LXVII (1952), 1036.

professing to be Aristotelian than upon those actually written by Aristotle, and although it tended to discredit Aristotle's late medieval disciples more than the master himself, it was nevertheless a radical doctrine, and it made Ramus seem impudent if not almost sacrilegious. The rest of his life was a struggle against the educational procedures of his time and against the hostility that the unorthodox always bring upon themselves. He sought reform throughout the field of the liberal arts, and he laid out a new program for grammar and rhetoric as well as for logic; but his own efforts were mainly bent upon the reform of the latter subject, and thus his work is perhaps best understood as a great protest against the scholasticism that I explained above in Chapter 2. His two earliest writings on logic were angrily criticized and even suppressed by royal edict, a part of the verdict against him being that he was to teach philosophy no more. Somewhat later, the whole of the verdict against him was reversed, thanks to his powerful friend, the cardinal of Lorraine, but this success made him more contentious than ever. Then came his conversion to Protestantism, his exile from Paris, his return, a second exile, a second return, and a series of troubles and misadventures that finally ended when he was killed by the mob as the St. Bartholomew massacre was in its third day.

As Ramus looked at the scholastic logic, the traditional rhetoric, and the conventional grammar of his day, he was troubled by what seemed to him to be redundancy and indecisiveness in the theories of these basic liberal arts. It seemed to him to be necessary for instruction in communication that students be trained to discover subject matter through a study of all the general wisdom behind a given specific issue or case. But was it strictly required that both logic and rhetoric offer this training, as they did when each of them sought to teach the doctrine of invention? Again, it seemed to him necessary that students be taught the principles of arrangement of subject matter through some sort of study of the degrees of generality of various statements and perhaps even through some study of the psychological habits of people who receive communications. But was it strictly required that both logic and rhetoric offer this training, as they did when each made the doctrine of arrangement into a major topic? And was it strictly required that rhetoric, having contracted to teach organization of material, should place the theory of the six parts of an oration under the heading of invention, with the result that the very crux of the problem of arrangement was disposed of before the topic of arrangement came up for discussion? Still again, it seemed to him to be necessary that students master the schemes and the tropes, since these departures from everyday speech were needed to give discourse the persuasive aura of aristocracy in an aristocratic society. But was it strictly required that the schemes and the tropes be handled both as a part of grammar and as a part of rhetoric in the existing curriculum?

Ramus's reform of the liberal arts was in fact a system of direct answers to these questions. He ordained that logic should offer training in invention and arrangement, with no help whatever from rhetoric. He ordained that the topic of arrangement should take care of all speculations regarding the method of discourse, with no help whatever from invention. He ordained that rhetoric should offer training in style and delivery, and that style should be limited to the tropes and the schemes, with no help whatever from grammar, which was to be assigned only subject matter derived from considerations of etymology and syntax. The subject of memory, which we have seen to be a recognized part of traditional rhetoric since the youth of Cicero, was detached by Ramus from rhetoric, and was not made a special topic elsewhere in his scheme for the liberal arts, except so far as logic helped memory indirectly by providing the theoretical basis for strict organization of discourse.

The closest associate of Ramus in his program of reform was Omer Talon, also known as Audomarus Talaeus, whose special task it was to write the reformed rhetoric, as Ramus was to write the logic. In the preface to his first work on rhetoric, the *Institutiones Oratoriae*, published at Paris in 1544, Talaeus says that Ramus's purpose in reforming the arts had already been proclaimed by his *Dialecticae Institutiones* and his *Aristotelicae Animadversiones*, his two earliest works on logic. And Talaeus adds that his own purpose is now proclaimed in this present work of his.[3] An even better and more specific declaration of the way in which Ramus and Talaeus had agreed to collaborate in revising logic and rhetoric is found in Talaeus's preface to his revised and more polished rhetoric, where he speaks as follows:

Peter Ramus cleaned up the theory of invention, arrangement, and memory, and returned these subjects to logic, where they properly

[3] *Petri Rami Professoris Regii, & Audomari Talaei Collectaneae Praefationes, Epistolae, Orationes* (Marburg, 1599), pp. 14-15. This preface is dated at Paris in the year 1544.

belong. Then, assisted indeed by his lectures and opinions, I recalled rhetoric to style and delivery (since these are the only parts proper to it); and I explained it by genus and species, (which method was previously allowed to me); and I illustrated it with examples drawn both from oratory and poetry. Thus these present precepts are almost wholly in words drawn from those authors; but as this first and rude outline has unfolded, the precepts have been tested by the judgment of both of us, and disposed in order, and ornamented and treated by kind.[4]

The notion that dialectic should consist of the procedures of invention and arrangement goes back to Aristotle's *Topics*, as I mentioned earlier, and was a recurrent feature of scholastic logic.[5] The great fifteenth-century advocate of this notion, Rudolph Agricola, was the one who led Ramus to base his own logic upon it. Agricola died many years before Ramus was born, but Johannes Sturm, the disciple of Agricola, lectured at the University of Paris when Ramus was a student there, and those lectures, as Ramus himself testifies, excited an incredible fervor for the study of logic, and gave Ramus his first real awareness of its applications.[6]

Ramus's reform of the liberal arts, however, involved more than Agricola's theory that logic should consist of the topics of invention and arrangement. After all, Thomas Wilson adhered to Agricola's bipartite division of logic without feeling it therefore necessary to exclude invention and arrangement from rhetoric and to limit rhetoric only to style and delivery. What Ramus did was to proceed beyond Agricola by fortifying himself with three general laws out of Aristotle's *Posterior Analytics*, and these laws explain his reforms better than anything else. Incidentally, the nature of these laws as Aristotle and Vincent of Beauvais conceived of them has already been indicated in my earlier chapter on scholastic logic.[7] Ramus was particularly impressed by these laws as the basic criteria for determining the subject matter and the organization of all science.[8] The importance he attached to them indicates that he was the sort of re-

---

[4] *Ibid.*, pp. 15-16. Translation mine. For Ramus's own statement of the way in which he returned the topic of memory to logic, see *P. Rami Scholarum Dialecticarum, seu Animadversionum in Organum Aristotelis, libri xx*, Recens emendati per Joan Piscatorem Argentinensem (Frankfort, 1581), p. 593.

[5] See above, pp. 15-16.

[6] *Collectaneae Praefationes, Epistolae, Orationes*, p. 67. See also Waddington, *Ramus*, pp. 384-385.

[7] See above, pp. 41-44.

[8] For a list of references by Ramus to these laws at various places in his writings, see Wilbur S. Howell, *Fénelon's Dialogues on Eloquence* (Princeton, 1951), p. 8, note 5.

former who used one part of the old order to revise that order as a whole, rather than the sort who abandoned the old order and adopted a new.

Although his laws came ultimately to be known among English Ramists as the law of truth, of justice, and of wisdom, and among Latin Ramists as *lex veritatis, lex justitiae,* and *lex sapientiae,* they were called "du tout," "par soy," and "vniuersel premierement" by Ramus himself in the famous first French edition of his *Dialectiqve,* after their original Latin forms "de omni," "per se," and "universaliter primum."[9] "Et bref," says Ramus, "toute enonciation marquée de ces trois marques, *Du tout, Par soy, Vniuersel premierement,* est vray principe d'art & science, & premiere cause de sa verité, comme nous dirons plus amplement au neufiesme des Animaduersions." "And in brief every statement marked by these three marks, 'of all,' 'in itself,' 'universal in the first instance,' is a true principle of art and science, and is the first cause of its truth, as we shall show more fully in the ninth book of the *Animadversions.*"[10]

One of the most suggestive of the explanations of the meaning assigned by the Ramists to these laws is found in the French version of the *Dialectiqve* published in 1576, four years after Ramus's death. This version is not to be confused with that just quoted, which Ramus prepared and published by himself at Paris in 1555 and at Avignon in 1556 as part of his program to make the learned arts available in his own native language.[11] The French version published after his death contains the following explanation of the three laws, the terminology being more fully developed than that of the version of 1555:

> Next, an axiom is true or false: true, when it pronounces as the thing itself is; false, when it pronounces to the contrary. The true axiom is necessary or contingent: necessary, when it is always true and cannot possibly be false. And this axiom is named and marked by Aristotle in the first book of his *Demonstration* [that is, the *Posterior Analytics*], the mark being "of all"; the impossible, on the contrary, can never be true. Axioms of the arts ought to be affirmed and true gen-

---

[9] *Dialectiqve de Pierre de la Ramee* (Paris: André Wechel, 1555), pp. 84-85. For these terms in Latin, see *P. Rami Regii Professoris Dialecticae Libri Duo* (Lvtetiae: Apud Andream Wechelum, 1574), pp. 52-53.

[10] *Dialectiqve* (1555), pp. 84-85. Translation mine here and below.

[11] For a warning against the confusing of the translation of 1576 with the earlier translation, see Waddington-Kastus, *De Petri Rami Vita, Scriptis, Philosophia,* p. 177. See also Waddington, *Ramus,* pp. 451-452.

erally and necessarily in this fashion, but beyond this they ought also to be homogeneous and reciprocal. A homogeneous axiom is one in which the parts are essential among themselves; as the form is essential to that which is formed; and as the subject is essential to its proper adjunct, and as the proper adjunct is essential to its subject in itself, and not through any other cause; and as the genus has its species to which it is essential. And this axiom is marked and termed "in itself." A reciprocal axiom is when the predicate is affirmed and true of its subject, not only "of all," and not only "in itself," but also reciprocally: as *Grammar is the art of speaking well; Rhetoric, the art of communicating well; Dialectic, the art of disputing well; Arithmetic, the art of computing well; Geometry, the art of measuring well*; also, *man is a reasonable creature; grammar is composed of two parts, etymology and syntax; number is even or odd; the wolf is born to howl.* And this axiom is called "universal in the first instance."[12]

The first of these axioms, the *lex veritatis*, permitted Ramus to sift out of the liberal arts any propositions that were true only at times. Such propositions were in the field of opinion rather than of science, and while they have to be reckoned with in our daily lives, where contingent truths, probabilities, and uncertainties surround us, they cannot claim to be demonstrable, and thus they cannot achieve the validity of necessary truth. Ramus wanted the learned arts to consist of universal and necessary affirmations—of affirmations in which the predicate was true of every case of the subject. For example, in the proposition that dialectic is the art of disputing well, every case of disputing according to artistic principle is a case of dialectic, and thus, according to him, the proposition is truly general, truly necessary, and to that extent is a candidate for admission into the dialectical science.

The second of these axioms, the *lex justitiae*, permitted Ramus to sift out of one liberal art any propositions that belonged to another. Suppose, for example, that you examined traditional grammar and traditional rhetoric, and found in the first the statement that schemes were grammatical and rhetorical, whereas in the second you found the statement that grammatical schemes were orthographical or syntactical, while rhetorical schemes were of words, of sentences, and of amplification. Here would be a case where the same statements appeared in about the same form in two different arts, and the subject

---

[12] *La Dialectiqve de M. Pierre de La Ramee Professevr du Roy, comprise en deux liures selon la derniere edition* (Paris: Guillaume Auuray, 1576), foll. 38v-49r. Translation mine here and below.

matter of the two arts seemed intermingled and confused. The law of justice, invoked at this point, required a decision to be made as to which of the two arts properly possessed the topic of schemes and tropes, and what was therefore left to the art which lost the decision. Ramus decided that schemes and tropes belonged to communicating well, rather than to speaking well, and that grammar was left with absolute dominion over etymology and syntax as the two essential properties of the art of serving oneself by means of articulate speech. The same fundamental decisions had to be made in relation to the ultimate ownership of statements having to do with invention and disposition. These statements were claimed by traditional rhetoric and scholastic logic, as we have seen; but Ramus, accepting Agricola (and Aristotle's *Topics*) as authority for the claim of logic to these procedures, decided that rhetoric had proper subject matter when it was left with style and delivery.

The third of these axioms, the *lex sapientiae*, permitted Ramus to clarify the organization of the subject matter of the liberal arts. In its original meaning, this law meant that the predicate of a scientific proposition must represent the nearest rather than the more remote class of things to which the subject could belong. Thus if we say that grammar is an art, our statement is scientific, since it places our subject in its proximate rather than its remote class. But if we say that grammar is a form, our statement places our subject in a class too remote from its scientific character, and thus the statement, although true, is not admissible into the grammatical science. Now Ramus saw the possibility of extending this law so that, instead of using it to place a given subject into its nearest class, we would use it to determine whether a given proposition belonged in the class of most general statements, or in the class of merely general statements, or in the class of concrete statements. And he also saw the possibility of proceeding to present a science in accordance with this classifying of propositions, the most general statements being placed first, the less general ones next, and the least general ones last. Thus the *lex sapientiae* appears to be the logical basis of Ramus's famous definition of method:

> Method is arrangement, by which among many things the first in respect to conspicuousness is put in the first place, the second in the second, the third in the third, and so on. This term refers to every discipline and every dispute. Yet it commonly is taken in the sense of a direction sign and of a shortening of the highway. And by this

metaphor it was practised in school by the Greeks and the Latins, who, speaking also of rhetoric, called method arrangement, from the term for its genus. And under this term there is no doctrine, whether of proposition, or of syllogism, that is taught in rhetoric, except only so far as rhetoric makes mention of method.[13]

The best short statement of Ramus's theory of logic, and thus of his major contribution to learning, is found in the French version of the *Dialectiqve* as published in 1555, although the Latin analogue of that work, the *Dialecticae Libri Duo*, first published one year later, is also a good summary of his logical teachings. Waddington calls the latter treatise Ramus's final word on logic, whereas he calls the former the first and most important philosophical work in French up to Descartes's *Discours de la Méthode*.[14] This verdict would have pleased Ramus in a very special way. For in the last preface which he wrote for his *Dialecticae Libri Duo*, he mentions Archimedes as having wished that his discourse on the sphere and cylinder might be engraved on his tomb; "and as for me," adds Ramus, "if you wish to inform yourself about my vigils and my studies, I shall want the column of my sepulchre to be taken up with the establishing of the art of logic or dialectic."[15] To Ramus, logic was the center of the program of liberal studies, and the chief instrument of man in the quest for salvation. In fact, the strength of Ramus's passion for this subject can be inferred from his own statement that God is the only perfect logician, that man surpasses the beasts by virtue of his capacity to reason syllogistically, and that one man surpasses another only so far as his address to the problem of method is superior.[16]

The *Dialectiqve* of 1555 is inscribed to Cardinal Charles of Lorraine, whom Ramus designates on the title page and in the dedicatory epistle as his Maecenas. The epistle thanks the cardinal for his protection of Ramus against the Aristotelians who sought to suppress his teachings, and offers the present book as a return for that favor. Dialectic, observes Ramus, deserves the great attention it has received from philosophers; "for if the special arts have been reduced to rule by the great labor of many men, grammar and rhetoric for speaking well and for ornamenting speech, arithmetic and geometry for computing and measuring well, what quantity of vigils and what

[13] *Dialectiqve* (1555), p. 119.
[14] *Ramus*, pp. 9, 106.
[15] *Dialecticae Libri Duo* (Lvtetiae, 1574), p. 2; *La Dialectiqve de M. Pierre de La Ramee* (Paris, 1576), sig. A2r. Translation mine.
[16] *Dialectiqve* (1555), pp. 118-119, 135-136, 139.

great number of men worked together to fashion dialectic, the general art of inventing and judging all things?"[17] The epistle proceeds to give a brief history of speculations upon dialectic or logic, Aristotle being credited with one hundred and thirty books on the subject, of which thirty-five deal with the true dialectic inasmuch as they speak of arguments and of the disposition and judgment of arguments.[18] The last great name in this brief history is Galen, after whom, says Ramus, the true love of wisdom ceased, and the servile love of Aristotle began. As for himself, Ramus believes it his mission to cull from the works of the past, and particularly from the dialectical works of Aristotle, such precepts and rules as are strictly germane to dialectic, and then to arrange them in the fashion required by his own regulations for method. Upon this mission, he says, I have spent almost twenty years, and not merely the nine which Horace had recommended as the proper interval between composition and publication.

Book I of the *Dialectiqve* opens with the definition that dialectic is the art of disputing well, and that logic is to be used in the same sense. Its rules are derived from the workings of the human reason. Man ought to study dialectic in order to dispute well, "because it proclaims to us the truth of all argument and as a consequence the falsehood, whether the truth be necessary, as in science, or, as in opinion, contingent, that is to say, capable both of being and not being."[19] Ramus observes later:

But because of these two species, Aristotle wished to make two logics, one for science, and the other for opinion; in which (saving the honor of so great a master) he has very greatly erred. For although articles of knowledge are on the one hand necessary and scientific, and on the other contingent and matters of opinion, so it is nevertheless that as sight is common in viewing all colors, whether permanent or changeable, so the art of knowing, that is to say, dialectic or logic, is one and the same doctrine in respect to perceiving all things, as will be seen

[17] *Ibid.*, fol. 2v. This preface is also printed in Waddington, *Ramus*, pp. 401-407.

[18] By thirty-five books of Aristotle on "la vraye dialectique," Ramus means, as he himself indicates, not thirty-five separate works, but some nine works divided into thirty-five main sections. Thus he counts the six separate titles in the *Organon* as containing seventeen main sections or books; he counts the *Metaphysics* as containing fourteen main sections or books; and he counts the *Rhetoric* as containing four sections or books, three of which he would reckon as belonging to the work now accepted as Aristotle's, and the other, as belonging to *De Rhetorica ad Alexandrum*, now usually regarded as the work of someone else.

[19] *Dialectiqve* (1555), p. 2.

by its very parts, and as the *Aristotelian Animadversions* explain more fully.[20]

Thus does Ramus indicate his belief in one system of logic for both science and opinion, and in one theory of invention and arrangement for both logician and rhetorician, whereas the scholastics, following Aristotle and Cicero, preferred two systems of logic, one for science and the other for opinion, and two systems of invention and disposition, one in the field of scientific and the other in the field of popular discourse. Nowhere is the issue between scholastic and Ramist indicated more sharply than it is in the words just quoted. Nowhere is the essential point in Ramus's reform of scholastic logic and traditional rhetoric stated more firmly than it is right here.

Ramus's next main point is that dialectic has two parts, invention and judgment or arrangement. These are not severely insulated from each other, he goes on, but rather are involved in each other, the first being devoted to the separate parts of reasoning, and the other, to the arranging of those parts into discourse. The separate parts of reasoning offer a problem in terminology, and Ramus proceeds carefully to review the various terms for those parts in traditional Aristotelian logic. One traditional term, he says, is categorem; another is category; still another is topics, that is, places and notes. The doctrine of topics or places or localities, he goes on, indicates that the parts of reasoning dwell in seats or habitats. But these parts should more properly be called principles, elements, terms, means, reasons, proofs, or arguments. These two last terms seem to Ramus to be the most appropriate for his purposes. "We shall use the terms of reasoning, that is, proof and argument, as being the most widely received and the most customary in this art."[21]

The basic distinction in Ramus's treatment of invention is that between artistic and non-artistic arguments—a distinction which he expressly credits to Aristotle's *Rhetoric*, and which has been discussed earlier in these pages.[22] Having established argument as the term for the thing produced by invention, Ramus proceeds to define the two great types of argument thus:

Argument then is artistic or non-artistic, as Aristotle partitions it in the second of the *Rhetoric*: artistic, which creates belief by itself and by its nature, is divided into the primary and the derivative primary.

[20] *Ibid.*, pp. 3-4. See above, p. 16.   [21] *Dialectiqve*, p. 5.
[22] *Ibid.*, p. 5. See above, pp. 68-69.

Non-artistic argument is that which by itself and through its own force does not create belief, as for example the five types which Aristotle describes in the first of his *Rhetoric*, laws, witnesses, contracts, tortures, oaths. Thus it is always that these arguments are interchangeably called authorities and witnesses.[23]

To artistic arguments, Ramus devotes fifty-five pages, and to the non-artistic, five. Since one of the great differences between the ancient and the modern theory of proof is that the ancients stressed the discovery of artistic proofs, and correspondingly neglected the non-artistic, whereas the moderns have done almost exactly the reverse, it can be seen that on this point Ramus is hardly a modern in his emphasis.

Artistic arguments, as distributed between the category of primary and the category of derivative primary, involve nine basic terms. The six of these which are primary comprise causes, effects, subjects, adjuncts, opposites, and comparatives; the three which are derivative comprise reasoning from name, reasoning from division, and reasoning by definition. Since the class of non-artistic arguments is composed, not of generals, but of particulars, it can be argued that Ramus intended it as a class to rank with the nine basic terms just enumerated to form a theory of invention of ten topics. In other words, it can be argued that he wanted to preserve ten basic entities out of respect for Aristotle's ten categories and thus give his reformed logic a traditional flavor. By splitting some of these ten topics into subdivisions (for example, by speaking of cause as the final, the formal, the efficient, and the material), he succeeded in preserving other traditional terms while effecting a neat reorganization of the accepted subject matter.

The ten basic entities in Ramus's theory of logical invention are in reality the ten basic relations between predicate and subject in the logical proposition, or the ten basic relations among the objects of knowledge in the human environment.[24] This means in a way that if you set yourself to making truthful declarations about an object, those declarations will inevitably concern the object's causes, or its effects, or its subjects, or its adjuncts, or its opposites, or its analogues, or its name, or its divisions, or its definition, or its witnesses. Thus a discourse on man might be made up of declarations on man as

[23] *Dialectiqve*, pp. 5-6, 61. For Aristotle's discussion of this distinction, and of the five types of non-artistic arguments, see *Rhetoric*, 1.2,15.
[24] *Dialectiqve*, pp. 71-72.

the product of causes, man as the producer of effects, man as the subject of many circumstances, man as the circumstance of certain subjects (the earth, for example); of declarations on things opposite to man, and things analogous to man; and of declarations about words that signify man, about wholes that include him, or parts that make him up, or definitions that exactly characterize him, or witnesses who testify to something he has or does not have.[25] When Thomas Wilson, Ramus's contemporary, wanted to show how the topics of logic worked, he indicated that some nineteen different basic topics were to be applied to a given concept, and he listed those topics as a miscellany not only of some of the predicaments and all of the predicables, but also of additions created by splitting certain other old terms asunder.[26] It was the indeterminate number of these topics in the scholastic theory that Ramus objected to, as he also objected to the fact that the scholastics mentioned the predicaments and predicables under invention as well as under arrangement, as if redundancy could not or should not be avoided. He wanted to make logic rigidly scientific by reducing the theory of logical invention to its universal kinds, not to a mixture of universals and particulars; and by treating these kinds in one of the two divisions of logic, not in both. As he brings his account of invention to a close, he observes:

> Consequently, then, although man may be ignorant of all things, this is not in any sense to declare that he should not seek or that he cannot invent, in view of the fact that he has naturally in himself the power to understand all things; and when he shall have before his eyes the art of invention by its universal kinds, as a sort of mirror reflecting for him the universal images and the generals of all things, it will be much easier for him by means of these images to recognize each single species, and therefore to invent that which he is seeking; but it is necessary by very many examples, by great practice, by long use, to burnish and polish this mirror before it can shine and render up these images.[27]

John Seton, Thomas Wilson, and Ralph Lever treated arrangement or judgment by making it the first rather than the second grand division of logic, as if the problem of arranging thought were of primary importance in the theory of learned discourse.[28] Ramus re-

[25] In his "Peroration de L'Invention," *Dialectiqve*, pp. 65-70, Ramus sketches a discourse upon man derived from the basic terms of his theory of topics.
[26] See above, pp. 25-28.   [27] *Dialectiqve*, p. 69.
[28] See above, pp. 16, 51, 60.

verses this emphasis, although little significance should be attached to his decision. What is really significant is that his treatment of arrangement does not include any mention of the categories or predicaments, any mention of the predicables, but is devoted instead to three other aspects of scholastic logic, expounded in the ascending order of complexity. After defining judgment as "the second part of logic, which shows the ways and means of judging well by means of certain rules of arrangement," and after indicating Aristotle's *Prior Analytics* and *Posterior Analytics* as the great source of these rules, Ramus adds, "The arrangement of logic has three species, the proposition, the syllogism, method."[29] This sentence gives an exhaustive inventory of his second book, and that second book is the most influential of all his contributions to logic.

The proposition, or in Ramus's French the "Enonciation," "is arrangement by means of which something is stated of something else."[30] This is the simplest unit of arrangement, the most elementary way of ordering what has been invented; and its parts are the subject (or antecedent) and the predicate (or consequent). It is at this point, by the way, that Ramus designates his theory of invention as a theory of the generic relations between antecedent and consequent, those relations being that of cause to effect, of effect to cause, of subject to adjunct, of adjunct to subject, and so on. But Ramus's main interest now is to show what the proposition is as a unit of discourse. Thus he discusses the simple proposition (which consists of one subject and one predicate) and the compound proposition, where the predicate is composite, or relative, or conditional, or disjunctive. The distinguishing feature of this part of his work is that, in concluding his analysis of the proposition, he mentions the three laws by which one can judge whether or not a given proposition is scientific. Since these three laws have already been explained as Vincent of Beauvais and Ramus conceived of them,[31] I shall say nothing further about them here, except to suggest that they stand in the structure of Ramistic logic as the five predicables stood in scholasticism. That is, a statement became properly scientific in the eyes of scholastic logic when it could be classed as having a predicate of genus, of species, of difference, of property, or of accident.[32] In the eyes of Ramus, who ignored the five predicables as a topic in logic, a statement became

[29] *Dialectiqve*, p. 71.
[30] *Ibid.*, p. 71.
[31] See above, pp. 41-44, 149-153.
[32] See above, pp. 17-18.

properly scientific only when it satisfied simultaneously each one of the three laws.

"Syllogism," says Ramus in beginning his discussion of the second aspect of judgment, "is arrangement by means of which a question under examination is ordered along with the proof and brought to a necessary conclusion."[33] Ramus's attendant discussion is conventional. He speaks of the three parts of the syllogism; the three figures of the simple syllogism, with their various moods; the composite syllogisms, conditional and disjunctive. He does not bother to speak of induction as a possible alternative to the syllogism; and thus he departs from scholastic logic, which usually recognized induction as a species of argument.[34] If his procedure in this respect seems far from progressive, it should be remembered, not only that the time was not yet ripe for sciences based upon experiment, observation, and the minute description of particulars, but also that a logic of induction in advance of that time would have had no influence. Moreover, Ramus's conception of science was that it began, not with the particulars that might one day yield universals, but with the universals that could be tested by his three laws. For such a science, the syllogism was the master instrument, while the judgment of particulars was a preliminary matter. Thus he says in his concluding remarks on the syllogistic judgment:

> When the judgment of the major premise and of the minor premise will then be well guaranteed, and the syllogistic collocation of these elements well set out, the question under examination will also be well judged to be true or false; for at the second judgment the first is presupposed, and from the first is borrowed that double light to clarify the conclusion. And in brief the art of the syllogism does not inform us of any other thing than that of resolving a stated question by the manifest truth of two well-arranged parts.[35]

Ramus later allows the process of induction, which arrives at a preliminary judgment by a survey of particulars, to be a common possession among all forms of life, whereas the syllogism is the property only of the highest form of life and the expression only of the highest intelligence. He phrases this thought in the following words:

> Finally let us remember that the syllogism is a law of reason, truer and more just than all the laws which Lycurgus and Solon once

---

[33] *Dialectiqve*, p. 87.   [34] See above, pp. 22-23, 54, 60.
[35] *Dialectiqve*, pp. 113-114.

fashioned, through which the judgment of the doubtful proposition is established by a necessary and immutable verdict—I say, a law of reason, proper to man, not being in any sense shared with the other animals, as the preliminary judgment can be in some sense shared, but solely in things pertaining to sense and belonging to the body and the physical life.[36]

Then he goes on to say that lower forms of life like spiders and ants, despite their sensory adjustment to their environment, can conceive of nothing by using a middle term, and can draw no conclusion by properly comparing and disposing such a term in the figure of a syllogism. Certainly, he adds, "—certainly this part in man is the image of some sort of divinity."[37]

The final section of Ramus's *Dialectiqve* is given over to the discussion of method, his definition of which has already been quoted as an application of the *lex sapientiae*. What Ramus has to say on method is the most important part of his contribution to the theory of communication, and it exercised such influence that a century-long debate on that subject ensued, one masterpiece of which was Descartes's *Discours de la Méthode*. The enthusiasm of Ramus's disciples and the malice of his opponents conspired, however, to distort this aspect of his own teaching, and to narrow his recommendations to the one that struck everybody as most unusual. Thus it is necessary to approach these recommendations through his own words rather than through the words of his later critics and admirers.

"Method," says Ramus, "is natural or prudential."[38] This view of method as twofold follows upon his definition of method as that in which ideas in any learned treatise or dispute are to be arranged in the order of their conspicuousness, the most conspicuous things being given first place, and less conspicuous things being given subordinate places. While both the natural and the prudential methods, as explained by Ramus, fall under his definition, and are governed by it, the natural method attempts to arrange ideas according to their degree of conspicuousness in an absolute sense, whereas the prudential method attempts to arrange them according to their degree of conspicuousness in the consciousness of the inexpert listener or reader.

The natural method, or as Ramus later implies, the method of arranging a scientific discourse, proceeds upon the assumption that some statements are naturally more evident or more conspicuous

---

[36] *Ibid.,* p. 118.   [37] *Ibid.,* p. 119.   [38] *Ibid.,* p. 120.

than others, as for example, a statement of the cause of a thing is more evident than a statement of its effect, or a general and universal is more evident than a particular or singular.[39] However true it is, argues Ramus, that any authentic discipline must consist of general and universal rules, those rules nevertheless possess different degrees of generality, and to the extent that they are more general, they should outrank the less general in the order of presentation. Thus propositions of utmost generality will be placed first; propositions of lesser generality will be placed next; subalterns will be placed next; "and finally the examples, which are most particular, will be placed last."[40] After tracing the origins of this method to the works of Hippocrates, Plato, and Aristotle, Ramus observes:

> And in a word this artistic method to me appears as a sort of long chain of gold, such as Homer imagined, in which the links are these degrees thus depending one from another, and all joined so justly together, that nothing could be removed from it, without breaking the order and continuity of the whole.[41]

Although Ramus's own *Dialectiqve* exemplifies the natural method as well as any work could, he is not content to rest the case there. Instead, in his discussion of this phase of method, he fabricates an illustration to show what it means, and the illustration is valuable as a precise description of the procedures he himself followed in reforming the liberal arts. His illustration consists in asking us to assume that all the definitions, divisions, and rules of grammar have been discovered and tested; and that each one is then inscribed upon its own paper and is mixed with the others in a jug, like tickets in a lottery. Now, Ramus demands, what part of logic will be able to teach one to arrange these papers in their rightful order as I draw them forth? Not the first part, surely, for here is a case where all materials have already been found, and where no need exists for the use of the places of invention. Not the doctrine of proposition or of syllogism, for here is a case where all the materials have been stated in proper form and tested by the first and by the second operation of judgment. No, of all the parts of logic, only method can help in this case. Accordingly, the logician, by invoking the natural method, will draw the papers from the jug, and when he comes upon the paper saying, "Grammar is the doctrine of speaking well," he will

---

[39] *Ibid.*, pp. 120, 128. See below, pp. 164, 168-169.
[40] *Dialectiqve*, pp. 120-121.   [41] *Ibid.*, p. 122.

recognize this as the most general statement he can possibly encounter about grammar, and he will put this paper first. When later
he comes upon another paper saying, "The parts of grammar are
two, etymology and syntax," he will recognize it as the next most
general statement he can possibly encounter, and he will rank it
second. He will rank third the statement that defines etymology. He
will then rank under etymology all statements belonging to it, keep-
ing the proper order from general to particular. Then he will repeat
the same operation for the second part of grammar, putting first the
definition of syntax, then less general statements about it, and finally
the examples. Between each topic in the entire treatise, as at last
assembled, he will then insert transitional elements to indicate what
the preceding topic has been, and what the following will be. "For,"
says Ramus, "by means of these notes of transition the spirit is re-
freshed and stimulated."[42]

Ramus's habit of dividing a subject into two main parts, as illustrated by this discourse on grammar, and by his treatment of logic
and rhetoric, led to the assumption that for him the natural method
is essentially the method of dichotomies—of proceeding always to
separate a logical class into two subclasses opposed to each other by
contradiction, and to separate the subclasses and the sub-subclasses
in the same way, until the entire structure of any science resembled
a severely geometrical pattern of bifurcations. Actually, however,
the natural method as used by Ramus himself is better defined as the
concept of arranging ideas in the descending order of generality than
as the concept of dividing invariably by twos. Not only does Ramus's
own definition of the natural method stress the former concept,
without reference to the latter; but his procedure tends also in the
same direction. For example, although he divides logic into invention and arrangement, and invention into artistic and non-artistic
proofs, he proceeds to discuss the latter under five headings, not two;
and of course his treatment of arrangement falls, not into two parts,
but three. Again, he divides artistic proofs into primary and derivative primary, but he proceeds to discuss the former class under six
headings, and the latter, under three. Even his original distribution
of logic into invention and arrangement is not based upon the assumption that the principle of contradiction is involved, for he expressly
notes the presence of invention in an act of arrangement, and the

[42] *Ibid.*, p. 126.

presence of arrangement in an act of invention.[43] His followers tended to construe the natural method and the law of justice to mean the severest kind of dichotomizing, as if any given idea had only two members, one completely insulated from the other. But it is worth noticing that Ramus himself did not take the habit of dichotomies as seriously as that.

Nor did he limit the use of the natural method to learned writing or to the kind of discourse in which the expert talks to the expert. He expressly says that it is used also in poetry and oratory, and his discussion of this point is worth quoting as an indication of the relation of logic and criticism in Ramistic philosophy:

> Now this method is not solely applicable to the material of the arts and doctrines, but to all things which we intend to teach easily and clearly. And consequently it is common to orators, poets, and all writers. The orators in their introductions and narrations, their proofs and perorations, like to follow this order, and they call it then the order of art and of nature. And sometimes they practice it most assiduously, as Cicero did in the accusation, first stating, then distributing.
> [This reference to Cicero's speech against Verres, II.1.12.34, is then explained by Ramus as an example of the natural method.]
> Thus do the poets, if sometimes they treat matter of learning and doctrine. As Virgil in the *Georgics* first divides his matter into four parts, as I have said. And in the first book he treats the things common to all parts, as astrology and meteorology; and the threshing of the wheat and its husbandry, which was the first part proper. He writes in the second book of trees in general and then of vines in particular. In the third book he writes of cows, horses, sheep, goats, dogs. And in the fourth, of bees.[44]

As a result of Ramus's belief in the applicability of the natural method to all types of discourse, popular as well as learned, it came to be assumed in the course of time that his theory of communication advocated nothing except the natural method. But this is hardly the case. He devotes eight pages of the *Dialectiqve* to the prudential method, which he defines as that "in which things are given precedence, not altogether and absolutely in terms of their being the most conspicuous, but in terms of their being still the most convenient for him whom we must instruct, and of their being most amenable for inducing and leading him whither we purpose."[45] He adds:

---

[43] *Ibid.*, pp. 4-5. See also above, p. 155.
[44] *Dialectiqve*, pp. 123-125.   [45] *Ibid.*, p. 128.

It is termed prudential disposition by the orators, because it lies largely in man's prudence rather than in art and in the precepts of doctrine, very much as if the natural method were arrangement for science, and the prudential method were arrangement for opinion.[46]

In his discussion of the prudential method, Ramus indicates that it is taught and practiced by philosophers, poets, and orators. Aristotle, he says, had implied it in his references to the procedures of hidden and deceitful insinuation, where the speaker or writer begins in the middle, without declaring what he intends to do, or what the parts of his subject are, as when he indulges in analogy or parable. As for the use of this method by philosophers, Ramus mentions Plato as the supreme example. Poets, who propose to teach the people, have to accept their auditors as a beast of many heads, says Ramus, and thus have to begin their stories in the middle, and explain later how things got to be as they are. The wisdom of this method, Ramus goes on, has particularly appealed to orators in their attempts to gain initial attention of their hearers. He then sums up this phase of his discussion:

And in brief all the tropes and figures of style, all the graces of action, which make up the whole of rhetoric, true and distinct from logic, serve no other purpose than to lead this vexatious and mulish auditor, who is postulated to us by this [i.e., the prudential] method; and have been studied on no other account than that of the failings and perversities of this very one, as Aristotle truly teaches in the third of the *Rhetoric*.[47]

These words, written as the *Dialectiqve* is close to its final page, may be taken as Ramus's best statement of the reasons behind the rhetorician's special interest in the prudential method. The troublesome and stubborn auditor, who is present in body but not in mind· as the orator speaks, will not follow ideas arranged exclusively in a descending order of generality, and thus will not be captivated by the natural method, as would the scientist and philosopher. What the popular audience needs is the casualness and variety of the prudential method, the flattery of the tropes and figures, the graces of delivery. One might wonder at this point why Ramus, believing these things, would not allow rhetoric to have something to say of

[46] *Ibid.*, p. 128. I have corrected the misprint in the last clause, which reads: "comme si la methode de nature estoit iugement de science, la methode de science [that is, de prudence] estoit iugement d'opinion."
[47] *Ibid.*, p. 134.

arrangement as well as of style and delivery—why he would not concede rhetoric three parts or possibly even four, instead of two, on the assumption that invention, like arrangement, style, and delivery, is one process in scientific discourse and quite another in discourse addressed to the people. Had he gone that far, he would have been closer to the Aristotelian and Ciceronian opinion than he turned out to be. In fact, his real break with Aristotle and Cicero was in ordaining that rhetoric must cease to speculate upon invention and arrangement as well as style and delivery, as if the two former processes had little relevance except in scientific discourse. To Aristotle and Cicero, dialectic was the theory of learned communication, rhetoric of popular communication, and thus both arts needed the two former processes, while rhetoric needed the two latter in particular. To Ramus, dialectic was the theory of subject matter and form in communication, rhetoric the theory of stylistic and oral presentation. By his standards, invention and arrangement were the true property of logic, and must be treated only in logic, even if arrangement had to have two aspects, one for the learned auditor and the other for the people. By his standards, style and delivery were the true property of rhetoric, and must therefore be treated only in rhetoric, even if the popular audience which demanded them had to have also a special theory of method that rhetoric was not allowed to mention.

The dictate that style and delivery are the whole of rhetoric was given concrete formulation by Ramus's good friend and colleague Audomarus Talaeus, as mentioned before.[48] Talaeus is said to have been born around 1510 in Vermandois, the region of Ramus's birth five years later; and he died at Paris in 1562, ten years before the massacre of St. Bartholomew's Day.[49] There seems to be no evidence that Talaeus shared Ramus's views towards ecclesiastical reform, but the whole body of his work is witness that in the field of educational reform he and Ramus were the closest and most friendly of collaborators. His *Institutiones Oratoriae*, published at Paris in 1544, is declared in its preface to do for the field of rhetoric what Ramus's *Dialecticae Institutiones* of the preceding year had done for the field of logic. An even fuller explanation of the nature of his collaboration with Ramus has already been quoted above,[50] and that explanation accompanied his *Rhetorica*, which had reached its fifth edition by

[48] See above, pp. 148-149.
[49] See *Biographie Universelle*, s.v. Talon, Omer; also *Nouvelle Biographie Générale*, s.v. Talon, Omer.
[50] pp. 148-149.

1552, and which was intended to reduce Ramistic rhetoric to its briefest Latin expression, as Ramistic logic was reduced to its briefest Latin expression by Ramus's *Dialecticae Libri Duo* of 1556.

A very good indication of Talaeus's adherence to the reforms of Ramus is found in a now-forgotten work, *La Rhetoriqve Francoise*, published at Paris in 1555. This work is a French translation of Talaeus's *Rhetorica*, done in the very year of Ramus's own French translation of his *Dialecticae Libri Duo*, and plainly intended to represent Ramistic rhetoric in vernacular learning, as the *Dialectiqve* represents Ramistic logic. The translator of Talaeus's *Rhetorica* into French was Antoine Foclin, who also called himself Foquelin or Fouquelin. Like Ramus and Talaeus, Foclin was a native of Vermandois. His edition of the satires of Persius, published at Paris in 1555, is dedicated to Ramus, under whom he had studied for the preceding nine years.[51] Thus he had ties of discipleship and place to bind him to Ramism and to dispose him to forward Ramus's reforms according to his own special talents.

La Rhetoriqve Francoise d'Antoine Foclin de Chauny en Vermandois is dedicated to Mary Queen of Scots, then twelve years of age and the darling of the French court, wherein she was being educated as the future bride of the dauphin and the future queen of France.[52] Foclin's dedicatory letter runs to six pages. It is full of enthusiasm for his generation's crusade to translate all the liberal arts into French and thus to save youth from having to master alien languages as a first step in education. It is also full of compliments for the young Scottish queen who would one day have the opportunity not only to assist native French writers to work in their own tongue, but also to support all learning and science. One passage indicates the nature of the education the young queen is receiving at the French court. Foclin mentions that Mary had recently pronounced a Latin oration in the presence of the king and queen and most of the princesses and nobles of the royal circle, and had then translated it into French. The oration had defended the unorthodox thesis, remarks Foclin, that it was becoming to women to know letters and the liberal arts; and it aroused admiration on all sides, and would

---

[51] See *Biographie Universelle*, s.v. Foquelin, Antoine.

[52] The title page of Foclin's work reads: "La Rhetoriqve Francoise d'Antoine Foclin de Chauny en Vermandois, A Tresillvstre Princesse Madame Marie Royne d'Ecosse. A Paris, De l'imprimerie d'André Wechel. 1555. Avec Privilege."

The Huntington Library holds this work in microfilm, and upon that copy my present discussion is based, all translations from it being mine.

have served him in the present work on rhetoric as a storehouse of examples of all the tropes and figures, had the French translation fallen sooner into his hands. Incidentally, the education of the young queen, as seen in this passage, is more conventional than that which Foclin is aiming for in his effort to make the learning of Latin unnecessary. In still another passage, Foclin apologizes to the queen because the French tongue is still too young and too poor to have a vocabulary of its own for the terms of the liberal arts, and must therefore borrow from the Greek or Latin, not only a basic term like rhetoric, but also the terms for all the tropes and figures.

So far as Ramism is concerned, the most important part of Foclin's dedicatory letter is that in which he identifies his work as a translation of the Latin rhetoric of Talaeus, and credits Talaeus with authorizing and even assisting in that translation. With reference to the enterprise of rendering the learned arts into French, Foclin says:

> In order to advance and patronize which in my own way, I have translated the precepts of rhetoric, as faithfully assembled from the books of the ancient Greek and Latin rhetoricians and arranged in unique order of disposition by Omer Talon, a man no less excellent in this art than perfect in all other disciplines. With the authorization and advice of whom, I have adapted the precepts of this art to our tongue, omitting at all times that to which her natural usage seemed repugnant; adding also that which she has of the proper and particular in herself, beyond Greek and Latin; and setting forth each precept by examples and evidences from the most approved authors of our language—which, I saw, had been done most methodically and ingeniously by that same author in Latin. In which (Madame) all that I can claim as mine (if I can claim anything mine in a work assembled by the labors of so many good men), all that, say I, which I can claim as mine, you have been the first to whom I have esteemed that it must needs be avowed and dedicated.[53]

Immediately after the dedicatory letter, which is dated at Paris, May 12, 1555, the text of Foclin's French version of Talaeus begins. It runs to 139 numbered pages, whereas Ramus's French *Dialectiqve* of that same year had run to 140 pages.[54] Such parallelism as this, by the way, is not hostile to the spirit of Ramism, which gave equal emphasis to the two arts, and made the arrangement of one cor-

[53] *La Rhetoriqve Francoise*, sig. A3r-A3v.
[54] Foclin's *Rhetoriqve* appears to contain 138 pages, but actually it contains one page more than that, because of the mistake of having two pages numbered 112.

respond almost mathematically to that of the other. But in one sense the mathematical proportions of Ramus's *Dialectiqve* and of Foclin's *Rhetoriqve* do not coincide. The former allocates seventy pages to invention and seventy to arrangement, thus maintaining an absolute equality of emphasis between the two parts of logic. The latter allocates one hundred and thirteen pages to style and only twenty-six to delivery, as if the second part of rhetoric, however important it is in practice, did not have the theoretical interest that the first part has.

The opening words of Foclin's *Rhetoriqve* are a perfect illustration of the natural method described by Ramus. Says Foclin:

Definition of rhetoric.
Rhetoric is an art of speaking well and elegantly.

The parts of rhetoric.
Rhetoric has two parts, style and delivery.

Style and its species.
Style is not anything but the ornamenting and the enriching of speech and discourse; the which has two species, the one being called trope, the other, figure.

Trope.
Trope is a style by means of which the proper and natural meaning of the word is changed to another, as is indicated by the word trope, which in French means interchange.

The species of trope.
There are four sorts of trope: metonymy, irony, metaphor, and synecdoche.[55]

Having descended through these progressively less general statements to a cluster of four basic terms, as Ramus commanded, Foclin proceeds to discuss each term in the order of his enumeration. This part of his discussion turns out also to have a Ramistic bearing. One of the dictates of Ramus's natural method was that causes should be placed before effects.[56] Ramus himself observed this dictate by arranging his discussion of the first part of logic so that the topic of cause not only preceded the topic of effect but also came first among the ten basic topics of logical invention. Foclin's arrangement of tropes follows this very pattern, cause being first, effect second, subject third, adjunct fourth, and so on down Ramus's basic list. Thus metonymy, the first trope in Foclin's cluster, has four distinct kinds.

[55] *Ibid.*, pp. 1-2.   [56] See above, p. 161.

The first kind consists in stating a cause as a means of implying an effect. The second kind consists in stating an effect in order to imply a cause. The third kind consists in stating a subject in order to imply an accident or adjunct. The fourth kind consists in stating an accident in order to imply a subject. Irony, the second trope in Foclin's list, is defined as implying a contrary by its contrary, and this reminds us that Ramus's fifth concept in invention is that of opposites. Foclin's third trope, metaphor, is defined as implying a like by a like—again a reminder that Ramus's sixth concept is that of comparatives or similitudes. Synecdoche, the fourth trope in Foclin's cluster, is defined as implying the whole by naming the member, or as implying the genus by naming the species, or as doing the reverse of either of these two operations. Here again it is easy to see that Foclin has Ramus's eighth and ninth topic of invention in mind, that of division, which concerns wholes and parts, and that of definition, which concerns genus and species.

Foclin devotes thirty-four pages to these four tropes, managing under metaphor to discuss catachresis, allegory, enigma, and hyperbole. Much of his space is given over to illustrations of these stylistic devices from the works of French authors of the time. Thus he quotes from Tahureau, Baïf, and Clément Marot, the latter being cited from his translation of Virgil's first *Eclogue*. But his chief illustrations are drawn from Ronsard, Joachim du Bellay, and Jacques Amyot. In 1547 Amyot had published a French translation of the *Aethiopica* of Heliodorus under the title, *L'Histoire aethiopique de Heliodorus, contenant dix livres*; and it was this Greek romance from the early centuries of the Christian era which provided Foclin with almost as many illustrations as did Ronsard and Bellay, although in his dedicatory letter he expresses the belief that there is much of the contrived and the artificial about the tropes and figures of Heliodorus, whereas those in the Scottish queen's French version of her own Latin oration are by contrast true and natural.[57]

Figure, the second part of style in Ramistic rhetoric, is given seventy-nine pages of analysis and illustration by Foclin. His definition and division of this topic make no reference to grammatical figures, as did the older stylistic rhetoricians:

Figure is then a species of style, by means of which the language is changed from the simple and popular manner of speaking. For just

[57] *La Rhetoriqve Francoise*, sig. A4r.

as in reference to words, some are literal, and others metaphorical, so in reference to language and manner of speaking, one kind is simple and popular, the other, figured—that it to say, a little changed from the popular and customary manner of speaking, as happens primarily when we wish to plan and discourse upon anything. Not that the vulgar do not sometimes use these ornaments of rhetoric, but that these lights do not shine as often in the language and speech of the unlearned.

Division of figure.

There are two sorts of figure: the one is in the word, the other in the sentence.[58]

Under these two headings, Foclin arranges his entire discussion of the uncustomary forms of speech. His analysis of figures of the word involves the topic of number, which leads him to speak of the measure and quantity of syllables in French poetry, and of resonance and rhythm in poetry and prose. Figures of the sentence involve such devices as prosopopoeia, apostrophe, and exclamation, each device being illustrated from the authors already named. Like a good Ramist, Foclin remembers that transitional elements in literary structure refresh and stimulate the spirit,[59] and thus he concludes his discussion of style with a model transition:

> The precepts of style, the first part of rhetoric, have been set forth in the tropes and figures. Let us go on to delivery, the second part of the doctrine and art proposed.[60]

Delivery, as Foclin defines it from Talaeus's Latin, becomes the external manifestation of style, the projection of style to the hearer. His text reads at this point:

Delivery.

Delivery is a part of rhetoric which teaches how to express conveniently and how to put forth the style and the speech as conceived in the mind. So that it differs from style in nothing except that in the latter one thinks and conceives of what figure and elegant manner of speaking one will use, whereas in the former one takes pains that the utterance may be such as the conception and the thought of the mind have been.

Parts of delivery.

Delivery has two parts, the voice, which is called the pronouncing, and the gesture, which is called the action. Of which parts, the first relates

---

[58] *Ibid.*, pp. 34-35. [59] See above, p. 162.
[60] *La Rhetorique Francoise*, p. 112, i.e., 113.

to the hearing, the second to the sight. For by these two senses, all knowledge comes into the mind.[61]

Foclin recommends that correct speech be learned in infancy and childhood as a part of grammar, but that rhetoric, as a later study, will show what voice and inflection should be used in all sentences, figures, and moods of speaking. He observes:

> For each thing that is said has some proper sound, some sound different from other things, and the voice sounds like the string of a lute, according as it has been touched as by the movement of things which must need be pronounced.[62]

Having made these general observations, Foclin quotes a long passage from *L'Histoire aethiopique*, and intersperses directions as to its pronunciation. After other quotations to the same effect, he turns to gesture, which he discusses in relation to the head, the face, the arms, and the hands. He mentions that gesture has great efficacy as a language that can be understood where spoken words are unintelligible. He recalls that Demosthenes strengthened his own delivery by diligent practice, even speaking against the roar of the sea to develop his voice. And, like most writers on this aspect of rhetoric, he cannot refrain from retelling the familiar story of how Demosthenes, when asked what he deemed the first requisite of eloquence, replied, "Delivery," only to repeat that same answer when he was then asked what was the second and what the third requisite.[63]

Thus did Foclin's *Rhetoriqve Francoise* bring into native French speech the Latin rhetoric of Talaeus in the very year of the first French version of Ramus's *Dialectiqve*. It would be idle to pretend that Foclin's translation is absolutely faithful to Talaeus's original, especially as Foclin himself acknowledges omissions, additions, and changes.[64] It would also be idle to pretend that Talaeus's *Rhetorica* was absolutely faithful to itself from one of its many versions to another in and out of France during the last half of the sixteenth century. Still again, it would be idle to pretend that Ramus's own *Dialectiqve* corresponds exactly to its later Latin and French versions, before and after Ramus's death. The truth is, Ramism as a system of logic and rhetoric in Latin, French, and English, is not a single

---

[61] *Ibid.*, pp. 112-113, i.e., 113-114.   [62] *Ibid.*, p. 114, i.e., 115.

[63] *Ibid.*, p. 137, i.e., 138.

[64] See above, p. 167. For a discussion of differences between Foclin's translation and Talaeus's original, see Walter J. Ong, S.J., "Fouquelin's French Rhetoric and the Ramist Vernacular Tradition," *Studies in Philology*, LI (1954), 127-142.

unvarying doctrine but a pattern of uniformities as to general frame-work and a pattern of variations as to many of its details. Perhaps the best statement of the pattern of uniformities in Ramism is to be found by the comparative study of Ramus's *Dialectiqve* of 1555 and Foclin's *Rhetoriqve Francoise* of the same year. At any rate these are authentic versions done by Ramus himself and by his leading collab-orators for their own nation at the same moment of time and in the same stage of the development of their doctrine as a whole. With these versions in mind, we are now prepared to see what happened when Ramism crossed the English Channel and invaded the domain of John Seton, Richard Sherry, Thomas Wilson, and Ralph Lever.

II. Ramus's Dialectic in England

On April 4, 1550, Roger Ascham, public orator of the University of Cambridge, wrote a letter to his friend Johannes Sturm, master of the grammar school at Strasbourg. The letter was in Latin, as befitted correspondence of that era between learned men of different countries of the European community. One notable thing about that particular letter is that it contains an enthusiastic account of the literary accomplishments of a young lady named Elizabeth, whom Ascham had been tutoring for the preceding two years, and who was one day to be the most famous queen in English history. "The praise which Aristotle gives," remarks Ascham to Sturm, "wholly centres in her—beauty, stature, prudence, and industry." He adds: "She has just passed her sixteenth birthday, and shows such dignity and gentleness as are wonderful at her age and rank."[1] Her conversational ability in French, Italian, English, Latin, and Greek, her delight and skill in music, her restrained elegance of dress, and her gift for perceiving what makes literary style good or bad, are all described in glowing phrases by Ascham.

Another notable thing about that letter is that it refers to Joachim Périon, a learned French Benedictine, and to one Cephas Chlononius. What Ascham says of the former indicates his awareness that Périon has recently been translating Aristotle into Latin and recently speaking in defense of Aristotle and Cicero, while industriously collecting meanwhile a vast number of theological topics for use in controversy. Périon's defense of Aristotle and Cicero, by the way, had been directed against Peter Ramus, and had been published at Paris in the form of three orations, two of which bear the date of 1543, and the third, 1547. Ascham does not designate these particular publications nor does his letter anywhere refer to Ramus by name. But the Cephas Chlononius whom he mentions in his reference to Périon, and whom he allusively describes as an overbold critic of the leading philosopher of Greece and the leading teacher of Rome, is unquestionably to be identified as Ramus.[2]

Ascham's veiled censure of Ramus in this letter of 1550 has been tentatively established as the earliest reference by an Englishman

---

[1] These quotations are from the translation of part of this letter in *The Whole Works of Roger Ascham*, ed. John Allen Giles (London, 1864-65), vol. I, pt. I, pp. lxii-lxiv. For the complete Latin text of the letter, see the same place, pp. 181-193.

[2] See M. Guggenheim, "Beiträge zur Biographie des Petrus Ramus," *Zeitschrift für Philosophie und Philosophische Kritik*, CXXI (1903), 141-142, where there is a convincing demonstration that Cephas Chlononius means Ramus in Ascham's letter.

to Ramus's philosophy.[3] Another very early reference, much more detailed, much more sympathetic, and not at all difficult to identify, is also the work of Ascham, and can be found in the letter which he wrote to Sturm on January 29, 1552, from Halle, when he was in the midst of a period of travel on the continent.[4] On this occasion, Ascham asks with some urgency that Sturm write him at once on a piece of news he has just heard. Some English friends of mine, says Ascham, inform me that Peter Ramus has written something critical against you and me as a result of your publication at Strasbourg of our correspondence.[5] You know what I think of Ramus from my previous letters to you, Ascham goes on; how much I approve of the spirit of his teaching, and of his general plan, which I take to be that of tearing to pieces some inept and insipid Aristotelians rather than that of refuting Aristotle himself. Unless you have forgotten my words or have torn up my letter, he continues, you will remember how much I prefer Ramus to Périon, the Ciceronianisms of whom I laughed at with Martin Bucer, as Philipp Melanchthon and I have laughed at his inept planning and bad arranging. Ramus appears to me, he says in an illuminating passage, to feel rightly concerning the doctrine of Christ, and to conceal his true opinions as the times may dictate, showing his zeal meanwhile by writing against those whom he perceives as deliberate adversaries of the true religion. And this judgment of mine concerning Ramus, he adds, has been confirmed by our Jerome Wolf, who has been in Paris and afterwards in Augsburg.

Ascham turns next to a more detailed exposition of his view of Ramism. I hope, he writes, that my former letters, and this present one, contain nothing in the way of license of expression; and yet my praise of the talent and the teaching of Ramus has been expressed both openly and silently, and my approval of his general position has been set forth in the following words:

> The excellent doctrine of Aristotle seems too devoid of adornment, too obscure, for delight in reading it to be able to arouse the zeal of the many, or for the usefulness of it to be able to compensate for the labors involved, because almost everywhere it is taught without the accurate use of examples.

[3] On this point see Wilson and Forbes, *Gabriel Harvey's "Ciceronianus,"* p. 19.
[4] For the complete Latin text of this letter, see Giles, *Works of Ascham*, vol. I, pt. II, pp. 318-322; for a translation of two brief excerpts, see vol. I, pt. I, pp. lxxvi-lxxvii.
[5] The reference is to *Rogeri Aschami et Joannis Sturmii Epistolae Duae de Nobilitate Anglicana* (Argentorati: Richelius excudebat, 1551). There is a copy of this work in the Bibliothèque Nationale.

This declaration, by the way, is the copy of a sentence which Ascham had already used in his letter to Sturm of April 4, 1550, in connection with his reference to Cephas Chlononius.[6] The fact that it is linked to Chlononius in the earlier letter, and to Ramus in the present one, permits us to be sure that Chlononius and Ramus are one and the same. Moreover, it permits us to see that Ascham and Ramus are together in insisting upon example or practice as the final confirmation of theory. Lest we miss his dedication to this tenet of Ramism, Ascham not only underlines now what he had said earlier, but he adds that he himself had always required theory to be accompanied by practice, lest studies appear uselessly involved in obscurity or rashly guided into error.

At this point in the letter of 1552, Ascham feels justified in re-asserting his friendly disposition towards Ramus and in mentioning his regret at the latter's recent attack upon the Sturm-Ascham correspondence. I suspect, says Ascham, that certain Englishmen from Cambridge, who disagree somewhat with us in religion, have turned Ramus against us out of religious hostility, although they themselves have left England and now live in Paris for religious reasons.

Ascham goes on to remark that Ramus's intelligence is shown nowhere to better advantage than in his having selected as his adversaries the three greatest of men, Aristotle, Cicero, and Sturm. As for his present attack upon me, says Ascham, "I am not astonished nor greatly distressed, if I displease Ramus, whom the Aristotles, the Ciceros, and the Sturms are not able to please."[7] Then he makes a remark which is not only calculated to drive a wedge between Sturm and Ramus, but also is destined to be the earliest reaction by an Englishman to Ramus's reform of dialectic and rhetoric. Says he to Sturm:

> Ramus, I believe, will press you and rush at you with the greater violence, since he knows that you refer invention in the first instance to the art of speaking, whereas he removes it from his own course in rhetoric; and since he also knows that delivery, which these very Ramists make much of, is rightly regarded by you, by Aristotle, and by the learned generally, as belonging more in the realm of practice than of theory.

[6] This declaration and my subsequent quotations from the letter of 1552 are in my translation. For the two versions of the declaration as given by Ascham, see Giles, *Works of Ascham*, vol. I, pt. I, p. 186, and vol. I, pt. II, p. 319.

[7] Giles, vol. I, pt. II, p. 320.

He now asks Sturm to assess the attack that Ramus has made upon their letters, and to refute it at some apt place in his next work, unless silence seems the better course. Apparently Ascham thinks himself unworthy of the task of defending his famous friend Sturm against an opponent as notable as Ramus; at any rate, he expresses his willingness to hide behind Sturm's shield, since, as he says, I myself have never written anything in the spirit of publicly refuting Ramus.

There is much else in this particular letter, but nothing that adds substantially to Ascham's opinion of Ramus. The letter is proof that Ascham wanted in 1552 to explain his earlier ambiguous estimate of Cephas Chlononius, and to make it very clear that he approved much more highly of Chlononius or Ramus than he ever had of Joachim Périon. The letter is also proof that Ascham had heard but the vaguest rumors about Ramus's attack upon the Sturm-Ascham correspondence—"some friends of mine write me from England" (these are his exact words), "that Peter Ramus has written I know not what against my letters and yours, published by you at Strasbourg."[8] Perhaps Ascham's English friends were only passing on to him the merest recent gossip. At any rate, the work in which Ramus attacks these letters has thus far remained unidentified beyond Ascham's excited little reference.[9]

As for the subsequent disposition of the two men towards each other, there is proof that it was friendly in the letter which Ramus wrote to Ascham from Paris on February 25, 1564, when Ascham was serving as Queen Elizabeth's secretary.[10] From what that letter says, it appears that one day, in the palace of the French king, Ramus chanced to meet a certain English nobleman, who thereupon gave him greetings in the name of Ascham. Ramus asked at once to know who was so interested in him in England that he would thus send a sign of his friendship across the sea to Páris. The nobleman replied with an account of Ascham's virtues and learning, and Ramus was so impressed that he began to consider ways of returning the compliment implied in Ascham's message of greeting. Now, Ramus goes on, a way has presented itself—a young man named Matthew

[8] Ibid., p. 318.

[9] See Charles Schmidt, La Vie et les Travaux de Jean Sturm (Strasbourg, 1855), p. 292. Among biographers of Ramus, the belief has persisted that Sturm and Ascham on their side were not unfriendly to Ramism; see Waddington, Ramus, pp. 393, 396; and Graves, Peter Ramus, pp. 93, 212, 214.

[10] For the text of this letter, see Giles, II, 96-97.

Scyne, of the staff of the English ambassador at Paris, Thomas Smith, is returning to England and has consented to bear my greetings to you. He has also consented, adds Ramus, to ask you about a certain book of Archimedes, περὶ ᾿ισομέτρων, which I have heard to be in the possession of a learned physician of your court.[11] If that physician could supply me with a copy, Ramus continues, I would be glad to supply him in turn with a certain rarer thing of Pappus and Apollonius and Serenus in that same field. Ramus concludes with the promise that if the mathematical studies to which he is now giving himself are benefited by the manuscript in question, he will feel himself perfected by the great fruit of Ascham's mind.

Despite these blandishments, or perhaps because of their faintly patronizing air, Ascham had not become a convert to Ramism at the time of his death in 1568. In his famous *Scholemaster*, first published in 1570, he takes the side of Aristotle in logic and Cicero in rhetoric against anyone who criticizes them, and he specifically mentions Ramus and Talaeus as their critics, although Quintilian is singled out as the chief culprit in that vein. Says Ascham:

> *Quintilian* also preferreth translation before all other exercises: yet having a lust to dissent from *Tullie* (as he doth in very many places, if a man read his Rhetoricke over advisedlie, and that rather of an envious minde, than of any just cause) doth greatlie commend *Paraphrasis*, crossing spitefullie *Tullies* judgement in refusing the same: and so do *Ramus* and *Talaeus* even at this day in *France* to.[12]

Such singularity in dissenting from the best men's judgment, Ascham goes on, is not popular with discreet and wise learning. He adds:

> For he, that can neither like *Aristotle* in Logicke and Philosophie, nor *Tullie* in Rhetoricke and Eloquence, will from these steppes likelie enough presume by like pride to mount hier, to the misliking of greater matters: that is either in Religion, to have a dissentious head, or in the common wealth, to have a factious hart.[13]

[11] Ramus is apparently asking here for a copy of Heron's *Mensurae*, the final section of which in its original Greek text is headed περὶ μέτρων. In a certain Paris manuscript of a work of Archimedes (Paris 2361), Heron's *Mensurae* is attached to Archimedes's *Quadratura Parabolae*, and in another Paris manuscript of Archimedes (Paris 2360), the *Mensurae* does not appear. Possibly Ramus wants to satisfy himself about this item by looking at other manuscripts, particularly that belonging to the English physician. For a discussion of these two Paris manuscripts of Archimedes, see *The Works of Archimedes*, ed. T. L. Heath (Cambridge, 1897), pp. xxiv-xxv.

[12] Roger Ascham, *The Scholemaster*, ed. John E. B. Mayor (London, 1863), p. 101.

[13] *Ibid.*, pp. 101-102.

At this point Ascham recalls the case of a Cambridge student who had begun by dissenting from Aristotle and had ended by adopting the Arian heresy. Then comes Ascham's parting shot at Ramus:

> But to leave these hye pointes of divinitie, surelie, in this quiet and harmeles controversie, for the liking or misliking of *Paraphrasis* for a yong scholer, even as far as *Tullie* goeth beyond *Quintilian*, *Ramus* and *Talaeus* in perfite Eloquence, even so moch by myne opinion cum they behinde *Tullie* for trew judgement in teaching the same.[14]

In 1569, the year before these words were first published, a Cambridge student named Gabriel Harvey chanced to buy a copy of Ramus's *Ciceronianus*. That copy, now in Worcester College Library at Oxford, contains a note by Harvey himself which says: "I redd ouer this Ciceronianus twise in twoo dayes, being then Sophister in Christes College."[15] By the year 1573, having meanwhile become master of arts at Cambridge, Harvey was appointed Greek reader in Pembroke Hall, and soon was referring publicly to Ramus as "not indeed that branch, but, if I may so speak, a most flourishing tree, not merely of both the grammars, but of every last one of the arts."[16] This mention of Ramus as a branch is, by the way, Harvey's little pun, since "ramus" is the common Latin term for the branch of a tree; and the witticism calls to mind Thomas Drant's similar word-play in his verse preface to Carter's edition of Seton's *Dialectica* in 1572.[17] But Harvey's completely serious recognition of Ramus as an authority on the liberal arts, and his earlier undergraduate absorption in Ramus's *Ciceronianus*, are indications that Ascham and his generation were beginning in the first years of the fifteen-seventies to lose the struggle to keep Aristotle and Cicero supreme in logic and rhetoric.

Indeed, so far as instruction in rhetoric at Ascham's own Cambridge is concerned, the supremacy of Cicero was challenged as early as April 23, 1574. That was the date when Harvey was appointed praelector in rhetoric at his alma mater and began the preparation of the lectures which, as delivered in the spring of 1575 and 1576, and as published in 1577, are the first heavy commitment by an Eng-

---

[14] *Ibid.*, p. 102.

[15] See Wilson and Forbes, *Gabriel Harvey's "Ciceronianus,"* p. 18.

[16] *Ibid.*, p. 20. Harvey's words as quoted by Wilson and Forbes are: "Ramus, non ille quidem Ramus, sed arbor, vt ita dicam, cunctarum Artium, non modo vtriusque Grammaticae, florentissima." Translation mine.

[17] See above, pp. 55-56, and note 76.

lishman to the rhetorical thinking of Ramus and Talaeus.[18] Those lectures will be discussed later when I speak of Ramistic rhetoric in England.

As for Ramistic logic, it was established as a part of English learning before the date of Harvey's lectures. Its earliest expounder at Cambridge was Laurence Chaderton (or Chatterton), older than Harvey by several years, but like him a member of Christ's College. Chaderton was fellow of Christ's between 1568 and 1577, and thus was in a position to influence Harvey at the very time when the latter became enamored of Ramus's *Ciceronianus*. During Chaderton's period of service as fellow of Christ's, he held the office of reader in logic in the public schools of the university, and, "lecturing on the *Ars logica* of Peter Ramus, roused a great interest in that study," as his biographer puts it.[19] But Chaderton's lectures were never published. The earliest published advocacy of Ramistic logic in England was not from a Cambridge man, but from a Scot named Roland MacIlmaine of the University of St. Andrews.

MacIlmaine's life seems to have escaped the prying eyes of biographers. So far as I know, only three main facts can confidently be asserted of him. The first is that he took his master's degree from St. Mary's College of the University of St. Andrews in 1570, after having enrolled in that college in 1565 and graduated as bachelor of arts on March 7, 1569.[20] The second is that he published at London in 1574 the earliest Latin text of Ramus's *Dialecticae Libri Duo* to be printed on English soil, the publisher being Thomas Vautrollier, who was given a patent on June 19 of that year to bring out MacIlmaine's edition for a ten-year period.[21] Thirdly, MacIlmaine pub-

---

[18] The best authorities for the dates of these lectures are Wilson and Forbes, *Gabriel Harvey's "Ciceronianus,"* pp. 5-10.

[19] E. S. Shuckburgh, *Laurence Chaderton, D. D. (First Master of Emmanuel) Translated from a Latin Memoir of Dr. Dillingham* (Cambridge, 1884), p. 5. Harvey himself has been called "the earliest English advocate of Ramus" by Harold S. Wilson, "Gabriel Harvey's Orations on Rhetoric," *English Literary History,* XII (September 1945), 180. But it seems more accurate to think of him only as the first English Ramist in rhetoric. Chaderton was probably earlier than Harvey in advocating Ramus publicly, and MacIlmaine certainly was.

[20] See James Maitland Anderson, *Early Records of the University of St. Andrews* (Edinburgh, 1926), pp. 164, 165, 273.

[21] See Arber, *Transcript of the Registers,* II, 746, 886.

The title page of this edition reads: "P. Rami Regii Professoris Dialecticae Libri Dvo. Exemplis omnium artium & scientiarum illustrati, nō solùm Diuinis, sed etiam mystisis, Mathematicis, Phisicis, Medicis, Iuridicis, Poëticis & Oratoriis. Per Rolandum Makilmenaeum Scotum. Londini, Excudebat Thomas Vautrollerius. 1574. Cum Priuilegio Regiae Maiestatis." A second edition of this work came from the same press in 1576. Waddington, *Ramus,* p. 454, lists two later editions at Frankfurt, one in 1579 and the other in 1580.

lished in 1574 at the same press the earliest English translation of Ramus's chief work, calling it *The Logike of the moste Excellent Philosopher P. Ramus Martyr, Newly translated, and in diuers places corrected, after the mynde of the Author.*[22]

MacIlmaine's translation, which I should like now to consider in some detail, is introduced by an epistle to the reader, wherein he comments with obvious enthusiasm upon several aspects of Ramus's reform of logic. If the translation is to be regarded as the first English exposition of Ramistic logic in words derived from Ramus, the introduction becomes not only the first parallel effort in an Englishman's own words, but also the official opening salvo in the battle to convert Englishmen to that logic and to Ramism as a whole.

MacIlmaine begins his campaign of exposition and persuasion by stressing the classical origins of Ramistic logic. He says that this logic comes from Aristotle's *Organon*, *Physics*, and *Metaphysics*, as well as from Cicero's rhetorical works and from Quintilian's *Institutio Oratoria*. What Ramus had done, MacIlmaine implies, was to take these basic writings and distill from them their fundamental logical precepts. Here are MacIlmaine's own words about the sources of Ramus's work:

> As fore the matter whiche it containethe, thou shalt vnderstand that there is nothing appartayning to dialectike eyther in Aristotles xvij. booke of logike, in his eight bookes of Phisike, or in his xiiij. bookes of Philosophie, in Cicero his bookes of Oratorie, or in Quintilian (in the which there is almost nothing that dothe not eyther appartayne to the inuention of arguments a [sic] disposition of the same), but thou shalt fynde it shortlie and after a perfecte methode in this booke declared.[23]

By way of elaboration, he remarks that no argument in practical life can be found which is not classifiable either under Ramus's nine types of artistic argument or under his tenth type, the non-artistic argument. He emphasizes next that there exists "no sort of disposition whiche dothe not appartayne eyther to the iudgement of the proposition, sylogisme or methode." In these two statements he indicates his belief in Ramus's ten topics of invention as an exhaustive

[22] The rest of the title page reads: "Per M. Roll. Makylmenaeum Scotum, rogatu viri honestissimi, M. Aegidij Hamlini. Imprinted at London by Thomas Vautroullier dwelling in the Blackefrieres. Anno. M. D. LXXIIII. Cvm Privilegio." A second edition of this work was produced at the same press in 1581. My references are to the first edition.

[23] pp. 7-8.

account of the problem of analysis in learned or popular composition, and his belief that the problem of synthesis consists only in framing ideas into the three structural units, that is, into propositions, syllogisms, and treatises.

The next large point of emphasis in MacIlmaine's advocacy of Ramism is that the character of Ramistic logic or of any discipline built upon it is determined by the famous three laws. If you marvel, he says, that my short volume contains everything I have indicated, the best explanation is that "in this booke there is thre documents or rules kept, whiche in deede ought to be obserued in all artes and sciences." These three documents are then explained each in turn.

The law of justice, which ordinarily is ranked second by the Ramists, is given the primary place in MacIlmaine's discussion, possibly because it would seem to Englishmen to have produced the most spectacular of the results which Ramus had achieved. MacIlmaine explains it thus:

> The first is, that in setting forthe of an arte we gather only togeather that which dothe appartayne to the Arte whiche we intreate of, leauing to all other Artes that which is proper to them, this rule (which maye be called the rule of Iustice) thou shalt see here well obserued.[24]

In my book, adds MacIlmaine, are all the things which pertain to logic, and not one of the things which pertain to grammar, rhetoric, physics, or any other discipline. Many years ago, he continues, a shoemaker criticized the clothing that Apelles had drawn on a figure in one of his pictures; and Apelles replied that the shoemaker should keep to his own art and criticize only the figure's shoes. Thus did Apelles teach the law of justice. Any writer on any art breaks this law when he digresses from his purpose. Concluding this part of his explanation of Ramism, MacIlmaine observes:

> Is he not worthie to be mocked of all men, that purposethe to wryte of Grammer, and in euery other chapiter mynglethe somthing of Logicke, and some thing of Rethoricke: and contrarie when he purposethe to write of Logicke dothe speake of Grammer and of Rethoricke?[25]

The law of truth, as another great principle in the Ramistic criticism of knowledge, is given its first English formulation in the following words of MacIlmaine:

[24] p. 8.   [25] p. 9.

The seconde document (which diligently is obserued in this booke) is that all the rules and preceptes of thine arte be of necessitie tru, whiche Aristotle requirethe in the seconde booke of his Analitikes and in diuerse chapiters in his former booke.[26]

Like Ramus, MacIlmaine is interested in applications. Thus he cautions that writers or teachers violate this second law whenever their precepts are mingled with anything false, ambiguous, or uncertain—"as if in theaching me my logicke, which consistethe in rules to inuente argumentes, and to dispone and iudge the same, thou shouldest begyn to tell me some trickes of poysonable sophistrie."[27] And he adds, with special reference to the world of use, that the law of truth should be planted in all hearts, particularly in the hearts of ministers.

As for the law of wisdom, MacIlmaine formulates it to apply in the first instance to the problem of organizing discourse. Thus he says:

> The third documente which thou shalt note herein obserued, is, that thou intreate of thy rules which be generall generallye, and those whiche be speciall speciallie, and at one tyme, without any vaine repetitions, which dothe nothing but fyll vp the paper. For it is not sufficient that thou kepe the rule of veritie and iustice, without thou obserue also this documente of wisedome, to dispute of euery thing according to his nature.[28]

Observing that one plays the sophist's part if he treats general matters particularly, or particular matters generally, and that one falls thereby into tautologies and redundancies, which of all things are most hostile to the arts and sciences, MacIlmaine proceeds to illustrate what the violation of this third law means to him. If I ask what logic is, he declares, and you reply that it teaches how to invent arguments, your answer is in accord with the law of truth but not the law of wisdom, for you have treated a general thing particularly. "I aske the," he explains further, "for the definition of the whole arte, and thow geuest me the definition of inuention, which is but parte of the arte."[29]

Thus does MacIlmaine advocate Ramism by stressing its classical origins and its characteristics as determined by the three laws. His next step is to lay emphasis upon its theory of method. The method followed in my work, says he, is that of placing first what is most clear, and next what is next most clear, and so on. "And therfore,"

[26] p. 9. [27] pp. 9-10. [28] p. 10. [29] p. 11.

he remarks, "it continually procedethe from the generall to the speciall and singuler."[30] His immediate elaboration of this principle of structure is thoroughly Ramistic:

> The definition as most generall is first placed, next folowethe the diuision, first into the partes, and next into the formes and kyndes. Euery parte and forme is defined in his owne place, and made manifest by examples of auncient Authors, and last the members are limited and ioined togeather with short transitions for the recreation of the Reader.[31]

This, remarks MacIlmaine, is the perfect method. This is the method observed by Plato, Aristotle, and all the ancient historians, orators, and poets. This is the method which was lost to view for many years and is now raised as it were from death by that most learned man and martyr to God, Petrus Ramus.

MacIlmaine in his introduction and translation does not stress method in Ramistic philosophy in the terms that Ramus had insisted upon. We know that Ramus thought of method as either natural or prudential.[32] We also know that, while his special affection was bestowed upon the natural method, which he considered to be applicable to scientific discourse and also to poetry and oratory, he gave at least a respectable amount of space to the prudential method, and made it the strategy of presenting material to the unread populace. In his introduction MacIlmaine says nothing to suggest his awareness of the prudential method as Ramus conceived of it. The final chapter of his translation, which is brief, hurried, and even contemptuous, has something that might pass for an account of the prudential method, although his comments at that point would limit it to the uses of deceit and to the procedures of irrelevance, digression, and inversion. In thus allowing the prudential method to become almost completely inactive as an element in Ramism, MacIlmaine is lending support to the notion that Ramus advocated only the natural method, and this notion gradually became influential in England.

The final point of emphasis in MacIlmaine's advocacy of Ramism is that the new logic is intended to serve the preacher, the scientist, the lawyer, the orator, the mathematician, and indeed all writers, teachers, and learners. In other words, it is the theory of communication, so far as any communication must have subject matter and form, and thus it reaches into the practical world at the points where com-

---

[30] p. 12.   [31] p. 12.   [32] See above, pp. 160-165.

[183]

munications are necessary parts of the pattern of culture. We are fortunate in having from MacIlmaine an account of the uses of Ramistic logic, if only to give our expectations on this score a precise Elizabethan formulation.

If you are a divine, says MacIlmaine, you will have to accommodate the principles of Ramistic logic to your own special needs. Thus, instead of beginning your sermon with a definition, as the strict method of logic would dictate, you begin instead with a statement of the sum of the text you have taken in hand to interpret. Next you divide the text into a few heads, so that the hearer may better remember your discourse. Next you treat each head in terms of the ten places of invention, showing causes, effects, adjuncts, comparisons, and so on. Lastly, you make your matter plain and manifest with familiar examples and authorities from the word of God.

MacIlmaine next supposes his reader to be a doctor of medicine about to deliver a lecture upon the subject of a fever. I shall quote this passage in full for its interest to students of the theory of communication and to students of Elizabethan science:

Yf thou be a Phisition and willing to teache (as for example) of a feuer, this methode willethe thee to shewe first the definition, that is, what a feuer is, Next the deuision, declaring what sorte of feuer it is, whether the quartane, quotidian, hecticke, or what other: thirdly to come to the places of inuention, and shewe fyrst the causes of the feuer euery one in order, the efficient, as maye be hotte meates, the matter as melancolie, choler, or some rotten humor, and soforthe with the formale causes and finall. The seconde place is theffecte, shewe then what the feuer is able to bring forthe, whether deathe or no. The third place wishethe thee to tell the subiecte of the feuer, whether it be in the vaines, artiers, or els where. The fowrthe to shewe the signes and tokens which appeare to pretende lyfe or deathe: and to be shorte, thou shalt passe thoroughe the rest of the artificiall places, and do that which is requyred in euery of them: And last come to the confirmyng of thy sayinges by examples, aucthorities, and (as Hippocrates and Galen haue done) by histories and long experience. After this Methode Heraclitus the Philosopher examyned the phisitions whiche came to heale hym, and because they were ignorant and could not aunswere to his interrogations he sent them away, and woulde receyue none of their Medicens: for (sayd he) yf ye can not shewe me the causes of my sicknes, much lesse areye able to take the cause awaye.[33]

After this extended reference to the scientist in his relation to the

[33] pp. 13-14.

inventional scheme of Ramistic logic, MacIlmaine turns next to the lawyer, the orator, and the mathematician, all of whom are expected to find their own problems of communication better solved in the new logic than in the old. "So the lawyer," says MacIlmaine, "shall pleade his cause, in prouyng or disprouyng after as his matter shall requier, with these ten places of Inuention, and dispone euery thing orderlie into his propositions, syllogismes, and methode."[34] "So shall the Orator declayme," he remarks. So shall the mathematicians set forth their demonstrations. And, to be brief, he says, "bothe in wrytyng, teaching, and in learnyng, thou mayest alwayes kepe these thre golden documentes in intreatyng thy matter, and this most ingenious and artificial methode for the exacte forme and disposition of the same."

The final steps in MacIlmaine's advocacy of Ramism consist in his statement that it brings more profit to the reader in two months than would a four-year study of Plato and Aristotle as they were then available to the public; and in his further statement that, in being offered in English, Ramistic logic is a rebuke to those who "woulde haue all thinges kept close eyther in the Hebrewe, Greke, or Latyn tongues." Like a true son of the Reformation he says of the hostility to translations that "I knowe what great hurte hathe come to the Churche of God by the defence of this mischeuous opinion."[35] He reminds his readers that Aristotle and Plato wrote in their native tongue, not in Hebrew or Latin, and that Cicero wrote in his native tongue, not in Greek. "Shall we," he demands, "then thinke the Scottyshe or Englishe tongue, it not fitt to wrote any arte into?" And he answers his question with a resounding "No in dede."

In the pages that follow his introductory epistle, MacIlmaine proceeds to set forth the ten places of invention and the three aspects of disposition, thus bringing into English the basic concepts of his source. But he does more than that. His translation manages to keep Englishmen reminded of the zeal with which the Ramists viewed their own accomplishments. This zeal is figured forth in his way of presenting the account of the logician using Ramus's theory of method to classify the various precepts of grammar as they are drawn on individual slips of paper from a disordered mass of slips containing in sum the whole body of grammatical knowledge.[36] This zeal is also displayed in his fondness for illustrating logic by repeated refer-

[34] p. 14.   [35] p. 15.
[36] pp. 95-96. For Ramus's use of this example, see above, pp. 161-162.

ences to the liberal disciplines as reformed by Ramus. Thus he illustrates perfect definition by calling grammar "an Arte which teachethe to speake well and congruouslye," rhetoric, to speak "eloquentlye," dialectic, "to dispute well," and geometry, "to Measure well."[37] Thus he illustrates distribution by describing one of its forms as follows:

> So Grammer is parted into Etimologie and Syntaxe. Rethoricke, into Elocution and Action: Dialecticke, into Inuention and Judgemente.[38]

One additional illustration of this zeal is found in his translation of Ramus's three laws, where his words seem to contain a note of triumph and finality. He says:

> And here we haue three generall documentes to be obserued in all artes and sciences. The first is that all the preceptes and rules shoulde be generall and of necessitie true: and this is called a documente of veritie. The seconde that euery arte be contained within his owne boundes, and withholde nothing appartaining to other artes, and is named a documente of iustice. The third, that euery thing be taught according to his nature, that is: generall thinges, generally: and particuler, particulerly: and this is called a documente of wysdome.[39]

It has already been pointed out that MacIlmaine does not translate with adequacy what Ramus said about the prudential method. In fact, he converts Ramism into English with this part almost completely missing. On the other hand, he occasionally adds material to that found in Ramus's own writings, his apparent purpose being to reclassify certain subheads of doctrine under still stricter dichotomies. For example, Ramus himself divides artistic arguments into primary and derivative primary; and under the one heading he handles six, and under the other, three, of his ten basic places of invention. MacIlmaine adds some complications to this procedure by subdividing primary arguments into two classes, and by subdividing those two classes so that the first yields five of the ten places of invention, and the other, one, whereas the remaining four places are left where Ramus had originally put them. In other words, MacIlmaine introduces some organizational flourishes into a doctrine already organized within an inch of its life. The new ingredients act, of course, to make Ramus's natural method seem more heavily addicted to dichotomies than it had been in his own works.

---

[37] p. 62. See also pp. 28, 96. For these definitions and partitions in Ramus, see above, p. 151.

[38] p. 55.   [39] p. 74.

In one other respect, MacIlmaine's translation changes the original direction of Ramism. While discussing effect as the second of the ten places of invention, Ramus's *Dialectiqve* of 1555 uses illustrations from Virgil and Horace, whereas MacIlmaine's translation deletes the Virgilian lines and substitutes for them a quotation made up from the first six verses of the eleventh chapter of Matthew.[40] Again, in discussing subject as the third of the places of invention, the *Dialectiqve* uses illustrations from Virgil, Cicero, and Propertius, whereas MacIlmaine confines himself to a single illustration from the thirteenth chapter of Numbers.[41] Still again, in discussing similitudes as one of the aspects of the sixth place of invention, the *Dialectiqve* draws examples from Cicero, Ovid, and Virgil, whereas MacIlmaine drops Ovid and adds passages from Matthew and Genesis.[42] These are not isolated instances of MacIlmaine's tendency to mix sacred with secular illustrations at points where Ramus remains coolly secular.[43] The shift towards a concern for scriptural illustration indicates that logic is being specifically emphasized by MacIlmaine as a tool of the preacher and the theological controversialist, although of course it always had had its obvious application to religious advocacy. Scriptural illustrations were to become still more prominent in the second English translation of Ramistic logic ten years later.

It is needless at this moment to give an analysis of the Latin text of the *Dialecticae Libri Dvo* as edited by MacIlmaine and published at London in 1574 and 1576. But that text should never be forgotten in any historical evaluation of the English Ramists. MacIlmaine intended his Latin version for the learned world, even as he intended his translation for the general public. Thus he established two distinct trends in English scholarship, and each was to have consequences in the period between 1574 and 1700, as the following discussion will indicate in detail. Either trend by itself makes Ramus into an important influence on English logic and rhetoric during the late sixteenth and the entire seventeenth centuries. Both trends considered together amount almost to a complete monopoly for Ramus's logical and rhetorical theory in England in the early part of that epoch and to a position of considerable weight throughout.

The beginnings of MacIlmaine's interest in Ramism cannot be

---

[40] Compare *Dialectiqve*, pp. 20-22, with *Logike*, pp. 29-30.

[41] Compare *Dialectiqve*, pp. 22-23, with *Logike*, pp. 30-32.

[42] Compare *Dialectiqve*, pp. 41-44, with *Logike*, pp. 46-48.

[43] Compare *Dialectiqve*, pp. 34-37, 44-46, 46-48, 55-56, 61-62, with *Logike*, pp. 43-44, 49, 51-54, 60, 67-69.

exactly accounted for. Two probabilities may be cited, however, to link the reforms of the French logician with Scotland and the Scots at the time of MacIlmaine's residence at St. Andrews. Chief of these probabilities is that the dedication of Foclin's *Rhetoriqve* to Mary Queen of Scots would be likely to give Ramism some special prestige in Scottish universities in the period between 1555 and 1567. The other probability is that James Stewart, Earl of Mar and of Moray, who became regent of Scotland in 1567, after the abdication of Queen Mary and the succession of her one-year-old son to the throne, had once studied under Ramus when the latter was principal of the College of Presle,[44] and would be likely, as an alumnus of St. Andrews and a person of real authority in its affairs, to impart some prestige to Ramism at his alma mater, particularly during his regency, which covered the last three years of MacIlmaine's student life.

An attempt has been made to link George Buchanan with the Scottish interest in Ramus,[45] and on the surface this distinguished poet and humanist seems well suited to the task of transporting Ramism from France to Scotland. After all, Buchanan had more contacts with European scholars than did any of his Scottish contemporaries, and he served as principal of one of the colleges at St. Andrews in the period when Ramistic influences of some kind were effectively at work upon the very generation to which MacIlmaine himself belonged. But against the acceptance of Buchanan as a Ramist is the fact that his plan for the reform of St. Andrews, as composed in the middle fifteen-sixties, advocates Cicero for rhetoric and Aristotle for logic.[46] And against it also is the fact that, during his two lengthy periods of residence on the continent between 1526 and 1561, Buchanan was a close associate of the family of Gouvea, the most celebrated of whom was the legal scholar Antonio, Ramus's implacable foe.[47]

[44] See David Irving, *Memoirs of the Life and Writings of George Buchanan* (Edinburgh, 1817), p. 100; also Waddington, *Ramus*, p. 396. Ramus was principal of the College of Presle in Paris between 1545 and 1551. See Waddington, *Ramus*, pp. 62-79. James Stewart was in France in 1548 and again in 1550. See *Dictionary of National Biography*, s.v. Stewart, Lord James. One of those years is no doubt the date of his studies under Ramus.

[45] See for example Waddington, *Ramus*, p. 396; Mullinger, *University of Cambridge*, II, 410; Graves, *Peter Ramus*, p. 213.

[46] See "Mr George Buchanan's Opinion anent the Reformation of the Universitie of St Andros," in *Vernacular Writings of George Buchanan*, ed. Peter Hume Brown (Edinburgh and London, 1892), pp. 9, 12.

[47] For an account of the controversy between Ramus and Gouvea, see Waddington,

Andrew Melville, another distinguished Scottish educator of the second half of the sixteenth century, has also been linked with his country's interest in Ramism.[48] But he could hardly have influenced MacIlmaine in any real sense, since he left St. Andrews before MacIlmaine entered, and lived on the continent between 1564 and 1573, his advocacy of Ramism in Scotland being a matter of importance only after he became principal of the University of Glasgow in the very year when MacIlmaine published the works which have just been discussed.

Although St. Andrews appears to have been the first center of Ramism in the British Isles, Cambridge was not far behind, as mentioned earlier. But what of Oxford? The view has been widely stated that that university remained loyal to Aristotle and gave Ramus no real reception.[49] Was that its actual attitude between 1574 and 1618? There is evidence to support a mild negative answer.

The first piece of evidence is provided by the story of John Barebone as told by Anthony à Wood. Barebone, a member of Magdalen College at Oxford, bachelor of arts in 1570, and a fellow of Magdalen for seven years after 1571, had a reputation as a noted and zealous Ramist when he applied for his master's degree in April, 1574. In his disputations and daily colloquies he had given great offense by his manner of rejecting Aristotle, of practicing the logical method of Ramus, and of indulging on every possible occasion in bitter controversy. Accordingly, he was told that his application for a master's degree would be denied unless he agreed to undergo certain exercises in addition to those prescribed under the new statutes. These special exercises were to consist in his defending against all opposition the three Aristotelian theses that would be propounded to him publicly at the proper time, and in his confessing publicly in his introductory remarks that he had given his teachers offense by disputing against them with too much acrimony.[50]

Ramus, pp. 39-42. For a brief sketch of Buchanan's relations with the family of Gouvea, see Irving, *op. cit.*, pp. 67-71, 79-83, 188.

[48] *Dictionary of National Biography*, s.v. Melville or Melvill, Andrew (1545-1622), says that Melville went to France in 1564, where he "came under the direct influence of Peter Ramus, whose new methods of teaching he subsequently transplanted to Scotland."

[49] See Waddington, *Ramus*, p. 396; Mullinger, *University of Cambridge*, II, 410-411; Graves, *Peter Ramus*, p. 212; Charles Edward Mallet, *A History of the University of Oxford* (New York, 1924-1928), II, 147-148; Wilson and Forbes, *op. cit.*, p. 19.

[50] For Wood's two versions of this story, see his *Historia et Antiquitates Universitatis Oxoniensis* (Oxford, 1674), Lib. I, p. 292, and his *The History and Antiquities of the University of Oxford*, ed. Gutch, II, 176.

This episode does not reflect hostility to Ramus on the part of Barebone's examiners. It reflects instead their lack of enthusiasm for a contentious young colleague who had already spent three years among them as fellow. It also reflects their conviction that no master of arts should be allowed to be wholly ignorant of Aristotle. Barebone apparently met the special requirements imposed upon him, for he is recorded as having received his master's degree on July 9, 1574. He later served as vice-president of Magdalen, was awarded his bachelor's degree in divinity, and became chaplain at Merton.[51]

Another piece of evidence bearing upon the interest in Ramus at Oxford is provided by John Case's *Specvlvm Moralivm Qvaestionvm*, published at Oxford in 1585, and accepted as the earliest book at the new Oxford press.[52] In his record of the doings of the year 1585, John Strype speaks of this book as follows:

> In the other university of Oxford was a new printing press erected about this year, (whether any before, I know not,) given as a suitable present to that university by the earl of Leicester, their high chancellor. And the first book printed there was a book of Ethics, made by one Case, a learned man there, entitled, *Speculum Quaestionum Moralium*. Which book the author dedicated to the said earl of Leicester, and to the lord Burghley, chancellor of the other university.[53]

Strype describes part of the contents of Case's dedicatory letter to the two chancellors in these words:

> And whereas at this time and somewhat before, another great contest arose in both universities, concerning the two philosophers, Aristotle and Ramus, then chiefly read, and which of them was rather to be studied; he gave them both their commendations and characters in his said epistle . . .[54]

Strype's immediate quotation from Case to illustrate what the latter says of Ramus and Aristotle is somewhat truncated and does not exactly represent its source. Case himself speaks thus:

> Still I cannot but acknowledge that the youthful ardor of mind in both universities has of late been fighting it out to determine whether in the mastering of the arts the great acuteness of Aristotle is of more worth than the flowing genius of Ramus. But, as I expect, the young

---

[51] See Joseph Foster, *Alumni Oxonienses* (Oxford, 1891), I, 68.

[52] See Madan, *Oxford Books*, I, 14-15.

[53] John Strype, *Annals of the Reformation and Establishment of Religion* (Oxford, 1824), vol. III, pt. I, p. 499.

[54] *Ibid.*, p. 500.

exalt such apostasy from the true experience of age and from the wise old custom of philosophizing, because beardless youth often does what white hair denies to have been rightly done . . . . I do not blame Ramus in this, for he was learned; I rather exalt Aristotle, for he stands out above all. But perhaps the young men will hold my work the poorer because I name in it the old interpreters of Aristotle.[55]

This is testimony from a former fellow of St. John's College in Oxford that the interest in Ramus in the years before 1585 was high at his university as well as at Cambridge, and that Oxford undergraduates were more inclined to the new logic than to the old. It is also an indication from a Catholic (for Case owed allegiance to Rome) that Ramism was respected outside of Protestant circles, and was not subject to a purely denominational preference. Case even allows an apologetic note to appear in his mention of his own present book and its alignment on the side of Aristotle—there is regret rather than scorn in his fear that the undergraduates will prefer Ramus to himself. And he knew the undergraduate temper, too. When this book appeared, he was privately teaching logic and philosophy to Roman Catholic undergraduates in his own home in Oxford, having left his fellowship at St. John's sometime before.

It must be recorded that on another occasion Case was again not so much an open opponent of Ramism as a neutral with some leanings towards Aristotle. He published in 1584 at London a companion-piece to the work just quoted. It too was in Latin, and its title page as it would read in English describes it as *The Sum of the Ancient Interpreters of the Entire Aristotelian Dialectic, showing what Ramus attacks truly or falsely in Aristotle, by the author John Case, formerly fellow of the college of St. John the Baptist of Oxford, Useful and Necessary to everyone attached to the Socratic and the Peripatetic Philosophy.*[56] Case's willingness to admit truth as well as error in Ramism is not the usual sign of the confirmed anti-Ramist of the fifteen-eighties. Indeed, a spirit of moderation in men-

[55] John Case, *Specvlvm Moralivm Qvaestionvm* (Oxford, 1585), fol. 5. Quoted by Mullinger, *University of Cambridge*, II, 411, note 1. Translation mine.

[56] This quotation is my translation of a substantial portion of the title page of the second edition of this work as published at Oxford in 1592. The Latin title page in the part covered by my quotation reads as follows: "Svmma vetervm Interpretvm in vniversam Dialecticam Aristotelis; qvam vere falsoue Ramus in Aristotelem inuehatur, ostendens. Auctore. Ioanne Case Oxoniensi, olim Collegii D. Ioannis Praecursoris socio. Omnibus Socraticae Peripateticaeque philosophiae studiosis in primis vtilis ac necessaria." See Madan, *Oxford Books*, I, 32-33.

tioning Ramus at that time is almost equivalent to a qualified endorsement of his position.

The great Richard Hooker, who received his bachelor's and master's degrees from Corpus Christi College at Oxford some seven years after Case's similar degrees from St. John's, saw faults rather than virtues in Ramism; but his criticism of Ramus is at least a sign that his alma mater did not neglect to consider that philosopher. In his treatise *Of the Lawes of Ecclesiasticall Politie*, published in a first installment of four books about 1593, Hooker speaks of Aristotle as having come closer by true art and learning to the parts of natural knowledge than any man since, and has this to add on a subject which he identifies as "Ramystry":

> In the pouertie of that other new deuised ayde two things there are notwithstanding singular. Of marueilous quicke dispatch it is, and doth shewe them that haue it as much almost in three dayes, as if it dwell threescore yeares with them. Againe because the curiositie of mans wit, doth many times with perill wade farther in the search of things, then were conuenient: the same is thereby restrayned vnto such generalities as euery where offering themselues, are apparent vnto men of the weakest conceipt that neede be. So as following the rules & precepts thereof, we may define it to be, an Art which teacheth the way of speedie discourse, and restrayneth the minde of man that it may not waxe ouer wise.[57]

Still another piece of evidence concerning the interest in Ramus at Oxford belongs to a period some twenty-five years after the first appearance of the treatise just quoted. On May 9, 1618, a young man named Richard Mather entered Brasenose College, Oxford, and was set the task of reading the works of Peter Ramus by his tutor, Dr. Thomas Worrall. Samuel Clark, who had personally known Mather, records the episode thus:

> Soon after his coming to *Oxford*, by a good providence, he came into acquaintance with learned Doctor *Woral*, who was very helpful to him by directing him in the course of his private Studies; and among other things, he advised him to read over the Works of the Learned

---

[57] Richard Hooker, *Of the Lavves of Ecclesiasticall Politie* (London, [1593?] 1597), pp. 58-59. This edition, a copy of which is in the Huntington Library, advertises itself as containing "Eyght Bookes," but in reality it contains only five, the fifth having its own title page, the date 1597, and separate pagination. The title page of the first four books bears no date, but the work was entered in the Stationers' Registers January 29, 1592 [i.e., 1593], and thus it was probably first published that year. See Arber, *Transcript of the Registers*, II, 625.

Peter Ramus; which Counsel he followed, and saw no cause to repent of his so doing.[58]

Mather spent only a few months at Oxford, however, and then left to become minister at Toxteth Park near Liverpool. During the next few years he identified himself with the puritans, was twice suspended from his ministry for nonconformity, and at length emigrated to New England, where he was preacher at Dorchester in Massachusetts from 1636 till his death in 1669. One of his sons, Samuel, was a member of the second graduating class at Harvard; another, Increase, was father of Cotton. Thus Richard Mather is a link not only between Ramism and the Oxford undergraduate of the second decade of the seventeenth century but also between Ramism and the religious leadership of early New England.[59]

This account of the influence of Ramus in Oxford has omitted his most influential follower at that institution, Charles Butler, of Magdalen College, who received his master's degree in 1587, and who may have been one of the young men that John Case had in mind in his reference to the debate over Aristotle and Ramus among students of both universities around 1585. It was to become Butler's function to prepare the books that carried Ramism into the public schools of England throughout the seventeenth century. Like Gabriel Harvey, however, he is mainly associated with Ramistic rhetoric and thus can be considered to good advantage later rather than now.

While Butler and his Oxford associates were at work in these various ways, successive generations of Cambridge men devoted themselves to the cause of Ramism and produced an astonishingly large number of treatises in the process. In fact, the influence of Ramus at Cambridge was more fruitful and more persistent even though no more actual than at Oxford. This will become incidentally apparent in the following account of the later stages of Ramism in England.

Debates in the learned world often had Ramism as an ingredient at the turn of the sixteenth century, and when they did so, they acted of course to perpetuate the interest which MacIlmaine had

---

[58] Samuel Clark, *The Lives Of sundry Eminent Persons in this Later Age* (London, 1683), pt. I, p. 128. For an account of Mather's tutor, and for Mather's dates at Oxford, see Foster, *Alumni Oxonienses*, s.v. Worrall, Thomas (Wirrall, Wyrell), of Cheshire, and Mather, Richard.

[59] For an authoritative discussion of the influence of Ramus in New England during the seventeenth century, see Perry Miller, *The New England Mind*, pp. 111-180, 312-330, 493-501.

introduced. Sometimes these debates concerned a cardinal tenet of Ramistic logic; sometimes the name of Ramus was bandied back and forth by the contending parties in the course of disputes upon themes outside of logical theory. History affords some good illustrations of each of these aspects of English Ramism.

Strype is the best authority for the opening stages of a controversy which involved Ramus's theory of method as its major issue. In his survey of literary events of the year 1580, he says:

> Let me add here the mention of a book writ against Everard Digby; the same with him, I suppose, that was fellow of St. John's college in Cambridge: against whom Dr. Whitaker, the master, took occasion by some branches of statute, to expel him the college: especially suspecting him to be a papist. Of which matter see the Life of Archbishop Whitgift.[60] This Digby had writ somewhat dialoguewise against Ramus's *Unica Methodus*: which in those times prevailed much; and perhaps brought into that college to be read; the rather, Ramus being a protestant, as well as a learned man. Whereupon one Francis Mildapet, a Navarrois, writ against Digby, in vindication of Ramus, a small book, entitled, *Admonitio ad Everardum Digby, Anglum, de Unica P. Rami Methodo, rejectis caeteris, retinenda.*[61]

Strype's reference to the dialogue against Ramus points at a Latin work by Digby, the title of which if translated would read thus: *Two Books on the Bipartite Method, in Refutation of the Unipartite Method of Peter Ramus, elucidating from the Best Authors a Plain, Easy, and Exact Way towards the Understanding of the Sciences.* This work was published at London by Henry Bynneman in 1580, having been entered in the Stationers' Registers under the date of May 3 of that year.[62] As Francis Bacon was to do some twenty-five years later in his *Advancement of Learning,* Digby advocated two methods, not one alone, for the organization of scientific discourses.[63] Immediately after his work appeared, it evoked a reply from the

---

[60] This is a reference to John Strype's *The Life and Acts of the Most Reverend Father in God, John Whitgift, D. D.* (London, 1718), pp. 271-273, where an account is given of Digby's expulsion by Whitaker and his subsequent reinstatement as a result of the intervention of Archbishop Whitgift. The latter's investigation indicated that Whitaker had suspected Digby of being a papist, but had removed him from his fellowship, not on that issue, but on a minor charge.

[61] Strype, *Annals,* vol. II, pt. 2, p. 405.

[62] Arber, *Transcript of the Registers,* II, 370. Digby's title reads: "De duplici methodo libri duo, unicam P. Rami methodum refutantes; in quibus via plana, expedita et exacta, secundum optimos autores, ad scientiarum cognitionem elucidatur."

[63] For this aspect of Bacon's theory of method, see below, pp. 369-370.

author mentioned by Strype. This author, Francis Mildapet, signed himself from Navarre in order to recall Ramus's student days at the College of Navarre in Paris, while his reply, as its title indicates, is intended as *An Admonition to Everard Digby, the Englishman, seeking the Preservation of the Unipartite Method of Peter Ramus, and the Rejection of Other Methods.*

Mildapet's *Admonition* is dedicated to Philip, Earl of Arundel. Its general position toward Digby's *Two Books* is indicated at the very outset in a Latin passage quoted and thus paraphrased by Strype:

> That is, that this dialogue was thought by some to be more boldly sent abroad than learnedly composed: and this writer esteemed it framed with no great judgment; and more wit than reason appeared throughout in it. So that Digby seemed to oppose Ramus's philosophy chiefly out of a prejudice against him upon the account of religion. But that which Digby's adversary did, was, as he said, that he thought it not amiss to unravel the artifice of that book; and to admonish Digby freely, and yet modestly, of retaining that *only method.*[64]

Strype has nothing further to say about the controvery between Digby and Mildapet. But it did not end at this point. By November 3, 1580, exactly six months after the entry of his *Two Books* for publication, Digby had contrived a reply to Mildapet, and had licensed it in the Stationers' Registers.[65] Its title, as it would be construed in English, is *A Response to the Admonition of F. Mildapet of Navarre concerning the Preservation of the Unipartite Method of P. Ramus.* This in turn provoked a reply from Mildapet early in 1581. In that reply we learn for the first time that Digby's opponent now and before was William Temple, a Cantabrigian of King's College. Temple was younger than Digby by some six or seven years, and the occupant of a fellowship in his college, though barely yet a master of arts. His rejoinder to Digby advertises itself as *A Dissertation of William Temple of King's College, Cambridge, on behalf of a Defense of Mildapet concerning the Unipartite Method, directed against the Lover of the Double Way; to which is added an Explanation of Some Questions in Physics and Ethics, along with a Letter concerning the Dialectic of Ramus, addressed to Johannes Piscator of Strasbourg.*[66] Not simply the opening dissertation against

---

[64] *Annals*, II, 2, 406.

[65] Arber, *Transcript of the Registers*, II, 381.

[66] The Latin title page reads: "Pro Mildapetti de vnica methodo defensione contra diplodophilum, commentatio gvlielmi tempelii, e regio collegio cantabrigiensis. Huc

Digby but the entire work is concerned with Ramism, the *Questions in Physics and Ethics* being directed at Georgius Lieblerus, a European defender of Aristotle against Ramus, whereas the *Letter concerning the Dialectic* is addressed to that Johannes Piscator who appears to have been at once a critic of Ramus's dialectic and a zealous editor of that philosopher's more discursive works.[67] Thus ended Temple's controversy with Digby. The whole affair gave the latter some reputation as a conservative philosopher; but it made Temple a leading exponent of Ramism in England and on the continent as well.[68]

Another controversy in which Ramus figured was that between Gabriel Harvey and Thomas Nash. During the last decade of the sixteenth century, these two Cantabrigians took offense at each other and exchanged insults in a series of printed works that reflect little credit upon either man. Robert Greene, also a Cantabrigian, was an ally of Nash in the early stages of this campaign of vilification, but he died before the pens of the main contestants had been half

accessit nonnvllarum e physicis & ethicis quaestionum explicatio, una cum Epistola de Rami dialectica ad Joannem Piscatorem Argentinensem. Londini, Pro Thoma Man. Anno 1581."

[67] On December 12, 1580, the following work was entered in the Stationers' Registers: *In. P. Rami. Dialecticam. animaduersiones Joanis Piscatoris Argentinensis. exemplis sacrarum Litterarum passim illustratae.* See Arber, *Transcript of the Registers*, II, 384. This work was published by Henry Bynneman at London under the date of 1581, and by Henry Middleton in a second edition at the same place under the date of 1583. An earlier edition at Frankfurt bears the date of 1580 and probably was the direct occasion for Temple's *Letter concerning the Dialectic*. Piscator's *Animaduersiones* along with Temple's letter and Piscator's reply were republished later at Frankfurt, whereas the two letters without the *Animaduersiones* appeared also at London in 1582. See the *Short-Title Catalogue*, s.v. Piscator, John; also *Dictionary of National Biography*, s.v. Temple, Sir William (1555-1627); also *Catalogue Générale des Livres Imprimés de la Bibliothèque Nationale*, s.v. Piscator, Johannes, Argentinensis. Piscator, also called Jean le Pêcheur, was a Calvinist theologian at Strasbourg. See Waddington, *Ramus*, p. 393. Bibliographers have attempted to distinguish between a Piscator of Herborn, a Piscator of Wittenberg, and a Piscator of Strasbourg. But these three are in reality one and the same man. See Walter J. Ong, S.J., "Johannes Piscator: One Man or a Ramist Dichotomy?" *Harvard Library Bulletin*, VIII (1954), 151-162.

[68] Temple wrote a preface for *De prima simplicium et concretorum corporum generatione disputatio* (Cambridge, 1584), a pro-Ramist work by James Martin (or Jacobus Martinus) of Dunkeld, Scotland. Martin had been professor of philosophy at Paris and Turin. To Martin's work and Temple's Preface, Andreas Libavius responded with his *Quaestionum physicarum controversarum inter Peripateticos et Rameos tractatus* (Frankfurt, 1591). Libavius, a German chemist, identified himself later with the attempt to combine Ramus's dialectic with that of Philipp Melanchthon; see his *De Dialectica aristotelica a Philippo Melanchthone et P. Ramo perspicue selecta et exposita* (Frankfurt, 1600); also his *Dialectica philippo-ramaea* (Frankfurt, 1608); and also Waddington, *Ramus*, p. 394. The men who sponsored this combination became known as the "Philippo-Ramists." See below, pp. 282-284.

emptied of poison. This is not the place for an account of the charges and countercharges that these masters of invective hurled at each other. It should be noted, however, that they attacked wherever they felt they could gain advantage, and that Ramus, as one of Harvey's idols, was not wholly spared.

In 1589, a year before this controversy had gotten under way, Nash contributed a preface to a printed version of *Menaphon*, the pastoral tale which his friend Greene had composed. His preface, addressed to "the Gentlemen Students of both Vniuersities," contains an approving reference to Gabriel Harvey as one of the four or five living authors of creditable Latin verse.[69] But elsewhere in the same work, after praising his own St. John's College at Cambridge "as an Vniuersitie within it selfe," Nash laments that the precepts of her learned men have not prospered, and that instead, especially in the training of preachers, "those yeares which shoulde bee employed in *Aristotle* are expired in Epitomes."[70] The Ramists, of course, were responsible not only for the popularity of epitomes of the liberal disciplines but also for the wide use of what Nash in the same passage calls "Compendiaries" and "abbreuiations of Artes." That Nash has Ramus specifically in mind as he wrote this preface is fully shown when he speaks of the superiority of Greene's "extemporall vaine" over "our greatest Art-masters deliberate thoughts." Invention like that of Greene is quicker than the eye, he declares, and its results are more admirable than those obtained by the proverbial seven years of labor. A perfection that requires the work of years owes more to time than to talent, more to industry than to inspiration. At least, Nash implies as much in the following words:

> What is he amongst Students so simple that cannot bring forth (*tandem aliquando*) some or other thing singular, sleeping betwixt euerie sentence? Was it not *Maros* xij. years toyle that so famed his xij. *Aeneidos*? Or *Peter Ramus* xvj. yeares paines that so praised his pettie Logique? Howe is it, then, our drowping wits should so wonder at an exquisite line that was his masters day labour?[71]

An even sharper slur upon Ramus occurs in Nash's *Anatomie of Absurditie*, also published before the Harvey-Nash controversy was

---

[69] See the text of Nash's preface as printed in G. Gregory Smith, *Elizabethan Critical Essays* (Oxford, 1904), I, 316.

[70] *Ibid.*, I, 313-314.

[71] *Ibid.*, I, 309. For Ramus's own estimate of the time he spent in composing his *Dialectiqve*, see above, p. 154.

fairly launched. Here Nash speaks of artificers who discredit art by their ignorance, who bring shame upon their office by their own impudence and presumption. Within this context he fits the following remarks:

> But as hee that censureth the dignitie of Poetry by *Cherillus* paultry paines, the maiestie of Rethorick by the rudenesse of a stutting *Hortensius*, the subtiltie of Logique by the rayling of *Ramus*, might iudge the one a foole in writing he knewe not what, the other tipsie by his stammering, the thirde the sonne of Zantippe by his scolding: so he that estimats Artes by the insolence of Idiots, who professe that wherein they are Infants, may deeme the Vniuersitie nought but the nurse of follie, and the knowledge of Artes nought but the imitation of the Stage.[72]

Shortly after these words were published, Richard Harvey, brother of Gabriel, made some slighting references to Greene and to his friend, Nash. Greene replied in *A Quip for an Upstart Courtier* by sneering at the humble parentage of the Harveys. To this Gabriel replied in *Fovre Letters and certaine Sonnets* (London, 1592). In the fourth of these letters, he takes pains to set Ramus in a better light than Nash had done:

> The vayne Peacocke with his gay coullours, and the prattling Parrat with his ignorant discourses (I am not to offend any but the Peacocke and the Parrat) haue garishly disguised the worthiest Artes, and deeply discredited the profoundest Artistes, to the pitifull defacement of the one and the shamefull preiudice of the other. *Rodolph Agricola, Philip Melancthon, Ludouike Viues, Peter Ramus*, and diuers excellent schollers haue earnestly complaned of Artes corrupted, and notably reformed many absurdities; but still corruption ingendreth one vermine or other, and still that pretious Traïnement is miserably abused which should be the fountaine of skill, the roote of vertue, the seminary of gouernment, the foundation of all priuate and publike good.[73]

Greene died a few months before the publication of Gabriel's *Fovre Letters*, and Nash was left to carry on the controversy alone. He answered Gabriel in a pamphlet called *Strange Newes* (London, 1592). Gabriel delivered an immediate reply in *Pierce's Supererogation*, which contains a passage mischievously hailing Nash as the

---

[72] The *Anatomie of Absurditie* is given by extract in Smith's *Elizabethan Critical Essays*, I, 321-337, the above quotation being on p. 334.

[73] In Smith, II, 236.

greatest confuter in an era of strenuous debates, particularly that between Peripatetics and Ramists.

> There was a time [writes Gabriel] when I floted in a sea of en-countring waues, and deuoured many famous confutations with an eager and insatiable appetite; especially Aristotle against Plato and the old Philosophers, diuers excellent Platonistes, indued with rare & diuine wittes (of whome elsewhere at large); Iustinus Martyr, Philoponus, Valla, Viues, Ramus, against Aristotle; oh, but the great maister of the schooles and high Chauncellour of Vniuersities could not want pregnant defence, Perionius, Gallandius, Carpentarius, Sceggius, Lieblerus, against Ramus; what? hath the royall Professour of Eloquence and Philosophy no fauourites? Talaeus, Ossatus, Freigius, Minos, Rodingus, Scribonius, for Ramus against them; and so foorth, in that hott contradictory course of Logique and Philosophy.[74]

Gabriel now turns the weapon of sarcasm against Nash as he continues:

> But alas, silly men, simple Aristotle, more simple Ramus, most simple the rest, either ye neuer knew what a sharpe-edged & cutting Confutation meant, or the date of your stale oppositions is expired, and a new-found land of confuting commodities discouered by this braue Columbus of tearmes and this onely marchant venturer of quarrels, that detecteth new Indies of Inuention & hath the winds of Aeolus at commaundement. Happy you flourishinge youthes that follow his in-comparable learned steps, and vnhappy we old Dunses that wanted such a worthy President of all nimble and liuely dexterities.[75]

Sterile as these invectives between Nash and Harvey are, they serve to indicate that Ramus is a familiar presence in the consciousness of the Elizabethans, and that the learned world of the fifteen-nineties, like the world of Temple and Digby ten years earlier, was still divided concerning him. In fact, his enemies and his friends continue to identify themselves before and after 1600 in other heated controversies. The case of William Gouge at Cambridge in the late fifteen-nineties, as related by Samuel Clark, gives us a view of a college debate over Ramus and of partisan feeling that ended in blows and a near riot. Says Clark:

> From the School at *Eaton* he was chosen to Kings Colledge in *Cambridge*, whither he went *Anno Christi* 1595; and at the first entrance

---

[74] *Ibid.*, II, 245-246. For Smith's notes on the cast of characters in this debate, see II, 431-432.
[75] *Ibid.*, II, 246.

of his studies, he applied himself to *Peter Ramus* his *Logick*, and grew so expert therein, that in the publick Schools he maintained and defended him, insomuch as when on a time divers *Sophisters* set themselves to vilifie *Ramus*, for which end the Respondent had given this question, *Nunquam erit magnus, cui Ramus est Magnus* [Never will he be great to whom Ramus is great], which some of the *Sophisters* hearing, and knowing the said *William Gouge* to be an acute disputant, and a stiff defender of *Ramus*, they went to the *Divinity* Schools, where he was then hearing an *Act*, and told him how in the other Schools they were abusing *Ramus*, he thereupon went into the *Sophisters* Schooles, and upon the Moderators calling for another Opponent, he stepped up, and brought such an argument as stumbled the Respondent, whereupon the Moderator took upon him to answer it, but could not satisfie the doubt: This occasioned a *Sophister* that stood by to say with a loud voice, *Do you come to vilifie* Ramus, *and cannot answer the Argument of a* Ramist? Whereupon the Moderator rose up, and gave him a box on the ear, then the School was all on an uproar; but the said *William Gouge* was safely conveyed out from amongst them.[76]

Gouge survived to take four degrees from Cambridge, to serve as fellow of his college for six years, to lecture there on logic and philosophy, and to hold a post as puritan divine during much of the period between 1607 and 1653. In addition to the anti-Ramists whom he successfully "stumbled" in the debate described by Clark, it is quite certain that he knew Richard Montagu during his life at Cambridge. At any rate, Montagu's years at King's College overlapped those of Gouge. Montagu became one of the antagonists of John Selden in a controversy during the early years of the seventeenth century on the question whether tithes are due by divine or by ecclesiastical law. Selden, an eminent legal scholar, whose collegiate education was begun at Hart Hall, Oxford, and continued at Clifford's Inn, argued against the justifying of tithes under divine law, his famous work on this subject being *The History of Tithes*, published in London in 1618. Montagu, a staunch defender of the Church of England against puritanism on one side and Catholicism on the other, replied to Selden by asserting that tithes are an obligation under divine law. During his reply, Montagu took occasion to censure Ramus and thereby to attack argumentative positions occupied by Selden.

[76] Samuel Clark, *Lives of Thirty-two Divines* (London, 1677), p. 235, as quoted in Mayor's edition of Ascham's *The Scholemaster*, p. 231.

Selden, for example, had said that he followed Scaliger in condemning Paulus Diaconus for his ignorant abridging of Sextus Pompeius Festus. Montagu retorted that few would defend Paulus for that act any more than one would defend Festus in turn for his abridging of the great lost encyclopedia of Verrius Flaccus. Yet Paulus had made his abridgment, not to supersede Festus, nor to take credit for another man's work, but for his private use and for the use of students. "He was, if not the last, yet one of the last," says Montagu, "that vndertooke in this gelding kind."[77] Festus would have perished utterly, Montagu observes a bit later, if Paulus had not made an epitome of him. As for the modern habit of epitomizing masterpieces, however, Montagu attributes it to Lipsius and Ramus, and speaks thus of them and their work:

> The Abridgements that haue beene made long since, and of late, are held to be one of the chiefe plagues of Learning, and learned men. It maketh men idle, and yet opiniatiue, and well conceited of themselues. He that can carry an Epitome in his pocket, . . . imagineth mightily, that he knoweth much, and yet indeed is but an *ignaro*. In a day he is taught, but to little purpose, as much as others can learne in a whole yeere. Lately the World went a madding this way, for *Systemaes, Syntagms, Synopseis*, and I know not what, both for the Handmaids and Mistresses of Arts. *Lipsius* and *Ramus* swayed all: but soone they, perceiuing their owne folly, left them, *turbidos rivulos, & foeculentos* [sic], and retyred, with some losse of time and trauell, vnto the Fountaines.[78]

Selden had also condemned those who spoke of three or of four sorts of tithes in disregard of the rigorous exactness of the modern theory of division. His own position was that "Tithes are best diuided into the first, and second Tithe." This statement provokes Montagu to retort:

> And why best? Belike, because it is a *Dichotomie*, which being the darling of the Father of Nouellists in *Grammar, Philosophie*, and vnlesse hee had died opportunely, *in Theologie*, must needs be the dotage of all such as he. But as great an *Artist*, (no dispraise to *Ramus*) that great *Dictator* of Learning, *Alexanders* Master, approueth not this best diuision in euery subiect, much lesse that vniuersall title, *Best*. Doubtlesse it is the *best*, which includeth all of that

[77] Richard Montagu, *Diatribae vpon the first part of the late History of Tithes* (London, 1621), p. 417.

[78] *Ibid.*, pp. 415-416.

[201]

kinde: where the *membra diuidentia* be so full, that nothing is exorbitant, or without the verge of that diuision: else there is, sure there may be, a better diuision than that. . . .[79]

Montagu's strictures against abridgments of knowledge and dichotomous divisions are reminiscent of Francis Bacon's remark that, while Ramus deserved well of learning for reviving the three laws, he was not equally happy in introducing the "canker of Epitomes" and the "uniform method and dichotomies."[80] Indeed, Bacon's whole response to Ramus is relevant in a very immediate sense to the history of Ramism in England during the first quarter of the seventeenth century. But Bacon also belongs to the party that sought a more forward-looking reform of scholasticism than that advanced by the Ramists, and thus his opinion of Ramus will be reserved for the chapter presently to be devoted in part to his position in the history of English logic and rhetoric.

The Montagu-Selden controversy, like that between Harvey and Nash and the still earlier one between Digby and Temple, provided effective publicity for Ramism in England from 1580 to 1621. In the same period, and for a half-century thereafter, various scholars of English or continental origin contributed even more directly to England's awareness of Ramus's logic. The efforts of these scholars were devoted to propagating the reforms of Ramus through successive editions of his *Dialecticae Libri Duo*, through learned commentaries upon its text, and through learned adaptations of its precepts to the problems of orators and preachers. These scholarly works are mainly in Latin, and they amount, of course, to a direct continuation of MacIlmaine's pioneering effort to make the Latin text of the *Dialecticae Libri Duo* available to English learning.

Friedrich Beurhaus, a German Ramist, deserves mention among English scholars of that same persuasion. Beurhaus was vice-rector of the school of Dortmund at the time when three of his textbooks on Ramus were published at London. The first of these consists of the Latin text of the *Dialecticae Libri Duo* with questions and answers in Latin at the end of each chapter to guide students to Ramus's full meaning. The title in English would read like this: *Inquiries of an Expository Sort upon the Two Books of Dialectic of Peter Ramus, most famous Royal Professor, as brought forth at Paris without*

[79] *Ibid.*, pp. 341-342.
[80] See *The Works of Francis Bacon*, ed. James Spedding, Robert Leslie Ellis, and Douglas Denon Heath (Boston, 1860-1864), VI, 294; IX, 128.

Commentaries in the Recent Year 72; These being Part One of the Logic Scholar for the Teaching and Learning of Dialectic (London, 1581).[81] A year later another learned work by Beurhaus appeared at the same press, advertising itself under a Latin title as *Scholastic Disputations upon the Main Heads of Peter Ramus's Dialectic, as well as Comparisons between It and Various Logics, These being Part Two of the Logic Scholar, in which Truth of Art is investigated.*[82] One of the most interesting features of this volume is a history of logic from ancient times to Beurhaus's day, with special attention to the sixteenth century. Three chapters of the Introduction are devoted to this subject.[83] The third and last contribution of Beurhaus to English Ramism was published at London by G. Bishop in 1589 as a text and defense of the *Dialecticae Libri Duo*, the defense being described as a tissue of scholastic disputations.[84] This and the two previous works gave Beurhaus a larger representation in English publishing houses than any continental Ramist enjoyed during the sixteenth or seventeenth century.

Wilhelm Adolf Scribonius, a doctor of medicine from Marburg in Prussia, gains a place among English Ramists by virtue of a work which was published in two editions at London by Vautrollier in 1583. Its title translated into English reads: *The Triumph of Ramistic Logic, Wherein a Very Great Many Censures and Observations are set forth, first in the Self-same Augmented Precepts of Ramus, and then in all his Interpreters and Observers.*[85] Gabriel

---

[81] The title page in Latin reads: "In P. Rami, Regii Professoris Clariss. Dialecticae Libros Dvos Lvtetiae Anno LXXII. Postremo sine Praelectionibvs Aeditos, Explicationvm Quaestiones: quae Paedagogiae Logicae De Docenda Discendaqve Dialectica. Pars Prima. Auctore Frederico Bevrhvsio Menertzhagensi Scholae Temonianae Prorectore. Londini Ex Officina Typographica Henrici Bynneman. CIƆ. IƆ. LXXXI. Cum serenissimae Regiae Maiestatis Priuilegio."

[82] The title page reads in part: "De P. Rami Dialecticae Praecipvis Capitibvs Dispvtationes Scholasticae, & cum ijsdem variorum Logicorum comparationes: quae Paedagogiae Logicae Pars Secvnda, qua artis veritas exquiritur . . . . Londini, Ex Officina Typographica Henrici Bynneman. CIƆ. IƆ. LXXXII."

[83] Chapters iv, v, and vi. Chapter vi is especially detailed on the logic of the Renaissance.

[84] I have not seen a copy of this work. The Cambridge University Library lists its copy as follows: "P. Rami . . . Dialecticae libri duo. Defensio eivsdem per Scholasticas . . . disquisitiones: avthore Frederico Bevrhvsio . . . 1589. Londini, Impensis G. Bishop." See *Early English Printed Books in the University Library Cambridge* (Cambridge, 1900-1907), I, 347. This work was entered in the Stationers' Registers December 9, 1588. See Arber, *Transcript of the Registers*, II, 510.

[85] The title page of the second edition, as listed in the *British Museum General Catalogue of Printed Books*, s.v. Scribonius, Gulielmus Adolphus, is as follows: "Triumphus Logicae Rameae, ubi tum in ipsa praecepta P. Rami addita, tum in universos ejus interpretes & animadversores animadversiones observationesq[ue] plurimae proponuntur . . .

Harvey had this work in mind, no doubt, when he listed Scribonius among the defenders of Ramus in "that hott contradictory course of Logique and Philosophy."[86]

Next to MacIlmaine, the greatest Ramistic logician among sixteenth-century Englishmen is William Temple, whose debate with Digby on the subject of Ramus's theory of method has already been discussed. Soon after that debate, Temple published at Cambridge a Latin text of the *Dialecticae Libri Duo*, together with his commentary; and in the same volume he placed not only a disputation of his own upon Porphyry's *Isagoge*, but also a rebuttal under twenty-nine heads to the letter which Johannes Piscator had addressed to him after he had addressed a letter to Piscator on the subject of the latter's criticism of Ramus's dialectic.[87] Piscator's criticism of Ramus had already been published at English presses, as had Temple's response to it and Piscator's response to Temple.[88] Thus it is certain that, when Temple's edition of the *Dialecticae Libri Duo* was published in 1584, no Englishman was known as a better Ramist than he, thanks to that published correspondence with Piscator, and to the earlier controversy with Digby.

Temple inscribed his edition of 1584 to Sir Philip Sidney, addressing him in the dedicatory epistle in part as follows:

> So that you may begin to love this discipline which was saved as from ruin by the genius of P. Ramus and quite splendidly elucidated by him, it is something which has now spread itself throughout Europe, and however inelegantly taken up at first, has nevertheless begun to be put to use by a very great many in the best universities.[89]

With his characteristic warmth and generosity, Sidney wrote at once to Temple to thank him for the book and the inscription. His letter is brief and in every other respect qualified for quotation at this time:

Editio secunda. Londini, 1583." The first edition is listed in the *Short-Title Catalogue*, s.v. Scribonius; see also Arber, *Transcript of the Registers*, II, 429.

[86] See above, p. 199.

[87] The volume containing these three works by Temple bears the following title: "P. Rami Dialecticae Libri Dvo, Scholiis G. Tempelli Cantabrigiensis illustrati. Qvibus accessit, Eodem authore, De Porphyrianis Praedicabilibus Disputatio. Item: Epistolae de P. Rami Dialectica contra Iohannis Piscatoris responsionem defensio, in capita viginti novem redacta. Cantabrigiae, Ex officina Thomae Thomasij. 1584." This work was also published at Frankfurt in 1591; see Waddington, *Ramus*, p. 454.

[88] See above, p. 196, note 67.

[89] This section of Temple's dedicatory epistle is quoted by Mullinger, *University of Cambridge*, II, 409, note 5. Translation mine.

Good Mr Temple. I have receaved both yowr book and letter, and think my self greatly beholding unto yow for them. I greatly desyre to know yow better, I mean by sight, for els yowr wrytings make yow as well known as my knowledg ever reach unto, and this assure yourself Mr Temple that whyle I live yow shall have me reddy to make known by my best power that I bear yow good will, and greatly esteem those thinges I conceav in yow. When yow com to London or Court I prai yow lett me see yow, mean whyle use me boldli: for I am beholding. God keep yow well. At Court this 23th of Mai 1584.

Your loving frend
Philip Sidnei

To my assured good frend
Mr William Temple[90]

It must have been pleasant for Temple to be thus assured that his works were already well known in London and at Court, and that men like Sidney were reaching into them for a knowledge of the new logic. It must also have been pleasant for him to have received this invitation to meet Sidney in person. Not long after the invitation was issued, such a meeting took place. Its result was that when Sidney went abroad in 1585 at the head of an expedition to aid the Netherlands in her war against the persistent aggression of Spain, Temple accompanied him as private secretary. When Sidney died on October 17, 1586, at Arnheim, from a poisoned battle wound, a codicil in his will bequeathed "to Mr. Temple the yearly Annuity of thirty Pounds by Year"[91]—a clear proof that his esteem for Temple never waned. Nor did Temple's for Sidney. According to one report, he held Sidney in his arms as his distinguished patron lay dying.[92] Moreover, he paid tribute to Sidney's poetical theory by writing a Latin comment on the *Defence of Poesie*, and to Sidney's genius by composing a Latin elegy in his honor for one of the several volumes lamenting his death.[93]

It is quite possible that Temple's interest in Ramism had begun during his earliest years at Cambridge, when he could have attended

---

[90] *Sir Philip Sidney The Defence of Poesie Political Discourses Correspondence Translations*, ed. Albert Feuillerat (Cambridge, 1923), p. 145.

[91] *Ibid.*, p. 376. For mention of Sidney's companions on his expedition to the Netherlands, see Mona Wilson, *Sir Philip Sidney* (London, 1950), p. 237.

[92] See *Dictionary of National Biography*, s.v. Temple, Sir William (1555-1627).

[93] Temple's analysis of the *Defence* is preserved in manuscript at Penshurst. I am indebted to Professor William Ringler of Washington University in St. Louis for letting me see his photostat of it. For a brief description of it, and for the titles of the three foremost volumes in Sidney's honor, see Wilson, *Sir Philip Sidney*, pp. 307, 319.

Gabriel Harvey's lectures on the rhetoric of Talaeus or Laurence Chaderton's lectures on Ramus's logic. At any rate, Temple became bachelor of arts from King's College in 1578, whereas Harvey had lectured on rhetoric in the spring of 1575 and 1576, and Chaderton had been engaged in arousing interest in Ramus's logic during the years between 1571 and 1577.[94] This same Chaderton is also certain to have had a part in the development of our next Ramist scholar, William Perkins, who took his degree of bachelor of arts from Christ's College, Cambridge, in 1581, and his master's degree in 1584, the very year of Temple's edition of Ramus's *Dialecticae Libri Duo.*[95]

Perkins's contribution to the cause of Ramism in England occurred during the period of his appointment as fellow of Christ's College between 1584 and 1595. This contribution consisted of a treatise on preaching, which was published originally in Latin in 1592 and translated into English after Perkins's death.[96] The English translation, as done by Thomas Tuke in 1606, is called *The Arte of Prophecying, or, A Treatise concerning the sacred and onely trve manner and methode of Preaching.* Perkins divides his subject into two parts, preaching and praying. He then divides preaching into preparation for the sermon and promulgation or uttering of the sermon, whereas praying is later made to consist of considering, ordering, and uttering. He divides preparation for the sermon into interpretation and right division or cutting; he divides right division into resolution or partition and application; and so on. This prevailingly dichotomous structure is of course Ramistic, and so far as I know, Perkins is the first Englishman to write of preaching in terms of that kind of structure.

There are two other evidences of Ramus's influence upon Perkins. One presents itself when Perkins, in speaking of resolution or partition as the process of making a biblical text unloose its true doctrine, mentions two means to this end, the second of which, he says, "is done by the helpe of the nine arguments, that is, of the causes, effects, subiects, adiuncts, dissentanies, comparatiues, names, distribution,

---

[94] See above, p. 179; see below, p. 248.

[95] See *Dictionary of National Biography*, s.v. Perkins, William (1558-1602).

[96] The first edition of the Latin text is titled *Prophetica, sive de sacra et vnica ratione concionandi*, ([Cantabrigiae]: ex officina Johannis Legate, 1592). A second edition bearing the same date as the first is listed in the catalogue of the Bibliothèque Nationale at Paris. The English translation is entered in the Stationers' Registers under the date of December 10, 1606. See Arber, *Transcript of the Registers*, III, 334, 338.

and definition."[97] These "nine arguments" are of course the nine places for the invention of artistic arguments according to Ramus's dialectic, and Perkins was thinking of that very work when he penned this passage. He was also thinking of that same work when, in his brief chapter on memorized sermons, after rejecting "artificiall memorie, which standeth vpon places and images," he says: "It is not therefore an vnprofitable aduice, if he that is to preach doe diligently imprint in his minde by the helpe of disposition either axiomaticall, or syllogisticall, or methodicall, the seuerall proofes and applications of the doctrines, the illustrations of the applications, and the order of them all."[98] These words in part recall the second division of Ramus's dialectic, which he named disposition, it will be remembered, and which he divided into three parts, propositions, syllogisms, and method.

Although Perkins has to be counted among the English Ramists on account of the organization of his theory of preaching, and on account of his two references to what we must identify as Ramus's dialectic, he is not a thoroughgoing disciple of that master. He does not mention Ramus as one of his authorities. Instead, at the end of his treatise, he mentions the "Writers which lent their helpe to the framing of this Art of Prophecying," and the only ones he enumerates are Augustine, Hemingius, Hyperius, Erasmus, Illyricus, Wigandus, Jacobus Matthias, Theodorus Beza, and Franciscus Junius.[99] As would be expected from this list, Perkins derives his doctrine from sources closer to Ciceronian rhetoric and scholastic logic than to the logic and rhetoric of Ramus. In fact, Ramus under his law of justice did not allow preaching to be a separate art but assigned its precepts to logic or to rhetoric—a position which Perkins refuses to defend. He remarks instead in his preface that preaching "would remaine naked and poore, if all other arts should call for those things, which are their owne."[100] His own effort is to restore to preaching those grammatical, rhetorical, and logical rules that belong to it, and to ignore Ramus's opposition to such an amalgam. Thus he must be regarded as a traditionalist in respect to most of his subject matter, and as a Ramist only in respect to method of presentation and to a few points of doctrine.

[97] Tuke's translation in *The VVorkes of That Famovs and VVorthy Minister of Christ, in the Vniversitie of Cambridge M. VVilliam Perkins* (London, 1613-1616), II, 663.

[98] *Ibid.*, p. 670.   [99] *Ibid.*, p. 673.   [100] *Ibid.*, p. 645.

As Chaderton is to be reckoned an influence upon Perkins and Temple, so did Temple and Perkins undoubtedly influence George Downham, the next scholarly Ramist after Perkins. Downham, whose father was bishop of Chester, graduated bachelor of arts at Cambridge in 1585, one year after Perkins was appointed fellow of Christ's College, and one year after Temple first published his text and elucidation of the *Dialecticae Libri Duo*. Thomas Fuller speaks thus of Downham:

> He was bred in *Christs-colledge* in *Cambridge*, elected Fellow there-of 1585. and chosen Logick-professor in the University. No man was then and there better skill'd in *Aristotle*, or a greater Follower of *Ramus*, so that he may be termed the *Top-twig* of that *Branch*.[101]

This pun on the Latin meaning of the word "ramus" permits Fuller to share with Harvey and Drant whatever honors one may allow to wordplay.[102] Perhaps Fuller deserves a special award for implying further that Downham's name, downward looking as it is, offers an amusing contrast to his upward position on the tree of English Ramism.

The activity of Downham as professor of logic at Cambridge can be equated with a treatise which he published some years later when he was soon to begin his term as bishop of Derry in Ireland. That treatise appeared in Latin at Frankfurt in 1605 and again at the same place in 1610.[103] The title of the second of these editions would read thus in English: *Commentaries on the Dialectic of P. Ramus, in which both generally and severally the Perfection of the Ramistic Doctrine is demonstrated from the Better Authors, the Sense explained, the Use exhibited*. In this work Downham proves himself a master of the tightfisted style of the logician and of the openhanded style of the orator. So Fuller believed, at any rate, when he borrowed Zeno's ancient metaphor to speak as follows about Downham's logical treatise:

> It is seldome seen, that the *Clunch-fist* of *Logick* (good to *knock* a man down at a blow) can so open it self as to *smooth* and *stroak* one

---

[101] Thomas Fuller, *The History of the Worthies of England* (London, 1662), p. 189.

[102] See above, pp. 55, 178.

[103] There is a copy of the 1605 edition in the Columbia University Library; see Frank Allen Patterson, *The Works of John Milton* (New York, 1931-1938), XI, 521, 523. The 1610 edition has the following title: *Commentarii in P. Rami dialecticam, quibus ex classicis quibusque auctoribus praeceptorum Rameorum perfectio demonstratur, sensus explicatur, usus exponitur* (Francofurti, 1610).

with the *Palme* thereof. Our *Dounham* could doe both, witness the Oration made by him at *Cambridge*, (preposed to his book of Logick) full of *Flowers* of the *choicest eloquence*.[104]

Commentaries in Latin and English on Ramus's *Dialecticae Libri Duo*, and Latin editions of that same work, continued to be produced in England for more than sixty years after the date of Downham's "book of Logick." Alexander Richardson, who was a member of Queen's College, Cambridge, when Downham resided at Christ's, delivered a course of lectures on various subjects at his alma mater after he became master of arts in 1587, and evidently was so well regarded by his hearers that many of them took down what he said and passed his teachings on to others in the form of notes. These notes were published twice at London during the seventeenth century under the title of *The Logicians School-Master*.[105] Samuel Thomson, a London bookseller, who brought out the second of these editions with many items that had not been included in the first, devotes a preface to Richardson, acknowledging his insight into all the branches of learning, and his dedication to the arts. These arts Richardson would have greatly improved, observes Thomson, had his health been better, and had he claimed for himself what was really his. As a tribute to his lectures at Cambridge on many subjects, Thomson remarks upon the happiness of the student "who could make himself Master of *Richardson's* Notes." He adds:

> But among many other Notes of his those of his Commentary on *Ramus* Logick were most generally prized and made use of by young Students: whereof (though long since printed) there are many Copies in Manuscript still in being; and indeed it was his Logick whereby, as by a Key, he opened the secrets of all other Arts and Sciences, to the admiration of all that heard him.[106]

---

[104] Fuller, *Worthies*, p. 189.

[105] The title page of the first edition reads thus: "The logicians School-Master: or, a comment vpon Ramvs Logicke. By Mr. Alexander Richardson sometime of Queenes Colledge in Cambridge. London, Printed for Iohn Bellamie, at the three golden Lyons in Cornhill. 1629." There is a copy of this edition in the Cambridge University Library.—The title of the second edition indicates the items that had not been printed in the first: "The Logicians School-Master: or, A Comment upon Ramus Logick. By Mr. Alexander Richardson, sometime of Queenes Colledge in Cambridge. Whereunto are added, His Prelections on *Ramus* his *Grammer; Taleus* his *Rhetorick*; Also his Notes on *Physicks, Ethicks, Astronomy, Medicine*, and *Opticks*. Never before Published. London: Printed by *Gartrude Dawson*, and are to . . . by *Sam. Thomson* at the *White-Hor* . . . *Paul's* Church-yard. 1657." (The title page of the copy which I used at the Harvard Library is torn off at the corner and thus my transcript of it is incomplete as indicated by the dots.)

[106] *The Logicians School-Master* (1657), sig. A3v-A4r.

Richardson's sense of the value of Ramistic logic in relation to the other arts upon which he lectured is shown by the fact that in the second edition of his notes some 351 pages are devoted to a commentary upon Ramus's *Dialecticae Libri Duo*, whereas the comments on grammar, rhetoric, physics, ethics, astronomy, medicine, and optics cover a total of 159 pages, more than 50 of which are given to rhetoric. Richardson's method in respect to logic is to quote a few lines of Ramus's doctrine in Latin and to explain them in Latin-studded English. Quite often his explanations proceed by stating and answering objections which other scholars, such as Keckermann, for example, had urged against Ramus.[107] If Thomson is correct in implying that many manuscript copies of Richardson's notes on Ramus were still circulating when the second edition of *The Logicians School-Master* appeared, then 1657 must be accepted as a date well before the end of Ramus's influence in England.

There is also evidence of an active scholarly interest in Ramus in the decade before that in which the second edition of Richardson's notes was published. A good indication of this interest is provided by a vest-pocket edition of the *Dialecticae Libri Duo* made at Cambridge in 1640. Its editor is not identified, but it contains Ramus's Latin text and his preface to the reader, "recently brought out in this more distinctive and more correct form for use in schools."[108] Six years later, as posthumous publications of William Ames, who had learned Ramism from William Perkins and George Downham at Christ's College in the middle fifteen-nineties, there appeared two little works from the Cambridge press entitled *Demonstratio Logicae Verae* and *Theses Logicae*.[109] The first of these is made up of six-

[107] *Ibid.*, pp. 42, 57, 61, etc.

[108] The title page of the copy at the Folger Shakespeare Library reads thus: "P. Rami Veromandui, Regii Professoris, Dialecticae Libri duo: Rècens in usum Scholarum hâc formâ distinctius & emendatiùs excusi. Cantabrigiae, Ex officina *Rogeri Danielis*, almae Academiae Typographi. CIƆDCXL. Et veneunt per *Petrum Scarlet*."

[109] The Yale University Library has a volume in which these two works are bound with four other treatises by Ames. The first two treatises in this volume are paged together, and are called *Technometria* and *Alia Technometriae*. The third treatise is the *Demonstratio Logicae Verae*. It has its own pagination, and a title page which reads: "Gulielmi Amesii Demonstratio Logicae Verae. Cantabrigiae, Ex officina *Rogeri Danielis*, almae Academiae Typographi. 1646." Next after it is the *Disputatio Theologica adversus Metaphicam*, with its own title page and date (1646), but with pagination continued from the preceding treatise. The fifth treatise is the *Disputatio Theologica, De Perfectione SS. Scripturae*, with its own title page, dated at Cambridge in 1646, and its own pagination. Last is the *Guilielmi Amesii Theses Logicae*, with no title page or date of its own, and with its pagination continued from the preceding treatise.—The *Demonstratio Logicae Verae* was first published at Leiden in 1632, but I have not seen that edition. A copy of it is listed in *Gesamtkatalog der Preussischen Bibliotheken*, s.v.

teen introductory and 129 later propositions, along with a conclusion, the whole being an explanation of Ramus's *Dialecticae Libri Duo*. The *Theses Logicae* is devoted to the same end, and it proceeds by setting forth a sequence of more than 350 short logical definitions, principles, and laws.

Ames's *Demonstratio Logicae Verae* and the vest-pocket text of the *Dialecticae Libri Duo* reappear once more in the history of Ramism in England. The latter work was combined with George Downham's Latin commentary upon Ramus's Latin logic and published at the press of John Redmayne at London in 1669.[110] Some idea of the relation between Ramus and his scholarly commentators is indicated by the fact that in this volume the *Dialecticae Libri Duo* occupies only 54 pages, whereas the Downham commentary runs to 481 pages of text and several pages of introduction and supplement. Included in the introductory matter is the address which Downham delivered at Cambridge in 1590 as professor of logic, and which Fuller thought to be a splendid example of discourse at once tight and open.[111] As for Ames's *Demonstratio Logicae Verae*, it was republished at Cambridge in 1672 in combination with the text of Ramus's *Dialecticae Libri Duo*, the Amesian propositions being on this occasion distributed at appropriate intervals throughout the parent work.[112]

Much of our story of the Ramist scholars in England has thus far involved Christ's College at Cambridge. The line of Ramists who studied and in almost every case taught at Christ's extends backward in time from Ames, Downham, and Perkins to Gabriel Harvey and Laurence Chaderton. After Ames, the line runs to William Chappell and thence to his illustrious pupil, John Milton, who may be

---

Ames, William, Puritaner.—Apparently the *Theses Logicae* was first published in the edition at Cambridge in 1646.

[110] The title page reads: "P. Rami Veromandui Regii Professoris Dialecticae Libri Duo: *Recèns in usum Scholarum hâc formâ distinctiùs & emendatiùs excusi*. Cum Commentariis Georgii Dounami Annexis. Londini, Ex Officina *Johannis Redmayne*, & veneunt per *Robertum Nicholson & Henricum Dickinson* Cantabrigiae Bibliopolas. MDCLXIX." This work is mistakenly listed by Donald Wing, *Short-Title Catalogue of Books Printed in England, Scotland, Ireland, Wales, and British America and of English Books Printed in other Countries 1641-1700* (New York, 1945-1951), s.v. La Ramée, Pierre de. Wing places its publication at Cambridge.

[111] See above, pp. 208-209.

[112] The title page reads: "P. Rami Veromandui Regii Professoris, Dialecticae Libri duo: Quibus loco Commentarii perpetui post certa capita subjicitur, Guilielmi Amesii Demonstratio Logicae Verae, Simul Cum Synopsi ejusdem, quâ uno intuitu exhibetur Tota Ars bene Disserendi. Cantabrigiae, Ex Officina *Joann. Hayes*, Celeberrimae Academiae Typographi. 1672. Impensis *G. Morden*, Bibliopolae."

counted not only the most celebrated but also the last of England's Ramist scholars.

Chappell was a student at Christ's when Ames was serving there as tutor and fellow. Thus these two men were thrown together in the first few years of the seventeenth century. Ames was forced to resign his fellowship in 1610, his withdrawal being occasioned by the intemperance of his advocacy of puritanism.[113] Not long before that date, Chappell was appointed to a fellowship at Christ's, and he held that position for twenty-seven years, after which he became bishop of Cork. In 1648, just one year before his death, he published at London an anonymous Latin treatise on preaching, the *Methodus Concionandi*. This was published in an English version under Chappell's name in 1656 as *The Preacher*.[114] The person who made the English translation cannot be certainly identified, but he may well have been the original author himself. Indeed, the "Phil. Christianus" who signed the preface to the translation implies that Chappell alone was responsible for its authorship.

Chappell's procedure in *The Preacher* is not unlike that already described above in the discussion of Perkins's *Arte of Prophecying*. That is to say, Chappell arranges his materials by definition and by dichotomies, and on one occasion makes direct use of the places of Ramus's theory of dialectical invention; but he does not otherwise incur obligations to Ramistic logic and rhetoric. Thus he defines the "Method of Preaching" as "a discourse upon a Text of Scripture, disposing its parts according to the order of nature, whereby, the accord of them, one with the other may be judged of, and contained in memory."[115] He divides this method into two parts, that of doctrine and that of use.[116] He divides doctrine into preparation and handling.[117] He divides preparation into entering the place where the doctrine is and placing the doctrine itself.[118] After he has sufficiently

---

[113] Mullinger, *University of Cambridge*, II, 510-511.

[114] The title page reads: "The Preacher, or the Art and Method of Preaching: shewing The most ample Directions and Rules for Invention, Method, Expression, and Books whereby a Minister may be furnished with such helps as may make him a Useful Laborer in the Lords Vineyard. By William Chappell Bishop of *Cork*, sometime Fellow of Christs College in *Cambridge*. . . . *London*, Printed for *Edw. Farnham*, and are to be sold at his shop in Popes-head Palace neer Corn-hill, 1656." There is a copy of this work in the McAlpin collection in the Union Theological Seminary.— No translator is mentioned in connection with the entry of this work in the Stationers' Registers. See [George E. B. Eyre and Charles R. Rivington], *A Transcript of the Registers of the Worshipful Company of Stationers; from 1640-1708 A. D.* (London, 1913-1914), II, 92. The entry is dated October 23, 1656.

[115] *The Preacher* (1656), p. 1.   [116] *Ibid.*, p. 3.
[117] *Ibid.*, p. 4.   [118] *Ibid.*, p. 4.

considered doctrine as his first main topic, he turns to the topic of use, and this he discusses both in general and in particular, the latter head being broken down into the concerns of the mind and the concerns of the heart. Of those uses "which have respect to the heart, or will, and affections,"[119] he mentions what bears upon the present state of feelings and what bears upon their future state. He speaks of reproving and of comforting as procedures to be followed in respect to present distempers of feeling; and as a method for reproving someone, he recommends the standard places of Ramus's program for dialectical invention. True, he covers eight of these standard places,[120] where Ramus had covered ten. But it takes no great ingenuity to see that Ramus's ten places are covered by Chappell's eight. Both men agree upon causes, effects, subjects, adjuncts, opposites, and comparatives as the first six of what Ramus calls arguments and what Chappell calls "heads of the aggravations of sin."[121] After that point Chappell begins to take liberties with Ramistic doctrine, as most Ramists were certain sooner or later to do. Thus he combines under his seventh heading the topics of name, division, and definition, whereas these three in Ramus had been discussed as the seventh, the eighth, and the ninth places. But agreement prevails between Chappell and Ramus at the end of the list, nevertheless, for both give last place to testimony.

One of Chappell's chief claims to fame among literary historians is that he is reputed to have whipped his pupil John Milton towards the end of the latter's freshman year at Christ's College.[122] The actuality of this incident has been questioned by the friends and defended by the detractors of Milton, but there seems to be no doubt that Chappell was Milton's tutor from April 1625 to March 1626 and that some trouble between them terminated their relationship and caused Milton to be transferred to the supervision of another tutor, Nathaniel Tovey.[123]

Milton's interest in Ramistic logic probably began during his association with Chappell. After all, the latter can be proved to be a moderate Ramist, and logic is one of the subjects which Milton would have had to study during his first years at the university. Moreover, it is highly likely that Tovey was also a Ramist and

---

[119] *Ibid.*, p. 153. [120] *Ibid.*, pp. 166-179. [121] *Ibid.*, p. 166.
[122] For a discussion of this episode, see David Masson, *The Life of John Milton* (Cambridge and London, 1859-1880), I, 135-145.
[123] *Ibid.*, I, 141.

would not have changed the direction of Milton's logical studies when the latter became his pupil. Tovey is known to have been lecturer in logic at Christ's in 1621, the first year of his tenure as fellow of that college.[124] Thus he would certainly have been acquainted with the contemporary movements in logical theory, and would certainly have been impelled to regard favorably the enthusiasm of his own college and university for Ramus. Unfortunately, however, Tovey left no publications to establish his Ramism as fact. Anyway, it is certain that Milton knew of Ramus's logic as early as 1627, when he was completing his sixth college term. On March 26 of that year, as scholars now fix the date, Milton wrote a letter to his childhood preceptor, Thomas Young, remarking that "to express sufficiently how much I owe you were a work far greater than my strength, even if I should ransack all those hoards of arguments which Aristotle or which that Dialectician of Paris has amassed, or even if I should exhaust all the fountains of oratory."[125] The reference to "that Dialectician of Paris," as Masson originally suggested,[126] is of course a reference to Ramus, and it not only establishes Milton's knowledge of that author but it also suggests his contemporaneous familiarity with the practical applications of Aristotelian and Ramistic inventional theory in the problem of composing a discourse.

Forty-five years were to elapse before Milton published a Latin text and his own Latin exposition of Ramus's *Dialecticae Libri Duo*. That work, as it appeared at a London press in 1672, is called *Joannis Miltoni Angli, Artis Logicae Plenior Institutio, Ad Petri Rami Methodum concinnata*.[127] On the only occasion when it was translated into English, its title was rendered as *A fuller institution of the Art of Logic, arranged after the method of Peter Ramus, by John Milton, an Englishman*.[128] As for its date of composition, it doubt-

---

[124] *Ibid.*, I, 106. See also *Alumni Cantabrigienses*, Pt. I, s.v. Tovy, Nathaniel.

[125] Patterson, *The Works of John Milton*, XII, 5. The date of this letter is usually given as March 26, 1625, but opinion now supports a date exactly two years later. See William R. Parker, "Milton and Thomas Young, 1620-1628," *Modern Language Notes*, LIII (1938), 399-407.

[126] *Life of Milton*, I, 123.

[127] The title page continues: "Adjecta est Praxis Annalytica & *Petri Rami* vita. Libris duobus. Londini, Impensis *Spencer Hickman*, Societatis Regalis Typographi, ad insigne Rosae in Caemeterio, *D. Pauli*. 1672." There is a copy of this work in the Princeton University Library.

[128] The translator is Allan H. Gilbert in Patterson, *The Works of John Milton*, XI. All of my English quotations from Milton's *Artis Logicae Plenior Institutio* are in Gilbert's translation, which I cite as Gilbert and use with the kind permission of the Columbia University Press.

less belongs among Milton's early works. Masson is almost certainly right in his guess that it was "sketched out in Milton's university days at Cambridge, between his taking his B.A. degree and his passing as M.A."[129] Two anti-Trinitarian statements in the work have been cited to suggest that it was written after 1641, since at about that time Milton is believed to have lost faith in the doctrine of theTrinity.[130] But of course those statements could have been inserted during the sixteen-forties into a work mostly finished at an earlier date. Masson's conjecture, which would place the composition of the work between the years 1629 and 1632, is supported by the reflection that a treatise like *The Art of Logic* belongs to a university environment, as the whole history of Ramistic scholarship in England demonstrates time and again; and that, with Milton as author, the treatise would thus be the direct product of his recent undergraduate training in Ramus and of a tradition at Christ's in his day to carry on Ramistic studies as part of one's advanced scholarship. In fact, Downham's *Commentaries* represented to Milton's generation at Christ's the best previous scholarship on Ramus by an alumnus of that college, and Downham's *Commentaries* are Milton's only domestic source for his *Art of Logic*.[131]

But Milton wished to improve Downham, not to copy him. The latter, as we have seen, initially published his *Commentaries* without giving his readers the benefit that would have come if he had also included the text of Ramus's *Dialecticae Libri Duo*. Milton determined to avoid that sort of thing. At the same time, he determined to avoid publishing a mere text of Ramus's logic, since that was too brief to be clear. He begins the preface to his *Art of Logic* by saying that he together with Sidney believed Peter Ramus to be the best writer on this art. He observes, with a hidden reference to Ramus's law of justice, that "other logicians, in a sort of unbridled license, commonly confound physics, ethics, and theology with logic."[132] He goes on to say that Ramus, as the many commentaries on him will testify, sought too earnestly for brevity and thus fell short "not exactly of clarity but yet of copiousness of clarity, for in the presentation of an art it should not be scrimped but full and abun-

---

[129] *Life of Milton*, VI, 685.

[130] This view is adopted and explained by Franklin Irwin, "Ramistic Logic in Milton's Prose Works" (unpubl. diss., Princeton, 1941), pp. 29-33. See also G. C. Moore Smith, "A Note on Milton's *Art of Logic*," *The Review of English Studies*, XIII (1937), 335-340.

[131] Gilbert, pp. 520-521.   [132] *Ibid.*, p. 3.

dant."[133] Then he explains how his present work is designed to give the precepts of Ramus along with such aids to their understanding as can be found in Ramus's *Scholae Dialecticae* and in the Ramistic commentaries. In this connection he says:

> So I have decided that it is better to transfer to the body of the treatise and weave into it, except when I disagree, those aids to a more complete understanding of the precepts of the art which must of necessity be sought in the *Scholae Dialecticae* of Ramus himself and in the commentaries of others. For why should we insist on brevity if clarity is to be sought elsewhere? It is better by producing one work to put together in one place a rather long exposition of a subject with clarity than with less clarity to explain in a separate commentary a work that is too brief, although this last has up to the present been done with no less trouble and much less convenience than if, as now, the treatise itself was so detailed as to furnish its own explanation.[134]

A recent interpreter of Milton's attitude towards Ramism, P. Albert Duhamel, argues that Milton "was never a Ramist except superficially," and uses as proof, among other considerations, the opening words of the quotation just given, where Milton promises to explain Ramism "except when I disagree."[135] It is true that Milton like every other English Ramist disagrees in some particulars with Ramus's own logical doctrine, and Duhamel gives a good brief list of those disagreements as they apply in Milton's case.[136] But it must always be remembered that Ramus had encouraged disagreement between himself and his disciples by launching a movement of disagreement between himself and the scholastics. Moreover, it must be insisted that, while Milton availed himself of opportunities to disagree with Ramus, he did not therefore become either a superficial Ramist or a covert Peripatetic. Had he wanted to write an Aristotelian logic, he would have modeled his work upon such neoscholastic logics of his day as Blundeville's *The Arte of Logicke*, Smith's *Aditvs ad Logicam*, or Sanderson's *Logicae Artis Compendivm*. These works show how the scholastics reconstructed Aristotelian logic in the light of the reforms of Ramus.[137] If Milton, as Duhamel contends, is closer to the Peripatetics than to Ramus, he would obviously have followed these neo-scholastics of the early

[133] *Ibid.*, p. 3.   [134] *Ibid.*, pp. 3-5.
[135] See P. Albert Duhamel, "Milton's Alleged Ramism," *PMLA*, LXVII (1952), 1043.
[136] *Ibid.*, p. 1045.
[137] For a discussion of this point, see below, pp. 285-308.

seventeenth century rather than the *Dialecticae Libri Duo* and Downham's *Commentaries*.

A hidden reference to Ramus's law of justice has already been pointed out in Milton's preface to his *Art of Logic*. There is also a hidden reference in the same place to Ramus's law of wisdom and law of truth.

The law of wisdom, as we know, applied in part to the method of organizing a discourse; and it required in this context that subject matter be arranged in a descending order of generality. Milton protests that certain expounders of Ramus had forgotten this law, but that he will not. His actual words are as follows:

> Since many of these expositors, perhaps drawn on by too much zeal for commenting, reveal a neglect of all proper method astonishing in them by mixing everything together, the last with the first, and are accustomed to heap up the axioms, syllogisms, and their rules in the early chapters that deal with simple arguments, thus necessarily covering students with darkness rather than furnishing them light, I have decided first of all to take care that I treated nothing prematurely, that I mentioned nothing before its proper time as though it were already explained and understood, and that I dealt with nothing except in its place, without fear that any one might judge me too narrow in my explanation of the precepts of Ramus, while I was trying to set them forth by lingering over rather than rushing through them.[138]

Milton's reference to the law of truth is quite fugitive, so far as his preface is concerned. This law, we remember, required all precepts of a science or body of knowledge to be universally true as opposed to partly true. Milton promises to exclude from his work all precepts that are not universal or certain. He says:

> Yet I should not easily agree with those who object to the paucity of rules in Ramus, since a great number even of those collected from Aristotle by others as well as those which they have themselves added to the heap, being uncertain or futile, impede the learner and burden rather than aid him, and if they have any usefulness or show any wit, it is of such a sort as any one might more easily understand by his native ability than learn by means of so many memorized canons.[139]

A recurrent theme of the Ramists is that they were seeking to reform Aristotelianism, not to destroy it.[140] Thus they protested that

---

[138] Gilbert, p. 5.   [139] *Ibid.*, p. 5.
[140] See for example MacIlmaine's view as quoted above, p. 180.

their views were not really novel, that in fact they used Aristotle as their authority. Milton is no exception to this general practice. He says in his preface:

> Our common addition of the authority of Aristotle and other old writers to the separate rules of logic would be wholly superfluous in the teaching of the art, except that the suspicion of novelty which until now has been strongly attached to Peter Ramus ought to be removed by bringing up these testimonies from ancient authors.[141]

After his preface, Milton sets forth Ramus's logical precepts, book by book, and topic by topic, adding his own comments, registering his own disagreements, and citing a few of his own examples from such sources as Francis Bacon, Christian history, and the Bible.[142] Of particular interest in the work as a whole is his direct explanation of Ramus's three laws and of Ramistic method.[143] At the end of the treatise he adds "An Analytic Praxis of Logic from Downham" and a brief "Life of Peter Ramus" from John Thomas Freigius.[144] The latter item tells of Ramus's ancestry, his audacious criticism of Aristotle, his academic troubles, the suppression of his two earliest works, the intervention of the cardinal of Lorraine on his behalf, his temporary triumph, and the agitations of his final years; but his conversion to Protestantism is treated by Freigius only in guarded references, as if it were completely disconnected from the development and formulation of Ramus's dialectic.

The influence of Ramus upon Milton's habits as controversialist and poet has been in part explored. Franklin Irwin's unpublished Princeton dissertation, "Ramistic Logic in Milton's Prose Works," identifies Ramistic characteristics in Milton's tractates and pamphlets and in his *De Doctrina Christiana* above all. Leon Howard has shown the parallelism between Milton's *Art of Logic* and the theme and purpose of *Paradise Lost.*[145] Then, too, as I mentioned before, there is at least one modern critic who speaks of Milton's alleged Ramism and who considers it important to detach Milton from Ramistic influences almost entirely, as if his prose were deliberately Aristotelian and his *Art of Logic* a redaction of the work of scholastic logicians rather than of Ramus's reformed scholasticism.[146] Whatever may be

---

[141] Gilbert, pp. 7-9.   [142] *Ibid.*, pp. 25, 37, 43.
[143] *Ibid.*, pp. 317-323, 471-485.   [144] *Ibid.*, pp. 487-495, 497-515.
[145] Leon Howard, " 'The Invention' of Milton's 'Great Argument': A Study of the Logic of 'God's Ways to Men,' " *The Huntington Library Quarterly*, IX (February 1946), 149-173.
[146] This critic is P. Albert Duhamel in the article cited above, p. 216, note 135.

the ultimate view, however, of the connection between Milton's great eloquence and the canons of Ramistic dialectic, it is safe to say that his *Art of Logic* shows a scholar's basic support of Ramus's canons, and a scholar's awareness of the dependence of those canons upon the final authority of Aristotle, Cicero, and Quintilian. Thus Milton belongs among the learned Englishmen who kept Ramism alive in their native intellectual circles between 1574 and 1672.

It remains for us to look at the frequent attempts in that same period to keep Ramism alive for the Englishmen who read no Latin or who preferred their learning in the vernacular. On their behalf seven free versions of Ramus's *Dialecticae Libri Duo* appeared during the sixteenth and seventeenth centuries, and these must be added to the learned works just described if the full extent of Ramism in England is to be understood. These seven, of course, include MacIlmaine's *Logike*, and that has already been sufficiently discussed. But the others have also their points of interest and eccentricity.

In the year 1584, just three years after the second edition of MacIlmaine's translation had been published, Dudley Fenner brought out at a continental press an anonymous work called *The Artes of Logike and Rethorike*.[147] The logical doctrine in this treatise is an unacknowledged translation of the main heads of Ramus's *Dialecticae Libri Duo*, although these heads are illustrated, not from the classical authors whom Ramus used, but from the Bible. As for Fenner's rhetorical doctrine, it will be explained in the next section of this chapter as the first English translation of the main heads of Talaeus's *Rhetorica*. On this latter account alone, Fenner's work possesses special interest in the history of Ramism in England. But it also possesses special interest as the first attempt to join together in one English volume the reformed logic and the reformed rhetoric of the Ramists. Here between two covers the unlearned Englishman could read for the first time the entire Ramistic theory of communication, even as Thomas Wilson had made it possible for the

---

[147] The title page reads thus: "The Artes of Logike and Rethorike, plainlie set foorth in the English tounge, easie to be learned and practised: togither vvith examples for the practise of the same for Methode, in the gouernement of the familie, prescribed in the word of God: And for the whole in the resolution or opening of certayne partes of Scripture, according to the same. 1584." This work was published at Middelburg by Richard Schilders about the time when Fenner began serving as chaplain to the English merchants of that city.—A second edition, probably published in 1588, bears the imprint of Schilders and identifies the author as "M. Dvdley Fenner, late Preacher of the worde of God in Middlebrugh."

unlearned of the previous generation to read within two volumes the whole of scholastic logic and Ciceronian rhetoric.

Since Fenner had entered Peterhouse College at Cambridge in 1575, he may be numbered among the Cambridge Ramists, although he did not complete his college course, thanks to his expulsion for puritan tendencies.[148] No man of his time had a greater desire than he to unlock the learned arts from the iron enclosure of Greek and Latin. In the preface to the first edition of *The Artes of Logike and Rethorike* he defends himself against the criticism of those who deem it inexpedient to popularize matters "which are wonte to sit in the Doctors Chayre."[149] Let not learned men strive, he warns, to keep learning rare and excessively dear, "least the people *curse them*."[150] Since it is true, he adds, that "the common vse and practise of all men in generall, both in reasoning to the purpose, and in speaking with some grace and elegancie, hath sowen the seede of these artes, why should not all reape where all haue sowen?"

Fenner next defends himself in this preface against the charge that his treatises will seem "newer then the newest" and will invite objection because he has made changes in the accepted body of doctrine. He does not openly name Ramus as his authority at this point or elsewhere in his work. But he did not need to, so far as his own contemporaries were concerned. They would have seen, as modern scholars have not always done, that Fenner was working within the accepted body of Ramistic doctrine, and that the changes which his preface refers to and discusses are not unlike the minor changes made by most other good Ramists when they were seeking to promulgate their master's teachings.

One change which Fenner justifies in his preface and incorporates in his first treatise concerns the definition of logic. "Logike," he says, "is an arte of reasoning."[151] This definition, he earlier remarks, satisfies the requirements by having "an arte" as its true general, and "of reasoning" as its true full difference.[152] It does not need the addition of "well" to make it more perfect, he argues, inasmuch as the end of anything is not a necessary part of its definition. Another change which he argues for in the preface and inserts later in his *Logike* consists in the arrangement of arguments into two categories, "firste and arising of the firste," the latter category being then di-

---

[148] Thomas Alfred Walker, *A Biographical Register of Peterhouse Men* (Cambridge, 1927-1930), II, 6-7. See also *Dictionary of National Biography*, s.v. Fenner, Dudley.
[149] Sig. A2r.   [150] Sig. A2v.   [151] Sig. B1r.   [152] Sig. A2v.

vided into "more artificiall and lesse artificiall."[153] Ramus, it will be remembered, had been content merely to divide arguments into artificial and inartificial, or more accurately into artistic and non-artistic.[154] Still another change which Fenner records in his preface and in his *Logike* concerns the argument of cause. Ramus had listed four types of this argument, that of final cause, of formal cause, of efficient cause, and of material cause.[155] Fenner lists two types, one of which contains Ramus's first and third collapsed into a single heading, and the other, Ramus's second and fourth.[156] Fenner says that this difference between himself and the accepted tradition is a distinct gain in logical theory, and he certainly believes that the same thing is true of his other changes. But now all his changes seem less like improvements than like capricious variations in a pattern that refuses to lose its dominant familiar contours.

What Fenner does with the subject of method is a good example of his adherence to the familiar outlines of Ramism. He recognizes, as MacIlmaine had scarcely managed to do,[157] that the Ramistic theory of method involves an analysis of "the best and perfectest" as well as "the worst & troublesomest" ways of handling matter. According to the perfect way, which would be that followed in learned writing, "the definition of that whiche is to bee handled, must be firste set downe, and then the diuision of the same into the members, and the generall properties of the same, and then the diuerse sortes of it, if there be anie; so proceeding vntill by fitte and apte passages or transitions, the whole be so farre handled, that it can be no more deuided."[158] This kind of arrangement, called by Ramus the natural method, is said by Fenner to be "so agreeable to reason, and easie to be practised" that it "is for the most parte followed of all writers or speakers." Yet writers or speakers may change, alter, or hide it according to their subject, the time, the place, and such circumstances. When they do change it, they adopt what Ramus called the prudential method, and what Fenner calls "the hyding or concealing, or crypsis of Methode." Those who follow this latter way, adds Fenner, "leaue out the former orderly placing of Definitions, Diuisions, and Transitions, and do take in diuers repetitions, declarations, makings lightsome, enlargings, or amplifications, prouings of the thing, preuenting of obiections, outgoing from the matter, called digressions, as it shall make most fitte for their purpose."

[153] Sigs. A2v-A3r, B1r. [154] See above, p. 155. [155] *Dialectiqve* (1555), pp. 6-20.
[156] Sig. B1v-B2r. [157] See above, pp. 182-183. [158] Sig. D1r.

While Fenner was an undergraduate at Cambridge, or shortly thereafter, a young man named Abraham Fraunce entered St. John's College of the same university. Fraunce took the degree of bachelor of arts in 1579-80, and was at once appointed fellow of his college. During the next three years, as he worked towards his master's degree, he began to write what was ultimately to become the third English version of the main doctrine of Ramus's *Dialecticae Libri Duo*.

Fraunce's earliest steps in this direction consisted in a little treatise in praise of logic, and another which compared Ramus's logical theory with that of Aristotle. These two works were followed almost at once by a third, which Fraunce called *The Sheapheardes Logike*. Fraunce never published these early works, but the British Museum has them all in a manuscript dating from the early fifteen-eighties.[159] The manuscript reveals that the comparison between Ramus and Aristotle is dedicated by Fraunce to "his verye good Master and Patron M^r. P. Sydney." It reveals also that *The Sheapheardes Logike* contains three things: "the praecepts of that art put downe by Ramus; examples fet owt of the Sheapheards Kalender; notes and expositions collected owt of Beurhusius, Piscator, Mr. Chatterton and diuers others." The fact that *The Sheapheardes Logike* derives many quotations and even its title from Edmund Spenser's *The Shepheardes Calender*, at that moment a very recent new book, gives the Fraunce manuscript a special literary interest. But it also has special interest for the historian of Ramism in England. The Chatterton mentioned in connection with its notes and expositions is none other than Laurence Chaderton, one of the earliest expounders of Ramus at Cambridge. As indicated above,[160] Chaderton never published anything on Ramistic logic under his own name; but he was still lecturing on that subject to the students of Fraunce's undergraduate generation, and doubtless to Fraunce himself. Thus it is highly probable that the only surviving fragments of his widely popular lectures are now to be found in Fraunce's logical writings, particularly *The Sheapheardes Logike*.

Fraunce's interest veered from literature to law after he took his master's degree in 1583, and so he changed his abode from St. John's College to Gray's Inn. For the next few years he worked upon the

[159] For a description of this manuscript, see *Catalogue of Additions to the Manuscripts in the British Museum in the years MDCCCLXXXVIII-MDCCCXCIII* (London, 1894), pp. 321-322.
[160] See above, p. 179.

English common law. In 1588, some five years after he left Cambridge, and almost seven years after his first attempts to write on logical theory, he published his version of the precepts of Ramus, adding many legal illustrations to his previous quotations from Spenser, and calling his work *The Lawiers Logike*.[161] This book is the first systematic attempt in English to adapt logical theory to legal learning and to interpret Ramism to lawyers.

The union of law and logic is proclaimed in Fraunce's title, but this is merely the beginning of his efforts to keep his readers aware of his novel combination of disciplines. A twelve-line stanza on the page that precedes his preface celebrates the same union. This stanza dedicates the work to Henry, Earl of Pembroke, and speaks in part as follows of its author's basic design:

> I say no more then what I saw, I saw that which I sought,
> I sought for Logike in our Law, and found it as I thought.

The preface that immediately follows these verses is addressed to "the Learned Lawyers of England, especially the Gentlemen of Grays Inne," and it supports in full what has just been said of the history of Fraunce's concern for logic. But it adds several circumstances of interest. For example, it says that the two short treatises which came before *The Sheapheardes Logike* were begun "when I first came in presence of that right noble and most renowmed knight sir Philip Sydney."[162] "These small and trifling beginnings," adds Fraunce, "drewe both him to a greater liking of, and my selfe to a further trauayling in, the easie explication of Ramus his Logike." In addition to this fact about Sidney, the preface also tells us that the present work has been redone six times in the past seven years, thrice while Fraunce was still at St. John's, and thrice during his residence at Gray's Inn. The preface also tells us something of the concern of a university man about to embark upon a legal career—something of his doubt that his eight years at Cambridge would turn to profit at an inn of court, something of his anxiety as to "wheather Law were without Logike or Logike not able to helpe a Lawyer."[163] "VVhich when I prooued," he remarks, "I then perceaued, the prac-

---

[161] His title page reads: "The Lawiers Logike, exemplifying the praecepts of Logike by the practise of the common Lawe, by Abraham Fraunce. At London, Imprinted by William How, for Thomas Gubbin, and T. Newman. 1588." For a brief comparison between the manuscript version and the printed version of this work, see the catalogue cited above in note 159.

[162] *The Lawiers Logike*, sig. ¶r.   [163] *Ibid.*, sig. ¶v.

tise of Law to bee the vse of Logike, and the methode of Logike to lighten the Lawe." Thus the preface reconciles Fraunce's two educations. But with an instinct for the appeasement of readers who would not want to encumber their minds with law as the price for mastering Ramus's logic, Fraunce reassures them by saying, "I haue reteyned those ould examples of the new Shepheards Kalender, which I first gathered, and therevnto added thease also out of our Law bookes, which I lately collected."[164]

This observation prompts Fraunce to defend himself now quite openly for abandoning philosophy at St. John's in favor of law at Gray's Inn. It is plain from what he says that philosophy is deemed the more glamorous and aristocratic pursuit, law the more bourgeois. In an effort to correct the errors within this attitude, he emphasizes that philosophy, especially in its logical branch, is illustrated repeatedly in the law, as Cicero had amply demonstrated in the *Topics*; and he urges that philosophy, ordinarily counted a delicate, conceited, and elegant learning by people who did not distinguish "betweene the brauery of a Midsommers Comencement, and the seauen yeares paynes of a Maister of arts," was in sober fact a taxing and difficult study, capable of producing a "perpetuall vexation of Spirite, and continuall consumption of body, incident to euery scholler."[165] Turning next to the other side of his case, Fraunce defends the law against the charge that it is hard, unsavory, rude, and barbarous. He believes it to be only in need of good teachers, good discipline, and good students recruited from the universities.

The concluding section of Fraunce's preface is devoted to a defense of Ramistic logic against what he characterizes as "the importunate exclamations of a raging and fireyfaced Aristotelean." This Aristotelian, seeing Ramus's logic to be highly esteemed, cries out against it in arguments that are in one sense the ageless outcry of old men against the innovations of the young, and in another sense a lament for the decline of Aristotle, for the spread of education to the masses, and for the profanation of the temple of learning by the lower middle class. Fraunce reports this Aristotelian thus:

Good God, what a world is this? VVhat an age doe wee now lyue in? A Sopister in tymes past was a tytle of credite, and a woord of commendation; nowe what more odious? Aristotle then the father of Philosophy; now who lesse fauoured? Ramus rules abroade, Ramus

164 *Ibid.*, sig. ¶v.   165 *Ibid.*, sig. ¶2v-¶3r.

at home, and who but Ramus? Antiquity is nothing but Dunsicality, & our forefathers inuentions vnprofitable trumpery. Newfangled, youngheaded, harebrayne boyes will needes bee Maysters that neuer were Schollers; prate of methode, who neuer knew order; rayle against Aristotle assoone as they are crept out of the shell. Hereby it comes to passe that euery Cobler can cogge a Syllogisme, euery Carter crake of Propositions. Hereby is Logike prophaned, and lyeth prostitute, remooued out of her Sanctuary, robbed of her honour, left of her louers, rauyshed of straungers, and made common to all, which before was proper to Schoolemen, and only consecrated to Philosophers.[166]

Under Fraunce's satirical distortions this argument may seem less persuasive than amusing at first; but still it cannot be disposed of simply by ridicule, or deprecated as unable to rally conservative learning to new resistance against the radicals. Thus Fraunce does rightly to answer it with partial seriousness:

Coblers bee men, why therefore not Logicians? and Carters haue reason, why therefore not Logike? *Bonum, quò communius, eo melius*, you say so your selues, and yet the best thing in Logike you make to be the woorst, in thinking it lesse commendable, because it is more common. A spytefull speach, and a meaning no lesse malitious, to locke vp Logike in secreate corners, who, as of her selfe shee is generally good to all, so will shee particularly bee bound to none. Touching the gryefe you conceaue for the contempt of Aristotle, it is needles and vnnecessary: for, where Aristotle deserueth prayse, who more commendeth him then Ramus? VVhere he hath too much, Ramus cutteth off, where too little, addeth, where any thing is inuerted, hee bringeth it to his owne proper place, and that according to the direction of Aristotle his rules. Then, whereas there can bee no Art both inuented and perfected by the same man, if Aristotle did inuent Logike, as hee perswadeth you, hee did not perfect it, if hee did not finish it, there is some imperfection, if there bee any want, why then allow you all?[167]

After these words Fraunce immediately closes his preface with the hope that his readers will derive as much profit from practising as he has had pleasure in going through "this last explication of Ramus his Logike." In such a mood he turns from promise to performance and begins the first legal logic in the English language.

His explication of Ramus follows the general pattern of the latter's *Dialectiqve* and its Latin counterpart, the *Dialecticae Libri Duo*.

---

[166] *Ibid.*, sig. ¶¶2v.   [167] *Ibid.*, sig. ¶¶3r.

Indeed, Fraunce openly stresses that he had these two works before him as he notes that the second is somewhat differently arranged from the first. Speaking of the topic of final cause, he thus refers to both these classics:

> *Ramus* in his *French* Logike placeth the end first, sith, according to *Aristotle* in the second of his *Physikes*, the ende is first in conceipt and consideration, though last in execution. But in the last edition of his Latine Logike hée setteth it in the last place, respecting rather *finem rei*, then *efficientis scopum & intentionem*, which last resolution of his I follow at this present, yet not so resolutely, but that I can bée content to heare their aduise, who bid vs take héede that we confound not the finall cause with the thing caused.[168]

"I haue in my text kept my selfe," says Fraunce in his second chapter, "onely to such maximaes both in Inuention and Disposition, as are put downe orderly by *Ramus*, and are essentially belonging to this art: yet for the satisfiyng of the expectation of some yoong Logicians, somewhat vnacquainted with this newfound Logike, as it pleaseth some to tearme it, I will héereafter, as occasion shall serue, put downe in the annotations, some of the other stampe."[169] These words are accurate as the statement of a part of Fraunce's procedure in *The Lawiers Logike*. His most extensive chapters consist of as many as five sections. A first section contains Ramist doctrine stated in English, and this is a continuing element throughout the entire work. Another section consists of illustrations of Ramus's doctrine, both from Spenser's English poetry and from the Latin and "Hotch-pot French"[170] of England's early legal literature. Still another section consists of annotations. These are in English or in Latin. Sometimes an annotation will appear to be Fraunce's commentary on Ramus when in reality it is merely Fraunce's translation of Ramus's French text.[171] At other times the annotations will be clearly credited

---

[168] *Ibid.*, fol. 25r. For later references by Fraunce to Ramus's "French Logike," see foll. 110r and 113r.

[169] *Ibid.*, foll. 7v-8r.

[170] This is Fraunce's own phrase, *ibid.*, sig. ¶3r.

[171] A good illustration of this occurs at fol. 24r, where Fraunce appears to be annotating Ramus's doctrine concerning the formal and final cause. Says Fraunce: "So euery naturall thing hath his peculiar forme, as a lyon, a horse, a trée, &c. the heauen, the earth, the sea, &c. So euery artificiall thing also, as a house, a shippe, &c. So things incorporall, as vertue, vice, &c. So in a woord, whatsoeuer is, by the formall cause it is that which it is, and is different from all other things that it is not."
Here is the passage in Ramus's *Dialectiqve* (Paris, 1555), p. 8, from which Fraunce translates this annotation: "Ainsi toute choses naturelles ont leur forme, comme le Lyon, le Cheual, l'Arbre, le Ciel, la Terre: Ainsi les choses artificielles, comme vne maison,

to their sources, as when open reference is made to such Ramists as Piscator, Beurhaus, Scribonius, and Talaeus, or to such scholastics as Sturm, Hotman, Agricola, and Melanchthon. Hotman is cited as often as any of these, perhaps because his known interest in logic and his European reputation in the field of legal scholarship provided Fraunce with a contemporary model for his pioneering attempt to bring logic and law together in England.[172] It is obvious that Fraunce intended his annotations to be as important a contribution to Ramism as were his illustrations. In addition to these two sections, and of course the actual statement of Ramist doctrine, his chapters contain nothing that needs to be mentioned, except perhaps for an occasional section headed canons or rules, and another headed elenchs or rebuttals. These two sections, however, usually occupy little space in comparison to the other three.

Like many other Ramists, Fraunce does not reproduce his master's doctrine without additions and changes. Thus at the end of his fourth chapter in Book I, he inserts a discussion of logical abuses, which, as he says, deceive the simple "with a glorious shew of counterfeit rea-

---

vne nauire: Ainsi semblablement les choses incorporelles, comme la couleur, la chaleur, la vertu & le vice a sa forme: Ainsi generallement toute chose est ce qu'elle est par sa forme, & par icelles est separée des autres."

There are many other passages in Fraunce which seem to be his own commentary on Ramus's doctrine but are in reality translations from Ramus's *Dialectiqve*. The following table indicates where many of them fall:

The Lawiers Logike		*Dialectiqve*
fol. 5r	Reference to Aristotle's *Elenchs*	p. 2
fol. 5r	Reference to Plato's *Timaeus*	p. 3
fol. 5r	Quotation from Parmenides	p. 3
fol. 5v	Aristotle made two logics	pp. 3–4
fol. 16r	Aristotle on the Efficient Cause	p. 9
fol. 16r	Ancient philosophers on Efficient Cause	p. 17
fol. 16v	Virgil quoted on advantage of knowing causation	p. 20
fol. 16v	Importance of efficient cause in daily affairs	p. 17
fol. 17r–17v	Aristotle on Fortune & Chance; and also Ovid, and Cicero, and Epicurus, and Cicero again, and a pagan poet	pp. 15–17
fol. 24r	Aristotle on the two properties of form	p. 7
fol. 24v	Aristotle on Pythagorean idea that number is the cause, Plato on idea as cause	pp. 8–9
fol. 31r	Parmenio, Philotas, Lentulus, etc.	p. 21
fol. 39v	Propertius & Ronsard	p. 25
foll. 66v–67r	Plato's complaint against the use of authority	pp. 64–65
fol. 81r–81v	Socrates and Aristotle on Menon's dilemma*	pp. 66–69
fol. 98v	The syllogism as an arithmetical deduction	p. 89

* This borrowing is placed by Fraunce under "Elenchs," not "Annotations."

[172] For Hotman's logical theory, see his *Dialecticae Institutionis Libri IV* (1573), a copy of which is in the Bibliothèque Nationale of Paris. For a brief discussion of it, see Rodolphe Dareste, *Essai sur François Hotman* (Paris, 1850), p. 33.

sons, commonly called Fallacians."[173] Fraunce found this doctrine, not in Ramus's French *Dialectiqve*, but in the older scholastic logics. Again, after his chapter on logical effects, when he would normally take up next the concept of subject, Fraunce defines and discusses instead the doctrine of the whole, the part, the genus, and the species.[174] Readers of Ramus know that he places the doctrine of these four terms under the category of derivative primary arguments, and deals with them when he speaks of dividing wholes into parts.[175] Fraunce thus opposes himself to Ramus by placing the four terms under primary arguments. In his discussion of them, Fraunce recognizes that it is expedient for him to give some reason "why I seuer the generall, speciall, whole and parte from the tractate of diuision, where *Ramus* placed them."[176] The reason, as he there states it, is that Talaeus had suggested the primary, as opposed to the derivative primary, character of the doctrine belonging to these four terms. This suggestion Fraunce himself elects to follow, even though Talaeus had ended by not following it. Still again Fraunce departs from Ramus by discussing the topic of comparatives in a kind of appendix to the doctrine of invention, not as the last element in the category of primary arguments. This departure has the effect of placing such matters as quality, quantity, like, unlike, equal, greater, and less between the twentieth and twenty-four chapters of Fraunce's first book rather than between the twelfth and the sixteenth chapters, as a strict adherence to Ramus would have required. No one should attach particular importance to this or other discrepancies between these two logicians. Fraunce did not make changes with the idea of becoming a renegade Ramist, nor would any of his contemporaries have thought him one. Discrepancies between one Ramist and another are always in evidence, as I have often suggested, and they are to be accepted only as a reminder that they can exist and flourish without thereby creating any serious divisions within Ramism as a movement.

Fraunce's attempt to interpret Ramus for lawyers would normally be expected to suggest the desirability of performing the same task for preachers. To some extent, of course, Dudley Fenner had had preachers in mind when he published his translation of Ramus's *Dialecticae Libri Duo* in 1584, although he did not particularly emphasize sacred logic beyond providing biblical illustrations for the

[173] *The Lawiers Logike*, fol. 26v.   [174] *Ibid.*, foll. 31v-37v.
[175] See above, p. 156.   [176] *The Lawiers Logike*, fol. 35r.

doctrines in his source. In the decade following Fenner's work and Fraunce's *The Lawiers Logike*, William Perkins, as we have seen,[177] took up the challenge of writing about pulpit oratory in terms reminiscent of Ramus; but while he made preaching his central subject, as Fenner had not done, he failed to emphasize Ramus's doctrine in such a way as to make his learned Latin treatise a full commitment in that direction. The first author to compose in English a full Ramistic logic for preachers, and to appear to be trying to do for divines what Fraunce had done for lawyers, published his work in 1620, when Perkins had been dead for eighteen years, and Fraunce was sixty years old or more. That author was Thomas Granger, himself a preacher, who had studied at Peterhouse College, Cambridge, between 1598 and 1605, and had received in that time both his bachelor's and master's degrees.

Granger's Ramistic treatise on preaching is called the *Syntagma Logicvm*, that is, *The Logic Book*, or (to quote the author's own explanatory subtitle) *The Divine Logike*.[178] A Latin preface of seven pages dedicates the work to Francis Bacon, "a most honorable, most sagacious, and most learned man." In the main, however, Granger keeps to his own native language and loses no time in identifying the text of his work with Ramistic logic. On his title page he sets forth in Latin an aphoristic definition of each member of the trivium, and immediately adds in connection with the third definition a pithy comparison between the logic of Aristotle and that of Ramus. This comparison would read thus in English:

> From ancient minerals did pagan Aristotle polish the golden organon. First to the uses of theology did Christian Ramus with rare judgement accommodate it.

The same comparison, carried somewhat further, is the theme of an English laudatory stanza that precedes Granger's actual text.

---

[177] See above, pp. 206-207.

[178] Its title page reads as follows: "Syntagma Logicvm. or, The Divine Logike. Seruing especially for the vse of Diuines in the practise of preaching, and for the *further helpe of iudicious Hearers, and* generally for all. By Thomas Granger Preacher of Gods Word.

Grata quidem ratio est concordi voce relata, Gram.
Gratior est ratio veniens ratione venusta, Rhet.
Grata ter est ratio veniens ratione polita. Logic.
E veterum mineralibus organon aureum expoliuit Aristoteles *ethnicus.*
Ad vsum inprimis Theologicum summo cum iudicio accommodauit Ramus *Christianus.*
London, Printed by *William Iones*, and are to be sold by *Arthur Iohnson*, dwelling in *Pauls* Church-yard at the signe of the white Horse. 1620."

This stanza is one of six appearing at the head of Book I, and it is first of two English stanzas, the previous four having been in Greek or Latin. This English stanza reads as follows:

> This book's a *Garden* where doth grow a *Tree*,
> Cal'd Logike, fruitfull for Theologie.
> The *Roote*, whose sappe doth vegetate the rest,
> Is *Aristotle* height, because the best.
> The *Boughes & Branches* growing thence, are *Ramus*,
> *Douname, Beurhusius, Temple,* and *Polanus,*
> And here and there, some other fruits doe grow,
> Of pleasant taste, and of delightfull show.
> Each reader may this *Garden* make his owne,
> (And many will no doubt, when it is knowne.)
> Then giue the price, (but small) to them that sell,
> And thanke the Gardner dressing it so well.[179]

It is impossible to say that this description of *The Divine Logike* reflects Granger's own exact view of the connection between his work and that of the Ramists. After all, the stanza just quoted is unsigned, and the one just before and just after it bear the name of John Jones of Cambridge.[180] But Granger's similar view is available, nevertheless, in his own signed English preface to his work, where he addresses his readers on the subject of his relation to contemporary logic. He speaks there of the ancient change that had occurred in logical theory when logicians, ceasing to be occupied exclusively with philosophical disputation and its rewards of applause, began to concern themselves with fashioning logic in such a way "that it might be as apt an instrument for Oratours in pleading, and Rhetoricians in declaming, as for Philosophers in disputing."[181] Just as the ancient logicians had adapted logic to philosophers and orators, Granger goes on, "so the *moderne,* and newest (according to the necessitie, condition, and exigence of times) to the practise of Diuines also, both for the composing of common places, and other tractates, and also for the interpretation, explication, amplification, and illustration of the

---

[179] *The Divine Logike*, sig. a4v. The Polanus referred to here is Amandus Polanus von Polansdorf, a Prussian, who served as professor of theology at Basel, and whose work, the *Syntagma Theologiae Christianae* (Geneva, 1612), probably suggested Granger's title.

[180] This Jones, a member of Caius College, and a bachelor of arts in 1618-19, was son of Granger's printer, William Jones. See *Alumni Cantabrigienses,* Pt. 1, s.v. Joanes, John.

[181] *The Divine Logike*, sig. a2r.

Diuine text, or any other worke for the benefite of Gods Church."[182] Having thus identified the trend in the logic of his day towards the needs of the preacher, Granger states his own ambition:

> To this end also haue I perused the chiefest and best in this facultie, and out of their Texts, and Commentaries (as the learned may easily see) as also from myne owne practise, and experience haue I composed this worke, therein directly ayming at the benefite, and helpe of Preachers, and hearers, which haue some vnderstanding alreadie in the rules of this Art, or that are desirous to attaine to some knowledge, and practise thereof.[183]

The "chiefest and best" logicians to whom Granger here refers do not remain entirely anonymous throughout his preface. In fact, he mentions at once the one who to his mind apparently qualifies for recognition above all other contemporaries—Ramus. Speaking of Ramus as too epitomized to be understood by the unlearned without a lengthy commentary, and characterizing lengthy commentaries as too verbose to be useful to the learned who have already mastered them in epitome, Granger thus defines his special aim:

> Therefore I haue heere walked in the middle path, that neither the skilfull might iustly taxe me with prolixitie, nor the vnskilfull with breuitie. For this worke is in very deede an Epitome of the best Expositions, and Logicall tractates both old, and new; and againe, *Ramus* is an Epitome of this: which being well perused thou shalt finde him (that seemes so obscure to all) as plaine, and easie, as the a b c. So that this worke may serue insteed of all commenters, and *Ramus* himselfe for an Epitome.[184]

The Divine Logike adheres to this statement of purpose. It emerges as an English epitome of the standard commentaries on Ramistic logic, to which it adds dashes of scholastic doctrine for good measure; and it also emerges as an English commentary on the logical system epitomized in Ramus's *Dialecticae Libri Duo.* Of the two parts of logic it says that the "former is of the purpose, or matter propounded, whether it bee in minde, word, or writing: the second is of iudgement."[185] Argument, an aspect of matter, is considered as to invention and disposition.[186] Under invention are given the familiar Ramistic classifications: arguments are "artificiall" or "inartificiall", artificial arguments are "prime" or "primortiue"; prime

---

[182] *Ibid.,* sig. a2r-a2v. [183] *Ibid.,* sig. a2v. [184] *Ibid.,* sig. a3r.
[185] *Ibid.,* p. 2. [186] *Ibid.,* p. 11.

arguments lead ultimately to the consideration of "Cause," "Effect," "Subiect," "Adiunct," opposites, comparatives; primortive arguments lead ultimately to the consideration of reasoning from name, from divisions, and by definitions; and at last inartificial arguments lead to the consideration of divine testimonies, human testimonies, and the like.[187] Books II, III, and IV discuss disposition under the Ramistic headings of axioms, syllogisms, and method, as Book I had discussed invention.

Like Fraunce and the other English Ramists, Granger does not hesitate to take liberties with his basic source. The best illustration of this, and the only one I shall mention, is to be found in Book V of *The Divine Logike*. Here Granger turns to the subject of judgment and fallacies. Ramus did not treat fallacies as a part of logic when he wrote his *Dialectiqve*, and judgment was in his view not only the second grand division of logic but also an exact synonym of disposition. Granger follows Ramus in making judgment the second part of logic, while he departs from Ramus by considering disposition as a kind of subdivision of the first part, that is, the part belonging to the content or matter of discourse. Thus the act of judging becomes for Granger the act of evaluating a discourse already devised and arranged. Here is what he says at the very beginning of Book V on the relations between judgment and disposition:

> *Ivdgement*, is the second part of Logicke, whereby euery proposite, or oration, is iudged, and censured, whether it be according to Truth, and sound Reason, or otherwise. It is the Consequent, Effect, and End of Disposition.

This concept permits Granger to discuss in a subsequent chapter Ramus's famous three laws, which of course are a standard part of the second grand division of Ramistic logic. And it permits Granger also to introduce the subject of fallacies and refutations for the closing pages of his work, with the result that he like Fraunce is able to give his readers the most attractive feature of scholastic logic as an entity within the system of Ramus.

Six years after the publication of Granger's *Divine Logike* there appeared at London a translation of Ramus's *Dialecticae Libri Duo* under the name of Antony Wotton. This work is unusual in being the first English translation of Ramus's logic since MacIlmaine's to advertise itself on its title page for what it is. It is also unusual in

[187] *Ibid.*, pp. 11-233.

having its title page state that Ramus's logical system is basically a reorganization of scholastic logic. Here are the words used by Wotton to convey these and other points:

> The Art of Logick. Gathered out of *Aristotle*, and set in due forme, according to his instructions, by *Peter Ramus*, Professor of *Philosophy* and *Rhetorick* in *Paris*, and there Martyred for the Gospell of the *Lord Iesus*. With a short Exposition of the Praecepts, by which any one of indifferent *capacitie, may with a little paines*, attaine to some competent knowledge and vse of that noble *and necessary Science*. Published for the Instruction of the vnlearned, by Antony Wotton.[188]

It turns out in his preface that Antony Wotton had studied Ramus's logic more than forty years before, and had found it continuously useful since. Hence he had appointed his son in Cambridge to do a translation of it and had given the latter a set of Latin notes on Ramus's text as a general guide to the whole undertaking. Those notes appear in the present book, says Wotton, as the basis of the exposition of Ramus's doctrine, whereas the present translation of that doctrine, and the scriptural illustrations, are the work of the son. The preface does not add that the son's name is Samuel, and that Samuel was even then a fellow of King's College, having taken his bachelor's degree in 1625.[189] Nor does the preface expressly acknowledge that Antony had been student and fellow at King's in the days of William Temple's appointment at the same college,[190] and probably had acquired from that distinguished scholar not only his initial interest in Ramus but also the material for the Latin notes which Samuel had been given as a way of preparing him to do his translation. No blame should be attached to Antony, however, for his failure to mention these facts. After all, what he does say in his preface makes it sufficiently possible to determine them. Moreover, his own attainment in years, the nearness of his death, and the quality of his learning in logic are reasons why the son no doubt preferred to have the father's name by itself upon the title page of their joint work on Ramus.[191]

Another English translation of the main ideas of Ramus's logic

---

[188] The imprint reads: "London Printed by I. D. for *Nicholas Bourne*, and are to be sold at his shop at the *Exchange*. 1626."

[189] See *Alumni Cantabrigienses*, Pt. 1, s.v. Wotton, Samuel.

[190] See *Dictionary of National Biography*, s.v. Wotton, Anthony (1561?-1626).

[191] Antony Wotton died December 11, 1626. The preface to his *Logick* is dated May 2 of that year.

appeared at London two years after the one just discussed, and was unusual in being accompanied by a commentary that attempted to reconcile Aristotle and Ramus, then to correct the shortcomings of Ramus wherever he did not agree with Aristotle, and finally to expound both authors from the writings of the Scholastics. The author of this ambitious undertaking was Thomas Spencer, and his own title page is in fact a statement of these three very purposes:

> The Art of Logick, Delivered in the Precepts of *Aristotle* and *Ramvs*. VVhwerein 1. The agreement of both Authors is declared. 2. The defects in *Ramus*, are supplied, and his superfluities pared off, by the Precepts of *Aristotle*. 3. The precepts of both, are expounded and applyed to vse, by the assistance of the best Schoolemen. By Tho: Spencer.[192]

In the work lying under this title, Spencer has followed the method of placing within each chapter, usually at the beginning but sometimes elsewhere as well, an English translation of doctrine conspicuously identified in the adjacent margin as from Ramus; and of proceeding then to confirm and explain that doctrine by reference to ancient and recent logicians. Aristotle's *Organon* is his chief ancient source, although he also refers many times to Porphyry's *Isagoge*.[193] As for the "best Schoolemen" promised by his title, they turn out to be important figures in medieval and Renaissance philosophy. Two of them are Peter Fonseca and Sebastian Couto, Portuguese commentators on Aristotle, and authors of the widely known *Commentarii Collegii Conimbricensis e Societate Jesu in vniuersam Dialecticam Aristotelis*, which Spencer cites on several occasions as the logic of "the Iesuites."[194] Another schoolman is Pierre d'Ailly, French ecclesiastic and philosopher of the late fourteenth and early fifteenth centuries.[195] Still another is the medieval English logician, William Ockham.[196] Still another is Saint Thomas Aquinas, whom Spencer

---

[192] The imprint reads: "London Printed by *Iohn Dawson* for *Nicholas Bourne*, at the South entrance of the *Royall Exchange*. 1628."

[193] See *Art of Logick*, pp. 59, 60, 63, 69, 70, 71, 129, 130, 131, for a sample of Spencer's references to Porphyry. His references to Aristotle are so numerous as to make it inexpedient to list them here.

[194] *Ibid.*, pp. 3-8. For an account of this Jesuit commentary, see *The Catholic Encyclopedia*, s.v. Conimbricenses.

[195] *Art of Logick*, pp. 78, 97, 100, 167, 173, 175, 185, 262. Spencer refers to him by his Latin name Aliaco.

[196] *Ibid.*, pp. 8, 27, 33, 50, 53, 107, 109, 118, 119, 130. For an analysis of Ockham's contribution to logical theory, see Boehner, *Medieval Logic An Outline of Its Development from 1250 to c. 1400*, pp. 36-44.

cites more often than any of the other schoolmen.[197] In the ideas and words of these and lesser authorities, Spencer sets forth the topics and subtopics of the theory of invention and disposition, featuring only the name of Ramus in the marginal notations, adhering in general to the order prescribed by Ramus, and emphasizing everywhere Ramus's main points, including the famous three laws.[198]

One of the defects in Ramus to be corrected by Spencer from the precepts of Aristotle concerns the doctrine of the ten categories. The ten categories were part of the machinery of invention in scholastic logic. Ramus, in redesigning that machinery, had kept to the notion of ten basic seats of argument, but had not named those seats as Aristotle named his categories. It thus turned out that, whereas under invention the scholastic logicians talked of substance, quantity, quality, relation, place, time, posture, apparel, doing, or suffering, the Ramists made invention consist of cause, effect, subject, adjunct, and six other places of predication. Spencer combines these two systems. He gives one chapter to Aristotle's categories, and pays special attention to the category of primary substance, under which he discusses what Ramus calls effect and subject.[199] Then he devotes twenty-five chapters to Ramus's other places of invention, finding Aristotelian authority for them, of course. As to his inclusion of effect and subject under primary substance, he has this to say:

> This Doctrine is peculiar to *Aristotle: Ramus* doth not acknowledge it; for, he hath not a word of it: It may bee, he conceived, that, 1. To set downe all the seats of arguments in one place together, would breed a needles repetition. 2. These single termes did not appertaine to *Logick.* 3. The first substance, or thing subiected, in every sentence, hath not the nature of an argument. It is very likely, that, he thought thus: because, this doctrine of *Aristotle* hath beene anciently receiued; therefore, hee would not depart from it vnles hee had some reason for it: and I conceiue, he had no reason, but these 3.[200]

Although Spencer proceeds to reject each of these three reasons, he does so without a trace of disrespect for Ramus's Aristotelian learning. He seems, indeed, to argue his case more to justify his restoring

---

[197] *Art of Logick*, pp. 2, 16-18, 22, 23, 25, 26, 29, 33, 39, 43, 45, 47, 48, 50, 53, 54, 56, 60, 77, 81, 83, 85, 86, 93, 97, 112, 130, 134, 168, 185, 195, 201, 202, 203. Spencer's references are for the most part to the *Summa Theologica.*

[198] *Art of Logick*, pp. 11-147 (for invention), 149-311 (for disposition) and 179-181 (for the three laws).

[199] *Ibid.*, pp. 14-23.

[200] *Ibid.*, p. 19.

of the ten categories to logical theory than to explain what logicians should do with them once they were restored.

The chief superfluity which Spencer sees in Ramus, and hence abandons on the authority of Aristotle, is the doctrine of method. This doctrine occupied the third and last position in Ramus's treatment of disposition or judgment. As Spencer finishes his analysis of propositions and syllogisms, the two other parts of Ramistic disposition, he suddenly says without preamble:

> Now we are come to an end of all the precepts of *Logicke*: so as, there is no more required, to make a Logician, then what hath beene sayd alreadie. But that seemes not enough to *Ramus*, for he brings another member of this art, and calls it *Methode*: but I omit the same of purpose; for divers reasons.[201]

Only the last of Spencer's four reasons appears to be the one which could have moved him to omit from his Ramistic treatise what is in effect the very hallmark of Ramism. He gave that reason as the concluding statement of his work:

> He [Ramus] alledges *Aristotles* authoritie for method; but altogether without cause; for he alledgeth no place, nor words, and I am sure he cannot. *Aristotle* calls all the precepts of *Logicke* a Method, whereby wee come to know, how to discusse. *Top. lib.* I. *cap.* 2. *lib.* 8. *cap.* 12. *prior. lib.* I. *cap.* 31. therfore he did neuer meane to make *Method*, one member of his Art, distinct from the rest: seeing therefore we haue nothing to say touching *Method*, I must here put an end to the whole Worke.[202]

Now, this reasoning ignores the fact that Ramus had conceived of his logic as in one sense the ancient science of dialectical invention and judgment, and in another sense the ancient science of rhetorical invention and disposition. Thus he had drawn into logic a distillation of such theories of argument as Aristotle's *Topics* and Cicero's *Topics*, as well as a distillation of what Aristotle's *Rhetoric* and Cicero's voluminous rhetorical writings had to say on invention and disposition in oratory. At the same time, Ramus had restricted rhetorical theory to the subjects of style and delivery, on the assumption that the other subjects of ancient rhetoric were adequately covered in logic. So when Spencer says that Ramus has no authority in Aristotle for making method a division of the theory of discussion,

[201] *Ibid.*, pp. 309-310.   [202] *Ibid.*, p. 311.

he is thinking only of Aristotle's *Organon*, not of Aristotle's *Rhetoric*; for in the latter work method as the theory of arrangement of persuasive discourse is explicitly treated.[203] It is true that Ramus's theory of the natural method as the strict arranging of propositions in a descending order of generality has no authority in Aristotle's *Rhetoric* or *Organon*. But Ramus's theory of the prudential method can claim some authority in Aristotle's *Rhetoric*, and his theory of method as a part of logic is not an unwarranted deduction from the ancient dialecticians.[204] What Spencer's reasoning does is to bring out unwittingly that Ramus, bound as he was to Plato, Aristotle, and Cicero, managed nevertheless to give the ancient theory of arrangement a novel twist and to emerge as the first thinker of the modern era to insist upon adding to the ancient doctrine of persuasive arrangement the concept of expository or learned discourse as having its separate theory of form.

The last English translation of Ramus's *Dialecticae Libri Duo* ever to be printed appeared in 1632 and several times thereafter during the course of the seventeenth century. It was the work of Robert Fage, and its title page is an exact description of its contents:

> Peter Ramus of Vermandois, The Kings Professor, his Dialectica in two bookes. Not onely translated into English, but also digested into questions and answers for the more facility of understanding. By R. F. *Gent*. London. Printed by W. J. 1632.

The dedicatory letter identifies the "R. F." of the title page as "Ro. Fage," and assigns the book to the author's uncle, Bestney Parker, indicating also that the translation had been first done for the latter in the form of a continuous discourse, and then altered to become a dialogue. Since there was a Robert Fage who studied at St. Catharine's College, Cambridge, between 1621 and 1627, and received in that period both his bachelor's and master's degrees, it is almost a certainty that he is the "Ro. Fage" of the Ramus translation. If so, the last Englishman to translate Ramus's *Dialecticae Libri Duo* became vicar of Fulbourn in Cambridgeshire in 1632, the year when his translation appeared, and was later made vicar of Wilburton, where he died in 1669.[205]

As for the later editions of Fage's translation, there would seem

---

[203] See the closing words of Book II of the *Rhetoric*, as well as the opening chapter and the seven closing chapters of Book III.

[204] See for example Plato's *Phaedrus*, 265-266.

[205] See *Alumni Cantabrigienses*, Pt. I, s.v. Fage or Fagge, Robert.

to have been six in all. Walter J. Ong, S.J., calls attention to an apparently unique copy of an edition bearing the date of 1635, and to another apparently unique copy of an edition of 1636.[206] He has also identified Fage's translation as the first unit in a work published at London in 1651 under the title, *A Compendium of the Art of Logick and Rhetorick in the English Tongue, Containing All that Peter Ramus, Aristotle, and Others Have Writ Thereon: with Plaine Directions for the More Easie Understanding and Practice of the Same.*[207] This particular edition of Fage's translation does not bear its author's name, and thus cannot easily be recognized for what it is. The same observation applies to the next three editions. John Milton's nephew and pupil, Edward Phillips, published a miscellany at London in 1658 and 1685 under the title, *The Mysteries of Love & Eloquence*, and at London in 1699 under the title, *The Beau's Academy*. There is a treatise on logic in this miscellany, and it was J. Milton French who first identified it as the work of Ramus and Fage.[208] Thus at the very end of its career in translation in England, as at the very end of its career there in scholarly Latin text and commentary, Ramus's *Dialecticae Libri Duo* manages to get itself associated with the name of Milton, though Phillips, who probably became interested in Ramism when Milton was tutoring him in the early sixteen-forties, hardly qualifies as an English Ramist in any but a passive sense.

The concluding topic in this history of Ramistic logic in England brings Ramus into the English theater and makes him a figure in English drama. Two playwrights of the late sixteenth century deserve special mention in this connection. One of them has not been identified, although the play of his in which Ramus is mentioned survives. The other is Christopher Marlowe, whose undergraduate days at Corpus Christi College in Cambridge occurred at the time when William Temple of nearby King's was rising to fame as the leading Cambridge Ramist and was engaging Everard Digby in controversy on the question of Ramus's theory of method.

Marlowe's *The Massacre at Paris*, probably composed in the very early fifteen-nineties, and performed a number of times before Lon-

---

[206] See his "Hobbes and Talon's Ramist Rhetoric in English," *Transactions of the Cambridge Bibliographical Society*, I (1949-1953), 261, note 1.

[207] *Ibid.*, pp. 260-261. For a discussion of the other items in this compendium, see below, pp. 276, 279, 384.

[208] J. Milton French, "Milton, Ramus, and Edward Phillips," *Modern Philology*, XLVII (November 1949), 82-87.

don audiences in the following decade,[209] makes use of the massacre
of St. Bartholomew for its titular materials, although the play as a
whole dramatizes French history between 1572 and 1589, with
leading emphasis upon the murderous struggles among Henry of
Anjou, Henry of Navarre, and Henry of Guise for the throne of
France. This war of the three Henries came to a climax in the assassination of Henry of Guise at the command of Anjou, who was
reigning as Henry III. Thereafter, Henry III was assassinated by
a fanatic monk of the Catholic faction which Guise had headed, and
Henry of Navarre, a Protestant and the son of Antoine de Bourbon
and Jeanne d'Albret, ascended the French throne as Henry IV to
place the Bourbon dynasty in its long tenure of power.

At the beginning of Marlowe's play, the marriage of Henry of
Navarre and Margaret, Anjou's sister, is being celebrated, and
Henry of Guise is beginning to lay plans to kill Navarre's mother,
and Navarre himself, as well as Admiral Coligny, the greatest
Protestant leader in France. Guise's agents proceed at once to murder
Navarre's mother by giving her a pair of poisoned gloves, and to
attempt Coligny's life by shooting him with a musket ball. In actual
historical fact the death of Navarre's mother under circumstances
suggesting that she was poisoned occurred some two months before
the marriage of Navarre and Margaret.[210] Thus at this point Marlowe is guilty of an anachronism, but his error is dramatically effective, nevertheless, and it lays no undeserved amount of extra guilt
upon Guise. After the attempted assassination of Coligny, Guise is
driven into an alliance with the queen-mother of France, Catherine
de' Medici, and with Anjou, the result of which is the massacre of
St. Bartholomew. Marlowe traces this tragic occurrence from the
fatal stabbing of Coligny to Guise's preoccupation with Protestant
victims of the humblest sort. From that point the scene of the play
widens to permit the development of the dynastic themes that the
blood and violence of the massacre have endowed with tragic values.

One of the episodes in Marlowe's dramatic version of the massacre
is that in which Ramus meets his death in the presence of Anjou and
Guise. Of all the victims of the actual massacre as depicted by Marlowe, Ramus is the most important historical personage, Navarre's
mother and Coligny having fallen before the signal for the beginning

---

[209] On these points, see *The Works of Christopher Marlowe*, ed. C. F. Tucker Brooke
(Oxford [1925]), p. 440. This edition is cited below as *Works of Marlowe*.

[210] For the sequence of these events, see *La Grande Encyclopédie*, s.v. Saint-Barthélemy.

of wholesale slaughter was given, and the other victims being obscure Protestants. As if to underline the importance of Ramus, he is the only victim to be killed by Anjou. Perhaps Marlowe thought it an ironic comment upon royalty that the king's professor of logic should be murdered without provocation by one who was soon to become King Henry III.

The actual scene of the murder is swift and intense. As Ramus is sitting in his study, against the background of frightened cries from the oncoming horror, his friend and collaborator Talaeus enters and begs him to fly for his life if he would escape the Guisians. Then Talaeus leaps out of the window and disappears through the ranks of the assassins, as they recognize him for a Catholic and suffer him to go. Perhaps he does not hear Ramus's plea, "Sweet *Taleus* stay."[211] Or perhaps he does and chooses not to heed. In either event, the historical Talaeus should not be blamed at all, for he was dead when Ramus met his violent end, and had been dead ten years. Here is a case where Marlowe's anachronism, if allowed to stand for fact, as it has stood in some editions of *The Massacre at Paris*,[212] would identify Talaeus with the crime of having deserted his best friend at a moment of crisis. At least Talaeus's sins cannot be expanded to include that of abandoning Ramus in the latter's final hour.

The indictment which Guise in Marlowe's play directs at Ramus before Anjou strikes Ramus down is surely reminiscent of attacks upon Ramism at Cambridge during Marlowe's student days. And what does that indictment consist in? It consists in the charge that Ramus is superficial as a thinker, irreverent as a student of Aristotle, injudicious as an advocate of dichotomies and epitomes, and rash as a disputant against the axioms of the doctors. Says Guise when Ramus asks wherein he had offended:

> Marry sir, in hauing a smack in all,
> And yet didst neuer sound anything to the depth.
> Was it not thou that scoftes the Organon,
> And said it was a heape of vanities?
> He that will be a flat dicotamest,
> And seen in nothing but Epitomies:
> Is in your iudgment thought a learned man.

[211] *Works of Marlowe*, p. 456.

[212] See *The Jew of Malta and The Massacre at Paris*, ed. Henry Stanley Bennett (London, [1931]), p. 203, where Talaeus is said to have survived the massacre and to have died in 1610.

And he forsooth must goe and preach in Germany:
Excepting against Doctors axioms,
And *ipse dixi* with this quidditie,
Argumentum testimonii est inartificiale.
To contradict which, I say *Ramus* shall dye:
How answere you that? your *nego argumentum*
Cannot serue, sirra: kill him.[213]

At Ramus's plea for a hearing, Anjou bids him speak, and the ensuing response may be considered to have been composed in Cambridge rather than Paris. Ramus says that he wants a hearing, not to prolong his life, but to cleanse himself of malicious misrepresentations like those of James Schegk. His defense of himself is that he had sought to improve the arrangement of Aristotle's logical writings, and that the man who hates Aristotle or loves his own works better than he loves God can never be a good logician or philosopher. Marlowe's words sound thus as Ramus speaks them:

Not for my life doe I desire this pause,
But in my latter houre to purge my selfe,
In that I know the things that I haue wrote,
Which as I heare one *Shekius* takes it ill,
Because my places being but three, contains all his:
I knew the Organon to be confusde,
And I reduc'd it into better forme.
And this for *Aristotle* will I say,
That he that despiseth him can nere
Be good in Logick or Philosophie.
And thats because the blockish Sorbonests
Attribute as much vnto their workes
As to the seruice of the eternall God.[214]

It is fitting that these last words should be a taunt at his enemies, for Ramus had offended many people in his time, and it was too late now for him to pretend diplomacy. Guise asks why Anjou should suffer this peasant to declaim, and Anjou stabs Ramus, saying, "Nere was there Colliars sonne so full of pride." Thus does Marlowe memorialize the murder of one of the chief influences behind the intellectual life of that time.

[213] *Works of Marlowe*, p. 457.
[214] *Ibid.*, p. 457. For further information about Shekius, that is, Schegt, see Waddington, *Ramus*, pp. 198-199, 216, 366, 394. The reference to Ramus's three places means that the ten fundamental terms of Ramus's theory of invention are grouped under three wider headings, that is, 1) artistic primary arguments, 2) artistic derivative primary arguments, and 3) non-artistic arguments. See above, pp. 155-156.

Ramus enters in less spectacular fashion into another drama of the late sixteenth century, *The Pilgrimage to Parnassus*.[215] This was a college play performed at St. John's College, Cambridge, in connection with the Christmas festivities of 1598.[216] Since no edition of this play was printed until 1886, and no second performance is known to have occurred,[217] the number of people to have been aware of it in its own time is limited, and thus it cannot claim to have made England conscious of Ramus to any appreciable extent. But it reflects the success of the English Ramists in making their cause a matter of familiar reference within their halls of learning, even if it did not contribute to the spread of that cause or to its impact upon the general public.

Under the image of a devout journey to the mountain of Apollo and the Muses, the *Pilgrimage* represents the struggle of undergraduates for their bachelor's degree. The play represents the students as passing through four realms of knowledge and as having to surmount four obstacles. The heroes are Philomusus and Studioso, that is, Muse-Lover and Zeal, who are sent on their way by Consiliodorus, that is, Hellenic Wisdom. Consiliodorus is father of Philomusus and uncle of Studioso. His words of advice and warning to the two young men occupy a large part of the first act, which is quite short, as are the other four.

The two pilgrims journey first through the land of logic, where they meet the student's first obstacle, Madido, the Moist One, or the Sot. Madido has never completed his journey to the sacred mountain, being addicted to wine, to Horace, and to the idea that the tavern is a better source of inspiration for the aspiring poet than is learning. Philomusus and Studioso are not greatly impressed with him, although perhaps Philomusus has a momentary desire to accept his invitation to a pint of wine.

Next after logic comes the sweet land of rhetoric, through which the pilgrims pass during Act III, and where they meet the student's second obstacle, Stupido, or Stupidity. Stupido has been on the pilgrimage for ten years, and has decided to go no further—a change of mind that appears essentially unprecipitate. Perhaps his being a puritan has something to do with his renunciation of rhetoric, poetry,

---

[215] For the text of this play, see *The Three Parnassus Plays* (*1598-1601*), ed. J. B. Leishman (London, 1949), pp. 95-132.

[216] *Ibid.*, pp. 24-26.

[217] *Ibid.*, pp. 8, 26.

and philosophy as vain and useless arts. Or perhaps, as Philomusus suggests, Stupido is one

> Who, for he cannot reach vnto the artes,
> Makes showe as though he would neglect the artes
> And cared not for the springe of Hellicon.[218]

In Act IV the pilgrims come to the land of poetry, where they meet the student's most dangerous obstacle, Amoretto, Little Cupid, or Love. His delight is in the verses of Ovid, his design is to remain forever in his present state, and his advice to Philomusus and Studioso is that they spend not their wanton youth "In sadd dull plodding on philosophers."

> *Studioso*   Yea but our springe is shorte, and winter longe:
> Our youth by trauellinge to Hellicon
> Must gett prouision for our latter years.
> *Amoretto*   Who thinks on winter before winter come
> Maks winter come in sommers fairest shine.
> There is no golden minte at Hellicon.
> Cropp you the ioyes of youth while that you maye,
> Sorowe and grife will come another daye.[219]

This argument proves irresistible, and the pilgrims decide as if to renounce their quest and to remain with Amoretto. But in Act V they are on their way again, this time in the land of philosophy, where they meet the student's last obstacle, Ingenioso, or Cleverness. Ingenioso is the crafty lad who knows more than the masters and the masterpieces. He has learned that there is no gold on Parnassus, and only the prospect of a vicarage or a schoolroom for those who reach the land of the Muses. But our pilgrims are now safe from further delay, and they come soon to the end of their four-year journey.

Ramus enters this play, not as a character, but as a reference. As Philomusus and Studioso begin the first stage of their journey in the land of logic, Studioso remarks that he has gotten hold of "Iacke Setons mapp" to guide them.[220] Thus it is plain that St. John's College, which had previously produced such anti-Ramists as Everard Digby, Robert Greene, and Thomas Nash, and such an ardent Ramist as Abraham Fraunce, was again in the camp of the scholastics in 1598, and could find no better guide than Peter Carter's edition of John Seton's *Dialectica*.[221] But it is Madido, the Sot, who mentions

[218] *Ibid.*, p. 117.   [219] *Ibid.*, p. 119.   [220] *Ibid.*, p. 101.
[221] See above, pp. 194, 197, 222.

that, when he first came to the land of logic on his way to Parnassus, he had begun "to reade Ramus his mapp, *Dialectica est,* &c.," and had thrown it away when "the slouenlie knaue presented mee with such an vnsauorie worde that I dare not name it, vnless I had some frankensence readie to perfume youre noses with after."[222] We may be sure that Madido is here referring to some word which had a prominent place in Ramus's *Dialecticae Libri Duo* as a scientific term and an equally prominent place in current undergraduate slang as a scatological term. Perhaps that word is "ars," the third term in Ramus's famous definition of dialectic, and the term which Madido would have had to mention next if he had completed his Latin quotation from the first chapter of the *Dialecticae Libri Duo.* At any rate, "ars" as a Latin term would at that time be part of every undergraduate's learned vocabulary, while as an English term for the buttocks it would not be used in polite speech, and it would suggest not only a certain untidiness in anyone who did use it but also certain characteristics that make Madido's reference to frankincense inelegant though understandable.

Ramus figures once more in the intellectual background of the *Pilgrimage.* When Philomusus and Studioso meet Stupido in the land of rhetoric, they find him a disciple of Ramus as well as a puritan and a scorner of "these vaine artes of Rhetorique, Poetrie, and Philosophie."[223] Stupido's first words to the pilgrims are these:

> Welcome my welbeloued brethren, trulie (I thanke god for it) I haue spent this day to my great comfort; I haue (I pray god prosper my labours) analised a peece of an homelie according to Ramus, and surelie in my minde and simple opinion Mr Peter maketh all things verie plaine and easie. As for Setons Logique, trulie I neuer looke on it but it makes my head ache.[224]

Since Philomusus and Studioso have already passed through the land of logic with the assistance of "Iacke Setons mapp," and since Stupido, who regards Seton as difficult, has by now spent ten years in getting through that same land under the guidance of Ramus, we have to conclude, of course, that the author of the *Pilgrimage* is making Ramus seem helpful only to the stupid, and is representing him as essentially beneath the notice of the wise and successful scholar. We have also to conclude that this same author is implying

[222] Leishman, *Three Parnassus Plays*, p. 108.
[223] *Ibid.*, p. 113.   [224] *Ibid.*, p. 112.

an adverse judgment against the puritans, with whom Stupido is repeatedly identified, and that he is expressing a favorable judgment toward the established church, which had its historical roots in John Seton's kind of Catholicism and scholasticism. But it is difficult to conclude, as Leishman does, that the Stupido of this play is a caricature of William Gouge.[225] When the *Pilgrimage* was performed at St. John's College in 1598, Gouge had been an undergraduate at nearby King's for only three years, whereas Stupido is caricatured as a slow undergraduate of ten years' standing. Moreover, Gouge was a good student, who stayed on at Cambridge to take the bachelor's and the master's degrees and to occupy a fellowship until 1604, whereas Stupido seems not to be headed in those directions. To be sure, Gouge was known as an undergraduate for his ability to defend Ramus, and his connection with puritanism is conspicuous.[226] But Ramists and puritans at Cambridge in the fifteen-nineties include William Perkins, Antony Wotton, and William Ames, as well as Gouge, and thus in a general way there are at least four possible candidates for the honor of being Stupido's counterpart. It is certain, therefore, that the audience which saw the *Pilgrimage* performed in 1598 would have had more than Gouge in mind as they speculated upon the identity of Stupido. It is also certain that they would have known all about Ramus, and that they would have applauded the historical accuracy of the *Pilgrimage* in representing the puritans in the person of Stupido as exempting both Ramistic and scholastic logic, but not rhetoric, poetry, and philosophy, from the catalogue of vain and useless arts.

As we turn now to Talaeus's rhetoric, which deserves to be ranked next to Ramus's logic among the important branches of Ramism in England, it might be well to mention in passing that these two liberal arts are not the only aspects of my present subject; for Ramus was accepted by Englishmen as an authority on grammar, arithmetic, and geometry as well. This fact is borne out by various publications in England in the period under discussion in this chapter. As early as 1581, Ramus's *Rudimenta Graeca* was given a printing at London; four years later *The latine grammar of P. Ramvs Translated into English* was published in an edition at London and in another at Cambridge; and in 1594, a Cambridge graduate student named Paul Greaves, of Christ's College, brought out at Cambridge his *Gram-*

[225] *Ibid.*, pp. 70-71.   [226] See above, pp. 199-200.

matica Anglicana, which described itself in its subtitle as "ad vnicam P. Rami methodum concinnata." Ramus's mathematical writings were meanwhile receiving attention from Englishmen. Thomas Hood, a graduate of Trinity College, Cambridge, and the first lecturer in mathematics under a foundation established by Thomas Smith for the instruction of citizens of London, published at London in 1590 *The Elementes of Geometrie,* a translation of Ramus's Latin treatise on this subject.[227] William Kempe, also a graduate of Trinity College, Cambridge, and master at Plymouth grammar school, published at London in 1592 *The Art of Arithmeticke in whole numbers and fractions,* this work being likewise translated from Ramus. William Bedwell, distinguished Arabic scholar and mathematician, as well as a graduate of Trinity College, Cambridge, and a friend of Thomas Hood, left behind when he died a work called *Via Regia ad Geometriam,* which was later published at London in 1636 under the editorship of John Clerke, and was offered to the public as Bedwell's translation and enlargement of Ramus. Bedwell, along with Kempe, Hood, and Greaves, offers further evidence of the influence of Ramus upon the intellectual life of Cambridge in the last quarter of the sixteenth century. In addition, these men illustrate how far Ramus's influence spread in England beyond the boundaries of logic and rhetoric.

[227] See *Dictionary of National Biography,* s.v. Hood, Thomas (*fl.* 1582-1598).

III. Ramus's Rhetoric in England

To Gabriel Harvey belongs the credit of being the first Englishman to interpret Ramistic rhetoric to his countrymen. Harvey was a student at Christ's College, Cambridge, during the early years of Laurence Chaderton's tenure as fellow at that very hall of learning, when Chaderton was arousing great interest by what may be regarded as the first lectures on Ramus's logic at an English university. Thus Chaderton was in a position to influence Harvey, as pointed out above,[1] and may even have done so. Years later, when Harvey was attacking Thomas Nash, he mentioned Chaderton's sermons, and described them as "methodicall"[2]—a particularly appropriate term if this is an instance of its being applied by a Ramist pupil to the work of his former Ramist master. But when Harvey himself described his original conversion to Ramism, he did not mention Chaderton among the influences that played upon him. He mentioned instead how he once came upon the *Ciceronianus* of Johannes Sambucus, an author connected by marriage with the prestige of Italian learning; and how in that work he found a eulogistic reference to Ramus's *Ciceronianus*, which he immediately proceeded to buy and to devour, reading "all of it in one day" and all of it again the next day.[3] This explanation may be more for the sake of impressiveness than of exactitude, inasmuch as it occurs when Harvey is addressing undergraduates and is working to give Ramus the glamor of a foreign as opposed to a local endorsement. But nevertheless it stands in the way of the confident assertion that Harvey was converted to Ramism by his older contemporary Chaderton.

The date of Harvey's reading of Ramus's *Ciceronianus* has been fixed as 1569.[4] Five years later, when Harvey was appointed praelector in rhetoric at Cambridge, he was presented with the opportunity of doing for Ramistic rhetoric in the English academic world what Chaderton had been doing already for Ramistic logic. Harvey's appointment as praelector occurred on April 23, 1574, two months before MacIlmaine's Latin text of Ramus's *Dialecticae Libri Duo* was registered for publication at the company of stationers in London. During the spring of 1575, while Englishmen were reading

---

[1] See p. 179.
[2] See Harvey, *Pierce's Supererogation* (London, 1593), in Smith, *Elizabethan Critical Essays*, II, 281.
[3] See Wilson and Forbes, *Gabriel Harvey's "Ciceronianus,"* pp. 18, 69-71.
[4] *Ibid.*, pp. 18, 20.

MacIlmaine's recent works on Ramistic logic, Harvey delivered his first course of lectures under his praelectorship, the two inaugural discourses being subsequently published at London in 1577 as the *Rhetor*.[5] He gave a second course of lectures in the spring of 1576, and the work which we know under the title of his *Ciceronianus*, also published at London in 1577, is the inaugural lecture of that series.[6] The *Rhetor* and the *Ciceronianus* are in Latin, and were no doubt in the first instance delivered as Latin lectures. Taken together they constitute an admirable statement of the basic philosophy of Ramistic rhetoric.

The *Rhetor* discusses natural inclination, theory, and practice as the three means to oratorical effectiveness. Natural inclination and theory are the topics of the first of the two lectures in the work, and practice is the topic of the second. Harvey often refers to the rhetorical learning of his day, and mentions such traditionalists as Agricola, Susenbrotus, Mosellanus, Sturm, and Erasmus;[7] but his favorite authorities are Ramus and Talaeus, as we would expect, while such Ramists as Foclin, Freigius, and Rodingus receive various degrees of attention.[8] All of these authors contribute more or less to Harvey's development of the Ramist view that rhetoric consists exclusively of style and delivery.

Early in his discussion of the topic of theory, Harvey sets forth the standard Ramist conception of the way in which the five parts of Ciceronian rhetoric should be detached from their traditional surroundings and redistributed between rhetoric and dialectic. The following passage speaks to that effect:

> For of that fivefold division, which has almost alone prevailed among our ancestors, how many now do not see that invention, disposition, and memory are not the property of speech but of thought, not of tongue but of mind, not of eloquence but of wisdom, not of rhetoric but of dialectic? Therefore two sole and as it were native parts re-

[5] The title page reads: "Gabrielis Harveii Rhetor, Vel duorum dierum Oratio, De Natura, Arte, & Exercitatione Rhetorica. Ad suos Auditores. Londini, Ex Officina Typographica Henrici Binneman. Anno. 1577."

[6] For a careful discussion of the dates of these two courses of lectures, see Wilson and Forbes, *Gabriel Harvey's "Ciceronianus,"* pp. 5-10. The title page of Harvey's *Ciceronianus* reads as follows: "Gabrielis Harveii Ciceronianvs, Vel Oratio post reditum, habita Cantabrigiae ad suos Auditores. Quorum potissimùm causa, diuulgata est. Londini, Ex Officina Typographica Henrici Binneman. Anno. CIꓱ. Iꓱ. LXXVII." See Wilson and Forbes, p. 35.

[7] *Rhetor*, sigs. h1v, h2r, h2v, h3v, k4r, o2v, o4r.

[8] *Ibid.*, sigs. e1r, e1v, e2v, e4v, f1r, f1v, f2r, h2v, h3v, k4r, l1r, l1v, n1r, o4r, q1r, q1v.

main as proper and germane to this art, like the two eyes in the body, style and delivery; the former bright in the splendors of tropes and the involutions of schemes; the latter agreeable in the modulation of voice and the appropriateness of gesture; each exciting a singular love for itself whether in public orations or in private communication.[9]

Practice or exercise as the topic of the second lecture in the *Rhetor* involves Harvey in a discussion of two terms that were to be prominent in English Ramism, not so much in connection with logical or rhetorical theory, as with the applications and uses of that theory. These two terms are analysis and genesis.[10] Analysis is the process by which the student takes the composition of somebody else and subjects it to scrutiny in an effort to discover how far it incorporates within itself the principles of logic and rhetoric. Genesis is the process by which the student brings a composition of his own into being through the application of the machinery of invention, of arrangement, of style, and of delivery. Harvey devotes almost the whole of his second lecture to these two terms; and since at the very end he promises to take up next the subject of Cicero's *Oration to the People upon his Return*, we may assume that the subsequent lectures in his first series were themselves an example of the exercise which Ramus called analysis.

A good vernacular expression of the meaning of analysis and genesis is afforded by Fraunce's *Lawiers Logike*, the dialectical theory of which has already been discussed.[11] Speaking of the value of dialectic "in discoursing, thinking, meditating, and framing of thine owne, as also in discussing, perusing, searching and examining what others haue either deliuered by speach, or put downe in writing," Fraunce proceeds to identify these two procedures by saying that "this is called *Analysis*, that *Genesis*, and in them both consisteth the whole vse of Logike."[12] Later, Fraunce illustrates genesis by an example which he borrows from Sturm. This example consists in taking the word *nobilitas* and drawing it through the places of cause, effect, subject, adjunct, opposites, comparatives, and so on, to indicate how rich a store of arguments may come to the writer or speaker who applies inventional theory to the problem of devising subject matter. Fraunce then illustrates analysis by taking the word *amicitia*

---

[9] *Ibid.*, sigs. e4v-f1r. Translation mine.

[10] *Ibid.*, sigs. k4v-q2r. For Harvey's discussion of Ramus's doctrine of analysis and genesis, see *ibid.*, sig. l1r. For another account of this doctrine in Ramus, see Graves, *Peter Ramus*, pp. 117, 140-141, 165.

[11] See above, pp. 222-228.   [12] *Lawiers Logike*, fol. 3r-3v.

in Cicero's *Laelius* and identifying the places of invention as they appear to have been used in the framing of that composition.[13]

Fraunce's examples of genesis and analysis relate only to invention, the first part of logic, and he carries them no further. But we may easily see their application in other fields. A strictly rhetorical exercise of genesis, for instance, would require the student to draw his previously acquired subject matter through the tropes and the schemes, in order to clothe thought in every appropriate stylistic garment. Rhetorical analysis, on the other hand, would require him to identify the stylistic garments of trope and scheme in the work of any author chosen for study.

Towards the end of his *Ciceronianus*, as he prepares to invite his Cambridge auditors to his coming lectures on another of Cicero's orations, this time the *Oration in the Senate upon his Return*, Harvey indicates that his method will be to conduct an analysis of this Ciceronian work by applying to it the principles of Ramistic logic as well as Ramistic rhetoric. Thus once again he indicates what Ramistic analysis means to him. Here are his words to the undergraduates:

> Let us return, then, dear Cantabrigians, to that interrupted but not abandoned exercise of Ciceronian exegesis. Let us weigh on their appropriate scales all his ornaments of speaking and his main points of disputing. . . . And since amplitude of content supports his harmony of diction, as the soul supports the body, let us also employ the double analysis which we have hitherto been using and apply both rhetoric and dialectic continually in all his writings and with special care in every period. Let us make rhetoric the expositor of the oratorical embellishments and the arts which belong to its school, and dialectic the expositor of invention and arrangement. Both these methods of analysis will be very pleasant for me to teach and, believe me, they will be very useful for you to learn.[14]

Harvey's *Ciceronianus* is interesting not only as a plain indication of the methods of rhetorical analysis in process of being demonstrated to Cambridge undergraduates of the fifteen-seventies but also as an expression of a Cambridge man's idea of the change that was occurring in the intellectual climate of England. In one sense, this

[13] *Ibid.*, foll. 81v-85v.

[14] This passage is quoted from Clarence A. Forbes's excellent translation of Harvey's *Ciceronianus* in Wilson and Forbes, *Gabriel Harvey's "Ciceronianus,"* pp. 85-87. All of my quotations from this work are used with the permission of the University of Nebraska Press.

change meant the renunciation of a counterfeit Ciceronianism and the adoption of a true one. In another sense, it meant the end of a literary school devoted only to style, and the beginning of a school devoted to subject matter as well. In still another sense, it meant a realignment of English learning towards France and Germany as opposed to Italy. And finally it meant an endorsement of Cambridge as the brightest future star in the firmament of European as well as strictly English scholarship.

These various ideas are all involved in Harvey's account of his own spiritual progress from a counterfeit to a true Ciceronianism. At one time, he had thought himself a simon-pure devotee of Cicero, and had carried his devotion so far that he "virtually preferred to be elected to the company of the Ciceronians rather than to that of the saints."[15] He thus describes what this devotion entailed:

> This will give the sum of the matter: I valued words more than content, language more than thought, the one art of speaking more than the thousand subjects of knowledge; I preferred the mere style of Marcus Tully to all the postulates of the philosophers and mathematicians; I believed that the bone and sinew of imitation lay in my ability to choose as many brilliant and elegant words as possible, to reduce them into order, and to connect them together in a rhythmical period. In my judgment—or perhaps I should say opinion rather than judgment—that was what it meant to be a Ciceronian.

This sort of Ciceronian, as Harvey had earlier explained, was sponsored in Europe by Italian learning. In that connection he had said:

> I had among my favorites the most elegant and refined Italians; and especially Pontanus, Cortesius, and those whom I have just mentioned—Bembus, Sadoletus, Longolius, Riccius, Nizolius too, and Naugerius—I ever cherished in my bosom and embrace. One who named them seemed to be naming not men but heroes and heavenly beings.

> As for Erasmus and those who clove to his views, Budaeus, More, Aegidius, Glareanus, Vives, and all the others who are not considered Ciceronians, I not only scorned them as perfectly infantile, but even pursued them with hate as utter enemies. To tell the truth, it seemed to me a wicked offence to touch Erasmus.[16]

As a sharp contrast to his former idea of the meaning of Ciceronianism, Harvey offers to his undergraduate hearers the idea he now

[15] *Ibid.*, p. 69. [16] *Ibid.*, p. 61.

holds to be wise and true. This new idea had come to him as the result of his reading of Johannes Sambucus and Ramus. Harvey explains this new idea in various ways, even using at one point the very words Ramus had used in a similar connection.[17] But the following direct appeal to his students is perhaps as good a place as any in which to see what his present conception of sound literary learning is:

> Do you wish, then, to be honored with the glorious and magnificent appellation of "Ciceronians"? I shall open my thoughts to you more than ever before. Read the artistically and carefully elaborated *Ciceronianus* of Ramus, that of Erasmus, and that of Freigius. Follow with the utmost diligence the footprints of Marcus Tully, your supreme commander. Complete the laborious but splendid course of eloquence and philosophy, which Cicero completed with noble mind and lofty intellect. . . . Consider not merely the flowering verdure of style, but much rather the ripe fruitage of reason and thought. . . . Remember that words are called by Homer πτερόεντα, that is, winged, since they easily fly away, unless they are kept in equilibrium by the weightiness of the subject matter. Unite dialectic and knowledge with rhetoric, thought with language.[18]

These instructions, adds Harvey, will make a Ciceronian, "if not of the Roman sort, yet of the French, German, British, or Cisalpine sort." He had earlier sounded a sharp note of scorn against the refusal by Italians to admit any northern Europeans to the ranks of the eloquent. "As for us," he had then declared, "let us admit one Frenchman, and three Germans: Ramus, Erasmus, Sturmius, and Freigius."[19] These, then, are the true Ciceronians—the men who follow, not so much the superficial characteristics of Cicero's style, but the profundities of his insight into knowledge as the principle of form.

The standing of any university, Harvey makes plain, is determined only by its ability to produce these true Ciceronians. He promises his students that, "if I navigate with you in this harbor as did my preceptors with their auditors and students in their respective universities—Sturmius at Strassburg, Ramus at Paris, Freigius at Basel and Freiburg, Erasmus in all these cities and very many others of Germany, France, Italy, and England, especially here in our own Cambridge—, perhaps you will one day see me not among the hindmost, and doubtless I shall very soon see you among the foremost Ciceronians."[20] Harvey predicts, indeed, that Cambridge will be the place

[17] *Ibid.*, p. 73.   [18] *Ibid.*, p. 83.   [19] *Ibid.*, p. 81.   [20] *Ibid.*, pp. 79-81.

to produce such an expositor of Cicero as he has been describing in his lecture. "Already this long time," he says, "the standing of a learned university, the majesty of a mighty queen, the tranquil peace of a flourishing realm, the splendor of a cultured age, and the expectation of men beyond the seas have been summoning such a man."[21] He adds:

Were he to step forth in our midst, resolved to inspire the exalted and heroic spirits of noble characters to cultivate the aforesaid studies, I should not hesitate to rank the University of Cambridge above the most illustrious schools of all of Europe. Others may contend about their venerable age, but I would rather hear that Cambridge is preeminent for the number and fame of her learned men. Then some day, just as of yore Athens was called the School of Greece, so Cambridge may rightfully be known as the School of Britain; and to be a Cantabrigian may mean among us what it meant among the Greeks to be an Athenian.

Harvey is aware, of course, that the new learning which he wishes to make victorious at Cambridge had powerful opponents in England as well as in Italy. One of these opponents was Ascham, who had died some eight years before Harvey delivered the lecture now under discussion. Harvey mentions Ascham and specifically disclaims any intention of casting aspersions upon the latter's *Scholemaster*,[22] although Ascham, as we have seen, had cast some aspersions of his own upon Ramus.[23] Harvey proceeds to acknowledge Ascham's learning and eloquence, as if only compliments were in his mind; but then he changes his tone, and criticizes the *Scholemaster* for being defended as a treatise on grammar when in reality it discusses not only metaphors, which are properly within the sphere of rhetoric, but also contraries, which are properly within the sphere of dialectic.[24] In other words, Harvey finds that Ascham fails to observe Ramus's law of justice, which requires the liberal arts to keep to fixed boundaries. Immediately after this criticism, Harvey avows his own dedication to Ramism in these words:

But let others decide about the *Scholemaster* of Ascham, who is eminently refined, elegant, and even, if he be compared with the schoolmasters of others, truly most excellent and polished. In my schoolmaster I not only require these same qualities in still richer measure,

---

[21] *Ibid.*, p. 101.   [22] *Ibid.*, pp. 91-93.   [23] See above, pp. 173, 177-178.
[24] Wilson and Forbes, *Gabriel Harvey's "Ciceronianus,"* p. 93.

but I desiderate many others not less fruitful. I even dare boast, all arrogance aside, that in my schoolmaster I distinguish, separate, and divide the three subjects—rhetoric from grammar and dialectic from both; that I assign its due to each subject in geometrical proportion, as they say; that, in short, I heed the well-known Aristotelian doctrine of the categories. Ascham has not done this; if he had, he could not have got so far outside his circumscribed limits nor digressed so frequently from his purpose.

Harvey's *Ciceronianus* and *Rhetor* were respectively published in June and November of 1577, and thus are almost certainly the earliest interpretations of Ramistic rhetoric to be printed in England.[25] Talaeus's *Rhetorica* and a volume called *Rethorica Rami* were licensed for publication with the society of stationers in London on November 11, 1577,[26] but even if these got into print before the *Rhetor*, they were clearly later than the *Ciceronianus* by some five months, and they may even not have been published that year at all, since no copy of an edition of a *Rhetorica* by Talaeus or Ramus under an imprint dated at London in 1577 is now extant.[27]

Ramistic rhetoric in Harvey's interpretation may claim to be first in England not only in time but also in quality. Harvey followed Ramus exactly in restricting rhetoric to style and delivery, but he also followed Ramus in denying vigorously that style and delivery are the only two subjects that a speaker has to master or an oratorical critic has to teach. The movement which he founded in England upon Ramus's authority did not mean that the presentational aspects of Ciceronian rhetoric, alone and by themselves, constituted the whole of the speaker's art, although certain modern writers, among them Sandford, have interpreted that movement in these exact terms.[28] Neither Harvey nor Ramus ever believed that speechmaking could be limited in such a way as that. They believed instead that speaking is made up of logic, so far as any discourse must have subject matter and form, and is also made up of rhetoric, so far as any discourse must be clothed in words and uttered as speech. Their biggest dispute with scholastic logic and traditional rhetoric was that those subjects were

---

[25] The month in which each of these works was published is indicated in its colophon. See also Ronald B. McKerrow, *The Works of Thomas Nashe* (London, 1904 [-1910]), V, 163-164.

[26] Arber, *Transcript of the Registers*, II, 319.

[27] See Baldwin, *William Shakspere's Small Latine & Lesse Greeke*, I, 521.

[28] William P. Sandford, "English Rhetoric Reverts to Classicism, 1600-1650," *The Quarterly Journal of Speech*, XV (1929), 504.

gravely redundant in covering invention and disposition twice over. Their basic program of reform was to have logic handle the processes of invention, disposition, and in a minor sense memory, wherever these arose as a problem in learned or popular discourse, whereas rhetoric would handle the processes of style and delivery, with grammar limited to considerations of etymology and syntax. This exact program is behind everything that Harvey says throughout the *Rhetor* and the *Ciceronianus*. And it is expressed elsewhere in his writings. For example, it is pretty completely stated in one of the marginal comments made by him in his own copy of Quintilian's *Institutio Oratoria*, where he delineates the perfect orator in these Ramistic words:

> A most excellent Pleader and singular discourser in any Civil Court, or otherwyse; not A bare Professor of any one certain faculty or A simple Artist in any one kynde: howbeit his principall Instrumentes ar Rhetorique, for Elocution and Pronunciation; and Logique, for Invention, Disposition, and Memory.[29]

Harvey's program of reform had not long to wait before it found a supporter in Dudley Fenner's *The Artes of Logike and Rethorike*. As I mentioned before, Fenner's work is made up of an unacknowledged translation of the main heads of Ramus's *Dialecticae Libri Duo*, and an unacknowledged translation, the first in English, of Talaeus's *Rhetorica*.[30] Fenner entered Peterhouse College, Cambridge, in 1575, and thus was in a position to hear and heed Harvey's lectures on rhetoric.[31] It is probably Harvey, indeed, who gave Fenner the idea for a work in which logic and rhetoric would on the one hand be severely separated into two arts, on the basis of Ramus's law of justice, and on the other would be united between two covers of the same volume, on the basis that both were requisite for perfection in the art of communication. At any rate, Harvey emphasized this Ramistic paradox in his lectures at Cambridge, and Fenner illustrated it in his *Logike and Rethorike*.

"Rhetorike," says Fenner at the beginning of the second of his two works, "is an Arte of speaking finelie. It hath two partes, Garnishing

---

[29] G. C. Moore Smith, *Gabriel Harvey's Marginalia* (Stratford-upon-Avon, 1913), p. 123.

[30] See above, p. 219.

[31] Fenner entered Peterhouse for the Easter Term of 1575 and thus may have heard the lectures making up Harvey's *Rhetor*. For Fenner's dates at Cambridge, see Walker, *Register of Peterhouse Men*, II, 6-7; for the date of Harvey's first course of lectures on rhetoric, see Wilson and Forbes, *Gabriel Harvey's "Ciceronianus,"* p. 6.

of speache, called Eloqution. Garnishing of the maner of vtterance, called Pronunciation."[32] The second of these parts is later dismissed altogether from consideration—"bicause [says Fenner] it is not yet perfecte (for the preceptes for the most parte pertaine to an Oratour) which when it shalbe perfect, it shall eyther onely conteyne common preceptes for the garnishing of vtterance in all, or also proper preceptes for the same in Magistrates, Embassadours, Captaynes, and Ministers, therefore vntill it be so perfitted, wee thinke it vnnecessarie to be translated into Englishe."[33] But Fenner's treatment of style as the first part of rhetoric is in the exact Ramistic tradition.

After dividing style into the tropes and the figures, Fenner proceeds to define and discuss each of these forms of language. Tropes, he says, are "a garnishing of speache, whereby one worde is drawen from his firste proper signification to another. . ."[34] His subsequent discussion of these forms involves allegory, metonymy, irony, synecdoche, and metaphor, each of which is illustrated from the Bible. Next come the figures, which are defined as follows:

> A Figure is a garnishing of speache, wherein the course of the same is chaunged from the more simple and plaine maner of speaking, vnto that whiche is more full of excellencie and grace. For as in the finenesse of wordes or a trope, wordes are considered asunder by them selues: so in the fine shape or frame of speach or a figure, the apte and pleasant ioyning togither of many wordes is noted.[35]

Fenner's analysis of the figures is more extensive than that of the tropes, as we would naturally expect in any rhetoric. He defines such unusual forms of language as rhyme, blank verse, anadiplosis, anaphora, paronomasia, exclamation, apostrophe, and prosopopoeia, preferring always the biblical illustration to other possibilities.

The *Logike and Rethorike* was published in 1584 and again near 1588 at Middelburg in the Netherlands.[36] Midway between these two dates, William Webbe brought out at London his *Discourse of English Poetrie*, in which he has something to say that indicates the influence of Talaeus's *Rhetorica* upon poetical theory. Webbe, by the way, had taken a bachelor's degree from Cambridge in 1573, his college being St. John's; and thus he would as an undergraduate have heard something of the new rhetoric of Talaeus. In his *Dis-*

[32] *Artes of Logike and Rethorike* (1584), sig. Dıv.
[33] *Ibid.*, sig. Eıv.   [34] *Ibid.*, sig. Dıv.   [35] *Ibid.*, sig. D3r.
[36] See above, p. 219, note 147.

course of English Poetrie he speaks of "the reformed kind of English verse,"[37] that is, of verse built upon quantity rather than rhyme—an issue that Gabriel Harvey and Edmund Spenser had discussed with each other and the public several years before in a famous series of published letters.[38] In explaining the verse-forms of Greek and Latin poetry, Webbe lists twelve measures or feet, each by its technical name, and then he adds: "Many more deuisions of feete are vsed by some, but these doo more artificially comprehende all quantities necessary to the skanning of any verse, according to *Tallaeus* in hys Rethorique."[39] Webbe means this reference to indicate that he is here borrowing and translating from Chapter 16 of Book I of Talaeus's *Rhetorica*, where under the heading *De Metro* Talaeus lists and discusses these same twelve feet.[40] Webbe could not have borrowed these terms from Fenner's *Rethorike*, for Fenner does not include them in his short discussion of feet and measures, his excuse being that English literature contains no worthy examples of them, and hence the handling of them would be more curious than necessary.[41]

In the year 1588, as Fenner's translation of Talaeus was achieving its second edition on the continent, Abraham Fraunce published his *Arcadian Rhetorike* at London.[42] This work is also a translation of Talaeus, the second in the English language, the first on English soil. Fraunce obviously intended it and his *Lawiers Logike* to serve together as the means of introducing his countrymen to Ramus's complete theory of communication. But by publishing his two works separately, and by giving no open indication that his *Rhetorike* had its origins in Ramism, he inadvertently fostered the early twentieth-century belief that the latter treatise was in one sense a continuation of the stylistic pattern of traditional rhetorical theory and in another sense, a seemingly capricious renunciation of invention and disposition as concerns of the man of eloquence.[43]

---

[37] I quote from the text of Webbe's *Discourse* as printed in Smith, *Elizabethan Critical Essays*, I, 278.

[38] These letters between Harvey and Spenser are reprinted by Smith, I, 87-122.

[39] *Ibid.*, I, 280. It should be remarked that Puttenham's famous *Arte of English Poesie* (London, 1589), Bk. II, Ch. 14, also limits the number of metrical feet to twelve, and with three exceptions names the twelve with the terms used by Webbe and Talaeus. See below, pp. 327-329.

[40] See *Avdomari Talaei Rhetorica e P. Rami Praelectionibus observata*, ed. Claudius Minos (Frankfurt, 1582), pp. 80-81.

[41] *Artes of Logike and Rethorike*, sig. D3r.

[42] For an excellent modern edition, see *The Arcadian Rhetorike By Abraham Fraunce*, ed. Ethel Seaton (Oxford: Published for the Luttrell Society by Basil Blackwell, 1950).

[43] Smith, *Elizabethan Critical Essays*, I, 303-306, 422, quotes a chapter of *The Ar-*

Fraunce's *Rhetorike* differs in two main ways from Fenner's. First of all, it deals in some detail with delivery as the second part of Ramistic theory, whereas Fenner had thought it unnecessary to translate this part into English. Here is Fraunce's approach to it:

> Of *Eloquution* which was the first part of Rhetorike, wee haue spoken alreadie: it now remaineth to talke of Vtterance or Pronunciation the second part. *Vtterance* is a fit deliuering of the speach alreadie beautified. It hath two parts, *Voyce* and *Gesture*, the one pertaining to the eare, the other belonging to the eye.[44]

The second way in which Fraunce differs from Fenner is that Fenner relies upon the Bible for his illustrations, whereas Fraunce in the very spirit of Ramus borrows his from secular classics. Thus in his discussion of voice and gesture he provides illustrative passages from Homer in Greek, Virgil in Latin, Sidney in English, du Bartas in French, Tasso in Italian, and Boscán Almogaver and Garcilasso in Spanish. These authors, indeed, are the seven main sources of illustration in the whole *Arcadian Rhetorike*, as Fraunce's original title page indicates.[45] Each illustration is designed, of course, to exhibit a trope, a figure, a kind of voice, or a motion of head, eyes, lips, arms, hands, and feet. Thus the work as a whole may be characterized as a collection of Ramistic precepts for style and delivery, and as a collection of model passages to show how the precepts actually work in the writings of the great ancients and moderns. Ramus and Talaeus had prided themselves upon deriving the principles of composition from the practice of the masters, and Fraunce adheres to this same procedure in the *Arcadian Rhetorike* as he had in the *Lawiers Logike*.

William Kempe, already mentioned as a Cambridge Ramist and a translator of Ramus's *Arithmetic*,[46] published at London in 1588, at the very press where *The Arcadian Rhetorike* was produced, a treatise called *The Education of children in learning*.[47] This work

---

cadian Rhetorike, and supplies notes about Fraunce, without mentioning Ramus or Talaeus in that connection. He suggests a family relation between Fraunce's *Lawiers Logike* and *Arcadian Rhetorike*, on the one hand, and Thomas Wilson's *Rule of Reason* and *Rhetorique*, on the other; also between Fraunce's *Rhetorike* and Sherry's *Treatise of Schemes and Tropes*. Clark, *Rhetoric and Poetry in the Renaissance* (1922), pp. 58-61, discusses Sherry, Peacham, Fenner, Fraunce, Charles Butler, John Barton, and John Smith as partners in a single movement towards limiting rhetoric to style and delivery.

[44] *Arcadian Rhetorike*, ed. Seaton, p. 106.

[45] *Ibid.*, pp. xx-li, lviii. In these pages Miss Seaton has a full discussion of all the authors used by Fraunce for illustrative purposes.

[46] See above, p. 246.

[47] The title page reads: "The Education of children in learning: Declared by the

deserves mention here as an account of the way in which Ramus's logic and rhetoric were beginning to enter into English elementary education during the late sixteenth century. Kempe was a master in the Plymouth grammar school when he wrote the *Education*, and thus it is probably a reflection of his own practice. Avowedly seeking to arouse public interest in his profession, he dedicated his work to the mayor and the other officials of Plymouth, and in a preface to the reader announced his intention of reaching, not the learned schoolmasters, but "all other sort of people," and of setting forth "the dignitie and vtilitie of the matter, with such holie and ancient Histories, with such plaine and sensible reasons, as may teach the vnlearned with some delight, and not be tedious to those that are learned."[48] "I suppose," he confessed of his work, "that it will seeme altogether a strange and a new Booke." After his preface are printed four Latin epigrams to the author from his friends, one of whom signs himself "Io. Sw." and thus begins:

> Sturmius and Ramus, Freigius, Manutius, Ascham,
> Beheld each thing in this kind that they might explain it.
> Kempe has what they had, well collected, for teaching the English,
> His diligence being at one with his motive of duty.[49]

Ramus's influence is seen after Kempe has talked of "The Dignitie of Schooling," as established by its pedigree, and "The Vtilitie of Schooling," as established in part from a long speech by Alfred the Great. Appropriately enough, Ramus is the obvious source of what Kempe has to say about the liberal arts under his third major topic, "The Method of Schooling." Kempe's theory of method is stated as follows:

> Wherefore first the scholler shall learne the precepts: secondly, he shall learne to note the examples of the precepts in vnfoulding other mens workes: thirdly, to imitate the examples in some worke of his owne: fourthly and lastly, to make somewhat alone without an example. Now, all these kindes of teaching are seene in euery speciall sort of the things taught, be it Grammar, Logike, Rhetorike, Arithmetike, Geometrie, or any other Arte.[50]

Dignitie, Vtilitie, and Method thereof. Meete to be knowne, and practised aswell of Parents and Schoolemaisters. . . . Imprinted at London by Thomas Orwin, for Iohn Porter and Thomas Gubbin. 1588."

[48] *The Education of children in learning*, sig. A3r.

[49] *Ibid.*, sig. A4r. Translation mine.

[50] *Ibid.*, sig. F2r.

After this preview of the curriculum, Kempe traces the child's progress year by year until at the age of twelve he has mastered elementary grammar and is ready for the study of logic and rhetoric. As Kempe describes the teaching of these latter two subjects and of advanced grammar, we find ourselves in the presence, not of scholasticism and traditionalism, but of Ramus's own doctrine.

The Ramists assigned the tropes and figures to style, as traditional rhetoric had done; but style, as we have noticed, is always the first part of rhetoric to a thorough Ramist, whereas traditional rhetoric counted it the third part, even in treatises where no other part was discussed. Not only does Kempe adhere to Ramism in this particular, but he also approves of Ramistic analysis and genesis as educational procedures, and he exactly follows Ramus's prescription as to the contents of the second part of rhetoric, the first and second part of logic, and the two parts of grammar. The following quotation, long as it is, displays these aspects of Kempe's Ramism, and gives us an amazing picture of the fatiguing discipline of Elizabethan elementary education:

> First the scholler shal learne the precepts concerning the diuers sorts of arguments in the first part of Logike, (for that without them Rhetorike cannot be well vnderstood) then shall followe the tropes and figures in the first part of Rhetorike, wherein he shall employ the sixth part of his studie, and all the rest in learning and handling good authors: as are *Tullies Offices*, his Orations, *Caesars Commentaries, Virgils Aeneis, Ouids Metamorphosis*, and *Horace*. In whom for his first exercise of vnfolding the Arte, he shall obserue the examples of the hardest poynts in Grammar, of the arguments in Logike, of the tropes and figures in Rhetorike, referring euery example to his proper rule, as before. Then he shall learne the two latter parts also both of Logike and Rhetorike. And as of his Grammar rules he rehearsed some part euery day; so let him now do the like in Logike, afterwards in Rhetorike, and then in Grammar agayne, that he forget not the precepts of arte, before continual vse haue ripened his vnderstanding in them. And by this time he must obserue in authors all the vse of the Artes, as not only the words and phrases, not only the examples of the arguments; but also the axiome, wherein euery argument is disposed; the syllogisme, whereby it is concluded; the method of the whole treatise, and the passages, wherby the parts are ioyned together. Agayne, he shall obserue not only euery trope, euery figure, aswell of words as of sentences: but also the Rhetoricall pronunciation and gesture fit for euery word, sentence, and affection.

And so let him take in hand the exercise of all these three Artes at once in making somewhat of his owne, first by imitation; as when he hath considered the propertie of speach in the Grammaticall etymologie and syntaxis: the fineness of speach in the Rhetoricall ornaments, as comely tropes, pleasant figures, fit pronounciation and gesture: the reason and pith of the matter in the Logicall weight of arguments, in the certeyntie of the axiomes, in the due fourme of syllogismes, and in the easie and playne method: then let him haue a like theame to prosecute with the same artificiall instruments, that he findeth in his author.[51]

This procedure of mastering the precepts, of analyzing master-pieces, and finally of producing themes of the student's own was to continue, says Kempe, for three years, that is, from the twelfth year of the student's age to the fifteenth. Thereafter would follow a half-year of arithmetic and geometry; and so "before the full age of six-teene yeers," the student would "be made fit to wade without a schoolemaister, through deeper mysteries of learning, to set forth the glorie of God, and to benefite his Countrie."[52] Kempe, as he said, was writing both to encourage parents to educate their children and to describe educational methods for the inexpert schoolmasters outside and inside the professional system.[53] But there can be no doubt that the procedures recommended to his readers were followed in his grammar school at Plymouth and elsewhere in schools of the period. If his program for the last year or so of grammar school seems to overlap the work of the first year of college, no one should be surprised, for that sort of duplication has been in the school system throughout history.

The exact identity of the earliest edition used to acquaint English schoolboys with Talaeus's Latin *Rhetorica* has not been satisfactorily determined. I have already mentioned that a work under such a title, and another called *Rethorica Rami*, were licensed for publication with the company of stationers in London on November 11, 1577, but that a copy of neither of these works from that date survives.[54] Nor does a copy of Claudius Minos's edition of Talaeus's *Rhetorica* survive in an imprint dated at London in 1582, although that work, and a now-vanished edition of Ramus's *Dialecticae Libri Duo*, were licensed for publication on December 5 of that year.[55] Also not pre-

---

[51] *Ibid.*, sig. G2v-G3r.   [52] *Ibid.*, sig. H1r.   [53] *Ibid.*, sig. A2r-A3v.
[54] See above, p. 254. See also Arber, *Transcript of the Registers*, II, 319.
[55] See Arber, II, 417.

served is any 1586 imprint of a London edition of Talaeus's *Retor-ike* or of Ramus's Latin *Logike*, although both of these works were received by the stationers that year on August 22 for printing.[56] And finally there is no surviving copy of a 1588 London edition of Talaeus's *Rhetorica* accompanied by Ramus's commentary, despite the fact that such a work was entered with the stationers as that year was drawing to an end.[57]

A less negative record exists for editions put out in the fifteen-nineties. Charles Butler, one of the few Oxonians to become an ardent Ramist, published for schoolboys a Latin text of Talaeus in 1597. Since this work contains a dedicatory letter dated from Oxford on May 5, 1593, it can be assumed that its first edition appeared in that year, although no copy under such a date survives. The 1597 text is something of a curiosity, not only on account of the date on the letter, but also because the work bears the title, *Rameae Rhetoricae Libri Dvo*.[58] The obvious similarity between this title and the one already mentioned as having been licensed in the stationers' registers on November 11, 1577, would suggest at first glance that Butler's work had originally appeared as many as twenty years before 1597. But against this is the fact that Butler would have been only sixteen years of age in 1577, and not yet an undergraduate at Oxford. A more likely explanation of the registration of Talaeus's *Rhetorica* under Ramus's name in 1577 is that everyone accepted the latter as the primary authority behind the new rhetoric and as the more famous personality of the two, whereas Talaeus was considered as a secondary figure, and his name was even regarded in some quarters as a pseudonym under which Ramus had published certain of his works.[59] Butler did not subscribe to the view that Talaeus was Ramus's pseudonym. But he did publish Talaeus's *Rhetorica* under Ramus's name in 1597, confining himself to style and delivery, as did Talaeus, and allotting to the first topic the thirty-seven chapters and sixty-three pages of his Book I, and to the second topic, the ten chapters and seventeen pages of his Book II.

A somewhat expanded edition of Butler's work, titled the *Rhetoricae Libri Dvo*, appeared at Oxford in 1598, and it is this which became the most famous textbook in the history of Ramistic rhetoric

[56] Arber, II, 455.

[57] Arber, II, 509. The exact date of this entry is December 6, 1588.

[58] The title page reads: "Rameae Rhetoricae Libri Dvo. In vsvm Scholarvm. Oxoniae, Excudebat Josephus Barnesius. 1597."

[59] See Waddington, *Ramus*, pp. 464, 475.

in England.[60] It no longer bore Ramus's name on its title page, but it made no secret of its origins. Its dedicatory letter proclaims its sources in veiled terms by saying that "whatever the ancients or moderns have written anywhere in this line, the whole is set forth here, accommodated to a legitimate method, and made clear by distinguished examples from poets and orators."[61] Whenever the word "method" appears in the writings of the late sixteenth century in England, it amounts almost to a confession of the author's awareness of Ramus. But Butler acknowledges his indebtedness to Ramus in much more definite terms when he comes to address his readers in the preface that follows his dedicatory epistle.

This preface opens with a eulogy of Ramus as the greatest of the entire company of ancient and modern philosophers. Says Butler:

As to the place which Peter Ramus may rightly hold among the philosophers whom distinguished wisdom, as allotted to later times, has celebrated throughout the entire circle of the earth, let that be the judgment of the pre-eminent in learning and equity who are best able and willing to decide. Indeed, according to my opinion, if you would have regard either for truth in precepts, or for brevity in method, or for clarity in examples, or for use and utility in all things, he will stand out second to none in that most celebrated and most honored chorus. Surely (that I may freely speak what I mean)
—so far towers his head above the heads of all others
As cypresses are wont to tower above the pliant viburnum.[62]

Virgil had used this image of the cypress to express the superiority of Rome to all other cities.[63] Butler uses it and the Virgilian glorification of Rome to cap his tribute to Ramus. Then he continues:

I offer this little book to you (O candid reader) in the name of that one [i.e., Ramus]. If it should bring anything of fruit and profit, you

---

[60] Its title page reads: "Rhetoricae Libri Dvo. Qvorvm Prior de Tropis & Figuris, Posterior de Voce & Gestu Praecipit. In vsvm scholarum accuratiùs editi. . . . Oxoniae, Excudebat Josephvs Barnesivs. M. D. XCVIII." Editions of this work appeared at Oxford in 1600 and 1618; at London in 1629, 1642, 1649, 1655, and 1684; at Cambridge in 1642; and at Leiden in 1642.
[61] *Rhetoricae Libri Dvo*, sig. ¶3r. Translation mine here and below.
[62] *Ibid.*, sig. ¶3v.
[63] See Virgil, *Ecloga I*, lines 25-26. Virgil's lines are:
> Verum haec tantum alias inter caput extulit urbes,
> Quantum lenta solent inter viburna cupressi.
Butler adapts these lines to his context by making some slight changes in wording. Thus he says:
> —tantùm alios inter caput extulit omnes,
> Quantum lenta solent inter viburna cupressi.

may credit it all as having been learned from him. In truth, he himself studiously sought out the material, traversing completely the broad forests of the most tested authors; he cut the choice cuttings with active hand as one cuts to a rule, and he hewed, and smoothed, and shaped them all.

Now if this seems to imply that Butler was attributing direct authorship of the present work to Ramus, as his title of the preceding year had done, he immediately corrects that impression in the following words:

> Having thus prepared all of this, he himself, occupied with grander buildings, commended to Audomarus Talaeus, certainly a skilled master in all phases of this subject, the work of joining the pieces together into perfection. And the latter, indeed, the task having been entrusted to him, brought it to completion, Minerva being not unwilling, as they say.

The bare definitions in Butler's *Rhetoricae Libri Dvo* have the familiar wording of all such elements in Ramistic rhetorical theory. "Rhetoric is the art of speaking well," he begins. Comment follows this general observation. Then comes the organizing remark for the whole treatise: "The parts of rhetoric are two, style and delivery."[64] "Style," it turns out, "is that of trope or that of figure," whereas delivery as "the appropriate declaring of style" has two parts, voice and gesture.[65] "Trope," we are told, "is style in which a word is changed from its native meaning to some other," and "figure is style in which the character of speaking is changed from its straight and artless idiom."[66] The several figures and tropes are illustrated from classical authors, the orations of Cicero and the poetry of Virgil being of course the sources most often cited by Butler and by Talaeus as well.

Butler's one English illustration is worthy of notice, not only as a departure from the text of Talaeus, but also as an indication of the regard in which Edmund Spenser's poetry was held in the closing years of the sixteenth century. Speaking of rhyme-scheme in poetry as one of the forms of change from the straight and artless idiom of ordinary talk, Butler remarks that rhymes have been used by all nations and peoples, but that "today they mostly consist in a recurrence connected with sound"; and then he illustrates with the following poem "of our Homer":

[64] *Rhetoricae Libri Dvo*, sig. A1r.   [65] *Ibid.*, sigs. A1r, F3v-F4r.
[66] *Ibid.*, sigs. A1r, A3r.

Deedes soone doe die how ever noblie donne,
And thoughts of men doe as themselues decay;
But wise wordes taught in numbers for to rūne,
Recorded by the *Muses*, liue for aye:
Ne may with storming showres be washt away:
Ne bitter breathing windes ẃ boist'rous blast,
Nor age, nor envie shall them ever wast.

For not to haue beene dipt in *Lethe* lake,
Could save the sonne of *Thetis* from to die:
But that blinde bard did him immortal make,
With verses dipt in dewe of *Castalie*:
Which made the easterne conquerour to crie,
  O fortunate yongman whose vertue found
  So brave a trumpe thy noble actes to sound.[67]

Butler was serving as master of the free school of Basingstoke, Hants, when his famous edition of the *Rhetoricae Libri Dvo* was published. Two years later, that is, in 1600, he became vicar at Wootton St. Laurence, and he remained in that post until his death in 1647.[68] Thus he did not belong to the company of educators during the larger part of his long life. But he must have maintained enough contact with his former profession to know that his *Rhetoricae Libri Dvo* became one of the leading textbooks of the seventeenth century.

This work, indeed, was paid the signal honor in 1612 of being recommended by the prominent educator, John Brinsley. Brinsley published that year at London a treatise entitled *Lvdvs Literarivs: or, The Grammar Schoole*, which on its title page declared itself to be intended "for the helping of the younger sort of Teachers, and of all Schollars, with all other desirous of learning." The *Lvdvs* is made up of a lengthy dialogue between Spoudeus and Philoponus, two schoolmasters, the former of whom prefers traditional methods of teaching, and the latter, newer methods. In their discussion they intimate that English and penmanship are to be taught as prerequisites to the work of the Latin grammar school, and that Latin grammar itself is next given full emphasis. As the student progresses, he

[67] *Ibid.*, sig. C3v-C4r. Butler quotes here from Spenser's "The Rvines of Time," lines 400-406, 428-434. This poem was published at London in 1591 in a volume entitled *Complaints.* Butler's quotation differs in minor ways from Spenser's text. See *The Works of Edmund Spenser A Variorum Edition*, ed. Edwin Greenlaw, Charles Grosvenor Osgood, Frederick Morgan Padelford, Ray Heffner (Baltimore: The Johns Hopkins Press, 1932-1949), [VIII], 48-49.
[68] See Foster, *Alumni Oxonienses*, s.v. Butler, Charles, of Bucks.

must be taught to write themes in Latin, and it is Spoudeus, the traditionalist, who wants to accomplish this object by reading his students the rules out of Aphthonius, and then by having them compose themes not only in accordance with those rules but also in imitation of Aphthonius's models, especially those of the fable and the *chria*.[69] Philoponus indicates that he teaches Latin composition in a less rigid way. Thus it is not surprising, when the talk turns to rhetoric, that Philoponus emphasizes the new doctrines of Talaeus, and proceeds to pay a handsome compliment to Butler. The words of Philoponus deserve quotation at some length:

> For answering the questions of Rhetoricke, you may if you please, make them perfect in Talaeus Rhetoricke, which I take to be most vsed in the best Schooles; onely to giue each definition and distribution, and some one example or two at most in each Chapter: and those of the shortest sentences out of the Poets: so that they can giue the word or words, wherein the force of the rule is. . . . Claudius Minos Commentary may bee a good helpe to make Talaeus Rhetoricke most plaine, both for precepts and examples. . . .
>
> Or in stead of Talaeus, you may vse Master Butlars Rhetoricke, of Magdalens in Oxford, printed in Oxford; which I mentioned before: being a notable abbridgement of Talaeus, making it most plaine, and farre more easie to be learned of Schollars, and also supplying very many things wanting in Talaeus. . . . It is a booke, which (as I take it) is yet very little knowne in Schooles, though it haue beene forth sundry yeares, set forth for the vse of Schooles; and the vse and benefit will be found to be farre above all that euer hath beene written of the same.[70]

The success of his *Rhetoricae Libri Dvo* prompted Butler to make another textbook in a related field when he had reached the age of sixty-eight. This new work he called the *Oratoriae Libri Dvo*, and it was first published at Oxford in 1629.[71] Here he defines *oratoria* as the faculty of putting a speech together on any question whatever, and *oratio* as a structure of words and thoughts designed to per-

[69] *Lvdvs Literarivs* (London, 1612), pp. 172 ff. For a brief discussion of Aphthonius, see above, pp. 140-143.

[70] *Lvdvs Literarivs*, pp. 203-204.

[71] Its complete title page reads: "Oratoriae Libri Dvo. Qvorvm Alter ejus Definitionem, Alter Partitionem Explicat: In vsvm Scholarvm recèns editi. Authore Carolo Bvtlero, Magd. Oxoniae Excudebat Qvilielmvs Tvrner, *impensis Authoris*. 1629." This work did not achieve the popularity of Butler's *Rhetoricae Libri Dvo*, but it nevertheless was given four later editions—in 1633, 1635, 1642, and 1645. See Lee S. Hultzén, "Charles Butler on Memory," *Speech Monographs*, VI (1939), 45.

suade.[72] Here he speaks of persuasion as the process of doing three things—gaining favor, moving, teaching.[73] Here he discusses the six parts of the classical oration, the positions of argument, the kinds of oratory. These matters he treats in Book I, whereas Book II deals with the five ancient parts of rhetoric, that is, with invention, arrangement, style, memory, and delivery.[74]

The fact that Butler's *Rhetoricae Libri Dvo* deals exclusively with style and delivery, while his *Oratoriae Libri Dvo* covers not only these two fields to some extent, but also the great fields of memory, arrangement, and invention, may be a bit bewildering at first glance. It may be bewildering because Butler, living in an age when Ramists and traditionalists held opposing views on rhetoric, would seem in his earlier work to have been thoroughly Ramistic, and in his later work to have been thoroughly traditional. Is he then to be explained as a man who was a Ramist in his youth and a traditionalist in his old age? Must we cross him off the roster of English Ramists in the period between 1629 and the date of his death in 1647, and enroll him for those eighteen years in the ranks of traditional rhetoricians? Must we say that he renounced Ramus and embraced Cicero as an old man, and that his conversion to Ciceronian rhetoric is merely part of a general shift in the seventeenth century from the rhetoric of style and delivery to the rhetoric of subject matter and arrangement?

These questions have to be answered in the negative.[75] They have to be answered in the negative because Butler believes himself as much of a Ramist in the *Oratoriae Libri Dvo* as he was in the

[72] *Oratoriae Libri Dvo* (1629), sig. A1r, A2r. These definitions read: "Oratoria est Facultas formandi Orationem de qualibet Qvaestione"; "Oratio est Dictionū & Sententiarū structura, ad persuadendū accōmodata."

[73] *Ibid.*, sig. B1v. Butler's terms are *conciliando, concitando, docendo.*

[74] Butler deals first with style in Bk. I, Ch. 2, of the *Oratoriae Libri Dvo*, where he speaks of the traditional three kinds of style, grand, medium, and plain. He also deals with style in Bk. II, Ch. 4, and that entire chapter is brief enough for quotation:

Caput 4. De Elocutione & Pronunciatione.
De Elocutionis & Pronunciationis ornamētis,
vide Rhetoricam. Quae vt Poësin, Historiam,
Philosophiam, Epistolas, adeoque ipsum familiare
Colloquium, exornant; ita in Oratione praecipuè
locū habēt, & cuilibēt Dicendi generi asserunt
tum gratiam, tum dignitatem. (sig. P2v).

[75] I am aware that my negative answer runs against previous opinion on this matter. Sandford, in particular, explains Butler's *Oratoriae Libri Dvo* as a phase of the shift from an anticlassical to a classical attitude. See William Phillips Sandford, "English Rhetoric Reverts to Classicism, 1600-1650," *The Quarterly Journal of Speech,* xv (1929), 503-525. See also by the same author, *English Theories of Public Address, 1530-1828*, pp. 104-107.

Rhetoricae Libri Dvo. For example, in treating invention in the *Oratoriae Libri Dvo*, Butler uses the same materials that Ramus had used in treating invention as the first part of logic. That is to say, Butler reduces arguments to artistic and non-artistic; artistic arguments he classifies as primary and derivative primary; the ultimate distinctions drawn by him among artistic arguments are that they concern cause, effect, subject, adjunct, opposites, comparatives, and so on. These are terms out of Ramus's logic, as we know. And if Butler seems at times to depart from that source, his terms are nevertheless from commentaries by the later Ramists.

That Butler is here following Ramus as a devoted and deliberate disciple, there can be no doubt, for he says as much. Here are his words as he turns from diagramming Ramus's inventional system, and prepares to comment upon it:

> These brief and methodical precepts concerning the places or kinds of arguments are supplied from Peter Ramus, whose singular acuteness in rebuilding the arts I am never able to admire enough; and they are not so much assembled in part as adopted in full. Except some in Ramus are brought forth somewhat differently here, to the end that they may be adapted to the use of oratory. But not of course in any wrong sense. For whatever cannot be set forth in a better fashion, why should it be made worse by change?[76]

Now if Butler is a Ramist in both of his works in the field of oratory, why is it that those works differ so radically? The answer is that in the earlier work he was writing on rhetoric, which as a Ramist he had to limit to style and delivery, while in his later work he was in reality writing on logic, and as a Ramist he had to develop this subject under the headings of invention and arrangement. Thus his two works differ more as Ramistic rhetoric differs from Ramistic logic than as Ramistic rhetoric differs from traditional rhetoric.

But that is not the whole story. For, having claimed Butler as a Ramist both in his youth and old age, we must now admit that his later Ramism is not all it should have been. That he wrote on logic in 1629 and called his subject *oratoria* is a liberty that Ramus would never have allowed himself, for Ramus believed that there could be no faculty of forming an oration except so far as that faculty was governed by logic or by rhetoric, and thus there could be no treatise on that faculty unless it was called logic or rhetoric. Nor would

---

[76] *Oratoriae Libri Dvo* (1629), sig. L1r. Translation mine.

Ramus have allowed himself to approve of Butler's final decision to treat memory as a part of logic. To Ramus, memory was not a division of logic or of rhetoric. It was a faculty developed from nature, not from science; or rather, it was not proper material for a science, although it was assisted by the science of dialectical method. Butler knows of Ramus's opinion in this matter, but he does not heed it.[77] He gives instead a competent analysis of the ancient theory of memory.[78]

In one other instance he proves himself in 1629 to be an adulterated Ramist. His master would never have used in a scientific work what Butler uses in speaking of the parts of the oration, the positions of argument, and the kinds of oratory. These materials were not acceptable to Ramus because, if they appeared in rhetoric, they made rhetoric overlap logic in violation of the law of justice; and if they appeared in logic, either they violated the law of truth or else they duplicated materials already established in logic by prior claim. For example, the theory of the six parts of an oration was to Ramus a loose variant of the theory of method in logic. Thus it deserved only a bare mention in that science, and no mention at all in rhetoric, where anything of that sort was an intruder. For another example, the theory of the positions of argument was a loose variant of the theory of the ten places of Ramistic logic. Thus it duplicated what logic already contained, and so it lost its place in logic, whereas it too was an intruder in rhetoric. Now, these arguments constitute almost the sum of what Butler admires as Ramus's "singular acuteness in rebuilding the arts"; but still they did not seem to have the acuteness in 1629 to convince Butler of the necessity of perpetuating Ramus's basic distinctions.

In the year 1648, when Butler had been dead for only a few months, and his *Rhetoricae Libri Dvo* was a venerable work with more than a half-century of popularity behind it, a schoolmaster named William Dugard, of the Merchant Taylors' School in London, published at his own commercial press in that city a little work called *Rhetorices Elementa*, which was in fact an elementary version of the text of Butler's edition of Talaeus arranged in the form of

[77] *Ibid.*, sig. K3v. Butler's words are: "Oratoriae partes numerantur quinque: Inventio & Dispositio, Elocutio & Pronunciatio, atque Memoria. E quibus primum par Dialecticae, alterum Rhetoricę, acceptum refert: partem quintam non ab Arte, sed à Natura traditam, vt sibi, prae caeteris artibus necessariam, & quasi peculiarem, assumit; & praeceptis perficit."

[78] For a translation of Butler's chapter on memory, see Lee S. Hultzén, "Charles Butler on Memory," *Speech Monographs*, VI (1939), 47-65.

questions and answers. Dugard, who was also to publish at his press the famous reply of John Milton to Salmasius, gave his version of Butler a second edition in 1651.[79] Its Latin title declares it to be so formed that, if the questions are omitted or neglected altogether, the answers alone would present the entire theory of rhetoric to beginners. And in his preface to those beginners, Dugard speaks thus of Butler:

> Butler improved Talaeus in very many ways. Little questions of the kind presented here (unless my prediction deceives me) render Butler himself easier and more adaptable by far to the capacity of those of tender years. . . . Therefore, these having been sampled, you are to consult Butler himself if you shall have been at a loss in any way concerning this matter.[80]

The work which follows this declaration presents the rhetoric of Talaeus in the form of a catechism, style being given twenty-six pages of text, and pronunciation, five, while at the end the figures of style are summarized in neat tabular form.

Dugard's *Rhetorices Elementa* reached a fifth edition by 1657. Three years later, Charles Hoole, writing a treatise for the indoctrination of young schoolmasters, mentioned Dugard along with Butler and Talaeus when he came to speak of the study of rhetoric in grammar schools. Hoole's treatise, called *A New Discovery Of the old Art of Teaching Schoole*, invites comparison with Kempe's *Education of Children* and Brinsley's *Lvdvs*. Like them, it is a description of contemporary education, and like them it indicates the popularity of Ramistic rhetoric in English education. Hoole addresses himself first to the curriculum of the petty school, where children of the age of four or five were taught to read English; and then he speaks of the grammar school itself, where in successive years the emphasis is upon Latin, "forasmuch as *speaking Latine is the main end of Grammar.*"[81] Pupils of the fourth form are expected

---

[79] The title page of this second edition reads: "Rhetorices Elementa, Quaestionibus et Responsionibus Explicata: Quae ità formantur, ut, Quaestionibus prorsus omissis, vel neglectis, Responsiones solummodo integram *Rhetorices* Institutionem Tironibus exhibeant. Per Guil. Du-gard, In usum Scholae *Mercatorum-Scissorum*. Editio Secunda. . . . Londini, Typis Autoris. *Anno Domini* 1651. Veneunt apud *Fr. Eglesfield* in *Caemeterio Paulino.*" I have not seen a copy of the first edition.—For a discussion of Dugard's connection with the publication of Milton's reply to Salmasius, see F. F. Madan, "Milton, Salmasius, and Dugard," *The Library*, IV (1923), 119-145.

[80] *Rhetorices Elementa* (1651), p. 6. Translation mine.

[81] Charles Hoole, *A New Discovery Of the old Art of Teaching Schoole*, ed. E. T. Campagnac (Liverpool and London, 1913), "The Usher's Duty," p. 50. Italics are Hoole's.

to reach perfection in grammar and to begin to study the elements of rhetoric. In mastering the latter subject, they make their first contact with Talaeus and Butler through Dugard. Says Hoole:

> And to enter them in that Art of fine speaking, they may make use of *Elementa Rhetorices*, lately printed by *Mr. Dugard*, and out of it learn the Tropes and Figures, according to the definitions given by *Talaeus*, and afterwards more illustrated by *Mr. Butler*. Out of either of which books, they may be helped with store of examples, to explain the Definitions, so as they may know any Trope or Figure that they meet with in their own Authours.[82]

Another honor was paid in 1671 to Butler's version of Talaeus— it was partly converted into English by John Newton. Newton was a loyalist during the Protectorate, and a clergyman and educational reformer after the Restoration. What he wanted above all in education was to have young people taught "all the Sciences in their own Tongue," and to have the Latin School reserved for those who, being already familiar with the liberal arts in the vernacular, were intent upon entering a learned profession.[83] In furtherance of this design, he published English versions of the seven liberal arts, one version being entitled *An Introduction to the Art of Rhetorick* (London, 1671).[84] Newton is an eclectic. His rhetorical theory recognizes invention, arrangement, style, memory, and delivery as the five common heads of that science; but his sources are not as purely Ciceronian as these divisions suggest. He indicates instead that his borrowings are from a Neo-Ciceronian rhetorician and from a Ramist—"the truth is," he says, "the form and Method of this our Rhetorick, in respect of Elocution, some examples only excepted, is the same with Butler, and as for invention and disposition, I have very much followed the first part of that excellent piece of Oratory, which *Michael Radau* hath published under the title of *Orator Extemporaneus*,

[82] *Ibid.*, p. 132.

[83] These ideas are stated in the dedicatory epistle and preface of his *Introduction to the Art of Logick* (London, 1678). This work was first published in 1671. For a discussion of it, see below, pp. 316-317.

[84] For Newton's complete writings on the trivium and quadrivium, see his *The English Academy: or a brief introduction to the seven liberal arts* (London, 1677). There was a second edition of this work at London in 1693. The title page of his *Art of Rhetorick*, as published in 1671, reads as follows: "An Introduction to the Art of Rhetorick. Composed for the benefit of young Schollars and others, who have not opportunity of being instructed in the Latine tongue; and is very helpful to understand the figurative expressions in the holy Scriptures. Published for a Publick Advantage, By *John Newton*, D. D. *London*, Printed by *E. T.* and *R. H.* for *Thomas Passenger* at the three Bibles on *London-Bridge*, and *Ben. Hurlock* over against St. *Magnus* Church. 1671."

from whence I might have taken much more than I have, but that I was afraid of being too prolixe and over burthening my young English Rhetorician. . . ."[85] As for memory and delivery, the other two parts of Newton's present subject, "I purposely omit them," declares he, "as being natural endowments, which may be better improved by constant practice, than by any precepts which can be given."[86]

In the chapter which concludes his analysis of invention, Newton makes use of material from Radau to give us an insight into the cultural conditions that produce and are produced by the Ramist conception of rhetoric. At that point he is speaking of the sharpness of an oration.[87] Now sharpness as he discusses it is a stylistic phenomenon, even though invention is his present subject, and even though style will be treated after he has talked of disposition or arrangement. His own definition of sharpness is that it consists in an agreeing discord or a disagreeing concord in an oration, as when a beautiful and chaste maiden is said to be a fire that scorches and chills, or when the sun is called a fountain of light. These concords and discords, he explains, are produced in various ways. But what really gives them authority with listeners is that the public has a strong appetite for them. Says Newton:

> Such is the Curiosity of this age in which we live, as that it is grown weary of these plain and ordinary waies, and requireth or expecteth in the very style something more than ordinary; insomuch that now a daies he is not worthy the name of an *Orator*, that knowes not how to brandish an Oration, by some sharp and witty flourishes. And therefore, that we may comply with the present times, we will also speak something of that sharpness or ingenuity, with which an oration should be adorned.[88]

The history of Ramistic rhetoric in Britain would not be complete without mention of various Latin editions of Talaeus in addition to those that I have already indicated as having possibly preceded Butler, and those that grew directly or indirectly out of Butler. Andrew Hart, a famous Scottish printer and bookseller of the Elizabethan and Jacobean period, published at Edinburgh in 1621 a little work entitled *Avdomari Talaei Rhetorica*, which is the earliest surviving British reprint of that treatise to acknowledge Talaeus as its author

---

[85] *Introduction to the Art of Rhetorick* (London, 1671), sig. A1or-A1ov.

[86] *Ibid.*, p. 130. For a discussion of Michael Radau's *Orator Extemporaneus*, see below, p. 326.

[87] *Introduction to the Art of Rhetorick*, pp. 28-36.   [88] *Ibid.*, p. 28.

and Ramus as its source.[89] Ten years later the same work was published in England at the Cambridge University press, and there were also two printings of it at London, one of which belongs to the year 1636, and the other probably to the same year, though it is undated.[90] Finally, in 1651 at the press of William Dugard in London there appeared a little work entitled *Rhetoricae Compendium, Latino-Anglice*, by Thomas Horne, an Oxonian who had become headmaster of Eton.[91] The Latin section of Horne's compend runs to twenty-two pages and is followed by seventeen pages of English, the latter being a translation of the former, and having as title, "A Short Epitome of Rhetorick." The work does not advertise its origin, but it consists in reality of a very short disquisition upon six of the ten major terms in Ramus's theory of logical invention, and a much longer disquisition upon the doctrine of style as set forth by Talaeus. Delivery, the second phase of Talaeus's rhetoric, is mentioned but not discussed.

Horne's version of Ramistic doctrine and Newton's adaptation of Butler are not the only vernacular versions of the reformed rhetoric to be published in England during the seventeenth century. As a matter of fact, there are five other versions, two of which are respectively a schoolboy digest and a scholarly English commentary, whereas three are closely identified with Dudley Fenner's sixteenth-century translation of Talaeus.

John Barton, master of the free school in Kinfare, Staffordshire, brought out at London in 1634 a work consisting of a short English

[89] There is a copy of Hart's reprint at the Folger Shakespeare Library. Its title page reads: "Avdomari Talaei Rhetorica. E P. Rami Regii Professoris Praelectionibvs observata. Edinburgi, Excudebat Andreas Hart. 1621." A work of similar title was entered with the company of stationers on December 6, 1588. See Arber, *Transcript of the Registers*, II, 509. No copy of it appears to have survived.

[90] The title page of the Cambridge edition reads: "Avdomari Talaei rhetorica e P. Rami, Regii professoris praelectionibus observata. Cui praefixa est epistola, quae lectorem de omnibus utriusque viri scriptis, propediem edendis commonefacit. Cantabrigiae, Ex Academiae celeberrimae Typographeo. 1631." There is a copy of this edition in the University Library, Cambridge.—The dated London edition as held in the University Library, Cambridge, has the same title as that just quoted, and its imprint reads, "Londini: Excusum impensis Societatis Stationariorum. 1636." The undated London edition, a copy of which I have seen in the Huntington Library, has the same title but not quite the same imprint as that in the dated London edition. Its imprint reads, "Londini: Excusum pro Societate Stationariorum." The Huntington copy has perhaps been cropped in such a way as to have had its date removed. At any rate, the card catalogue of that library identifies it as "perhaps the 1636 ed. with date cut off."

[91] The title page reads: "Rhetoricae Compendium, Latino-Anglice. Opera Thomae Horn, A. M. Scholae Etonensis Archididascali. Londini, Typis *Guil. Du-gardi*. Veneunt apud *Franc. Eglesfield* in Caemeterio Paulino. 1651."

summary and a shorter following Latin summary of Ramistic rhetoric, these two parts being published as *The Art of Rhetorick Concisely and Compleatly Handled*, although the Latin section is separately titled "Rhetorices Enchiridion."[92] In the dedicatory letter
Barton refers to his double summary as "these two-languag'd twins,"
and his letter to the reader implies that these twins are descended
from such previous rhetoricians as Keckermann, Aristotle, Cicero,
Dietericus, Molinaeus, Butler, and Isidore. He even mentions that,
since grammar and logic are necessary to an orator, men who "formerly wrote Rhetoricks, put in the Topicks of Logick and Figures
of Grammar, as essential parts of Rhetorick."[93] But his own work is
not descended from those who gave rhetoric something beyond the
procedures of style and delivery. True, he objects to "elocution"
and "pronunciation" as terms for the two parts of the proper rhetoric, on the ground that they both mean about the same thing, and
that neither includes the concept of gesture.[94] True, he proposes
"adornation" and "action" as substitutes for these two terms. At this
point, however, his originality ends. For the rest, he devotes himself
to the Ramistic convention, and varies from it only by giving the
topic of action almost no space at all. Here are his essential statements on the subject of adornation, and the full text of his chapter
on action:

> Rhetorick is the skill of using daintie words, and comely deliverie,
> whereby to work upon mens affections. It hath two parts, *Adornation*
> and *Action*. *Adornation* consisteth in the sweetnesse of the phrase, and
> is seen in *Tropes* and *Figures*. A *Trope* is an affecting kinde of speech,
> altering the native signification of a word. . . .[95]

> A *Figure* is an affecting kinde of speech without consideration had of
> any borrowed sense. . . .[96]

> Thus much of Adornation; a word of Action. *Action* is a part of Rhet-
> orick exercised in the gesture and utterance.

> *Gesture* is the comely carriage of the bodie; whereof nothing is need-
> full to be spoken.

[92] The complete title is as follows: "The Art of Rhetorick Concisely and Compleatly
Handled, Exemplified out of holy Writ, and with a compendious and perspicuous Comment, fitted to the capacities of such as have had a smatch of learning, or are otherwise
ingenious. By J. B. Master of the free-school of *Kinfare* in *Staffordshire*. . . . [n.p.]
Printed for *Nicolas Alsop*, and are to be sold at the *Angel* in *Popes-head-alley*. 1634."
[93] *Art of Rhetorick*, sig. A3v.   [94] *Ibid.*, sig. A3v.
[95] *Ibid.*, p. 1.   [96] *Ibid.*, p. 23.

Utterance is the sweet framing of the voice; of which we will note onely that which we call *Emphasis*, which is the elevation of some word or words in the sentence, wherein the chief force lies. *Psal. 76.7. Thou, thou,* art worthy to be praised.[97]

Another vernacular version of Talaeus's *Rhetorica* appeared in 1657, when the second edition of Alexander Richardson's *Logicians School-Master* was published. This work has already been described in an earlier section of this chapter where English commentaries upon Ramus's *Dialecticae Libri Duo* were under examination.[98] Richardson's notes on "Taleus his *Rhetorick*" run to some fifty-six pages, and cover only the subject of the tropes and figures. The basic philosophy behind his analysis of these components of style can be grasped from what he has to say about grammar and rhetoric:

> For whereas Grammer is the garment of Logick, and would cover every thing as Logick layes it down, the Nominative case before the Verb, and the Accusative after the Verb: *Figura* comes and sets this speech otherwise, and so changeth the habit of it; so that I may compare Grammer to a trubkin, and Rhetorick to a fine handsome fellow; and in Rhetorick I may compare a Trope to one cut or jag, and a Figure to all the jags, or the whole shape thereof.[99]

The images suggested by these partly obsolete terms would appear to be that of a small squat woman to represent grammar, and a fine handsome fellow to represent rhetoric, whereas a trope would be one slash in a garment to show the color of a garment underneath, and a figure would be the pattern that all such slashes make, or the shape of the garment as a whole. These metaphors were valid parts of the Ramistic concept of grammar and rhetoric. And by virtue of its preoccupation with unusual patterns of language, Ramistic rhetoric naturally assumed jurisdiction over much of what we would today consider to be poetical theory. Says Richardson, speaking of metrical language: "So that here comes in Poetry, so that 'tis not a distinct art by it self, and therfore not to be handled by it self, but is a branch of Rhetorrck [sic]. . . ."[100] Nevertheless, as Richardson makes plain a moment later, poetry has one characteristic of its very own—it con-

---

[97] *Ibid.,* p. 35. Following these words there is a half page devoted to commentary. The quotation from Psalms actually reads: "Thou, *even* thou, *art* to be feared." For Barton's reasons for not discussing gesture, see his preface, sig. A7r.

[98] See above, pp. 209-210.

[99] *The Logicians School-Master* (1657), "Rhetorical Notes," p. 66.

[100] *Ibid.,* p. 70.

veys its meaning through the medium of fiction. He places this restriction upon poetry thus: "For the most part," he says, " 'tis used in fables; and *fabula* is the subject of Poetry. . . ."[101]

The three remaining seventeenth-century English versions of Talaeus's *Rhetorica* stem more or less directly from the second part of Dudley Fenner's *Artes of Logike and Rethorike*. As we have already observed, Fenner was the first Englishman to translate Ramistic rhetoric into his native language.[102] No doubt because the first edition of his work was published anonymously, it tended in time to become an item that could easily be attributed to another author or that could be freely appropriated as unowned material. The three rhetorics remaining to my present discussion belong to one or the other of these two categories.

Fenner's *Rethorike* is one of the three anonymous units of a work published in 1651 under the title, *A Compendium of the Art of Logick and Rhetorick in the English Tongue*. I have already mentioned that the first unit of this *Compendium*, as Walter J. Ong, S.J., has demonstrated, is to be identified as Robert Fage's translation of Ramus's *Dialecticae Libri Duo*.[103] Now it should be added that the other two units, likewise identified by Father Ong, are Thomas Hobbes's English abstract of Aristotle's *Rhetoric*, and the main heads of Talaeus's *Rhetorica* in Fenner's translation, the latter treatise being said on its title page in the *Compendium* to be "By a concealed author."[104]

Fenner's *Rethorike* is also the unacknowledged source of part of the rhetorical doctrine in John Smith's *The Mysterie of Rhetorique Unvail'd* (London, 1657).[105] Smith's *Rhetorique* is in general a compilation wherein some 138 tropes and figures are listed, not only by Greek, Latin, and English names, but also by English definitions, and by Latin and English illustrations. The English illustrations, says Smith, "are most of them streams from Sir *Philip Sidneys* fountain."[106] As for his Latin illustrations, he is also explicit about their intermediate source, for he credits them repeatedly to Thomas Far-

---

[101] *Ibid.*, p. 71.   [102] See above, p. 219.   [103] See above, p. 238.

[104] See Walter J. Ong, S.J., "Hobbes and Talon's Ramist Rhetoric in English," *Transactions of the Cambridge Bibliographical Society*, I (1949-1953), 260-262. For a discussion of Hobbes's abstract of Aristotle's *Rhetoric*, see below, pp. 384-385.

[105] Smith signs his preface "From my Chamber in Mountague Close, Southwark March 27. 1656. John Smith." Wing, *Short-Title Catalogue*, lists this work under the name of John Sergeant and indicates editions in 1657, 1665, 1673, 1683, and 1688. The Huntington Library has a copy of the ninth edition, dated at London in 1706.

[106] *Rhetorique* (1657), sig. A5r.

naby. But he does not tell us that his quotations from Sidney, and certain of his definitions as well, are borrowed from Thomas Blount's *Academie of Eloquence*, and he probably did not know that Thomas Blount in turn had as silently borrowed the same quotations and definitions from John Hoskins's *Directions for Speech and Style*, then an unpublished manuscript. The relations between Smith, Blount, and Hoskins were brilliantly identified by Hoyt H. Hudson.[107] According to Professor Lee S. Hultzén, Smith also borrows definitions and a few illustrations from Henry Peacham's *Garden of Eloquence* in its edition of 1593.[108] Now, since Peacham, Hoskins, Blount, and Farnaby are all committed for the most part to the old Ciceronian tradition rather than to Ramism, it is a surprise to find that Smith is enough of an eclectic to borrow as cheerfully from the latter as from the former source. But so it is. As the beginning of his *Rhetorique* are twelve pages of logical and rhetorical doctrine as an introduction to the main work, and of these pages, three contain a glossary of terms from Ramistic logic, whereas nine are closely parallel to Fenner's translation of Talaeus.

A few passages from Fenner and Smith will show how strikingly the latter follows the former in these nine pages of rhetorical doctrine.[109] After each author has defined rhetoric in somewhat the same fashion, they both have this to say of its parts:

> [Fenner] It hath two partes, Garnishing of speache, called Eloqution. Garnishing of the maner of vtterance, called Pronunciation.

> [Smith] It hath two parts, *viz.* 1. Garnishing of speech, called *Elocution*. 2. Garnishing of the manner of utterance, called *Pronunciation* (which in this Treatise is not principally aimed at.)

They both have also the same frame of language for the definition of elocution and the mention of its parts:

> [Fenner] Garnishing of speache is the firste parte of Rhetorike, whereby the speache it selfe is beautified and made fine. It is eyther

---

[107] John Hoskins, *Directions for Speech and Style*, ed. Hoyt H. Hudson (Princeton, 1935), pp. xxx-xxxviii.

[108] *Ibid.*, p. xxxvii, note 38.

[109] The passages quoted here can be found in Fenner's *Rethorike* (1584) and Smith's *Rhetorique* (1657) as follows:

1) Naming of the parts of rhetoric: Fenner, sig. D1v; Smith, p. 1.
2) Definition and parts of elocution: Fenner, sig. D1v; Smith, p. 2.
3) Definition of a trope: Fenner, sig. D1v; Smith, p. 2.
4) Definition of a figure: Fenner, sig. D3r; Smith, p. 4.
5) Definition of *figura sententiae*: Fenner, sig. D4r; Smith, pp. 7-8.

the fine maner of wordes, called a Trope. The fine shape or frame of speache, called a Figure.

[Smith] *Elocution*, or the garnishing of speech, is the first and principal part of Rhetorique, whereby the speech it self is beautified and made fine: And this is either
> The fine manner of words called a *Trope*: or,
> The fine shape or frame of speech, called a *Figure*.

Again they both use similar words to define the nature of the trope:

[Fenner] The fine maner of wordes is a garnishing of speache, whereby one worde is drawen from his firste proper signification to another. . . .

[Smith] A *Trope*, is when words are used for elegancy in a changed signification; or when a word is drawn from its proper and genuine signification to another.

Still again, they both use similar, at time identical, words to define the nature of the figure:

[Fenner] A Figure is a garnishing of speache, wherein the course of the same is chaunged from the more simple and plaine maner of speaking, vnto that whiche is more full of excellencie and grace. For as in the finenesse of wordes or a trope, wordes are considered asunder by them selues: so in the fine shape or frame of speach or a figure, the apte and pleasant ioyning togither of many wordes is noted.

[Smith] A *Figure* is an ornament of elocution, which adornes our speech, or a garnishing of speech when words are used for elegancy in their native signification. And as in a *Trope*, or the finenesse of words, words are considered asunder by themselves, so in a *Figure*, the apt and pleasant joyning together of many words is noted.

And once again, they both use the same language to define the figure of sentence as the second type of figure:

[Fenner] Garnishing of the frame of speache in a sentence, is a garnishinge of the shape of speache, or a figure, which for the forceable mouing of affections, doeth after a sorte beautifie the sence and verie meaning of a sentence. Because it hath in it a certayne manlie maiestie, which farre surpasseth the softe delicacie or dayntines of the former figures.

[Smith] Secondly. Garnishing of the frame of speech in a sentence, called *Figura Sententiae*, is a figure, which for the forcible moving of affections, doth after a sort beautifie the sense and very meaning of a sentence: because it carries with it a certain manly majesty, which far surpasses the soft delicacy of the former Figures, they being as it were effeminate and musical, these virile and majestical.

The final episode in the history of the anonymous first edition of Fenner's *Rethorike* is that it was published under the name of Thomas Hobbes in 1681.[110] Thus it was established among that distinguished philosopher's authentic writings, and received without question as one of his works, until October 1951, when an article in *The Quarterly Journal of Speech* announced its true identity. That article, which I myself prepared as a preliminary digest of this present chapter, had scarcely appeared in America when Walter J. Ong, S.J., in an article published in England in the *Transactions of the Cambridge Bibliographical Society*, also announced the true identity of the work attributed to Hobbes.[111] In one important respect Father Ong's article reached beyond mine. Whereas I had been unable to explain why William Crook, Hobbes's literary executor, had been willing, two years after the latter's death, to attribute to him a work already printed in the previous century under its rightful author's name, Father Ong offered what seems to be the true explanation of this mystery. According to him, Hobbes's executor must have come upon the work published at London in 1651 as the *Compendium of the Art of Logick and Rhetorick in the English Tongue*; and noticing that it contained an anonymous *Art of Rhetorick* as a kind of appendix to what he would of course recognize as Hobbes's condensed version of the *Rhetoric* of Aristotle, the executor must have concluded that Hobbes was the author of the appendix as well as the main work. At any rate, he attributed Fenner's *Rethorike* to Hobbes in 1681, and it was thereupon accepted in the Hobbes canon for almost three hundred years, although at the same time it was accepted in its own orbit as one Dudley Fenner's English rhetoric, and an English rhetoric, moreover, which oddly violated Cicero's laws by limiting rhetoric to two parts, style and delivery.

[110] The title page of the work in which Fenner's translation of Talaeus is published under the name of Hobbes reads as follows: "The Art of Rhetoric, with a Discourse of The Laws of *England*. By *Thomas Hobbes* of *Malmesbury*. London, Printed for *William Crooke* at the Green Dragon without *Temple-Bar*, 1681." For the work belonging to Fenner, see pp. 135-168. For other details concerning it, see Wilbur S. Howell, "Ramus and English Rhetoric: 1574-1681," *The Quarterly Journal of Speech*, xxxvii (October 1951), pp. 308-309.

[111] Walter J. Ong, S.J., "Hobbes and Talon's Ramist Rhetoric in English," *Transactions of the Cambridge Bibliographical Society*, I (1949-1953), 260-269.

So ends the history of Talaeus's *Rhetorica* in seventeenth-century England. Hobbes's involuntary association with it did not give it a new lease on life after 1681, nor had Milton's association with Ramus's *Dialecticae Libri Duo* prolonged its life after 1672. But these dates are not to be taken as marking the complete end of Ramism in England. They are instead the dates that mark the retirement of Ramism from active competition with other logical and rhetorical theories. Even after its retirement in 1672, as we have seen, Ramus's *Dialecticae Libri Duo*, in Fage's translation, made two public appearances in the closing years of the seventeenth century, thanks to Edward Phillips, Milton's nephew.[112] And Talaeus's *Rhetorica* also made some public appearances after the Fenner-Hobbes version of 1681. There was, for example, a final edition of Butler's *Rhetoricae Libri Dvo* at London in 1684, and John Smith's *Mysterie of Rhetorique Unvail'd* was reprinted in 1683 and 1688.

Even in the eighteenth century, evidence of the persistence of Ramistic rhetoric can be found. Smith's *Rhetorique* had a ninth edition at London in 1706, and one "J. H., Teacher of Geography," published an abridgement of it in 1739.[113] Also, a treatise which, by its own acknowledgment, depended upon Smith's *Rhetorique* as well as upon Farnaby's Latin *Rhetoric*, appeared anonymously at London in 1706 under the title, *The Art of Rhetorick, As to Elocution; Explain'd*, and it, too, was based ultimately upon Talaeus.[114] For example, it divides rhetoric into two parts, "*Elocution* and *Pronunciation*," adding "We shall treat only of the *Former* here."[115] It defines elocution as "the *adorning* of Speech either with fine *Words* or *Expressions*."[116] It goes on to treat of the tropes and the figures, as a Ramistic rhetoric would. As for the value of that rhetoric, it has this to say in some complimentary verses by "M. N." to the author just before the first page of the text:

[112] See above, p. 238.

[113] See above, p. 276, note 105. See also Hoskins, *Directions for Speech and Style*, ed. Hudson, p. xxxvii.

[114] The title page reads: "The Art of Rhetorick, As to Elocution; Explain'd: And Familiarly Adapted to the Capacityes of *School-Boys*, by way of *Question* and *Answer*; in English. . . . London. Printed, for *S. Sturton* at the Corner of *Gutter-Lane* in *Cheap-side*, 1706."

The anonymous author thus acknowledges his sources towards the end of his preface to the reader: "I do not deny but I have been hugely Oblig'd to the Learned *Farnaby's Rhetorick* in Latin, and the Ingenious *Mr. Smith's Mystery of Rhetorick Unveil'd* in English, for the *substance of This Treatise*."

[115] *Art of Rhetoric, As to Elocution; Explain'd*, p. 1.

[116] *Ibid.*, p. 2.

Our Infant Poets taught by Rules like these,
Shall Learn with *Dreyden's* strength, and *Otway's* Ease,
The Happy Secret to instruct, and please.
Thus *Rhet'rick* by thy Artful Pen restor'd,
Such Just Renown shall to thy Name afford,
That *Greece* and *Rome* shall be no more Ador'd.

But these words are more of an epitaph than a prophecy. For the rules that represented this rhetoric were fast losing authority, and another sort of rhetoric was emerging, even as a new era in logic was at hand. What constituted that new logic and rhetoric will be the subject of a later chapter.

CHAPTER 5

Counterreform: Systematics and
Neo-Ciceronians

I. Middle Ground between Contradictions

RAMUS's reform of scholastic logic encountered two sorts of opposition during the late sixteenth and early seventeenth centuries. The first sort may be described as the opposition of denial; the second, as the opposition of compromise. During his own lifetime, and particularly in the period between 1543 and 1560, he was opposed by the supporters of the logic he had attacked, and those adversaries confined themselves largely to denying the validity of his revision of the traditional system. Prominent in that group of anti-Ramists were Périon, Gouvea, Galland, Charpentier, and Turnebus, each of whom spoke out sharply against his reform, although by 1561 all of them except Charpentier were on friendly terms with him.[1] After Ramus's death in 1572, his teachings spread rapidly throughout northern Europe, their popularity in England being related to their popularity in provincial France, Holland, Belgium, Denmark, Switzerland, and Germany. Now in these countries his logical system came into collision not only with the entrenched scholastic logic but also with the logic of Melanchthon. An older contemporary of Ramus, Melanchthon too had tried his hand at improving the liberal arts, and his writings on logic and rhetoric were particularly esteemed among his own religious sect, the Lutherans.[2] As a result of the competition between his system and that of Ramus, a disposition to work out a compromise acceptable to these two schools and to the older scholasticism came into existence, and a logic compounded of elements from all three schools was born. The English aspects of that compromise will be the subject of the present chapter, first as regards logic, and next as regards rhetoric.

In the field of logic, three terms were applied during the period between 1590 and 1640 to the logicians who helped to promote the compromise. Some of them were called Philippo-Ramists, a word

[1] For an account of this early criticism of Ramism, see Waddington, *Ramus*, pp. 39-58, 70-80, 102-106, 121-122; see also Graves, *Peter Ramus*, pp. 30-47, 63-70.
[2] For brief reference to Melanchthon's writings on rhetoric and logic, see above, pp. 92, 94-95.

suggested in part by Melanchthon's given name and by the popular designation of his religious sect as Philippists. Others of the compromisers were called Mixts, after a term in the old chemistry meaning "compounds." Still others were called Systematics, the reference being to the Latin word "systema" as used in the titles of their works on the liberal arts, and particularly as used in the works of Bartholomew Keckermann, a learned German of Danzig.

Keckermann contributed several works to the critical revision of Ramism. His *System of Logic*, published in Latin at Hanau in 1600, and his *Three Tractates of Logical Precognitions*, published at the same place four years later, are especially important to my present subject, because of their influence upon the chief English Systematic, Robert Sanderson.[3] Other works of Keckermann to be counted as influential in England are his *Two Books of Ecclesiastical Rhetoric* and his later *System of Rhetoric*. To them, indeed, even the devoted English Ramists occasionally refer, as we have seen.[4]

The other chief continental Systematics were Heizo Buscherus, Andreas Libavius, John Henry Alsted, and Clemens Timplerus. Buscherus, rector of the school at Hannover, Germany, published in 1595 at Lemgo a Latin work in two books called *The Philippo-Ramistic Logical Harmony*, and this is one of the earliest works to use the term "Philippo-Ramistic."[5] Somewhat earlier Buscherus had composed *Two Books concerning the Theory of Solving Fallacies, soundly and clearly deduced and explained from the logic of P. Ramus*, thus showing his interest in giving Ramistic logic an explicit claim to a topic less emphasized by Ramus than by the scholastics. The next Systematic, Andreas Libavius, wrote chiefly upon medicine and chemistry. Indeed, he is credited with being perhaps the first doctor to suggest the possibility of blood transfusions.[6] As early as 1591 he brought out at Frankfurt *A Treatise of Disputed Physical Questions between Peripatetics and Ramists*, and one interesting thing about this work is that it has a preface by the English Ramist, William Temple.[7] Libavius also wrote a treatise upon various vexing

[3] See below, p. 303. The Latin titles of these two works are respectively as follows: *Systema Logicae* (Hanoviae, 1600) and *Praecognitorum Logicorum Tractatus Tres* (Hanoviae, 1604).

[4] See above, p. 274.

[5] Its Latin title is as follows: *Harmonia Logica Philippo-Ramea* (Lemgoviae, 1595). There is a copy of it at the Bodleian.

[6] *Biographie Universelle*, s.v. Libavius, André.

[7] Its title reads: *Quaestionum Physicarum Controversarum inter Perapeteticos et Rameos tractatus: cum Praefatione Gul. Tempelli.*

controversies of his own day among physicians of the Peripatetic, Ramistic, Hippocratic, and Paracelsic school.[8] But somehow he found time to write considerably on logic. At Frankfurt in 1600 he published a Latin work called *First and Second Dialogue of Andreas Libavius concerning Aristotelian Dialectic, clearly selected and explained from Philipp Melanchthon and P. Ramus*,[9] this treatise being third in time among his strictly logical writings. He also published at Frankfurt in 1608 what he called *The Philippo-Ramistic Dialectic*. This characterized itself as based upon the descriptions and commentaries of Melanchthon, Ramus, and other logicians; and as an added feature it contained Talaeus's *Rhetorica*.[10] As for John Henry Alsted, he wrote on the philosophy of Aristotelians, Lullians, and Ramists before publishing at Herborn in 1614 his *Harmonious System of Logic, in which the Universal Mode of Disputing Well is handed down from Peripatetic and Ramistic Authors*.[11] At about the same time Clemens Timplerus of Steinfurt in Luxembourg was also contributing to the cause of the Systematics by writing his *Methodical System of Logic* and *The Methodical System of Rhetoric*.[12]

The influence of the Systematics can be seen in England among the devoted Ramists whose work has just been described. Whenever the strict limits of logic as Ramus conceived of it are relaxed by his followers to permit scholastic elements to return to their traditional home, the counterreform is at work, even if it may not reach very far. For example, the *Syntagma Logicum* of Thomas Granger, although it belongs among England's Ramistic treatises, as I have indicated, has certain traits that come to it from the Systematics, its division into five books rather than two being a scholastic influence, as is its inclusion of the ancient rhetorical idea that there are three kinds of subject matter, demonstrative, deliberative, and judicial.[13] For another example, Thomas Spencer's *Art of Logick*, already discussed

---

[8] The Latin title, as quoted in the *Nouvelle Biographie Générale*, s.v. Libavius, André, reads thus: *Variarum Controversiarum inter nostri saeculi medicos peripateticos, Rameos, Hippocraticos, Paracelsicos, Agitatarum, Libri Duo* (Frankfurt, 1600).

[9] That is, *De Dialectica Aristotelica a Philip. Melanchthone et P. Ramo perspicue selecta et exposita, Andrea Libavii. . . . Dialogus Primus [-Secundus].*

[10] The title reads thus: *Dialectica Philippo-Ramaea, ex Descriptionibus et Commentariis P. Melancthonis et P. Rami, aliorumque Logicorum. . . . Addita est Rhetorica Descriptionis A. Thalaei.*

[11] The title reads thus: *Logicae Systema Harmonicum, in quo universus bene disserendi modus ex authoribus Peripateticis juxta et Rameis traditur.*

[12] Their respective Latin titles are: *Logicae Systema Methodicum* (Hanau, 1612) and *Rhetoricae Systema Methodicum* (Hanau, 1613).

[13] See above, pp. 229-232; see also Thomas Granger, *Syntagma Logicum* (1620), p. 3.

as a Ramistic treatise, seeks to combine the precepts of Aristotle with those of Ramus and to explain both by the assistance of the best scholastics—an ambition that almost makes Spencer a Systematic.[14] There are many other indications of the same general ambition among English Ramists, particularly the later ones, and each indication may be counted as a softening of the Ramistic reform by the counter-reformers.

But the true work of the English counterreformers is most clearly seen in the logics that were written in England to restore scholasticism while preserving some of Ramus's innovations. These logics belong bibliographically to the period between 1599 and 1673, although the most influential ones had all been published before 1620. The three that may be said to have been so important as to have taught logic to all England during the seventeenth century are the product of Oxford men, even as Cambridge men had claimed the same distinction during the sixteenth century, both before and after the birth of the English Ramists. Latin is the language in which almost all of the work of the English counterreformers was published. Nevertheless, their story begins with a vernacular work of limited popularity and of non-academic appeal. This work is Thomas Blundeville's *Art of Logike*.[15]

Blundeville published his *Logike* at London in 1599, but there is some reason to suppose that he wrote it around 1575. The evidence for a considerable interval between its date of composition and of publication comes from Blundeville himself. In his edition of 1619 he tells us that the *Logike* was written "many yeeres past" and withheld from publication a long time, until, as he says, "I was fully perswaded by diuers of my learned friends, to put it in print, who hauing diligently perused the same, and liking my plaine order of teaching vsed therein, thought it a most necessary Booke for such Ministers as had not beene brought vp in any Vniuersitie."[16] If this statement is open to the interpretation that his *Logike* could have been written more than two decades before he published it first, an-

---

[14] See above, pp. 234-237.

[15] The lengthy title page reads in part: "The Art of Logike. Plainely taught in the English tongue, by M. *Blundeuile* of Newton Flotman in Norfolke, aswell according to the doctrine of Aristotle, as of all other moderne and best accounted Authors thereof. . . . London Imprinted by *Iohn Windet*, and are to be sold at Paules Wharfe, at the signe of the Crosse Keyes. 1599." The second edition, which I have not seen, was published in 1617. The third edition, as published at London by William Stansby in 1619, is entitled, *The Arte of Logicke*, etc. It contains a preface with a postscript attached, neither of which is found in the edition of 1599.

[16] *Logike* (1619), sig. ¶3v.

other statement in the edition of 1619 would seem to place its date of composition in the middle fifteen-seventies. That other statement is one in which he says that his treatment of logic in English accepts Latin terms after a due explanation of their meaning, and that it is much better to proceed thus "then to faine new words vnproper for the purpose, as some of late haue done."[17] Now this remark seems to be able to refer only to Ralph Lever's *Witcraft*, published in 1573; for that work is the sole English logic of the sixteenth century to make an issue of preferring to construct an English logical vocabulary out of native rather than Latin elements.[18] Thus Blundeville appears to suggest that he could not have written his *Logike* before *Witcraft* was published, and that he could well have written it when *Witcraft* was still a recent book. At that time, say in 1575, he would not have been likely to foresee that Ramistic logic as advocated by MacIlmaine and others was destined to drive traditional logic from the presses and book markets of England for an entire generation, and that his own *Logike* would thus not be in demand for many years. At any rate, the great popularity of Ramism in England between 1575 and 1600 may well explain why he did not publish his work for a long time after its date of composition. That he was active as a writer as early as the fifteen-sixties is well known.[19] Moreover, one of his most attractive publications, *The true order and Methode of wryting and reading Hystories*, not only is dated in 1574, but also is derived in large part from a treatise by Jacobus Acontius, an Italian philosopher, while another treatise by Acontius, the *De Methodo*, first published in 1558, is an important influence behind the very *Logike* now under discussion.[20] Blundeville would have been more likely in 1575 to use Acontius as an anti-Ramist authority on method than he would after 1580, when he could have found that sort of authority nearer home.[21]

One obvious mark of the influence of scholastic logic upon Blundeville can be seen in the way his treatise is organized. Like many of

[17] *Ibid.*, sig. ¶2v.
[18] See above, pp. 59-60.
[19] See *Dictionary of National Biography*, s.v. Blundeville, Thomas.
[20] The title page of Blundeville's work on reading histories is worded as follows: "The true order and Methode of wryting and reading Hystories, according to the precepts of Francisco Patricio, and Accontio Tridentino, tvvo Italian writers, no lesse plainly than briefly, set forth in our vulgar speach, to the great profite and commoditye of all those that delight in Hystories. By Thomas Blundeuill of Nevvton Flotman in Norfolke. Anno. 1574. Imprinted at London by VVillyam Seres."
[21] For a controversy in England in 1580-1581 on the subject of Ramistic method, see above, pp. 194-196.

the scholastic logicians, and indeed like Ramus, for that matter, Blundeville divides logic into two parts, and he calls those parts invention and judgment. His definitions of them are standard:

> Inuention findeth out meete matter to proue the thing that yee intend, and Iudgement examineth the matter, whether it be good or not: and then frameth, disposeth, and reduceth the same into due forme of argument.[22]

Now at this point it was the practice of the Ramists to limit themselves to invention and judgment, and to include under these two topics all that could be said on the subject of logic. But Blundeville does not do this. He goes back instead to the more elaborate practice of the scholastics, and he proceeds to organize his treatise by speaking respectively (1) of words, (2) of definition, division, and method, (3) of propositions, (4) of places, (5) of arguments, and (6) of fallacies. These parts of logic are roughly parallel to the six treatises making up Aristotle's *Organon,* and thus Blundeville and the scholastics seem so far as organization is concerned to be purer Aristotelians than do the Ramists, inasmuch as the latter tended to organize the materials of the *Organon* around the two main headings of Aristotle's *Topics.*

Another obvious mark of the influence of scholastic logic upon Blundeville is evident in his treatment of the predicables, the predicaments, and the places. Ramus had felt the redundancy involved in discussing these three matters in the traditional scholastic way; and his reform of logic had in an important sense consisted of the absorption of the predicaments by the doctrine of the places, and of the predicables both by the doctrine of the places and by the doctrine of the three laws. Hence the predicables and the predicaments are not explicit terms in Ramus's logic, whereas the places are explicit to the point of being conspicuous. What Blundeville does is to make all of these three terms important once again in logic. He devotes one chapter to the predicables, thirteen to the predicaments, six to additional scholastic refinements like forepredicaments and postpredicaments, and three to the places.[23] Thus does he show his preference for scholasticism upon a very crucial issue indeed.

Still another indication that Blundeville is a scholastic can be seen

---

[22] *Logike* (1599), p. 1.
[23] *Ibid.,* Bk. I, Chs. 4-23, Bk. IV, Chs. 1-3. The chapters devoted to the places (in Bk. IV) are scheduled as six chapters in the table of contents of Blundeville's *Logike,* but are printed as three.

in his insistence upon restoring to logic the doctrine of confutation and fallacies. These topics were included in Aristotle's *Organon* and in such scholastic logics as that of Thomas Wilson.[24] Ramus had felt it unnecessary to discuss them explicitly, since to his view they were already amply covered in everything logic had to say about valid proof and sound arguments, and so would lead to redundancy if treated as a new and distinct heading. Blundeville is apparently more eager to have confutation and fallacies represented in logic than he is to avoid redundancy. At any rate, he devotes Book VI of his treatise to the theory of rebuttal and to the discussion of logical errors. His coverage of these errors, by the way, is so reminiscent of what Thomas Wilson had formerly said on the same point in *The rule of Reason* that there can be little doubt of his having borrowed his organization and some of his materials from his predecessor; indeed, there is even better evidence to the same effect in other parts of his treatise.[25] But while he does not mention Wilson either in his discussion of fallacies or in previous matters, he makes it clear at least once that he relies upon Melanchthon's logic. Speaking of the "Fallacia Accidentis," Blundeville mentions its three forms, the last of which he describes as follows:

> Thirdly, as (*Melancthon* saith) when an accidentall cause is made a principall cause, as thus: *Elias* was an holy prophete, but *Elias* was cladde with Camelles haire, *ergo* I being cladde with Camelles haire am an holy prophet.[26]

[24] See above, pp. 28-29.

[25] Wilson discusses thirteen "deceiptfull argumentes," six of which are "Subtilties in the worde," and seven, "Subtilties without the word." See his *The rule of Reason* (London, 1552), foll. 128r-162v. Blundeville adopts the same division for his treatment of "Fallaxes," and his thirteen items are close to those of Wilson. See his *Logike* (London, 1619), pp. 190-197. For other close parallels between Wilson and Blundeville, consult the following passages in each, using the third edition of the latter's *Logike*, and the first or second edition of the former's *Rule of Reason* as indicated:

1) The four principal kinds of argument: Wilson (1552), fol. 46; Blundeville (1619), p. 133.
2) The example of Induction—all wines are hot: Wilson (1551), sig. h5v; Blundeville, p. 173.
3) The common jest to illustrate Sorites: Wilson (1552), fol. 69v; Blundeville, p. 177.
4) The dilemma of the man who marries: Wilson (1552), fol. 70r-v; Blundeville, p. 178.
5) The inversion—Pythagoras (?) & Euathlus: Wilson (1552), fol. 171r; Blundeville, p. 178.
6) Crocodilites, Ceratinae, Asistata, Pseudomenos: Wilson (1552), foll. 170v-175v; Blundeville, p. 179.

[26] *Logike* (1599), p. 167.

In referring to the compromise between Ramistic and Melanch-
thonian logic, Graves says that, like most compromises, it "was unsatisfactory and led rather to the preservation of Aristotle than of
Ramus."[27] This opinion seems conclusively demonstrated by what I
have been saying about Blundeville. Nevertheless, there is at least
one aspect of his *Logike* that can hardly be explained as an over-
shadowing of Ramism by scholasticism. That aspect has to do with
Blundeville's discussion of method. Method is a topic in scholastic
logic, and indeed Blundeville treats it just after the topic of definition and division, as Thomas Wilson had done.[28] But Blundeville's
analysis of method goes far beyond Wilson's. What he does is to
take for granted not only that method is now a more important topic
than it was in the old logic, but also that it cannot be discussed without some reference to Ramus, who of course was responsible for the
new interest in it. Thus Blundeville's chapter on method draws its
materials from Galen, from Acontius, and from the scholastics, with
an acknowledgment that the three kinds of method endorsed by
these sources are in effect what Ramus had insisted upon reducing
to one kind.

Blundeville begins his chapter on method by defining his terms
and dividing his subject into parts. "Methode," he remarks, "is a
compendious way of learning or teaching any thing: and it is three-
fold, that is to say, Compositiue, Resolutiue, and Diuisiue or defini-
tiue."[29] To each of these divisions of the subject he devotes explicit
and concrete attention.

The compositive method as he conceives of it is the procedure
followed when a learner or teacher begins with the smallest division
of a given thing and proceeds to understand or explain it by going
on to the next larger division, and so on, until the whole thing has
been accounted for. This kind of method, says Blundeville, is illustrated by my present treatise; "for first we treate of words or tearmes,
then of a proposition, and last of al of a Syllogisme."[30] The neatness
of this example cannot be questioned; but when Blundeville attempts
to show how the compositive method may be expressed in spatial
terms, the image he chooses is less fortunate. He says:

> . . . so likewise he that will teach the nighest way from Norwich to

[27] *Peter Ramus*, p. 217.
[28] See Wilson, *The rule of Reason* (London, 1551), sig. E4v-E6r. See also above,
pp. 21-22.
[29] *Logike* (1599), p. 55.   [30] *Ibid.*, p. 55.

London by order compositiue will bidde him first goe to Windham, from Windham to Atleborough, from Atleborough to Thetford, from Thetford to Newmarket, from Newmarket to Barkway, frō barkway to Ware, frō Ware to Londō.[31]

The resolutive method involves the same procedure in reverse. In other words, it consists of understanding or explaining a thing by beginning with the thing as a whole and by resolving it progressively into smaller and smaller divisions. Thus we might go from whole to part, or from effect to cause. Blundeville illustrates this method by suggesting a logic organized in terms of the syllogism, the proposition, and at last the subject and predicate. Nor does he decline to reverse his geographical example for our benefit:

> If ye will teach the way from Norwich to London by Methode resolutiue, ye must say that there is a town called Ware twenty myles from London: next to that is a Towne called Barkway, and so till yee come to that which was first in methode compositiue.[32]

Blundeville credits Galen with being the one to add to the two methods just discussed a third and final one—the divisive or definitive method. This consists of an orderly definition and division of general, less general, and particular elements, as when a given thing is understood or explained by successive descriptions of its generic, its special, and its individual characteristics. If, for example, we have to speak of quality, says Blundeville, we define it, then we divide it into its four kinds, and next we divide these kinds into their parts and members, until we can go no further. It is at this point that Blundeville elects to incorporate into his *Logike* a two-page summary of *De Methodo* of Acontius, this being his way of fully explaining the divisive or definitive method, despite his having credited its identification to Galen. Blundeville's summary of Acontius defines method as the right way of searching out or teaching knowledge of a thing, and defines that right way as an inquiry into what the thing is, what its final end is, and what are the causes of that end.[33] "And these," says Blundeville as he finishes the summary, "are all the chiefest poynts contayned in the Latine treatise which my freend *Acontius* wrote *de Methodo*: and though that *Petrus Ramus* maketh but one kynd of Methode, that is to say, to proceede from the first principles or elements: yet I am sure he will not deny but that to goe forwarde and backward be two diuers things, though not contrary,

---

[31] *Ibid.*, p. 55.   [32] *Ibid.*, p. 55.   [33] *Ibid.*, pp. 56-57.

as doth well appeare by the Compositiue and Resolutiue Methode before defined."[34]

The rest of Blundeville's discussion of method is borrowed from the scholastics, and is in large part a statement of the matters which Thomas Wilson had suggested as embracing the whole of this aspect of logic.[35] In other words, Blundeville proceeds to treat such subjects as the nine questions that should be asked in methodically handling a simple logical inquiry. Had he confined himself to these questions, his theory of method would have wholly belonged to the stable world of scholastic logic. The fact that he did not confine himself to them, but went beyond to espouse a more comprehensive theory, may be said to be the measure of the influence of Ramus upon scholasticism, even though Blundeville does not accept Ramus's exact methodology.

No more than three editions of Blundeville's *Logike* appear to have been published, and those fell within the twenty years between 1599 and 1619. It is odd that the work did not have a larger number of editions in that period. In the first place, it had the vernacular market to itself from the date of its first appearance until 1620, when Thomas Granger's *Syntagma Logicum* began to offer competition by presenting a new English adaptation of Ramus to readers interested in logic. In the second place, it was intended to fill a professional need, being designed, as the title page of its first edition declares, "specially for such zealous Ministers as haue not beene brought vp in any Vniuersity, and yet are desirous to know how to defend by sound argumentes the true Christian doctrine, against all subtill Sophisters, and cauelling Schismatikes. . . ." Perhaps the class of ministers not educated in any university was too small to sustain more than three editions of Blundeville's work. Perhaps its sale in other quarters was gradually choked off by the several popular Latin logics that appeared at English presses in the first two decades of the seventeenth century. At any rate, these Latin logics achieved about a dozen separate printings between the dates of Blundeville's first and third edition, and are the next topic in this chapter.

The least influential of these Latin logics is John Sanderson's *Institvtionvm Dialecticarvm Libri Qvatvor*, which was given three editions at Oxford between 1602 and 1609 after an earlier one at Antwerp in 1589.[36] Twenty-seven years before the date of that Ant-

[34] *Ibid.*, p. 58.
[35] Compare *Rule of Reason* (London, 1551), sig. E4v-E6r, with Blundeville, pp. 58-59.
[36] The title page of the first edition reads thus: "Institvtionvm Dialecticarvm Libri Qvatvor, A Ioanne Sandersono, Lancastrensi, Anglo, Liberalium artium Magistro, &

werp edition, Sanderson had served as logic reader at Cambridge, where he had previously earned a bachelor's and a master's degree. Afterwards he had been expelled from his academic position because of his adherence to the Catholic faith, and had ultimately settled in France as teacher in the English college at Rheims and as canon of the cathedral at Cambrai.[37] His *Institvtionvm Dialecticarvm Libri Qvatvor*, virtually his only surviving work, is rooted in the scholastic tradition and slightly marked with the reforms of Ramus. Like the scholastics of the early sixteenth century, Sanderson divides logic into invention and judgment, the latter topic being then subdivided into terms, propositions, and arguments, and being treated part by part in the first three books of his treatise, whereas Book IV is allotted to invention. But like the Ramists, Sanderson emphasizes his transitions as he goes from one part of his subject to the next; like them he divides many of his chapters into a text and a following commentary; and in his preliminary chapter on syllogism, induction, enthymeme, and example, he speaks of the principles of demonstration, and discusses what he calls their three aspects, and what Ramus had heralded as the three laws of propositions.[38]

Samuel Smith's *Aditvs ad Logicam*, that is, *Approach to Logic*, which declares itself in its Latin title to be "for the use of those who first greet the university," turned out to be much more popular than Sanderson's *Libri Qvatvor*. The *Aditvs* was originally published at London in 1613, and went through three other editions at Oxford by 1619, remaining thereafter a steady seller until 1685.[39] Smith attended Magdalen College in Oxford, where he became bachelor of arts in 1609, master of arts in 1612, and bachelor of medicine in

---

sacrae Theologiae Doctore, Metropolitanae Ecclesiae Cameracensis Canonico, conscripti. Antverpiae, Ex officina Christophori Plantini, Architypographi Regij. M. D. LXXXIX." Two of the three Oxford editions are dated 1602; the third, 1609. See *Short-Title Catalogue*, s.v. Sanderson, John.—Despite three English editions, this work did not exert great influence. It is not once mentioned in T. W. Baldwin's *William Shakspere's Small Latine & Lesse Greeke*, which is one of most thorough of the published studies of English education in the age of Shakespeare.

[37] See *Dictionary of National Biography*, s.v. Sanderson, John.

[38] For Sanderson's emphasis on transitions, see *Institvtionvm Dialecticarvm Libri Qvatvor* (Antwerp, 1589), pp. 91, 155; for his treatment of the three laws, see p. 131.

[39] My discussion of this work is based upon a copy of the "fourth" edition in the Huntington Library. Its title page reads: "Aditvs ad Logicam. In vsum eorum qui primò Academiam Salutant. Autore Samvele Smith *Artium Magistro*. Quarta editio, de nouo correcta, & emendata. Londini Per Guilielmum Stansby. 1627." For an inventory of the fourteen printings of this work during the seventeenth century, see Madan, *Oxford Books*, III, 448. The original fourth edition appeared at Oxford in 1618. The London reprint of 1627 also advertises itself as the fourth edition.

1620. After he took the last of these degrees, the university appointed him junior proctor. At that time, says Wood, he was "accounted
the most accurate disputant, and profound philosopher in the university."[40] What seems to have been a career of unusual promise was
cut short abruptly when he died on June 17, 1620, about two months
following the start of his proctorship. He is said to have written several works on logic, but his single published work in this field is the
Aditvs, and thus his contribution to the work of the Systematics can
be seen only in it.

Smith's general conception of logic is more like that of the scholastics than of the Ramists. For example, his definition emphasizes
disputation and argumentation as the chief ends of logic, more or less
as Ramus was inclined to do, but he carefully indicates that logic
teaches us to argue probably and closely, while Ramus always preferred to insist that it teaches us to argue well. Says Smith:

> *Logic is the science of disputing in a probable and close way upon any
> subject whatever.* Or, as I would put it more plainly, *logic is the
> artistic and methodical understanding of precepts by which we know
> how to use reasoning concisely for establishing trust in any probable
> case whatever.*[41]

Another example of the way in which Smith's general conception of
logic parallels the scholastic conception is found in the relation he
sees between logic and rhetoric. Ramus had thought of logic as the
inventional and organizational aspect of discourse, whereas rhetoric
was the stylistic and the oral aspect. To Smith, the two arts differ as
the technical discourse differs from the popular, and he echoes Zeno's
ancient metaphor to suggest this kind of contrast:

> [Logic] differs . . . from rhetoric because the latter teaches how to
> prove by means of the expanded palm, that is, copiously and with
> ornament, whereas the former teaches how to prove by means of the
> closed fist, that is, strictly and narrowly.[42]

When Smith comes to divide logic into its parts, he proves himself once again to be on the side of scholasticism rather than Ramism.
Thus he ignores the theory that logic is limited to invention and
arrangement, and accepts instead a tripartite logic, the first division

---

[40] Anthony à Wood, *Athenae Oxonienses*, ed. Bliss, II, 283. For other details concerning him, see under Smith, Samuel (1587-1620) in the *Dictionary of National Biography*.
[41] *Aditvs ad Logicam* (1627), sig. A2r. Translation mine here and below. The
italics parallel those in Smith's Latin text.
[42] *Ibid.*, sig. A2r.

being terms, the second, propositions, and the third, clusters of propositions or, in a word, discourses. His statements on this point are worth quoting at some length:

> Logic as a whole is divided into three parts; the first treats of simple terms; the second of terms compounded; and the third, of discourse. For as boys ought first to be taught to recognize letters and syllables of the alphabet, then to combine characters, and at last to read the combinations, so beginners in logic ought at first to be taught what is a term, in what manner it should be formed, and what uses it has in logic, then in what manner a proposition is made from simple terms, and what are its structures, and finally, from what propositions is erected the syllogism. All this we now begin (God willing) to show in three books, and we follow the order of building, and take the position of beginning with the simple term, and of going on to the proposition, and thence to the discourse.[43]

The major topics covered by Smith in carrying out his program are of course scholastic, not Ramistic. Thus he speaks of the term as "the sign of a thing and of a concept, written or spoken in a certain configuration of letters or syllables, according to an arrangement divine or human."[44] Thus also he speaks of the predicable as "a general term begotten to be properly applied to many things, as 'animal' is applied to 'man' and to 'beast' "; and he proceeds at once to list and discuss the predicables of genus, of species, of differentia, of property, and of accident.[45] Thus again he defines the predicament or category as "a certain fixed series of words expressing simple states," this series being of course the ten famous terms in Aristotle's *Categories*.[46] And thus finally he speaks of the proposition and its kinds; of the syllogism, the enthymeme, the induction, the example; of the places belonging to persons and to things; and of fallacies within and outside of language. His treatment of these matters is devotedly conventional and shows little concern for the reforms of Ramus some seventy years earlier. But there is precision and brevity in his style and comprehensiveness in his scope—qualities which no doubt contributed to the long popularity of the *Aditvs*.

In two distinct respects, however, the *Aditvs* shows the tendency of the Systematics to incorporate silently into logic the doctrines of Ramus. First of all, Smith devotes some space to those Aristotelian principles which Ramus had made his own and had repeatedly em-

---

[43] *Ibid.*, sig. A2v-A3r.   [44] *Ibid.*, sig. A3r.
[45] *Ibid.*, sig. A4v-A5r.   [46] *Ibid.*, sig. A11r.

phasized as the three laws. Secondly, Smith follows Ramus in giving the subject of method a larger emphasis and a more concentrated treatment than it had had in scholastic logic.

Smith's treatment of the three laws does not once mention Ramus, but it would be ingenuous to suppose that he would have discussed them if Ramus had not popularized them throughout the learned world by explaining them repeatedly and by making them the basis of his reform of the liberal arts. To Ramus the three laws are derived from Aristotle as three tests that any proposition has to meet before it can be accepted as scientific.[47] To Smith the three laws are also derived from Aristotle, but now they constitute the three marks which an argument must have if it is to meet the first of the five requirements laid down in the *Organon* for apodictic as opposed to probable or to sophistical arguments.

Smith's general view is that any argument qualifies as science if it is in the form of a syllogism and if its materials meet Aristotle's five requirements. These requirements are that the constituent propositions of the argument must be true or necessary, primary and immediate, more knowable than is the conclusion arrived at, earlier in time than is that conclusion, and causal in the sense of having a middle term as cause of the condition which the conclusion predicates of the subject.[48] The first requirement obviously interests Smith most, for he devotes more space to it than to the others; and as we read what he says about it, we are in the presence of ideas that owe to Ramus their position in seventeenth-century logic.

The first of the three marks of a genuinely necessary proposition, says Smith, is that the proposition must be "$\kappa\alpha\tau\dot{\alpha}\ \pi\dot{\alpha}\nu\tau\sigma\varsigma$," or "de omni," or "suitable to everything at all times." In other words, the predicate must be true at all times of all cases of the subject. Here are Smith's own words:

> $\mathrm{K}\alpha\tau\dot{\alpha}\ \pi\dot{\alpha}\nu\tau\sigma\varsigma$, De Omni, is that which suits everything and at all times. Therefore two conditions are required if the proposition is to be "de omni": universality of subject, in order that it may be predicated for the subject on behalf of its entire contents, as, *truly it is a fact that every tree is green*; universality of time, in order that the predicate may be attributed to the subject without any exception as to time or place, as, *every man is an animal*. If the former condition is alone

[47] See above, pp. 149-153; also pp. 41-44.
[48] For Smith's definitions of these five conditions, see *Aditvs ad Logicam* (1627), sig. E1r, E3r, E3v, E4r, E4v.

fulfilled, it is called antecedently universal; if the latter condition is added, it is called posteriorly universal. This κατά πάντος differs from the dictum "de omni" in the rules of the syllogism, because this refers to a single proposition, whereas the dictum "de omni" refers to the entire syllogism. Moreover, the dictum "de omni" requires only universality in the subject, but κατά πάντος adds perpetuity of time to universality of subject.[49]

The second mark of the genuinely necessary proposition is that the proposition be "καθ' ἀυτο," or "per se," or self-consistent. Thus when we say "man is rational," we have a proposition that is self-consistent, inasmuch as the predicate is a part of the definition of the subject. Smith distinguishes three other subject-predicate relations that exhibit this mark of self-consistency. If, for example, the proposition is "man is one who laughs," it has self-consistency, because its predicate cannot be defined except in relation to its subject. If again we say "Socrates is," we have predicated existence of substance, and our proposition is self-consistent; or if we say, "having had his throat cut, he died," we have predicated an effect of its own cause, and thus have achieved self-consistency.[50]

The third mark of the necessary proposition is that the predicate and subject be in a primary, immediate, and reciprocal relation. As Ramus had done before him, Smith uses the Greek terms "καθόλου πρῶτον," and the Latin terms "quatenus ipsum," to describe this type of proposition. He says:

> Καθόλου πρῶτον, quatenus ipsum, is that in which an attribute is predicated concerning a subject, not so much universally, not so much through itself, as primarily, immediately, and reciprocally; as, *all living things take nourishment*. Now this sort of necessity is met with when the predicate belongs to the subject so far as the subject is thus, or else it belongs to the extension of the subject. Thus "flying" and "croaking" belong to the crow, but "flying" belongs to him so far as he is a bird, "croaking" so far as he is a crow. Hence, the proposition, *the crow croaks*, is "quatenus ipsum"; but not so the proposition, *the crow flies*.[51]

The influence of Ramus upon Smith in the field of method is not so well defined as in the field of the three laws, but it is nevertheless unmistakable. Method was the last topic in Ramus's logic, and thus it was in the position of greatest emphasis, so far as the strategy of

[49] *Ibid.*, sig. E1r-E1v. [50] *Ibid.*, sig. E1v-E2r. [51] *Ibid.*, sig. E2r.

presentation is concerned. Smith also gives the last place in his *Aditvs* to this topic. Moreover, as if to emphasize its importance still more, he makes his chapter on method occupy the entire third section of his third book, whereas the preceding two sections of that book had each contained several topics. It is the acceptance of method as a very important part of logic that betrays the influence of Ramus in the seventeenth century, and Smith's logic agrees with this rule, even if his actual theory of method is closer to Blundeville than to Ramus.

Smith gives his chapter on method the title, "De Ordine," but leaves no doubt that he intends this term to refer to what the Ramists called "methodus." He says as much at the very outset:

> As discourse in its inferential aspect teaches how to prove something from something else, so in its organizational aspect it shows in what manner definitions, divisions, and the other parts of any art or science whatever should be correctly linked together among themselves so that some may precede and others follow. This popularly is called order or method; for we may seize hold of both terms indiscriminately so long as according to them things are arranged that we may know them the more easily.[52]

As for the parts of the theory of method, Smith finds them by distinguishing between the contemplative and the practical sciences. The former examine things in and for themselves, without direct consequences in action. The latter examine things in order that what is discovered may be used as the basis of action. Smith's distinction between these two types of intellectual endeavor is equivalent to our distinction between theoretical and applied science, if by applied science we mean all applications of knowledge to actual affairs, whether in the field of technology or in law, medicine, politics, ethics, or communication. In harmony with the idea of contemplative and applied sciences, Smith defines two sorts of order to be followed in arranging discourses, one of which he calls "synthetical, that is, unitive," and the other, "analytical, that is, divisive." Here are his own definitions of these terms, and his opinions about their connection with the two orders of science:

> The synthetical or compositive order is that which proceeds from elements towards what rests upon the elements, in order that a perfect examining of things may be made. This alone is solely perceived in the sciences. . . .

[52] *Ibid.*, sig. G1v.

The analytical order is that which, from an ultimate proposed end or action, or from an act by us, progresses towards investigating the primary elements by which that end may be achieved. This is solely perceived in the practical sciences. . . .[53]

Incidentally, the method of proceeding from elements towards what rests upon elements is illustrated by the *Aditvs* itself, as Smith explicitly recognizes in his account of the three divisions of logic.[54] Thus his work indicates what the synthetical or unitive order is, and this kind of order approximates what Blundeville had called the "methode compositiue." Also, of course, Smith's conception of analytical order is close in terminology and intent to Blundeville's "methode resolutiue."

Scarcely less popular during the seventeenth century than Smith's *Aditvs* was Edward Brerewood's *Elementa Logicae*, first published at London in 1614, and often reprinted up to 1684.[55] Brerewood died the year before this work originally appeared, and at the time of his death he was serving as first professor of astronomy at Gresham College, London. His *Elementa Logicae* had probably been written some twenty-five years before it was published, for it belongs among the interests he would have had between 1581 and 1590, when he was a student at Brasenose College, Oxford, and was taking his bachelor's and master's degrees.[56] At any rate, he was interested in natural philosophy by 1592, and was appointed to his professorship at Gresham in 1596, so that a work on logic would not particularly belong to his later years. No doubt one reason why he did not publish it soon after he wrote it was that Ramistic logic was dominant in England in the fifteen-eighties and nineties, and there was little or no market for the older doctrine. But by the time of his death in 1613, interest in the older doctrine was reviving, and his publishers may on that ground have been impelled to bring out his *Elementa Logicae* when it came to them later with a preface by William Baker of Oxford.

[53] *Ibid.*, sig. G3r. Smith's Latin terms for these two kinds of order are respectively "Ordo Syntheticus seu compositivus" and "Ordo Analyticus seu resolutivus."

[54] See above, p. 294.

[55] My discussion of this work is based upon its third edition, a copy of which is at the Huntington Library. Its title page reads: "Elementa Logicae, In gratiam Studiosae inventutis in Academia Oxoniensi. Authore Edovardo Brerevvood, olim Collegij *Eneanasenser* alumno dignissimo. Londini, Apud Ioannem Billivm, 1619." There were 10 separate printings during the seventeenth century, as follows: London, 1614, 1615, 1619, 1621, 1628, 1638, 1649, 1684; Oxford, 1657, 1668. All but three of these printings are listed in Madan, *Oxford Books*, III, 448.

[56] See *Dictionary of National Biography*, s.v. Brerewood or Bryerwood, Edward.

In essence the *Elementa Logicae* is a version of two topics of scholastic logic and is arranged in such fashion that chapters of doctrine are followed by chapters in which questions about the doctrine are raised and answered. The first topic concerns propositions. It is given twenty-four of the twenty-nine chapters making up the work as a whole, Aristotle's *De Interpretatione* being cited several times as the authority for this part of the discussion.[57] Brerewood defines a proposition as "an indicative, suitable, and complete statement signifying truth or falsity without ambiguity,"[58] and in his analysis of it he deals with the individual words that make it up and with its various kinds as found in logic. His second topic, argumentation, covers in five chapters the syllogism, the enthymeme, the induction, and the example, his sources at this point being Aristotle's *Prior Analytics*, *Posterior Analytics*, *Topics*, and occasionally the *Categories*.[59]

Two other topics of scholastic logic, that is, the predicables and the predicaments, are treated by Brerewood in his *Tractatus quidam logici de praedicabilibus et praedicamentis*, which was edited by Thomas Sixesmith and published at Oxford in 1628. This work did not achieve any spectacular popularity, but it nevertheless went through four editions by 1659, and it combined with the *Elementa Logicae* to round out Brerewood's adaptation of the scholastic system, and to. make him a familiar name in seventeenth-century education.

Brerewood and Samuel Smith, as two of the foremost English Systematics, held their influence among their learned countrymen until the time when *The Port-Royal Logic* in French, Latin, and English versions became widely popular in England during the latter part of the seventeenth century. But the chief English Systematic, Robert Sanderson, has the distinction of composing a logic that was popular not only before the work of the Port-Royalists appeared, but for more than a half-century thereafter. Called in everyday speech Sanderson's *Logic*, this Latin treatise bears the actual title of *Logicae Artis Compendivm*.[60]

---

[57] See in particular *Elementa Logicae* (1619), Chs. 9, 10, 11, 15.
[58] *Ibid.*, p. 1.　　　　　　　　[59] *Ibid.*, Chs. 25, 27.
[60] First published at Oxford in 1615, this work was reissued eight times in the seventeenth, three times in the eighteenth, and once in the nineteenth centuries. In addition, there is an issue that bears no date. Madan, *Oxford Books*, III, 448, lists all dated editions as follows: 1615, 1618, 1631, 1640, 1657, 1664, 1668?, 1672, 1680, 1705, 1707, 1741, 1841. My discussion is based upon the Huntington Library copy of the second edition. Its title page reads: "Logicae Artis Compendivm. Secvnda Hac Editione recognitum, duplici *Appendice auctum, & publici iuris factum* à Rob. Sanderson Collegij

Robert Sanderson was educated at Lincoln College, Oxford, in the first few years of the seventeenth century.[61] After taking his bachelor's degree in 1606, he became fellow and later the lecturer in logic at his college, this second post being awarded to him upon his graduation in 1608 as master of arts. He was ordained deacon and priest in 1611, held several ecclesiastical positions, including that of chaplain to Charles I, and at length became regius professor of divinity at Oxford. He was deprived of his professorship during the civil war, but at the Restoration he regained it, and was then made bishop of Lincoln. He died in 1663 at the age of 76, as his *Logic* was about to receive its sixth edition, and not long after a young Cambridge undergraduate named Isaac Newton had given it careful study.[62]

The second edition of Sanderson's *Logic* contains two appendixes not found in the first edition. An unusual feature of the "Appendix Posterior" or "Later Appendix" is a chapter devoted to the history of logic, and it is here that we can form an estimate of the way in which seventeenth-century logicians regarded themselves in relation to their predecessors.

The first of the seven headings into which Sanderson divides the history of logic would be translated as "Logicians before Aristotle."[63] These logicians, among whom Sanderson mentions Pythagoras, Parmenides, Zeno, Socrates, Plato, and others, are accorded some praise for their pioneering work, although Sanderson follows the usual practice of naming Aristotle as the inventor of logic. So far as Sanderson divides these logicians into schools, he speaks of them as Stoics and Academics, and he has one interesting thing to say about each school. The Stoics, he says, created a logic that was in one sense confused and in another sense ostentatious; and as an example of this latter characteristic, he cites their fondness for such outlandish arguments as the ones they called "Antistrephon," "Crocodilites," "Utis," and so on. This remark may be interpreted as indirect criticism by Sanderson of Thomas Wilson and Blundeville, both of whom had

---

Lincolniensis in almâ Oxoniensi Socio. Oxoniae, Excudebant Iohannes Lichfield & Iacobvs Short. 1618."

[61] See *Dictionary of National Biography*, s.v. Sanderson, Robert (1587-1663).

[62] On this point see David Brewster, *The Life of Sir Isaac Newton* (New York, [1831]), p. 27.

[63] *Logicae Artis Compendivm* (1618), pp. 117-118. The pagination of the two appendixes is independent of that of the main work.

given some space to these terms.[64] As for the Academics, Sanderson thinks their logic more serious than that of the Stoics, but he nevertheless criticizes them, and in particular their leader, Plato, for failing to teach logic methodically, and for failing to teach it esoterically. These two shortcomngs in Plato were rectified by Aristotle, Sanderson adds, the latter being methodical and completely opposed to anything heterogeneous and exoteric. Now, the belief that Plato wrote for the general public and Aristotle for the initiated is not self-evident, as Sanderson seems to think. Rather, it is self-evident that the works of Plato, as transmitted to us, are more nearly prepared for ultimate public consumption than are the works of Aristotle, which have come down to us as the cryptic notes upon which Aristotle based academic lectures. But the really interesting thing about Sanderson's comment is that logic to him is somehow better as an esoteric science than it is when it is made exoteric. This attitude becomes more prominent when he speaks later of Ramus.

The second heading in Sanderson's history of logic would be translated as "From Aristotle to the Scholastics."[65] He speaks here of two schools, one of which sought to divert logic to the uses of the market place, and to make it an instrument for moving the affections, whereas the other school sought to keep it for its proper and native end of contemplation, understanding, teaching, and ministering to the intellect. Sanderson recognizes that orators were largely responsible for the former school, and in describing it he mentions such men as Cicero, Augustine, Jerome, and Chrysostom. The other school belonged to the philosophers, and here Sanderson enumerates several names, chief of whom are Porphyry, Avicenna, and Averroës.

Sanderson devotes his next two sections to the scholastics.[66] These logicians include Englishmen, of course, and Sanderson indeed names an Englishman, Alexander of Hales, as father of this group. The famous thirteenth-century textbook on logic, the *Summulae Logicales*, is credited with having an unfortunate influence for a hundred years, although its author, Petrus Hispanus, is given a place at the end of Sanderson's list of the twelve leading scholastics, and is identified by his special name, "Magister Summularum," as each of the other scholastics are identified by theirs.

---

[64] See Wilson, *Rule of Reason* (1552), foll. 170v-175v, and Blundeville, *Logike* (1619), pp. 178-179.

[65] *Logicae Artis Compendivm*, pp. 118-119.

[66] *Ibid.*, pp. 119-121. Sanderson's Latin headings are "Scholastici" and "Quorundā Scholasticorum Cognomenta."

Coming to the three centuries immediately preceding his own, Sanderson speaks of the Lullians and the Ramists as the outstanding logicians, and he devotes to each of these sects a section of his history.[67] The Lullians were followers of Ramon Lull, who died in the early fourteenth century, and whose work, *The Great, General, and Ultimate Art*,[68] is an attempt to simplify logic and indeed all learning. Sanderson speaks of Lull with some contempt and lets it be known that his attitude is derived from Keckermann's *Three Tractates of Logical Precognitions*. But the Ramists receive from Sanderson the sort of respectful treatment that permits us to see at a glance what Ramus's influence upon logic was conceived at that time to be.

Introducing Ramus as a more polished and cultivated scholar than Lull, and citing Vives as the authority for this estimate, Sanderson mentions Ramus's daring assaults upon Aristotle, his criticism of the peripatetic philosophy, and his success in gaining for his *Dialecticae Libri Duo* a following among those who worshipped eloquence and whose status as Ciceronians led them to dislike the diction and style of scholasticism. Nor were Ramus's followers unproductive. "Certainly," says Sanderson, "the industry of Ramus brought to the republic of logic the benefit of inducing good genius to improve more diligently the theory of method."[69] Thus does a Systematic characterize Ramus's major contribution to logical theory, and indicate what there is in Ramism that is most deserving of lasting notice.

What criticisms do the Systematics make of Ramus's reforms? The answer is supplied in some specific charges developed briefly by Sanderson as he refers his readers to Keckermann for further indictments. Here is what Sanderson says:

> But nevertheless there are in Ramistic logic many things that justly displease the learned: to wit, 1) its alteration of the terms of the art and of the expressions long current in the schools of logic; 2) its manifold mutilation of logic, which the Ramists have limited to excessively narrow boundaries and deprived of some integral parts; 3) its illustration of the uses of logic from the writings of poets and orators, although these men have treated things not logically but exoterically; 4) its prescription of a single method everywhere, and its

---

[67] *Ibid.*, pp. 121-122.

[68] As edited by C. Sutorius at Frankfurt in 1596, this work bears the title, *M. Raymundi Lullii, . . . Ars magna generalis et ultima, quarumcumque artium et scientiarum ipsius Raymundi Lullii assecutrix et clavigera, et ad eas aditum facilem praebens*, etc. See *Catalogue Général des Livres Imprimés de la Bibliothèque Nationale*, s.v. Lulle, Raymond. For a brief comment on Lull, see above, pp. 7, 9.

[69] *Logicae Artis Compendivm*, p. 122. Translation mine here and below.

prescription for using it—a method excessively meagre and painful, to which the Ramists wished all disciplines to be confined by the mere process of definition and dichotomies. And there are justly a very great many other vices or defects under most worthy censure against the Ramists; which Keckermann has set forth accurately and weightily in the entire fourth chapter of Tractate Two of his *Logical Precognitions.*[70]

Sanderson's emphasis upon these four defects in Ramism is a good statement of the platform of the English Systematics. He turns next to the Systematics, whom he calls "Systematici," and speaks of them in such fashion as to indicate some of the alterations he himself proposes to make in their doctrine:

> The newest century has produced several logicians who have rejoiced in marching by a certain middle course between the Peripatetics and the Ramists. These very ones publicly inveigh against the Ramists while praising the Peripatetics; but nevertheless in their systems of logic they are more Ramist than Peripatetic. For they transform the boundaries accepted in the peripatetic schools, and they indulge too much in method, while thus they cut everything to pieces in dividing and subdividing piecemeal and in vain, so that meanwhile they lose the sap and substance of things. These logicians can be called the Philippo-Ramists, or the Systematics; of whom the pre-eminent one is Keckermann, for Timplerus, Alsted, and several others have not kept equal pace with him. He has his great use, indeed, his very great use, but to those who are of mature judgment and excellently trained in the peripatetic school. For whoever shall be able skilfully to unite the writings of that man with the writings of the scholastics, after having made a selection of boundaries and of method, will in my opinion do the most skilful thinking of anyone in philosophy. Nevertheless, I would wish that Keckermann be not rubbed often into the hands of youth. Youth ought to be accustomed more to the peripatetic boundaries, and instructed in a simpler method, not being of such power of judgment as to know how to separate the useless from the useful.[71]

It is not too farfetched to conclude from this analysis of the Systematics that Sanderson conceives it to be his mission to unite their doctrine with that of the older logic and thus to produce a better amalgam of Ramism and scholasticism than had yet been made. That mission is rather well accomplished in his *Logic*, which may be considered the best work of its kind to have been produced in England.

[70] *Ibid.*, p. 122. [71] *Ibid.*, pp. 122-123.

One of the scholastic elements in Sanderson's amalgam appears in his conception of the relation of logic and rhetoric. This conception is stated in the second chapter of the "Later Appendix," where there is a discussion of the circle of disciplines. The liberal disciplines, he says, are either instrumental studies or master-studies; that is, some of them are equivalent to servants, and the others, to sovereigns.[72] The servant-studies, or the instrumentals, consist of grammar, logic, and rhetoric, these being what scholasticism called the discursive or the rational part of philosophy, since they are concerned either with speech or with reason. After explaining why in barbarous times these studies were called the trivium, Sanderson adds:

> Of these, logic directs the reason, and is charged with perfecting the mind; grammar directs speech, and is charged with forming discourse; rhetoric in its own way directs both one and the other, yet speech the more, and is charged with moving the affections.[73]

This conception of the relation between logic and rhetoric is clearly scholastic rather than Ramistic, and indicates that, if Sanderson had written on rhetoric, he would have done something with invention and arrangement as well as style and delivery. But he would not have made memory a topic of rhetoric or of logic, and in this respect his procedure is close to the Ramists. His reason for rejecting the theory of memory is that it belongs more to quackery than to science. On this point he says, as he brings his discussion of the relation of grammar, logic, and rhetoric to a close:

> Some add mnemonics to these same arts. Of course it does not aid memory in any way except as logic aids the mind. But I fear that mnemonics may be more of an imposture than an art, if indeed it propounds anything distinct from the method which is taught in logic.[74]

The chief scholastic elements in Sanderson's *Logic* are found in his definition of his subject and in his division of it into parts and terms. He rejects the Ramistic idea that logic or dialectic is the theory of disputing, and says instead, "Logic, which by synecdoche is dialectic, is an instrumental art directing our minds to the understanding of everything intelligible."[75] His enumeration of the parts of logic is accompanied by explicit references to the corresponding works in Aristotle's *Organon*. His own words are:

[72] *Ibid.*, p. 102.　　　　[73] *Ibid.*, p. 102.
[74] *Ibid.*, pp. 102-103.　　[75] *Ibid.*, p. 1.

Its parts are three, by virtue of the number of mental operations directed by it. Of these parts, the *first* directs the first operation of the mind, that is, *simple conceiving*, and is *about simple terms*; to which pertain Porphyry's *Introduction*, and Aristotle's *Book of Categories*.

The *second* part directs the second operation of the mind, that is, *connecting* and *dividing*, and is *about propositions*; to which pertains the *Book on Interpretation*.

The *third* part directs the third and final operation of the mind, that is, *discoursing*, and is *about argumentation* and *method*; to which pertain the *Two Books of Prior Analytics*, the same number of books of *Posterior Analytics*, the *Eight Books of Topics*, and lastly, the *Two Books of Sophistical Elenchi*.[76]

As we would expect from this description of the three parts of logic, the major terms with which Sanderson deals in his treatise are the five predicables, the ten predicaments, the various aspects of propositions, the four kinds of argument, the places of invention, and the fallacies within and outside of language. Incidentally, he provides a Latin distich to aid students in remembering the ten predicaments, and the following words as arranged in relation to their corresponding logical terms may help to suggest what the distich means:

[Substance]	[Quantity]	[Relation]	[Quality]	[Acting]
A tree	six	servants	in violent heat	cools off

[Suffering]	[Where]	[When]	[Situation]	[Apparel]
scorched	In the country	tomorrow	I shall remain	nor shall I be tunicked.[77]

As for Ramistic elements in Sanderson's *Logic*, three chief things may be said. First of all, Sanderson devotes two chapters of his "Appendix Prima" or "First Appendix" to genesis and analysis as aspects of the uses of logic;[78] and these terms, as I said earlier, designate important procedures in Ramus's discussion of the contribution that practice as distinct from natural inclination or the study of theory

---

[76] *Ibid.*, pp. 2-3. Except for titles of works in the *Organon*, the italics are Sanderson's. *The Sophistical Elenchi* is occasionally printed as two books rather than one. On this point see Owen, *The Organon, or Logical Treatises, of Aristotle*, II, 540, 575.

[77] *Logicae Artis Compendivm*, p. 27. Sanderson's distich is arranged thus in Latin:

1	2	3	4	5
Arbor	*Sex*	*Servos*	*Fervore*	*Refrigerat*
6	7	8	9	10
Vstos	*Ruri*	*Cras*	*Stabo*	*nec Tunicatus ero.*

[78] *Ibid.*, pp. 67-88.

may make in the development of logical ability.[79] In his discussion of analysis Sanderson refers explicitly to the tenth book of John Henry Alsted's *Harmonious System of Logic*, thus showing his close awareness of the work of one of the very Systematics whom he had mentioned in his account of the history of logic.[80] Secondly, Sanderson devotes some attention to the discussion of the laws of scientific demonstration, and at this point he is covering ground that Ramus had heavily emphasized when he spoke of the famous three laws.[81] Thirdly, Sanderson discusses at some length the theory of method, not as a Ramist, to be sure, but as one of the logicians who accepted Ramus's thesis that method was more important than the scholastics had allowed it to be.

Sanderson's two chapters on order and method—he uses these words interchangeably—make an initial distinction between the method of discovering knowledge and the method of presenting or teaching it by discourse.[82] He calls the first of these the method of invention, and the second, the method of doctrine. Here is his general description of the two:

> Each proceeds from that which is more known by us to that which by us is less known; but one and the other in a different manner, nevertheless. For we discover precepts by ascending, that is, by progressing from the concrete and the particular, which to us are more directly known, towards the intelligible and universal, which are more known by nature. But we transmit precepts by descending, that is, by progressing from the universal and intelligible, which are more known by nature, and more clearly known by us also, to that which is less universal, and closer to the senses, and as it were less known.

Invention conceived as the discovery of new precepts may have been suggested to Sanderson by Bacon's *Advancement of Learning*, for Bacon in that work speaks influentially of such a concept.[83] At any rate, the idea is an important development in the history of logic, and it points to the thesis that Descartes was to enunciate in his *Discours de la Méthode*. It might even be said that, while John Stuart Mill's canons of induction were a long way ahead when Sanderson wrote his *Logic*, Sanderson's work, nevertheless, is spiritually closer

[79] See above, pp. 248-250.
[80] *Logicae Artis Compendivm*, p. 79; for my previous references to Alsted, see above, pp. 283-284, 303.
[81] *Logicae Artis Compendivm*, pp. 174-179.
[82] *Ibid.*, p. 226.
[83] See below, p. 367.

to Mill than to Ramus, so far as it conceives of a distinctive formula for the discovery of knowledge. Here is what Sanderson says of this formula:

> The method of invention has four means, and as it were four stages through which we ascend. First is the perception, by the help of which we assemble some notion of individual things. Second is the observation or the seeing accurately, in the course of which we collect and arrange what we have assimilated at different times by the perceptions. Third is the proof by trial, wherein we subject the multitude of assembled observations to fixed tests. Fourth and last is induction, in which we summon the multitude of collected and tested proofs so as to make up a universal conclusion.[84]

As for the method of doctrine, Sanderson divides it into two procedures, one of which he calls the "Compositiva," that is, the compositive, and the other, the "Resolutiva" or resolutive.[85] There can be little doubt that these terms and the meanings assigned to them by Sanderson are parallel to the similar terms and meanings in Blundeville's *Logike* and Smith's *Aditvs*.[86] For example, Sanderson, like Smith, applies the compositive method of presentation to the theoretical sciences, whereas the resolutive method applies to the practical arts; and Sanderson, like Smith and Blundeville, thinks of the former method as a progress from smaller to larger units, while the latter is a progress from large to small.

One feature of Sanderson's discussion of these two methods is that he assigns five laws as common to each, two laws as peculiar to one, and two laws as peculiar to the other. Thus he has a total of nine laws to regulate the two methods of transmitting knowledge to readers or listeners. These laws are given such names as "Lex brevitatis," "Lex Harmoniae," "Lex vnitatis," and "Lex Generalitatis," thus recalling the procedure of Ramus in enumerating his famous three principles of reform. Here are the nine laws as stated by Sanderson:

[The Five Laws Common to Both Methods of Presentation]

    I Lex brevitatis. *Nothing should be left out or be superfluous in a discipline. . . .*

    II Lex Harmoniae. *The parts of each individual doctrine should agree among themselves. . . .*

---

[84] *Logicae Artis Compendivm*, pp. 226-227.   [85] *Ibid.*, p. 227.
[86] See above, pp. 289-291, 296-298.

III Lex vnitatis, sive Homogeniae. *No doctrine should be taught that is not homogeneous in subject or end.* . . .

IV Lex Generalitatis, sive Antecessionis, & consecutionis. *That should precede in teaching, without which something else cannot be understood, provided that it can be understood itself without something else.* . . . .

V Lex Connexionis. *The individual parts of doctrine ought to be connected by apt transitions.* . . .

[The Two Laws for the Compositive Method of Presentation]

I Lex vnitatis. *The unity of a science depends upon unity of subject.* Unity of subject is, to wit, unity of matter or at least of form. . . .

II Lex Generalitatis. *The more universal should precede the less universal.* . . .

[The Two Laws for the Resolutive Method of Presentation]

I Lex vnitatis. *The unity of an instrumental discipline depends upon unity of end.* . . .

II Lex Generalitatis. *The more universal precedes the less universal.* . . .[87]

Now that Sanderson has fully revealed his respect for the Ramists and his devotion to the scholastics, we may pass on to the later Systematics. These will not detain us long, for their work was not as influential in England as that of the Systematics already considered. Still, they are of some interest, and their logics should not be entirely omitted from the present discussion.

One of these logics, the *Fasciculus Praeceptorvm Logicorum*, by Christopher Airay, was published at Oxford in 1628 and reprinted at the same place in 1633, 1637, and 1660.[88] Airay was educated at Queens College, Oxford, in the seven years immediately preceding the publication of his *Fasciculus*; in fact, he probably composed that work just after his appointment as fellow of Queens in 1627. Like the other Systematics, Airay displays a strong interest in scholastic logic and a mild tendency to adopt some of the favorite ideas of the Ramists. He is scholastic in dividing logic into the simple term, the proposition, and the discourse, and in finding justification for this

---

[87] *Logicae Artis Compendivm*, pp. 227-231.

[88] The present discussion of this work is based upon the Huntington Library copy of the edition at Oxford in 1633. Its title page reads: "Fasciculus Praeceptorvm Logicorum: In Gratiam juventutis Academicae compositus & typis donatus. Editio altera limatior operâ secundâ C. A. Oxoniae, Excudebat *Guilielmus Turner*, An. Dom. 1633."

tripartite division in the mental operations of conceiving, connecting (or dividing), and discoursing.[89] He is also scholastic in arranging his work into six books, and in progressing from the predicables to the predicaments, and onward to propositions, arguments, places, and fallacies. Needless to say, Aristotle's *Organon* is frequently cited as the authority for these doctrines.[90] Incidentally, the distich Airay proposes as a device for remembering the predicaments is different from that of Sanderson, and would be translated more or less as follows in relation to Aristotle's ten terms:

[Situation]	[Quantity]	[Acting]	[Quality]	[When]
On plain	vast	fought	valiantly	long ago

[Relation]	[Substance]	[Where]	[Suffering]	[Apparel]
The son	of Arnesti	standing immovable	& heated	in armor[91]

Despite all these marks of scholasticism, however, Airay's *Fasciculus* shows in one place that it belongs in the period of the Ramists. That place is where the laws of demonstration are discussed. Airay treats the three laws called "de omni," "per se," and "quatenus ipsum," and he makes it plain that his discussion of them is based upon Aristotle's *Posterior Analytics*.[92] Nevertheless he must have been aware, not only that Aristotle had explained them, but that Ramus had given them a new and important emphasis in logic and had made it almost a requirement that his immediate successors give them some attention.

Another logic belonging to the school of Systematics is Franco Burgersdijck's *Institutionum Logicarum Libri Duo*. Burgersdijck, a Dutchman, was professor of logic at the University of Leiden, and his *Libri Duo* was published in that city in 1626 and again in 1634.[93] Thus it belongs primarily to the history of continental logic, but it

---

[89] *Fasciculus* (1633), p. 4.   [90] *Ibid.*, pp. 2, 19, 145, etc.

[91] *Ibid.*, p. 38. Airay designates the categories by numbers above the words of the distich, as follows:

8	2	5	3	7
In Campo	Magno	Pugnabat	Fortiter	Olim
4	1	9	6	10
Filius	Arnesti	Stans	& Calefactus	in Armis

[92] *Ibid.*, pp. 145-152.

[93] There is a copy of the edition of 1626 at the Edinburgh University Library. The British Museum has a copy of the edition of 1634. Burgersdijck was born in 1590 and died in 1636. He was professor of logic and ethics at Leiden after 1620, and his treatise on the former subject enjoyed great popularity in the schools of the Netherlands during the seventeenth century. See *Allgemeine Deutsche Biographie*, s.v. Burgersdyk, Franco B.

has to be mentioned here because it was given an edition at Cambridge in 1637 and some seven later editions at the same place by 1680.[94]

One interesting thing about this work is that its preface to the reader contains an account of recent developments in logical theory and indeed classifies all contemporary logicians as adherents of Aristotle, adherents of Ramus, or adherents of the compromise being made between those two leaders.[95] The members of the first group, says Burgersdijck, "follow Aristotle . . . and abridge his *Organon*, and distribute by the same method the precepts drawn from that place, and illustrate them with suitable examples."[96] "In this class," he adds at once, "can be numbered Hunnaeus, Crellius, Bertius, Molinaeus, and very many others."[97] After a discussion of this group, Burgersdijck turns to his second class, "in which," he says, "Peter Ramus is leader of the family, a man elegantly learned indeed, but audacious, indiscreet, and how very hurtful to antiquity."[98] This statement leads Burgersdijck to evaluate Ramism. As for his third class, he mentions that he places within it "Keckermann and a great many others, who have mixed the doctrine of Aristotle with that of Ramus, and from the teachings of these two have arranged logical materials from Aristotle while allowing Ramus to supply the method —and what they lacked in one, they supplied from the other."[99]

Despite the slight disapproval implied in this judgment of the Systematics, Burgersdijck is certainly a member of that class himself. In his *Libri Duo* he deals with the logical materials of Aristotle's *Organon*. Thus he speaks of the predicaments, the predicables, the types of logical proposition, the four kinds of argument, the places,

[94] These editions are dated as follows: 1637; 1644; 1647; 1651; 1660; 1666; 1668; 1680.

[95] My present discussion of this work is based upon the Princeton University Library copy of the Cambridge edition of 1668. This copy has lost its title page, and the following title has been written on the flyleaf: "Fr. Burgersdicii Institutionum logicarum libri duo Cantabrigiae Apud Joann. Field 1668." The dedicatory epistle in this copy is signed "Franco Burgersdicius" and is dated at Leiden September 15, 1626. The "Praefatio ad Lectorem" is undated and unsigned.

[96] *Institutionum Logicarum Libri Duo* (1668), sig. A2r. Translation mine here and below.

[97] Hunnaeus is also known as Augustin Huens (1522-1577). For a brief judgment of his logical writings, see Eug. De Seyn, *Dictionnaire des Ecrivains Belges*, s.v. Huens, Augustin. Crellius is Fortunatus Crellius, whose *Isagoge Logica* (Neustadt, 1592) is referred to here. Bertius, known as Petrus Bertius, published at Leiden in 1604 *Petri Bertii Logicae Peripateticae Libri Sex*. Molinaeus, that is Pierre Du Moulin, published at Paris in 1603 his *Elementa Logica*, which went through several Latin editions, was translated into French as *Éléments de Logique* (Sedan, 1621), and appeared in an English version at London in 1624 as *The Elements of Logick*.

[98] *Institutionum Logicarum Libri Duo*, sig. A3v.

[99] *Ibid.*, sig. A4v.

and the fallacies. Although he does not arrange these materials according to Ramus's theory of method, he does nevertheless show some inclination to follow Ramus as well as Aristotle. For example, he divides logic into two parts, that having to do with themes, and that having to do with instruments; he follows the practice of presenting his doctrine in terms of a text interspersed with commentary; and he devotes the last section of his work to the theory of method. In these respects, at least, he shows that Ramus has practices of which he approves, even if in respect to such things as the theory of method he is closer to the Systematics than to the Ramists.

Two other logics of the counterreform are by John Prideaux, a scholar, churchman, and bishop. Prideaux was educated at Oxford in the seven years between 1596 and 1603; he served as fellow and later as rector of his college, Exeter; he became regius professor of divinity at Oxford in 1615 and bishop of Worcester in 1641.[100] Among his writings are treatises on both rhetoric and logic, as we might expect from a man who was successively a teacher, a preacher, a propagandist, and an ecclesiastical executive. The term "propagandist" is used advisedly in this case, by the way, for Prideaux belonged to that unique institution, the controversy college at Chelsea, which was established in the reign of James I to offer argumentative resistance to the cause of the Catholics.[101] Prideaux's writings on rhetoric will be mentioned again in the next section of this chapter. As for logic, he wrote a work which would be called in English *The Easiest Start towards the Constructing of Correct Syllogisms and the Unraveling of Sophisms*, and another work called *Heptades Logicae*, that is, *The Sevens of Logic*. The first of these was originally published at Oxford in 1629, and the second at the same place in 1639, the two being in the same volume on the latter occasion.[102] Both were combined to form the first treatise in Prideaux's later work, a Latin

---

[100] For further details of his life, see *Dictionary of National Biography*, s.v. Prideaux, John (1578-1650).

[101] A brief account of this institution can be found in *Dictionary of National Biography*, s.v. Sutcliffe, Matthew (1550?-1629).

[102] My discussion of *The Easiest Start* and the *Sevens of Logic* is based upon the Huntington Library copy of the 1639 edition. That copy contains the following three items by Prideaux, each with its own title page:

1) *Tabvlae ad Grammatica Graeca Introductoriae. . . .* Editio tertia. Oxoniae, 1639. 34 pp.

2) *Tyrocinivm ad Syllogismvm Legitimum contexendum, & captiosum dissuendum, expeditissimum. . . .* Oxoniae, 1639. 18 pp.

3) *Heptades Logicae. Sive Monita ad Ampliores Tractatus Introductoria. Pugnus quo compressior eò ferit fortius.* Oxoniae. 1639. 16 pp.

account of various sciences, the English title of which would be *Notes on Logic, Rhetoric, Physics, Metaphysics, Pneumatics, Ethics, Politics, and Economics.*[103]

Prideaux is fond of the figure seven as a way of indicating what is important in a science. Thus in the *Heptades Logicae* and in the *Notes on Logic* he presents all logical doctrine under seven heads. The *Heptades Logicae* contain the Latin equivalents of seven terms denoting respectively the processes of intellectualizing, objectifying, stating, reasoning, methodizing, analyzing, and synthesizing. Corresponding terms in the *Notes on Logic* have the ring of the compromise between scholasticism and Ramism, and are the Latin equivalents, not of terms for seven mental operations, but of terms for the seven results of those operations, so far as logic is concerned. Thus intellectualizing is equated in the *Notes on Logic* with the predicables, objectifying is equated with the predicaments, stating, with the proposition, reasoning, with the syllogism, methodizing, with method, analyzing, with analysis, and synthesizing, with synthesis. So in the end the same seven scholastic-Ramistic concepts control Prideaux's entire logical theory.[104]

Another original feature of Prideaux's two treatises on logic is that they contain questions and answers designed to induce students to form preferences in respect to the competing logical theories of the day. Here are examples, some of which offer additional proof of Prideaux's fondness for sevens, and some of which provide direct indications that English Systematics sometimes called themselves Mixts:

> Q. Is it true that the seven dialectical theories of method in use today, to wit, 1) the Aristotelian, 2) the Lullian, 3) the Ramistic, 4) the Mixt, whether indeed in the manner of Keckermann or of Alsted,

---

[103] This work is undated. Madan, *Oxford Books*, II, 487, argues that it was probably published in 1650. Its title page reads: "Hypomnemata Logica, Rhetorica, Physica, Metaphysica, Pneumatica, Ethica, Politica, Oeconomica. Per Jo: P: Coll: Exon: Oxoniae Excudebat Impensis suis Leonar: Lichfield Academiae Typographus." There is a copy at the Huntington Library.

[104] The following parallel lists indicate Prideaux's Latin terms:

Heptades Logicae, p. 1	*Hypomnemata*, p. 2.
1. Noematica	1. Praedicabilibus
2. Thematica	2. Praedicamentis
3. Axiomatica	3. Propositionibus
4. Dianoetica	4. Syllogismis
5. Methodica	5. Methodis
6. Analytica	6. Analysi
7. Genetica	7. Genesi

5) the Forensic of Hotman, 6) the Jesuitic, and 7) the Socinian, differ mostly in respect to manner of treatment, not in respect to purpose?

A. Yes.[105]

Q. Is it true that a Mixt ought to be preferred to a Peripatetic, a Ramist, a Lullian, and the others?

A. Yes.[106]

Q. Is it easier and more useful to teach through seven heads, or through five, or through three, than through the more current dichotomies of the moderns?

A. Yes.[107]

Q. Is it true that the Ramistic dichotomies of the moderns overload the memory rather than inform the intellect?

A. Yes.[108]

Q. Is it true that the scholastic and Ramistic methods of breaking a subject down insist too much at various times upon trifles?

A. Yes.[109]

Q. Are the Aristotelian and the Ramistic methods one and the same?

A. Yes.[110]

Q. Is it not true that the 359 places of Aristotle's *Topics* overload the memory of the learner more than they instruct methodically?

A. Yes.[111]

Q. Is it true that the ten places of Ramus ought to be esteemed good throughout?

A. No.[112]

Q. Is it not true that the places of the *Topics* can be accommodated equally to rhetorics and to logics for the purpose of treating simple and complex themes?

A. Yes.[113]

---

[105] *Hypomnemata*, p. 94. For the same question in slightly different form, see *Heptades Logicae*, p. 13. Translation mine here and below. Prideaux's reverent attitude towards sevens appears to have led him to devise seven contemporary schools of logic, when three would have been adequate. For brief reference to Lull, Hotman, and the Jesuits, see above, pp. 7, 9, 227, 234, 302. Socinian logic is identified with the Socinians, a continental religious sect of the sixteenth and seventeenth centuries. The Socinians were anti-Trinitarians, their leaders being Laelius Socinus and his nephew Faustus.

[106] *Heptades Logicae*, p. 2. The passage reads: "An Mixta à Peripatetica, Ramea, & Lulliana sit caeteris praeferenda. Aff."

[107] *Ibid.*, p. 2.

[108] *Hypomnemata*, p. 32.

[109] *Heptades Logicae*, p. 14; *Hypomnemata*, p. 99.

[110] *Heptades Logicae*, p. 13.

[111] *Hypomnemata*, p. 76.

[112] *Ibid.*, p. 76.

[113] *Ibid.*, p. 76.

Q. Is it true that the Ramistic method of disclosing fallacies is easier than that of the Aristotelians?

A. No.[114]

Prideaux's theory of method reveals once again his fondness for dividing a subject by sevens, and it also shows his persistent eclecticism. In this section of his treatise he speaks of those who place the theory of method within the third grand division of logic, that is, within the division which deals with discourses as distinguished from propositions and terms. Then he mentions those who divide logic into two parts, that is, into invention and judgment, and who proceed to regard the theory of method as an aspect of the latter branch.[115] Although he does not attach names to either of these two groups of logicians, it is obvious that he is here describing the respective practices of the Systematics and the Ramists. As for himself, he does not at this point identify his doctrine with either of these schools; but earlier he had shown how the first five of his seven heads of logic could be construed either as belonging to the topics of invention and judgment or to the three divisions of the Systematics.[116] Thus he wants his readers to feel at home with him, no matter what school of logic they attend. But he mildly insists upon offering them some things they would not get from the usual Systematic or Ramist; for when he comes to explain what methods are available for discovering knowledge or for presenting it, he falls back upon his heptades and enumerates seven possible methods, referring here to the authority of the *Institutiones Logicae* of Julius Pacius.[117] These seven methods are the "Euretic" or Inventive, the Synthetic, the Analytic, the Topical, the Dramatic, the Historical, and the Cryptic.[118]

The first three of these methods as Prideaux describes them can be identified with conventional Systematic doctrine. That is to say, the Inventive Method is useful in the discovery of new knowledge, says Prideaux, and it proceeds through sense perception, observation, experiment, and induction—the very steps which Sanderson outlines for the method of invention, although Prideaux does not

[114] *Ibid.*, p. 89. [115] *Ibid.*, p. 90. [116] *Ibid.*, p. 2.

[117] *Ibid.*, p. 91. The *Institutiones Logicae* of Julius Pacius was published at Cambridge in 1597. Pacius, also called Pace or Pacio, was an Italian jurisconsult and scholar who taught at various continental universities in the late sixteenth and early seventeenth centuries. He translated Aristotle, expounded the logic of Ramon Lull, and was well known as an authority on civil law. I have not examined his *Institutiones Logicae*.

[118] For Prideaux's discussion of them, see *Hypomnemata*, pp. 91-93.

mention him.[119] Prideaux's Synthetic Method and Analytic Method are easily recognizable as the compositive and resolutive procedures advocated by Blundeville, Smith, and Sanderson. In explaining the Synthetic Method, by the way, Prideaux refers briefly to the three laws that govern it, and these are exactly the three Aristotelian principles borrowed by Ramus for his reform. Prideaux finds it unnecessary, however, to comment upon their origin, feeling no doubt that his readers were aware of that matter.

The last four methods summarized by Prideaux may be called rhetorical rather than logical, if by rhetorical we understand methods useful in popular as distinguished from scientific discourse. At the beginning of his *Notes on Logic*, Prideaux speaks of the logic of the fist and the logic of the palm, and he explicitly recognizes that this distinction is suggested to him by Zeno's metaphorical summary of the difference between logic and rhetoric.[120] The logic of the palm, as Prideaux explains it, includes dialogues, panegyrics, forensic dissertations, and other similar forms; and he likens it not only to the Socratic, Platonic, and Ciceronian mode of antiquity but also to the forensic mode among the moderns.[121] This kind of logic is to be understood as a background for Prideaux's later discussion of what he calls the Topical, the Dramatic, the Historical, and the Cryptic Method. The Topical Method, he says, is that in which material is presented in terms of its mainheads or topics. The Dramatic Method is that in which material is presented dialogue-wise, or by catechism, as in the works of Plato. The Historical Method is that in which material is presented in the order of chronology. The Cryptic Method is that in which material is presented in some arbitrary order for the sake of the pleasure of the listeners and the emotional effect upon them. Prideaux refers this method to oratory and poetry. His description of it is worth quoting in full:

> Lastly, the Cryptic Method is entirely arbitrary. On account of its genius and natural capacity, poets and orators are the chief ones to appropriate it rather freely in some noteworthy matter, so that they may delight or variously move the auditors or readers concerned. Of such is the art of Homer (praised by Horace) when he shows Ulysses reflecting anew upon past happenings for Alcinous. Of such also is the imitation of Virgil in the story told by Aeneas at the request of Dido. More recent fragments of this method are seen in the *Biblidos*

[119] See above, p. 307.   [120] *Hypomnemata*, pp. 1-2.
[121] This forensic mode Prideaux characterizes as one of the seven logics of his day. See above, p. 313.

[315]

of Calagius, in the *Hebraidos* of Frischlin, in Du Bartas's description of the brazen shield received by Barak from Deborah, and among us in Chaucer's *Canterbury Tales* and in Spenser in the records found through Britomart in the library of memory; and in others everywhere.[122]

Next after Prideaux in the roster of English Systematics is John Newton. Newton has already been mentioned as an educational reformer who wanted all the sciences to be available in English and who translated Butler's Ramistic rhetoric as part of that plan.[123] He also prepared an English version of the logic of the Systematics. This work, called *An Introduction to the Art of Logick*, was published at London in 1671 and again in 1678.[124] Addressing himself at the beginning of this work to all teachers of vernacular learning, he presents logic as the seventh and last part of an English Academy, and says that his present work was composed "from those well known, and yet received Compendiums of this Art, which have been heretofore published by the late Learned Prelate Bishop *Saunderson*, Mr. *Airy*, Mr. *Smith*, *Burgersdicius*, and Others."[125] Had Newton included Brerewood in this list of sources, he would have been able to suggest that his vernacular logic had been influenced by every important work published in Latin by the English Systematics. In sober fact, however, Newton appears to have relied more upon Burgersdijck's *Institutionum Logicarum Libri Duo* than upon Sanderson, Airay, or Smith. For example, his division of logic into two parts, one called the thematical, and the other, the instrumental, is directly borrowed from Burgersdijck, as is his entire discussion of method.[126] But he doubtless relied to some extent upon all the authors whom he named. At any rate, he follows the familiar plan of discussing such other great topics of Systematic logic as the predicables, the predicaments, the types of propositions, the kinds of argument, the

---

[122] *Hypomnemata*, p. 93.

[123] See above, pp. 271-272.

[124] My present discussion is based upon the Harvard University Library copy of the second of these editions. Its title page reads: "An Introduction to the Art of Logick: Composed for the Use of English Schools, and all such who having no Opportunity of being Instructed in the Latine Tongue, do however Desire to be Instructed in this Liberal Science. By *John Newton*, D. D. *The Second Edition Enlarged and Amended by the Authour*. London, Printed by *A. P.* and *T. H.* for T. Passinger, at the Three Bibles, on the middle of *London-Bridge*, 1678."

[125] *Introduction to the Art of Logick* (1678), sig. A6r. For a further reference to Newton's *English Academy*, see above, p. 271, note 84.

[126] Compare Burgersdijck, *Institutionum Logicarum Libri Duo* (1668), pp. 4, 206-211, with Newton, *Introduction to the Art of Logick* (1678), pp. 3, 170-171.

places, and fallacies, nor does his treatment of these terms depart from the essential doctrine of Smith, Sanderson, and Airay.

By way of bringing to a close this account of the English Systematics, I should like to mention a treatise by Obadiah Walker entitled *Of Education Especially of Young Gentlemen*, published at Oxford in 1673, and reprinted on five later occasions in the seventeenth century. This work was designed to indicate how an education could be acquired and how it could be used in the conduct of life. Chapters xi, xii, and xiii of Part I introduce the faculties of memory, style, invention, and judgment, since of course these faculties must be trained by the educational process. For the improvement of memory, Walker recommends the use of the memory system devised by the ancient rhetoricians; and he shows how that system could be applied in his day to the streets of London as a network of places into which images could be stored and thus remembered. For the improvement of style, he recommends the figures of speech. As for invention, he turns from rhetoric to logic, and discusses Aristotle's ten predicaments and the other devices used in providing oneself with a store of arguments. What he actually says about the predicaments and the other devices is conventional and unimportant; but his inclusion of them in his treatise is a reminder that, despite the conventionality of the doctrine associated with them, they stood for important objectives in seventeenth-century education, as this account of the English Systematics has continuously demonstrated.

II. The Reappearance of the Three Patterns

THE work of the Systematics in effecting a compromise between
scholasticism and Ramism during the later sixteenth and earlier
seventeenth centuries had a close parallel at the same time in the field
of rhetorical theory. The Ramistic reform of rhetoric had consisted
in limiting that subject to style and delivery, while ordaining that
the ancient rhetorical procedures of invention and arrangement
should be purged of redundancies, combined with the similar procedures of ancient dialectic, improved in certain respects, and transferred with utter finality to logic. This reform, of course, had caused
some hostility among the traditional rhetoricians, Ascham's attitude
being a good case in point.[1] Yet later traditional rhetoricians saw that
Ramus's criticism of their doctrine had real justification, even if he
had been too emphatic or arbitrary in some of his views. Thus they
attempted to answer him not by hostility but by compromise. In
other words, they sought to restore Ciceronian concepts to rhetoric,
even as the Systematics were restoring Aristotelian concepts to logic;
but at the same time they sought to purge those concepts of redundancy and to arrange them methodically, as the Ramists were effectively advocating. The rhetoric which resulted from this compromise
as worked out by English rhetoricians in the period between 1586
and 1700 will be the subject of this final part of the present chapter.

The English rhetoricians who formulated this compromise were
not as historical-minded as their opposite numbers in logic, and thus
they did not identify themselves as a distinct school or give themselves a name to correspond with their effort at counterreform. It is
a good thing, of course, that they did not call themselves Philippo-
Ramists or Systematics or Mixts, for they would then have been
easily confused with the counterreform in logic, as if they too were
followers of Aristotle instead of Cicero. In the absence of a name invented by themselves, it seems wise to call them Neo-Ciceronians.
Not only did they take the Ciceronian position that rhetoric had
the duty of providing a machinery for invention, arrangement, and
memory, as well as for style and delivery, even though logic might
also claim some jurisdiction over the first three of these processes;
but also they recognized that the late medieval interpretation of
Ciceronian rhetoric was often wordy, poorly arranged, and difficult

[1] See above, pp. 173, 177-178.

to teach. Thus they certainly deserve to be known as Ciceronians of a new vintage.

My discussion of the English Ramists has already provided two examples of strong Neo-Ciceronian tendencies in English rhetorical theory of the seventeenth century. Those examples involve practicing Ramists who did not seem to adhere with due strictness to Ramistic rhetorical doctrine. The outstanding case of this sort is of course Charles Butler. Butler published the most famous of England's Latin versions of style and delivery as formulated by Ramus's colleague Talaeus in the latter's *Rhetorica*; and some thirty years later, Butler published a Latin treatise devoted mainly to invention, arrangement, and memory, his purpose on this second occasion being to give these concepts a better adaptation to oratory than they had in the strict logical theory of Ramus.[2] In other words, Butler limited rhetoric severely to style and delivery with the Ramistic right hand of his youth, and with the less Ramistic left hand of his old age he sought to broaden Ramus's logic by applying it to oratory and by showing that there was for the orator an extra-logical theory of invention, arrangement, and memory. Ramus would have denied that invention and arrangement had an extra-logical as well as a logical context; but Butler registered no such denial, although he fancied himself a devoted Ramist in his later as in his earlier work. The truth is, no doubt, that the thirty years between those two works had convinced him of the necessity of modifying Ramism as a way of preserving it against those who wanted to revive Cicero, and that thus his thinking had meanwhile acquired a Neo-Ciceronian aspect. Another seventeenth-century English rhetorician with the characteristics of a Ramist and a Ciceronian is John Newton. Newton belongs with the Ramists because he published in 1671 a rhetoric made up in part of Charles Butler's chapter on style; but he identifies himself with the Ciceronians by including in that same rhetoric Michael Radau's discussion of invention and arrangement.[3] By Newton's time, such a mixture may have seemed almost commonplace, so far had Ramus's doctrine lost its original compulsiveness. Thus Newton may possibly be a Ramist by mistake or a counterreformer by accident; but Butler has to be counted as primarily a Ramist and only secondarily as a part of the counterreform.

Turning now to those English rhetoricians who belong more completely to the counterreform than do Butler or Newton, I should like

[2] See above, pp. 262, 266.   [3] See above, pp. 271-272.

to speak first of Thomas Vicars. Vicars was awarded the degree of bachelor of arts at Oxford in 1611, and the master's degree four years later. Thereafter he served for a time as fellow of his college, Queens.[4] During this period he became interested in the German Systematic, Bartholomew Keckermann, and published around 1620 a translation of one of Keckermann's works under the title, *A Manuduction to Theologie*. "Manuduction" means "a leading by the hand" or "a hand guide," and this word was a favorite with Vicars, for it appeared a year later in its Greek and Latin form in the title of another of his works, the Χειραγωγια *Manuductio ad Artem Rhetoricam*, that is, the *Manuduction to the Rhetorical Art*.[5] This treatise is a good example of rhetoric formulated in the Neo-Ciceronian style, as can be seen to best advantage in its third edition, published at London in 1628.

The compromise proposed by Vicars between the Ciceronians and Ramists is anticipated by the title page of that third edition.[6] Not only does the Latin title contain the words "genesis" and "analysis" as a reminder of the famous Ramistic operations of composing and criticizing oratory; it also contains John Owens's Latin epigram in which the time-honored Ciceronian (and Zenonian) analogy of palm and fist is used to differentiate rhetoric and dialectic. Here is Vicars's title as it would read in English:

A Hand Guide or Manuduction to the Rhetorical Art. In which are taught Genesis and Analysis, that is, the theory of artistically composing and of skilfully, clearly, and methodically analyzing orations. Third edition augmented by a second part. For the use of schools. By the author, Thomas Vicars, of Carlisle, lately Fellow of Queens College in Oxford. John Owen:
Rhetoric is like unto the palm, Dialectic to the fist.
The latter wages war; but yet the former carries off the palm.[7]

[4] See *Dictionary of National Biography*, s.v. Vicars, Thomas (*fl.* 1607-1641).
[5] (London, 1621). There is a copy of this work at the British Museum.
[6] The title page of the copy in the Folger Shakespeare Library reads: "Χειραγωγια Manvdvctio ad Artem Rhetoricam. In qua Genesis & Analysis, h.e. ratio artificiosè componendi & dextrè resolvendi orationes perspicuè & methodicè docetur. Editio tertia altera parte auctior. In usum Scholarum. Auctore Thoma Vicarsio, Carleolensi, nuper Collegii Reginensis apud Oxonienses Socio. Joan. Audoen. Rhetorica est palmae similis, Dialectica pugno; Haec pugnat, palmam sed tamen illa refert. Londini, Typis Joannis Haviland, impensis Roberti Milbovrne. CIƆ. IƆC. XXIIX."
[7] This epigram is numbered 105 in Book 1 of *Epigrammatum Ioannis Owen Oxoniensis, Cambro-Britanni, Libri Tres. Ad Henricvm Principem Cambriae Dvo* (London, 1612). The text of this epigram in that source is as follows:
Ratio & Oratio.
Rhetorica est palmae similis, Dialectica pugno;
Haec pugnat; palman sed tamen illa refert.

As for the actual execution of this design, Vicars devotes Book I to "genesis," and discusses the five main parts of Ciceronian rhetoric, whereas Book II is devoted to "analysis," and contains an application of Cicero's rhetorical terminology to three of that orator's speeches. It has to be emphasized, however, that Vicars defines "analysis" at the beginning of Book II by a direct and open quotation from Ramus's *Scholae Dialecticae*.[8] Thus does he reconstruct Ciceronian rhetoric upon a plan borrowed from Ramus. He could, of course, have been more Ramistic than Ciceronian in his work, had he omitted the discussion of memory, as the Ramists did, and had he treated invention and arrangement in terms of Ramus's logical doctrine, while giving style and delivery an exposition from Talaeus. But in fact he discusses these terms in the manner of Cicero, and he yields to Ramus only as he feels the need to adopt a new organizing principle for rhetorical doctrine.

Although Vicars appears to be the first English rhetorician since Ludham to use Cicero's five great terms as the basic concepts for a theory of rhetoric, his *Manuduction to the Rhetorical Art* did not achieve the highest degree of influence in the Neo-Ciceronian movement. It was given only one other edition after 1628.[9] A much more successful Neo-Ciceronian rhetoric is Thomas Farnaby's *Index Rhetoricus*, first published at London in 1625, and given ten later editions in the seventeenth and several in the eighteenth centuries.[10] In fact, even if Farnaby's work in its original Latin title calls itself "the rhetorical indicator adapted to schools and to the instruction of the tenderer ages"—even if, in short, it is a schoolboy rhetoric—there is no work in the Neo-Ciceronian tradition to compare with it in the

---

[8] See *Manvdvctio ad Artem Rhetoricam* (London, 1628), p. 101, for this reference to Ramus.

[9] See Wing, *Short-Title Catalogue*, s.v. Vicars, Thomas.

[10] The copy of the first edition at the Bodleian Library bears the following title and date: *Index Rhetoricus, Scholis et Institutioni tenerioris aetatis accommodatus* (London, 1625). According to Pollard and Redgrave, *Short-Title Catalogue*, and Wing, *Short-Title Catalogue*, editions of this work occurred at the following dates: 1625, 1633, 1634?, 1640, 1646, 1654, 1659, 1672, 1682, 1689, 1696. Raymond E. Nadeau refers to an edition of 1704; see Clyde W. Dow, "Abstracts of Theses in the Field of Speech and Drama, VII," *Speech Monographs*, XIX (1952), 128. The Huntington Library holds a copy of an edition dated at London in 1713, and the *Dictionary of National Biography*, s.v. Farnaby, Thomas (1575?-1647), identifies a fifteenth edition in 1767.—My present discussion is based upon the Huntington Library copy just mentioned. Its title page reads: "Index Rhetoricus et Oratorius, Scholis, & Institutioni tenerioris Aetatis accommodatus. Cui adjiciuntur Formulae Oratoriae, et Index Poeticus. Opera & Studio Thomae Farnabii. Editio Novissima prioribus emendatior. . . . Londini, Typis excuduntur pro Mat. Wotton, ad Insigne *Trium Pugionum*, in vico vulgo dicto *Fleet street*; & G. Conyers, ad Insigne *Annuli Aurei*, in vico vulgo dicto *Little-Britain*. 1713."

durability of its appeal. As one of the most famous schoolmasters of his time, Farnaby was ideally suited to write such a popular textbook as the *Index Rhetoricus* turned out to be. And as a good classical scholar he was well equipped to handle not only the several Roman poets whose works he edited but also the Latin rhetoricians who formulated the tradition behind his textbook in rhetoric. At the head of that tradition, of course, were Cicero and Quintilian. Farnaby refers often to these two, and to a great many of their descendants, including Agricola, Sturm, Vossius, and Keckermann.[11]

The *Index Rhetoricus* is a clear and compact discussion of most of the chief terms in Ciceronian rhetoric. Farnaby defines rhetoric as the faculty of speaking well and in a manner calculated to persuade, no matter what the speaker's subject may be. He assigns to this faculty the three specific duties of delighting, teaching, and moving. He indicates that speakers deal with all matters under dispute, but that in practice they limit themselves to demonstrative, deliberative, and forensic questions. He acknowledges that ability in speaking comes from nature and from the study of theory; but it is the latter topic, of course, which interests him most. In treating it, he indicates that all rhetorical theory can be referred to the headings of invention, arrangement, style, and delivery. Under the first of these terms he discusses the discovery of materials for the three kinds of oratory and for the various positions of argument, as well as for the three duties of rhetoric. Under the second term, arrangement, he enumerates the six parts of an oration, and discusses them as a pattern of organization for the material previously invented. Style is then explained in terms of elegance, orderliness of verbal units, and dignity, the last quality being finally broadened into an analysis of the tropes and figures. Then follows a section on delivery, and here Farnaby talks of practice, imitation, reading, and precepts.

Ramistic influences in the *Index Rhetoricus* are not strongly visible, but they can nevertheless be detected. For example, Farnaby omits the subject of memory when he seeks to restore the Ciceronian rhetorical system, and this part of his procedure is a tribute to the

[11] According to Raymond E. Nadeau's doctoral dissertation, "The Index Rhetoricus of Thomas Farnaby" (University of Michigan, 1951), the primary sources of the *Index Rhetoricus* are the *Commentariorum Rhetoricorum . . . Libri vi* (1605) and the *Rhetorices Contractae* (1621) of Vossius, the *Systema Rhetoricae* (1606) of Keckermann, and the *Institutio Oratoria* of Quintilian. Nadeau indicates some fifty-nine other sources, Cicero being of course one of the most outstanding. See Clyde W. Dow, "Abstracts of Theses in the Field of Speech and Drama, VII," *Speech Monographs*, XIX (1952), 128.

success of one of Ramus's reforms. For another example, Farnaby discusses the six parts of an oration under the heading of arrangement, although these materials were placed under invention by the older Ciceronians. Here again his procedure shows a concern for the observance of Ramus's law of justice, by which each division of knowledge was awarded what lawfully belonged to it. Thus does Farnaby respond to the influences created by the Ramists, as we would expect a rhetorician to do who owed much to Keckermann, the Systematic. In fact, Farnaby's *Index Rhetoricus* stands in relation to Neo-Ciceronian rhetoric in England as Sanderson's *Logicae Artis Compendivm*, likewise a product of Keckermann's influence, stands in relation to the logic of the English Systematics. That is to say, both of these treatises were very popular, very long-lived, and very cognizant of the determination to effect a compromise between the ideas of Ramus and those of the medieval tradition.

Another work in the Neo-Ciceronian movement is William Pemble's *Enchiridion Oratorivm*, published at Oxford in 1633.[12] Pemble had prematurely died ten years earlier, after having taken two degrees at Oxford and after having served brilliantly at Magdalen Hall in that university as lecturer in divinity.[13] His *Enchiridion Oratorivm*, which in English would be called the *Oratorical Manual*, defines rhetoric as "the art of treating any matter whatever in an ornamental and copious way for the people's knowledge and persuasion."[14] It proceeds to divide rhetoric into invention, arrangement, style, and delivery, although it deals only with the first two of these terms. Under invention, which Pemble defines as "the devising of arguments true or apparently true for rendering a cause probable,"[15] there is a discussion of the discovery of arguments in simple and complex themes, in the three kinds of oratory, and in the four argumentative positions of the legal case. Arrangement, defined as "the distribution of invented materials in an order showing what ought to be collected into what places,"[16] is made to deal with the six parts of the oration. In respect to this topic, the *Enchiridion Oratorivm* conforms to the same pattern as that of the *Index Rhetoricus*, although

[12] The title page of the Harvard University Library copy reads as follows: "Enchiridion Oratorivm. A Gvlielmo Pembelo Avlae Magdalenensis non ita pridem Alumno facundissimè pio concinnatum. . . . Oxoniae Apud *Iohannem Lichfield* Academiae Typographum pro *Edvardo* Forrest. A. D. 1633."

[13] *Dictionary of National Biography*, s.v. Pemble, William (1592?-1623).

[14] *Enchiridion Oratorivm*, p. 1. Translation mine here and below.

[15] *Ibid.*, p. 2.

[16] *Ibid.*, p. 2; see also p. 57.

the latter work was published after Pemble's death and thus could not have influenced him. Pemble likewise conforms to the pattern of the *Index Rhetoricus* in omitting memory from the list of necessary rhetorical subjects. As he does this, he says that memory is not any more proper to rhetoric than to the other arts[17]—an ancient idea, and also, of course, an echo of Ramus's reform.

The Neo-Ciceronian movement was given additional support by Obadiah Walker in 1659 with the publication at London of a work called *Some Instrvctions concerning the Art of Oratory*.[18] Walker's treatise *Of Education* has already been briefly noticed in the first part of the present chapter, and at that time he was seen to be identified to some extent with the English Systematics.[19] Walker was a product of Oxford, where he studied at University College and took the degrees of bachelor of arts in 1635 and of master of arts in 1638. He stayed on at his college as tutor after he had received his second degree, and thereafter his life was associated with academic pursuits. In 1676 he became master of University College.[20] *Some Instrvctions concerning the Art of Oratory* may thus be said to have a sound pedigree and to proceed from well-informed quarters. Moreover, the work is to be regarded as an interesting interpretation of four of the main terms of Ciceronian rhetoric.

Walker arrives at these four terms by dividing oratory into invention and style, and by subdividing each of these subjects so that the first covers both invention and arrangement, whereas the second covers both style and delivery. Here are his own statements to indicate his major and subordinate divisions:

> The Parts of Oratory are 1. *Invention*, taking care for the Matter; and 2. *Elocution*, for the *Words*, and *Style*.[21]
>
> In all your Compositions, especially those of any length, upon all your Materials revised, a Division, and distribution of them under certain Heads, such as best fits them, is alwayes to be cast, and contrived;

[17] *Ibid.*, p. 2.

[18] The title page of the Huntington Library copy reads as follows: "Some Instrvctions concerning the Art of Oratory. Collected for the use of a Friend a Young Student. London, Printed by F. G. for R. *Royston*, at the Angel in *Ivy lane*, 1659." This work was given a second edition "very much Corrected and Augmented" at Oxford in 1682. The second edition differs from the first by having 150 pages of text rather than 128, but even so the two editions are virtually identical in content for the first 100 pages of each. Thereafter the second edition shows some additional material.

[19] See above, p. 317.

[20] See *Dictionary of National Biography*, s.v. Walker, Obadiah (1616-1699).

[21] *Some Instrvctions concerning the Art of Oratory* (1682), p. 1.

though not necessary alwayes to be mentioned; yet, in many also not to be concealed.[22]

Thus much of 1. *Invention,* and *Arguments*; and of the partition of them; Now 2. of *Elocution.* . . . And in it 1. concerning *Words.* 2. Then of *Periods*; and of the various artificial *placing* of the words in them. 3. Next, of the several *figures* and *modes* of livelier and more passionate expression. 4. of *Stiles.* After which I shall adde something, 5. of *Recitation.* 6 of *Pronuntiation.* and 7. of *Action.*[23]

Walker draws the major part of his doctrine from Ciceronian authors, and betrays the influence of Ramus only in the way in which he distributes his emphasis upon the various headings of his subject. His chief authority is Quintilian's *Institutio Oratoria,* this work being cited over and over again.[24] He refers to Cicero's orations for examples of rhetorical practices, and on one occasion he uses a passage from Cicero's *De Inventione* to illustrate etiology.[25] When he is finishing his discussion of rhetorical topics as a source of arguments, he mentions that Aristotle's *Rhetoric* may be consulted for additional information on this point.[26] The only well-known modern rhetorician to whom he refers is Farnaby, although he names such modern writers as Scaliger, Hooker, Bishop Andrews, and Francis Bacon.[27] Despite the Ciceronian tendency of his chief rhetorical authorities, however, there is one major respect in which Walker differs from them: he devotes only one-tenth of his total space to the subject of invention, whereas the true Ciceronian who deals with invention at all would regard it as worthy of a much heavier emphasis. Walker's tendency to slight it may be regarded as an indirect result of Ramus's insistence that rhetoric had no right to speculate upon that aspect of the theory of communication. As a natural corollary, Walker's overemphasis on style is probably a reflection of the exclusive concern of Ramistic rhetoric for the verbal and oral aspects of writing and speaking.

Walker and Farnaby, along with Pemble and Vicars, are the chief English rhetoricians of the Neo-Ciceronian school during the seventeenth century. Their effort to revive most or all of the major terms of Ciceronian rhetoric, and also at the same time to accept some of

---

[22] *Ibid.,* p. 15.   [23] *Ibid.,* p. 24.

[24] *Ibid.,* pp. 2, 7, 10, 16, 22, 25, 41, 43, 75, 82, 95, 104, 105, 107, 130, 134, 135, 136, 137, 142.

[25] *Ibid.,* pp. 22, 72, 80-81, 91, 93.   [26] *Ibid.,* p. 7.

[27] *Ibid.,* pp. 2 (for Farnaby); 143 (for Scaliger); 46-48 (for Hooker); 77, 89 (for Andrews); and 12, 60, 75, 106 (for Bacon).

Ramus's reforms, was aided by a similar endeavor on the continent and by an occasional edition of a continental rhetoric in England. For example, Michael Radau's *Orator Extemporaneus*, already mentioned as the source of certain non-Ramistic features of John Newton's otherwise Ramistic rhetoric, first entered the English Neo-Ciceronian movement in 1657 when it was given an edition at London.[28] It contains a bipartite summary of the oratorical art, one section being devoted to a theoretical treatment of invention, arrangement, style, and memory, while the other section presents exercises for training students in the three kinds of oratory, particularly the demonstrative. Radau, by the way, was professor of sacred theology in the Jesuit college at Brunsberg, Prussia, and had had the misfortune to see his *Orator Extemporaneus* published as if it were largely the work of one George Beckher before it was finally presented to the public under its rightful auspices.[29]

My account of the Neo-Ciceronian movement in England would not be adequate without some recognition of the English rhetoricians of the later sixteenth and the earlier seventeenth centuries who sought to maintain a stylistic rhetoric looking back to the old Ciceronian tradition rather than to Ramus. That is to say, there were a few English rhetoricians in those years who confined rhetoric to style, as if they were partly Ramists, but who nevertheless treated style in the manner of such old-fashioned Ciceronians as Richard Sherry and Henry Peacham. A characteristic of the work of these rhetoricians is that they heavily emphasized the tropes and the figures while omitting various features of the Ramistic treatment of these devices of style.

A good case in point has already been covered in my discussion of John Smith's *Mysterie of Rhetorique Unvail'd* (1657).[30] This compilation of some 138 tropes and figures owes much to John Hoskins and Henry Peacham, as well as to Thomas Farnaby, and thus it belongs in part to the Ciceronian school; but it also owes several pages of doctrine to Dudley Fenner's first English version of Talaeus's

---

[28] See above, pp. 271-272. This work was given a second edition in England in 1673, two years after Newton published an English version of much of it. The Princeton University Library has a copy of this second edition. Its title page reads as follows: "Orator Extemporaneus seu Artis Oratoriae Breviarium bipartitum, Cujus Prior pars praecepta continet generalia, Posterior praxin ostendit in triplici dicendi genere praesertim Demonstrativo. Nec non supellectilem Oratoria, Sententias, Historias, Apophthegmata Hieroglyphica suppeditat. Auctore R. P. Michaele Radau Societatis Jesu. S. Theologiae Doctore ejusdemque Professore. Londini, Typis *Iohannis Redmayne*, MDCLXXIII."

[29] For an account of Beckher's plagiarized edition of the *Orator Extemporaneus*, see the edition of this work at Amsterdam in 1673, sig. *5r-*5v.

[30] See above, pp. 276-279.

Rhetorica, and thus it partakes in part of Ramus's reforms. Its Ramistic characteristics serve to identify it interestingly with the work of the English Ramists. At any rate, I placed it in that school rather than in the Neo-Ciceronian school, although it would not be out of place in the latter.

George Puttenham's *The Arte of English Poesie*, published at London in 1589, will begin my discussion of the stylistic rhetorics of the counterreform. This famous work is, to be sure, a treatise on poetry rather than on rhetoric, but it handles the doctrine of style as a work on rhetoric would, and thus it belongs in part to the history of rhetorical theory in England. Moreover, it treats style, not according to the Ramistic formula that Abraham Fraunce used in the *Arcadian Rhetorike* in 1588, but according to the older Ciceronian formula. That is to say, Puttenham devotes some twenty-three chapters of the third book of his treatise to style, and these chapters consist of recognizable topics from traditional rhetoric. There is, for example, an elaborate analysis of the figures of grammar and rhetoric; and there is also an examination of such other matters as the grand, medium, and familiar style, the principal deformities of expression, and the nature of decorum as a stylistic virtue.[31] Only in one place does Puttenham show an awareness of Ramistic rhetorical theory, and that is in his second book, where he discusses the whole subject of prosody, and includes a particular description of the twelve kinds of ancient metrical feet. His enumeration of these feet is obviously influenced either by the corresponding passage in Talaeus's *Rhetorica* or by William Webbe's version of that passage in Talaeus's *Rhetorica*.[32] In other respects, however, Puttenham appears to pay no attention to the Ramists.

Puttenham's theory of style in respect to oratory and poetry may be said to consist in the belief that, as oratory achieves persuasiveness only by transcending the speech patterns of ordinary daily converse, so does poetry achieve persuasiveness and delightfulness only by transcending the speech patterns of oratory. In other words, Puttenham acknowledges ordinary conversation to be a step below the level that oratory must achieve, whereas oratory is a step below the level that poetry must achieve. And he takes the position that, if the language used on any of these levels be well-bred, ordinary conversa-

[31] George Puttenham, *The Arte of English Poesie*, ed. Edward Arber (London, 1869), pp. 149-282. For a recent edition of this work, see Gladys Doidge Willcock and Alice Walker, *The Arte of English Poesie by George Puttenham* (Cambridge, 1936).
[32] *The Arte of English Poesie*, ed. Arber, pp. 133-137. See also above, p. 257.

tion is at the lowest point on the scale because it does not use figurative language at all, while oratory and poetry are progressively higher in value because of their progressive concern for the right use of figures. This view amounts to a denial that the language of ordinary life can be a medium for oratory or poetry. It also amounts to an affirmation that the medium for oratory and poetry can be found only by dressing up the language of ordinary life with such violations of our daily speech as the tropes and the figures represent.

The requirement that the language of effective literature must be well-bred, as opposed to rustic, uncivil, or pedantic, is the first part of the theory just stated, and Puttenham openly commits himself to it. His words are addressed to the poet, but he has the orator also in mind. Here is what he says of the poet's use of language:

> This part in our maker or Poet must be heedyly looked vnto, that it be naturall, pure, and the most vsuall of all his countrey: and for the same purpose rather that which is spoken in the kings Court, or in the good townes and Cities within the land, then in the marches and frontiers, or in port townes, where straungers haunt for traffike sake, or yet in Vniuersities where Schollers vse much peeuish affectation of words out of the primatiue languages, or finally, in any vplandish village or corner of a Realme, where is no resort but of poore rusticall or vnciuill people: neither shall he follow the speach of a craftes man or carter, or other of the inferiour sort, though he be inhabitant or bred in the best towne and Citie in this Realme, for such persons doe abuse good speaches by strange accents or ill shapen soundes, and false ortographie.[33]

Given a well-bred pattern of language to start with, the would-be orator and poet proceed then to take the position, according to Puttenham, that good utterance "resteth altogether in figuratiue speaches,"[34] and that figurative speech is "a noueltie of language euidently (and yet not absurdly) estranged from the ordinarie habite and manner of our dayly talke and writing."[35] In fact, like all his predecessors in the study of figurative language, Puttenham acknowledges the figures to be "but transgressions of our dayly speech."[36] When these transgressions are absent altogether, then our writings or our public speeches become "but as our ordinary talke, then which nothing can be more vnsauourie and farre from all ciuilitie."[37] Puttenham illustrates such unfigured talk by citing the case of the Yorkshire knight

---

[33] *The Arte of English Poesie*, ed. Arber, pp. 156-157. [34] *Ibid.*, p. 152.
[35] *Ibid.*, p. 171.   [36] *Ibid.*, p. 269.   [37] *Ibid.*, p. 151.

in Queen Mary's reign who was chosen speaker of parliament and whose speech to the queen was so marred by his lack of teeth and his inability with unusual language that a gentleman contemptuously called the effort an "alehouse tale"—"because the good old Knight made no difference betweene an Oration or publike speach to be deliuered to th'eare of a Princes Maiestie and state of a Realme, then he would haue done of an ordinary tale to be told at his table in the countrey, wherein all men know the oddes is very great."[38] On the other hand, when figures or transgressions of our daily speech are not only present in our writings or orations, but are present in such a way as to be enclosed within a metrical pattern, then our literary effort becomes poetry or "speech by meeter," and this kind of utterance is "more cleanly couched and more delicate to the eare than prose is, because it is more currant and slipper vpon the tongue, and withal tunable and melodious, as a kinde of Musicke, and therfore may be tearmed a musicall speech or vtterance, which cannot but please the hearer very well."[39] Puttenham immediately adds:

> It is beside a maner of vtterance more eloquent and rethoricall then the ordinarie prose, which we vse in our daily talke: because it is decked and set out with all maner of fresh colours and figures, which maketh that it sooner inuegleth the iudgement of man, and carieth his opinion this way and that, whither soeuer the heart by impression of the eare shalbe most affectionatly bent and directed.

The difference between figured metrical language and figured prose is not the only difference that Puttenham sees between poetry and oratory, as the whole first book of his treatise demonstrates. In fact, if his entire theory on this matter were worked out, it would be necessary to recognize that he occasionally uses terms like "imitation" and "counterfeiter" in his discussion of poetry, but does not imply their similar use in the analysis of oratory. Thus he does not regard the poem as being a kind of metrical oration. He does regard the two, however, as being alike persuasive, and he believes they owe their persuasiveness, so far as style is concerned, to the presence within them of figurative language.

Two other stylistic rhetorics of the Neo-Ciceronian school were produced in England before the end of the sixteenth century, although one of them was not published in its own right until the present era. Angel Day's *The English Secretorie* was the earlier of

---

[38] *Ibid.*, p. 151. [39] *Ibid.*, p. 24.

the two. When this work appeared at London in 1592 in its third edition, it contained directions to be heeded and models to be followed in letter writing, as it had in its two earlier editions; but it also contained a new element in the form of "A declaration of such Tropes, Figures, and Schemes, as either vsually or for ornament sake are therin required."[40] In other words, this third edition of Day's work is both a formulary and a stylistic rhetoric. It is a formulary rhetoric because it contains models of descriptive, laudatory, vituperative, deliberative, dehortatory, conciliatory, consolatory, amatory, judicial, and familiar letters, as well as of many other kinds. It is a stylistic rhetoric, of course, because of its section on the figures, which Day classifies as tropes and schemes. His treatment of these contrivances of style is distinctly non-Ramistic. To begin with, he classifies schemes as grammatical and rhetorical,[41] whereas a Ramist would have insisted that schemes must belong wholly to rhetoric under Ramus's law of justice. Secondly, he includes in his program a brief mention of invention and arrangement,[42] whereas Ramus would have regarded these matters as the property of logic and as unsuitable for discussion elsewhere in the world of learning. For the rest, Day's treatise on style is like the many others of its kind, and it need not detain us longer.

The later of the two rhetorics mentioned at the beginning of the preceding paragraph is John Hoskins's *Directions for Speech and Style*. This work was not published under Hoskins's name until the nineteen-thirties, when it received two editions, one by Hoyt H. Hudson and the other by Louise Brown Osborn.[43] Nevertheless, it had something of a history in print before it achieved these two editions. First of all, a few pages of it were silently embodied in Ben Jonson's *Timber* and were published in that work in 1641, some four years after Jonson's death. Thanks to Miss Osborn, these pages were

---

[40] *The English Secretorie* was published at London as follows: 1586, 1590?, 1592, 1595, 1599, 1607, 1614, 1618, 1626, 1635. My present discussion is based upon the Huntington Library copy of the 1599 edition. Its title page reads: "The English Secretary, or Methode of writing of Epistles and Letters: with A Declaration of such Tropes, Figures, and Schemes, as either vsually or for ornament sake are therin required. Also the parts and office of a Secretarie, Deuided into two bookes. Now newly reuised and in many parts corrected and amended: By Angel Day. At London Printed by P. S. for C. Burbie and are to be sold at his shop, at the Royall Exchange. 1599."

[41] *The English Secretary* (1599), p. 81.

[42] *Ibid.*, p. 9.

[43] See Hoskins, *Directions for Speech and Style*, ed. Hudson; Louise Brown Osborn, *The Life, Letters, and Writings of John Hoskyns 1566-1638* (New Haven, 1937), pp. 115-166.

publicly identified in 1930 as the property of Hoskins.[44] Secondly, almost all of the *Directions* was borrowed without acknowledgment and published by Thomas Blount as a principal part of his *Academie of Eloquence*. Thirdly, many of Blount's borrowings were in turn lifted from him without acknowledgment and published by John Smith as part of his *Mysterie of Rhetorique Unvail'd*. The pillaging of Hoskins by Blount and Smith was publicly exposed in 1935 by Hoyt H. Hudson, as I indicated earlier.[45] Thus two of the most famous stylistic rhetorics of the second half of the seventeenth century must be regarded as in part the work of Hoskins.

The *Directions for Speech and Style* deserves the compliment that these imitators paid it. It is a treatise on letter-writing, and it recognizes invention, arrangement, and style as the main divisions of its subject. Style is, however, the great point of interest for Hoskins. Thus he devotes most of his treatise to the four qualities of the good epistolary style, and to the figures that provide for variety, amplification, and illustration. His definition of a metaphor provides an excellent example of the ease and attractiveness of his treatise as a whole:

> A Metaphor, or Translation, is the friendly and neighborly borrowing of one word to express a thing with more light and better note, though not so directly and properly as the natural name of the thing meant would signify.[46]

Metaphor and the other tropes, as well as certain figures or schemes, are lumped together by Hoskins and discussed as devices "For Varying"; all the other figures considered by him are arranged to show his readers how "To Amplify" or how "To Illustrate."[47] Thus he does not classify tropes and figures according to the bipartite scheme of Ramus and Talaeus, even though Talaeus is mentioned by him as one of his recent sources.[48] In fact, he owes little to Ramistic rhetoric, and his reference to Talaeus may well have no purpose except to arouse interest by associating his work with a strong popular trend in the same general direction. His main sources are Cicero and Quintilian among the ancients, and Lipsius and Pierre de la Primaudaye

---

[44] See Louise B. Osborn, "Ben Jonson and Hoskyns," *The Times Literary Supplement*, May 1, 1930, p. 370.

[45] See Hoskins, *Directions for Speech and Style*, ed. Hudson, pp. xxvii-xxxviii. See also above, pp. 276-277.

[46] *Directions for Speech and Style*, ed. Hudson, p. 8.

[47] *Ibid.*, pp. 8-17, 17-40, 41-50.

[48] *Ibid.*, p. 3.

among the moderns.[49] One indication, for example, of his reliance upon the Ciceronian tradition is that he begins his rhetorical treatise with a few words about invention and arrangement—two subjects which a Ramist would have deemed out of place in a work devoted to the figures of style. But it should be emphasized that Hoskins does not rely upon the Ciceronian tradition in any servile way. He interprets rather than copies it, and thus his *Directions for Speech and Style* is (in Miss Osborn's phrase) "essentially original."[50]

The next author in the ranks of English stylistic rhetoricians of the Neo-Ciceronian school is Thomas Blount, whose borrowings from Hoskins have just been mentioned. Blount's *Academie of Eloquence*, first published at London in 1654, contains so much of Hoskins's *Directions* that it hardly deserves special mention as an independent stylistic rhetoric.[51] Of the four parts into which it is divided, the first is described by Blount as "a more exact *English Rhetorique*, then has been hitherto extant."[52] But Hudson calls this part "nothing but a copy of the second, third, fourth, and fifth sections of Hoskins's *Directions*, with such omissions and changes as Blount's fancy, reason, or inadvertence dictated."[53] Again, the fourth part of the *Academie of Eloquence* contains, as Blount says, "A Collection of Letters and addresses written to, for, and by severall persons, upon emergent occasions; with some particular *Instructions* and Rules premised for the better attaining to a Pen-perfection."[54] But once more, as Hudson points out, the instructions and rules premised by Blount are nothing but passages from Hoskins.[55] True, the collection of letters in this fourth part of Blount's work cannot be traced to the *Directions*, nor can the *formulae majores* and *formulae minores* of the second and third parts. But neither can these elements be classed as the property of stylistic rhetoric. What they are, in actuality, is a

[49] *Ibid.*, pp. xxii-xxvii.

[50] *The Life, Letters, and Writings of John Hoskyns*, p. 109.

[51] The *Academie of Eloquence* was given other editions as follows: 1656, 1660, 1663, 1664, 1670, 1683, 1684. See Wing, *Short-Title Catalogue*, s.v. Blount, Thomas. See also Hoskins, *Directions for Speech and Style*, ed. Hudson, p. xxx, note 35. My present discussion is based upon the Huntington Library copy of the second edition. Its title page reads: "The Academy of Eloquence: Containing a Compleat English Rhetoriqve, Exemplified; *Common-Places*, and *Formula's* digested into an easie and Methodical way to speak and write fluently, according to the *Mode* of the present Times: with Letters both Amorovs and Morall, Upon emergent Occasions. By Tho. Blount Gent' The second Edition with Additions . . . . London, Printed by T. N. for *Humphrey Moseley*, at the Prince's Arms in S. Pauls Churchyard. 1656."

[52] *Academy of Eloquence* (1656), sig. A4r.

[53] Hoskins, *Directions for Speech and Style*, ed. Hudson, p. xxxi.

[54] *Academy of Eloquence*, sig. A4r-A4v.   [55] Hudson, p. xxxi.

contribution to the formulary rhetoric of the seventeenth century. They are interesting on that score; and the *formulae majores* and *minores*, which Blount respectively calls "Common-places" and "lesser forms," are interesting because Blount attributes his belief in the importance of such collections to Francis Bacon's similar belief as expressed in the *Advancement of Learning*.[56] Still, these formulas need not be considered further. As for the rest of Blount's *Academie*, nothing may be said of it that would not be better said in reference to Hoskins.

I shall close this account of Neo-Ciceronian stylistic rhetoric with a brief comment upon John Prideaux. Prideaux has been mentioned already as one of the English Systematics.[57] Thus it is not strange to find him also among the Neo-Ciceronians, although he never sought to cope with Ciceronian rhetoric as a whole.

Prideaux's earliest work on stylistic rhetoric appeared in Latin as the second treatise in his *Hypomnemata*, which was published at Oxford around 1650. This second treatise runs only to three short chapters, one dealing with the tropes, one with the figures, and one with the schemes.[58] Prideaux defines rhetoric as "the art of speaking ornamentally, or, as Aristotle holds (*Rhetoric*, Bk. 1, Ch. 2), it is the faculty of seeing whatever aims to be suitable to the creating of belief in any thing."[59] In other words, Prideaux appears to identify the tropes, figures, and schemes with what Aristotle meant by all the modes of persuasion in any given case. This interpretation of Aristotle is of course subject to criticism, for Aristotle describes the modes of persuasion as the whole operation of creating trust in our own character as speakers, of putting our hearers in the right frame of feeling, and of proving the truth or probability of our cause by resort to argument.[60] But at any rate Prideaux is not completely wrong in his reference to Aristotle, inasmuch as Aristotle in a later chapter of the *Rhetoric* talks of language as one of the key factors in creating trust in ourselves, arousing emotion in others, and making people believe in the truth of what we say.[61] What Prideaux does is to confine himself to the stylistic aspect of a problem that Aristotle had not

---

[56] *Academy of Eloquence*, sig. A4r.

[57] See above, pp. 311-316.

[58] *Hypomnemata*, pp. 103-111.

[59] *Ibid.*, p. 104. Translation mine. Prideaux's words are as follows: "*Rhetorica* est *Ars ornatè* dicendi. vel ut habet *Arist. Facultas* in qua[que] *re videndi* quid contingit esse *Idoneum* ad faciendam *fidem*. Rhet. L. 1. c. 2." (Prideaux's italics).

[60] See Aristotle, *Rhetoric*, 1356ª 1-35.

[61] *Ibid.*, Bk. 3, Ch. 7.

confined to style. Incidentally, as Prideaux discusses the tropes, figures, and schemes, he falls into the habit of dividing each of these topics into seven parts, even as he had divided logic into heptades when he first wrote upon it in 1639. Thus he speaks of seven varieties of tropes, seven of figures, and seven of schemes.

Prideaux's *Sacred Eloquence*, published at London in 1659, is more important than the treatise just discussed, and it represents a further development of his theory of stylistic rhetoric.[62] Prideaux defines sacred eloquence as "a Logicall kind of Rhetorick, to be used in Prayer, Preaching, or Conference; to the glory of God, and the convincing, instructing, and strengthning our brethren."[63] He divides his subject into heptades or sevens, and proceeds to speak of Tropes, Figures, Schemes, Patheticks, Characters, Antitheses, and Parallels. In discussing each of these topics, he divides his doctrine under seven heads, indicating at one point that such organization makes the points easier to remember, and that there is biblical authority for sevenfold divisions of things.[64] His conception of the rhetorical importance of the tropes, figures, and schemes is well illustrated by what he says as schemes come up for analysis: "To teach, to delight, and throughly [sic] to perswade, are the scopes of Oratory. After teaching—Tropes therefore, and delighting—Figures, convincing and perswading—*Schemes* may be well enquired after."[65] As for "Patheticks," Prideaux identifies them with the passions, and he discusses the seven most prominent ones—love, hatred, hope, fear, joy, sorrow, zeal.[66] "Characters" turn out to be characterizations of men or situations. For example, Prideaux enumerates the seven steps in sin's genealogy, the seven qualities of a good bishop, the seven traits of old age, the seven arms of a Christian soldier.[67] "Antitheses" and "Parallels," as the terms suggest, are devices for building sermons upon a series of seven contrasts or of seven similitudes.[68] Throughout the treatise Prideaux cites such authorities on rhetoric as Cicero, Quintilian, St. Augustine, and the author of the *Rhetorica ad Herennium*, thus preserving the content of the Ciceronian tradition; but there can be little doubt that his use of heptades as a structural

---

[62] Its title page reads: "Sacred Eloquence: Or, the Art of Rhetorick, As it is layd down in Scripture. By the Right Reverend Father John Prideavx late Lord Bishop of VVorcester . . . . London, Printed by *W. Wilson*, for *George Sawbridge*, and are to be sold at his Shop at the signe of the *Bible* on Ludgate-Hill. 1659."

[63] *Sacred Eloquence*, p. 1. [64] *Ibid.*, pp. 106-117.
[65] *Ibid.*, p. 58. [66] *Ibid.*, pp. 76-105.
[67] *Ibid.*, pp. 108, 110-112, 114-115, 117.
[68] *Ibid.*, pp. 118-123, 124-134.

principle in presenting doctrine is partly a repudiation of Ramistic dichotomies and partly an acceptance of Ramus's desire for a clearer organization of the learned arts.

In the period under discussion in this chapter England produced several formulary rhetorics designed to exemplify rhetorical theory by presenting students with model compositions for imitation and study. In fact, the preceding review of Neo-Ciceronian rhetoric has involved some reference to these formularies. For example, the second and all later editions of Thomas Farnaby's *Index Rhetoricus* contains a section entitled "Formulae Oratoriae," and thus Farnaby belongs in part to the formulary school.[69] So indeed do Angel Day and Thomas Blount, as I mentioned earlier.[70] There are in this school a few others, however, who deserve a brief moment of attention.

The chief English authors of formulary rhetorics in the closing decades of the sixteenth century are Anthony Mundy and Lazarus Piot, if we except Angel Day, who need not be discussed further. Mundy published at London in 1593 a work called *The Defence of Contraries*, which advertised itself in its subtitle as "Paradoxes against common opinion, debated in forme of declamations in place of publike censure: only to exercise yong wittes in difficult matters."[71] Although it proclaims itself on its title page as "Translated out of French," it is in fact a translation of a French version of Ortensio Landi's Italian work, the *Paradossi*, first published at Lyon in 1543. Landi's *Paradossi* contains thirty declamations.[72] Mundy translates twelve of these and promises at the end of his work to do fourteen others, twenty-six paradoxes having been in the French version that he used.[73] His paradoxes are argumentative compositions in defense of such unpopular conditions as poverty, physical ugliness, ignorance,

[69] See above, p. 321, note 10.   [70] See above, pp. 330, 332.

[71] The title page continues thus: "Wherein is no offence to Gods honour, the estate of Princes, or priuate mens honest actions: but pleasant recreation to beguile the iniquity of time. Translated out of French by A. M. one of the Messengers of her Maiesties Chamber. *Patere aut obstine.* Imprinted at London by Iohn Winder for Simon Waterson. 1593." There was a second edition in 1616.

[72] For a good bibliographical account of this work, see Jean George Théodore Graese, *Trésor de Livres Rares et Précieux* (Dresden, 1859-1869), V, 130-131.

[73] The French version published at Paris in 1561 contains twenty-six paradoxes. Its title reads: "XXV paradoxes ou sentences débatues et . . . deduites contre le commune opinion. . . . Plus adjousté de nouveau le paradoxe que le plaider est chose très utile et nécessaire à la vie des hommes. Paris, 1561." This French version is credited to Charles Estienne.—My colleague, Dr. Henry K. Miller, Jr., informs me that, although the first twenty-five of the paradoxes in this volume are from Landi's *Paradossi*, the twenty-sixth—the one in defense of lawyers—is apparently Estienne's own, or at any rate is not in Landi.

blindness, foolishness, loss of worldly honors, drunkenness, sterility, and want. The paradoxes promised for his second volume are to include, he says, a defense of the wounded, the illegitimate, prisoners, women, and lawyers.[74] As for his intention in preparing the volume for publication, he paraphrases what his French source had said to justify itself. Thus he recalls in his address "To the friendly Reader" that a knight is prepared for the field by exercises in arms; and he adds:

> In like manner, for him that woulde be a good Lawyer, after he hath long listened at the barre; he must aduenture to defend such a cause, as they that are most imployed, refuse to maintaine: therby to make himselfe more apt and ready, against common pleaders in ordinarie causes of processe. For this intent, I haue vndertaken (in this book) to debate on certaine matters, which our Elders were wont to cal Paradoxes . . . to the end, that by such discourse as is helde in them, opposed truth might appeare more cleere and apparant. Likewise, to exercise thy witte in proofe of such occasions, as shall enforce thee to seeke diligentlie and laboriously, for sound reasons, proofes, authorities, histories, and very darke or hidden memories.[75]

Lazarus Piot's *The Orator* is very similar in purpose to Mundy's *Defence of Contraries,* but there is no truth in the old belief that "Piot" is one of Mundy's pseudonyms and that *The Orator* is merely an expansion of Mundy's earlier collection of paradoxes. In fact, Mundy and Piot are two quite different persons, and these two works are quite unlike in content, as Celeste Turner was the first to emphasize.[76]

The Orator is made up of a hundred exercises, each of which contains a speech made in accusation and a speech made in reply.[77] Declamation 81, for example, concerns a surgeon who murdered a man

---

[74] *Defence of Contraries,* pp. [102-103].

[75] *Ibid.,* sig. A4r-A4v. The fact that Mundy's preface "To the Reader" is a paraphrase of Estienne's "Au Lecteur Salut" was also called to my attention by Dr. Miller.

[76] See Celeste Turner, *Anthony Mundy An Elizabethan Man of Letters* (Berkeley, 1928), pp. 98-102, 196.

[77] Its title page reads: "The Orator: Handling a hundred seuerall Discourses, in forme of Declamations: Some of the Arguments being drawne from *Titus Liuius* and other ancient Writers, the rest of the Authors owne inuention: Part of which are of matters happened in our Age. Written in French by Alexander Siluayn, and Englished by L. P. London Printed by Adam Islip. 1596."—The French work upon which Piot based *The Orator* is by Alexandre van den Busche, also called Le Sylvain. The copy of it in the British Museum has the following title: "Epitomes de cent histoires tragicques, partie extraittes des Actes des Romains & autres, de l'inuention de l'autheur, auecq[ue] les demandes, accusations & deffences sur la matiere d'icelles." (Paris, 1581.)

"to see the mouing of a quicke heart."[78] The surgeon was a resident
of Padua, enjoyed a reputation for great skill, and had the desire to
open a living man in order that he might observe how the human
heart beats. The government would not give him a condemned malefactor for experimental purposes, however, and thus the surgeon
had to make his own arrangements. One night a poor soldier came
to his door. The surgeon took him in, kept him three days in secret,
and then had him taken to a cave, where, with the help of hirelings,
the surgeon bound him and opened him alive, and "saw that in him
which he so greatly desired." But one of the hirelings confessed his
part in the crime. The surgeon was brought to trial. Declamation 81
consists of his statement in defense of his act, and of the attorney
general's reply. The surgeon's statement in defense pled that he
killed this one man to save many, and that he had been forced to do
as he did because the Senate would provide him with no condemned
malefactor for his purpose. He also argued that the murdered man
was probably a bad lot, being a soldier. But he said nothing of what
he had seen when he observed a living heart at work. The reply of
the attorney general accused the surgeon of egotism, and argued that
he might have tried his experiment on an animal "whose entrals had
not beene much vnlike vnto a mans." The attorney general also said
that the surgeon was guilty of slandering as well as murdering the
victim, and that his crime would incite others to similar atrocities.

This is one of the most interesting of the cases in *The Orator*. Of
greater literary interest, perhaps, is Declamation 95, which concerns
a Jew who lent a Christian money, and was promised a pound of
flesh from the Christian's body if the debt was not paid on time.[79]
The speeches in this case may have suggested something to Shakespeare for his famous trial scene in *The Merchant of Venice*. If so,
the argument runs, Shakespeare's play could not have been written
before 1596, when *The Orator* was published.[80]

Piot wants these declamations to be used to develop rhetorical
skill. In his address to the reader at the beginning of his work, he
speaks as follows:

> In these thou maiest learne Rhethoricke to inforce a good cause, and
> art to impugne an ill. In these thou maiest behold the fruits and
> flowers of Eloquence, which as *Tully* saith in his Orator, *Bene con-*

[78] *The Orator*, pp. 326-332.   [79] *Ibid.*, pp. 400-406.
[80] For a brief reference to this matter, see William Allan Neilson and Charles Jarvis
Hill, *The Complete Plays and Poems of William Shakespeare* (Boston, 1942), p. 116.

stitutae ciuitatis est quasi alumna: Vse them to thy profit good Reader, and accept them with as good a mind as I present them with a vertuous intent. If thou studie law, they may helpe thy pleadings, or if diuinitie (the reformer of law) they may perfect they [sic] persuasions. In reasoning of priuate debates, here maiest thou find apt metaphors, in incouraging thy souldiours fit motiues . . . briefly euery priuate man may in this be partaker of a generall profit. . . .

Two formulary rhetorics of the seventeenth century will close my account of this branch of the counterreform. One of them was the work of John Clarke, the other, of Thomas Horne. Both were intended to circulate within the world of the schoolboy rather than in the world of the adult student as envisaged by Piot, Mundy, and Angel Day. Thus it should occasion no surprise that Clarke and Horne make more of an attempt than did Piot, Mundy, and Day to preserve important parts of the terminology of Ciceronian rhetoric in connection with their publishing of models for study and imitation.

Clarke's earliest contribution to formulary rhetoric was published at London in 1628 under the title, *Transitionum rhetoricarum formulae, in usum scholarum*; but that work was supplanted the next year by his *Formvlae Oratoriae*, a third edition of which was entered in the stationers' registers on June 1, 1629, with John Clarke designated as author and Thomas Farnaby as editor.[81] Clarke was master of the free school at Lincoln, and his *Formvlae Oratoriae* makes use of that circumstance by including a series of salutatory, valedictory, and eristical orations as given by students at that school.[82] The work also includes other types of speeches, as well as a series of formulas for introducing orations, for winning good will, for conciliating, for addressing one's adversary, for insinuating, moderating, explaining, partitioning, proving, citing testimony, objecting, refuting, concluding, recapitulating, arousing feeling, and making transitions.[83] In addition to these models, there is a preliminary section headed

[81] The earliest edition that I have seen is the fourth. Its title page reads: "Formvlae Oratoriae in usum scholarū concinnatae uná cum orationibvs Declamationibus &c Dé[que] collocatione oratoria et artificio demum Poetico, praeceptiunculis. Quarta Editio. . . . Impē Roberti Mylbourn in Caemiᵒ Paulino ad Insigᵉ. Canis Leporary. 1632." For the entry of the third edition with the Stationers, see Arber, *Transcript of the Registers*, IV, 212.—Clarke's *Transitionum Formulae* was entered with the stationers on March 31, 1628. See Arber, *Transcript of the Registers*, IV, 195.

[82] See *Formvlae Oratoriae* (1632), pp. 190 ff.

[83] For a comparison of Clarke's formulas with those of Lipsius, Alsted, and Farnaby, and for a sketch of formulary rhetoric in the seventeenth century, see Ray Nadeau, "Oratorical Formulas in Seventeenth-Century England," *The Quarterly Journal of Speech*, XXXVIII (1952), 149-154.

"Methodvs" in which epistles, themes, and declamations are classified and discussed. Epistles, for example, are classed as demonstrative, deliberative, and judicial, whereas demonstrative epistles are classed as narration-descriptions, laments, eulogies, and so on. Towards the end of the work as a whole, there is a section on making verses. With variety of this sort, we need not wonder that the *Formvlae Oratoriae* found a continuing place for itself in schoolboy life, and that by 1673 it was in its eleventh edition.[84]

Thomas Horne, whose *Rhetoricae Compendium* was mentioned in connection with my account of the English Ramists,[85] also made a contribution to formulary rhetoric in England by publishing at London in 1641 a work called Χειραγωγία *sive Manuductio in Aedem Palladis*.[86] The *Manuductio* is divided into three parts, one dealing with rhetorical preliminaries, another with precepts, and the third with examples.[87] The examples concern such themes as "On the Birthday of Christ, Savior of Humankind," "Lamentations on Christ's Passion," "In Annual Remembrance of the Consecration of Charles," "Virtue shines in Adversity," "Elizabeth Queen of the English," "Envy as Nurse of Evil," "A Friend as Another Self," and so on. But the section on precepts also contains examples of a briefer sort in the shape of formulas for such rhetorical operations as introducing speeches, expressing gratitude, rebuking an adversary, providing connections and transitions, exhorting, dissuading, supplicating, citing examples, referring to authorities, and stating conclusions.[88] In the first section of his work Horne maintains contact with the Ciceronian tradition by talking about invention and about the parts of the classical oration.[89] For the rest, there is nothing about the work to require attention, except for the interesting circumstance that Horne's Latin text is at one point interrupted so that for study and imitation he can present a few English models of sententious remarks, letters, and short speeches.[90]

John Newton, whose work on logic and rhetoric has been men-

[84] See Wing, *Short-Title Catalogue*, s.v. Clark, John.

[85] See above, p. 273.

[86] Its title page reads: "Χειραγωγία sive Manuductio in Aedem Palladis, Quâ utilissima methodus *Authores* bonos legendi indigitatur: Opera Th. Horne Art. Mag. Scholae Tunbridgiensis Archididascali . . . . Londini, Excudebat Rob. Young. 1641." My present discussion is based upon the Princeton University Library copy of the edition of this work at London in 1687.

[87] *Manuductio* (1687), pp. 1-54, 55-152, 153-208.

[88] *Ibid.*, pp. 71-92.

[89] *Ibid.*, pp. 26-29, 30-33; also p. 99.

[90] For these English examples, see pp. 102-110.

tioned above,[91] and who wanted to make the liberal arts available in English, expressed in 1671 an interesting verdict upon the formulary rhetorics of Clarke and Farnaby, and upon certain other aspects of rhetorical education in the seventeenth century. In the preface of his *Introduction to the Art of Rhetorick*, he castigates teachers who disparage the teaching of English to children, and he mentions the difficulty he himself had had as a schoolboy with rhetorical instruction as conducted in Latin. He observes: "I thought it hard my self, that I should be commanded to make a Theam before I had any other instructions for framing thereof than what *Clark's Formulae* or *Farnabie's Rhetorick* did afford me: As for the Oratorical part of *Butler's Rhetorick* it was to us like *terra incognita*, and it is well if it be otherwise yet. . . ."[92] Newton then speaks disparagingly of the things he had been forced to read in order to find subject matter for his themes. As he recalls how thoroughly he had neglected the books assigned to him, he remarks that he cannot but smile now at the cheats perpetrated by the boys against their masters. The boys, it would seem, went to Clarke's *Formulae* or Farnaby's *Index Rhetoricus* whenever they had to write a composition; and they proceeded to copy out an exordium from this place, a narration and confirmation from that, concealing their source in each case by some changes in phraseology. The remedy for such cribbing, Newton thought, was to teach boys to write in their own tongue and to delay their use of the formularies until they had some grounding in histories and moral discourses.

In concluding this sketch of Ciceronian rhetoric as it was adapted to the needs of Englishmen in the seventeenth century, I should like to mention two additional treatises that belong to my subject, not as formularies or as works upon Cicero's full program or upon style, but as works upon gesture and memory. Gesture is the sole concern of John Bulwer's *Chirologia . . . Chironomia*, published at London in 1644.[93] "Chironomia" is a word out of Quintilian meaning

---

[91] See pp. 271-272, 316-317.   [92] Sig. A5r-A5v.

[93] Its title page reads: "Chirologia: or the Natvrall Langvage of the Hand. Composed of the Speaking Motions, and Discoursing Gestures thereof. Whereunto is added Chironomia: Or, the Art of Manvall Rhetoricke. Consisting of the Naturall Expressions, digested by Art in the Hand, as the chiefest Instrument of Eloquence, By Historicall Manifesto's, Exemplified Out of the Authentique Registers of Common Life, and Civill Conversation. With Types, or Chyrograms: A long wish'd for illustration of this Argument. By J. B. Gent. Philochirosophus. *Manus membrum hominis loquacissimum.* London, Printed by *Tho. Harper,* and are to be sold by *R. Whitaker,* at his shop in Pauls Church-yard. 1644." The dedicatory epistle is signed "John Bulvver." The *Chirologia* covers 191

"the law of gesture,"[94] and Bulwer characterizes this law as "The Art of Manuall Rhetorique." Thus he sets forth, as he says, "the Canons, Lawes, Rites, Ordinances, and Institutes of Rhetoricians, both Ancient and Moderne, Touching the artificiall managing of the Hand in Speaking."[95] As for the "Chirologia," Bulwer interprets that as the natural language of the hand and body—that is, the meanings that writers have fixed upon such gestures as wringing the hands, shaking hands, kissing the hands, and so on. One of the most interesting things about Bulwer's work as a whole is that he attributes to Francis Bacon's *De Dignitate et Augmentis Scientiarum* the inspiration that produced it.[96] Another interesting thing about it is its connection with contemporary theories of acting.[97] Still another interesting thing about it is its illustrations, one of which precedes the title page and pictures "Eloquentia" as an open hand, "Logica" as a fist. An adaptation of this illustration appears on the title page of this present book.

The other additional treatise is called *The Art of Memory*, written by Marius D'Assigny, and published at London in 1697.[98] D'Assigny, who was of French extraction, had a considerable interest in rhetoric. In fact, his *Rhetorica Anglorum*, put out in 1699, was composed of oratorical exercises in sacred and ordinary rhetoric and of certain rules for the strengthening of weak memories.[99] His *Art of Memory*, dedicated "To the Young Students of both Universities," is a rather quaint treatise on man's faculty for remembering, and it contains much medical and psychological lore of its own day; but its final chapter, "Of Artificial or Fantastical Memory or Remembrance," is a restatement of the Ciceronian theory of places and images as an aid to recollection.[100] Thus did Ciceronian rhetoric continue to exert its influence to the very end of the period of my present study.

---

pages. The *Chironomia* has its own title page and separate pagination. It covers 147 pages.

[94] See *Institutio Oratoria*, I.11.17.

[95] These words are from the separate title page of the *Chironomia*.

[96] See *Chirologia* . . . . *Chironomia*, sig. A4v-A5v.

[97] For a discussion of this matter, see B. L. Joseph, *Elizabethan Acting* (Oxford, 1951). Joseph prints from Bulwer's *Chirologia* . . . . *Chironomia* several pages of illustrations of gestures; see pp. 4, 40, 42, 44, 46, 48.

[98] Its title page reads: "The Art of Memory. A Treatise useful for such as are to speak in Publick. By Marius D'Assigny, B. D. . . . London, Printed by *J. D.* for *Andr. Bell* at the Cross-Keys and Bible in *Cornhil*, near Stocks-market. 1697."

[99] See *Dictionary of National Biography*, s.v. D'Assigny, Marius (1643-1717), for the complete Latin title of this work.

[100] *Art of Memory*, pp. 82-91.

CHAPTER 6

New Horizons in Logic and Rhetoric

I. Descartes and the Port-Royalists

Ramus's campaign against the citadel of scholasticism was not conducted in the modern spirit, even if it is tempting to regard him as a direct forerunner of Bacon and Descartes. He was on the side of the moderns, to be sure, in his fervent belief that the scholastic theory of communication needed drastic revision if it was to satisfy the needs of a new era in human affairs. But when he came to formulate his conception of what those revisions should be, he hardly assumes the role of prophet of things to come. Indeed, his revisions seem now to be little more than a scholasticism with certain redundancies eliminated, certain terms discarded, certain procedures newly emphasized, and certain reorganizations effected. Thus he cut out of rhetoric all material that had previously received a logical as well as a rhetorical coverage, and he gave that material to logic alone. Thus also he cut out of grammar all things previously included in both rhetoric and grammar, and he gave those things entirely to rhetoric. Having made these three liberal arts severely independent of each other, he reorganized their precepts by using dichotomies as a presentational device and by adopting a descending order of generality as the grand principle of structure. In the field of logic, which was his own favorite subject, he gave new emphasis to the separation of that art into invention and arrangement; he discarded the predicables and the predicaments from logical theory; he reduced invention to a neat and convenient system of ten places; and finally he gave prominence to his own version of Aristotle's three laws of the proposition and to his own rigorous revision of the scholastic theory of method. These reforms are not unreasonable or unhelpful, nor did they prove unpopular. But nevertheless they do not provide a clue to the direction that logic was to take in the eighteenth and nineteenth centuries. In short, they are not the instruments of revolution.

The same observation holds true for the Systematics. They were on the side of the moderns in their belief that something had been wrong with the old scholasticism, and that Ramus had not entirely corrected it. But in their vision of reform they saw only the alternative of proceeding to improve scholasticism in the direction taken by Ramus or of proceeding to improve Ramism by a retreat towards scholasticism. Thus they accepted Ramus's emphasis on the theory of method and sought to improve and extend what he had done in that field. Thus they rejected his rejection of the predicables and the predicaments, with the result that these celebrated terms were restored to logical theory. Thus also they rejected Ramus's division of logic into invention and arrangement, preferring instead a scholastic division into terms, propositions, arguments, and fallacies. So far as the Systematics began to emphasize logical method as investigative no less than presentational, they were showing their awareness of the intellectual revolution that was taking place in the seventeenth century. But otherwise they were looking to the past, not the future.

Apart from the English Ramists and Systematics, who between themselves were responsible for most of the logical treatises produced in England during the seventeenth century, there was a movement that now demands some attention. That movement stemmed from one of the great works of the modern world, René Descartes's *Discours de la Méthode*; and it became influential in England when one of the most popular textbooks of all time, *The Port-Royal Logic*, began to appear at London presses in the closing decades of the seventeenth century. The *Discours de la Méthode* and *The Port-Royal Logic* are not the only forces behind the development of modern English logic, but they are the most important new forces to reveal themselves in logical treatises printed in England before 1700; and the earlier of them is perhaps the most illuminating of all the books that have to be read if we are to understand the nature of the difference between the medieval and the modern world. Speaking of Descartes's philosophy as a whole, and of the *Discours de la Méthode* in particular, Leon Roth well summarizes the importance of that work as follows: "It marks an epoch. It is the dividing line in the history of thought. Everything that came before it is old; everything that came after it is new."[1] These words, by the way, apply with special aptness to the *Discour de la Méthode* as a protest against the Ramists and the scholastics and as an anticipation of the logic of Port-Royal.

The *Discours de la Méthode* or *Discourse on Method* was pub-

[1] Leon Roth, *Descartes' Discourse on Method* (Oxford, 1937), p. 3.

lished in 1637,[2] when Descartes was forty-one years of age, and thus we may say that the new logic had its official beginning at that time. But Descartes tells us in that treatise that he was twenty-three when he first evolved his famous method and decided to make it the rule of his life.[3] Since Descartes became twenty-three on March 31, 1619, the new logic may be said to have been in existence for eighteen years before it finally reached the public, and to have had some kind of form before the publication of that great similar revolutionary document, Francis Bacon's *Novum Organum.*[4]

More of a spiritual autobiography than a formal exposition, the *Discourse* recounts how Descartes had become dissatisfied with the literary education he had received, and with the entire system of opinions which he (and the surrounding European community) held. That education had embraced the usual subjects: languages, fables, histories, eloquence, poetry, mathematics, morals, theology, jurisprudence, medicine, and philosophy.[5] As he describes these for us, and expresses his continuing respect for them and for his Jesuit teachers, we recognize an active note of distaste only in his account of philosophy, by which he obviously meant logic. He says of it that it "affords the means of discoursing with an appearance of truth on all matters, and commands the admiration of the more simple."[6] As for the respected beliefs which his education had given him, they seemed to him to rest more upon example and custom than upon reasoned conviction, and his faith in them began to wane. At this point (he was sixteen at the time and the year was 1612) he made a decision which might stand as the symbol of the decision made by mankind in turning from the medieval to the modern world: he decided to abandon old beliefs and to reconstitute his knowledge. Speaking of this decision and of the events that led to it, he says:

> For these reasons, as soon as my age permitted me to pass from under the control of my instructors, I entirely abandoned the study of letters, and resolved no longer to seek any other science than the knowledge of myself, or of the great book of the world. I spent the remainder of my youth in travelling, in visiting courts and armies, in holding

[2] *Ibid.*, pp. 13-16.
[3] René Descartes, *Discours de la Méthode*, ed. Étienne Gilson (Paris, 1925), p. 22.
[4] For a comparison of Bacon and Descartes on the subject of method, see Roth, *op. cit.*, pp. 52-71.
[5] John Veitch, trans. *The Method, Meditations, and Selections from the Principles of Descartes* (Edinburgh and London, 1887), pp. 5-11.
[6] *Ibid.*, p. 7.

intercourse with men of different dispositions and ranks, in collecting varied experience, in proving myself in the different situations into which fortune threw me, and, above all, in making such reflection on the matter of my experience as to secure my improvement.[7]

Descartes's reflection upon the matter of his experience during the next seven years produced at length his famous method. That method was his personal prescription for the reconstituting of his own knowledge, and it consisted of four maxims. He states them thus:

The *first* was never to accept anything for true which I did not clearly know to be such; that is to say, carefully to avoid precipitancy and prejudice, and to comprise nothing more in my judgment than what was presented to my mind so clearly and distinctly as to exclude all ground of doubt.

The *second*, to divide each of the difficulties under examination into as many parts as possible, and as might be necessary for its adequate solution.

The *third*, to conduct my thoughts in such order that, by commencing with objects the simplest and easiest to know, I might ascend by little and little, and, as it were, step by step, to the knowledge of the more complex; assigning in thought a certain order even to those objects which in their own nature do not stand in a relation of antecedence and sequence.

And the *last*, in every case to make enumerations so complete, and reviews so general, that I might be assured that nothing was omitted.[8]

As a prudent reformer, who understood that man cannot live without belief and that the abandonment of belief is not something to be casually undertaken or irreverently executed, Descartes sought to caution the public against the injudicious application of his method to their own lives. "I have never contemplated anything higher," he insists, "than the reformation of my own opinions, and basing them on a foundation wholly my own."[9] "The single design to strip one's self of all past beliefs," he adds, "is one that ought not to be taken by every one."[10] He even acknowledges that he had to protect himself against the chaos of disbelief by evolving and using a provisory code of morals for his own guidance during the interval between his rejection of the old and his acceptance of the new. That provisory code is his subject in Part III of his *Discourse*, and its first article is that he did not permit himself to abandon his faith in God.[11]

[7] *Ibid.*, p. 10. [8] *Ibid.*, p. 19. [9] *Ibid.*, pp. 15-16.
[10] *Ibid.*, p. 16. [11] *Ibid.*, p. 23.

The remaining sections of the *Discourse* represent Descartes's attempt to build a new world for himself. Part IV, it will be recalled, contains his celebrated argument, "je pense, donc je suis," which becomes the first principle of his new philosophy and also the basis for his proof of the existence of God.[12] In Part V he presents a summary of a treatise he had prepared in the course of applying his four maxims to the study of the world and man; and this summary is an interesting indication of the structure and content of the new science he is working to create. A memorable feature of this section of the *Discourse* is his tribute to Harvey for the latter's discovery of the circulation of the blood.[13] In Part VI, his concluding section, Descartes explains at some length why his *Discourse* and the three treatises accompanying it in its first edition are being offered to the public in place of the treatise which he had presented in summary. At moments during this explanation he seems particularly close to the modern world, as for example when he mentions that the new science will have the power to "render ourselves the lords and possessors of nature."[14] Most prophetic of all are his remarks about the future of medicine.

> It is true [he says] that the science of Medicine, as it now exists, contains few things whose utility is very remarkable: but without any wish to depreciate it, I am confident that there is no one, even among those whose profession it is, who does not admit that all at present known in it is almost nothing in comparison of what remains to be discovered; and that we could free ourselves from an infinity of maladies of body as well as of mind, and perhaps also even from the debility of age, if we had sufficiently ample knowledge of their causes, and of all the remedies provided for us by Nature.[15]

Turning now to the consideration of the *Discourse* as a pivotal event in the history of logic, I should like to point out that it breaks with the past in at least three important ways. A discussion of each of them at this point will introduce us to several of the unusual aspects of *The Port-Royal Logic* and will indicate much of what the new logic was to be.

In the first place, Descartes's *Discourse* calls for a logic that will accept experiment rather than disputation as the chief instrument in the quest for truth. The logic of the scholastics and the Ramists had

---

[12] For Descartes's statement of his first principle, see *Discours*, ed. Gilson, p. 32.
[13] *Ibid.*, pp. 50, 407-408.   [14] Veitch, *op. cit.*, p. 61.
[15] *Ibid.*, p. 61.

been a logic of learned disputation. That is to say, it had been a logic for the conduct of disputes, and its great unwritten assumption was that by conducting disputes man could detect error and establish truth. Descartes's disagreement with this assumption is sharp and uncompromising. In considering whether the scientist gains an advantage from publishing his discoveries and having them subjected to controversy, Descartes indicates that in his own case his critics had not been of assistance. Of disputation in general he then says this:

> And further, I have never observed that any truth before unknown has been brought to light by the disputations that are practised in the Schools; for while each strives for the victory, each is much more occupied in making the best of mere verisimilitude, than in weighing the reasons on both sides of the question; and those who have been long good advocates are not afterwards on that account the better judges.[16]

But the scientist does gain an advantage from publishing his discoveries and having them verified and extended by the experiments that others will thereupon be induced to make. In fact, Descartes reveals that this very consideration is a powerful factor in impelling him to publish the *Discourse* and the three treatises that accompany it.[17] Private and personal as this decision may appear to be, it stands nevertheless in relation to the great intellectual change that took place in the seventeenth century—a change in which disputation lost its monopoly as an instrument for the pursuit of truth, and came rather to be regarded as an adjunct to the experimental approach.

In the second place, Descartes's *Discourse* calls for a logic that will be a theory of inquiry rather than a theory of communication. The logic of the scholastics and the Ramists had been formulated as an instrument for the transfer of knowledge from expert to expert. Thus invention was construed, not as the process of discovering what had been hitherto unknown, but as the process of establishing contact with the known, so that the storehouse of ancient wisdom would yield its treasures upon demand, and would bring the old truth to bear upon the new situation. The ten places of Ramus, and the ten categories of Aristotle as interpreted by the scholastics, were devices for establishing contact between the new case and the old truth. Once he had established systematic contact between these two sets of realities, the learned man had the materials for communication,

<hr>

[16] *Ibid.*, p. 67.   [17] *Ibid.*, p. 73.

and his next problem was to arrange those materials for presentation. This problem was solved by the scholastic and the Ramistic theory of method. Method to these logicians was not a method of inquiry but a method of organization. Thus Ramus's natural method required that the more general statement should have precedence over the less general whenever ideas were arranged into formal treatises. But how were those general statements found in the first place? Ramus found them in custom and example, but Descartes could not find them there, inasmuch as his original loss of belief occurred because all knowledge found in custom and example seemed to him doubtful or erroneous. Thus Descartes had to evolve a new sort of method—a method of inquiry. In evolving this method, he had turned first, he says, to the logicians, only to find them inadequate. Of their science he has this to say:

> But, on examination, I found that, as for Logic, its syllogisms and the majority of its other precepts are of avail rather in the communication of what we already know, or even as the Art of Lully, in speaking without judgment of things of which we are ignorant, than in the investigation of the unknown; and although this Science contains indeed a number of correct and very excellent precepts, there are, nevertheless, so many others, and these either injurious or superfluous, mingled with the former, that it is almost quite as difficult to effect a severance of the true from the false as it is to extract a Diana or a Minerva from a rough block of marble.[18]

This criticism provides the context for Descartes's announcement of the four maxims that make up his method. These four maxims bear upon the investigation of the unknown, but the third in particular embodies Descartes's whole concept of investigative procedure, and that maxim requires the investigator to proceed from the simplest and easiest truths towards the more complex. Such a procedure stands in sharp contrast to Ramistic method, which began with the most general and proceeded towards the most particular. It should be noticed, however, that Descartes's theory of method, although opposed to Ramus's theory, is not unlike that of Smith, Sanderson, and certain other Systematics, who, as I have shown, thought of method in its investigative aspects.[19] Nevertheless, Descartes differs from the Systematics in refusing to allow presentational method a place in logic. In this respect he was more modern than they—and indeed more modern than the Port-Royalists.

[18] *Ibid.*, p. 18.   [19] See above, pp. 289, 297, 306.

In the third place, Descartes's *Discourse* calls for a logic of practical as distinguished from speculative science. By practical he meant actually usable in life. Speaking of his new notions in the field of physics, and remarking upon the difference between them and the principles employed up to his time, he gives the following account of the meaning of his notions to science:

> For by them I perceived it to be possible to arrive at knowledge highly useful in life; and in room of the Speculative Philosophy usually taught in the Schools, to discover a Practical, by means of which, knowing the force and action of fire, water, air, the stars, the heavens, and all the other bodies that surround us, as distinctly as we know the various crafts of our artizans, we might also apply them in the same way to all the uses to which they are adapted, and thus render ourselves the lords and possessors of nature.[20]

A further indication of Descartes's conception of the science that would emerge from the use of his method is afforded when in the *Discourse* he speaks of the new science of man, and indulges immediately in a minute description of the functioning of the heart and arteries.[21] A practical science composed of minute descriptions of this sort would postulate induction as the basic logical procedure, and induction was to become the chief intellectual operation as discussed in the new logic. The chief intellectual operation of the old logic was syllogistic, even though induction was recognized as one of the forms of reasoning. And of course the science envisaged by the old logic was speculative rather than practical. For example, in Samuel Smith's *Aditvs ad Logicam*, which I examined as a specimen of the work of the Systematics, method is divided into two branches, the compositive and the resolutive, and the former of these, which is the method of going from part to whole, and which is not unlike Descartes's procedure from simpler to more complex, is useful only in what Smith calls the contemplative sciences, where things are examined for themselves, not for the sake of action.[22] Smith does not overlook the practical sciences, to be sure. In fact, he specifically applies the resolutive method to them. The difference between him and Descartes is that he sees speculative sciences emerging from the method of proceeding from the particular to the general, whereas Descartes sees practical sciences emerging from that same method.

[20] Veitch, *op. cit.*, pp. 60-61.
[21] *Ibid.*, pp. 46-54.
[22] See Smith, *Aditvs ad Logicam* (1627), sig. G2v-G3r.

It took many years for logic to change so as to incorporate within itself the three requirements that Descartes wanted it to have. Indeed, so far as English logic is concerned, these three requirements are completely met for the first time only when John Stuart Mill published his *System of Logic* at London in 1843. Mill's logic emphasizes experiment rather than disputation as the chief instrument in the pursuit of truth, his famous description of the four experimental methods of inquiry being an adequate illustration of that emphasis.[23] Mill's logic also stresses that this science is the instrument of inquiry rather than communication. Such stress appears first when Mill defines logic as "the science which treats of the operations of the human understanding in the pursuit of truth."[24] But it appears even more openly when he adds almost at once: "The sole object of Logic is the guidance of one's own thoughts: the communication of those thoughts to others falls under the consideration of Rhetoric, in the large sense in which that art was conceived by the ancients; or of the still more extensive art of Education."[25] As for an emphasis upon practical science and the inductive procedure, Mill's logic, with its celebrated denial that the syllogism is an adequate description of the process of inference, and with its corollary assertion that "All inference is from particulars to particulars,"[26] is more completely inductive, and more completely directed towards the practical and empirical than any preceding logic had been. In this respect, and indeed in the two others that I have just mentioned, Mill was influenced by many forces: by his opposition to Whately's *Logic*; by his acquaintance with the works of Newton, Whewell, and Herschel; by his discipleship in the utilitarian philosophy of his father and Bentham; and by his intimate familiarity with the development of English thought since Bacon. Thus his logical theory is not to be explained as a direct descendant of Descartes's *Discourse on Method*. But Descartes may be explained, nevertheless, as Mill's collateral ancestor, and the *Discourse*, as a necessary step in the transition from scholastic to modern logic.

Twenty-five years after the date of the first publication of the *Discourse*, a work called *La Logique, ou L'Art de Penser* appeared anonymously at Paris. This work came ultimately to be called the

---

[23] For that description, see John Stuart Mill, *A System of Logic, Ratiocinative and Inductive*, 4th edn. (London, 1856), I, 419-466.

[24] *Ibid.*, I, 4.

[25] *Ibid.*, I, 4-5.

[26] *Ibid.*, I, 206-231. The quotation is from p. 218.

Logique de Port-Royal in its own country and *The Port-Royal Logic* in England. Mill mentions it respectfully under the last of these titles, and credits it with having given logic a focus upon thinking, as distinguished from the old scholastic focus upon argumentation.[27] It enjoyed an almost unparalleled success in France and on the continent from 1662 to 1878, receiving a great many editions at Paris, and numerous others at Lyon, Amsterdam, Utrecht, Leiden, Halle, Basel, and Madrid. "One can say of this *Logic*," remarks an enthusiastic eighteenth-century editor, "that it put into oblivion all those produced up to its time, and that not one of those produced afterwards has put *The Art of Thinking* into oblivion, although some of them have been very good."[28] Its great popularity in Europe, and its interesting connection with Descartes's *Discourse*, entitle it without question to a place in the history of continental logic. What makes it of interest in the history of English logic is that it had a great success in Britain before the seventeenth century had ended, and it was still being published at British presses two hundred years later. Between 1664 and 1700 it received eight London editions, one in its French text, four in Latin, and three in English.[29] Thereafter it was frequently reprinted in English up to the closing years of the nineteenth century.

The authors of this celebrated work were Antoine Arnauld and Pierre Nicole, the former of whom composed the first draft for circulation in manuscript, and the latter of whom helped to prepare the first printed edition and to expand the text for subsequent editions.[30] These two men were close associates in a group of mystics and reformers congregated at Port-Royal near Paris. Theologically this group subscribed to the principles of Jansenism, and thus they sought to live by a high moral code and to spread such doctrines as that of the complete depravity of man, the actuality of predestination, and the impossibility of full atonement. The most famous of the Port-Royalists was Pascal. By his *Provincial Letters* and his *Thoughts on Religion* he made Jansenism an impressive force in France during

---

[27] *Ibid.*, I, 3-4.

[28] [G. Du Pac de Bellegarde and J. Hautefage], *Œuvres de Messire Antoine Arnauld* (Paris, 1775-1781), XLI, iv. Translation mine. Cited below as *Œuvres de Arnauld*.

[29] The French edition was published at London in 1664 as *Logique, ou l'Art de Penser*. There is a copy of it in Dr. Williams's Library, London. The Latin editions were published at London in 1674, 1677, 1682, and 1687, under the title, *Logica, sive ars cogitandi*. So far as the seventeenth century is concerned, the English editions appeared under the title, *Logic; Or, The Art of Thinking*, as follows: London, 1685, 1693, 1696.

[30] *Œuvres de Arnauld*, XLI, iv-v, 101-104.

the seventeenth century. In addition to their accomplishments in theology, the Port-Royalists believed in the reform of education, and to this end they arranged themselves against the methods used by the Jesuits and by the universities. The schools which they established came to be known as the little schools of Port-Royal, and two of the textbooks written to demonstrate their reforms became celebrated.[31] One was the *Grammaire Générale et Raisonnée*, later known as the *Grammaire de Port-Royal*, written by Antoine Arnauld and Claude Lancelot. The other was the work under consideration here.

The first English translators of *The Port-Royal Logic* are conscious of a certain originality in the work which they are making available to their countrymen. They emphasize this attitude in their first edition in a preface headed "The Translators to the Reader."[32] Here they mention how obscure, tedious, and useless logic has become; how the schoolmen have clogged and fettered reason with vain misapplications; how ordinary works on logic are shelters for the obstinate and vainglorious who refuse either to be beaten or convinced by argument; and how the remedy is provided by the famous author of the present treatise. He has recovered this art from night and confusion, continue the translators, and has cleared away the rubbish, the underbrush, the superfluous boughs, "so that now Logic may be said to appear like Truth it self, naked and delightful, as being freed from the *Pedantic* Dust of the Schools."[33] These sentiments, which might at first be mistaken for the self-interested exag-

[31] For a study of the educational methods and accomplishments of the Port-Royalists, see H. C. Barnard, *The Little Schools of Port-Royal* (Cambridge, 1913).

[32] Who these translators were I do not know. The title page of their first edition indicates that, "For the Excellency of the Matter," the *Logic* has been "Printed many times in *French* and *Latin*," and is "now for Publick Good translated into *English* by Several Hands." The best I can do is to suggest that one of the translators bears the initials J. L., and another, H. C. The initials J. L. appear in the stationers' registers under the date of April 2, 1674, where *The Art of Thinking* is entered for publication as "*a new System of Logick, written originally in French by Monsieur* le Bon *and done into English by* J. L." See *Transcript of the Registers*, ed. Eyre and Rivington, II, 479. Monsieur Le Bon was the person originally granted the privilege of publishing the *Logic* in its French text in Paris. See Graesse, *Trésor*, s.v. Logique. But J. L. remains unidentified. As for the initials H. C., they appear as the signature on the dedicatory epistle of the translation of Aristotle's *Rhetoric* published at London in 1686; and they connect their owner with our *Logic* because the title page of that translation of Aristotle says that the *Rhetoric* was "Made English by the translators of the Art of Thinking." H. C., however, does not reveal anything about himself in his dedicatory epistle, which is addressed to Henry Sydney, once ambassador to Holland, and later a prominent figure in the government of William and Mary.—The second English translation of the *Logic* was done by John Ozell and was published at London in 1717. The third translation, by Thomas Spencer Baynes, appeared at Edinburgh in 1850.

[33] *Logic; Or, The Art of Thinking* (London, 1685), sig. A3v.

gerations of commerce, turned out to correspond with the detached judgment of scholarship.

One dominant feature of *The Port-Royal Logic* is its lack of enthusiasm for the logical theory of the scholastics. It pays a tribute to Aristotle by acknowledging his "very vast and comprehensive mind," and by admitting the debt of all subsequent logicians to his analysis of the syllogism and of demonstration. In this latter connection the Port-Royalists say: "And whatever confusion may be found in his Analytics, it must be confessed, nevertheless, that almost all that we know of the rules of logic is taken thence; so that there is, in fact, no author from whom we have borrowed more in this Logic than from Aristotle."[34] But the borrowings of the Port-Royalists from Aristotle are not always complimentary. Here and there they cite Aristotle's definitions and reasonings as examples of things to avoid.[35] And while they deny that it is their intention to do him dishonor by such means,[36] they refuse throughout their work to defer to his authority upon any matter when reason counsels otherwise. Indeed, they state as a kind of thesis that "there is no ground whatever in human sciences, which profess to be founded only on reason, for being enslaved by authority contrary to reason."[37] And in accordance with it they contend that the ten categories, those great concepts of scholastic logic, "are in themselves of very little use, and not only do not contribute much to form the judgment, which is the end of true logic, but often are very injurious, for two reasons, which it is important to remark."[38] Their two reasons are to the effect that the categories are arbitrary man-made conventions rather than ultimate truths, and that they lead men to be satisfied with verbal formulations rather than with a distinct knowledge of things. Despite these objections, however, the Port-Royalists admit the ten categories into their logic as being "short, easy, and common";[39] and they devote a brief perfunctory chapter to them.[40] They also devote a brief perfunctory chapter to another great concept of scholastic logic, the five predicables, saying as they dismiss them, "This is more than sufficient

---

[34] Thomas Spencer Baynes, trans. *The Port-Royal Logic,* 8th edn. (Edinburgh and London [188?]), p. 21. Here and below I have cited Baynes's translation rather than that of 1685. Baynes took his duties as translator much more seriously than the original translators did, and thus his text can be used with almost no amendments, whereas many amendments and various time-consuming explanations would have to be made in connection with any conscientious use of the earliest English version.

[35] For examples, see Baynes, pp. 168-169, 252.

[36] *Ibid.,* pp. 20-21.   [37] *Ibid.,* p. 23.   [38] *Ibid.,* p. 40.

[39] *Ibid.,* p. 8.   [40] *Ibid.,* pp. 39-42.

touching the five universals, which are treated at such length in the schools."[41] As for the rules of the syllogism, the figures and modes of the syllogism, and the grand principle for judging the correctness of a syllogism, these topics are also included, but are admitted by the Port-Royalists to be of little use, despite the traditional emphasis upon them.[42] If to these examples of reluctance on the part of the Port-Royalists to endorse scholastic logic we add their slighting references to such favorite terms of the Systematics as "second intentions" and the like,[43] we get the impression that in their view a great part of traditional logical theory has lost its utility.

Another dominant feature of the logic of the Port-Royalists is their firm but respectful rejection of several important features of the logical theory of the Ramists.[44] In fact, the references of Arnauld and Nicole to Ramus and his disciples are so numerous as to indicate that Ramism had made a profound impression in logical circles in France, and that its influence was still felt by Frenchmen in the second half of the seventeenth century. Some of these references are concealed, but many are open and direct, as if the Port-Royalists wanted their criticisms of Ramism to be more than an attempt to slay the slain.

The concealed rejection of one feature of Ramism occurs when the Port-Royalists justify the definition of logic implied in the original title of their work. This original title, *La Logique, ou L'Art de Penser*, shocked certain persons when the work appeared at Paris in 1662, their objection being that they considered logic to be the art of reasoning well rather than the art of thinking. In the second and all later editions of the work appears a preliminary chapter headed

[41] *Ibid.*, p. 55.

[42] *Œuvres de Arnauld*, XLI, 258. For some reason Baynes does not include in his translation a reference to the note in the French text at the beginning of Part III, Ch. 3, saying, "This chapter and the following, up to the twelfth, are among those which we mentioned in the Discourse [that is, in the first of the two discourses prefixed to the text of *The Port-Royal Logic*] as containing things which are subtle and necessary for logical speculation but which are of little use." These nine chapters are devoted to the rules, the figures, and the modes of the syllogism.

[43] For these slighting references, see Baynes, pp. 10-11. "Words of the first Intention are those, whereby any thing is signified or named by the purpose and meaning of the first Author or Inuentor thereof, in any speech or language whatsoeuer it be: as the beast whereon wee commonly ride, is called in English a *Horse*, in Latine *Equus*, in Italian *Cauallo*, in French, *Cheual*. Words of the second Intention are termes of Art, as a Noune, Pronoune, Verbe, or Participle, are termes of Grammar: likewise *Genus*, *Species*, *Proprium*, and such like, are termes of Logicke." Thus speaks Thomas Blundeville, *The Arte of Logicke* (1619), pp. 3-4.

[44] My present discussion of this matter parallels that in my *Fénelon's Dialogues on Eloquence* (Princeton, 1951), pp. 25-33.

"Second Discours," in which the authors reply to their critics and
have this to say of the objection just stated:

> We have found some persons who are dissatisfied with the title, *The
> art of thinking,* instead of which they would have us put, *The art of
> reasoning well.* But we request these objectors to consider that, since
> the end of logic is to give rules for all the operations of the mind,
> and thus as well for simple ideas as for judgment and reasonings,
> there was scarcely any other word which included all these operations:
> and the word *thought* certainly comprehends them all; for simple
> ideas are thoughts, judgments are thoughts, and reasonings are
> thoughts. It is true that we might have said, *The art of thinking well*;
> but this addition was not necessary, since it was already sufficiently
> indicated by the word *art,* which signifies, of itself, a method of doing
> something well, as Aristotle himself remarks. Hence it is that it is
> enough to say, the art of painting, the art of reckoning, because it is
> supposed that there is no need of art in order to paint ill, or reckon
> wrongly.[45]

Reasoning or arguing had been a component of the scholastic and
the Ramistic conception of logic, and thus the insistence of the Port-
Royalists upon thinking is an answer to both of these schools; but
their insistence upon the exclusion of "well" suggests by its length
and seriousness that something had happened to give this adverb a
special place in the theory of logic, and that special measures are
necessary to dislodge it. What had happened, of course, was that
Ramus had made the word a part of all of his definitions of the liberal arts.[46] Indeed, his emphasis upon it had taken such a hold that
the Port-Royalists used the heavy artillery of Aristotle's authority
against it, even though they did not always defer in their own minds
to that authority.

A second feature of Ramistic logic, and a very important feature
indeed, is rejected quite openly by the Port-Royalists. This feature
comprehends Ramus's interpretation of the doctrine of places. As we
know, Ramus had equated the doctrine of the places or seats of
argument with the doctrine of invention, and had made invention
first of the two parts of logic. The Port-Royalists say that these
places, like the ten categories of scholastic logic, are of little use.[47]

[45] Baynes, pp. 14-15.   [46] See above, p. 151.

[47] They make this remark about the categories and the places in the first of their two
preliminary discourses. Their words are: "Il y avoit d'autres choses qu'on jugeoit assez
inutiles; comme les catégories & les lieux. . . ." See *Œuvres de Arnauld,* XLI, 111.
Baynes's translation of this passage (*op. cit.,* p. 8) is inaccurate so far as the word

Moreover, they reject Ramus's argument for treating the places as the first part of logic. Their words are:

> Ramus, on this subject, reproached Aristotle, and the philosophers of the schools, because they treated of places *after* having given the rules of argumentation, and he maintained against them that it was necessary to explain the places, and what pertains to invention, *before* treating of these rules.
>
> The reason Ramus assigns for this is, that we must have the matter found, before we can think of arranging it.
>
> Now the exposition of places teaches us to find this matter, whereas the rules of reasoning can only teach us arrangement.
>
> But this reason is very feeble, for although it be necessary for the matter to be found, in order to [arrange it], it is nevertheless not necessary that we should learn how to find the matter before having learnt how to dispose it.[48]

The Port-Royalists then widen their attack on the places so as to include Cicero, Quintilian, and Aristotle among those who advocated that method of finding subject matter. Despite the celebrity of such sponsors, say Arnauld and Nicole, general experience proves the places to be of little real value. Here is the supporting argument:

> We may adduce, as evidence of this, almost as many persons as have passed through the ordinary course of study, and who have learned, by this artificial method, to find out the proofs which are taught in the colleges. For is there any one of them who could say truly, that when he has been obliged to discuss any subject, he has reflected on these places, and has sought there the reasons which were necessary for his purpose? Consult all the advocates and preachers in the world, all who speak and write, and who always have matter enough, and I question if one could be found who had ever thought of making an argument *a causa, ab affectu, ab adjunctis*, in order to prove that which he wished to establish.[49]

As if the doctrine of the places were so firmly entrenched in men's minds as to require still more drastic assaults, the Port-Royalists

---

"lieux" is concerned. He renders the passage thus: "There are other things which we deem sufficiently profitless; such as the categories and the laws. . . ."

[48] Baynes, pp. 236-237. The amendment in brackets is dictated by the French text. See *Œuvres de Arnauld*, XLI, 302. Baynes's "in order to its arrangement" seems less well adapted to the original.

[49] Baynes, p. 238.

narrow the attack once more to the sector occupied by Ramus. They
quote the speech that Virgil in the *Aeneid* puts into the mouth of
Nisus as the latter's friend Euryalus stands surrounded by enemies
bent on vengeance. Then they observe sarcastically:

> "This is an argument," says Ramus, "*a causa efficiente.*" We may,
> however, judge with certainty, that Virgil, when he wrote these verses,
> never dreamt of the place of efficient cause. He would never have
> made them had he stopped to search out that place; and it was neces-
> sary for him, in order to produce such noble and spirited verses, not
> only to forget these rules, if he knew them, but in some sort also to
> forget himself, in order to realize the passion which he portrayed.[50]

After this bombardment of Ramus and the scholastics, during which
we can plainly see that the doctrine of the places is doomed to ultimate extinction, the Port-Royalists suddenly cease their firing, and
allow the places to come back into logic under a flag of truce. But
Arnauld and Nicole explain the doctrine with cold brevity, and they
specifically refuse to treat it according to the plan followed by Cicero,
by Quintilian, and by Ramus. They say that the plan of Cicero and
Quintilian is not methodical enough, whereas "that of Ramus is too
embarrassed with subdivisions."[51] Instead of these, they choose to
follow the very recent plan proposed by the German philosopher
Clauberg.[52]

A third feature of Ramistic logic is rejected by the Port-Royalists
in connection with the method they follow in their own work and
recommend for others. Ramus had decreed that a subject should be
divided into distinct parts, and that material belonging more to one
part than another should not be allowed to appear except in that one
part. This rule is rejected by the Port-Royalists when they explain
in the first of their preliminary discourses what method they themselves have followed. They say:

> It is right, also, to mention that we have not always followed the
> rules of a method perfectly exact, having placed many things in the
> Fourth Part which ought to have been referred to the Second and
> Third; but we did this advisedly, because we judged that it would
> be useful to consider in the same place all that was necessary in order
> to render a science perfect; and this is the main business of method,
> which is treated of in the Fourth Part. For this reason, also, we re-

[50] *Ibid.*, p. 239.   [51] *Ibid.*, p. 241.
[52] For a note on the Port-Royalists and Clauberg, see Baynes, p. 416.

served what was to be said of axioms and demonstrations for the same place.[53]

Later, when the Port-Royalists speak of the problem of dividing wholes into parts, they accept Ramus's view as merely advisory rather than compulsive. Here are their exact words:

> Ramus and his followers have laboured very hard to show that no divisions ought to have more than *two members*, [dichotomy]. When this may be done conveniently, it is better; but clearness and ease being that which ought first to be considered in the sciences, we ought not to reject divisions into three members, and especially when they are more natural, and when it would require forced subdivisions in order to reduce them to two members. For thus, instead of relieving the mind, which is the principal end of division, we should load it with a great number of subdivisions, which it is much more difficult to retain than if we had made at once more members in that which we divide. For example, is it not more short, simple, and natural, to say, *All extension is either line, or superficies, or solid*, than to say with Ramus, *Magnitudo est linea, vel lineatum; lineatum est superficies, vel solidum?*[54]

The theory that a subject may be divided into as many as four parts rather than the two advocated by the Ramists is espoused by the Port-Royalists themselves when they speak of logic as made up of conceiving, judging, reasoning, and disposing.[55] And when they come to discuss method, they divide it into analysis and synthesis, making the former relate to the discovery of truth, the latter, to the presentation of truth to others.[56] Ramus, it will be recalled, spoke also of two methods, but both of his related to the presentation of truth.[57] Thus the Port-Royalists extend Ramus's theory by adding something to it, and that something consists explicitly in their mentioning Descartes and in their recommending as a foundation of all method the four rules propounded in his *Discourse*.[58] In fact, Descartes is given credit for much of the rest of what the Port-Royalists say on the subject of method in inquiry.[59] It must be conceded that the Port-Royalists are not so far committed to Descartes as flatly to reject the idea of a logic that speculates upon the method of presenting truth to others. Instead, they tend to retreat in this respect from the advanced outpost of Cartesianism—they tend, in other words, to go back to

[53] *Ibid.*, p. 12.   [54] *Ibid.*, pp. 165-166. The bracketed word is in Baynes.
[55] *Ibid.*, p. 25.   [56] *Ibid.*, pp. 308-323.   [57] See above, pp. 160-165.
[58] Baynes, pp. 315-316.   [59] See *Œuvres de Arnauld*, XLI, 362, note (a).

the Systematics when they allow logical theory to deal with the method of presentation as well as with the method of inquiry. Thus they show signs of conservatism and caution. They show signs of not yet being willing to limit logical method to the discovery of new truth, of not yet being willing to require rhetorical theory to take charge once more of the theory of presentation; but while in each of these respects they are not in line with the later views of Mill, they are still in the forefront of the logical speculation of the seventeenth century.

A fourth feature of Ramistic logic is rejected by the Port-Royalists when they refuse to follow the dictates of Ramus's law of justice. This law, as we know, required that each science should keep rigidly to its own subject matter and should touch nothing belonging to other sciences.[60] In applying this law, Ramus had refused to allow both logic and rhetoric to speculate upon invention and arrangement, or to allow both rhetoric and grammar to speculate upon the tropes and the figures. He had decreed instead that logic must be the sole science of invention and arrangement, rhetoric the sole science of style and delivery. And when he and Talaeus carried out this decree, they were careful to exclude all logical content from the theory of rhetoric, all rhetorical content from the theory of logic. The Port-Royalists show their impatience with this rule in the first of the two preliminary discourses which are attached to their work. Speaking there of certain subjects not treated within their logical theory, they remark that those subjects belong properly to metaphysics. As if this statement implied a conformity to Ramus's law of justice, they go on to explain that the subjects in question are omitted as being held in low esteem by everyone. In the course of this explanation, they affirm their own belief in mentioning in logic any subject whatever that is useful in forming the judgment. And they say the following with Ramus expressly in mind:

> The arrangement of our different knowledges is free as that of the letters in a printing office,—each has the right of arranging them in different classes according to his need, so that, in doing this, the most natural manner be observed. If a matter be useful, we may avail ourselves of it, and regard it, not as foreign, but as pertinent to the subject. This explains how it is that a number of things will be found here from physics and from morals, and almost as much of metaphysics as it is necessary to know, though in this we do not profess to have

[60] See above, pp. 151-152.

borrowed anything from any one. All that is of service in logic belongs to it; and it is quite ridiculous to see the trouble that some authors have given themselves—as Ramus and the Ramists—though otherwise very able men, who have taken as much pains to limit the jurisdiction of each science, and to prevent them from trespassing on each other, as might be taken in marking out the boundaries of kingdoms, and determining the jurisdiction of parliaments.[61]

While the Port-Royalists were thus taking a stand against certain important aspects of Ramism, and were at the same time showing their reluctance to accept some of the most hallowed concepts of scholasticism, they did not lose the opportunity to express their profound indebtedness to Descartes. As I said a moment ago, they made open mention of his writings as they were propounding their theory of the method of inquiry. But on other occasions they refer to him almost as openly, even if our lack of familiarity with his works makes those references seem much less direct to us than to seventeenth-century readers. At one point the Port-Royalists identify him under a reference to "a celebrated philosopher of this age," and at once acknowledge his books as the source of much that was new in their own logic.[62] At another point, they cite him as "an author of the present time," quoting him there as having said "with great reason, that the logical rules of Aristotle serve only to prove to another that which we already know, but that the art of Lully only enables us to talk, without judgment, of that which we do not know."[63] At still another point, they refute the philosopher Gassendi by quoting against one of his views the celebrated proposition, "je pense, donc je suis," although they do not openly identify these words with Descartes.[64] This and the preceding references are sufficient evidences of the Cartesianism of the authors of *The Port-Royal Logic*. But there are many others. For example, the acceptance by the Port-Royalists of reason rather than authority as the court of highest appeal in science is not only the pervasive theme of their whole logical theory but also that of Descartes's intellectual life after he had lost faith in the sciences produced by authority. And, for another and final example, the Port-Royalists's use of the words "idea," "thought," and "thinking," is thoroughly Cartesian, as Baynes has indicated.[65]

What was the actual logic derived by the Port-Royalists from their reluctance towards scholasticism, their respectful repudiation

---

[61] Baynes, pp. 10-11. [62] *Ibid.*, pp. 7-8. [63] *Ibid.*, p. 41. Cf. Veitch, *op. cit.*, p. 18.
[64] *Œuvres de Arnauld*, XLI, 132; also Baynes, p. 33. [65] *Op. cit.*, pp. xxxvi-xxxvii.

of Ramus, and their warm admiration for Descartes and the new philosophy? This question can be answered only by a complete reading of *The Port-Royal Logic* itself. Anyone who undertakes that task will find himself rewarded, for the Port-Royalists have not lost their significance for us. In Part I of their work, they discuss the operation of the mind in conceiving, that is, in forming ideas and in attaching words to them. The student of what we call semantics will find this section of *The Port-Royal Logic* refreshingly modern. Part II deals with the mental operation of judging, that is, of putting ideas together, of affirming or denying one thing of another, of expressing ourselves in propositions. Part III deals with the act of reasoning. This operation involves the syllogism, which the Port-Royalists doubt to be as useful as it is generally supposed to be.[66] However, in their analysis of fallacies, particularly those common in civil life and ordinary discourse, they make perhaps their finest contribution to logical theory, and are as modern as today's newspaper.[67] Of the second of their two chapters on fallacies Baynes says:

> It contains a fine analysis of the inward sophisms of interest, passion, prejudice, and self-love, through which we are continually deceived, and is characterized throughout by a tone of high moral thoughtfulness, and a truly humane, just, and noble spirit. It is a part, therefore, which has naturally excited general attention, and called forth universal praise.[68]

Immediately after this remarkable chapter on fallacies stands Part IV, which describes the mental operation of disposing, that is, of ordering ideas, judgments, and reasonings, so as to obtain knowledge and to establish it for others. Here, too, there is much to command the attention of the modern reader, although we no longer regard logic as the science of the method of explaining all the other sciences, and thus as a branch of the art of communication.

By way of concluding my analysis of *The Port-Royal Logic*, I should like to say that it comes closer to the three requirements laid down by Descartes for this science than does any other logic of its time, whether French or English, and thus it deserves what its authors say of it when they offer it to the public as "this new logic."[69]

As for Descartes's strongly implied stipulation that logic must speculate upon the experimental as distinguished from the disputa-

[66] Baynes, p. 179.   [67] See Part III, Ch. 20; Baynes, pp. 266-297.
[68] Baynes, p. xxxv.   [69] *Ibid.*, p. 1.

tious approach to truth, the Port-Royalists are on his side. They do not mention disputation when they speak of the four operations that logic reflects upon, and of the three services that logic performs.[70] But they do mention the spirit of debate as an injurious vice, although they add that discussions cannot in general be censured and that, "provided they be rightly used, there is nothing which contributes more towards giving us different hints, both for finding the truth, and for recommending it to others."[71] Moreover, their attitude towards the value of the experimental approach to truth is well illustrated in their discussion of their own opinion of Aristotle. "And where is the philosopher," they ask at that point, "who is hardy enough to affirm that the swiftness of heavy things increases in the same ratio as their weight, since there is no one now who may not disprove this doctrine of Aristotle by letting fall from a high place very unequal weights, in the swiftness of which, nevertheless, there will be remarked very little difference?"[72]

Descartes's explicit stipulation that logic must speculate upon the method of finding truth rather than upon the method of imparting truth to others is accepted by the Port-Royalists only in part, as we have seen. They devote some time to the method of imparting truth to others, calling it the method of synthesis or composition or doctrine.[73] In this emphasis, at least, they are closer to the old outlook than to the new. But they reverse the situation in their discussion of the method of inquiry. There, instead of borrowing their precepts from the Systematics, who also had recognized this method, they borrow openly from Descartes, and quote his four famous rules in detail. Thus they give new impetus to the tendency that was to lead to Mill's removal of the theory of communication from logic. In other words, they emerge on this issue as more modern than the Systematics, even if they are less modern than Mill.

Descartes's requirement of a logic for practical as distinguished from speculative science is of real influence with the Port-Royalists, although their own professional interests are in theology and education rather than in physics or medicine, and thus they do not have the scientific learning necessary for a logic heavily illustrated from the inductive sciences. They insist that traditional logic is soon forgotten by students who have had to learn it, and they attribute this situation to the failure of logic to relate itself to common use. They

[70] *Ibid.*, pp. 25-26.   [71] *Ibid.*, p. 276.   [72] *Ibid.*, p. 23.
[73] *Ibid.*, pp. 309, 316-318.

observe at the same time that logic "exists for the very purpose of being an instrument to other sciences." They state their own intention of illustrating logic from the solid knowledges, "to the end that we might learn to judge of these sciences by logic, and to retain logic by means of these sciences."[74] Later they describe common logic as having the defect "that those who study it are accustomed to find out the nature of propositions or reasonings, only as they follow the order and arrangement according to which they are fashioned in the schools, which is often very different from that according to which they are fashioned in the world and in books—whether of eloquence, or of morals, or of other sciences."[75] They even express doubt in the value traditionally attached to the rules of the syllogism, as we have seen; and of induction they remark, "It is in this way that all our knowledge begins, since individual things present themselves to us before universals, although, afterwards, the universals help us to know the individual."[76] But this and other statements by the Port-Royalists do not make their logic an inductive practical logic as was that of Mill. For example, the excellent observation just quoted does not lead them to include induction under the analysis of reasoning. They include it instead as a topic in their first chapter on fallacies. Still, they are on the side of the future rather than the past in the inductive aspect of their logic, as in the other aspects, and thus they gave the seventeenth century a real intimation of things to come, and its best intimation, so far as England's logical theory is concerned, although they were conservative in the formulation of the new design.

[74] *Ibid.*, p. 16, for this and the previous quotations and paraphrases of this paragraph.
[75] *Ibid.*, p. 144.　　[76] *Ibid.*, p. 265.

II. Bacon, Lamy, Hobbes, and Glanvill

SEVENTEENTH-CENTURY England did not witness the publication of a rhetorical theory that could engage in serious competition with the two major theories described in the preceding chapters. In the period between 1600 and 1621, the English Ramists had almost no rivals among their own countrymen in the dissemination of rhetorical ideas; and from 1621 to 1700 the Neo-Ciceronians became more and more successful, at first as the competing, and later as the dominant, faction. But at the end of the century these two theories were still in possession of the field, and no new rhetoric had emerged in any well-formulated single treatise to declare itself the herald of a new era. Thus the history of English rhetoric in the seventeenth century does not openly present a development to match in modernity and freshness of approach the event that occurred in English logic when the famous work of the Port-Royalists began to appear at London presses and to assimilate itself into English learning. In fact, the last major episode in a history limited to my present subject and period would appear to have been already recorded, and the attempt to chronicle the emergence of a new rhetoric would seem to lack a sound factual basis.

Nevertheless, a new rhetoric that offers some parallel to the new logic of the Port-Royalists was in the making in England during the seventeenth century. It did not come into being as a single distinct work under single authorship, but it did emerge in outline in various English publications brought out between 1600 and 1700. Some of these publications were devoted directly to rhetoric. They have been reserved for this chapter of my history, not because they would have been completely out of place under earlier classifications, but because they offer some interesting hints as to a new rhetorical attitude and thus do not entirely belong to the old systems. Others of these publications were devoted to subjects not specifically rhetorical, among them being a famous appraisal of learning, a history of the new movements in science, some works in the field of logic, and some sharp criticisms of the contemporary English pulpit. All of these works, and the new rhetorical attitude suggested in them, will be my subject in the concluding pages of this book.

First of all, this new attitude consisted in the recognition that rhetoric must make herself the theory of learned as well as of popular communication, and that therefore rhetoric must become a fuller, a more inclusive, discipline than it had been with the Ciceronians. In Ciceronian terms, of course, rhetoric was limited to popular, and logic to learned, converse. Thus both sciences undertook to survey invention and arrangement, while rhetoric was forced also to survey style and delivery, her followers being required to face the public, and the public being in need of such aids to ready understanding as spectacular patterns of language and dramatic delivery. Zeno's comparison of logic to the closed fist and rhetoric to the open hand was in itself a way of saying that logic constituted the theory of discourse for the world of learning as rhetoric did for the world of practice and use. But there came a time when logic under the impetus of Descartes's teachings began to renounce its obligation to the theory of communication, and to affirm its obligation to the theory of inquiry. At that point it became inevitable that rhetoric would take over the obligation renounced by logic, for society always needs a complete theory of communication, and rhetoric always possesses some special equipment for the meeting of that need. Thus the new rhetoric of the seventeenth century is a development towards the idea that learned exposition as well as popular argument and exhortation is within its proper scope.

Francis Bacon, ordinarily considered as Descartes's only rival for the honor of being the father of modern philosophy, published his first great work, *The Advancement of Learning*, when Descartes was nine years of age. This work is one of the most remarkable of the modern era. It undertakes to defend learning against all those who discredit it; and it undertakes also to survey all branches of learning so that the strong disciplines may be identified, and the weaker ones carefully marked for further study and improvement. Bacon refers to this survey as "a general and faithful perambulation of learning, with an inquiry what parts thereof lie fresh and waste, and not improved and converted by the industry of man."[1] His inventory of the learned disciplines, his comments upon their adequacies and inadequacies, became the greatest native influence in English learning during the seventeenth century. So far as English logic of that period is concerned, Bacon is a less immediate influence than Descartes, because no English logic based directly upon his thinking appeared before 1700, whereas *The Port-Royal Logic* with its strong Cartesian outlook repeatedly appeared in England after 1664. Nevertheless, *The Advancement of Learning* contains suggestions which could have led

[1] See *The Works of Francis Bacon*, ed. Spedding, Ellis, and Heath, VI, 181. Cited as *Works of Bacon* hereafter.

to the same kind of logic that the Port-Royalists produced from Descartes's *Discourse*, had English logicians been inclined to move in that direction. In other respects, Bacon's work had tremendous consequences at home, particularly in its call for an experimental approach to knowledge and in its frank request for the development of new arts and sciences. Although it cannot be said to have proposed a complete new rhetoric, as distinguished from the Ciceronian and Ramistic systems then in existence, it did take a fresh look at the theory of communication, and it did indicate that rhetoric had obligations to learned as well as to popular discourse—obligations more comprehensive and vital than it had in the older systems.

According to *The Advancement of Learning*, all knowledge can be divided into history, poesy, and philosophy, the last of these categories being the complement of the human reason and the general head for all sciences, theological, natural, and humanistic.[2] When Bacon comes to speak of the humanistic sciences, and those in particular which concern man's mind as distinguished from his body, he dwells at some length upon four great intellectual arts, and these arts he calls invention, judgment, memory, and elocution.[3] These are four of the five great arts that Cicero had associated with rhetoric. But to Bacon they are not so much the parts of a single discipline as the disciplines underlying all the various knowledges. In other words, as each scientist gains knowledge in his own field, and judges it, and records it, and transmits it, he deals not only with the knowledge of that field, but with the knowledges of gaining, judging, recording, and transmitting; and sooner or later he builds up wisdoms connected with these four processes as well as knowledge connected with his field. These four processes and the wisdoms built up from the contemplation of them are what Bacon discusses under the arts belonging to the four terms which he borrows from Ciceronian rhetoric. It is profoundly apparent that, while he is in one sense a traditionalist bent upon preserving these terms in a spirit of respect, he is in another sense an innovator bent upon enlarging their reference, revitalizing their meanings, and making them relate, not to the mere desire of a speaker to command subject matter, organization, memory, and delivery, but to the larger desire of scholarship to contribute to "the glory of the Creator and the relief of man's estate."[4] Thus Bacon's discussion of the four arts has a wider context than did the Ciceronian or scholastic discussion of them.

[2] *Ibid.*, VI, 182, 202, 207.   [3] *Ibid.*, VI, 260-261.   [4] *Ibid.*, VI, 134.

The wideness of this context is apparent when Bacon discusses invention as the first of these intellectual arts.[5] He sees at once that there must be two kinds of invention, one of which brings new arts and sciences into being, and the other of which helps us to find materials for speech and arguments. In other words, there must be one technique of invention for the discovery of something not known before, and another technique for the rediscovery of something previously known but temporarily forgotten. Bacon sees this second technique as a means of getting through to the traditional beliefs of the race, but not as a means of discovering new worlds. He says:

> The invention of speech or argument is not properly an invention: for to invent is to discover that we know not, and not to recover or resummon that which we already know; and the use of this invention is no other but *out of the knowledge whereof our mind is already possessed, to draw forth or call before us that which may be pertinent to the purpose which we take into our consideration.* So as, to speak truly, it is no *Invention*, but a *Remembrance* or *Suggestion*, with an application; which is the cause why the schools do place it after judgment, as subsequent and not precedent. Nevertheless, because we do account it a Chase as well of deer in an inclosed park as in a forest at large, and that it hath already obtained the name, let it be called invention: so as it be perceived and discerned, that the scope and end of this invention is readiness and present use of our knowledge, and not addition or amplification thereof.[6]

In his subsequent discussion of the invention of speech and arguments, Bacon speaks respectfully of promptuaries and topics as aids to the resummoning of the knowledge we already have; and although he recognizes that logic as well as rhetoric has claimed the former as well as the latter of these aids, he does not hesitate to give the promptuaries or rhetorical places back to rhetoric.[7] In this particular he is siding with Ciceronian rhetoric against the Ramists. But in his vision of invention as the discovery of something hitherto undiscovered, and in his promise to do a subsequent work on the invention of sciences,[8] he is anticipating Descartes and the Port-Royalists, and is taking the side of the new logic against Ramism and scholasticism.

Bacon's discussion of judgment as the second of the four intellectual arts is in fact a brief discussion of logic. He speaks here of

[5] *Ibid.*, VI, 261-272.   [6] *Ibid.*, VI, 268-269.   [7] *Ibid.*, VI, 269-270.
[8] *Ibid.*, VI, 268.

induction, syllogism, and fallacies.[9] The last of these subjects is so handled by him as to constitute the beginnings of what came to be famous as his doctrine of Idols. As for induction and syllogism, he speaks of the former as being the process of judging immediately from the evidence of the senses, whereas the latter is the process of judging through a middle term.

Two observations may be made at this time about Bacon's discussion of memory, the third of the great intellectual arts.[10] First of all, he thinks of memory in a wide sense as the whole process of storing up what has been invented and judged, and thus he includes within it the art of making written records. Secondly, he thinks of memory in the narrow sense as the process of storing up knowledge in the human mind. As he discusses this latter aspect of the custody or retaining of knowledge, he mentions with some contempt the artificial memory system of ancient rhetoric, with its places and images. His comment upon that system runs as follows: "It is certain the art (as it is) may be raised to points of ostentation prodigious: but in use (as it is now managed) it is barren; not burdensome nor dangerous to natural memory, as is imagined, but barren; that is, not dexterous to be applied to the serious use of business and occasions."[11]

The final one of the four great intellectual arts is first mentioned by Bacon as the art of elocution or tradition.[12] "Elocution" as he uses the term has initial reference to *elocutio*, that is, style, the third part of Ciceronian rhetoric, where the speaker or writer seeks to cover with words the thoughts that invention and arrangement have taught him to find and to organize. But in line with his policy of widening the context in which he uses the ancient terms, Bacon makes "elocution" the synonym of "tradition" in his first reference to the fourth intellectual art, and while it is not at once clear what he means by this second term, the reader naturally expects that it will turn out to mean more than style in rhetoric. In his later discussion of this art of elocution or tradition, he specifies that it covers the entire process of communication. The opening words of that discussion can be construed in no other way: "There remaineth the fourth kind of Rational Knowledge, which is transitive, concerning the expressing or transferring our knowledge to others; which I will term by the general name of Tradition or Delivery."[13] Delivery, as the fifth part

---

[9] *Ibid.*, VI, 272-280.   [10] *Ibid.*, VI, 280-282.   [11] *Ibid.*, VI, 281.
[12] *Ibid.*, VI, 261.   [13] *Ibid.*, VI, 282.

of Ciceronian rhetoric, means oral presentation or pronunciation. By using that term here, after having used elocution before in a similar connection, Bacon is saying that the fourth intellectual art takes over the functions of two parts of Ciceronian rhetoric, but that those functions are now conceived, less as style and delivery in the speech intended to persuade, than as the whole enterprise of expressing or transferring our knowledge to others in speech, in writing, in exposition, or in controversy. Here, then, is a concrete and eloquent recognition of an enlarged art of tradition or communication.

"Tradition," says Bacon, "hath three parts; the first concerning the *organ* of tradition; the second concerning the *method* of tradition; and the third concerning the *illustration* of tradition."[14] This partition requires him to speak of the organ of tradition as language, and he broadens language to mean spoken words, written words, hieroglyphics, gestures, and cyphers. The main discipline connected ·with this aspect of communication is grammar, to which Bacon devotes some attention. He then goes on to speak of the method and the illustration of tradition, and these two parts of communication as he explains them deserve a moment of attention in any history of English logic and rhetoric.

"For the Method of Tradition," remarks Bacon as he comes to this subject, "I see it hath moved a controversy in our time."[15] The controversy to which these words refer was undoubtedly that between Everard Digby and William Temple in the early fifteen-eighties over the question of Ramus's theory of method.[16] That controversy, of course, was merely one episode in the great European debate on the same question during the second half of the sixteenth century, and thus Bacon's words have a double reference. To Bacon, that debate had been unproductive. Remarking that "where there is much controversy there is many times little inquiry,"[17] he proceeds at once to announce that "this part of knowledge of method seemeth to me so weakly enquired as I shall report it deficient."

In remedying the deficiency which he finds in the theory of method as set forth in the controversy over Ramism, Bacon allows method to stand as a part of judgment in logical theory, and even gives the reasons for his stand, thus obviously implying his agreement with Ramus on this point. But Ramus had thought of method exclusively in terms of the delivery of knowledge from one expert to another or

---

[14] *Ibid.*, VI, 282-283.   [15] *Ibid.*, VI, 288.   [16] See above, pp. 194-196.
[17] *Works of Bacon*, VI, 288.

from expert to public, and had therefore committed himself to two divisions of method, the natural and the prudential. It is in respect to these cardinal tenets of Ramism that Bacon expresses disagreement, and his disagreement is made manifest, not by an open refutation of Ramus, but by the expression of a theory that urges method to consider how it may contribute to the advancement as well as to the mere delivery of learning. He says:

> Neither is the method or the nature of the tradition material only to the *use* of knowledge, but likewise to the *progression* of knowledge: for since the labour and life of one man cannot attain to perfection of knowledge, the wisdom of the Tradition is that which inspireth the felicity of continuance and proceeding. And therefore the most real diversity of method is of method referred to Use, and method referred to Progression; whereof the one may be termed Magistral, and the other of Probation.[18]

Thus does Bacon recommend two methods of presentation, one for the delivery of knowledge on the more elementary levels of instruction, and one for the delivery of knowledge between the scientist and the more adult section of the community. The words that immediately follow this recommendation have something to say of each method.

> For as knowledges are now delivered [Bacon adds], there is a kind of contract of error between the deliverer and the receiver: for he that delivereth knowledge desireth to deliver it in such form as may be best believed, and not as may be best examined; and he that receiveth knowledge desireth rather present satisfaction than expectant inquiry; and so rather not to doubt than not to err: glory making the author not to lay open his weakness, and sloth making the disciple not to know his strength.

Although Bacon's main theory of method is set forth in terms of his distinction between a magistral and a probationary presentation, he enumerates several other choices open to the deliverer of knowledge.[19] One of these choices is between the enigmatical and the exoteric method; another, between the aphoristic and the conventional method; another, between the method of assertion and proof and that of question and answer. In the course of his explanation of these

[18] *Ibid.*, VI, 289. For Bacon's earlier comment upon these two methods of delivery of knowledge, see VI, 133.
[19] *Ibid.*, VI, 290-296.

and other aspects of method, he pauses momentarily to praise and criticize Ramus in words to which I referred above;[20] and he takes pains to condemn as an imposture the method taught by Ramon Lull.[21] This entire section of *The Advancement of Learning* is important for rhetoric, because as rhetoric took over learned as well as popular communication, it needed a theory of expository organization to supplement its ancient theory of the six parts of the persuasive discourse, and Bacon's theory of the method of delivery tends to be an original contribution to the theory of exposition, as Ramus's had been in its day. It must be remembered, however, that Bacon did not consider method to be within the scope of rhetoric. He accepted instead the Ramistic belief that the method of presentation belonged to logic. Thus his contributions to expository method were not intended by him to contribute to the future of rhetoric, and in this respect he did not see beyond his time.

But he did see beyond his time when he discussed what was left to rhetoric after grammar had supplied the organ of communication and logic had supplied the method. Bacon saw rhetoric as the instrument which contributed to the delivery of knowledge by illuminating what was to be transmitted. He refers to this aspect of the fourth great intellectual art as "the Illustration of Tradition, comprehended in that science which we call Rhetoric, or Art of Eloquence; a science excellent, and excellently well laboured."[22] When Bacon calls rhetoric the illustration of tradition, the image behind his words is that of shedding light so as to make anything visible to the eyes. In other words, illustration within the context of the theory of communication would mean the shedding of light so as to make knowledge visible and hence deliverable to an audience. "It is a figure called Illustration," remarks John Marbecke in 1581, "by which the forme of things is so set foorth in words, that it seemeth rather to be seene with the eies, then heard with the eares."[23] This is what illustration meant to Bacon, and his theory of communication assigned to rhetoric the task of presenting the form of things so that they could be seen as if in a great light.

Thus it is that, as Bacon says, "The duty and office of Rhetoric is *to apply Reason to Imagination* for the better moving of the

[20] *Ibid.*, VI, 294-295. See above, p. 202.
[21] *Works of Bacon*, VI, 296.
[22] *Ibid.*, VI, 296.
[23] John Marbecke, *A Booke of Notes and Common places* (London, 1581), p. 491. My quotation is from *A New English Dictionary*, s.v. Illustration.

will."[24] Of great interest is the theory of persuasion involved in these words and almost at once explained by Bacon. It is an adaptation of the famous theory set forth in Plato's *Phaedrus*. As Bacon expounds it, the human will is conceived as a kingdom subject to domination by a coalition between two of three powerful rival kingdoms. One of these rivals is reason, which has certain natural advantages in her struggle to possess the will, and so would ordinarily be victorious against any single rival. Another of the rivals is passion or affection, a vast, unruly force, capable almost of possessing the will unaided. The third rival is imagination. Bacon believes that a coalition between imagination and passion would give these two powers control over the will, despite the natural superiority of reason to either one alone. So also would a coalition between imagination and reason, or between passion and reason, although this last coalition would rarely be likely to take place, the two parties being suspicious of each other. Within this atmosphere of warfare, sedition, and conspiracy, Bacon places rhetoric as a kind of diplomacy exerted to contract an alliance between reason and imagination so that man may live the rational life. Here is the crucial passage of his exposition:

> Again, if the affections in themselves were pliant and obedient to reason, it were true there should be no great use of persuasions and insinuations to the will, more than of naked propositions and proofs; but in regard of the continual mutinies and seditions of the affections, . . . reason would become captive and servile, if Eloquence of Persuasions did not practise and win the Imagination from the Affection's part, and contract a confederacy between the Reason and Imagination against the Affections. For the affections themselves carry ever an appetite to good, as reason doth; the difference is, that *the affection beholdeth merely the present; reason beholdeth the future and sum of time*; and therefore the present filling the imagination more, reason is commonly vanquished; but after that force of eloquence and persuasion hath made things future and remote appear as present, then upon the revolt of the imagination reason prevaileth.[25]

One outstanding fact about this conception of rhetoric is that it does not limit its own application merely to discourse addressed to the people. In the passage just quoted, Bacon intimates that, if the passions were obedient to the reason, the only persuasions that would be necessary are naked propositions and proofs, or in a word, cold logic. But he does not assume cold logic to be more of a force between

[24] *Works of Bacon*, VI, 297.   [25] *Ibid.*, VI, 299.

the learned man and the learned audience than it is between the speaker and the populace. On either level he suggests that passions are unruly, the imagination errant, the reason in danger of defeat. Thus rhetoric cannot be restricted to the popular sermon, the popular appeal, the popular exposition. She must be present in learned discourse as well. Bacon indicates the need in the learned community for the appeals of rhetoric when he speaks of the derision heaped upon Chrysippus and many of the Stoics for believing that subtle arguments addressed to reason were sufficient to control human behavior, and that learning could "thrust virtue upon men by sharp disputations and conclusions, which have no sympathy with the will of man."[26] And much earlier in *The Advancement of Learning* he analyzes the weaknesses of learned men, showing there that they as a class are not exempt from tendencies towards unreason, emotion, and prejudice.[27] The best proof, however, that Bacon does not limit rhetoric to popular discourse comes from *The Advancement of Learning* as a whole. For this work is a learned work, written by a learned man, for a learned community; but yet it does not disdain to be rhetorical in Bacon's own sense of that term—it addresses itself to the imagination and reason, and it seeks to transmit its message by shedding a great light upon it, by making it visible to the eyes. Many of its passages illustrate this quality, and none better than that in which Bacon summarizes the value of learning.

We see then [he says] how far the monuments of wit and learning are more durable than the monuments of power or of the hands. For have not the verses of Homer continued twenty-five hundred years or more, without the loss of a syllable or letter; during which time infinite palaces, temples, castles, cities, have been decayed and demolished? It is not possible to have the true pictures or statuaes of Cyrus, Alexander, Caesar, no nor of the kings or great personages of much later years; for the originals cannot last, and the copies cannot but leese of the life and truth. But the images of men's wits and knowledges remain in books, exempted from the wrong of time and capable of perpetual renovation. Neither are they fitly to be called images, because they generate still, and cast their seeds in the minds of others, provoking and causing infinite actions and opinions in succeeding ages. So that if the invention of the ship was thought so noble, which carrieth riches and commodities from place to place, and consociateth the most remote regions in participation of their fruits, how much more are

[26] *Ibid.*, VI, 298-299.   [27] *Ibid.*, VI, 129-135.

letters to be magnified, which as ships pass through the vast seas of time, and make ages so distant to participate of the wisdom, illuminations, and inventions, the one of the other?[28]

The theory that the illuminations of rhetoric are pervasive in all discourse, learned as well as popular, leads Bacon to attach an important modification to the image that the Ciceronians had borrowed from Zeno to express the difference between rhetoric and logic. Bacon indicates that these two arts differ, not so much as the open hand differs from the closed fist, but more as the handling of ideas without reference to an audience differs from the handling of ideas with reference to an audience. His exact words in this connection are as follows:

> It appeareth also that Logic differeth from Rhetoric, not only as the fist from the palm, the one close the other at large; but much more in this, that Logic handleth reason exact and in truth, and Rhetoric handleth it as it is planted in popular opinions and manners. And therefore Aristotle doth wisely place Rhetoric as between Logic on the one side and moral or civil knowledge on the other, as participating of both: for the proofs and demonstrations of Logic are toward all men indifferent and the same; but the proofs and persuasions of Rhetoric ought to differ according to the auditors . . . which application, in perfection of idea, ought to extend so far, that if a man should speak of the same thing to several persons, he should speak to them all respectively and several ways . . . and therefore it shall not be amiss to recommend this to better inquiry. . . .[29]

In a way, this distinction, as Bacon conceives of it, amends Ramism and scholasticism, for those logics had assumed responsibilities towards audiences, especially the learned audience, whereas Bacon wants logic to remain indifferent to that consideration. At the same time, this distinction anticipates Descartes, who had wanted logic to ignore communication and focus upon inquiry. But it would not be accurate to press these interpretations of Bacon too far. After all, as we have already seen, he visualized logic as the sole custodian of method in communication, and thus he is not consistently committed to a logic that renounces all interest in audiences. His basic position seems rather to be that, as logic remains the custodian of method in the transmitting of knowledge, and as grammar remains the custodian of the verbal means of transmission, so rhetoric should keep to

---

[28] *Ibid.,* VI, 168-169.   [29] *Ibid.,* VI, 300.

her task of shedding light upon the subject of any learned or popular communication, and, in discharging that task, should realize that the greatest of light is shed upon a subject when it is connected with popular opinions and manners, and with the nature of the individual auditor. Thus Bacon stands as a composite of scholasticism, of Ramism, and of something that looks to the future. His call for an investigation of the problem of adapting subjects to audiences is particularly modern, although Plato in *Phaedrus* had also wanted rhetoric to investigate that problem, and Aristotle in his *Rhetoric* had actually begun the investigation.

Bacon has many other things to say about rhetoric in the course of his numerous writings, and whatever he says is stimulating. But I shall not dwell further upon him here. As I see it, his chief contribution to modern rhetoric consists in his theory of tradition, and in his emphasis upon rhetoric as the supreme illustrator of knowledge for any audience, learned or popular. That important segment of his total rhetorical theory seems more significant than any other as a prophecy of things to come. Anyone who wishes to see the whole of his rhetorical theory, and to judge what other values it holds for the modern world, should read Professor Karl Wallace's book on that theory.[30] Wallace's book is an excellent guide to materials that would otherwise be difficult to assemble and to examine.

Turning now to other writers of the seventeenth century, and to other works which involved rhetoric, I should like to say that their second large contribution to the new rhetorical theory consisted in a growing recognition of the inadequacy of artistic proof as a means of persuasion, and in the development of a belief in non-artistic proof as a better way to that goal. The nature of the distinction between these two kinds of proof has already been discussed in these pages.[31] In general, artistic proofs were so called because they were developed by systematic means from all of the truths already known and accepted about all of the patterns of behavior involved in any case handled by rhetoric, whereas non-artistic proofs were not subject to production by any systematic means, but had merely to be used if they existed or ignored if they did not exist. Thus when a series of reliable eyewitnesses testified that a given thing had happened, their testimony was considered non-artistic, or not subject to production by any predetermined plan or method. When on the other hand a

[30] Karl R. Wallace, *Francis Bacon on Communication & Rhetoric* (Chapel Hill, 1943).
[31] See above, pp. 68-69.

series of reasonings from the normal and predictable circumstances of a case tended to show that a given thing had happened, those reasonings were considered artistic, or subject to development by method. It is instructive to recall that Ramus advocated an inventional method made up of ten places or seats of argument, and that nine of his places produced artistic proofs, whereas the tenth existed to take care of any non-artistic proofs that might be there for use.[32] In an age which lacked the facilities to assemble and disseminate such non-artistic proofs as documents, confessions, eyewitness reports, contracts, laboratory analyses, statistics, and the like, it was inevitable that artistic proofs would receive special emphasis. It was also inevitable that interest in artistic proofs would decline with the development of science, with the expansion of facilities for the study and dissemination of facts, and with the growth of respect for direct observation and controlled experiment. When Descartes decided that he could no longer accept things as true merely because they were accepted generally as true, and when he determined to hold beliefs only if his reason clearly attested their validity, he was in effect deciding not only that the old science was forever gone and a new experimental science was on the way, but also that the old rhetoric with its formula for artistic proofs would soon disappear, and a new rhetoric based upon invention from observation and facts must one day develop. Descartes's attitude, as we have seen, was subsequently reflected in logical theory by the Port-Royalists' denunciation of the doctrine of places in logic. Throughout the seventeenth century a parallel attitude is shown in a disposition on the part of some writers to turn away from a rhetoric of invention by commonplace and to adopt a rhetoric of invention by research.

One early evidence of this attitude in England is provided in a little Latin essay by Nathaniel Carpenter on the subject of logic and rhetoric. Carpenter studied at St. Edmund Hall and Exeter College in Oxford in the early years of the seventeenth century, being awarded his bachelor's degree in 1610, his master's degree in 1613, and his bachelor's degree in divinity in 1620. During his residence at Oxford, he achieved some reputation as a preacher; and like John Prideaux, the future logician and bishop, he was designated a member of the controversy college at Chelsea, thus becoming a part of that unsuccessful effort to establish a propaganda center against the

---

[32] See above, pp. 155-156.

threat of Catholicism in England.[33] Carpenter's most famous work, the *Philosophia Libera*, published at Frankfurt in 1621, and republished three times at Oxford in the course of the seventeenth century, contains an essay refuting Zeno's claim that logic is to be understood as the closed fist, rhetoric as the open hand; and it is in the course of this essay that he suggests a theory of invention not dependent upon the places of logic or rhetoric.[34]

The complete argument of Carpenter's essay is addressed to the thesis that logical discourse is not necessarily compact, nor is rhetorical discourse necessarily diffuse, as Zeno's metaphor implies. Carpenter reasons syllogistically that diffuse discourse is the product of the procedure known as amplification, but that amplification is the work of logic. As evidence for the latter of these two premises (the former being accepted as indisputable), Carpenter turns first to the books on logic, and shows that they recognize three classes of argument, one class being designated as the argument for proof, another, as the argument for exposition or instruction, and still another, as the argument for amplification. Carpenter next turns to the theory involving the assignment of invention, arrangement, and style to the various academic disciplines, and he argues here as follows:

> Moreover, since three things are required for the fulness of a speech, namely, invention of subject matter, arrangement of arguments, and adornment, it is obvious that the first is supplied from the various fields of knowledge conformably to the speaker's end and purpose, the second from logic, and the third from rhetoric. Accordingly, it follows that the various fields of knowledge contribute substance or content, logic the tying together and arranging of arguments, and rhetoric merely the flower and spice of the speech. But no sane person denies that the faculty of amplifying is based upon the faculty of arranging arguments.

The final movement of Carpenter's argument is devoted to showing that even the tropes and figures depend basically upon logic as the science of arrangement, and thus that amplification cannot be made

---

[33] For previous mention of this institution, see above, p. 311. For other details about Carpenter, see *Dictionary of National Biography*, s.v. Carpenter, Nathanael (1589-1628?).

[34] For the Latin text of this essay, which is entitled "Logica pugno, Rhetorica palmae, non rectè à Zenone comparatur," see Nathaniel Carpenter, *Philosophia Libera* (Oxford, 1622), pp. 158-161. For an English translation, see Wilbur S. Howell, "Nathaniel Carpenter's Place in the Controversy between Dialectic and Rhetoric," *Speech Monographs*, I (1934), 20-41.

the property of rhetoric simply by classifying it among the tropes and figures. Anyway, says Carpenter, tropes and figures actually contract discourse on some occasions, and amplify it on others, and so cannot be said to be in essence an amplificatory device.

In the perspectives of history, Carpenter's argument is modern only in his emphasis that invention belongs to the various fields of knowledge, and that the speaker or writer does not find substance or content except in those fields. This theory amounts to a rejection of the places of Ramistic logic as aids to the discovery of subject matter; and to a rejection, as well, of the places of scholastic logic and Ciceronian rhetoric. In other respects, Carpenter draws his materials from traditional sources. Thus he accepts logic as the authority on the classification and the arrangement of arguments, and rhetoric as the authority on ornament, thereby identifying himself as something of a Ramist, although he goes on to reject the basic claim of Ramus that the tropes and figures are the absolute property of rhetoric. His belief in the falsity of Zeno's metaphor is of course antischolastic and anti-Ciceronian; but he does not advance therefrom to a modern position in any respect except that just specified.

A much later and more decisive evidence that rhetoric was turning away from invention by commonplace and was endorsing invention by external means is provided in a work called *The Art of Speaking*, published at London in 1676, and reprinted there in 1696 and 1708. This work is an English translation of a French treatise first published anonymously at Paris in 1675 under the title, *De l'Art de Parler*. Because the French treatise did not identify its author, and because it bore unmistakable resemblances to the thinking of the already famous Port-Royalist logicians, its English publishers indicated on its title page in 1676 that it was "Written in French by Messieurs du Port Royal: In pursuance of a former Treatise, Intituled, The Art of Thinking." Thus started a legend of a Port-Royalist rhetoric as a parallel of the Port-Royalist logic, and this legend was not impaired when the latter work achieved its first English translation nine years after the original appearance of the *Art of Speaking*. In its second printing at London in 1696, and in its third there in 1708, the *Art of Speaking* continued to advertise itself as the work of the "Messieurs du Port Royal." By then, of course, the *Logic, Or The Art of Thinking* of Arnauld and Nicole was so well known in England that a treatise definitely associated with those two authors would sell much better than it could have expected to otherwise. Thus there was an undoubted commercial advantage in continuing in 1696 and 1708 to sell the *Art of Speaking* as a Port-Royalist work. But by 1688 the work had appeared at Paris in its third edition, and that third edition had changed its title to *La Rhétorique, ou l'Art de Parler*, and had announced its author as Bernard Lamy. Bernard Lamy was not a Port-Royalist. He belonged instead to the Congregation of the Oratory, a religious order which like the Port-Royalists had interested itself in educational reform.[35] His *Art of Speaking* hardly deserves the title of a Port-Royalist rhetoric, for it is in many ways a compromise between Ramus and the Port-Royalists, not an important disavowal of the Ramists and the Neo-Ciceronians.[36] Nevertheless, it had a new spirit about it, and one aspect of that spirit had to do with its acceptance of the Port-Royalist opposition to artistic proof and the doctrine of the places of rhetoric as aids to invention.

The *Art of Speaking* is divided into four regular parts and a fifth part in the form of an appendix entitled "A Discourse, in which is given an Idea of the Art of Perswasion."[37] The first part deals with matters of speech, grammar, and usage; the second part, with tropes and figures; the third part, with speaking, pronouncing, articulating, breathing, reciting; and the fourth part, with style, considered not only in relation to its different kinds (the sublime, the plain, and the middle), but also in relation to its adaptability to oratory, history, philosophy, and poetry, and in relation to its power to make discourse beautiful. Thus far, the work is Ramistic in its restriction of rhetoric to style and delivery; and at the same time it is Ciceronian in its tendency to allow matters of grammar to creep into rhetoric, and in its treatment of style as something more than the

[35] For a comparison of the Oratorians and the Port-Royalists in this respect, see Barnard, *The Little Schools of Port-Royal*, pp. 205-207.

[36] The *Art of Speaking* is discussed as a compromise between Ramus and the Port-Royalists in Wilbur S. Howell, *Fénelon's Dialogues on Eloquence*, pp. 33-36. For another recent study of Lamy's work, see Douglas Ehninger, "Bernard Lami's *L'Art de Parler*: A Critical Analysis," *The Quarterly Journal of Speech*, XXXII (1946), 429-434.

[37] My discussion is based upon the first edition of the English translation. I am indebted to my colleague, Professor Alan Downer, for lending me his copy for my present purpose. The title page reads: "The Art of Speaking: Written in French by Messieurs du Port Royal: In pursuance of a former Treatise, Intituled, The Art of Thinking. Rendred into English. London, Printed by W. Godbid, and are to be Sold by M. Pitt, at the *Angel* against the little North Door of St. *Paul's* Church. 1676." Parts I, II, and III of this edition are paged together from p. 1 to p. 212, but the numbering of the pages is incorrect at several points. Parts IV and V are paged together from p. 1 to p. 164, and the numbering of this sequence is correct. Part V begins on p. 88 of the second sequence of pages.

tropes and the figures. In its fifth part, it becomes frankly Ciceronian, mentioning the five ancient divisions of rhetoric, the three ways of persuading, the places of proof, the means of insinuation, the appeals to passions, and the classical pattern of oratorical arrangement. The work ends by acknowledging that in its final part it had dealt with invention and arrangement, that in its first four parts it had dealt with style, and that in not treating memory or oratorical delivery, it had recognized these faculties to be more in the realm of practice than of precept.

The only section of this work that definitely belongs neither to the Ramists nor to the Neo-Ciceronians is that in which the places of invention are denounced as worthless after they have been briefly explained in two short chapters. This denunciation of the means of inventing artistic proofs is a mark of the influence upon Lamy of *The Port-Royal Logic* and its severe denunciation of the logical theory of places. "Thus in few words," says Lamy as he begins his similar attack, "have I shown the Art to find Arguments upon all Subjects of which the Rhetoricians are accustomed to Treat, which makes the greatest part of their Rhetorick."[38] He proposes at once "to judg of the usefulness of this method." He acknowledges that his respect for the authors who have commended it has obliged him to set it forth. He also acknowledges that the places have "some kind of use," and he specifies that use as follows:

> They make us take notice of several things from whence Arguments may be drawn; they teach us how a Subject may be vary'd and discovered on all sides. So as those who are skill'd in the Art of *Topicks*, may find matter enough to amplifie their discourse; nothing is barren to them; they speak of every thing that occurs, as largely and as oft as they please.[39]

Having stated the traditional defense of places, Lamy turns to those who attack this means of inventing proof, and he quotes them with approval:

> Those who reject these Topicks, do not deny their Fecundity; they grant that they supply us with infinite numbers of things; but they alledg that that Fecundity is inconvenient; That the things are trivial, and by consequent the Art of *Topicks* furnishes nothing that is fit for us to say. If an Orator (say they) understands the subject of which he treats; if he be full of incontestable Maxims that may inable him to

[38] *The Art of Speaking*, Pt. V, p. 103.   [39] *Ibid.*, Pt. V, p. 104.

resolve all Difficulties arising upon that subject; If it be a question in Divinity, and he be well read in the Fathers, Councils, Scriptures, &c. He will quickly perceive whether the question propos'd be Orthodox, or otherwise. It is not necessary that he runs to his Topicks, or passes from one common place to another, which are unable to supply him with necessary knowledg for decision of his Question. If on the other side an Orator be ignorant, and understands not the bottom of what he Treats, he can speak but superficially, he cannot come to the point; and after he has talk'd and argued a long time, his Adversary will have reason to admonish him to leave his tedious talk that signifies nothing; to interrupt him in this manner, Speak to the purpose; oppose Reason against my Reason, and coming to the Point, do what you can to subvert the Foundations upon which I sustain my self.[40]

Frank talk like this is a refreshing change in rhetorical theory, as the talk of the Port-Royalists against the places of logic was a refreshing change in that field. Lamy goes on to say that a "witty man speaking of the method of which *Raimondus Lullius* treated after a particular manner, calls it *An Art of Discoursing without judgment of things we do not understand.*"[41] This "witty man" is of course Descartes, and these words from his *Discourse on Method* were also quoted by the Port-Royalists.[42] Before Lamy thus covertly indicates the source of his condemnation of Lull, he takes up the argument that the places of rhetoric are of value in providing the speaker with proofs beyond those gleaned from the study of his own particular subject. He dismisses this argument thus:

To this it is answered, and I am of the same Opinion, That to perswade, we need but one Argument, if it be solid and strong, and that Eloquence consists in clearing of that, and making it perspicuous. All those feeble Arguments (proper as well to the accused, as the accuser, and as useful to refel as affirm) deriv'd from Commonplaces, are like ill Weeds that choke the Corn.[43]

So did Lamy introduce into French and then into English rhetoric a devastating attack upon the concept of artistic proofs and the places of invention. If modern rhetoric no longer believes in artistic proofs, and no longer teaches an elaborate system of places, the Port-Royalist logicians and their disciple Lamy are in large part respon-

[40] *Ibid.*, Pt. v, pp. 104-105. [41] *Ibid.*, Pt. v, p. 106.
[42] See Descartes, *Discours de la Méthode*, ed. Gilson, p. 17, lines 19-20; also *The Port-Royal Logic*, trans. Baynes, p. 41; also above, pp. 348, 360.
[43] *The Art of Speaking*, Pt. v, p. 106.

sible. They are responsible, that is, because their correct diagnosis of the weakness of the system of places, and their correct recommenda-- tion of an invention based upon an exhaustive study of the factual states in any case, happened to fall in the earlier part of the modern period, and happened to be expressed in works that were reprinted again and again during the seventeenth and eighteenth centuries in the most influential centers of European learning. But if the Port-Royalists and Lamy had not happened to speak as they did, the events set in motion by Bacon and Descartes would sooner or later have forced rhetoric to re-examine the whole question of persuasive methods in an age of science, and would have caused her to make the sort of changes that were actually recommended in *The Port-Royal Logic* and the *Art of Speaking*.

A third large contribution which seventeenth-century writers made towards the development of a new attitude in rhetoric consisted in the advocacy of a simpler theory of organization than the older rhet- oric and logic had taught. Ramistic rhetoric, of course, had involved no theory of organization whatever, since that subject was reserved by Ramus for logic and in particular for the doctrine of method. In Ramistic logic, as we know, the procedure recommended for all learned discourse was called the natural method, and it consisted of a severe arrangement of propositions in a descending order of gen- erality. As for discourse addressed to the people, Ramus allowed a less rigid procedure, called the prudential method, but his disciples tended not to advocate it. Ciceronian rhetoric, in the period before and after Ramus, taught arrangement in terms of the divisions rec- ommended by Cicero for the oration. And scholastic logic, particu- larly under the direction of the Systematics, taught various kinds of method, a few of which concerned inquiry, and the others, presenta- tion. Valuable as these theories were—and their importance has un- fortunately been forgotten—they still had to be modified somewhat in the modern era to foster rhetoric's continuing interest in discourse organized to persuade, and to meet her developing interest in dis- course organized to explain and teach.

The best contribution made in the seventeenth century towards a theory of expository method lies in Bacon's distinction between the magistral and the probationary types of transmission of knowledges, and his recommendation of the latter type for further use and de- velopment. As I have said, Bacon assigns to logic his entire discussion of method, and thus he does not consider his recommendations upon this subject to be part of a new rhetoric. But nevertheless they turned out to be that, as logic ceased to concern herself with the method of communication, and as rhetoric began to assimilate the methods taught by the Ramists and the Systematics, and to adapt those methods to her own necessities. The magistral and the probationary procedures have already been explained in my discussion of Bacon's theory of tradition as a whole. To those comments I should now like to add a passage in which Bacon describes in imaginative terms what he conceives his probationary method to be:

> But knowledge that is delivered as a thread to be spun on, ought to be delivered and intimated, if it were possible, *in the same method wherein it was invented*; and so is it possible of knowledge induced. But in this same anticipated and prevented knowledge, no man knoweth how he came to the knowledge which he hath obtained. But yet nevertheless, *secundum majus et minus*, a man may revisit and descend unto the foundations of his knowledge and consent; and so transplant it into another as it grew in his own mind. For it is in knowledges as it is in plants: if you mean to use the plant, it is no matter for the roots; but if you mean to remove it to grow, then it is more assured to rest upon roots than slips.[44]

As for the theory of method in persuasive discourse, there were tendencies at work in seventeenth-century English learning to require fewer parts for the deliberative, the forensic, and the demonstrative oration. These tendencies in learning were a reflection of tendencies in the surrounding society. England in that period was witnessing the decline in the power of the aristocracy, the growth of the political and social influence of the middle class, the lessening of the expectation for ceremony and formula in religion, and the development of a genuine need for the effects of religious persuasions, as distinguished from the former preference for verbal appeals confined largely to rituals. These social and political pressures had their consequences in the world of English learning, and one of those consequences was that rhetorical theory tended to become simpler and less ritualistic in all respects, the doctrine of arrangement being no exception.

But the tendency toward simplicity in the theory of rhetorical arrangement also received powerful support in seventeenth-century England from the authority of Aristotle's *Rhetoric*. In the year

[44] *Works of Bacon*, VI, 289-290.

1619, Theodore Goulston published at London his edition of that famous work, so arranged that the pages consist of three parallel columns, one of which contains the Greek text, the next, a Latin translation, and the third, a series of Latin notes and comment.[45] In or about the year 1637, Thomas Hobbes published at London an abridged English version of Aristotle's rhetorical theory under the title, *A Briefe of the Art of Rhetoriqve*.[46] Hobbes's version was reprinted at London in 1651 and 1681; and Goulston's Greek-Latin edition was republished at the same place in 1696.[47] Meanwhile, in 1686, a complete English translation of the *Rhetoric* appeared at London, announcing that it was "Made English by the translators of the Art of thinking."[48] Thus from first to last the seventeenth century in England saw much of this major work, and English learning had every opportunity to absorb Aristotle's theory of the arrangement of persuasive discourse.

Perhaps the best way to see how English learning conceived of that theory is to quote it in the words of Thomas Hobbes. In the

[45] The title page reads in part: "Ἀριστοτέλους Τέχνης ῥητορικῆς Βιβλία τρία. Aristotelis de Rhetorica seu arte Dicendi Libri tres, Graecolat. . . . Londini Typis Eduardi Griffini, cƆ. Ɔc. xix." No editor's name appears on the title page. The Latin dedicatory epistle is addressed to Prince Charles of Great Britain, and is signed "Theodor^{us} Govlston."

[46] There is a copy of this work in the Folger Shakespeare Library. Its title page reads: "A Briefe of the Art of Rhetoriqve. Containing in substance all that Aristotle hath written in his Three Bookes of that subject, Except onely what is not applicable to the English Tongue. London Printed by *Tho. Cotes*, for *Andrew Crook*, and are to be sold at the black Bare in *Pauls* Church-yard."
An entry in the stationers' registers for Feb. 1, 1636, i.e., 1637, attributes the work to "T. H.," i.e., Thomas Hobbes, and permits its first edition to be dated in or near that year. See Arber, *Transcript of the Registers*, IV, 372.

[47] Hobbes's *Briefe* appeared at London in 1651 in *A Compendium of the Art of Logick and Rhetorick in the English Tongue*. For an indication of other items in the *Compendium*, see above, pp. 238, 276. See also Walter J. Ong, S.J., "Hobbes and Talon's Ramist Rhetoric in English," *Transactions of the Cambridge Bibliographical Society*, I (1949-1953), 260-261.
The *Briefe* was reprinted in 1681 as "The Whole Art of Rhetorick" in Thomas Hobbes's *The Art of Rhetoric, with a Discourse of The Laws of England*. This volume also contains a little treatise called "The Art of Rhetorick Plainly set forth," as if it were the work of Hobbes. In reality, it is merely a reprint of the section on rhetoric in Dudley Fenner's *The Artes of Logike and Rethorike*. See above, p. 279.
The 1696 edition of Goulston's Greek-Latin version of Aristotle's *Rhetoric* bears the same title as the first edition of 1619. Its imprint reads: "Londini, Typis Ben. Griffini, Impensis Edvard. Hall Bibliop. Cantabr'. M DC XCVI."

[48] Its title page reads as follows: "Aristotle's Rhetoric; or, The true grounds and principles of oratory; shewing the right art of pleading and speaking in full assemblies and courts of judicature. Made English by the translators of the Art of thinking. . . London, Printed by T. B. for R. Taylor, 1686." This work contains the three books of Aristotle's *Rhetoric* and as Book IV the *Rhetorica ad Alexandrum*, formerly attributed to Aristotle. The identity of these translators has not been determined. See above, p. 352, note 32.

twelfth chapter of Book III of his *Briefe*, Hobbes drastically abridges the thirteenth chapter of Book III of Aristotle's *Rhetoric*, but he manages, nevertheless, to convey the essentials of Aristotle's doctrine. His entire chapter is brief enough for quotation here:

> The *necessary* parts of an oration are but two; *propositions* and *proof*; which are, as it were, the *problem* and *demonstration*.
>
> The *proposition* is the explication or opening of the matter to be *proved*. And *proof* is the *demonstration* of the matter *propounded*.
>
> To these *necessary parts* are sometimes added two other, the *proem* and the *epilogue*; neither of which is any *proof*.
>
> So that in some there be *four parts* of an oration; the *proem*; the *proposition*, or as others call it, the *narration*; the *proofs*, which contain *confirmation, confutation, amplification, and diminution*; and the *epilogue*.[49]

Aristotle's *Rhetoric* was destined, of course, to exert upon modern English rhetorical theory an influence not confined to the doctrine of arrangement. What Aristotle says of style undoubtedly affected what English rhetoricians of the seventeenth century came to advocate in that field, as I shall mention later. And there are many other ways in which Aristotle's penetrating eyes have helped modern rhetoric to understand her problems, as can be seen in the pages of Richard Whately's famous *Elements of Rhetoric*, first published at London in 1828. Nevertheless, modern theory has been particularly benefited by Aristotle's conception of the basic organization of persuasive discourse, and that benefit began to operate widely in English learning as the seventeenth century produced her Greek, Latin, and English versions of the *Rhetoric*.

The final contribution of seventeenth-century writers to a new attitude towards rhetoric came in their denunciation of the doctrine of the tropes and figures and in their advocacy of the principle that ordinary patterns of speech are acceptable in oratory and literature as in conversation and life. This change was accelerated in the eighteenth and nineteenth centuries by the rise of the democratic state, and by the consequent need on the part of the ruling class to develop new techniques for communication with the common man. But the change began in the Renaissance, and it received in the seventeenth century the support of the new science and the new spirit in religion.

---

[49] *The English Works of Thomas Hobbes*, ed. Sir William Molesworth (London, 1839-1845), VI, 500. Cited below as *Works of Hobbes*.

Scientific discourse, or the communication between one scientist and another in the scientific community, did not prove to be a natural medium for the tropes and figures of Ciceronian or Ramistic rhetoric. Nor could the preaching done in the churches of the later Reformation allow itself to be as indifferent to persuasion as it had been during the Middle Ages, when Catholicism had seemingly completed her task of conversion in the European community and appeared to need only to rely upon ceremonial forms to keep faith alive. Once preaching set out to convert commoners, style ceased to remain an exploitation of the ways in which verbal formulations can be made to depart from the patterns of ordinary speech, and at that moment the tropes and the figures tended to become obsolete in the pulpit, except as they contributed to the effectiveness of a simpler and plainer way of speaking.

The change from the tropes and the figures to a less unusual style began in the learned discourse of the seventeenth century with the publication of Bacon's *Advancement of Learning* in 1605. The influence of that remarkable work upon the theory of style in communication in the world of science, as upon the entire theory of the transmission of knowledges from man to man and from age to age, cannot be overemphasized. In his opening pages Bacon speaks of three vices or diseases that beset scholarship, and one of those vices turns out to be "delicate learning," that is, the concern for "vain imaginations, vain altercations, and vain affectations,"[50] or the excessive devotion to mannerism as distinguished from matter in the presentation of discourse. In a passage memorable for its acuteness in diagnosing the cultural distempers of the sixteenth century, Bacon remarks that the early Reformation had produced a need for ancient testimony as a support in the struggle against Rome, and that the need for ancient testimony had led to a revival of interest in ancient authors. A delightful appreciation of ancient language and style, he goes on, was produced as the result of that revival of interest, and was cherished, partly on aesthetic grounds, and partly as a means to a more effective presentation than that afforded by an imitation of the thorny style of Roman scholasticism. The delight of the scholars in the ancient style, Bacon continues, led them to a theory of preaching based upon the notion that the people could be won over to the Protestant cause by "eloquence and variety of discourse, as the fittest and forciblest access into the capacity of the vulgar sort."[51] Here,

---

[50] *Works of Bacon*, VI, 117.   [51] *Ibid.*, VI, 119.

then, is a brilliant explanation of the reasons behind the rise of stylistic rhetoric. Bacon caps his historical analysis with a famous passage in which he gives us some insight into the excesses created by the Ciceronian and Ramistic emphasis upon a study of the tropes and figures. He observes:

> So that these four causes concurring, the admiration of ancient authors, the hate of the schoolmen, the exact study of languages, and the efficacy of preaching, did bring in an affectionate study of eloquence and copie of speech, which then began to flourish. This grew speedily to an excess; for men began to hunt more after words than matter; and more after the choiceness of the phrase, and the round and clean composition of the sentence, and the sweet falling of the clauses, and the varying and illustration of their works with tropes and figures, than after the weight of matter, worth of subject, soundness of argument, life of invention, or depth of judgment.[52]

Bacon's implied distinction between a healthy and a pathological addiction to style is worth considering as a reminder that an early Ramist like Gabriel Harvey had associated the pathological addiction to style with a counterfeit Ciceronianism, and had tried to restore health to that branch of learning by endorsing Ramus's entire theory of communication.[53] Thus the early Ramists are on the side of the proper balance between content and style. Nevertheless, there is always danger that style, when abstracted from the other aspects of composition, will teach the unwary to value it above thought or to divorce it from thought, and it is that danger which the later Ramists tended to foster, simply because they could not keep their rhetoric close to their logic in an educational program which taught rhetoric at one stage of a pupil's development, and logic at another stage. The way to prevent the divorce of content from style is to teach style in company with invention and arrangement, as even the Ciceronians did not always do; and Bacon's attack upon stylistic rhetoric as a distemper of learning is therefore to be construed as a plea for the better integration of the mental and verbal aspects of communication, if the new science is to be properly transmitted.

The authority of Aristotle's *Rhetoric* is also on the side of a proper integration between content and style in the theory of communication, and thus the publication of that work in England during the seventeenth century tended to give Englishmen confidence in plain

---

[52] *Ibid.*, VI, 119.   [53] See above, p. 252.

ways of speaking or writing. For example, Hobbes's English abridgment of the *Rhetoric*, as published around 1637 and at two later dates in the century, contains the sort of stylistic doctrine that the times demanded.[54] Here are two passages to show how far Aristotle opposes a fine or an unnatural style for oratory:

> The virtues of a *word* are two; the first, that it be *perspicuous*; the second, that it be *decent*, that is, neither *above* nor *below* the thing signified, or neither too humble nor too fine.[55]

> To make a *poem* graceful, many things help; but few an *oration*. For to a *poet* it sufficeth, with what *words* he can, to set out his *poem*. But an *orator* must not only do that, but also seem not to do it: for else he will be thought to speak unnaturally, and not as he thinks; and thereby be the less believed; whereas *belief* is the scope of his oration.[56]

Thus Bacon, Aristotle, and Hobbes lent influence to the theory that the tropes and the figures, as a great system of violations of normal ways of speaking, were not an acceptable imperative for learned discourse. The Royal Society, as the center of the new scientific activity, went further—its members renounced the rhetoric of tropes and figures as a guide to scientific writing, and adopted a theory of style that belongs to the new attitude towards rhetoric.

We see the attitude of the Royal Society to best advantage in Thomas Sprat's fine work, *The History of the Royal-Society of London, For the Improving of Natural Knowledge*, published at London in 1667. This history deals with three subjects: the state of knowledge in the ancient and modern world; the actual procedures of the Royal Society in fostering the growth of experimental knowledge; and the values to be attached to experimental knowledge in general. In discussing the second of these subjects, Sprat describes what happens in the Royal Society as they meet to direct, judge, analyze, improve, and discuss experiments.[57] Each of these five activities is important in the history of seventeenth-century science. But for our present purpose, the happenings in the Royal Society as they discussed experiments are of crucial importance, for in these happenings we can see a new rhetoric of exposition emerging to replace the rhetoric of persuasion by tropes and figures.

The discussion of experiments, or transmission of descriptive and

---

[54] See above, p. 384. [55] *Works of Hobbes*, VI, 488.
[56] *Ibid.*, VI, 488-489.
[57] Thomas Sprat, *The History of the Royal-Society of London* (London, 1667), pp. 95-115.

argumentative materials from member to member, led the Royal Society, says Sprat, to become most solicitous about "the manner of their *Discourse*."[58] Unless they had taken pains about this, he adds, and had sought to keep it in due temper, "the whole spirit and vigour of their *Design*, had been soon eaten out, by the luxury and redundance of *speech*." What the Royal Society is objecting to when they express fear of luxury and redundance of speech is ornamental language—in short, the tropes and the figures. Maybe in the beginning, says Sprat, these ornaments were highly justified as being necessary "to represent *Truth*, cloth'd with Bodies; and to bring *Knowledg* back again to our very senses, from whence it was at first deriv'd to our understandings."[59] But now the ornaments of speaking are put to worse uses. Here is how Sprat elaborates his attitude towards the tropes and figures:

> They make the *Fancy* disgust the best things, if they come sound and unadorn'd: they are in open defiance against *Reason*; professing, not to hold much correspondence with that; but with its Slaves, *the Passions*: they give the mind a motion too changeable, and bewitching, to consist with *right practice*. Who can behold, without indignation, how many mists and uncertainties, these specious *Tropes* and *Figures* have brought on our Knowledg? How many rewards, which are due to more profitable, and difficult *Arts*, have been still snatch'd away by the easie vanity of *fine speaking*? For now I am warm'd with this just Anger, I cannot with-hold my self, from betraying the shallowness of all these seeming Mysteries; upon which, *we Writers*, and *Speakers*, look so bigg. And, in few words, I dare say; that of all the Studies of men, nothing may be sooner obtain'd, than this vicious abundance of *Phrase*, this trick of *Metaphors*, this volubility of *Tongue*, which makes so great a noise in the World.[60]

Had the Royal Society left matters here, history would have had a lively denunciation of the tropes and the figures, but no program of reform. As Sprat sees it, reform is difficult, because people labor so long to acquire an ornamental speech in the years of their education that "we cannot but ever after think kinder of it, than it deserves." Nevertheless, English science attempted to cope positively with the unfortunate effects of the ornamental style in science. "It will suffice my present purpose," Sprat observes, "to point out, what has been done by the *Royal Society*, towards the correcting of its excesses in *Natural Philosophy*; to which it is, of all others, a most

[58] *Ibid.*, p. 111.   [59] *Ibid.*, p. 112.   [60] *Ibid.*, p. 112.

profest enemy." And here is the outline of the new rhetoric, as Sprat describes it from the endeavors of the scientists:

> They have therefore been most rigorous in putting in execution, the only Remedy, that can be found for this *extravagance*: and that has been, a constant Resolution, to reject all the amplifications, digressions, and swellings of style: to return back to the primitive purity, and shortness, when men deliver'd so many *things*, almost in an equal number of *words*. They have exacted from all their members, a close, naked, natural way of speaking; positive expressions; clear senses; a native easiness: bringing all things as near the Mathematical plainness, as they can: and preferring the language of Artizans, Countrymen, and Merchants, before that, of Wits, or Scholars.[61]

These words, compared with those uttered by George Puttenham in 1589, enable us to measure the change that had occurred in England in the seventy-eight years that immediately preceded Sprat's *History*. Puttenham had warned writers against following "the speach of a craftes man or carter, or other of the inferiour sort, though he be inhabitant or bred in the best towne and Citie in this Realme. . . ."[62] Puttenham had advised the writer in all the intricacies of the tropes and figures of ornamental artistocratic speech. And now, less than a century later, the historian of the Royal Society is showing that English scientists were renouncing the tropes and figures and were preferring "the language of Artizans, Countrymen, and Merchants, before that, of Wits or Scholars." True, Puttenham was writing a rhetoric for the poet, whereas Sprat was recording a rhetoric for the scientist. But even so the change is striking, and it would still be noticeable, even if we confined ourselves to a strict comparison between poet and poet or scientist and scientist of the two eras. What lies between 1589 and 1667 is to be described, so far as rhetorical history is concerned, as the change from the medieval to the modern orientation. Nothing shows better how far that change had progressed than does the comparison between Puttenham and Sprat.

In the same period, a change was occurring in the theory of style in sermons, despite the tendency of formal homiletics to remain tied during the seventeenth century to Ramistic or Neo-Ciceronian doctrine. The change began in criticisms of ornamental style in pulpit oratory. At the very beginning of the sixteen-hundreds, William

[61] *Ibid.*, p. 113.   [62] See above, p. 328.

Vaughan's *The Golden-groue*, which deals with the arts of governing one's self, one's household, and one's country, contained under the last of these three heads a chapter on rhetoric, as well as chapters on grammar, logic, poetry, philosophy, and so on. In Vaughan's chapter on rhetoric there is a caustic reference to "our common lawyers, who with their glozing speeches do as it were lay an ambush for iustice, and *with their hired tongues think it not vnhonest to defend the guilty*, and to patronize vnlawfull pleas."[63] And just before this reference Vaughan condemns the unprofitable doctrine that rhetoric holds for preachers. "For although Rhetorical speeches do delight their auditory," he says, "yet notwithstanding, they make not much for the soules health."[64] Quoting then from the *Prometheus* of Aeschylus that "Simple and material speeches are best among friends," Vaughan adds this cautionary advice for the pulpit: "Preachers therfore must labour to speak and to vtter that, which the hearers vnderstand, and not go about the bush with their filing phrases."[65] He adds a bit later that "Caluine that zealous Preacher had, as many men know, an impediment in his speach, and in his sermons neuer vsed any painted rhetoricall termes."[66]

The use of painted rhetorical terms is decried later in the seventeenth century in William Pemble's *Vindiciae Gratiae*. Pemble has already figured in these pages as author of the *Enchiridion Oratorivm*, a Neo-Ciceronian manual published at Oxford in 1633.[67] Pemble lectured at Oxford on divinity until his premature death in 1623, and the *Vindiciae Gratiae*, first published some four years after his death, represents one series of those lectures. Although that series was devoted to the nature and properties of grace and faith, Pemble devotes much of his Preface to comments on preaching, and these indicate his desire for a double plainness in sermons, one being plainness of style and speech, and the other, plainness of matter. Plainness of style, he suggests, is his own ambition in the Preface he is now writing. He says in this connection:

> Vnto my apprehension, such Prologues, how euer sleeked ouer, doe yet feele rough and vneuen, and smell ranke of Lying or Flattery, when they are most seasoned with artificiall and trimme conueyance:

[63] William Vaughan, *The Golden-groue, moralized in three books: A worke very necessary for all such, as would know how to gouerne themselues, their houses, or their countrey* (London, 1600), sig. X8r. The italics are Vaughan's, and his note indicates that the quotation is from Martial.

[64] *Ibid.*, sig. X7v.   [65] *Ibid.*, sig. X7v.   [66] *Ibid.*, sig. X8r.

[67] See above, pp. 323-324.

but of all, most vnhandsomely doth this Rhetoricke suite with such as pleade Gods cause before mortall men, who, if they will acknowledge this alleageance, must yeeld attention vpon a *Sic dicit Dominus*, without further entreaty.[68]

As for what he means by plainness of style, that comes out in the following passage from a later stage of his Preface:

How many excellent discourses are tortured, wrested, and pinched in, and obscured through curiositie of penning, hidden alluions, forced phrases, vncouth Epithites, with other deformities of plaine speaking; your owne eares and eyes may be sufficient iudges. A great slauerie, to make the minde a seruant to the tongue, & so to tye her vp in fetters, that shee may not walke but by number and measure. Good speech, make the most on't is but the garment of truth: and shee is so glorious within, shee needes no outward decking; yet if shee doe appeare in a raiment of needle worke, its but for a more maiesticke comelinesse, not gawdy gaynesse. Truth is like our first Parents, most beautiful when naked, twas sinne couered them, tis ignorance hides this. Let perspicuitie and method bee euer the graces of speech; and distinctnesse of deliuery the daughter of a cleere apprehension: for my selfe, I must alwayes thinke they know not what they say, who so speake, as others know not what they meane.[69]

Perhaps the greatest of the seventeenth-century pleas for plainness of style in sermon-making came from the pen of Joseph Glanvill in 1678. Glanvill took his bachelor's degree at Oxford in 1655, and his master's degree three years later. Thereafter his life was spent in the church. But he was interested in the new movements in the science of his day; he enjoyed the friendship of the founders of the Royal Society; and on December 14, 1664, he himself was elected fellow of that distinguished organization.[70] Thus his theory of preaching grew out of his own professional concern for the needs of the pulpit and out of his acquaintance with the new rhetorical doctrine being evolved in the meetings of the Royal Society. It is no exaggeration to say that he brought the doctrine of plainness from the new theory of scientific exposition and planted it in the ancient theory of religious persuasion. He was not the first to advocate plainness in sermon-making; but his position in the seventeenth century

---

[68] William Pemble, *Vindiciae Gratiae. A Plea for Grace* (London, 1629), p. 1.

[69] *Ibid.*, pp. 22-23.

[70] *Dictionary of National Biography*, s.v. Glanvill, Joseph (1636-1680); also Foster, *Alumni Oxonienses*, s.v. Glanvill, Joseph.

as writer on homiletics and as member of the group advocating a new rhetoric for science gives his homiletical theory a double significance.

Glanvill's *A Seasonable Defence of Preaching*, published at London in 1678, is not primarily a work in the field of sacred rhetoric, but it must be mentioned as an indication of its author's interest in the problems of pulpit speakers, and it provides an excellent introduction to his more purely rhetorical doctrine.[71] The *Defence* is a dialogue on preaching by five laymen, identified as A, B, C, D, and E. The main speaker is A. He talks first with B on the question whether there is an excess of preaching in the modern church, his position being that there is not.[72] He next talks with C on the institution of preaching as distinguished from prayer.[73] C believes that preaching is outmoded in the modern era, inasmuch as there are no longer any heathens to convert; and thus he advocates more prayer and less preaching. A answers this argument by asserting that sermon-making is still essential, and that its success can be explained. In the course of this part of the dialogue, A mentions that the success achieved by the puritan preachers before the civil war depended not so much on the excellence of their sermons as on other factors. At this point D enters the argument. He turns out later to be a nonconformist, and his general contention is that preaching in the established church has not been effective of late, whereas preaching in the sects has shown both greater plainness and greater power.[74] In the course of A's objections to each of these theses, he pauses to exchange ideas with C on the relative merits of preaching, prayer, catechisms, and homilies.[75] The dialogue comes to an end in a conversation between A and E on the disadvantages of having a hired clergy and on the carelessness and looseness that might develop in sermons from the wrong kind of attempts to make them plain.[76]

It is Glanvill's *An Essay concerning Preaching: Written for the Direction of A Young Divine*, also published at London in 1678, that contains his chief contribution to rhetorical theory.[77] This work ana-

[71] The title page reads: "A Seasonable Defence of Preaching: and the Plain Way of it. London: Printed by *M. Clark*, for *H. Brome*, at the Gun in St. *Paul's* Church-yard. MDCLXXVIII."
[72] *A Seasonable Defence of Preaching* (1678), pp. 1-8.
[73] *Ibid.*, pp. 8-39. [74] *Ibid.*, pp. 39-50, 74-99.
[75] *Ibid.*, pp. 50-74. [76] *Ibid.*, pp. 99-112.
[77] Its title page reads: "An Essay concerning Preaching: Written for the Direction of A Young Divine; and Useful also for the People, in order to Profitable Hearing. London: Printed by A. C. for H. Brome, at the Gun in St. *Paul's* Church-yard. M. DC. LXXVIII."

lyzes first the different standards used by listeners to measure the effectiveness of sermons, some listeners being only in the mood for entertainment, others for instruction, still others for a pedantic show of learning, still others for plentiful biblical texts, still others for passion and vehemence, and still others for coldness and monotony. Glanvill then sets forth what he considers to be the true standard: "The *End* of preaching must be acknowledg'd to be the *Instruction* of the hearers in *Faith* and *Good Life*, in order to the Glory of God, and their present, and future happiness; and this ought to be the *Rule* and *Measure* of Preaching, and the exercise judg'd by this."[78] Having established this function as the true aim of the preacher, Glanvill proceeds to organize his theory of sermon-making into four main subjects. Let us let him describe them for us: "I shall handle the *Rules* of Preaching under these four Heads. It ought to be *plain, practical, methodical, affectionate*."[79]

Plainness to Glanvill is a broad characteristic, and he proceeds to explain it mainly in terms of its opposites. These are enumerated as "hard words," "deep and mysterious notions," "affected Rhetorications," and "Phantastical Phrases." Hard words are outlandish words used where ordinary English would serve. Deep and mysterious notions are hypotheses and speculative questions in theology and philosophy. Affected rhetorications are nothing less than the tropes and the figures of Ciceronian and Ramistic rhetoric. Of stylistic rhetoric in general Glanvill says: "There is a bastard kind of eloquence that is crept into the Pulpit, which consists in affectations of wit and finery, flourishes, metaphors, and cadencies."[80] Glanvill's objection to this sort of style is that it degrades the ministry. "If we would acquit our selves as such," he declares, "we must not debase our great, and important message by those vanities of conceited speech; plainness is for ever the best eloquence; and 'tis the most forcible."[81] As for fantastical phrases, they differ from the rhetorications in being not so much violations of accepted patterns of speech as exploitations of smart current colloquialisms. Thus, says Glanvill, if you teach men to believe Christ's doctrine, to obey his laws, and to conform to his example, you are counted dull and unedifying; "but if you tell the people, that they must roll upon *Christ*, close with *Christ*, get into *Christ*, get a saving interest in the Lord *Christ*: O, this is savoury, this precious, this is spiritual teaching indeed;

---

[78] *An Essay concerning Preaching* (1678), p. 10.
[79] *Ibid.*, p. 11. [80] *Ibid.*, p. 23. [81] *Ibid.*, pp. 24-25.

whereas if any thing more be meant by those phrases than what the other plain expressions intend, it is either falshood or nonsense."[82]

When Glanvill requires that, as a second consideration, sermons may be judged excellent only when they are practical, he means that sermons must actually improve the conduct of the listeners. "The main business of Religion," he avers, "is a good and holy life."[83] And the main design of the preacher, he adds, "should be to promote that." Thus sermons must contain pious doctrine, practicable directions, and forcible motives. Pious doctrine is of course made up of the basic tenets of the preacher's religion. Practicable directions concern the advice the preacher may give as to the way in which that doctrine transforms itself into duties and actions. Forcible motives are those hopes, those fears, and those preferences, "convincing mens understanding that their interest is in their duty."[84]

Glanvill's discussion of the requirement that preaching should be methodical is just as close to the spirit of the new rhetoric as is his discussion of plainness of style. Here is what he says at the outset of this part of his treatise: "Method is necessary both for the understandings, and memories of the hearers; when a discourse hath an order, and connexion, one part gives light to another; whereas the mind is lost in confusions."[85] These words remind us of the efforts of Ramus to give method a new significance in the theory of presentation. These words remind us, too, that Ramus believed order in discourse to be a great contributing factor in making it easy for the speaker and the hearer to remember what was being said. But Glanvill's general rules for method remind us, not of Ramus and the Ciceronians, but of the new rhetoric. The first of these rules is that method should "be *natural*"—"not strain'd and forced, but such as the matter, and the capacities, and wants of the auditors, require, and lead you to."[86] The second of Glanvill's rules for method is that "It should be *obvious*, and plainly laid down."[87] Those who advocate a cryptic method to surprise the hearers are vain and weak; "our business is not to surprise, but to instruct."[88] Glanvill's third rule is that the method should not be too intricate—"the main things to be said may be reduced to a small number of heads, which being thorowly spoken to, will signifie more than a multitude slightly touch'd."[89] Following these general rules, Glanvill talks of method in terms of the parts of the sermon, and proceeds to discuss the choice

[82] *Ibid.*, p. 26.   [83] *Ibid.*, p. 28.   [84] *Ibid.*, p. 37.   [85] *Ibid.*, p. 38.
[86] *Ibid.*, p. 39.   [87] *Ibid.*, p. 39.   [88] *Ibid.*, p. 39.   [89] *Ibid.*, p. 40.

of the text, the introduction, the body, and the application. Throughout this concluding portion of his discussion of organization, he keeps to the theme of plainness, common sense, and moderation. He also writes everywhere with an eye to the effect of a given procedure upon those who listen.

The fourth one of Glanvill's requirements is that a sermon should be affectionate. By this he means that it should express and arouse zeal. Affections, he says, "are the springs of the Soul, that move the Will, and put our powers into Action."[90] It is best, of course, he goes on, for our affections to be aroused by our understanding, by our knowledge of duty. But not everyone is capable of that kind of motivation. The common people, for example, "have not Souls for much knowledge, nor usually are they moved by this method."[91] For them, and for all others who lack the intellectual power to know what duty is, the tropes, figures, and schemes of style, and the inducements of vehemence in delivery, are necessary. Nor are these appeals illegitimate. God condescends to use them for us; "he speaks in our Language," says Glanvill, "and in such schemes of speech as are apt to excite the affections of the most vulgar, and illiterate."[92]

After concluding these four topics, Glanvill discusses faults in sermons, and then turns to a discussion "of the main circumstances of Preaching, which concern the *Voice* and the *Action*."[93] Thus does he manage to add delivery to his previous discussion of style, matter, and arrangement, as if he were thinking of the old Ciceronian divisions of rhetoric, and were trying to cover the four most often emphasized by the Neo-Ciceronians. His final step is to discuss the education of a preacher, and here too he reminds us of Cicero laying down a program of philosophical preparation for the duties of a pagan orator in a layman's world. He admits towards the end of the *Essay* that his doctrines may be out of step with his time. Some go to church, he remarks, to be entertained by fine language and witty sentences. "They come to Sermons with the same appetites and inclinations, as they go to see, and hear Plays."[94] Others go to church with a genuine zeal for religion but with a head full of false images and false expectations as to the language the preacher should use. The plainness and simplicity that I recommend, observes Glanvill, will not edify them; in fact, they will pretend they do not understand. They and the other group just mentioned, Glanvill declares, make up the greater part of those who judge sermons in this age. It

[90] *Ibid.*, p. 54.   [91] *Ibid.*, p. 55.   [92] *Ibid.*, p. 56.
[93] *Ibid.*, p. 78.   [94] *Ibid.*, p. 87.

is not often "that the true plain Preaching is popular."[95] To the young divine for whom he is writing the *Essay* Glanvill then says that one must be ready to hear affected triflers and ignorant canters extolled as rare men, while the truly excellent preachers are misliked. And upon this note he brings his theory of rhetoric to an end.

Glanvill's *Essay* concludes my discussion of the new rhetoric of the seventeenth century, and my analysis of the main currents in logical and rhetorical theory in England during the Renaissance. Glanvill is an excellent prophet of things to come in the theory of communication. His *Essay* summarizes most of the trends I have been discussing in this chapter. It stands as a refreshing change for the reader who proceeds chronologically to examine works on rhetoric in the period between 1500 and 1700. It points specifically towards the emergence in English rhetorical theory of that fine modern rhetoric, Fénelon's *Dialogues on Eloquence*, which was published in French in 1717 and 1718, and in English in 1722.[96] Fénelon's *Dialogues*, by the way, are supposed to have been composed in 1679, or thereabouts, and thus they are the product of the same era that produced Glanvill's *Essay* in England. They are a more complete rhetoric than Glanvill's, because Fénelon devotes as much space to the oration of the layman as to the sermon of the preacher, and he even gives his rhetorical theory a significance for the student of poetical communication.[97] Indeed, he goes farther than any rhetorician of his time towards creating a new rhetoric, even as the Port-Royalists went farther than contemporary logicians in creating a new logic. Although Fénelon was not a Port-Royalist, his *Dialogues* are a better Port-Royal rhetoric than that achieved by Lamy, who was given credit by seventeenth-century Englishmen for having completed in rhetoric the reform started by Arnauld and Nicole in logic. Thus Fénelon ought to be in my present chapter. But he cannot be claimed for English rhetorical theory until the eighteenth century was well under way, and that era lies outside my present limits. Glanvill's *Essay*, however, is almost as good an example of the new rhetoric as the *Dialogues* are, and it is an example which belongs naturally to England and to the seventeenth century. I am content to close these pages with Glanvill's name in the last sentence of my description of the new rhetoric.

[95] *Ibid.*, p. 91.
[96] On these points, see my *Fénelon's Dialogues on Eloquence*, pp. 36-37, 46, 49.
[97] See my "Oratory and Poetry in Fénelon's Literary Theory," *The Quarterly Journal of Speech*, XXXVII (1951), 1-10.

Index